THEY SAID THAT!

They Said That!

THE WIT AND WISDOM OF MODERN CELEBRITY CULTURE

LARRY ENGELMANN

RENAISSANCE BOOKS

Los Angeles

Library of Congress Catalog Card Number: 00-103617
ISBN: 1-58063-110-X
10 9 8 7 6 5 4 3 2 1

Design by Jesus Arellano

Published by Renaissance Books
Distributed by St. Martin's Press
Manufactured in the United States of America
First Edition

For

Marya Flood

Erika Erhart

Colleen Engelmann

Mao Lei

Hung Chen

and

Mitch Nelson,

who shared with me the days, both silly and somber, of the recent
past and kept me laughing through it all.

Contents

PART ONE
Artists, Entertainers, & Celebrities   11

PART TWO
Politics & Politicians   133

PART THREE
Sports   217

PART FOUR
Law & Order   263

Index   297

ARTISTS, ENTERTAINERS, & CELEBRITIES

ARTISTS, ENTERTAINERS, & CELEBRITIES

A

WILL ACKERMAN
(Founder of Windham Hill—
the New Age Record Company)
"If I could catch the guy who coined the phrase, 'I'm going to nail his forehead to the wall.' " *1992: On the term* New Age.

SCOTT ADAMS
(Author & Cartoonist)
"I discovered what I call the Bill Gates effect. That is, the more successful you are, the uglier you get." *1995*

"I'm in favor of the death penalty. I'm in favor of abortion. I'm in favor of euthanasia. I'm in favor of a strong military defense. What do all these things have in common? I'm basically in favor of killing." *1998*

"People wonder why employees at Microsoft work ungodly hours. It's not why you think. If you've got a good mix of the sexes at the office, you have about the same odds or better of scoring at work as you would at home." *1998*

ISABEL ADJANI
(Actress)
"To be a womanizer is fine if you love women, but you have to treat them with respect by telling them from the beginning you'll never be able to be faithful." *1996: On Daniel Day Lewis, father of the child she had with Lewis and whom she says he does not support.*

BEN AFFLECK
(Screenwriter & Actor)
"I never had so many women ask me, 'Can I touch it?' Sadly, they were talking about the statuette." *1998: On attaining instant stardom at the post-Oscar ceremony parties.*

SHANNON AHMAD
(Writer)
"As the truth stinks, I was forced to serve the stinking truth." *1999: Malaysia's National Laureate replying to criticism over his latest book* Shit, *a profanity-laden political satire.*

SHERMAN ALEXIE
(Writer)
"The two funniest groups of people I've been around are Indians and Jews. I guess that says something about the inherent humor of genocide." *1998*

KIM ALEXIS
(Model)
"I would rather exercise than read a newspaper." *1996*

HARRY ALLEN
("Director of Enemy Relations" for Public Enemy)
"Being assassinated, it's been said, will often change your political viewpoint." *1992*

JEFF ALLEN
(Agent)
"At his age, he shouldn't be doing a split. I'm sure he won't be trying it again." *1998: The agent for sixty-nine-year-old singer James Brown who was taking painkillers after injuring his back while performing in Florida.*

WOODY ALLEN
(Actor & Director)
"If I had known all this was going to happen, I would never have taken Mia to that first lunch years ago." *1992: When asked if he regretted his affair with Farrow's daughter, Soon-Yi Previn.*

"But I sit in the nonshooting section." *1994: On why he doesn't worry when he eats at Sparks Steak House in New York, site of the infamous Paul Castellano mob hit.*

"I was seeking Solomon but I wound up with Roy Bean." *1994: On the New York court decision that restricted his access to the two children he fathered with Mia Farrow.*

"Over the years I've learned a lot from negative criticism. How to start a fire with a flint and dry wood. Also the best restaurants in Fargo, North

WOODY ALLEN (CONT'D)

Dakota, and six ways to start your own business. One must always be open minded." *1995*

"A lady from Queens sitting next to me at *Cats* woke me before it was over." *1995: In answer to the question, Without naming any names—is there anyone in the theater who has hurt you so much that you want revenge? "Revenge is putting it mildly," Allen responded.*

"I would like definitely to know the time and place of my death and if a necktie is required." *1995*

"As I've said before when asked about the compensation of artistic immortality, rather than live on in the hearts and minds of an adoring public, I'd rather live on in my own apartment." *1995*

"She's a marvel. And she laughs at all my jokes. She thinks I'm hilarious, and that doesn't hurt the relationship one bit, I can tell you." *1995: On Soon-Yi Previn.*

"I'm astounded by people who want to 'know' the universe when it's hard enough to find your way around Chinatown." *1996*

"I hate reality, but, you know, where else can you get a good steak sandwich?" *1996*

"I've often said, 'The only thing standing between me and greatness is me.'" *1996*

"I was never a high-culture person. I don't spend every night hovering over Kierkegaard. I'm the guy who comes home from work, takes his shirt off, opens a bottle of beer and turns on the Knicks game." *1997*

"The gondolier could cut our throats and no one would know." *1997: Said to Soon-Yi Previn during their honeymoon in Venice.*

"You may be inflating my stature in France. To the best of my knowledge I have never received any personal honors there. Films of mine over the years have received some acclaim but I myself have never been awarded any medals, badges, ribbons, titles nor given any official dinners or state funerals. In short, while I would consider it an honor if your description of me were true, as I love the French, I remain there, as here, a total commoner unable to fix a parking ticket." *1998: In a letter to Alan Riding, cultural correspondent for the* New York Times *in Europe. Mr. Riding had written an article stating that Allen had received a medal from the French government.*

"Thank you very much for bringing this to my attention; it comes as a total surprise to me. I have no medal, certificate or loving cup nor am I invited to any meetings, dunned any dues or given deferential treatment at the Crazy Horse Saloon. I will have my press people check into this and as I said, thank you for uncovering this utterly esoteric piece of information." *1998: In a letter to Allen Riding after the* New York Times *cultural correspondent in Europe, who responded to Allen's denial by telling him that according to the Conseil de l'ordre des Arts et des Lettres, Allen had been made a Commandeur des Arts et des Lettres on March 31, 1989, which made him a Knight Commander, a superior form of Sir.) Riding's subsequent research indicated that something had gone wrong when the French government had given Allen the award and that it had never officially been presented to the American filmmaker and comedian. Riding suggested that Allen write to the French government in order to receive a copy of the award and, perhaps, a party. Riding concluded, "As you know, your love of the French is reciprocated: they'd jump at the chance to give you a party. It could even be at the Crazy Horse."*

"When asked why it is so important that the Knicks win . . . I can only answer that basketball or baseball or any sport is as dearly important as life itself. After all, why is it such a big deal to work and love and strive and have children and then die and decompose into eternal nothingness? (By now, the person who asked me why the Knicks winning is important is sorry)." *1998*

"In today's American film market, if my films don't show a profit, I know I'm doing something right." *1998*

ISABEL ALLENDE
(Novelist)

"It is given names of tools and weapons, and even said to have supernatural powers, but in fact it fits inside a tin of sardines." *1997: On the fragility of the male sex organ.*

KIRSTIE ALLEY
(Actress)

"That was the mental torture I was going through—would David [Crosby] be . . . mad at me, would my husband kill me, would my children die, would my dad be playing golf the next day and be really embarrassed, would my breasts look good enough?" *1994: On how she considered going topless at Woodstock '94.*

"I think Scientology makes you look younger." *1997*

ISADORA ALMAN
(Columnist)

"Besides straight, bi and gay, many people identify as 'unlabeled,' 'questing,' 'celibate' and a few other varieties of 'I don't know' and 'I'm not saying until I'm sure.' Sadie Sadie the Rabbi Lady, for example, describes herself as 'trisexual,' which in her particular case means she'll 'try anything twice.'" *1998: The sex columnist for the* Bay Guardian, *commenting on the controversial "Other" category in sexual preference surveys.*

BOB ALMOND
(Celebrity Rodney King Juror)

REPORTER: Mr. Almond, this is the Associated Press. I'm calling to get your reaction to Dean Martin's death.

ALMOND: [Long pause] Are you sure you have the right number?

REPORTER: Is this Bob Almond, the Rodney King jury foreman?

ALMOND: Yes.

REPORTER: I have the right number. What do you think of Dean Martin dying?

ALMOND: [Another long pause] I'm sorry, you have the wrong number.

REPORTER: Isn't this Bob Almond?

ALMOND: No.

REPORTER: But you said you were.

ALMOND: I lied. *1996: Telephone conversation between an inquiring AP reporter and Bob Almond, foreman of the Rodney King jury.*

ROBERT ALTMAN
(Director)

"You should see *Forrest Gump.* You'll be able to follow it." *1995: To French film critics who said they were confused by his movie* Ready to Wear, *when it opened in Paris.*

KINGSLEY AMIS
(Writer)

"Only all the fucking time!" *1995: When asked if he ever regretted leaving his first wife.*

MARTIN AMIS
(Writer)

"The People's Princess! If she'd lived another year, she would have lost it. Princess Anne does a lot more charity work than Diana ever did, but because she looks like a horse she doesn't get the attention. At least Grace Kelly was an actress, so there was some validity to why she was in the public eye. What did Diana do to deserve all the attention except look good?" *1998: On the late Princess Diana.*

JUKA AMMONDT
(Academic)

"The ancient Sumerians had big parties and drums and rattles. The roots of rock may go back to man's earliest efforts to get a grip on life." *1999: The Finnish academic plans to translate Elvis Presley songs into Sumerian.*

TORI AMOS
(Singer)

"Although I can see this world and a horrible situation, I also have a belief in other worlds. I just am a believer in the fairies. I just feel the fairies in my stomach." *1992*

"I'm really into weeing. If somebody's being a jerk, I like to go wee on their head and I do that, mentally. But pee is sterile, so you're not going to hurt anybody by peeing on his head. Some people really want to be wee'd on; they're begging you to do it so you just have to. And other than weeing on people's heads, I guess I'm OK. I was really queer as a kid but I'm all right now." *1992*

"You know, you're brought up as a Christian girl, with a nice dress on Sunday, nice shiny shoes. Then you put on thigh-high boots and snake pants, and you just feel like you want to take a ride on a bike with Jesus and that's your church service: no problem." *1992*

TORI AMOS (CONT'D)

"I have vivid memories of being a prostitute in another life. My New Age friends go, 'Oh, you really need some help.' I'm just like, 'No, you're full of shit if you don't talk to your own self.' I get tired of being judged by all my self-righteous, New Age women friends. I'm ready to stick my crystals up their ass." *1994*

"I think if you have big lips, you certainly don't belong in this country." *1994*

"I think our generation loves our pain, and if you dare take it away from us, we're going to kill you." *1994*

"I don't fall in love much. I mean, I fall in love every five seconds with something, but I don't go from boy to boy. I go from archetype to archetype." *1996*

"I know I'm an acquired taste. I'm anchovies, and not everybody wants those hairy little things." *1998*

"That everybody could have access to a really good red wine. And that everybody could have access to a good shrink." *1998: On how she'd like to change the world.*

"I hear the wine. It's like a structure. I see it as a piece. I hear it before I taste it. It's calling me. And then I start to hear it when I'm tasting it. Not that I put crystal suppositories up my ass. I'm not New Age." *1999: Explaining her passion for wine.*

LONI ANDERSON
(Actress)

"It was like experiencing a nuclear explosion in a very small place." *1995: Describing sex with her* WKRP in Cincinnati *costar Gary Sandy.*

PAMELA ANDERSON
(Actress)

"Everybody says I'm plastic from head to toe. Can't stand next to a radiator or I'll melt. I had [breast] implants, but so has every single person in Los Angeles." *1995*

"Move to Los Angeles, do a couple of *Playboy* covers, audition, get a part in a popular TV series, marry a rock star." *1995: On how to become famous.*

"I always say you want a man who can fix the toilet." *1996*

"I was not a big drug person. I couldn't smoke pot because it made me so paranoid that I couldn't tell if I had to pee or I was really cold." *1996*

"My grandfather was a logger, and they tell me he talked to the trees, and the trees talked to him, and he used to always say that if a tree falls in the forest, it doesn't make a sound. I kind of do have that belief then, because I do have that faith that things are going to happen the way they're going to happen, and they're out of your control." *1996*

"I have a certain presence that attracts people more than my legs and breasts." *1996*

"There's never going to be a great understanding of me. I think I'm a little whacked." *1996*

"Making love in the morning got me through morning sickness—I found I could be happy and throw up at the same time." *1996*

"It says '*Pamela*.' And when he gets excited it says, 'I love Pamela very, very much. She's a wonderful wife and I enjoy her company to the 10th degree!'" *1996: On the tattoo on her husband's penis.*

"They are like two balls of burning flame." *1999: On the residual pain caused by her surgery to remove breast implants.*

"I felt like I was Dolly Parton." *1999: On why she had breast reduction surgery.*

"No! Not at all! Tommy has been neutered or spayed. What do you call it?" *1999: Denying rumors that she's pregnant by husband Tommy Lee.*

PAUL THOMAS ANDERSON
(Director & Screenwriter)

"Mark Wahlberg came to me and said, 'I've got an inch on Leo.' And he showed it to me, so I hired him instead." *1998: The* Boogie Nights *director on why he changed his mind about casting Leonardo DiCaprio as porn star Dirk Digler.*

FRANCESCA ANNIS
(Actress)

"There is a good line in *Reckless*, when I say to [costar] Robson Green, 'What's attractive about older women?' and he says, 'I am not interested in older women, I am interested in you.' That says it all for me." *1998: Annis, fifty-two, star of the Masterpiece Theater miniseries* Reckless, *commenting on her romantic relationship with actor Ralph Fiennes, thirty-five.*

SUSAN ANTON
(Actress)

"Where is life? I have no child, I have no husband. Can I still get out there and work? Oh, my God, I'm fat. No I'm not, I'm fine. And then I start to think . . . I'm losing my mind. So I call my shrink." *1990: On her concerns.*

TOM ARNOLD
(Actor)

"I'm mad at Saddam. That bastard—he's after my wife." *1990: Commenting on a story in the* National Enquirer *that alleged that Saddam Hussein had written "long, rambling, passionate love letters" to Roseanne.*

"That's how I lost 85 pounds." *1991: When asked if his conversion to Judaism required circumcision.*

"I weighed 320 pounds. I was uncomfortable, and we were unable to have sex. We had sex, but it wasn't as good, you know, if you're that much farther away, if you got a big gut, you know, every inch counts." *1992: On why he and his wife Roseanne lost weight.*

"You know, we were stupid. We'd go to high schools in other towns and hang around." *1992: On what he did while skipping class in high school—and then not graduating.*

"Now we can try to have a kid in April. But the second part is that her breasts will get really big. They're big enough the way it is, and they really give her back and shoulders trouble. I see her on the treadmill when she works out. If a guy had that, if your nuts were that big, forget it. So she's had them shortened. I'd like to have the extra stuff put on my dick, but there's always the fear of tissue rejections." *1992: On problems he had with his wife Roseanne.*

"Rosie's always been Jewish. I was Methodist. Methodist is like religion lite. You got into the church, you see Jesus on the cross, he looks comfortable, he's smiling, got a little mousse in his hair.

Then you go in the Catholic church; he looks like he's been hit by a fucking truck. You go to the Jewish church, the mosque, or whatever it is, and you don't even see Jesus and you feel even more guilty." *1992*

"All right. I'm converted now. I send my food back in restaurants. I don't feel very good, I think I have diabetes, I take absolutely everything personally, and I don't like Jews anymore." *1992: On his conversion to Judaism.*

"If I read the columns that newspaper columnists and gossip columnists write, I would assume that people hated me and thought I was talentless." *1992*

"The nature of show business is people within the business feel that if someone else fails, they move up a notch." *1992*

"I love that she's a strong woman. I love that she's successful and that I can still get a hard on." *1992: On his wife, Roseanne.*

"At thirteen and a half I moved in with my mom and the day I arrived she popped open a beer and said, 'Here, have this. You have no curfew, you don't have to be home, you can grow your hair, you can screw girls here.'" *1992*

"When we redesigned our house, I got my own toilet. I get to have a phone in there, and I get to have my own literature, which is nice. *Life* from the 50s. And sports trivia books. And there might be a *Playboy*. You know, for the interviews." *1992*

"I think facing each other is the nice thing. When you lose the weight, you're closer in every way. The world's fattest man could have sex somehow. It's just easier if when you're on top of somebody, you don't kill them." *1992*

"I'm not a complete idiot!" *1993*

"We believe that a lot of judges are pedophiles." *1993: On the beliefs he shares with his wife, Roseanne.*

"Joan of Arc died. Only a few have risen above that and become millionaires." *1993: On his wife's comment that she was very much like Joan of Arc.*

TOM ARNOLD (CONT'D)

"He's racist as hell. Listening to him makes you hate Jews, because he's Jewish." *1993: On Howard Stern.*

"We've been married four years in January. Ironically, that's how long I've had a career." *1993: On life with his wife, Roseanne.*

"The truth is, when she was my age, she wasn't making as much money as I'm making now." *1994: When asked if he was jealous because his wife, Roseanne, earned more than he did.)*

"The greatest truth is honesty is the best policy. And if you're going to lie, you better be good at it." *1994*

"You poor people make me laugh!" *1994: To Ken McQuiston, a Michigan steelworker. Arnold stole McQuiston's girlfriend after meeting her at a party in Hollywood.*

"I read that Roseanne got the tattoo that said PROPERTY OF TOM ARNOLD covered up. It was on her butt. The joke was that it made me the fourth largest property owner in California." *1995*

"When we were married, she used to talk about how big it was. Anyway, things change. And, like I say, even a 747 looks small when it lands in the Grand Canyon." *1995*

"I know this sounds sick, but it was a lot of fun being famous back when Roseanne and I were together. I realized at the time that I was only famous because I was married to her, but that's better than being famous like John Hinkley." *1997*

"I thought we bonded—he talked about Vietnam, I talked about being married to Roseanne." *1999: Describing a meeting with Oliver Stone.*

PATRICIA ARQUETTE
(Actress)

"I know I have a big bust, but I don't feel that I'm better than anyone who's had implants." *1997*

ROSEANNA ARQUETTE
(Actress)

QUESTION: "You were in a long relationship with Peter Gabriel. Was there ever a point where you could see yourself staying home, washing diapers, frying chips?"

ARQUETTE: "I did it. Peter and I had a very big affair for many years, and it was very painful for a lot of people—including his wife." *1991*

BEA ARTHUR
(Actress)

"There are three things I've yet to do: Opera, rodeo and porno." *1994*

THE ARTIST
(Formerly Known As Prince)

"People are saying, 'Oh, this was Prince's big gamble.' What gamble? I made a $7 million movie with somebody's else's money." *1990: On his film Graffiti Bridge, a box office flop.*

"I would wake up nights thinking, 'Who am I?'" *1994: On why he changed his name to an unpronounceable symbol.*

"I was very ill and afraid for my sanity, but that was before I changed my name." *1995*

"People say I'm a crazy fool for writing 'Slave' on my face. But if I can't do what I want to do, what am I?" *1996*

"It's because I've got a record to sell." *1996: On why he shocked a press conference in England by behaving normally.*

"One time, George [Clinton] sent me a tape and said, 'You pee on it, send it back to me and I'll pee on it. Then we'll see what we've got.'" *1997*

ELIZABETH ASHLEY
(Actress)

"L.A. people, they're all health sissies and weather sissies. They're no fun in a crisis. There are people out there calling each other up in emotional support networking six months after the damned earthquake! Get over it! Hey, live in New York, where the subway goes underneath your building!" *1995*

"Where is it written that everyone has to have every skill? People wind up thinking that data is the same thing as knowledge. There have to be people that know the difference—those are the people that will, if not save civilization, at least when they write its obituary, will get it accurately." *1995*

JOHN L. ASHMAN
(Writer)

"Paul Revere had just discovered that someone in Boston was a spy for the British, and when he saw the young woman believed to be the spy's girl-friend in an Italian restaurant, he said to the waiter, 'Hold the spumoni—I'm going to follow the chick an' catch a Tory.'" *1995: This passage won Ashman the annual Bulwer-Lytton Ficton prize for the worst opening line of an imaginary novel.*

ED ASNER
(Actor)

"The decision by the Cincinnati jury on the Map-plethorpe exhibit was phenomenal! After all, I consider the Mapplethorpe picture—one man uri-nating into the mouth of another—(to be) merely a depiction of Ronald Reagan's trickle-down theory." *1990*

CHET ATKINS
(Musician)

"He went out to Texas and kind of uglified himself up and got smoking dope, and people started writing about him." *1998: On the rise of Willie Nelson.*

MILI AVITAL
(Actress)

"One of the first words I learned when I came to New York was 'whatever.' If you know only one word here, that should be it. *1998: The Israeli actress on her adjustment to New York when she arrived there at the age of eighteen.*

"One day when I was a waitress in New York, I was reading the specials to this woman who later became my manager. At the pasta, she interrupted me and said, 'Are you an actress?' Literally, two weeks after that, I got all these panicked messages from her. I called her back, and I'm like, 'Um, hello, I'm Mili the waitress. You know, from the restaurant?' And she's like, 'I know who you are! Pack your bags; you leave tomorrow for the shoot in Arizona. You landed the leading role in *Stargate*. I was like, 'I don't have a working visa. I don't have

a green card, I don't have anything, and where the hell is Arizona?'" *1998*

"I didn't understand the plot [of her first film *Stargate*]. I had no idea what people were saying to me half the time. I was doing one scene where I'm supposed to react to this guy who's morphing. How the hell do you explain morphing to someone who doesn't speak English?" *1998*

"Being a movie star makes you have very profound thoughts, as you can see." *1998*

B

BACKROADS
(Motorcycling Newspaper)

"Robbie Knievel, son of legendary stuntman Evel Knievel, made a world record jump by successfully launching his Honda CR500 231 feet, almost 2/3 of a football field, and clearing 30 hotel limousines. The jump took place at the Tropicana Hotel, on the Las Vegas strip.

"Before the jump Robbie left his trailer, kissed his dad Evel on the cheek and then soared into the record books.

"Upon finishing his jump the young Knievel gave thanks to Jesus, who now lives in South Park, Colorado, and was present in the huge crowd, but who had, unbeknownst to Robbie, placed a huge amount of cash against Knievel actually making the jump." *1998*

KEVIN BACON
(Actor)

"It was one of the hardest parts I've ever had to play, a guy who's unable to rise to the occasion. It was so completely unlike anything relating to my life." *1995: On playing an impotent character in the film* Murder in the First.

"Any idiot can get laid when they're famous. That's easy. It's getting laid when you're not famous that takes some talent." *1996*

SCOTT BAIO
(Actor)

"My parents called me, crying. They heard it from my brother, who heard it on the radio. And they're

SCOTT BAIO (CONT'D)

crying and I'm thinking, 'Someone died in my family!' Little did I know it was me." *1998: On the rumor that swept American newsrooms and the Internet saying that he'd died in a car accident.*

"After a while I started answering my phone, 'I'm not dead.' " *1998: On how he dealt with calls to his home after the news was broadcast that he'd been killed.*

ANITA BAKER
(Singer)

"We like to walk around naked. It's not pretty and we don't want people talking about us." *1995: On why she and her husband don't have live-in help.*

ALEC BALDWIN
(Actor)

"C'mon out here, you faggot!" *1992:Challenging a New York City hansom-cab driver to a fight. Baldwin had just testified at a hearing against the cruelty of horse-drawn carriages.*

"Kim says a nation is only as strong as it treats its animals. She's quoting Gandhi, I think." *1993: On Kim Basinger, his wife.*

"There's a lot more money to be made on Wall Street. If you want real power, go to Washington. If you want sex, go into the fashion business. But if you want the whole poison cocktail in one glass . . . go to Hollywood." *1994*

"You know, when I met my wife, I was living in New York and she was living in L.A. She lived by herself; she was divorced. It was just her and 11 dogs that she had. She had a big dog and 10 little dogs. When I first came to visit her, I was kind of taken aback. I said, 'It's just you and the 11 dogs in this little house in the valley?' And she was like, 'Yeah, that's it.' She lived this very simple life." *1997: On meeting his future wife, Kim Basinger.*

"Sexual promiscuity has always been the medicine of choice for the chief executive of the United States. What would you rather have him do: take drugs? Drink?" *1998: On the allegations of sexual behavior toward President Bill Clinton.*

CHRISTIAN BALE
(Actor)

"The only person I've ever sort of been a fan of was Steve McQueen, but he's been dead for, like, 15 years, so, not much chance of working with him." *1997: On the actor he'd most like to work with.*

BOB BARKER
(TV Host)

"She told me that I had been so straitlaced and that it was time I had a little hanky-panky in my life and she volunteered the hanky-panky." *1994: On his former female co-host on* The Price is Right, *who filed a sexual harassment suit against him.*

"I'm 70 years old. The sexual revolution in my life came when I was out of ammunition." *1994*

ELLEN BARKIN
(Actress)

"You know, I've never been able to even sit on a surfboard. Now, maybe that's because, you know, we don't really surf in the Bronx." *1990*

"I don't think it's fashionable to be Mickey Rourke now." *1990*

"Every actor in England would swim across the ocean to get a job in an American film. And I don't blame them. I would too if I were there because there's no work. Not that our movies are great. I obviously don't think that. But they would swim across shark-infested waters to get a job in a Hollywood movie." *1990*

"I've spent a lot of time watching English TV. And it is so bad. I mean, BBC dramas? They don't know what to do with the camera. I mean, I don't think these guys could take still photographs, let alone movie ones! I mean, it's really true!" *1990*

JULIAN BARNES
(Author)

"Good jokes are finally just jokes; whereas bad jokes are more revelatory of character and situation. Wonky puns, look-at-me one-liners, inappropriately perky comebacks: these don't necessarily denote lack of humor, more a chin-up flailing at the discovery that the world is not a clean, well-lighted place; or that it is for some, but not for you, as the light falls badly on you and mysteriously casts no shadow." *1998*

DAVE BARRY
(Humorist & Writer)

"Well, I didn't feel any bad effects until I woke up several days later in Finland." *1994: On drinking Akevitt, the potent Norwegian liquor he sampled at the Winter Olympic Games in Lillehammer, Norway.*

"I believe the reason why so many rock stars elected to die young is that, basically, it was better for their health." *1994*

"As a boy I never wanted to be president of the United States. I wanted to be Buddy Holly. I loved Buddy Holly, and not just because he was young and famous and hip and wrote great rock-and-roll music. I loved Buddy Holly because he wore glasses." *1994*

DREW BARRYMORE
(Actress)

"I think I have my best moments when I'm nude, asleep in bed. Now that I think about it, I have my most sensual thoughts in bed, my most creative thoughts in the bathroom, and when I'm in the shower, I come to conclusions about myself." *1992*

"Of course, I think it's Hollywood's responsibility to promote safe sex. . . . Maybe the movies could teach us how to deal with this better. People should be friends before they get intimate; that's how I am. I'm not the kind of person who goes to bed with a stranger." *1992*

"My philosophy of life is simple. I like to fuck with people just to fuck with them. I want people blown away when I do what they don't expect. It's not what's right or wrong but what's right for me." *1993*

"He's a Buddhist, I'm a total geek head, so somehow we seem to make this great combination." *1995: On her new boyfriend.*

"He is such an important part of my life that if I die before him I want a little bit of my ashes put in his food so that I can finally live inside him." *1997: On her cat.*

"He's brilliant and everything he says is everything you'd want to say, but articulated on the most eloquent level ever known to man." *1998: On Woody Allen.*

"I'm becoming that dork I couldn't stand when I was a kid. One Saturday night I found myself watching *The Capitol Gang* on CNN. I was like, 'Oh my God! What is going on, and what have I become?'" *1998*

"I try to stay in bed at least 10 minutes to ponder my place in the universe. Then I wash my face, check my karma and get my balance for the day." *1998: On her morning ritual.*

"Everyone looks at me like I'm a leper above the eyes." *1998: On her overplucked eyebrows.*

"I like to be around women who make me feel good about who I am, and what my body is like, and what I look like, and who I am inside, women that make me feel confident and excited and sexy and happy." *1998*

"I almost tattooed the Grinch on myself. I came so close. But I won't do characters on my body." *1998*

PETER BART
(Editor of Variety)

"Ali [MacGraw] was one of these people who felt like she had to decorate herself like a '60s person. She was about as much a '60s person as Leona Helmsley. She was materialistic, self-aggrandizing, and basically would fuck any actor she played opposite of." *1998: On actress Ali MacGraw, who married producer Robert Evans in 1969 and became a star in the film* Love Story.

KIM BASINGER
(Actress)

"There's nothing that makes me more passionate than protection for animals." *1993*

"Let him go on and lead the country so amazingly. Let's celebrate that [President Clinton's decision to have his dog Buddy neutered] and celebrate Buddy—he's doing a great job, too." *1998: On the president.*

"In the *Playboy* pictures, I wanted to make a small little art film for myself, and it worked brilliantly.

KIM BASINGER (CONT'D)

In fact it worked like clockwork. I wanted to shock, in a way, and the result of that story was that I literally sabotaged myself and heard the doors slam. Ultimately it helped me because I had to go into battle against *her*. She [the image of how people saw me] was up there. And it became me against her." *1998: Commenting on her spread for* Playboy *magazine in the early 1980s.*

"If anyone has a dream out there, just know that I'm living proof that they can come true." *1998: At the Academy Awards ceremony, accepting the Oscar for best supporting actress in* L.A. Confidential.

"Up until now, the only Oscar I knew was on *Sesame Street* or *The Odd Couple*." *1998*

ORSON BEAN
(Actor)

"I'm just going to miss the fun I had shooting the bull with the guy and ignoring the fact that there might be a few million people listening. It's something that doesn't exist anymore, like when a bush dies in your backyard." *1998: On why he's sorry Tom Snyder is leaving* The Late, Late Show, *where Bean had been a frequent guest.*

WARREN BEATTY
(Actor)

"Uh . . . let me say this. . . . Shirley and I are . . . um . . . ah . . . unusually famous. Where . . . uh . . . is Shirley at this . . . uh . . . point in her life? Well . . . uh . . . gee . . . I don't . . . uh . . . know . . . that I have . . . uh . . . anything of any consequence to . . . uh . . . say. I . . . I don't . . . feel I have the right to talk about . . . about . . . um . . . somebody else. I . . . uh . . . particularly don't talk about people . . . uh . . . uh . . . people I'm close to because my. . . um. . . credentials might be a little too, uh, potent." *1991: Commenting on his sister, Shirley MacLaine.*

"After I got established in films, it sometimes seemed I had very little interest in making a movie until I was romantically motivated. . . . If Diane Keaton had not made *Reds*, I don't know what I would have done. So, it had to be Diane, until it couldn't be Diane, and then it would be somebody else." *1991*

"I'll make an extremely good father because I want to." *1991*

"My notion of a wife at 40 is that a man should be able to change her, like a bank note, for two 20s." *1998*

PAUL BECKWITH
(Music Critic)

"Pat Boone is Tiny Tim's evil twin." *1997: On Pat Boone's heavy-metal album.*

BONNIE BEDELIA
(Actress)

"Sure, the body count in this movie bothers me, but what you gonna do? It's what everybody likes. At least it's not an awful body count—it's a fun body count." *1990: On the movie* Die Hard 2.

SAUL BELLOW
(Writer)

"Jack Nicholson's a very intelligent actor. That is to say, for an actor, he's quite intelligent. . . . I was impressed by the fact that he didn't throw the roaches of his marijuana away but kept them in a littler silver case." *1997*

"California is like an artificial limb the rest of the country doesn't really need. You can quote me on that." *1997*

ROBERTO BENIGNI
(Actor)

"I also want to thank my parents in Vergaio, who gave me the greatest gift: poverty." *1999: After winning Oscars for best actor and best foreign film.*

"This is a terrible mistake, because I have used up all my English." *1999: Accepting his second Oscar of the night, for best actor in* Life Is Beautiful, *which was named best foreign language film.*

"I jumped on top of him and kissed him all over." *1999: On meeting the pope.*

TONY BENNETT
(Singer)

"I like them because they're so nuts. Flea's a lot like Jimmy Durante." *1993: On the Red Hot Chili Peppers and the band's guitarist, Flea.*

"I was the Madonna of my day." *1994*

MILDRED AUGUSTINE WIRT BENSON
(Author)

"I'm so tired of Nancy Drew I could vomit." *1993: Benson, eighty-three, wrote twenty-three of the original thirty Nancy Drew mysteries.*

INGMAR BERGMAN
(Director)

"I have always avoided seeing my films. The times I have been forced to see any of them, I have always felt angry, sad, upset, shocked and have had to go to the toilet." *1990*

MILTON BERLE
(Comedian)

"Jews don't drink too much—it interferes with our suffering." *1997*

"I feel like a 20-year-old. But there's never one around." *1998: On life at eighty-nine.*

TOM BERNARD
(Film Studio Executive)

"We had eight groups of filmmakers interview *us* to see if we were worthy to view their movie, meet them at the back of the theater, and take a number, and give them millions of dollars." *1998: The copresident of Sony Pictures Classics on the arrogance, vulnerability, and charm evident in many filmmakers at the Sundance Film Festival.*

SANDRA BERNHARD
(Comedienne)

"As far as I'm concerned, sex ruins almost everything. . . . And Madonna feels this even more strongly than I do. We have spoken about it a lot and she is very down on sex at the moment." *1992*

"Being nice is a weak emotion. It's not even an emotion. It's just a weakness, period." *1998*

"There was so much I wanted to say about the princess, but when I saw Steven Segal speak so eloquently on CNN, I said to myself, 'What do *you* have to contribute to this moment?' It was such a rare and unique opportunity for so many stars and celebrities to express the repressed grief they've felt for things we can't even *begin* to imagine. When Tom Cruise described how many times he drove through that tunnel, it gave me the *chills.*

I said, 'It's the edgy shit that needs to go into your work, baby.'" *1998: On the outpouring of public grief following the death of Princess Diana.*

"My mother's an abstract artist, my father's a proctologist. That's how I view the whole world." *1998*

HALLE BERRY
(Actress)

"The truest cliché about Hollywood is that women have boobs and *everybody* wants to see them." *1994*

"It's like standing in a room buck naked and turning around very slowly. That's what singing is to me." *1998: On doing her own vocals for HBO's "Dorothy Dandridge."*

BERNARDO BERTOLUCCI
(Movie Director)

"I love the idea that things are in progress, that we are not stones." *1991*

BIG BIRD
(TV Personality)

"My heroes are Larry Bird, Admiral Byrd, Lady Bird, Sheryl Crow, Chick Corea, the inventor of birdseed and anyone who reads to you even if she's tired." *1997*

BJÖRK
(Singer)

"Women and men can meet anywhere. There's this thing in America called dates, right? We don't have those in Iceland. People just listen to music, get drunk and (do it)." *1998*

MR. BLACKWELL
(Fashion Critic)

"Let's be blunt, yesterday's *Evita* is today's Velveeta." *1998: On placing Madonna third on his worst-dressed-women list.*

VIRGINIA BLAIR
(Writer)

"Writing is nothing to be ashamed of as long as you do it in private and wash your hands afterwards." *1990*

YASMINE BLEETH
(Actress)

"What is Swedish?" *1995: Answering the question on Jeopardy's celebrity edition, "The language of the Netherlands."*

YASMINE BLEETH (CONT'D)

"Me, Cindy Crawford and Elvis Presley." *1998: On the perfect menage a trois.*

ROY BLOUNT JR.
(Humorist & Writer)

"I am not a member of Generation X. I don't know what my generation is, but it's probably back around P." *1994*

ROBERT BLY
(Author & Guru)

"We always say a few things that are true, but we don't know which ones they are." *1992: At the start of one of his men's gatherings.*

TOM BODETT
(Humorist)

"She said, 'Write about anything—what did you do today, for example.' And I said I'd had my dog castrated. She said, 'Well, that sounds like fun—write about that.' My dog was dumber than a box of rocks, but he would just never stop moving. It was this great big, husky, black Labrador who never stopped moving and I was told that if you take a dog's 'uhm' off, sometimes they calm down. Well, it didn't happen. It was like taking the steering wheel off your Ferrari. Alls it did is it took his sense of direction away. He had no point to his life at all, now, but he hadn't lost any of his energy." *1996: Recalling his first commentary.*

MICHAEL BOLTON
(Singer)

"You take a bunch of talented chimpanzees and give them a bucket of paint and they'll destroy a Rembrandt or Van Gogh. The critics, who are insensitive, rude people, can kiss my ass." *1992*

"Macho guys might feel threatened by me." *1992*

"[Bob] Dylan came in with lyrics like 'I could not bear what would materialize, but you, so ready to etherealize.' I said, 'Gee, I don't know, Bob. That's a lot of syllables for me.'" *1993*

"One woman claimed she orgasmed fourteen times at one of the concerts. She said now she doesn't have to see her husband for six months." *1993: On the response of a fan to his singing.*

"You get to meet important people from all walks of life—from Joe DiMaggio to Barry Bonds." *1994: On the advantages of being a celebrity.*

JON BON JOVI
(Musician & Singer)

"I'm a weird motherfucker." *1990*

"I am just getting old enough now that my friends are having kids. You call 'em up, say 'Let's go out,' and they go, 'Yeah, but no, I can't.' Kids change your life. Then they grow up, turn eighteen, and say, 'Fuck off, I'm out of here.' It's parents' great revenge for you to have kids." *1990*

"This is the first president who's not old enough to be my father. Who understood rock 'n' roll, who smoked dope, definitely fucked that blonde and avoided the draft. He did things that I can relate to. He called me last week. I spoke to him. That's pretty hip." *1993: On Bill Clinton.*

"I'd give up rock 'n' roll in a minute to be a quarterback." *1995*

"Politics is such a big, rotten, scummy business. Staggering. They're fuckin' rock & roll stars. You know what I mean?" *1995*

DANNY BONADUCE
(Actor)

"When I went into rehab, I was the only ex–child star among 48 patients. On the other hand, there were nine dentists. Nobody asked these guys if they were ex–child dentists." *1991: Bonaduce starred in TV's* The Partridge Family.

"You'd think I was one of the Kennedys." *1991: On the bad press he received after he was charged with assaulting a transvestite prostitute.*

BONO
(Singer)

"It's written in rock & roll that all you need is love. But you also need a great nose." *1990*

"Being a rock 'n' roll star is like having a sex change. People treat you like a girl. They stare at you, they follow you down the street, they hustle you. . . . I know what it feels like to be a babe." *1992*

"We're actually trying to make a kind of music that doesn't exist yet. That is a terrifying place to be." *1997: On his band's upcoming album.*

CHASTITY BONO
(Gay & Lesbian Activist)

"The show is not too gay for me, but we have to be realistic." 1998: *On the fact that TV's* Ellen *faced cancellation because it was too "gay specific."*

PAT BOONE
(Singer)

"Randy Wood wanted me to do 'Ain't That a Shame.' I had moved to New York in the fall of 1956 and enrolled in Columbia University as an English major. Well, the word 'ain't' was not acceptable English usage yet, so I asked Randy if I could change it to 'Isn't That a Shame.' He let me try it, but it didn't sound right." *1990*

"Either Lenin or Marx, I forget which of those early communist leaders it was, said, 'Give me the music of a people, and in one generation they'll be mine.'" *1990*

"I don't give a rip for rap and I feel they should have left some of the grunge in the garage. But I have found some terrific songs by Guns 'n' Roses, Alice Cooper, Ozzy Osbourne, Black Sabbath, even Megadeth—some of their songs have an Old Testament type of feel. I have had to pass on a number of songs I liked musically because of the lyrics—Judas Priest's 'Living after Midnight'—those lyrics wouldn't be right coming out of me." *1996*

"The prophesies in the Bible make it seem to millions of us all around the world that we are in that final countdown. We're heading to one-world government, one-world economy, and an Antichrist world dictatorship. Some say it's bleak, but to me it's not. I'm an optimist. It's like I just had a root canal the other day, and I detested the idea, but it had to be handled. It was going to get worse. And now I'm entering a new era in my mouth." *1997*

ANGELA BOWIE
(Wife of Singer)

"Even though I cared, there really wasn't much I was going to do about it. I made breakfast." *1990:*

The ex-wife of David Bowie on how she reacted when she found him naked in bed with Mick Jagger.

"He used sex the way a cat sprays, to mark his territory. It gets the job done." *1993: On her former husband.*

"Paul McCartney seems from the outside a puffed-up arrogant little snot, and he is. . . . I guess it's good that so much of his energy goes into accumulating and hoarding wealth. If he put his whole soul into his music, it would probably turn out actively nauseating, as opposed to merely mediocre." *1993*

"Those of us who are sexually aware enough and sexually adept enough, um, you know, barter with favors for sex. And why not? It's totally fair." *1993*

DAVID BOWIE
(Singer)

"I keep remembering works that cast their spell on my sponge-like mind." *1994: On the books he's read.*

"About 15 or 16 years ago, I really got pretty tired of fending off questions about what I used to do with my [penis] in the early '70s. My suggestion for people with prurient interests is to go through the 30 or 40 bios on me and pick out the rumor of their choice." *1995*

"I remember sitting at the same table with Iggy Pop and Lou Reed, listening to them not talk to each other." *1995: Remembering Max's Kansas City, a New York club.*

"I was never a child. I was born a rock god." *1996*

"The most frustrating thing about being an overachiever in terms of writing is that you have all this stuff and nobody gets a chance to hear it." *1997*

"To take a whole lot of jargonese out of the visual arts and make it more accessible to the people who are not touring academically and cannot plow through the reams of fairly elitist extrapolation of what is the heart and soul of minimalism." *1998: On his new goal in life.*

LARA FLYNN BOYLE
(Actress)

"Whenever I meet people whose parents are still together, I'm amazed. They're freaks. They make me nervous. Seeing people still married after twenty years is like watching a TV show." *1993*

"Love scenes are a pain in the ass. Ninety percent of the time they're manipulative, to make money, to make sure no one gets out of their seat. Doing a love scene is like scrubbing toilets." *1993*

"I want all of you in all of my weddings." *1993: To a group of her friends.*

"I just want to tell you that I admire you a lot because you've done so much for women." *1994: To Madonna at a party at the new House of Blues club in Los Angeles. "Ugh! That's even better than when Kevin Costner called me 'neat'!" Madonna responded moments later to the comment.*

RAY BRADBURY
(Writer)

"Writer's block . . . happens more often with TV and screenwriters who take jobs for money and then are astounded when their subconscious says, 'Nobody's home.'" *1995*

"Who do you want to talk to? All those morons who are living across the world? You don't even want to talk to them at home." *1997: Telling an audience that the Internet will never take the place of books.*

MARLON BRANDO
(Actor)

"There are so many of them I can't remember their names." *1991: When asked by reporters to name his children.*

"I've always been lucky with women. There have been many in my life though I hardly ever spent more than a couple of minutes with any of them." *1994*

"The four pillars of wisdom that support journalistic endeavors are: lies, stupidity, money-grubbing, and ethical irresponsibility." *1995*

BRANDY
(Actress & Singer)

"I'm nice to everybody. I'm like, 'Hi, my name is Brandy!' And I'll give people a hug. I'll go up to people and say things like, 'I like your hair.' Stuff like that." *1996: On how success hasn't gone to her head.*

SANDY BROKAW
(Publicist)

"There wasn't much demand for what he did. How many midgets do you see on TV?" *1993: On the suicide of his client, actor Herve Villechaize, ten years after* Fantasy Island *was canceled.*

TOM BROKAW
(TV News Anchor)

"You feel great sympathy for them. But you also envy the extra hour of sleep they're getting." *1999: On the homeless people he passed sleeping on the street when he came to work early in the morning to substitute for Matt Lauer on the* Today Show.

ALBERT BROOKS
(Actor & Director)

"I was trying to get him to be a little self-deprecating. The joke was, 'George Bush says it's time to give the country back to the little guy—here I am!'" *1991: On his efforts to give a comedy lesson to 1988 presidential candidate Michael Dukakis.*

"All over the hills near my house there are these coyotes and they laugh. You know the way they laugh? They're scary. Anyway, I woke up my girlfriend and I said, 'They're laughing with us, not at us.'" *1991*

"If you look in the Bible under Armageddon, one of the signs that the world is ending is an excessive number of lists and awards shows. Another sign is awards being given for performances on other awards shows. It's like brothers and sisters having children together—same thing. It's entertainment blood incest." *1999*

"He called me from his car. He asked, 'Do you promise it will be funny?' I said, 'I promise it will be funnier than *Titanic*.'" *1999: On how he got* Titanic *director James Cameron to make a cameo appearance in his comedy film* The Muse.

GARTH BROOKS
(Singer)

"I've got a long list of musicians I admire, but yeah, I've had the fantasy many times of getting in the makeup and going on stage with KISS." *1999*

MEL BROOKS
(Actor & Director)

"Critics are like eunuchs at an orgy—they just don't get it." *1996*

"Listen, you. I made 21 movies. I'm very talented. I'll live in history. I have a body of work. You only have a body." *1996: To film critic Roger Ebert.*

HELEN GURLEY BROWN
(Magazine Editor)

"There are people who say to Judy, 'Why don't you write something good? Something literary? Something you can be proud of?' Well, I'd like to put a bullet through those people's heads. No. First, I'd like to pull out their fingernails, one by one, then put a bullet through their heads. Because they're just pretentious jerks." *1990: On people who write to her friend, writer Judith Krantz.*

JAMES BROWN
(Singer)

"I've outdone anybody you can name—Mozart, Beethoven, Bach, Strauss. Irving Berlin, he wrote 1,001 tunes. I wrote 5,500." *1990*

"I didn't contest the charges because, being a hero and a legend like Martin Luther King, it would have been detrimental to the community here, and it would have just ruined this country. It was a sacrifice. I'm like a Kennedy—it's not what your country can do for you, it's what you can do for your country." *1991: On why he didn't fight harder against charges of aggravated assault and possession of a deadly weapon that landed him in prison for two years and two months.*

"Hair and teeth. If a man got those two things, he got it all." *1994: On feeling good at sixty.*

"I went to see the Pope, and the Pope told me I should never come to church, because I can do more out there [on the street]." *1998*

"DOWNTOWN" JULIE BROWN
(Veejay)

"Normally I'm just a talking head. Now *everything's* talking." *1998: On her photo layout in* Playboy.

TINA BROWN
(Editor)

"We tried it as a cover. In light of the Gulf crisis, we thought a brunette was more appropriate." *1990: On why she put Cher on the cover of* Vanity Fair *rather than Marla Maples.*

"I've always believed in lapses of taste." *1998: The departing editor of the* New Yorker *answering charges that she vulgarized the venerable weekly.*

TONY BROWN
(TV Host & Author)

"And the Greek army!" *1997: On television's* Tony Brown's Journal *completing a list of famous homosexuals in history provided by University of California Professor Peter Duesberg.*

STEPHANIE BROWNING
(Singer)

"I always felt like an alien in Colorado, where people were eating granola and riding bikes all the time. When I got to Chicago, I found there are so many people here like me, who preferred smoking cigarettes and listening to jazz." *1997: On moving from Denver to Chicago.*

CARLA BRUNI
(Model)

"He's a fossil. His wife can keep him." *1992: On her brief affair with Mick Jagger.*

PETER BUCK
(Musician)

"We're all smart and we're all assholes." *1993: On why his group, R.E.M., is so successful.*

SANDRA BULLOCK
(Actress)

"I get such a rush going to the store, standing in front of the condom counter and going through them. I love the gold-coin ones. Every time I undo one, it reminds me of the chocolate candies from my childhood." *1994*

SANDRA BULLOCK (CONT'D)

"I just want to act. I don't want to know about the money." *1996*

"Directing a film was a good education. I learned how disgusting actors are." *1999: On shooting her first short film,* Making Sandwiches.

DELTA BURKE
(Actress)

"I found that putting on weight gave my life wonderful things. People began to listen to me rather than look at me, to appreciate my work. That gave me a voice for myself, and I began to become a voice for others." *1995*

EDWARD BURNS
(Actor & Screenwriter)

"I don't work—I make movies. Ten years from now I might be working in a diner." *1998*

GARY BUSEY
(Actor)

"My weirdest appendage is my brain and the invisible aspect of it, which is the mind." *1991*

"We displayed our belt buckles to see whose was the biggest. It was Texas bonding of the highest degree." *1993: On meeting fellow actor Tommy Lee Jones.*

BRETT BUTLER
(Actress)

"The first thing I did was to send money to the people I knew who need it. The other thing I did was what I call the 'Grand Slam': new tits, a big stereo and a painting I've wanted for a long time." *1994: On achieving success.*

ROBIN BYRD
(TV Host)

"He came up to my breasts—just the right height." *1993: On Michael J. Fox.*

DAVID BYRNE
(Musician & Singer)

"I noticed that some of my drawings as a child had something in common with the art of the Northwest American Indians." (1990)

"I had a math teacher in high school who included Lewis Carroll and *Alice in Wonderland* in his higher math studies. I thought, 'This guy knows what he's doing.'" *1992*

GABRIEL BYRNE
(Actor)

"It was either Voltaire or Charlie Sheen who said, 'We are born alone. We live alone. We die alone. And anything in between that can give us the illusion that we're not [alone], we cling to.'" *1998*

JAMES BYRNE
(World Wide Wrestling Federation Official)

"Wrestling is 100 percent entertainment. There's no such thing as fake entertainment." *1999: When asked if pro wrestling matches are phony.*

JOHN BYRUM
(Screenwriter)

"Steven was sitting on the floor of his bungalow playing with a toy plastic helicopter. Battery-operated. It flew around in circles. I start telling him my notions about the script, and he said, 'Oh, great idea!' Like a 12-year-old. Then he said, 'I gotta have my think music on,' so he put on this James Bond album soundtrack." *1998: Byrum, who was hired to rewrite the script for* Jaws *after a Peter Benchley script was rejected, remembering presenting his ideas to the film's director Steven Spielberg. Byrum passed on the project, and the script was eventually passed on to three other individuals who each wrote part of the script.*

C

JAMES CAAN
(Actor)

"I went to a shrink once, but I caught him going to a fortune teller, so I quit." *1990*

"Forget absence makes the heart grow fonder. Absence makes them think you're dead." *1990: On giving up acting for a short time.*

"My idea of roughing it is watching TV without a clicker." *1990*

HERB CAEN
(Newspaper Columnist)

"I've loved this town before I was born, and I'll love it after I'm gone. One day if I do go to heaven, I'm going to do what every San Franciscan does who goes to heaven—he looks around and says, 'It ain't bad, but it ain't San Francisco." *1997: The celebrated columnist for the* San Francisco Chronicle, *who died February 1, 1997.*

NICHOLAS CAGE
(Actor)

"Let's talk about what drives America, what keeps it going. I've got the answer. Two words. Money and sex. Most men want sex. They need to make money to have sex. Most women want money. They need money to feather their nesting instincts, to raise a comfortable family. A rich man is as attractive to a woman as a beautiful woman is to a man. That, in a nutshell, is my interpretation of the American economy. Can you dig it?" *1991*

"If a rocket was going to planet Xenon to start a new world, I doubt there'd be a single actor in it. It's easy to be humble when you consider the actor's role in society—basically I'm a song-and-dance man." *1992*

"For a long time I felt like an anarchist, wanting to destroy everything which seemed in the way. But that's a hard label to live up to. I don't want to be wild every day. I want to sit at home and play fire truck with my son." *1993*

"I have enormous anxiety because I work so much and don't get to spend as much time with my [3-year-old] son as I'd like. I talked to my psychiatrist about it, and she said that soldiers go away for their jobs, so it's OK for me to go away, too." *1994*

"Let's just put it this way—I just don't want to come back as a dashboard. That I don't want to come back as. But I have a feeling that could be more likely than not." *1994: On what he hopes not to be in his next life.*

"I married the person that I would want to be if I was a woman. I have that much respect for her." *1995*

"I would have loved to be in *Dracula*. Dracula is one of my favorite characters in literature. Much of my lifestyle is modeled after him. I don't drink

blood, but otherwise . . . I just admire the sensibility. The Gothic decor of my homes is inspired by it. To me, Dracula is love in exile. I'm very inspired by that idea." *1996*

"There's a strange mixture of pride and competition that I feel in the Coppola family. Very intense. We come from a long line of robbers and highwaymen in Italy. Killers, even. There is also a lot of creativity." *1996: Cage was born Nicholas Coppola.*

"There always was this strange dynamic with my father. He's given me so much, but there's this thing. I don't know how to explain it, but I think it has something to do with my mother telling him I wasn't his kid." *1996*

"We take our afflictions and we transform them into a place where they can be . . . be glorified. When the fact of the matter is, historically, we're all street urchins. Gypsies. We came out of the gutter. We've become so glorified in the movie-star system that it's become this artificial royalty, which, if you look at the roots of it, is completely preposterous. The truth is that we're circus clowns." *1998*

DON CAGLIONE
(Makeup Artist)

"Look, Madonna must have the most valuable bust in the business. I'll bet each one of those honeys is worth six, maybe seven million. What if she has an allergic reaction to glue? What if we discolor a breast or inflict some kind of permanent damage? Not only will we be sued, we'll become known as the two schmucks who destroyed a national treasure." *1990: Caglione worked with Doug Drexel as makeup men on the set of* Dick Tracy *in charge of gluing down Madonna's breasts to keep them from popping out of her Breathless Mahoney décolletage.*

DEAN CAIN
(Actor)

"In football it was this: You're a piece of meat. And in acting it's this: You're a piece of meat." *1995: Cain was a football star at Princeton.*

DEAN CAIN (CONT'D)

"A lot of beautiful people are stupid. There's a tremendous amount of idiots who look so good it's frightening. But if people perceive me as some kind of idiot, that's their mistake." *1996*

MICHAEL CAINE
(Actor)

"People were always amazed at the success I had with women even though I wasn't handsome or had a great body. It's because I'm a talker. So, no, I'm not sexy, but I can talk sexy." *1992*

"If you're playing two lovers and the woman is holding up the bloody blanket, you're thinking, 'Why is she holding it up? She just slept with the guy, what's she trying to hide her breasts for?' She's hiding them because the actress has in her contract that she doesn't have to show her breasts or something. . . . Plus, if the woman's got breasts, who the hell is looking at me? I'm busting my butt here for nothing." *1999: On why he doesn't like to do topless love scenes.*

JAMES CAMERON
(Director)

"History is just a consensus hallucination." *1998: Cameron directed* Titanic.

"I told him it's a lot easier doing what you've been doing than to do Jimmy Stewart." *1998: On how he persuaded the reticent Leonardo DiCaprio to take the role of the dashing, upbeat Jack Dawson in* Titanic—*a role that seemed too easy and generic for an actor attracted to troubled, neurotic men. DiCaprio signed on and the rest is history.*

"Our female CFO, all female executives, the secretaries, I suddenly found everyone in the room [was looking at him]. I thought, 'Hmmm, this is a little odd.' " *1998: On how lead actor Leonardo DiCaprio initially caught his attention—not through his work in movies but for the electricity he generated the first time he visited Cameron's office.*

"I'm the king of the world." *1998: After winning an Academy Award for directing* Titanic.

"Forget about Clinton—how do we impeach Kenneth Turan?" *1998: In a letter to the* Los Angeles Times *about its film critic, who panned* Titanic.

"Leo has a questioning spirit. He's interested in the human condition." *1998: Praising Leonardo DiCaprio.*

"I felt that it was kind of a snub, not of the film per se, but of all the other people who did care and had sweated blood for the movie. So I kept calling and saying, 'You gotta go for the team, and frankly, you have to go for yourself, because the consequences of not going will be that you're gonna look like a spoiled punk.' So he didn't go, and he looked like a spoiled punk. And Leo knows I feel that way, so I'm not saying anything out of school. He agonized over it. . . . The message I got on my machine, like, the day before (was): 'It just ain't me, bro.' Apparently, getting $4 million to do a juice ad that airs only in Japan is him, going to the Oscars is not." *1998: On Leonardo DiCaprio's Oscar night no-show.*

"I've been to the bottom of the ocean, and I think Hollywood is stranger." *1998*

LUTHER CAMPBELL
(Rapper)

"That's the reason why we do two diff'rent versions. I mean, you know, we have a sense of mind. I mean, we all have kids here. That's why we make a clean version for the kids and an adult version for the adults. That's the reason why we do two different versions. I mean, you know, there's a lotta people that don't do two diff'rent versions. That's why we the first ones that adopt the sticker program. Some of you people might don't want to write that down in your newspapers and in your magazines and let these right-wing jerks know what's goin' on, y'know. But I would appreciate it if y'all do write that down: We were the first to make two diff'rent versions and the first to make a sticker to put on our album." *1990*

"There was a whole lot of artistic value in it." *1992: Admitting that during a concert a woman performed oral sex with him on stage.*

DANNY CANNON
(Director)

"I'd rather stick needles in my eyes." *1995: After directing Sylvester Stallone in* Judge Dredd, *responding to the question if he'd ever work with Stallone again.*

BEN CAREY
(Author)

"Firing up your erotic imagination is in some ways similar to concentrating on a memory, a dream or the threat of an intricate plot. Distractions lurk like land mines. One frame of the *McNeil/Lehrer News Hour* can bring down the whole rigging." *1995: Advice on how to improve your sex life.*

DREW CAREY
(Actor & Comedian)

"I know this sounds bizarre, but I think the world would be a safer place if everyone had a gun." *1997*

JUDY CARNE
(Actress)

"John Waters says he'll make me into a cult figure. I always thought I was a cunt figure." *1991*

CALEB CARR
(Author)

"I got stuck in a conversation with [George] Plimpton, who is a very nice man, but deeply enamored of his own stories. He couldn't give a damn about anybody else's stories, unless they happened to be fairly young and have very large breasts." *1997: Describing one of the few "industry" parties he attended. It was hosted by* The Paris Review *and its editor, George Plimpton.*

JIM CARREY
(Actor)

"I prayed to God that I would have depth as an artist and have things to say." *1994*

"Sometimes you find old jewelry." *1998: On the benefits of colonic irrigation.*

JOHNNY CARSON
(TV Talk-show Host)

"On the other hand, Jerry Brown smoked pot 25 years ago and forgot to exhale." *1992: On presidential candidate Bill Clinton's assertion that he smoked pot but never inhaled.*

HELENA BONHAM CARTER
(Actress)

"I don't actually think I'm very good. But I don't have very good judgment, and it's nice to think I might be wrong." *1998: Upon winning the Best Actress award at the National Board of Review ceremonies in New York.*

"It's like a wedding, but you have no idea if you'll be jilted at the altar—and he's only a 9-inch groom." *1999: On attending the Academy Awards ceremony as a nominee.*

NELL CARTER
(Singer & Actress)

"I've had diseases that lasted longer than my marriages." *1993*

BARBARA CARTLAND
(Writer)

"So many of my contemporaries are either dead or gaga." *1990*

JOHNNY CASH
(Singer)

"I thank God we live in a country where you have the right to burn the flag if you want to. And I thank God we live in a country where we have the right to keep and bear arms—so I can shoot you if you try to burn mine." *1990*

"I don't think there'll be any banjos." *1997: On what kind of music he expects to hear in heaven.*

DAVID CASSIDY
(Singer & Actor)

"You know what they say: 'He who laughs last, laughs last.'" *1998*

"Trip falling out of bed, crawl to the sink and peel residue of makeup from my eyes." *1998: On his typical morning.*

"It's lonely at the top. But it's lonelier at the bottom." *1999*

DICK CAVETT
(TV Talk-show Host)

"Tell us about the North Viet Cong." *1990: Asking Morley Safer about Vietnam. There was no such thing as a North Viet Cong.*

LACY CHABERT
(Actress)

"I've grown two inches." *1995: The twelve-year-old actress on how she's grown in her one year on the TV show* Party of Five.

VICTOR CHAO
(Club Owner)
"The bill can easily go up to 30 bucks for keeping your finger on the trigger for three seconds. Sometimes people cry when they see the bill." *1998: The owner of a club in Phnom Penh, Cambodia, where patrons can shoot machine guns and are charged by the bullet.*

RAY CHARLES
(Musician & Singer)
"I went to hear them one time in England. They had Billy Preston, who used to work with me. That's why I went there. The music, they had it so loud that when I came out, I literally scared myself to death because I couldn't hear. I thought I was losing my hearing . . . I'm already blind. I can't be no Helen Keller." *1999: On first hearing the Rolling Stones.*

HENG-MING CHEN
(Religious Cult Leader)
"God will come. Meat eaters might not be able to see Him." *1998: The wisdom of the Taiwanese spiritual sect leader, who believed God would arrive in Garland, Texas, at 10:00 A.M. on March 31, 1998. The first sign of God's appearance was to be on local access television channel 18.*

"The world of the spiritual is invisible. It's very difficult to explain what is going on." *1998: After God failed to appear in Garland, Texas, on March 31, 1998.*

"Because we did not see God's message on Channel 18 tonight, my predictions of God arriving on March 31 can be considered nonsense. But don't call us liars. Keep watching." *1998: After his predictions of God's appearance in Garland, Texas, proved premature.*

"I would rather you don't believe what I say anymore." *1998*

CHER
(Singer & Actress)
"The trouble with some women is that they get all excited about nothing—and then marry him." *1994*

"He was smart enough to turn an introverted sixteen-year-old girl and a scrawny Italian guy with a bad voice into the most beloved television couple of this generation." *1998: In a funeral eulogy for her former husband Sonny Bono, on his image as not terribly bright.*

"I hate my 50s. They suck. I never felt older until I hit 50. And the way I first noticed was through my work. When I was 40, I was playing opposite somebody who was 21, and nobody noticed. But at 45, as you start to look older, all you can do is look good for your age. There's a certain span of time—and I'm very much there—when you have to wait till you can play the Shirley MacLaine/Anne Bancroft roles. So what am I supposed to do. Like, go camping for 10 years?" *1998*

"You've been there, done that: bought the T-shirt, got the poster, *been* the poster." *1998: On fame.*

"I looked at myself onscreen and thought, shit, I'm all nose." *1999: On her motivation for plastic surgery.*

MEILIEN CHI
(Follower of Heng-Ming Chen)
"If God does come, you'd regret it for the rest of your life." *1998: Chi, thirty, who has a master's degree and studied in New York, on why she joined the religious sect headed by Taiwanese leader Heng-Ming Chen, and then moved to Garland, Texas. Chen believed God would land in the Dallas suburb on March 31, 1998, at 10:00 A.M. and she didn't want to regret not being there for the event for the rest of her life.*

JULIA CHILD
(Chef & Author)
"I just went to my 60th reunion at Smith College and hated every minute of it. Everyone was old and let their hair go gray and didn't wear any makeup. I hated it. I'm never going back to another one." *1995*

"Anything that says 'healthy' I stay away from . . . Giving up butter, for instance, means that in about two years you will be covered with dandruff." *1997*

MARGARET CHO
(Comedienne)

"I don't have his tapes but once I was on the Stair-Master next to him at the gym, and I felt his power." *1994: On infomercial guru Tony Robbins.*

"I've never been stopped by the police, but one time my Japanese friend and I were stopped by a group of kids who yelled, 'Chinos ruin everything!' We weren't angry because we weren't sure whether they were talking about us or the pants. See, they could have been really racist or just fashion conscious." *1999*

ANNABEL CHONG
(Porn Star)

"It's the best way to have lots of sex without commitment. These guys don't need to sleep over and they won't be calling me twenty-four hours a day." *1995: Chong, twenty-two, had sex with 251 men in one day in Los Angeles, breaking the old record of 120 set in 1991 by a sex worker in Amsterdam.*

DEEPAK CHOPRA
(Guru)

"Half the U.S. Congress has prostate cancer because they express their male energy only through predatory intelligence." *1996*

"Maybe I should be enlightened enough to say it doesn't matter." *1997: On filing a $10 million lawsuit against parties he claims conspired to defame him.*

MICHAEL CHOW
(Owner of Mr. Chow's Restaurants)

"Is this a star-system restaurant? *Yes.* But a regular can be a star. It's not literally about stars. Of course, that helps. The only restaurant that has no star system is McDonald's." *1998: On the Mr. Chow's restaurant in Los Angeles.*

"My motivation has never been money. It's an idea. When I started in restaurants, the whole idea of society people eating in a restaurant was fairly new. The good restaurants had formerly been in hotels, and you only went to them on birthdays and anniversaries. And still, not everyone sees glamour here. I'll never forget the night, not long ago, when Elizabeth Taylor looked around and suddenly pronounced, '*What a dump!*'" *1998*

CONNIE CHUNG
(Newswoman)

"Do you think John Kennedy Jr. is in heaven with his mother and father now?" *1999: Questioning Billy Graham following the death of JFK Jr.*

LA CICCIOLINA
(Italian Porn Star & Politician)

"When I die I want to be buried not in a wooden casket, but nude, standing up, close to the surface of the earth, so that I can change into a butterfly or I can give life to a flower." *1992*

TOM CLANCY
(Writer)

"What can you say about a country that tolerates homosexuals but not smokers? I never gave anyone AIDS." *1990*

"He reached into a pocket, moving his hand slowly and withdrawing a pair of food bars. Nothing he'd eaten by choice in any other place, but it was vital now. He tore off the plastic wrappers with his teeth and chewed them up slowly. The strength they imparted to his body was probably as much psychological as real, but both factors had their uses, as his body had to deal with both fatigue and stress." *1993: In his best-selling book* Without Remorse, *describing how his hero, John Kelley, eats plastic wrappers from food bars for physical and psychological nourishment.*

"Congress can't balance the budget or fix the economy, so what do they do? They ban smoking on all airplanes." *1994*

"This is America, and people are free to be idiots. But you have to really listen, because every now and then the idiot turns out to be right." *1994*

"Money has made me no different. For better or worse, I am the same jerk I always was." *1994*

"I don't want to sound commercial, but I'm in it for the money, not the awards. This is my job. It's how I feed my family. Shakespeare did the same thing. It's an honorable tradition. What do I care if someone reads my books a hundred years from now? I will be dead. I will not be walking the earth. And it's kind of hard to make money when you're dead." *1994*

ERIC CLAPTON
(Singer & Musician)

"After Jimi [Hendrix] died, I resented people liking Hendrix, because I felt so possessive about him. It was like, you're talking about my mother and you know what color her underwear are." *1994*

"It sounds strange for me to be saying this, but I've come around to the idea that sex is really just for procreation." *1994*

JIM CLARK
(Businessman, Founder of Netscape and Healtheon)

"Business is about making money and money better be the top objective. It is for me. I grew up poor and I've learned that money can make you a lot happier. No matter how much money you have, there's always the next thing you might enjoy." *1999*

ANDREW DICE CLAY
(Comedian)

"This is the greatest country in the world. We let everybody in, and that gives me more comedic material." *1990*

ADAM CLAYTON
(Musician)

"I think it was a period of deciding where being mega was any way I wanted to live my life." *1992: On his year of reflection on life.*

GEORGE CLOONEY
(Actor)

"You sit around on a TV series and say, 'Really, I'm a film actor. I'm just doing television.' After 10 or 11 years, you have to admit that what you are is a TV actor." *1999*

JAMES COBURN
(Actor)

"You can do all that when I'm gone!" *1999: On what the seventy-year-old tells his forty-five-year-old wife when she suggests having children.*

PAULA COLE
(Singer)

"Well, I do sip herbal tea. I am someone who likes to garden, talk to my cats and be a wacky hippie bird lady. I am intelligent. I am a feminist. I never wear a bra—it's too binding. And I do swear and smoke pot and shake my ass. So I'm all of that. I am all that." *1998*

JACKIE COLLINS
(Writer)

"People in Hollywood don't read. They have people who do it for them." *1990*

"It's the herbs and spices and my essence that make it so special." *1994: On her prize-winning meatloaf.*

JOAN COLLINS
(Actress & Writer)

"I can't work unless everything is neat and tidy; pencils sharpened, fresh tablets; even my makeup tray has to be just so." *1991: On the difficulties of writing.*

"A million dollars sounds like a lot, but actually it isn't." *1996: Explaining why she could not return the $1.3 million advance Random House had given her—because she'd already spent it.*

MICHAEL COLLINS
(Astronaut & Writer)

"Munching on a hot dog, I tried to digest what the president had said—and not said." *Writing in* Mission to Mars.

PHIL COLLINS
(Singer)

"I don't understand why critics give me such a hard time. I guess I was at the end of the line when credibility was dished out. A lot of writers call my music meaningless crap, then add, 'but most people will like it.' If I were a member of the public, I'd be offended." *1990*

SEAN CONNERY
(Actor)

QUESTION: "I have been told that after the age of 60, balding men are very sexual and sensuous—do you believe that?"

CONNERY: "I wouldn't know. It's been years since I've been in bed with anybody over 60 who's balding." *1990*

DANE COOK
(Comedian)

"My dad used to say, 'Life is like pinball: Sometimes you tilt, sometimes you're special and sometimes, like me, you get an extra ball.'" *1995*

ALICE COOPER
(Musician)

"The guy's got a girl's name, and he wears makeup. What an original idea." *1998: On Marilyn Manson.*

DAVID COPPERFIELD
(Magician)

"She is smart. She's been a top model for five years—that takes a lot of intelligence." *1994: On his girlfriend, model Claudia Schiffer.*

FRANCIS FORD COPPOLA
(Producer & Director)

"Four months later, after all this tension, I wound up with my cast, Brando and Pacino. If I hadn't fought, I would have made a movie with Ernest Borgnine and Ryan O'Neal set in the '70s." *1998: The director of* The Godfather, *on the difficulties he had at Paramount Studios in getting the cast he wanted for his film. Coppola wanted and eventually got Marlon Brando, Robert Duvall, James Caan, and Al Pacino. Robert Evans, producer of the film, thought Pacino was too short to play Michael in the film and referred to him as "the Italian dwarf."*

"I have no interest in the *Godfather* movies. I'm tired of—I do something that people want, that they love, they beg me to do. Then they start attacking me, second-guessing me. That's why I like to cook. You work hard in the kitchen, usually people say, 'Ummmm, that was good,' not 'There's mildew on the rigatoni.'" *1998: Recalling his reluctance to direct a sequel to* The Godfather.

RICHARD CORLISS
(Film Critic)

"Because critics are beneath contempt, they think they are above reproach." *1992*

BILL COSBY
(Comedian)

"What did he ever do for black people?" *1991: Commenting on Abraham Lincoln.*

"People will frighten you about a graduation . . . because they use words you don't hear often . . . 'And we wish you Godspeed.' It is a warning, Godspeed. It means you are no longer welcome here at these prices." *1995: In a commencement address at Southern Methodist University.*

"I didn't hear any ignoromics spoken this morning. There are about 100 people and nobody said 'liberry.' Nobody said 'We bein' here.'" *1997: Speaking on ebonics at a gathering of the Congressional Black Caucus.*

"Get people from anywhere in the world, and they all have this negative view of the black man, because of what they've seen, not what they know. We are a proud people in this country. You don't have a light bulb or a steamboat without us. But how can you impress anybody when all your shows or movies or songs are about the pursuit of the flesh?" *1997*

BOB COSTAS
(TV Broadcaster)

"When you see Barbara Walters sitting at the foot of a bed with Dennis Rodman, and naming him one of her 10 most fascinating people of whatever year that was, you know that Barbara Walters has long since sold out. Because Barbara Walters doesn't remotely believe that Dennis Rodman is fascinating. What she thinks is fascinating is an 18.6 rating instead of a 16.4 rating, and if Dennis Rodman can help her get it, she's willing to do that. That's her version of Jerry Springer letting people throw chairs at one another." *1998*

ELVIS COSTELLO
(Musician & Singer)

"I was extremely overserious until I was about 25 and the drugs kicked in." *1996*

"Rock and roll had two effects on music. One was of tremendous liberation, and the other was a license for a lot of idiots to decry the efforts of more craftsman-like writers." *1999*

KEVIN COSTNER
(Actor)

"I've had some things to cheer about. I've had some things that people should never have to have

KEVIN COSTNER (CONT'D)

happen to them. But don't cry for me, Argentina." *1996*

"It took people almost an hour to get comfortable with the movie, to realize that despite what they had read about it, it was a really good movie. By that time, it was too late. They kept waiting to see a movie that wasn't any good." *1996: On* Waterworld.

RONNIE COX
(Actor)

"They wanted me to be in it. I basically had read the script. Need I say more?" *1994: On why he didn't appear in* Beverly Hills Cop 3.

CINDY CRAWFORD
(Model)

"It's funny—I talk about this mole so much I feel like it has its own personality. If it had a little mouth, I'd let it talk to you." *1992: On the mole above her lip.*

"I am into fast food. I am. But it suits me really well right now." *1994*

"We were working on a love scene for three nights and I kept thinking, 'This is not like real life.' You know, where it'd be over in three seconds and thank you very much! Movies set up unreal expectations for how fabulous it should be." *1995*

"I don't want to keep proving myself to the world anymore. I've done that." *1996*

"I do try to have a thought in my head, so that it's not like a blank stare." *1998: Responding to a question about what goes through her mind when she's having her picture taken.*

"Really? Like what?" *1998: When asked if her ABC special's title,* Sex with Cindy Crawford, *might suggest something.*

"Obviously, some things aren't quite as high or as perky as they were, but my body is a result of how I treated it, as opposed to what I was born with. I am really pleased with the pictures." *1998: On her photo layout in* Playboy.

"Sex is such a huge topic. I mean, we only scratched the surface, but we hope that people watching it will maybe get inspired to talk or experiment. If teens are watching with their parents, maybe they'll get excited and be able to ask a question." *1998: On her hopes for her ABC program,* Sex with Cindy Crawford.

"One of the things that we all kind of kept talking about—and I don't know if this is a good thing or a bad thing—was sex. I mean, people were giggling and, you know, blushing and poking each other. I was blushing myself at some of the stuff that transpired." *1998: Remembering her meeting with ABC brass to discuss a program she might do for them. The program they finally agreed on is called* Sex with Cindy Crawford.

"I don't know if I would have the guts to walk around with that butt. . . . Is it cultural, or what was she given in self-confidence that I wasn't?" *1998: On how actress Jennifer Lopez flaunts her ample derriere.*

"In some of those sites, I morph into a dog. I didn't really think that was so great." *1999: On why she started her own Web site partly because there were dozens of unauthorized ones.*

MICHAEL CRICHTON
(Writer)

"Why did God invent man? Because it's too hard to get a vibrator to do the lawn." *1992*

"I used to think that Hollywood was fast women and fast cars, but it's really just fast food." *1996*

"I remember all the claims for television—about how it was going to produce universal education and there was going to be so much exposure to the world. Some of those claims have come true, but the overwhelming majority of the claims were just baloney. It's difficult now to make the claim that television is an educational medium. It's an advertising medium." *1999*

"People feel so enslaved by technology that they will stop having sex to answer the telephone. What could be so important? Who's calling, and who cares?" *1999*

"All professions look bad in the movies. Lawyers are all unscrupulous and doctors are all uncaring. Psychiatrists are all crazy and politicians are all corrupt." *1999: Defending himself against charges at a meeting of the American Association for the Advancement of Science, which stated that* Jurassic Park *had made scientists look bad.*

ROBERT X. CRINGLEY
(Writer)
"People in Silicon Valley are trapped in Silicon Valley. They can't afford to be away from the action. If they move away they're out of the buzz, they're no longer of the tribe. They have to stay. So you have all these smart, incredibly rich people with very marginal social skills crammed into a single peninsula, unable to leave. You have all these incredibly rich people, but there are no houses available, so you have the billionaire living down the street because he *has* to be on that street. So there it is. They leave, it's like leaving Shangri-La, and all of a sudden they age and die." *1998: On northern California's Silicon Valley.*

QUENTIN CRISP
(Writer)
"Sex was invented by the Beatles and was propagated by Madison Avenue." *1990*

"I hate music. There's too much music everywhere. It's horrible stuff, the most noise conveying the least information. Kids today are violent because they have no inner life; they have no inner life because they have no thoughts; they have no thoughts because they know no words; they know no words because they never speak; and they never speak because the music's too loud." *1997*

"I don't like to take a suitcase on an airplane because they always open it and steal all your clothes." *1997*

"They thought I went up and down the breadth of the land issuing manifestos. When they found out I never mentioned homosexuality at all, their love for me died in an instant. I'm afraid I also lost the love of the entire homosexual community when I said that Princess Diana was trash and got what she deserved." *1999: On reasons for the bad reviews he received in San Francisco for his performance of* An Evening with Quentin Crisp.

WALTER CRONKITE
(Retired News Anchor)
"What did Cronkite die of?" *1999: To his wife, Betsy, after a woman approached him in an airport and observed, "You know, you look a lot like Walter Cronkite before he died, only a bit heavier." Betsy Cronkite answered her husband's question with a single word—"thinness."*

DAVID CROSBY
(Singer & Musician)
"I'm not a total pacifist, you know. I've shot at people. I missed, but I shot at them. I'm sort of glad I missed." *1995*

"We changed the value systems in America substantially. . . . We stopped the war. And the only thing I would do differently is not waste all that time on the dope." *1995: On youth in the '60s.*

GARY CROSBY
(Celebrity Son)
"Wouldn't you know it? I finally got my shit together. I stopped drinking. I stopped smoking. I stopped fighting the fact that Bing Crosby was my father. And now look what's happened." *1995: Two weeks before his death from complications of lung cancer.*

SHERYL CROW
(Singer)
"If you want to turn on your boyfriend get naked and strap on an accordion." *1997: To a mostly thirteen-year-old-female audience at the Z-100 Jingle Ball benefit. Her remark was met with a confused silence.*

TOM CRUISE
(Actor)
"I've heard that I'm a misogynist. I'm a homosexual. I'm brainless. How can I be all of these things?" *1994*

"The guy who taught me to race cars would always say to me that he didn't know whether I was the smartest guy around or the dumbest." *1994*

TOM CRUISE (CONT'D)

"I have a theory—if it's meant for them, then it wasn't meant to be for me." *1997: On why he doesn't regret not taking certain film roles that other stars turned into hits.*

"People say: 'You've lost 40, 60, 80 million dollars. You've lost all this money. You've lost all this time.' I don't understand that kind of thinking. I've been doing this for 18 years. Yeah, I make money. I make a lot of money. And money's wonderful and nice. But that does not enter into why I make movies. There are some things you don't do for money. I know that's hard to believe. To have a chance to work with Stanley Kubrick, that's worth it for me." *1998: On the fifteen months he spent making the film* Eyes Wide Shut *with Stanley Kubrick.*

BILLY CRYSTAL
(Actor & Comedian)

"A year ago, the White House was complaining there was too much sex in Hollywood. Times change." *1998: At the Academy Awards ceremonies in March.*

MACAULAY CULKIN
(Actor)

"I'm not crazy about the stuff. But money is money." *1992*

"Whenever I need money, I just ask my mother and—bang!" *1993*

ALAN CUMMINGS
(Actor)

"Then Meryl Streep told me that she always admired my work. Meryl Streep admires my work. I had to go have a lie down after that." *1998: The Briton who plays the M.C. in a Broadway revival of the musical* Cabaret, *on his surprise at being visited backstage by a stream of celebrities.*

JANE CURTIN
(Actress & Comedienne)

"I don't watch it. I don't stay up that late, frankly." *1999: The original* Saturday Night Live *cast member when asked about the current show.*

JAMIE LEE CURTIS
(Actress)

"I did what anybody would do if they were going to dance around in a G-string and bra in front of 50 men for four days in a row: I didn't eat very much for a month." *1994: On her role in* True Lies.

"In some circles, I'm as famous for my Caesar salads as I am for my breasts." *1996*

TONY CURTIS
(Actor)

"I can't wait to find out how it ends." *1994: On reading his own autobiography.*

"Strippers don't screw any more than secretaries do. And I don't remember one occasion when I had a good time with an actress. They almost made you sign a paper: 'I hereby declare that since I let you screw me, you must make sure that I am introduced to Mr. Bob Goldstein, producer, Universal Pictures.' She'd let you have three screws, but if you didn't produce, you were out of there." *1996*

"Can you imagine me with a woman old enough to be my wife? No, really. I'm serious. Can you imagine me walking into Spago with a 70-year-old woman? Forget it. Fuck that! I don't have that spirit. My girlfriend is 25 years old—*perfect*." *1996: Curtis, at seventy.*

"I like you. You don't want to know how big my dick is, and you don't want to know who I fucked and who I didn't fuck. Although, just between you and me, my friend, I fucked them all." *1996: Speaking to Tom Junod, who was interviewing him for an article in* GQ.

"When you're making *Some Like It Hot* and Marilyn Monroe sticks her tongue in your mouth all the way down to your navel, that's not moviemaking, my friend, that's life." *1996*

"The doctor told me, 'This injection will give you an erection for two hours.' I said, 'Doctor, that will be one hour and fifty-seven minutes longer than I've ever had.'" *1996: On shots for impotence.*

JOHN CUSACK
(Actor)

"I think any actor can probably identify with being a professional liar. You don't always look at yourself that way, but I know on a lot of days I do." *1990*

BILLY RAY CYRUS
(Singer)

"Neil Diamond was saying how if you believe in yourself and believe in your dreams, then you will have everything you want. Just that second, my voice said to me, 'There's your answer. Use your music to do something positive.' And I knew, right then, this is my calling." *1993: On how at a Neil Diamond concert he received a revelation and decided to give up his dream of playing professional baseball and instead become a country-western singer.*

D

CHUCK D
(Rapper)

"If the racial situation isn't turned around you'll see mayhem in 5 or 10 years, you'll start seein' presidents, their heads bein' chopped off, you know, congressmen bein' slain." *1992*

"I think right now we're seein' a lot of strange things happen, especially to black leaders, people of importance, you know, Muhammad Ali, the speech problem; Richard Pryor, multiple sclerosis; the Magic Johnson incident. All the way down to Bo Jackson's hip injury. Who's to say, we're next or what? It just seems like one big government conspiracy." *1992*

MIKE D
(Rapper)

"I just don't understand white people. White people like stuff that is so overtly wack: Soul Asylum, Rush, *Sports Illustrated*." *1994: Beastie Boy Mike D is white.*

EVAN DANDO
(Musician & Singer)

"See, I've been smoking so much pot lately I can't remember." *1996: On how long he's been off heroin.*

CLAIRE DANES
(Actress)

"I keep asking people, 'It's really difficult to be kicked out of Yale, right?' " *1998: On being accepted to Yale University.*

TED DANSON
(Actor)

"I was told, 'The Mayor's coming, so be careful—don't do any political jokes—just do nigger jokes.' " *1993: While appearing in blackface at a Friar's Club Roast for Whoopi Goldberg. Danson made his comment shortly before the arrival of Mayor David Dinkins.*

"It's a great dance. Mary's masculine side and my feminine side get along fantastically and vice versa. We both like wearing pants, and we both get a thrill out of a garter belt once in a while." *1996: On his marriage to actress Mary Steenburgen.*

TERRENCE TRENT D'ARBY
(Singer)

"Every time I open my mouth I ruin my career." *1991*

"An artist should have his heart in one hand and his nuts in the other." *1993*

LARRY DAVID
(Writer)

"I've always loathed rich people, so I've become a person who I've loathed. And I loathed myself even when I wasn't that person, which makes it doubly difficult, if you can follow me." *1998: David is the co-creator of* Seinfeld.)

PATTY DAVIS
(Writer)

"At some point I'll just tell them, 'It's a generational thing' and hope they accept it. My father will probably say, 'That's what makes horse races' and I'll have no idea what he means. I don't think he does, either." *1994: On what she'll tell her mom and dad—Nancy and Ronald Reagan—about her nude layout in* Playboy *magazine.*

ELLEN DEGENERES
(Actress & Comedienne)

"Well, I drank a little too much before seeing Diana Ross, and I was so loaded, I thought the

ELLEN DEGENERES (CONT'D)

Supremes were with her. My friends said that there was no one else onstage. But I saw three women behind her, and they were moving so smoothly together." *1995*

"You have to stay in shape. My grandmother, she started walking five miles a day when she was 60. She's 97 today and we don't know where the hell she is." *1997*

DANA DELANY
(Actress)

"There's something about white Jockeys that's so male and gross that I like. There's something dirty-sexy about them. And if they have stains on them, that's better." *1994*

"The problem is, where do you find drama in condoms and diaphragms?" *1995: On playing Planned Parenthood founder Margaret Sanger in a television drama.*

DON DELILLO
(Writer)

"I didn't study much of anything. I majored in something called communication arts." *1991: On his years at Fordham University.*

JERRY DELLA FEMINA
(Advertising Executive)

"These media moguls really don't have many other games to play. . . . Years ago, they would have been content to buy themselves a Rolls-Royce." *1998: On media mogul Ted Turner's unsuccessful efforts to block Rupert Murdoch's purchase of the L.A. Dodgers.*

REBECCA DE MORNAY
(Actress)

"I get infuriated with men who don't do what you want them to do and then are surprised when they don't get what they want." *1993*

ROBERT DE NIRO
(Actor)

"I will never come back to France again. I'm going to tell my friends not to come either." *1998: Following a nine-hour interrogation by French officials who suspected him of involvement in a prostitution ring after finding his name in a seized address book.*

JUDI DENCH
(Actress)

"He'd literally sigh with relief every time I'd get off." *1998: On the horse she rode in her film* Mrs. Brown, *and the burden of the weight of her costume when she played Queen Victoria.*

BRIAN DENNEHY
(Actor)

"Sensitivity is a virtue of very low order, it seems to me, and we've all begun to pay too much attention to it." *1994*

GERARD DEPARDIEU
(Actor)

"Anytime I'm acting, I play with my feminine side. I'm much more open when I think as a woman than when I think as a man. Men are good only for going off to war, the idiots. I prefer to stay at home and do a bit of cooking." *1990*

"My wife. She told me that a guy who doesn't drink and who doesn't eat pork just because he's a Muslim is a real dud. I said, 'You know, you're absolutely right.'" *1990*

JOHNNY DEPP
(Actor)

"Baltimore is like a very magical belly button with this great suction and pulls all this really strange lint into it. That's my opinion. I love Baltimore." *1990*

"If I could have another mouth grafted onto my face to smoke more, I would." *1993*

"Part of me wants to walk a dog and change a diaper, and the other part wants to go and eat dirt somewhere." *1993*

"I made a decision when I was in my teens that my body is a journal. It's a journal of skin." *1993*

"Insanity and chain smoking." *1994: On what he inherited from his parents.*

"If someone were to harm my family or someone I love, I would eat them." *1995*

"I'm especially scared of boogers. Snot freaks me out. If someone ever showed me a booger, I'd smash their face." *1995*

"She's got that high-water booty. A high-water booty is important. And feet. Feet are very important." *1997: Counting the ways he loves Kate Moss.*

"It's demeaning when people talk about my looks. I think I usually look like shit, and most people would agree." *1998*

"I love people. And when you love people that much that you're disappointed in them every day, that love can turn to hate in a flash of a second." *1998*

"You can't be normal. You just can't hang out and have a cup of coffee and pick your nose, you know." *1999: On the price of fame.*

BO DEREK
(Actress)
"I have no experience, and I guess they're different from dogs and horses." *Reflecting on children for her new role as a TV mom.*

LAURA DERN
(Actress)
"He's a cool-cantaloupe cat and the most dedicated actor I've ever worked with. He has no problems traveling to Pluto." *1990: On actor Crispin Glover.*

"In *Wild at Heart* I met David Lynch on Jupiter, and we were on that planet together." *1990*

"You're gonna be scared by this movie [*Wild at Heart*]. I went to Jupiter with this one. It was so much fun. That's the other thing that's scary. I went to Jupiter, and it is cool on Jupiter." *1990*

"Probably the telephone. I know people who are really good at having five-minute conversations, but I can't do that. If it's a friend, I want to talk an hour. I spend a lot of time on the phone when I could be getting a degree or learning another language." *1998: On her worst habit.*

NEIL DIAMOND
(Singer & Musician)
"When I was a kid, I used to steal all the time. We were from Brooklyn. If my mom needed a turkey, you'd go and steal a turkey and keep the money and buy ice cream. . . . I just did normal things kids do in Brooklyn." *1994*

"Really, the only person who knows what kind of sex symbol I am is my wife. And she's not that impressed, between you and me." *1994*

IRMELIN DICAPRIO
(Mother of Actor)
"Why should he go? He wasn't nominated." *1998: The mother of Leonardo DiCaprio when asked if her son who did not receive one of* Titanic's *fourteen nominations, would attend the Oscars.*

LEONARDO DICAPRIO
(Actor)
"When you're my age your hormones are just kicking in and there's not much besides sex on your mind." *1998*

"I was expecting a little more from ol' Sharon, y'know? Actually, she hurt my lip." *1998: Recalling his screen kiss with Sharon Stone.*

"Luckily I outgrew the bed but, sadly, not before I developed dorsal spines on my penis." *1998: Describing how the bed he slept in during his boyhood years was merely a bed frame supported by cases of comic books. DiCaprio says he was a big fan of underground comics since boyhood, when his father was "in the Commix trade." As a result of reading underground comics, he says, "I found myself immune to the sophomoric antics of* Curious George *or the coy alliteration of* Cat in the Hat.*"

PHYLLIS DILLER
(Comedienne)
"My only original parts are my elbows." *1995: On her extensive plastic surgery.*

"Tony Randall and I were once doing a variety show together, and the first thing he said to me was something about fellatio. I don't think I'd ever heard that word before, and I said, 'I haven't read much Shakespeare.'" *1996*

SHANNEN DOHERTY
(Actress)

"Don't judge me for who I am, because everybody makes mistakes." *1993*

"Sometimes life sucks, but you can survive it. Turn it into a positive. People will let you down. In the end, you have yourself and your family. The rest of the time, just say, 'Whatever.'" *1995*

"She goes through something every woman goes through: having a boyfriend who sits around playing Sega all day and not paying enough attention to you. We've all been there." *1995: On a character she played in a film.*

"I love Dan Quayle. And he is not stupid—he's a very intelligent man who can definitely hold a conversation with your biggest intellectual you want to put up against him." *1996*

"I feel bad that I smoke now, but maybe you can do the right thing for only so long and then you try exactly what you said you never would, and you end up getting hooked." *1996*

"Doesn't every actor write poetry? I call it verbal vomit." *1996*

"I'm not a huge fan of tight short skirts that show your ass. And when I see a man in really tight jeans I cringe. I'm definitely worried about what it's doing to—I'm going to sound a little crass—doing to their balls." *1996*

"We're so damn conservative all day that when you finally get us in the bedroom, we're absolute animals." *1996: On why Republicans have better sex.*

BOB DOLE
(Politician)

"I've got to get to the airport." *1998: Upon declining to pause long enough to have his photo taken with Marilyn Manson, a fellow guest on David Letterman's* The Late Show. *"It's probably in his best interest not to have his picture taken with me," Manson responded sympathetically.*

MICKEY DOLENZ
(Drummer)

"It took a year to learn the drums. And, with all respect to great drummers, it isn't exactly brain surgery." *1993*

PHIL DONAHUE
(TV Talk-show Host)

"In 3,000 shows, I've only walked out three times with my fly open." *1990*

"Anyone can be a journalist, even me. You don't have to pee in a bottle. You don't have to pass a test. Do we do silly things? Do we throw spaghetti at each other? Do we wrestle with women in the mud? Yes. So what? Don't watch that day! Spare me this 'ain't it awful, we're all going to hell.'" *1996*

"In 1967, there were no automobile recalls. In 1967, you could smoke in an elevator. In 1967, we never thought we would lose a war. In 1967, AIDS was a verb, or a plural noun. In 1967, you could harass your secretary and there was nothing she could do about it." *1996: During the taping of his last show on how the world has changed since his first show.*

ERIC DOUGLAS
(Son of Kirk and Brother of Michael)

"If you can't be rude or annoying in a mental hospital, where can you be rude and annoying?" *1998: After being cleared of allegations that he harassed a young girl at a psychiatric hospital.*

KIRK DOUGLAS
(Actor)

"First Dan Quayle attacks Murphy Brown as if a television character were a real person. Then, of course, Murphy Brown attacked Dan Quayle as if he were a real person." *1992*

MICHAEL DOUGLAS
(Actor)

"At any given moment, any one of them could've become our proctologist." *1992: On the people present during filming of the sex scenes in* Basic Instinct.

ROBERT DOWNEY, JR.
(Actor)

"I don't know what to say except I hope they're all 100 percent correct." *1998: On the tendency of costars to refer to him as a genius.*

"When no girls were around, my best friend and I would make out with each other as a last resort." *1999: On his youthful high jinks.*

"After I got in a fight I was down in this discipline module, which is like a hole. Three times a day, you see a pair of hands and some food comes in. It's pretty awful. One day it opens and there was this lieutenant, with some deputy he'd brought to meet me. I hadn't had a shower in five days. I was sleeping in my clothes, my hair was all fucked up. But that Hollywood big-shot entertainer thing came in, and I thought, 'Well, I'd better come to. I have company.' And this guy came in and said, 'Listen, I know you don't have a lot to read in here. I hope I wouldn't be crossing the line if I brought a script for you. It's about unicorns. It's not what you think, there's a very human element to it.'" *1999: On his life in jail.*

RICHARD DREYFUSS
(Actor)

"We started the film without a script, without a cast, and without a shark." *1998: Remembering the first days of the making of the film* Jaws *in which he played a starring role.*

DAVID DUCHOVNY
(Actor)

"I haven't had any experience with UFOs. But paranormal life seems to be all around me. I grew up on the Lower East Side in New York." *1993*

"I think when I was younger, I wanted to tell everybody everything because I thought I was so damn interesting. Then I heard the snoring." *1995*

"Just total focus. Total concentration. Maybe one ear goes back to figure something out." *1998: On what he's learned about acting from his dog.*

"I really like gratuitous nudity. I hate when people go, 'I'll only do it if it makes sense for the movie.' That's such a crock. It never makes sense. So I like it—the more gratuitous, the better." *1998*

"He said he had watched *X-Files* but found the plots a bit convoluted and couldn't always understand them." *1998: The* X-Files *star, on meeting Prince Charles.*

ROBERT DUVALL
(Actor)

"I hear she spends 95 percent of her day in the bathroom. But once she's there, she knows what to do." *1998: Praising his* Apostle *co-star Farrah Fawcett.*

BOB DYLAN
(Singer & Musician)

"Don't stop doing what you're doing, man. We're all inspired by you." *1990: Speaking to Barry Manilow.*

E

CLINT EASTWOOD
(Actor & Director)

"But man, this romantic stuff can be really tough; I (couldn't) wait to go back to the shooting and the killing." *1997: After saying his role in* The Bridges of Madison County *was "closer to the real me than anything I've done."*

"I probably could have retired from acting a long time ago if somebody had said, 'OK, that's what you should do.' But there's always some fool out there who wants you." *1999*

ROGER EBERT
(Film Critic)

"I've got a seat-of-the-hunch pants." *1990*

"When you see *Casablanca*, does it depress you that all the people in it are dead?" *1995: Challenging Gene Siskel's comment that Hugh Grant's real-life fiasco influenced his impression of* Nine Months.

"It's kind of nuts, isn't it?" *1998: On the Academy Awards ceremonies, during an interview with Rosa Parks who accompanied documentary film nominee Spike Lee to the event.*

DR. DEAN EDELL
(Radio Talk-show Host, Physician)

"We are cutting off our noses to spite our faces, and this leaves us very shortsighted." *1991*

DR. DEAN EDELL (CONT'D)

"If a person with multiple personalities threatens suicide, is that a hostage situation?" *1997*

"Why are there interstate highways in Hawaii?" *1997*

"Why are there self help groups?" *1997*

ANITA EKBERG
(Actress)

"Why do they keep letting Sophia Loren into the country? She was in jail for a month for tax evasion!" *1999: Complaining about U.S. immigration policy during a visit to New York.*

JENNA ELFMAN
(Actress)

"I did an audition for [George Clooney's] next movie, and it was the first time I'd met [him]. We were doing this postcoital bedroom scene, and in the middle of it, I'm thinking if I don't get this part, this is probably my last chance to kiss George Clooney. It wasn't in the script, but I kissed him anyway. Thank goodness, because I didn't get the part." *1998*

BRET EASTON ELLIS
(Writer)

"We are clueless yet wizened." *1990: Defining the "twentysomething generation."*

"The thing that struck me about Kurt Cobain's suicide is not that I was sad but that it wasn't Kathie Lee Gifford." *1994*

NORA EPHRON
(Screenwriter)

"[The aim of films like *Silkwood* and *JFK* is to create] not the truth, but what it was like—sort of, maybe—in a way that journalism could never come close to." *1992: Ephron wrote the screenplay for* Silkwood.

GLORIA ESTEFAN
(Singer)

"If I'm going to eat a cow, I'd rather eat a happy one that had a quality life and doesn't mind being our food." *1996: Discussing how, if she were president, she would improve slaughterhouses and the quality of life for cows.*

EMILIO ESTEVEZ
(Actor)

"You know, they came up with a line for me: 'Let's show this big-lipped bastard!' And I said to the producers, 'You think this is a funny line, but I am not going to insult a physical characteristic of Mick Jagger, because I have too much respect for him.' I got a lot of raised eyebrows, but I said no way." *1992: On filming* Freejack *with costar Mick Jagger.*

"People come up to me on the street and say, '*Men at Work* is the funniest movie I ever saw in my life.' But you know, I do have to question how many movies these people have seen." *1992*

JOE ESZTERHAS
(Screenwriter)

"The notion that I can sit in a little room and play God and make up stories and characters out of my guts and heart and head is one that I love." *1998*

LINDA EVANGELISTA
(Model)

"It was God who made me so beautiful. If I weren't, then I'd be a teacher." *1997*

ROBERT EVANS
(Producer)

"The cause of the breakup was not infidelity—and that's only because I never got caught." *1994: On his failed marriage to Phyllis George.*

"[It] loosens the tongue and softens the weewee." *1994: On cocaine.*

RUPERT EVERETT
(Actor)

"It's no point, being a California corporate star, to me. All that happens is you end up making *Waterworld*, where you think that your fans like you so much that they want to see you drinking your own piss. Wrong." *1996*

"I'd like to be more of a bimbo if I could, because the less you think, the easier it is. Thinking is fatal in this business. It's better just to look nice, have your mouth a little bit open and say, 'Yeah.'" *1998*

ANGIE EVERHART
(Model & Actress)

"I'm with Ashley Hamilton. He's the most gorgeous man I've ever seen or been with in my life. He's as beautiful inside as he is outside. . . . He's a year sober." *1996*

F

J. P. FABER
(Writer)

"There is an old proverb I choose to believe; trust an olive, but tie up your camel." *1991: Faber was trying to quote John Phillip Law who said, "Trust in Allah, but tie up your camel."*

FABIO
(Model & Writer)

"I do the plot and subplot, and then I have someone help me finish." *1994: On how he writes his romance novels.*

"There is so much more to me than just the body. People photograph my chest the most, but I'm happiest with my brain. Unfortunately, we live in a superficial world." *1995*

MORGAN FAIRCHILD
(Actress)

"I'm a very eclectic personality. Right now I'm reading Garry Wills's book on the Gettysburg Address and I just finished a book on viruses." *1993*

HENRY FAIRLIE
(Writer)

"No scotch has ever been found to be contaminated. The God of Presbyterians, and He is a jealous God, would not countenance it." *1990*

ADAM FAITH
(Singer)

"Mum hated housework—a vacuum-cleaner bag is the last place she'd have chosen for her final resting place." *1996: Revealing that his mother's ashes were sucked up by his sister's vacuum cleaner.*

LINDA GUESS FARRIS
(Writer)

"He said he couldn't deny that in some cases some people might sleep their way into a job, but there was no way they were going to keep it unless they could do it well." *1995: Describing an interview with Fred De Cordova, former producer of* The Tonight Show *on whether Hollywood people have to sleep their way into jobs.*

LAURENCE FISHBURNE
(Actor)

"Why should I read all those words that I'm not going to get to say?" *1995: On why he read only the screenplay for Othello, from which two-thirds of Shakespeare's original lines were cut, rather than reading the entire play as written.*

"Will you turn off that fucking phone, please?" *1999: Interrupting his performance of* The Lion in Winter *in New York after an audience member's cell phone beeped for about twenty seconds. The rest of the theatergoers gave Fishburne a thunderous thirty-second ovation and the show went on.*

CARRIE FISHER
(Writer & Actress)

"What doesn't kill you makes you stronger . . . or puts you on a talk show." *1994*

"Do you know what your IQ is? I don't know what mine is. I don't even know what my bra size is." *1994*

HEIDI FLEISS
(Hollywood Madame)

"That's right, ladies and gentlemen, I am an alleged madame—and that is a $25 whore!" *1993: After a woman sitting in a booth next to her in a restaurant taunted her. After making this statement, Fleiss floored the woman with a right hook.*

"Everyone has their own definition of a prostitute. Even I'll say to a waitress who will take too long with my check, 'Stick it, whore,' under my breath. And every man calls every woman a whore. Big deal. I was probably born with a hooker's mentality because I do believe men should pay for everything. I think men should pay for girls' houses, cars, diamonds. I don't think girls should have to do anything. Girls should have fun, that's it." *1993*

HEIDI FLEISS (CONT'D)

"Why don't you do it yourself?" *1994: To Shannen Doherty after Doherty offered to pay $200 apiece for prostitutes for her fiance's bachelor party.*

"You look at any picture of a politician with some girls and three of them will be mine. If I really came out and talked I could have stopped NAFTA." *1994: "Maybe that's the sound Ross Perot said he heard," wrote Phil Rosenthal of the* Los Angeles Daily News, *after hearing this comment by Fleiss. Perot had referred to a "giant sucking sound" coming from Mexico if the NAFTA passed Congress.*

"I didn't lose my virginity until I was almost 18. I'm real slow." *1994*

"Want an idea of the kind of major Hollywood celebrities I serviced? Put it this way—Kevin Costner was on my C list." *1995*

"There is nothing worse than a half-truth." *1996*

CALISTA FLOCKHART
(Actress)

"I would like to take this opportunity to tell the press to kiss my skinny white ass." *1999: Lashing out at media speculation that she suffers from an eating disorder.*

LARRY FLYNT
(Publisher)

"I got over being a born-again Christian. I was fortunate enough to seek help. In my opinion, people who are born-again Christians are nothing other than manic-depressives. They get in a manic phase, and they do see the visions, they do hear the voices, and it's nothing more than a chemical imbalance that causes it. If these people would just take a little lithium, they would be OK." *1995*

"If you tell a girl that's working for you, 'If you don't sleep with me you're fired'—that's sexual harassment. Anything beyond that is just trying to get laid." *1998*

DAN FOLEY
(Actor)

"Not really, because kids are surprisingly stupid." *On whether young people recognize him for his voice work in "A Bug's Life."*

BRIDGET FONDA
(Actress)

"Every woman I know would rather have different breasts. They always think, 'If only they were a little different.'" *1992*

JANE FONDA
(Actress)

"You don't think I really meant all that, do you?" *1990: Commenting to Ted Turner on her trip to Hanoi and her broadcasts from the North Vietnamese capital in 1972.*

PETER FONDA
(Actor)

"I wasn't playing Dad, but I was playing that type of character. I'd lived with him. I knew I could go back and touch those things and find the moments and tell them perfectly." *1998: On playing the part of Ulysses Jackson in the film* Ulee's Gold. *The character reminded many people of Fonda's father, Henry Fonda.*

"'Fonda? *That* sonuvabitch? Isn't he up there in Montana just loaded on his ranch?' Well, no I wasn't. I took drugs but I wasn't a druggie. I made an average of 1.3 films a year. Some were, you know, bad. But I did my job well. My father took everything he was offered. I'm sure he wasn't thrilled with being in *The Swarm*, but there he was." *1998: Recounting the way some people thought he'd lived the past three decades, as opposed to the way he really lived.*

HARRISON FORD
(Actor)

"I came into a business that was completely fucked. They were trying to mold people to be some representation of some other success. I was supposed to be the new Elvis Presley." *1994*

"I've always wanted to be bald. I mean it, completely bald. Wouldn't it be great to be bald in the rain?" *1994*

"Why this sudden outpouring for geezers? I never feel sexy." *1998: Ford, fifty-six, on being named* People *magazine's "Sexiest Man Alive."*

"That's all part of my job—to be a focus for derision and to be mocked and taunted." *1999: On the abuse he received after being named "Sexiest Man Alive."*

DAVID FOSTER
(Producer)

"I have no fear. The boat sinks. Everybody drowns. The whole world knows the story." *1997: The producer of* The Mask of Zorro, *on a report that his film and the much-hyped $200 million movie* Titanic *would be released on the same weekend in December.*

JODIE FOSTER
(Actress)

"It doesn't take intelligence to be an actor." *1998*

PETER FRAMPTON
(Singer)

"In L.A. no one gives a shit, because everyone's famous. I even had a cab driver who'd just been on *Star Trek: The Next Generation* for two weeks." *1992*

ARETHA FRANKLIN
(Singer)

"I met Grant Hill once. I was outside the locker room after the game. I told someone to tell him Janet Jackson was outside." *1998: Franklin, fifty-five, on the wiles of age.*

DENNIS FRANZ
(Actor)

"You know, average working class guy with an average ass." *1998: On the appeal of his* NYPD Blue *nude scenes.*

CHARLES FRAZIER
(Author)

"Well, if by 'celebrity' you mean people you don't know yelling at you across the grocery store, I guess I don't mind it too much." *1998: The best-selling author of* Cold Mountain, *on becoming a celebrity.*

MICHAEL FUCHS
(HBO Chairman)

"[It will be] so great, people are going to want communism again." *1992: On HBO's movie* Stalin.

G

EVA GABOR
(Actress & Celebrity)

"It's so wonderful that we have 5½ presidents here." *1991: At the Ronald Reagan Presidential Library in Simi Valley, CA. Gabor explained later that what she really meant was that in addition to President Bush and ex-presidents Ford, Carter, Nixon, and Reagan, former first lady Lady Bird Johnson was present.*

ZSA ZSA GABOR
(Celebrity)

"I'm so damn famous, it's sickening." *1990*

"Don't expect me to sing, don't expect me to do anything, and then you'll be happy. Really, I am too rich to work too hard." *1990: On her proposed Las Vegas appearance.*

"I love animals and children. People I could do without." *1990*

"I realize that . . . I—who normally sleep naked except for diamond earrings—am not wearing them. In my dazed state I remember that jewelry is not allowed in jail." *1991: In her book* One Lifetime Is Not Enough.

"Henry [Kissinger] gave me the reason . . . : 'I can't fly down because we are invading Cambodia tomorrow. It is a big secret, you are the first person outside the White House who knows about it.'" *1991: In her book* One Lifetime Is Not Enough.

"I think she dresses much too flashy. I also think her hair is ridiculous, and her behavior with Donald was very stupid. All she cares about is money, money, money. I hate that." *1993: On Ivana Trump.*

"I can't help it if I have a big ass. I have done very well with it anyway." *1993*

"I am an excellent housekeeper: Every time I get a divorce, I keep the house." *1998*

NOEL GALLAGHER
(Musician & Singer)

"People tell me that whenever they hear *Wonderwall*, it transports them back in time to when they

NOEL GALLAGHER (CONT'D)

first heard it, which is all you can ask from a record. That and a big fucking car and house." *1999*

VINCENT GALLO
(Actor)

"I'm out here, honestly, because I love to look at women. Ugly, pretty—I'm here to take it all in." *1998: On why he attended the Sundance Film Festival.*

ANNABELLE GARCIA
(Daughter of Musician & Singer Jerry)

"We love each and every one of you because you put us through college. And we didn't have to work at Dairy Queen." *1995: At the memorial celebration for her father, thanking fans of the Grateful Dead on behalf of herself and her three sisters.*

"Dad never went to India, never studied Buddhism. He was more into UFOs." *1996*

DEBORAH KOONS GARCIA
(Widow of Jerry Garcia)

"Jerry died broke. We only have a few hundred thousand dollars in the bank." *1997*

JERRY GARCIA
(Musician & Singer)

"We made every effort not to scare them." *1992: On how Al and Tipper Gore were treated when they attended a concert by the Grateful Dead in Washington, D.C.*

"When we first started making records, I used to have ideas. Now I see our records as a long string of failures. I see it in terms of near misses. . . . For me, the big test is if I can perform a piece of music without being embarrassed by it." *1993*

"I've never felt that I have something to say that wasn't being said. I don't feel I have whatever it takes to be a writer. I've never been able to sustain an idea and get it down. It's hard for me to do it with music, too, as far as that goes. I feel like I'm swimming upstream. My own preferences are for improvisation, for making it up as I go along. The idea of picking, of eliminating possibilities by deciding, that's difficult for me." 1993

"I try to be who I am and do what I do, you know what I mean?" *1995*

"Every once in a while one pops out, all of a sudden it's there." *1995: On writing songs.*

ART GARFUNKEL
(Singer)

"When I go to the bass range with long *moo* sounds, I sense that I'm communicating. Taking them seriously makes them feel pregnant with a kind of moment, a quivering existential happening." *1993: On what happens when he sings to cows during his long walks.*

LESLIE GARNER
(Journalist)

"I'm sorry, but four children and a house in the suburbs looks pretty married to me." *1999: The* London *Evening Standard writer on Rolling Stone Mick Jagger's claim that Jerry Hall can't divorce him because they were never properly married.*

HENRY LOUIS GATES JR.
(Professor & Author)

"My father called me in to see him about a week before school started and we sat down and he said, 'Boy, you're going over to that white school,' as we called it, 'and there's an important thing you have to understand.' He said, 'There's two kinds of white people.' And I said, 'Two kinds of white people? How do you tell the difference?' He said, 'That's easy. There's two kinds of white people, the Irish and the Italian, and this is how you tell the difference.' He said the Irish have names that begin with 'o' and the Italians have names that end with 'o.' And that, ladies and gentlemen, has been the secret to my success all these years later." *1999: Speaking at commencement ceremonies at Hamilton College.*

DAVID GEFFEN
(Producer)

"Right now I'm completely 100 percent gay. [But] . . . every time I see Demi Moore walk in front of my beach house, I think, 'Whoa, she's really hot!' " *1994*

"Apparently you think more highly of him than I do." *1996: To NBC west coast president Don*

Ohlmeyer, upon reading Ohlmeyer's description of Michael Ovitz as the "Antichrist."

"Once in a while I'm in a situation where I end up having sex with a woman who wants to and I think, 'Try it, I can try this,' and it feels good and it really is no big deal for me." *1997*

"Let me put it this way: I am delighted to have a relationship with the president of the United States. I can't tell you I don't value that greatly. But, I mean, you know, I'm not blown away by anybody." *1998*

BOY GEORGE
(Singer)

"I wish him strength at this time, because when push comes to shove, we are sisters under the skin." *1998: The openly gay singer on singer George Michael's arrest after performing a lewd act in a Beverly Hills, CA, public restroom. Michael later apologized for the incident and came out to the public.*

RICHARD GERE
(Actor)

"If I am a cow and someone says I am a zebra, it doesn't make me a zebra." *1991*

"I don't think anyone starts doing creative work because they're serving humanity. They want to get laid; they want to get money; they want to get attention." *1994*

"People in monasteries deal with the same things people do making movies." *1995*

"You need to believe in the pristine nature of your innate mind." *1998*

"I am so tuned in to suffering that I have to make all my decisions based on that." *1999*

BALTHAZAR GETTY
(Actor)

"Me and my mom are real close. We give each other guidance. Just recently I made a big change for my mom in her life. I told her to get up off her ass, start doing things on her own, quit complaining about everything we have to go up against, and make it different." *1997*

ROBIN GIBB
(Singer)

"I dip in occasionally. It takes the pressure off me. It's just a way of life." *1997: On his wife, who has a female lover.*

MEL GIBSON
(Actor)

"I mean, it's a great story. It's got some great things in it. I mean, there's something like eight violent deaths." *1991: On* Hamlet.

"I'm terribly vindictive. If somebody ripped me apart in the press, I'd kill them. I would *have* them killed, and no one would ever know. I mean, I haven't done it, but I'm ready. There's this stuff in Australia; it's for pest eradication. It's odorless, colorless, tasteless, and one teaspoon will give you an instant brain hemorrhage. And it doesn't leave a single trace. It's perfect!" *1995*

"I read something about Disney having real problems with people saying [Pocahontas] is not historically accurate. I'm thinking, Historically accurate? My God, there's a fucking raccoon that talks in this. What do they want?" *1995*

KATHIE LEE GIFFORD
(Entertainer)

"Frank Gifford's been married 45 years. Too bad it took him three marriages to get there." *1998: Kathie Lee Gifford is the third wife of Frank Gifford.*

MALCOLM GLADWELL
(Journalist)

"In *Titanic* smoking is sexy and social and sophisticated and genuine and rebellious, and in the end virtually everybody dies—which is the most perfect touch of all." *1998*

DANNY GLOVER
(Actor)

"When I was at this luncheon for Nelson Mandela . . . I got so emotional, so nervous, that I found myself waving to Stevie Wonder." *1990*

"What I learned is not to spit when the camera is panning the dugout, and always look for the smallest guy on the opposite team when a fight

DANNY GLOVER (CONT'D)

breaks out." *1994: On watching televised baseball for his role in* Angels in the Outfield.

DAVID GOLDBERG
(TV producer)

"Left to their own devices, the three networks would televise live executions. Except Fox—they'd televise live naked executions." *1993*

LUCIANNE GOLDBERG
(Writer & Agent)

"I wrote Maureen Dean's book, *Washington Wives*, a big seller. And one day I picked up *The Washington Post* Style section to see a pic of Maureen— she's a looker, sort of candy-box looks. She was sitting on the deck of her Los Angeles house describing how she worked. 'Every morning,' she says, 'I have to have No. 2 pencils, very sharp. My housekeeper sharpens them. And I get a stack of legal pads and I write and write until I am exhausted.' I read this and I am thinking, I wore a window in the seat of three big flannel mommy nightgowns sitting at my computer in an Upper West Side apartment with kids screaming and a basset hound howling, while she's telling reporters about her pencils and foolscap. Talk about tacky." *1997*

WHOOPI GOLDBERG
(Actress & Comedienne)

"Stars don't get to do anything. They only are. They're a state of mind." *1992*

"Hollywood is one of the few places you can come from nowhere and be somebody. The scary thing is, Washington is the other place." *1992*

"Suddenly, at age 37, I have acquired sensuality and woman-ness." *1993: But not honesty. In 1983 Goldberg told an interviewer she was thirty-three years old.*

JOHN GOODMAN
(Actor)

"Yeah. They're all overweight." *1998: On the similarities of the characters he plays in the movies and on TV.*

"I got my education from *Mad*. If I didn't get a joke, I'd consult the encyclopedia." *1998: On how he became educated in Afton, MO.*

"We opened and closed in Springboro, Ohio. That's five miles from Ridgeville, which is four miles from Waynesville, which is one mile from Corwin, which is three miles from Harveysburg." *1998: On his experience in performing in the dinner-theater production of* 1776 *early in his acting career.*

"I did a lot of preparation for the part. I actually kept slaves for a while and grew my own hemp. One of the critics indicated I was a little too antic to be one of the founding fathers." *1998: On his early role in the musical* 1776.

"I was Oberon in *A Midsummer Night's Dream*. People didn't seem to like the play too much maybe because we did a disco version." *1998: On his New York stage debut in 1978.*

"I tried out for *Equus* here [pointing to the Plymouth Theater in New York]. I thought I had a good shot at being one of the horses." *1998: On his early acting career in New York.*

"Only later did I find out what part I'd played in *Barton Fink*'s genesis. According to Joel and Ethan (Coen), the film sprang from a mental picture they had of me and John Tuturro sitting on the edge of a bed in our underwear." *1998: On his appearance in Joel and Ethan Coen's* Barton Fink, *for which Goodman received a Golden Globe nomination.*

LOUIS GOSSETT JR.
(Actor)

"Half of the middle class is unemployed and homeless. It's touching more people than we think, and if we don't stop, everybody's gonna be homeless or something-less." *1993: On the U.S. economy.*

ELLIOTT GOULD
(Actor)

"As you know, I was once married to Barbra Streisand." *1998: When asked to name one of his worst jobs.*

BARBARA GRAHAM
(Writer)

"Poodles are descended from wolves. But they've progressed. They know the importance of a good haircut." *1994: In her book* Women Who Run with the Poodles.

HUGH GRANT
(Actor)

"I've always had a crush on cheerleaders." *1995*

"Oh, I think she's sex on a stick!" *1995: On Sharon Stone.*

"The trouble is, people aren't like characters in a film. I'm a bit of everything. It's like my libido. I find that for a month at a time I'm a eunuch, and then suddenly for the next month I'm a rapist. I never know which way it's going from day to day. There are days I feel quite aggressive and driven, and other days, I think, 'Why, it couldn't matter less. Bring me a chocolate-covered biscuit.'" *1995: Shortly before his arrest for having sex with a prostitute in his car in Los Angeles.*

"I did a bad thing, and there you have it." *1995*

"I dream about Princess Di but it is too kinky to go into." *1995*

"If my hangover isn't too bad I do sit ups." *1996: On his daily exercise.*

JOHN GRAY
(Writer)

"It's a control, it was really amazing, the semen comes out as perspiration." *1994: On what happens when a man practices celibacy—Gray says he was celibate for 9 years.*

"I remember very clearly sitting around the beach one night, there was a fire and these hobos gave me some of their beer. I was teaching them about God and one of them said, 'John, we love listening to what you say but we have no idea what you're talking about.' My reaction to that was, this is not the place for me." *1994: The author of* Men Are from Mars, Women Are from Venus, *on his unhappy past and his path to giving instructive seminars on love and sex to more affluent groups who think they do have an idea of what he is talking about.*

SPAULDING GRAY
(Actor)

"Anyone who plays sax like that is going to pull his pants down." *1997: After seeing a video clip of Clinton playing the saxophone.*

GRAHAM GREENE
(Actor)

"What am I but a speck of fly dung on the windshield of life?" *1992*

GERMAINE GREER
(Feminist Writer)

"God, I've spent my whole fucking life studying men, and they're still a mystery to me. I'm sick of myself, really. I'm heterosexual to the point of being a total pervert." *1999*

JENNIFER GREY
(Actress)

"Why a nose job? Because I was a very small girl attached to a very large nose." *1999*

PAM GRIER
(Actress)

"The characters are based on realism. I don't use the word [*nigger*], but I know people who use it all day long as an endearment—and that's how they talk. If people are offended by this word, they don't live in Compton." *1998: On her role and language in the film* Jackie Brown.

MELANIE GRIFFITH
(Actress)

"I didn't know that 6 million Jews were killed. That's a lot of people." *1992: On the Holocaust.*

"I did my breasts seven years ago, right after I had Dakota. But that's it. I don't want to feel like I have to look 20 anymore. . . . I'm not going to live a life where I have to have plastic surgery every 10 years. . . . Well, maybe every 20." *1998*

"Working with Jimmy is like being pregnant. In the beginning, you're happy and excited. Then you're thinking, I might have made the biggest mistake of my life. By the end, you just want it to be over with." *1999: On working with James Woods.*

MELANIE GRIFFITH (CONT'D)

"I had my tits done after my second child. But I didn't make them bigger. I just had them put back to where they were." *1999*

NICK GRIPPO
(Celebrity Caterer)

"Elizabeth invited me to partake in her private afternoon delight. Sensing my apprehension, she urged me to try these exquisite sapphires from the sea, and I'm glad she did. As we spent the afternoon in her boudoir, visiting, laughing and devouring spoonfuls of the most scrumptious thing I had ever tasted, I remember thinking to myself in between sips of champagne that life just couldn't get any better." *1998: Remembering an afternoon he shared with Elizabeth Taylor. The sapphires are caviar.*

NINA GRISCOM
(Model, TV Personality & Author)

"I'm always so surprised—although I guess by now I should be over it—when people look at me and just assume: She lives on Park Avenue, she must live in such-and-such a way." *1998*

JOHN GRISHAM
(Writer)

"If I wrote about honest lawyers, I wouldn't be able to give the books away." *1994*

"In our culture today we have a trial of the week, trial of the month, trial of the century, trial of the decade. . . . I get my ideas from CNN and *USA Today*." *1998*

"I don't like to read about relationships or about weird and strange people who do nothing." *1998*

MATT GROENING
(Cartoonist)

"One of the great things in the future, there's going to be 5,000 networks, but UPN will still be in last place. . . . The NRA is still around, but they're now crusading for the right to bear death rays. . . . *The Simpsons* is still on in the year 3000, but fans on the Internet are complaining that the last 500 years haven't been as good." *1999: The creator of* The Simpsons, *on the world of his futuristic new series,* Futurama.

"I think tattoos are the ultimate compliment for a cartoonist. However, I have mixed feelings when the people showing me their tattoos have the characters' names misspelled." *1999*

"Good taste is always decided by the richest person in the room. In cases of equal wealth, good taste is decided by the person whose normal facial expression most resembles that of someone getting a lingering whiff of a very disagreeable odor." *1990*

"Dan Quayle is more stupid than Ronald Reagan put together." *1992*

"How can you live with people you love but want to kill? That's the theme of *The Simpsons*." *1998: The creator of* The Simpsons *on the meaning of the show.*

DAVID GROHL
(Musician & Singer)

"I watched him during the entire performance, and I didn't know what to think, but afterward k.d. lang said, 'Take that as a compliment, my friend.' So I did." *1998: A member of the Foo Fighters, on seeing Woody Allen cover his ears while the group played.*

PETER GUBER
(Producer & Entertainment Excecutive)

"In Hollywood, it's all just the size of your dick." *1990*

"This is the first time a president is younger than Mick Jagger. The Beatles are older than Bill and Hillary Clinton. When you recognize that, you say to yourself that this is going to bring a completely different judgement to all the issues that are going to face the arts and communications." *1993*

BRYANT GUMBLE
(TV Personality)

"Maybe you've never had a great round of golf." *1997: After NBC weatherman Al Roker expressed surprise that Gumble would rather give up sex than golf.*

H

SHARYN HADDAD
(Celebrity Wife)

"He spanked me twenty-two times on my 22nd birthday. . . . His favorite sex fantasy was to have me dress up and pretend to be the wife of a United States senator." *1993: On her ex-husband Nick Nolte.*

JESSICA HAHN
(Church Secretary & Celebrity)
"I figured the snake knows if it goes anywhere it's not supposed to, it will suffocate." *1993: On posing naked with a snake for* Playboy.

DAVID HAINES
(Film Producer)
"I know it sounds odd, but after 14 years in the censorship office, I knew the industry." *1999: The, former chief deputy censor in Australian government, on how he ended up in his current career—producing and directing such X-rated films as* Buffy Down Under.

ARSENIO HALL
(Actor & TV Talk-show Host)
"Fat people weren't brought here from Fatland and forced to work [for] free and separated from their fat relatives and hung from large trees." *1990: Defending himself against an allegation from Roseanne that his comment "Remember the whales? Well, they're back," while showing a photo of her and husband Tom Arnold swimming, was tantamount to racism.*

"Excuse me, George Herbert, irregular-heart-beating, read-my-lipping, slipping-in-the-polls, do-nothing, deficit-raising, make-less-money-than-Millie-the-White-House-dog-last-year, Quayle-loving, sushi-puking Bush! I don't remember inviting your ass to my show." *1992: Responding to a statement by the White House press secretary that President George Bush might appear on the Arsenio Hall Show. He didn't.*

"Ross Perot has had more trouble entering a race than anybody since Michael Jackson." *1992*

"I saw Cecil B. de Mille's *The Ten Commandments* when I was a young child. The casting of legendary screen gangster Edward G. Robinson in a biblical film damaged me severely. It changed my life. I've been in therapy ever since." *1996: On what film had the greatest impact on his personal life.*

"[CBS TV president] Les Moonves said, 'We need a big mouth.' I don't know, who do you call? Me or Monica Lewinsky?" *1999: When asked how he'd landed a role on TV's* Martial Law.

BRAD HALL
(Producer)
"You'd be shocked. You've got to put in four- and five-hour days to do television." *1995: Producer of NBC series* The Single Guy *on how hard it is to work in TV.*

JERRY HALL
(Model & Celebrity Wife)
"Mick Jagger and I just really liked each other a lot. We talked all night. We had the same views on nuclear disarmament." *1995: On first meeting her future husband.*

ARGUS HAMILTON
(Humorist)
"No way! Most of our parents were married." *1996: On a federal survey showing that California leads the nation in illiteracy.*

ASHLEY HAMILTON
(Actor)
"I like to sit around and play guitar . . . and masturbate, but only on Tuesdays." *1994*

LINDA HAMILTON
(Actress)
"He was always a jerk, so there was no way to really measure." *1998: On her former husband, director James Cameron, when asked if the eleven Oscars won by his* Titanic *had changed him.*

"I was delivered by God when he left." *1999: On her divorce from* Titanic *director James Cameron, whom she called a "miserable, unhappy man."*

WILLIAM HAMILTON
(Playwright & Cartoonist)
"Since radios are to driving what tongues are to having sex, and driving in Los Angeles is what blood is to life, our radios are our blind poets." *1993*

HARRY HAMLIN
(Actor)
"One of the issues that I am currently involved with is the Greenpeace issue, to save the world." *1993*

BRUCE HANDY
(Journalist)

"Cheap gas, a strong economy, erection pills—what a country! What a time to be alive!" *1998*

TOM HANKS
(Actor)

"Usually when I'm in a hotel room, I strip down naked and walk around on the patio. That's as close as I can get to a feeling of anonymity and power." *1999*

PATTI HANSEN
(Model & Wife of Keith Richards)

"Change is so important. Otherwise, it's easy to get stuck." *1999*

CURTIS HANSON
(Film Director)

"It was also a foregone conclusion that the Titanic would get to New York." *1998: The director of* L.A. Confidential *when asked about a possible Oscar sweep by* Titanic.

ZACHARY HANSON
(Singer & Musician)

"I have to laugh when someone asks if we're missing our childhood. When I turn 16, I can flip hamburgers for five bucks an hour, or I can go around the world and perform for thousands of people and make a lot of money. What am I missing?" *1998: Hanson, twelve, plays with the pop group Hanson.*

WOODY HARRELSON
(Actor)

"When I meet a girl and I'm really deeply attracted to her, I go out of my mind. It's overpowering, just like someone reaching in and grabbing hold of my heart and my groin." *1993*

"People can be cynical when actors take stands, but the hemp movement's something I'm very passionate about." *1996*

"As my name will attest, I am a friend of the trees." *1996*

"Look, we are a society that deals with symptoms. We never deal with the root of anything, only facade. We all take drugs; everybody I know is a drug addict of some kind. How else could we live on this planet in its present condition? It's either pot or coffee or sugar or booze or sex." *1996*

"Thing I realized: When I let up from the weed—and the drinking, too—I cried every day! And I *liked* that! I like cryin'. And now I not only wanna cry and show my cryin' to other people—I wanna just split myself down the middle and open my guts and just throw *everything* out! To the world. Or to anyone unfortunate enough to bear it!" *1996*

"I'm a free thinker. Certainly, my thinking's somewhat conditioned. But I was kicked out of about a million schools when I was a kid. But I'm not tied to one school of thought. Not a particular ideology or deities or anything." *1996*

"I remember having this vision when I was 10. I was playing Monopoly, and I had this vision that life was no more or less than this game of Monopoly. The emotions you go through while sitting there—if you're at all passionate about living—it's *life*, man! I look at life like that—it's a game. It's a dream, and a game. I felt like that from the time I was really young—that I'm *dreaming* this." *1996*

"Poor white trash, that's me, all the way. You can't take that out of somebody, can you?" *1997*

"I'm glad that Gloria Steinem, you know, stated her mind, but I think that there's—if you want to look at pornography, uh, you know, what you resist, you empower. All of the mostly religious kind of fanaticism that, uh, talks about sexuality as a negative thing, you know, is what creates a space, you know, to me, for pornography." *1997*

MARK HARRIS
(Celebrity Widower)

"I know it sounds tasteless, but Martha's dentures were her trademark, and this is my way of immortalizing her." *1995: The widower of entertainment legend Martha Raye, on opening a nightclub in New York that will provide ashtrays shaped like false teeth.*

GEORGE HARRISON
(Musician)

"It was such a waste, some stupid person. If John had been killed by Elvis, it would have at least had meaning." *1990: Commenting on the murder of John Lennon.*

"Have you ever been raped? I'm being raped by all these people." *1993: Complaining in court about neighbors who walk across his Hawaii property to get to the beach.*

"As far as I'm concerned, there won't be a Beatles reunion as long as John Lennon remains dead." *1995*

"And we were the Spice Boys." *1998: The former Beatle on the evolution of British rock.*

DEBBIE HARRY
(Singer)

"This means more to me than a good bowel movement." *1992: On winning a "Jackie Award" at the Jackie 60 club in New York.*

"I'd probably go into the sex industry instead." *1999: On what she would do differently if she could relive her life.*

MARY HART
(TV Host)

"People today have an incredible interest in celebrities, and my legs are part of that." *1990*

NINA HARTLEY
(Porn Star)

"Is there anything more degrading than slave labor at McDonald's?" *1994*

SOPHIE B. HAWKINS
(Singer)

"I love Bob Dylan—especially when he was in the Beatles." *1992*

GOLDIE HAWN
(Actress)

"When it's a good time, I celebrate. When it's a bad time, I also celebrate. Know what I mean?" *1997*

SALMA HAYEK
(Actress)

"I'm sure the owner of the breasts, which are beautiful and larger than mine, must be really pissed off, because she paid a lot of money for them. And they're giving me the credit." *1999: On seeing nude photos of herself on the Web.*

ISAAC HAYES
(Musician)

"Artists are on another level. They are highly perceptive people, highly affected by aesthetics. They are very aware and giving off a powerful aura. Why do you think people can't get enough of celebrities? People crave highly evolved individuals." *1998*

LE LY HAYSLIP
(Writer)

"There is a heaven and I've found it. I can die now." *1994: The author of* When Heaven and Earth Changed Places, *which became the Oliver Stone film* Heaven and Earth, *commenting on Disneyland.*

"Without them there would be no book to tell or no movie. Those bad people put me on the path so I could progress. I can only be grateful to them. Without raping me, I would never have left my village; I would still be a little stupid farm girl." *1994: Responding to a reporter's question: "You were raped by the Viet Cong, tortured by the South Vietnamese, and led into prostitution by the Americans—but you don't seem angry at any of them. Why?"*

HUGH HEFNER
(Editor & Entrepreneur)

"It's a recreational drug! It takes the pressure out of sexuality! The street name for it should be Pfizer's Riser." *1998: On Viagra, which is manufactured by Pfizer.*

"The hiddenness of sex and the shame and guilt of it are increasingly eroding. Explicit sex is becoming part of the commonplace. Mass communication makes that a reality. Some of us who were raised in a more romantic time may miss the mystery that goes with that hiddenness, but I think that on this rather lonely planet, the celebration of sex is a very good thing." *1998*

KIMBERLY HEFNER
(Playboy Playmate)

"*Playboy* served as a light at the end of the tunnel for American servicemen during the Vietnam War." *1990*

KIMBERLY HEFNER (CONT'D)

"We just want to do whatever we can to help keep their spirits up." *1990: On sending* Playboy *to American soldiers serving in the Middle East.*

LEONA HELMSLEY
(Celebrity Hotelier)

"That miserable S.O.B., that little bastard. He gives away air; ice in the wintertime is what he gives away." *1990: On Donald Trump.*

"Trump's favorite charity is Marble Maple, Maple Marble, whatever. Maypo Marla. Marla Mipple." *1990: On Donald Trump & Marla Maples.*

"I wouldn't believe Donald Trump if he had his tongue notarized." *1990*

"I've cleaned toilet bowls in my life. . . . I wasn't born with any silver spoon." *1990*

MARILU HENNER
(Actress)

"Stop obsessing that you're not sexy for your man because you hate the way you look. Sexuality isn't just visual. It's in the mind, in your touch. Besides, you've always got your mouth." *1994: Advice to women who are unhappy with their appearance.*

"I've always found Danny [DeVito] incredibly sexy. After *Indecent Proposal* came out, everybody was saying, 'Of course, I'd do it for a million dollars with Robert Redford.' I was the opposite. Redford couldn't pay me enough; Danny wouldn't have to pay me." *1994*

CHARLTON HESTON
(Actor)

"I would feel very naked without a 12-gauge shotgun under my bed and a .38-caliber revolver in the drawer of my night table." *1992*

"As a husband you have to remember the crucial importance of three little words: 'I was wrong.' That will take you a lot further than 'I love you.'" *1998: On what he's learned during his fifty-four-year marriage.*

DON HEWITT
(TV Producer)

"You're telling me what people in the industry say? Most of them couldn't find their asses with both hands." *1996*

DAVID HILL
(President and CEO of Fox Broadcasting)

"Sweeps suck." *1999*

DUSTIN HOFFMAN
(Actor)

"I am obsessed with myself. I've always thought about myself. I get on the scale every day. I will look in the mirror—I've never been bored." *1993*

"I went to the proctologist last week and I got a thumb's up." *1998: When asked by Roger Ebert about his chances of winning an Oscar just before the Academy Awards ceremonies. "Oh, that* is *an inside joke," Ebert responded.*

"I want to be remembered as I always envisoned myself to be: taller, smaller nose, handsome, better teeth! Teeth like Matt Damon!" *1998*

DEXTER HOLLAND
(Singer)

"It's really inspired by wannabe gangsters. Guys who go to malls and get gangsta rap clothes. Guys on *Ricki Lake* who won't listen to their moms." *1999: Describing his band's hit* Pretty Fly (for a White Guy).

DENNIS HOPPER
(Actor)

"He's an ass. He was perfect for the part. He was an amoral drifter who will blackmail you and take everything he can from you. And you better watch yourself because when you turn your back, he might screw your wife." *1990: Telling how actor Don Johnson was similar to the character he played in the film* The Hot Spot.

"People keep asking me, 'What evil lurks in you to play such bad characters?' There is no evil. I just wear tight underwear." *1994*

"Seven of those days were pretty good. The eighth was the bad one." *1994: On his eight-day marriage to Michelle Phillips in 1971.*

"Sure, it comes from the same plant as marijuana, but industrial hemp has no value as far as its euphoric properties are concerned. I should know." *1996*

ANTHONY HOPKINS
(Actor)

"I think I would have eaten myself." *1992: On what he might have done had he not discovered acting.*

BOB HOSKINS
(Actor)

"Margaret Thatcher has done more harm to Great Britain than Hitler did!" *1990*

"If you look at Cher's tattoos they are absolutely brilliant. If you ever wound up in the situation where you took Cher to bed, it would be like going into an art gallery." *1993*

"We both said, 'It's not going to work.' The clothes were actually going to take away from the scene. They would have made it a completely different scene. It wouldn't have been believable." *1996: On playing J. Edgar Hoover in the Oliver Stone movie* Nixon, *and remembering why he and actor Brian Bedford, who played Hoover's aide Clyde Tolson in the movie, rejected Stone's suggestion that they play their movie roles dressed in women's clothing.*

ARIANNA HUFFINGTON
(Author & TV Commentator)

"If you happen to run across the Creep, tell him Soon-Yi says hello." *1998: In an imaginary conversation with Monica Lewinsky in her book* Greetings from the Lincoln Bedroom.

"Just One Orgasm Away from the Presidency." *1998: Title of a chapter dealing with Al Gore in Huffington's book.*

"I think politicians are really underestimating how many people are disgruntled with both parties and are willing to look at them without a partisan eye. I want to reach people who vote. And I really feel satire is a way to reach them." *1998: On her writing.*

"I think our tolerance of political platitudes has increased. I call it the guffaw threshold. We need to guffaw more at what politicians say." *1998*

"America is like a dysfunctional family going through denial. And I think the public will remain in denial until the proof is in." *1998: On the allegations over the secret sex life of President Clinton.*

"In a way it was the greatest gift. . . . You realize in the end how little it need affect you, then it gives you all the courage to speak your mind and not worry what everybody else is thinking. It's very liberating. Either you're crushed or you're liberated." *1998: On the criticism she's received over the years.*

ENGLEBERT HUMPERDINCK
(Singer)

"I've got more paternity suits than leisure suits." *1990*

HOLLY HUNTER
(Actress)

"Oh, plenty of times. Are you kidding—who hasn't? We're Americans." *1997: When asked if she'd ever had sex in a car.*

ELIZABETH HURLEY
(Model & Actress)

"I thought 70 percent of the people I met were idiots. Half of those were fools, and the other half were vile. . . .The other 30 percent are nice, though." *1995: On Hollywood.*

LAUREN HUTTON
(Model & Actress)

"What America has to offer is a more practical way of being. We're not bogged down with a castle on our back." *1990*

"[Irving Penn] would ask us these very pointed questions, and you'd have to think a lot about them. Penn was our Socrates, except that he was a good-looking Socrates and he liked girls." *1995: Penn is a photographer.*

"I have no secrets. All I can say is that I drink large quantities of water, I use a lot of hydrating creams and I make love once a day with an Italian." *1996*

DAVID HENRY HWANG
(Playwright)

"When I was a teenager, my father had the master bedroom extended into what had been a patio over

DAVID HENRY HWANG (CONT'D)

the garage. His Chinese friends told him this would bring bad luck, that according to the ancient necromancy of feng shui, building over your garage represented cutting off your head. My father, who had long since rejected the old-country ways in favor of new-world opportunity and English-only patriotism, pooh-poohed such superstition. Only a few years later he was kidnapped and briefly held for ransom." *1991*

CHRISSIE HYNDE
(Musician & Singer)

"Don't moan about being a chick, refer to feminism or complain about sexist discrimination. We've all been thrown down the stairs and fucked about, but no one wants to hear a whining female. Write a loosely disguised song about it instead and clean up." *1994: Her advice to "chick rockers."*

"If you sing, don't 'belt' or 'screech.' No one wants to hear that shit; it sounds 'hysterical.' Shave your legs, for chrissakes!" *1994: More advice to "chick rockers."*

"Don't think that sticking your boobs out and trying to look fuckable will help. Remember you're a rock and roll band. It's not 'fuck me,' it's 'fuck you.'" *1994: Still more advice to "chick rockers."*

"One of the reasons that I feel I even have a voice that I can sing with is because my purpose in life is to save cows." *1995: Hynde is a vegetarian.*

"I don't handle alcohol very well. One drink and I have to go to my bed. Two drinks and I have to go to *your* bed." *1995*

I

ICE-T
(Rapper)

"I never make love records. If I do a ballad it's *Let's Get Butt Naked and Fuck.* That was a spin-off of a love record. I never say, 'Ooh, baby.' If I say something to the ladies, it's real rowdy, the worst shit. And they get tickled." *1991*

"I been pulled out of my nice Mercedes Benz, laid out flat on the street, and humiliated in front of my girl, for nothing." *1992: On his persecution by the LAPD.*

"We just celebrated the Fourth of July, and that's like the 'fuck the police' holiday of America. That's the day we went head up with the rule of the Queen. Paul Revere was running around saying, 'Here come the pigs, here come the pigs!'" *1992*

"They told me in Italy, 'Oh, we have a custom in Italy—when we like you, we spit on you.' I'm like, 'We got a custom in L.A.—when you spit on us, we hit you in the head with hard objects.'" *1994*

BILLY IDOL
(Singer)

"Just because I've got spiked hair doesn't mean I'm not a loving, passionate person." *1990*

JULIO IGLESIAS
(Singer)

"I wouldn't have time to sing if I had to take a test every time a girl said I got her pregnant." *1992*

"I am like a natural amphetamine. I can be sitting in the recording studio for 10 hours without making wee-wee. Forgetting that I have to make wee-wee." *1992*

"The first time it gave me a headache. The second time it didn't activate very much. I make love better than I did in the past. But only in my head." *1998: On his experiences with Viagra and lovemaking.*

DON IMUS
(Radio Host)

"Watching Dan Rather do the news—he looks like he's making a hostage tape." *1996*

"I know [Phil Gramm] has a Ph.D. in economics, but you can't sound like you just walked out of the woods in *Deliverance* and not scare people." *1996*

MICHAEL INGHAM
(Secretary to the Primate of
the Anglican Church of Canada)

"While it is true that our primate occasionally enjoys bananas, I have never seen him walk with his knuckles on the ground or scratch himself publicly under the armpits." *1992: Responding to a questionnaire he received from the staff at the University of Wisconsin's Regional Primate Research Center requesting as much information as possible on their chosen study, primatology. The questionnaire was addressed to: "George Cram, Primates World Relief Development Fund, Toronto, Canada.*

JEREMY IRONS
(Actor)

"Why would deaf people attend a reading? It's like a blind person wanting to attend ballet." *1996: After asking a sign-language interpreter to move to one side so as not to distract the 300 members of his audience at a reading.*

CHRIS ISAAK
(Singer)

"My breath kept me out of the Army. The guy said, 'Chris, there just ain't enough Certs." *1993*

"I play my guitar a lot, work in the garden. The only thing that separates me from old people who stay at home is my healthy prostate gland." *1994*

"I'm wearing Hugo. Not Hugo Boss—Hugo Krotzlinger, the plumber that lives two houses away from me. We're the same size." *1998: On his attire at the VH1 Fashion Awards party.*

"I said, 'I just have one question: When you're using my music, is there nudity or violence?' They said yes to both. And I said, 'OK, we're a go!'" *1999: On why his 1995 song* Baby Did a Bad Bad Thing *is prominently featured in the late Stanley Kubrick's thriller,* Eyes Wide Shut.

MOLLY IVINS
(Columnist)

"If there are hookers in this town, they wear Rockports." *1998: On the dearth of high heels in San Franscisco.*

"Life's a funny female-dog, isn't she?" *1998*

J

JANET JACKSON
(Singer)

"I always wanted to work at McDonald's for a week." *1994*

KATHERINE JACKSON
(Mother of Singers)

"Michael's appearance makes people think he's gay, but he's not, because you can tell when a person is gay. . . . You look at a person's face, and you say, 'Oh, my God, that guy is gay.'" *1994*

LA TOYA JACKSON
(Singer)

"We're just like a normal family—we're dysfunctional." *1993: On the Jackson family.*

"What they're honoring, I really don't know." *1994: On* The Jackson Family Honors *television program.*

"I did it because I wanted people to see the real me." *1994: On her Playboy video.*

"I'm ecstatic—I thought I'd have to go to a sperm bank." *1996: On getting pregnant.*

MICHAEL JACKSON
(Singer)

"Most people don't know me, that is why they write such things, most of which is not true. I cry very often, because it hurts." *1990*

"I really believe that God chooses people to do certain things the way Michelangelo or Leonoardo da Vinci or Mozart or Muhammad Ali or Martin Luther King is chosen. And I think I haven't scratched the surface yet of what my real purpose is for being here." *1992*

"I can't think of a better way to spread the message of world peace than by working with the NFL and being part of Super Bowl XXVII." *1992*

"I wasn't aware the world thought I was so weird and bizarre." *1993*

"I made love to Lisa in my Mickey Mouse pajamas . . . then I asked her to marry me." *1994: On his proposal to Lisa Marie Presley.*

"I never met anybody who cared so much about children the way I do." *1994*

"Excuse me, I have to go to the bathroom." *1994: His immediate response upon hearing Lisa Marie Presley say she would marry him.*

"I'm in bliss 24 hours a day." *1997: On the joys of parenthood.*

"I want my son to live a normal life." *1997*

MICHAEL JACKSON (CONT'D)

"My doctor gave me the news. . . . I started to cry . . . I said, 'There's another one. Real soon, I feel it coming. . . . And I pray it's not me.' Then Mother Teresa came." *1997: Discussing Princess Diana's death with Barbara Walters.*

"Poland is the place which moved me most. . . . My dream of returning to the world of children can become real in this place." *1998: On his plans to build a $500 million World of Childhood amusement park in Bemowo, a suburb of Warsaw.*

"She used to confide in me. She'd just call me on the phone and we would talk about everything that was happening in her life. The press was hard on her in the same way they were hard on me and she needed to talk to someone who knew exactly what she was going through. She felt hunted in the way I've felt hunted. Trapped, if you like." *1999: On his relationship with Princess Diana.*

"I just want to go to Yugoslavia and hug every one of those children and tell them I love them. The TV footage just breaks my heart. It's just horrifying. I have to turn the set off—it makes me cry every day." *1999: On watching TV coverage of the Kosovo crisis.*

SAMUEL L. JACKSON
(Actor)

"I told Quentin [Tarantino] when we did *Pulp Fiction* that he was going to offend people when he said 'Dead nigger storage,' because there's something about saying 'nigger,' as opposed to 'niggeh,' that's like fingernails on a blackboard. It becomes an epithet when you put the 'er' on it, but with 'eh' it can be a term of endearment, a descriptive, it can be all kinds of things." *1998*

"I love wearing the clothes. The golf course is the only place I can go dressed like a pimp and fit in perfectly. Anywhere else, lime-green pants and alligator shoes, and I got a cop on my ass." *1999: On golf.*

MICK JAGGER
(Singer)

"It's hard to have a nine-to-five job as an opium addict; but if all you've got to do is toss off a chapter of a novel every month, you could find that the lifestyle suits you." *1993*

"You supposedly get different as you get older. I'm not so aggressive. I'm not so ready to punch people out as I used to be." *1993*

"What about all the beer you can drink and the girls down in front? There's other things than money." *1994: Responding to a journalist's assertion that touring was just about making money.*

"Very misunderstood." *1997: When asked what he thinks of Prince Charles.*

"Very understood." *1997: When asked what he thinks of Bill Clinton.*

"I started off with short dresses, which I knew I wouldn't get to wear. But I looked a lot better in a short dress, to be perfectly honest." *1998: On preparing for his role as a cross-dresser in the movie* Bent.

"After 20 years of taking coke, it's good to drink Pepsi!" *1998: Speaking at a Pepsi bottlers' convention in Hawaii.*

TINA JAKES
(Magazine Editor)

"Fabio has a very special magic. Just about every woman he meets loses weight." *1993*

JENNA JAMESON
(Porn Star)

"You have to be quite creative. Have you ever seen the things I can do with my spit?" *1997*

WAYLON JENNINGS
(Singer)

"I don't need a wheelchair; I don't use makeup, Viagra or Geritol. I don't have chronic fatigue—I can't even spell it. The only thing I've retired from is the road." *1998: On rumors of his retirement.*

STEVE JOBS
(Founder, Apple Computers)

"To people who ask me that question, I say, 'Fuck you! Fuck you!' " *1998: When asked what his commitment to Apple Computer was after he sold his stock in the company and then became its interim CEO.*

"I'm either going to be CEO or chairman of the company forever. I turned Apple over to a bozo once." *1998: Responding to a question about how long he planned to remain CEO at Apple.*

"I don't believe televisions and computers are going to merge. You go to your TV when you want to turn your brain off. You go to your computer when you want to turn your brain on." *1998*

"*Time* called me [in 1982] and said they wanted to make me Man of the Year. I was a little younger and had more hubris then. I thought, 'What a wise choice.' But this reporter they sent was the same age as me and had a giant problem with me. So he wrote this hatchet-job piece. When his editors saw the piece, they decided, 'We can't make this guy Man of the Year.' I remember I was off somewhere with a girlfriend and the magazine was delivered, and after I read it, I literally started crying. It wasn't long after that I decided that people like symbols and that I became one. I had to look at it as if I had a famous twin brother—but it ain't me." *1999*

"There used to be something magical here [in Silicon Valley]—scientific and cultural. You could smell it, feel it. When I was in high school, I would ride my bicycle to the Stanford artificial-intelligence lab on weekends and hang out. You could feel the magic in the air. I miss that time. People care more about material things now. When I was twenty-three I was worth a million dollars. When I was twenty-four, I was worth $10 million and, at twenty-five, over $100 million. But I never really cared that much about money." *1999: The co-founder and interim-CEO of Apple Computer, who considers himself, at the age of forty-four, an "old man."*

BILLY JOEL
(Singer & Musician)
"They maybe paid $200 for those tickets, and they sit there and expect me to deliver $200 worth of entertainment. I'll tell you, I'm not worth $200." *1994*

ELTON JOHN
(Singer & Musician)
"How hard is it to make a fuckn' white suit all the time?" *1996: On men's fashion designers.*

"I want to do a musical movie . . . Like *Evita* but with good music." *1996*

"I always wanted a machine that no one else had that you could switch on to see somebody naked." *1998*

"I've been through therapy and treatment, and I went to all my AA meetings. I went to three years of them and suddenly I found myself in a social situation only able to talk about the fact that I couldn't drink anymore and didn't take coke. And people were dying of boredom in front of my eyes. They would see me come into a room and throw themselves out the window." *1998*

DON JOHNSON
(Actor)
"It's like we're Ozzie and Harriet on acid." *1992: Describing his marriage to Melanie Griffith.*

ANGELINA JOLIE
(Actress)
"I had a therapist in school. I thought it was extra credit to take drug group and private therapy, so I took it." *1999: Describing her relationship with her family and her father Jon Voight.*

GRACE JONES
(Actress & Singer)
"I look actually more feminine when I'm dressed as a man." *1990*

"Forget all those health clinics and gyms. Sex is the best cure for everything, especially stress. If I have a good night of sex, all my problems are gone by 10 o'clock in the morning." *1999*

JAMES EARL JONES
(Actor)
"'I'm impressed with your poem, James Earl,' Professor Crouch told me after he read my ode to a grapefruit." *1993: In his autobiography,* Voices and Silences.

TOM JONES
(Singer)

"I did three shows in Moscow. Only thing was, the first night the audience was so polite. The promoter told me, 'If you want 'em to stand up, to have a good time, you've gotta tell 'em. because they're so used to being told what to do.'" *1994*

"I'm very, but not very, very." *1997: On the rumor that he is "very, very well endowed."*

ERICA JONG
(Writer)

"At the end of every book, I feel like killing myself. You think you'll never write one again. Until you use up the advance." *1995*

NEIL JORDAN
(Screenwriter & Director)

"I was brought up by priests—who tried to get me to sit on their knee, of course. I was told that the sky was full of these figures that look down on you and watch your every move. I was taught they spoke to you. I was an altar boy. But, no, I'm not a practicing Catholic. It kind of all went away without any particular trauma." *1998*

ASHLEY JUDD
(Actress)

"In 10 professional outings, [I was involved with] exactly two of my costars. Just 20 percent. Which, by the way, is well below the national average." *1997*

"I drink a lot of water. I happen to think that ponytails and water are the keys to happiness. It's amazing to me how little people drink. My grandfather didn't drink very much. The only time I remember him being sick was after my grandmother died and he got malnutrition. It happens a lot to men who've been cooked for all their lives. Isn't that sad?" *1997*

"To give me a sense of the country and the people, they took me to the central market, or marron. The women were dressed in all styles. . . . My favorite was the Pangi, or bright plaids worn on top of each other and secured with twists of the fabric. . . . A wonderful saleslady guided me to the brightest of the brights. We selected three eye-popping plaids (think Lilly Pulitzer amplified) and she advised me on how to choose clashing threads for sewing the hems. When next you see me looking very good in Nantucket, think Surinam . . . I could have done it when I was 22, joined the PC [Peace Corps] and flourished, but maybe by telling you about my experience, I have done even greater good." *1999: Revealing she wanted to be a Peace Corps volunteer after college, but instead became an actress, on her trek to Surinam, South America, as a pretend Peace Corps volunteer.*

K

SAM KEEN
(Author & Guru)

"Trace the history of your penis. When did you first become aware you had a dangling destiny?" *1991: In his best-selling book,* Fire in the Belly.

GARRISON KEILLOR
(Writer & Radio Host)

"You hear them at the grocery store deliberating the balsamic vinegar and olive oils, the cold-pressed virgin olive oil vs. the warm-pressed olive oil, and you think: These people probably subscribe to an olive oil magazine called *New Dimension*, people with too much money and very little character, people who are all sensibility and no sense, all nostalgia and no history, the people my Aunt Eleanor used to call 'a $10 haircut on a 59 cent head.'" *1994: On his generation of Americans.*

"I look upon the (bad poets) as ambitious, intelligent persons who deserve better teaching. Writing requires discipline, and it can be taught, but you don't find it in turgid poems about Bad Daddies and The Struggle to Be Me and all the other flat, morbid, narcissistic writing that is encouraged by bad teaching.

"The creative-writing industry is cranking out reams of stuff that nobody in his or her right mind would ever want to read. One genre it mostly ignores is satire and humor. It takes discipline to tell a joke." *1996*

"Watching [the movie *Fargo*] was like driving toward Bismarck, ND, at 10 miles an hour. You had a lot of time to see where you were going—and wishing you didn't have to." *1996*

CHRIS KELLY
(Rapper)

"That's, like, part of Kriss Kross, y'know what I'm sayin'? It might have been a fad to all of the people out there in the world, y'know what I'm sayin'? But y'know what I'm sayin', it wasn't no fad to us. We always said that we're gonna wear our pants backwards. When we came out from day one, we had 'em on backwards. We're going to wear 'em like this for the rest of our lives. Y'know what I'm sayin'? Putting our pants on backwards is like, y'know what I'm sayin', putting them on forward for you." 1996: *Kelly of the Atlanta duo Kriss Kross, which had the hit song* Jump *in 1992 and another—*Tonight's the Night*—in 1996, commenting on wearing his pants backward.*

MARGARET TRUDEAU KEMPER
(Ex-wife of former Canadian Prime Minister)

"I thought my usefulness was finished. After all, I believed my job on Earth was to procreate and be a pleasant sexual diversion for hardworking men." *1998: Blaming menopause for her deteriorating mental health.*

DOUGLAS KENNEDY
(Novelist)

"Somebody said writing for the movies is like the beginning of a love affair: It's full of surprises and you're always getting screwed." *1998: The author of* The Big Picture *and* The Job *on why he doesn't write the screenplays for his best-selling books.*

KERMIT
(Frog & Actor)

"I knew I wanted to be a performer even before my tail dropped off." *1996*

KEN KESEY
(Writer)

"I like being a famous writer. Problem is, every once in a while you have to write something." (*1992*)

CHAKA KHAN
(Singer)

"If you look at L.A. from a spiritual point of view, it's a cultivated desert, not meant for habitation

. . . How can you be motivated when the sun is out every damn day?" *1998*

JODIE KIDD
(Model)

"I love *The Tempest*, but I'm not sure I have enough guts to get in front of people and say, 'Romeo, Romeo,' so I'll just be a fairy in the back row." *1999: On her ambition to be an actress only in the plays of William Shakespeare and only in nonspeaking roles.*

MARGO KIDDER
(Actress)

"Out of the drug taking came a lot of creative thinking and breaking down of personal barriers and having a phony social persona. If that hadn't been the case, none of us would have developed our talents. But Steven Spielberg didn't take drugs. Brian [De Palma] didn't. Marty [Scorcese] didn't, until later when he got into trouble with coke. The directors who ended up successful were very protective of their own brains." *1998: Remembering drugs, directors, and Hollywood in the '70s.*

"I sat him down and went, 'OK, Steven, here's how you do it—you don't wear your socks and your T-shirt to bed. Get something besides the Twinkies in the fridge, and read her Dylan Thomas." *1998: Remembering teaching young director Steven Spielberg about the birds and the bees.*

NICOLE KIDMAN
(Actress)

"I worked it out: You sleep a third of your life, so if you can reduce that to a quarter, you have more time awake." *1993*

ANTHONY KIEDIS
(Singer)

"You can't go around taking your dick out. Some people don't like it." *1994*

"Golf is an extremely spiritual sport. It's visualization of the path. As you strike the ball, you—for the moment—own your own planet in orbit. You know, the green becomes a symbol of celestial heaven. It is extremely and intensely personal and revealing. It also shows a lot of sadness, hardship

ANTHONY KIEDIS (CONT'D)

and difficulty and coping with nature of life. But it's not dwelling in the tragic morosities of life. I think I made that word up. It's really about walking through the morosities of life." *1995*

CRAIG KILBORN
(TV Host)

"Most media analysts agree closed captioning for the *Jerry Springer* show is a ridiculous idea—because it implies his viewers can read." *1998*

"Mel Gibson apparently decided to go forward with a big-screen version of *Hogan's Heroes* after seeing *Saving Private Ryan* and *Schindler's List*, which Gibson said 'didn't really capture the zany, madcap comedy that was Nazi Germany.'" *1998*

"In the current *Ladies Home Journal*, Nicole Kidman describes hubby Tom Cruise as an avid outdoorsman who likes rock climbing and mountain biking, leading some to whisper that he may be a lesbian." *1998*

VAL KILMER
(Actor)

"It was the leather pants that killed Jim Morrison. It's like living in a wet suit. There is no circulation. I'm sure that's what did it to him." *1990: Kilmer played Morrison in a movie.*

"I don't make any pretense about being normal. I'm not." *1999*

"Even when I was a kid, I didn't like standing in line. Somehow with fame, you're exempt from line waiting. Maybe in hell you have to be the line keeper." *1999*

KIM SUN-JU
(South Korean Professor)

"Cultural life is something that is enjoyed only when there is economic prosperity. We can set it aside for better times." *1998: The Seoul University professor commenting on the fact that the film* Titanic *drew such huge crowds in his country that ticket sales for the movie drained precious cash from the country's depleted economy.*

CAROLE KING
(Songwriter & Singer)

"When do you guys ever pee?" *To members of the Grateful Dead on the unusual length of their songs.*

LARRY KING
(TV & Radio Talk-show Host)

"She's sexy. She does not photograph well. The television camera doesn't like her. It takes her chin down to a point. It doesn't do well by her eyes. But sitting next to her, hey, if I were single and she were single, and she's at the bar, I'd go over to her like that [he snaps his fingers]." *1990: On Marilyn Quayle, wife of the vice president.*

"They're inseparable, very hand-holding." *1991: On Ted Turner and Jane Fonda.*

"Mark, thank you. That was terrific." *1992: To John Lennon's killer, Mark David Chapman, following an interview.*

"It's wonderful that we have 8-year-old boys filling sandbags with old women." *1993: On efforts to stem the Mississippi river flood waters.*

"I can't believe the recognition I get. All over the world. I was in Israel, at the Wailing Wall, and this old rabbi is there praying. He looks up at me and says, 'So what's with Perot?' I have a nice franchise here and I totally enjoy it. I feel like I'm part of history." *1995*

"My reactions I don't keep in check. My feelings I do. They don't count. . . . You'll never hear me use the word 'I.'" *1995*

"He's an example of what's wrong with the '90s." *1997: On Howard Stern.*

"Is it boasting to say that I don't need Viagra?" *1998*

"I'm not gay. I respect gays, but I'm heterosexual. I don't know why. I didn't choose it. Trent Lott chose it." *1998*

STEPHEN KING
(Writer)

"I send 'em the book, they publish it. It's a great deal." *1996: On his relationship with his publisher.*

"Just never got around to [writing planned sequels to *Salem's Lot* and *The Shining.*] Things to do and people to kill, you know." *1996*

"Muse is a ghost. In a real sense, writing comes as it comes. It really is like ghostwriting. It's like it comes from someplace else. Maxwell Perkins, I think, said that Thomas Wolfe wasn't a writer, he was a divine wind chime. The wind blew through him and he just rattled. And I think that's true of a lot of writers. It's true of me." *1998*

"I think that writers are made, not born or created out of dreams or childhood trauma—that becoming a writer . . . is a direct result of conscious will. Of course there has to be some talent involved, but talent is a dreadfully cheap commodity. . . . What separates the talented individual from the successful one is a lot of hard work and study; a constant process of honing." *1998*

"To propose an advance is to keep a writer going when he says, 'I need to pay my rent, my mortgage. I need this to keep them from repossessing my car.' I already have the freedom to write. Elvis Presley once said something like 'I looked around myself when I was a teen-ager and saw I was in a tiny little pasture with all these other cows, chomping at grass and shitting. I broke through a fence somehow, I don't know how I did it, and I was in a bigger pasture. I looked and there were still fences all around, but I was by myself. So I grazed.'" *1998: On why he doesn't need advances from his writing and how he feels about it.*

"I have a real problem with bloat. I write like fat ladies diet." *1998: On the length of his books.*

"If I name names, I'll look like I'm slumming, or I'll look like I'm climbing, or I'll offend the people I leave out. So I better not say." *1998: When asked to name his peers.*

"I'm the geek. In the great carnival of American culture, I'm the big naked guy at the back of the midway biting the heads off chickens." *1998*

"Fifty is the age where you stop fooling yourself that if you just eat granola nobody will notice." *1998: On turning fifty.*

KATHY KINNEY
(Actress)

"Everyone has had a suggestion on what I should tell you. Everybody's life is different, so it doesn't work to compare. And everyone agreed the most important thing you should know is you will never, ever, ever, ever use any of that algebra." *1997: In a commencement address at Stevens Point (WI) Area Senior High School.*

BARBARA ANN KIPFER
(Writer)

"Pictures of mixed vegetables. Someone with boots on the wrong feet. Yarn lampshades. Nouns." *1990: Four items Kipfer lists in* The Happy Book *that should make you happy.*

AARON R. KIPNIS
(Writer)

"We discover our penises at a pretty early age. After all, there it is, just hanging out, right there within easy grasp." *1992: In his "men's movement" manual,* Knights Without Armor.

SALLY KIRKLAND
(Actress)

"To put it spiritually, all seven of my chakras were open." *1990: Explaining how she felt after receiving an Academy Award nomination.*

"The reason I'm on this planet is to give some insight into pain." *1990*

WALTER KIRN
(Editor)

"No one ever went broke underestimating the sexual satisfaction of the American people." *1995: Reviewing Robert James Waller's book* Border Music, *in* New York *magazine.*

"Never in publishing history has a romance writer gone farther faster with fewer dirty parts." *1995: On the phenomenon of Robert James Waller's megaseller,* The Bridges of Madison County.

EARTHA KITT
(Singer)

"I don't. What's there to think about?" *1999: On what she thinks of Madonna.*

CALVIN KLEIN
(Designer)
"We designed the underwear based on our ideas of what underwear should be." *1993: On his design secrets.*

KEVIN KLEIN
(Actor)
"I went to Indiana University, which we called the Harvard of the Middle of Nowhere." *1998: In Cambridge, MA, to accept an award from the university's Hasty Pudding Club.*

MARCI KLEIN
(Celebrity Daughter)
"My only complaint about having a father in fashion is that every time I'm about to go to bed with a guy I have to look at my dad's name all over his underwear." *1994*

EVEL KNIEVEL
(Daredevil)
"Women are the root of all evil. I ought to know. I'm Evel." *1999*

"When you're mad at someone, it's probably best not to break his arm with a baseball bat." *1999*

"You can be famous for a lot of things. You can be a Nobel Prize winner. You can be the fattest guy in the world. You can be the guy with the smallest penis. Whatever it is, enjoy it. It don't last forever." *1999*

"If God ever gives this world an enema, he'll stick the tube in the Lincoln Tunnel and he'll flush everybody in New York City clear across the Atlantic. And that would just be a start." *1999*

"I've done everything in the world I've ever wanted to do except kill somebody. There are a couple of guys I know who need shooting. They represent the rectums of humanity." *1999*

HERBERT KOHL
(Writer & Educator)
"It took me three years of grad school and a year of psychoanalysis to feel it was OK to be an elementary school teacher—to this day my family thinks I wasted my life." *1996*

JEFF KOONS
(Artist)
"I did a radio show this morning where that happened. But the interviewer was a little surprised and intimidated that I could tap my head and rub my stomach at the same time. He didn't know what to say. . . . I think it happens when people feel intimidated by art." *1993: On how he responds to interviewers who challenge him as an opportunist and a fraud.*

DEAN KOONTZ
(Writer)
"I'd give Charles Darwin videotapes of *Geraldo*, *Beavis and Butt Head* and *The McLaughlin Group*. I would be interested in seeing if he still believes in evolution. *1994: On what give he would give another writer, living or dead.*

MICHAEL KORS
(Designer)
"I think everyone wants to be 35, or at least the vision of 35. Stars in Hollywood who are 19 are very sophisticated. They look 35 to me. And then you see a star who's 60, she looks 35, too. Claire Danes and Goldie Hawn. Same clothes, same body, same hair." *1999*

MARTIN KOVE
(Actor)
"I was right there in the delivery room. I helped pull the babies out—the whole nine yards. *1990: Describing the birth of his twins.*

HILTON KRAMER
(Art Critic)
"Artists who work in video offer something that cannot be experienced as high art. They're basically offering you an amateur version of something people in the networks do much better." *1995*

JUDITH KRANTZ
(Writer)
"Shaking hands with Bill Clinton is, in and of itself, a full-body sexual experience, I promise you. He has the sexiest handshake of any man that I have ever experienced in my life." *1994*

STEVE KRAVITS
(Comedian)

"When they were hunting for Noriega, I kept thinking, 'He's a drug dealer? I could find him.' " *1990*

LENNY KRAVITZ
(Musician & Singer)

"I just smoke pot. That's all I need; my head is so fucking weird as it is, that does it for me." *1995*

KRIS KRISTOFFERSON
(Singer, Songwriter & Actor)

"[Memory lapses are] one of God's blessings. If I could remember everything, I'd be a mess." *1998*

"At least once in every film, I'm convinced that I'm uniquely unequipped to do the job, that I should never do another one. But I get over it." *1998*

NICOLE KRUK
(Groupie)

"He is skinny and really old. . . . I hope I'm not like him when I'm his age." *1996: Recalling her affair with Mick Jagger.*

MALCOLM KUSHNER
(Humor Consultant)

"This is a result of natural market farces." *1998: Saying his annual* Cost of Laughing Index, *which measures the price of such items as rubber chickens and scripts for half-hour sitcoms, went up 3 percent in one year.*

MARK KWIATKOWSKI
(Director of Warsaw's Royal Gardens)

"Behind the mask, there's a normal guy who must dress in all these clothes to keep up a convention, an act." *1998: On Michael Jackson and why he backs Jackson's plan to build a huge amusement park just outside Warsaw.*

L

LORENZO LAMAS
(Actor)

"There is no capital of Uruguay, you dummy—it's a country." *1999: Displaying his geographical genius on* The Daily Show *with Jon Stewart.*

ANN LANDERS
(Advice Guru)

"[Pope John Paul II] looks like an angel. He has the face of an angel. His eyes are sky blue, and his cheeks are pink and adorable-looking, and he has a sweet sense of humor. Of course, he's a Polack. They're very antiwomen." *1995*

"He [President Kennedy] was the womanizer from hell. I mean, this guy had women all over the place . . . Of course, he had a bum back, for one thing, and the women had to do all the work." *1995*

SHERRY LANSING
(Movie Studio Executive)

"Maybe sex in New York is different because it happens in smaller rooms." *1993: Comparing life in Los Angeles with life in New York.*

LOUIS LAPHAM
(Journalist)

"Dutiful attendance at the knee of privilege presupposes the capacity to endure long bouts of stupefying boredom. . . . Practice with inanimate objects. Look at a balloon for 90 minutes with an expression of close attention and profound respect; talk to a box of Cheerios about Martha's Vineyard and Monica Lewinsky; ask a fern for its view of the Mexican debt. The exercises will prepare you for an evening at the Council of Foreign Relations or an afternoon around the pool with Norman Mailer." *1999*

QUEEN LATIFAH
(Singer)

"I was the most popular in high school. I was voted Best All Round, Most Popular, Most Comical and Best Dancer. And it was only because I'm me." *1998*

CYNDI LAUPER
(Singer)

"I absolutely refuse to reveal my age. What am I? A car?" *1994*

LUCY LAWLESS
(Actress)

"Madeleine Albright. She's a tough chick. . . . I'd hate to meet her in a dark alley." *1999: Lawless, better known as Xena, the warrior princess, on who she thinks is most like her TV character.*

THUY THU LE
(Actress)

"I'm not an actress and I don't think I will be. I accepted the role because it was a true story. It showed the other side of the Vietnam War, the bad and ugly side of it." *1990: On her role in Brian de Palma's film,* Casualties of War.

TIMOTHY LEARY
(Guru & Celebrity)

"I am exploring for the first time in my life the amazing wonderland known as senility." *1991*

"But I've left specific instructions that I do not want to be brought back during a Republican administration." *1993: Discussing his plans to have his brain frozen.*

"I get really disgusted and despairing when I see young teenagers smoking grass and lying around listening to the Grateful Dead." *1994*

"I often don't remember what I did two days before. It makes life interesting." *1995: The seventy-five-year-old pop culture philosopher, on the senility sneaking into his mind, chasing out his memory.*

"I'm looking forward to the most fascinating experience in life, which is dying. You've got to approach your dying the way you live your life—with curiosity, with hope, with fascination, with courage and with the help of your friends." *1995*

"[Dr. Jack Kevorkian] is a tremendous hero, but he's treating himself like a victim. He hunches over when he's arrested. He should get himself a really elegant set of clothes and swagger around. He should stand up and tell everybody, 'No more victims, including me.' He should cover himself with Hawaiian flowers and have a champagne glass in his hand." *1995*

"I've led the league as a human being over the last 30 years, but I've only batted one out of three. The other two times, I went up there, and probably shouldn't have swung at that outside pitch. But look around—I'm still leading the league, I think." *1996: On living his life over again and doing things differently.*

MATT LEBLANC
(Actor)

"I'm not the guy the tabloids paint me out to be. I don't have enough time in my schedule to have all these addictions. But being dead was the worst. I hated that." *1998: On rumors in the press that he'd died.*

SIMON LEBON
(Singer)

"Because they can. It's the same answer to the question, 'Why do dogs lick their balls?' " *When asked, "What's your theory on why rock stars marry models?"*

FRAN LEBOWITZ
(Writer)

"It's like having to watch *Cats* for five days. It's like having Andrew Lloyd Webber for president. He has the soul and mind of Andrew Lloyd Webber and he's one Häagen-Dazs bar away from having his body." *1993: On Bill Clinton and his inauguration ceremonies.*

"I used to [read interviews with people who have made a lot of money], but they were so riddled with lies that I gave it up. They always said that the way to make a lot of money is not to think about money. Just do something you love. Clearly, what they love is making money. If what they said were true, then the richest people in the world would be good school teachers and bad poets." *1997*

"We live in a fantasyland where we value youth in a totally abstract way. What has value in this culture? Money. Who doesn't have any money? Youth. Did you ever hear anyone say, 'I'm going out with this 19-year-old guy. I don't really like him, but boy is he rich'?" *1998*

"My first exposure to adulthood was knowing that at every moment in your life when they're going to let you have all the ice cream you want, you will not be able to swallow it." *1998: Remembering when she was four years old and she was told that after having her tonsils out she could have all the ice cream she wanted.*

"Nothing is more telling of someone's age than who they think is glamorous. So, to me, Cary Grant looks like a movie star, Paul Newman looks like a movie star, Warren Beatty looks like a movie star, but Brad Pitt, to be perfectly frank, looks like a trick." *1998*

SPIKE LEE
(Director)
"This is Spike Lee. How you doing? Look, how in the hell are you going to write some bullshit that I don't have a fucking college degree? I got a fucking master's from NYU and an undergraduate degree from Morehouse College. How's the fucking *New York Times* gonna write some bullshit that I don't have a fucking college degree? You know you motherfuckers ought to do some fucking research or whatever you call that shit before you write some fucking bullshit, all right? I got a fucking Master of Fine Arts from fucking NYU. I want a motherfucking retraction. All right, motherfucker." *1992: Message left on the answering machine of the Campus Life editor of the* New York Times, *who had written incorrectly that Lee did not have a college degree.*

"That's before I get my breast implants." *1993: Amending an earlier statement that he ranks after only Madonna as the best self-promoter in America.*

"A lot of people will have to do a lot of explaining on AIDS one day. All of a sudden, a disease appears out of nowhere that nobody has a cure for, and it's specifically targeted at gays and minorities. The mystery disease, yeah, about as mysterious as genocide. I'm convinced AIDS is a government-engineered disease. They got one thing wrong; they never realized it couldn't just be contained to the groups it was intended to wipe out. So now, it's a national priority. Exactly like drugs became when they escaped the urban centers into white suburbs." *1993*

"They're blowing the whole black-Jewish thing up. There is no conspiracy among African Americans against Jewish people. I'm sorry, I mean the average black person doesn't know who's Jewish. It's just another white person." *1994*

"It bothers me, especially when a lot of these people might be members of the Klan." *1994: On the cut-out masks of his face that were printed in Indianapolis newspapers for fans to wear during the sixth Pacers-Knicks playoff game in Indianapolis.*

"He's a very interesting man. Dennis Rodman you could do a five-minute feature on." *1996*

"I be thinking that Ebonics be stupid!" *1997*

JENNIFER JASON LEIGH
(Actress)
"My mom told me that [director] Robert Altman told her I have no personality. I have one, I must have one, but I don't quite know what it is." *1993*

JACK LEMMON
(Actor)
"[Sylvester Stallone]'s got two bodyguards who look exactly like him walking around on the beach, so I guess he figures that cuts the odds of being assassinated to one in three." *1992*

SEAN LENNON
(Musician, Singer & Celebrity Son)
"No one understands the Beach Boys—like, they are the best band of all time." *1998*

"He was a countercultural revolutionary, and the government takes that kind of shit really seriously historically. He was dangerous to the government. If he had said, 'Bomb the White House Tomorrow,' there would have been ten thousand people who would have done it. These pacifist revolutionaries are historically killed by the government, and anybody who thinks that Mark Chapman was just some crazy guy who killed my dad for his personal interests is insane, I think, or very naive, or hasn't thought about it clearly. It was in the best interests of the United States to have my dad killed, definitely. And, you know, that worked against them, to be honest, because once he died his powers grew. So, I mean, fuck them. They didn't get what they wanted." *1998: On the murder of his father, John Lennon.*

"I had as close to a normal childhood as one could have if you were John Lennon's kid: the only thing

SEAN LENNON (CONT'D)

that was different was that I had two detectives with guns following me everywhere." *1998*

"If you go to a high school today and ask kids to tell you the difference between John Lennon and Paul McCartney, they don't even know what band they were in." *1998*

"If it wasn't for Michael Jackson, I probably wouldn't make music now. *Thriller* changed my life completely." *1998*

"It was a profoundly spiritual experience." *1998: Commenting on his appearance on an episode of TV's* Melrose Place.

JAY LENO
(TV Talk-show Host)

"[Ross] Perot is kind of like the car salesman on his honeymoon: Rather than make love, he just stands at the end of the bed and keeps telling the wife how great it's going to be." *1992*

"Former vice president Dan Quayle said he hopes to join an Indiana think tank called the Hudson Institute. I tell you something, if Dan Quayle gets in a think tank, I hope he's wearing a life preserver." *1993*

"He wanted to sing 'Where the Boys Are.'" *1994: On why Michael Jackson didn't perform in* The Jackson Family Honors.

"You know what other trial starts this week? Heidi Fleiss! It's one of the few cases where the defendant charges more per hour than the attorney . . . which is unusual, because essentially they are doing the same thing." *1994*

"A new study in Italy says some women are actually able to hear with their breasts. This is great for Italian men, because they talk with their hands." *1995*

"[Shirley MacLaine] once said she had a 10,000 year old man inside her. Big deal! So did Anna Nicole Smith." *1995*

"I wanted to have a career in sports when I was young, but I had to give it up. I'm only 190 pounds, so I couldn't play football. And I have 20/20 vision, so I couldn't referee." *1996*

"Some cows actually give more milk when they listen to other music—for example, when they listen to Elvis, like *Love Me Tender* increased in milk production. When they listened to Latoya [Jackson], found to produce sour milk. When they listened to Jerry Garcia, this makes the cows want more grass, apparently. Here's the most startling of all. When they played Michael Jackson, the cows would milk themselves." *1996*

"Look what's going on in Hollywood. First, Billy Joel and Christie Brinkley, they got a divorce. Then Kevin Costner and his wife. Richard Gere and Cindy Crawford. Tom and Roseanne. Now Lisa Marie and Michael. Do you realize the only strong stable relationship left in this town is Siegfried and Roy?" *1996*

"And Divine Brown, the woman who was caught with Hugh Grant—well, she announced she is now writing a book about her life as a hooker. I believe it's called *Waiting to Exhale*." *1996*

"Have you seen the Ensure commercial where the little girl is sitting on a bench with an old man and she says, 'Grandpa, can I marry you?' At first I thought it was a TV movie about Woody Allen and Soon-Yi." *1998*

"The rules for evacuating lifeboats in L.A. are women and children first, then men who dress like women, then women who dress like men, and then men." *1998: On what might happen if L.A. residents were on the* Titanic.

"The biggest commotion at last week's Grammys was caused by the pop group Hanson. They were getting grabbed, pieces of their clothing were being ripped off. Finally, they called a security guard and said, 'Look, keep Michael Jackson away from us.'" *1998*

"Many of the female artists [at the Grammy Awards] didn't shave under their arms. Did you see Paula Cole, who got a Grammy for her song, *Where Have All the Cowboys Gone?* I don't know where all the cowboys have gone, but I swear I saw a couple of prairie dogs under her arms." *1998*

"Maybe you have that on backwards." *1998: To guest Halle Berry who kept falling out of her low cut dress.*

"You know what they say when a supermodel gets pregnant: Now she's gonna be eating for one." *1999: On news of Cindy Crawford's pregnancy.*

"Researchers at Cornell University say studies prove that parents do in fact have a favorite child. I think Woody Allen proved that." *1999*

ELMORE LEONARD
(Writer)

"I started with a 29 cent Scripto. Now I use a $150 Mont Blanc." *1998: On how far he has come as a writer.*

"My first rule is, if it sounds like writing, re-write it. Another rule is try to leave out the parts people skip. Oh, and never start with the weather. With those rules you can go all the way." *1998: On his personal rules of writing.*

TEA LEONI
(Actress)

"I sort of thought I wanted to be an anthropologist. But my father suggested I go to a cocktail party full of anthropologists first. I did. He's a very wise man." *1997: On how she became an actress.*

"Men are like bulls; they gotta get the new cow. Maybe you've got to get the bull after he's had a lot of cows, so you might just be the last new cow." *1998: The wife of* X-Files *star David Duchovny, discussing her love life.*

DAVID LETTERMAN
(TV Talk-show Host)

"I hate waiting in lines, but I'd do it." *1991: When asked by Johnny Carson if he planned to firebomb NBC.*

"[Governor Bill] Clinton outspent the other candidates by at least 2-to-1 . . . on Valentine's Day gifts." *1992*

"The people on the plane actually had their choice between cannibalism and the regular airline food. They *chose* cannibalism." *1993: On the movie* Alive, *in which survivors of an Andes airline crash turn to cannibalism in order to stay alive.*

"The new host of the show will be Conan O'Brien. I don't know the man. Never met the man, but we certainly wish him all the success and happiness doing this show that we've had all these years. . . . He seems like a nice guy. The only thing I heard about the new guy, Conan O'Brien: I heard he killed a guy." *1993: On his successor on* Late Night.

"I look at stuff like Jon Stewart's talk show on MTV and the kind of television that kids are growing up on now and I might as well be living on Neptune. I don't get it." *1994*

"Coincidentally, as I understand it, this was also how Arnold Schwarzenegger asked Maria Shriver out on their first date." *1995: Referring to the film* Eat, Drink, Man, Woman.

"OK, sure there's gridlock, sure there's pollution, sure there's noise, but where else can you get a hot dog for $7?" *1995: On New York City.*

"Here now is the profile on the Unabomber. Turns out that the guy is a quiet loner—now there's a stunning surprise! Usually these guys are the life of the party. He lived in a shack in the hills that he built himself. He would go into town once a week on his bicycle for provisions. I want to tell you something, this is scary—it's like I have a twin!" *1996*

"Shirley [MacLaine]—she's nuts, isn't she?" *1996: To Ricki Lake, a guest on his show while promoting her film* Mrs. Winterbourne, *which starred MacLaine.*

"Listen to this, this will make you feel old. Corn Flakes is 100 years old today. I was thinking about this—the only other 100-year-old flake I know is Shirley MacLaine." *1997*

"How about this for irony? At the big victory party for *Titanic*, after the Academy Awards . . . they ran out of ice." *1998*

DAVID LETTERMAN (CONT'D)

"It's pretty exciting about that *Titanic*. I haven't seen so many people this worked up about a sinking ship since the night I hosted the Academy Awards." *1998*

"Congratulations to Kim Basinger. She won an Academy Award. . . . When she won her Academy Award, she said, 'I would like to thank everybody I've ever known.' And that reminds me of my own experience when I hosted the Academy Awards; I then had to apologize to everybody I'd ever known." *1998*

"Sad story about George Michael . . . Beverly Hills police caught Mr. Michael alone in a restroom in the middle of a lewd act. So apparently this is the second time he's decided to go solo." *1998*

"Did you remember to change your clocks this weekend? I think you spring ahead and you fall back. It's just like Robert Downey Jr. trying to get out of bed." *1998*

"Ellen DeGeneres, you know her show is also going off the air, but you'll be able to watch the Ellen DeGeneres show in reruns, and good news. The first 40 episodes have been digitally lesbianized." *1998*

"I worked for Don Ohlmeyer at NBC . . . and here's a guy who couldn't create gas after a bean dinner." *1998: To Norm Macdonald, whom Ohlmeyer fired from* Saturday Night Live's *"Weekend Update."*

"A street magician has buried himself in a six-foot-by-two-foot glass coffin—or as we refer to it here in Manhattan, a studio apartment." *1999*

Next week they're going to auction off an original boarding pass to the *Titanic*. I've got one of those—it's my contract with CBS." *1999*

"Congratulations are in order to Woody Allen—he and Soon-Yi have a brand-new baby. It's all part of Woody's plan to grow his own wives." *1999*

IVY LEUNG
(Porn Star)

"I don't know what you have to do to gain respect as an actress. If I did know, I'd be doing it now." *1996*

JERRY LEWIS
(Actor & Comedian)

"If ever there was a 'Point of Light'. . . I'm it!" *1992: In a letter to President George Bush.*

"The devil is a role made in heaven, for Christ's sake." *1995: Describing the role he plays of the devil in* Damn Yankees *on Broadway.*

"I've had great success being a total idiot." *1997*

JERRY LEE LEWIS
(Singer & Musician)

"You mention Elvis Presley to me again and I'm gonna kill you, so help me God!" *1995: To an interviewer from the music magazine* Q.

JULIETTE LEWIS
(Actress)

"I haven't figured it out yet, but movie life is a strange thing. People go kind of crazy sometimes. They cheat on their wives and ruin their diets." *1993*

"My concern was, having said 'No, I'm not going to go around the corner and meet up with Oliver,' that maybe I would get my ass kicked off the film, or that my life would become a living hell. I mean, you know, there are repercussions to saying no sometimes." *1995: The star of Oliver Stone's* Natural Born Killers, *on her refusal at night on the set to "go around the corner and 'meet' Oliver."*

"I don't get crushes on directors. I get these five-minute crushes on room-service guys, valets, grips, actors—but just for five minutes." *1996*

WENDY LIEBMAN
(Comedienne)

"They don't make effective birth control, but they can put a man on the moon. Oh, maybe that's a good method." *1994*

"My ex-husband was an animal in bed—a ferret. No, he was wild, actually, acrobatic. We had to have spotters. Not that I remember . . . I was asleep." *1994*

KERI LIZER
(TV Producer)

"I pursued a career. It eluded me." *1998: On giving up acting to become an executive producer for TV.*

HEATHER LOCKLEAR
(Actress)

"When I ask you how I look, just say, 'Beautiful, as always'. . . . And never mention my derriere." *1995*

"There are those who say, not without good reason, that if you think there is anything better than sex, then you've never really had good sex. That said, I'd put garlic, baked garlic, chocolate, chips and salsa, and definitely champagne at the top of my list." *1995*

"Lust is the sin that gets me excited. Very excited. Luckily, because I'm married, I also get really good jewelry out of it." *1996*

SHELLEY LONG
(Actress)

"The only reason I was not invited, the most important reason why I said it, is that I did not decline the invitation. I was not trying not to be there." *1993: On why she said she was not invited to the* Cheers *final cast party.*

PAMELA LONGFELLOW
(Author)

"Twenty-four hours—the Earth had traveled once around the sun, and Lizzie had simply gone along for the ride." *1990: In her novel* China Blues.

JENNIFER LOPEZ
(Actress & Singer)

"My mother would always say to other people, 'Oh, Jennifer? With that body? She's going to get pregnant.' " *1998: On growing up and dating.*

"All I can say is if they show my butt in a movie, it better be a wide shot." *1999*

TRACY LORDS
(Porn Star & Actress)

"I'd lock myself in a cage, swallow the key, and hope for constipation." *1992: On what she would do differently if she could be fifteen again.*

"Every teenage cheerleader runs around, screws half the football team and takes drugs. The major difference is that the evidence of my doing it existed on the shelves of video stores." *1993*

SOPHIA LOREN
(Actress)

"Actors who say, 'Oh, my God, I am so famous I cannot have a private life,' I say, 'What are you talking about? When you started you wanted to have the popularity, you wanted to be famous, be known, now you say how boring it is?' I think it's a mortal sin." 1999

COURTNEY LOVE
(Singer & Actress)

"We ate breakfast. We ate lunch. We ate dinner. We rented movies and ate ice cream. . . . We had some fucking dignity." *1995: Courtney Love, flamboyant widow of Nirvana lead singer Kurt Cobain, in a professed attempt to show she and Cobain engaged in pursuits other than drug use.*

"Testosterone is getting kicked out of rock. Part of rock is dick. It's like I'm the one in the dress that has to provide it!" *1995*

"If I was at home I'd be slamming drugs. When we are on the road, I don't get drugs—bad drugs, anyway." *1995: Talking about life on the road.*

"I don't think God necessarily put us here to be sober all the time, but I also don't think he put us here to be junkies." *1995*

"I don't mean to be a diva, but some days you wake up and you're Barbra Streisand." *1997*

"The more I chant and do yoga, drink raw juice and cut out chicken, which I've come to believe is truly evil, the less makeup I seem to need or want." *1998*

"If you love it, fuck you! If you hate it, fuck you!" *1998: On her group—Hole's—new album.*

"I don't want to play best friends and kooky villains. So I whacked it." *1999: On her nose job.*

"Once you've cleared a million bucks, excuse me, you're not a punk anymore." *1999: On how the success of her rock band, Hole, changed her life.*

LYLE LOVETT
(Musician & Singer)

"It's true that I did get the girl, but then my grandfather always said, 'Even a blind chicken finds a

LYLE LOVETT (CONT'D)

grain of corn every now and then." *1994: On marrying Julia Roberts.*

"Women like to eat outside." *1994: Explaining one of the "universal truths" of women.*

ROB LOWE
(Actor)

"I really used that time in Atlanta to learn more about Governor Dukakis." *1990: On a trip to Atlanta where he was charged with using his celebrity status to induce females to engage in sex and making pornographic films of those activities.*

"I had people come up to me on the street afterward and say, 'Hey, you know, I do it all the time. The difference is you got caught.'" *1990: On facing charges of filming himself engaged in sex with two young girls in Atlanta.*

"There's something in every woman that I find beautiful, and there's something in every guy that I find a reason to go watch *Monday Night Football* with." *1995*

GEORGE LUCAS
(Film Producer & Director)

"Bad movies have been around since the beginning of time." *1998*

"Before *American Graffiti*, I was working on basically negative movies. I became very aware of the fact that . . . the heritage we built up since the war [World War II] had been wiped out in the Sixties, and . . . now you just sort of sat there and got stoned. I wanted to preserve what a certain generation of Americans thought being a teenager was really about . . . from about 1945 to 1962." *The man who wrote and directed the 1972 film* American Graffiti, *on the genesis of the now-classic film.*

JOHN LYDON
(aka Johnny Rotten, Musician & Singer)

"My mum thought he was a bit retarded." *1994: Commenting on Sid Vicious, his bandmate in the Sex Pistols.*

"It [the movie *Sid and Nancy*] caused me quite a bit of annoyance at the time, people coming up to me and saying, 'Oh, you're Sid Vicious, aren't you dead?' That's the kind of audience it attracted." *1994*

"We have found a common cause, and it's your money." *1996: The lead singer of the Sex Pistols, explaining the motivation for their comeback.*

"I have nothing to say to *Rolling Stone*. It's as geriatric as the band it was named for." *1998: To a correspondent from* Rolling Stone.

M

NORM MACDONALD
(Comedian)

"I don't want to be maudlin or anything, but my dad, when I was a young boy, told me that, you know, life would not always be easy, and God knows he had hard times. And he said that in times of trouble, you should drink a lot of whiskey." *1999: Reflecting on getting fired from* Saturday Night Live.

"She said, 'Don't take acting classes. When you're happy in a scene, smile. And then when you're angry, frown.'" *1999: On getting advice from Roseanne.*

SHIRLEY MACLAINE
(Actress)

"I'm fighting bronchitis. And so in the middle of one of my numbers, I find that I have a big wad of snot between my nose and my throat, and I don't know what to do with it. You can't choreograph a moment to blow your nose. . . . This thing of what to do with my snot is really getting me down. . . . We're creating so much with our minds these days. It's amazing. Somebody was pressuring me in a personal situation. I couldn't say, 'Don't do this!' to him for certain reasons, and I know that's how I got all backed up and came down with bronchitis." *1990*

"You think you have a handle on God, the Universe and the Great White Light until you go home for Thanksgiving." *1991: In her book* Dance While You Can.

"You don't understand. I have to be on top." *1994: Explaining to a Santa Fe, NM, official why she wanted to build a house at the summit of sacred Atalaya Mountain and not lower down the slopes.*

"There's a definite arc to my career. I mean, I used to get married in films. Now I die." *1994*

"I think about who I was having an affair with at the time and how much I weighed." *1997: On what she thinks when she watches her old movies.*

"Marlene Dietrich taught me how to light myself . . . You have to know what you're doing with the filters and things like that. You get a thicker filter every five years. Pretty soon they're shooting you through linoleum." *1997*

"If I hadn't been an actress, I would have been a physicist—that's why I'm so interested in meta-physics—and would have been happy in research." *1998*

"Louise [Brooks] was a bundle of contradictions. She wanted to be successful—although she said she didn't care about success—and she wanted to express herself, but she had the habit of pulling the rug out from under herself. In the end, she said that she failed in everything—spelling, arithmetic, riding, swimming, tennis, golf; dancing, singing acting; wife, mistress, whore, friend. Even cooking." *1998: On '20s screen star Louise Brooks.*

MADONNA
(Singer & Actress)

"Why is it that people are willing to go to a movie and watch someone get blown to bits for no reason and nobody wants to see two girls kissing or two men snuggling?" *1990*

"You know how religion is. Guys get to do everything. They get to be altar boys. They get to stay out late. Take their shirts off in the summer. They get to pee standing up. They get to fuck a lot of girls and not worry about getting pregnant. Although that doesn't have anything to do with being religious." *1990*

"Sometimes I'm cynical and pragmatic and think it will last as long as it lasts." *1990: On her relationship with Warren Beatty.*

"If I was a writer, I think that's how I'd write." *1990: Discussing her favorite writer, J. D. Salinger.*

"I liked folding Sean's underwear. I liked mating socks. You know what I love? I love taking the lint out of the lint screen." *1991: On life with former husband Sean Penn.*

"I'm a revolutionary and, yes, it's a burden." *1992*

"I wouldn't want a penis. It would be like having a third leg. It would seem like a contraption that would get in the way. I think I have a dick in my brain. I don't want to have one between my legs." *1992*

"When I let my mind wander, when I let myself go, I rarely think of condoms." *1992*

"I have fantasies about being a suburban housewife." *1993*

"I don't think I have to introduce myself, unless you don't recognize me with my clothes on." *1993: To a theater audience in New York before the screening of her film* Body of Evidence.

"But if all I do is shock people, then why does everybody pay attention and why have I lasted so long? Because I've got something to say, that's why. When I don't have anything to say, I'll shut up and go away." *1993*

"When people say, 'What are you going to do next?' I laugh, because I'm just going to do what I'm going to do, and I'm going to keep doing it!" *1993*

"I tried to contact John Kennedy. I said, 'Show me a sign,' and then the girl I was playing [Ouija] with, like, her mascara started running. So I was sure he was in the room." *1993*

"I find it's easier to fart and blame it on someone else when you live in an urban area." *1993: On the advantages of urban life.*

"They send uptight, straight men to review me. They hate me. Don't they know I'm a gay man in a woman's body?" *1993*

"Everybody should run through the streets (naked) at least once. If you can do that, chances are you can have a lot of fun in other areas of your life." *1994*

MADONNA (CONT'D)

"Peeing in the shower is really good; it fights athlete's foot. I'm serious. Urine is like an antiseptic. It all has to do with enzymes in your body." *1994: To David Letterman, who replied, "Don't you know a good pharmicist? Get yourself some Desenex."*

"I definitely spent a couple of hours a day picking his brains." *1994: On life with Warren Beatty.*

"Evita basically robbed from the rich and gave to the poor. I identify with her on many levels." *1995: On Evita Peron.*

"It amazes me when I talk to people in their 20s and they've never read the classics. . . . When you don't have knowledge and understanding, then fear rises in you. Knowledge . . . gives people the tools to deal with change." *1995*

"If Princess Diana can take it, I can!" *1995: On criticism of her lifestyle and music.*

"Suddenly I was pigeonholed as this woman, this raving nymphomaniac who is obsessed with sex and with shocking people." *1995: On her public image.*

"I am fascinated by Courtney Love, but the same way I am by someone who's got Tourette's syndrome walking in Central Park." *1996*

"I have to work for someone in life. I needed something that's mine that I can be proud of. . . . My child will be a good Catholic like me." *1996: Unmarried Madonna commenting on her pregnancy.*

"I'm not interested in being Wonder Woman in the delivery room. Give me drugs." *1996*

"There are so many famous people everyone cancels everyone else out." *1996: On plans to raise her daughter in Los Angeles.*

"Goodbye, everyone. I'm going to get my nose job now." *1996: To nurses, doctors, and aides as she was wheeled into the operating room.*

"At least people read books here." *1997: On why she wants her daughter to go to school in Britain.*

ESPN'S CHRIS MEYER: "So, do you actually change your baby's diapers?"

MADONNA: "No. I never see the kid. I'm always out singing and dancing." *1997: An exchange between Chris Meyer and Madonna at a party thrown by Showtime in Las Vegas just before the Evander Holyfield–Mike Tyson fight.*

"I now realize that fame is not as important as I thought it was." *1998*

"It was the hardest thing that I've ever done, but it was really focused and there was a great simplicity to it as well. I'm a total perfectionist who beats up on myself when I don't get things right. And so I had to learn to a) not judge myself; and b) to let go of the idea that I had to accomplish this and master it in one day. Because you can't do that in yoga. So it taught me patience and judgment. It also taught me that you have to earn things, that just because you want to conquer something doesn't mean you're going to.

"Now I feel that yoga is a total metaphor for life. I had this notion that it was going to be easy, but it wasn't. And I also got really infuriated with my teacher because she would only teach me a little bit every time. And that was a huge lesson for me. I'd only get to learn the sun salutes, then the next day I could only learn one position. If you're in a hurry, you can't embrace or enjoy yoga. So that was another lesson for me—to enjoy the stillness of it." *1998: On her Ashtanga yoga classes, which she began in New York shortly after the birth of her daughter.*

"I love how anonymous I feel when I go to the (yoga) class. And I love how everybody's in one room . . . and no one's judging anyone. It's a wonderful feeling—and very inspiring." *1998*

"I went through a real metamorphosis when I did that movie. People were constantly attacking me and misunderstanding me and using me as their whipping girl in the press. I'd become this target, and I was feeling really sorry for myself. And suddenly, when I started playing Eva in the movie, I could get outside of myself and I realized that I wasn't a victim at all. To a certain extent, I had invited a lot of things. I hadn't really taken responsibility for my role in the whole thing. So I let go of a lot of bitterness.

"I thought of all the people who were upset at me for playing Evita and why they would have been upset and how their feelings were all intertwined with what she actually did in their country. And I suddenly saw how people could get confused. And then I had more compassion for everybody. It helped me have a whole new outlook.

"You have to work through the layers. That's what the whole creative process is. If where you're at is anger and rage, then that's what comes out of you. That's what informs everything you do. It might provoke people and get them to have discussions, and it might turn a few people's heads, but I don't know if it inspires anyone." *1998*

"I've got a lot on my plate right now. But I'm not complaining. It's a good problem to have." *1998*

"She doesn't know who 'Barney' is. Who cares? I mean, she can do without 'Barney.'" *1998: On how she is raising seventeen-month-old Lourdes.*

"I'll never have mainstream acceptance. I mean, I'm an unwed mother. I've kissed girls in public." *1998*

"Oh, God, it's so hard for me and my father to understand each other. I mean, his favorite female artist is Celine Dion." *1998*

"I am attracted to a thug. I like that quality, but I like the other side of it too. Because all the guys who go around behaving in macho ways are really scared little girls." *1999*

BILL MAHER
(TV Talk-show Host)
"David Helfgott said playing for the Academy audience reminded him of playing at the mental hospital. Half the people were on medication and half have delusions of grandeur." *1997*

"Drug kingpin Amado Carillo Fuentes . . . died from nine hours of liposuction and plastic surgery—or, as it's commonly known here in Beverly Hills, natural causes." *1997*

"Woody Harrelson said he would be willing to endorse a hemp colonic. Easy for him to say. He's a movie star. He's used to having people blow smoke up his ass." *1998*

"Today is Take Our Daughters to Work Day. This is when girls 9 to 15 go to work. Or, as it's called at the Nike factory, Thursday." *1999*

NORMAN MAILER
(Writer)
"The fact is they don't like long novels. It takes maybe six whole days. If they can get through it in an hour and a half, they get their money faster. It's hard work for a reviewer, this book. They can't skip-read it because there are no plot points. It could have been twice as long, and then they would have started comparing it with Proust and they know it's only half as good as Proust." *1991: On the unfavorable reviews by critics of his 1,328-page novel* Harlot's Ghost.

"This country is so complicated that when I start to think about it I begin talking in a Southern accent." *1992*

"One is tempted to argue that cubism grew out of the inside of the nose, for, indeed, its interior is often a cavernous, clotted, intricate web, full of bogs, stalactites, stalagmites, filamentlike hairs." *1995*

"Oh, there's so many people I want to kill." *1998: On his plans for the future.*

"Like the British when they lost India." *1998: On how he felt when the women's liberation movement first began to gather steam.*

"When I wake up in the morning and go over what I wrote the day before, I am a much better editor now, because I typically don't remember any of it. I feel totally impartial, as if I were reading the work of a stranger, so it makes it much easier to cut out stuff and to shorten it. I have to admit that most mornings I say to myself, what idiot wrote this mess? I see all the mistakes. So I guess there is one advantage to old age." *1999: On being seventy-five.*

DAVID MAMET
(Playwright)

"Cinema is a melodramatic medium. We go to it to exercise our emotions rather than our thoughts. I'd rather read a book than go to a movie that asks me to think." *1998*

BARRY MANILOW
(Singer & Composer)

"It's not really the noise that bothers me. It's just that I can't sunbathe in the nude as much as I'd like to." *1992: On his Bel Air Hills, CA, neighbors Ronald and Nancy Reagan, whose personal helicopter often carries them over his property.*

"I wanted to write music that would be played in elevators forever and ever. When you get played in elevators, you know you've made it!" *1993*

"I considered myself and still consider myself the hippest man on the planet." *1993*

"We're all here for the same reason: to love me." *1996: To fans at his concert in New York.*

"Who would've thought I'd become the sex god I've become today?" *1998*

MARILYN MANSON
(Singer & Musician)

"What happens someday if more people own my record than the Bible? Will that make me God because more people believe in me than Him?" *1998*

"My plan for the millennium is to save rock and roll from my senseless and unimaginative peers, and to look good while doing so." *1998*

"I think my lifestyle over the past few years has been a long form of suicide." *1998*

"He was wearing more makeup than me, and it scared me." *1998: On his* Late Show *appearance with David Letterman.*

MARLA MAPLES
(Actress & Celebrity Wife)

"A psychic told me I'm just a little girl inside a grown-up body. That's what makes me feel uncomfortable—I forget I have this body. I'm just a little girl." *1990*

"I've learned that you can't always take the Bible literally and be happy." *1991*

"I'm so excited to meet you. I've always modeled myself after Ginger." *1992: On meeting actress Tina Louise, better known as Ginger on* Gilligan's Island.

"I still love cartoons, and now that Donald [Trump] and I are going to have a baby, I'll have someone to watch them with." *1993*

"I have never really been that impressed by a celebrity, except the first time I saw Billy Graham. There is no other human being on this earth as charismatic." *1995*

"I've often wanted to sit down and share some thoughts with her. Be sure of who and what you are. . . . If you can keep your own sense of self, that will pull you through." *1997: On Princess Diana.*

JULIANNA MARGULIES
(Actress)

"When you're in New York, no matter what you do you have to pass the homeless person on the street, and you have to smell the urine coming up from the sidewalk. There's a reality to it. I don't ever want to get to a place where I don't know what the subway costs." *1998*

"I don't have dark secrets. You're not going to find out one day that I was a stripper and a heroin addict on Avenue B. And if I was, I probably would have told you." *1998*

MARIN INDEPENDENT JOURNAL
(CA Newspaper)

"When a social worker becomes curious about why the Brown parents are never seen, Charlie is forced to admit his involvement in their murder." *1997: Initial description of the TV program* A Charlie Brown Christmas. *It was changed in later editions.*

BRANFORD MARSALIS
(Musician)

"A lot of the bands we play with are just bad, especially those alternative-rock bands. I see the audience applauding while they're playing, and I wonder if it's just because they're fans of the band and don't care, or out of spite. Because it certainly isn't because they sound good." *(1994)*

STEVE MARTIN
(Comedian, Actor & Writer)

"I just start typing and then I do the spell check." *1995: On his writing technique.*

"It's completely doable, especially if there's a woman involved." *1995: On middle-aged men fathering children.*

JACKIE MASON
(Comedian)

"All the geniuses with computers love to tell you you can talk to people all over the world if you're on line. Who wants to? You want to talk to people all over the world? People don't talk to the guy next door. . . . People are standing in an elevator—do you talk to anybody? A guy calls you up and he's got the wrong number—do you start a conversation? Do you ever say, 'Sure glad you got the wrong number!' You're gonna holler, 'You got the wrong number!' And God forbid he calls you again: you think he's a stalker, you call the police." *1996*

JEFFREY MASSON
(Author)

"I walk around Berkeley with my three dogs off leash, and I really like that. It's just different, it really is different. It makes me feel that we are more equal." *1998: The author of* Dogs Never Lie About Love *on the egalitarian rush he gets from walking his dogs in Berkeley, CA, without using leashes.*

JOYCE MAYNARD
(Author)

"If you can imagine the effect of the voice of Holden Caulfield, then imagine Holden Caulfield sending you letters every day to your college mailbox." *1998: Remembering her relationship with author J. D. Salinger, the reclusive author of* Catcher in the Rye, *when she was eighteen and Salinger was fifty-three. Maynard details her subsequent affair with Salinger in her book* At Home in the World.

MERCEDES MCCAMBRIDGE
(Actress)

"Every time I come to San Francisco, I always head for the grand and spacious lobby at the St. Francis Hotel. I find one of those big plush couches to sit on, and then I meditate—a kind very particular to me. You see, I was conceived there." *1992*

JENNY MCCARTHY
(Actress)

"At 18, I went to a clinic in Arizona that specialized in boob jobs on young girls who didn't want their parents to know . . . and accepted payment on the installment plan. Isn't that the American dream? To purchase new breasts on credit?" *1998*

"My breast implants give me something to make fun of. If I take them out, I'm afraid they'll look like shrunken raisins. But I still have a feeling you'll see a dramatic decrease in my bust line in a couple of years." *1998: On her figure and her career plans.*

PAUL MCCARTNEY
(Musician & Singer)

"The money looks good." *1995: On the 100 million British pounds being offered for the reformed Beatles to tour.*

"When a lot of friends who are highly trained musicians sit down to a piano to compose, they have so much information in their heads from all the Bernstein, Beethoven, Mozart and whatever. I think it's inhibiting to have all that in your head. I'm lucky. I don't know much classical music at all. It's like a big black hole up there." *1997*

"You're up on your beautiful Appaloosa stallion. It's a fine spring day. We're riding through the woods. The bluebells are all out, and the sky is clear blue." *1998: His last words to his wife Linda, just before her death.*

FRANK MCCOURT
(Writer)

"Supermodels, with legs up to their shoulders . . . kept coming up and praising me. I said to my wife, 'If this had happened 30 years ago, I'd be dead of whisky and fornication.' " *1998: On his newfound fame as a Pulitzer Prize winner.*

NATASCHA MCELHONE
(Actress)

QUESTION: "You've acted in films opposite (Jim) Carrey, Anthony Hopkins, Brad Pitt, Harrison

NATASCHA MCELHONE (CONT'D)

Ford and Robert De Niro. That must be quite intimidating."

ANSWER: "When you're sitting opposite someone of that caliber, you relax. Because their face is so familiar, it feels like you're sitting with a relative. Then you realize that they're recognizable because you've seen them in the movies all the time." *1998*

BOB MCGRATH
(Theatrical Director)

"For the Manson family, God wasn't somebody you heard about on Sunday. He was right there with them. And they believed that revelations were coming down to them through the Beatles' *White Album.* It's twisted and negative but it's also inspiring in a way." *1990: McGrath directed* The Manson Family, *an opera that opened at the Lincoln Center.*

DUFF MCKAGAN
(Musician)

"I think the Bible's a good story, you know? I mean Jesus was . . . back in those times, the Romans were just squashing everybody and here came this guy who had positive thoughts. I think that's all there was to it. And he turned all these people on to these positive thoughts. All of a sudden all the people were going, 'This guy's fucking groovy.' And the Romans were like, 'Not that groovy, because he's fucking taking over all of our people we're squashing, so we're gonna kill him.' And there's no such thing as the Immaculate Conception. His mom got fucked to have him, you know? Come on. He was just a positive guy who wanted to spread love and goodness. And the Romans did not dig that. And they fucking squashed him like a grape." *1991*

IAN MCKELLEN
(Actor)

"If you want to get the girl, tell them you're gay. That's my advice." *1999*

ED MCMAHON
(TV Host)

"I saw him for lunch. I said to the waitress, 'What's your name?' and she said 'Monica,' so that took care of the first half-hour of the lunch. Johnny and I don't see each other as much, but when we see each other, we're right back where we were." *1998: Describing his relationship with Johnny Carson.*

TERRENCE MCNALLY
(Playwright)

"In Hollywood, the big expression is 'Take the money and run.' In New York, it's 'What money? And run where? I'm stuck here.' " *1995*

VAUGHN MEADER
(Comedian & Impersonator)

"Playing the president was easy, but playing God was a bitch." *1997: Meader, whose impersonation of President John F. Kennedy on the record album* First Family, *sold 10 million copies in 1962–63, describing how he handled his fleeting fame. Meader's career came to an end on November 22, 1963, with JFK's assassination.*

MATT MEAGHER
(Reporter)

"Anybody who thinks they're going to watch *Inside Edition* and be a well-informed person . . . is a moron." *1997: Meagher is the TV show's senior investigative reporter.*

RUSSELL MEANS
(Actor & Native American Celebrity)

"I've always thought it was arrogant to write about yourself, particularly when you're still alive." *1996*

"[Disney's *Pocahontas*] makes the stunning admission that the British came over here to kill Indians and rape and pillage the land." *1996*

JOHN COUGAR MELLENCAMP
(Singer & Musician)

"Acting is kind of like playing dress-up, like putting clothes on a Barbie." *1991*

GEORGE MICHAEL
(Singer)

"I've already kind of done that, haven't I?" *1998: Asking why he was outing himself after he was arrested for a "lewd act" in a bathroom in a park in Beverly Hills, CA.*

"I have no problem with people knowing that I'm in a relationship with a man right now." *1998: After he was arrested for masturbation in a public restroom in Beverly Hills.*

BETTE MIDLER
(Singer & Actress)

"I don't think she understands why they call it Neverland." *1994: On Lisa Marie Presley's marriage to Michael Jackson.*

"The picture we made had strong American values: divorce, alcoholism, plastic surgery and revenge." *1997: On the making of the movie* The First Wives Club.

"No way. There are a lot of damaged people out there." *1999: On why she won't ever move back to Los Angeles.*

DENNIS MILLER
(Comedian)

"A lot of people voting for Pat Buchanan say they are doing so to send a message. Apparently that message is, 'Hey, look at me, I'm an idiot!' " *1992*

"Reagan was 77 and he had access to the button [controlling America's nuclear weapons]. My grandfather is 77 and we won't even let him touch the remote." *1993*

"I think that's the worst thing about dying in a plane wreck: You have to check into eternity with all the same (bleeps) you couldn't stomach in the lobby at O'Hare." *1995*

"In New York City this week, the Fashion Cafe opened. It's a new restaurant owned by models Claudia Schiffer, Naomi Campbell, and Elle Macpherson. . . . The entire menu is specially prepared to taste as good on the way up as it does on the way down." *1995*

"Hollywood has always been screwed up with its take on women. Look at the movie *Pretty Woman*. This was a man's view of prostitution—Hey, tool down Hollywood Boulevard about 2 A.M. some Saturday and try to find a Julia Roberts look-alike." *1996*

"Everybody in this nation is an immigrant except for the Indians. I'm sorry, they're not called Indians anymore. They're called casino-owner Americans." *1996*

"Clinton said he chose to vacation in Utah because he always finds it soothes the soul to visit the last state in the Union to outlaw polygamy." *1998*

"Madonna this week ended negotiations with London producers and said she will not be appearing as Maggie in the play *Cat on a Hot Tin Roof*. The producers will now go with their second choice: an actress." *1998*

HELEN MIRREN
(Actress)

"[Cleopatra] is the best-written female role ever. She's full of fire and spark and has balls." *1990*

"I love Hollywood—it's such a whore. It just goes with the flow, the wind, the market. It never has a hidden agenda. But Hollywood is very much about manipulation and hype. In England there is a sense of the culture, a sense that the work we do is art, not a way of making money, and that we're carrying the torch into the next generation." *1996*

DENNIS MISCHER
(TV Producer)

"There's one year he told me he'd rather just sit in Malibu and watch the hummingbirds mate." *1998: On trying to persuade Johnny Carson to participate in the Emmy Awards.*

JONI MITCHELL
(Singer & Songwriter)

"I was at a cafe, smoking somewhere, and a girl came up to me and said, 'I'm a manic depressive. I love your music, but I hate pictures of you. Every time I see you, you're smiling, and it makes me mad.' So there's a person who thinks I'm suffering, she's suffering. If they see evidence otherwise, they feel I'm unauthentic." *1997*

ISAAC MIZRAHI
(Fashion Designer)

"I never walk the streets. I have people I pay to do that for me." *1998*

EDDIE MONEY
(Singer)

"They wanted me to do Howard Stern, but my wife can't stand him, so I can't do it. They also want me to do (VH1's) *Behind the Music*, but my wife doesn't want the kids to know I had a drug problem and she doesn't want pictures of the ex-wife on the screen. This is what I've got to deal with. I married my mother." *1999*

"I actually lost a rental car about 15 years ago. I must have had a blackout. Six years ago they found the car in a cornfield. It was all dusty, but it was a brand-new car. It only had 300 miles on it, even though it was nine years old. But the most important thing is they found my original saxophone in the trunk. True story. Shit like that happens to me all the time." *1999*

DARLA MOORE
(Investment Banker)

I think Southerners, women, and capitalists are overdue for some serious self-congratulations." *1998: Moore, forty-three, gave $25 million to the University of South Carolina, saying that her background, speech, and gender all were obstacles in the 1980s New York business scene.*

DEMI MOORE
(Actress)

"When you have a child you want to save everything. I saved my daughter's belly button." *1990*

"Clinton's economic plan scares me. It's going to put us in some jeopardy. They're going to punish people who have money (by getting them to pay for everything that isn't working for poor people). This plan is going to affect anybody who makes over $200,000 a year, which is not rich anymore." *1992*

"Not many people have read the book." *1995: She starred in the movie version of the literary classic* The Scarlet Letter, *and defended the film's new, upbeat ending.*

"[Deepak Chopra] is my guru now. Through his teachings I hope to live to a great age—even 130 years isn't impossible. I'm hoping that Chopra's advice will even help me produce the baby boy Bruce and I want so badly." *1996*

"Part of my drive is that I feel I am here for a purpose. There is something—I don't know what yet—but as I keep going it will become clearer where I can be of service. I believe we are all very connected, we are all one." *1997*

MICHAEL MOORE
(Documentary Filmmaker)

"I told my parents I was coming to see you and they asked me not to mention how old they are." *1994: To suicide doctor Jack Kevorkian.*

"Did J. Edgar Hoover ever say to you, 'I'm not in this dress because I'm spying on you, I'm wearing it because I love you'?" *1994: To Gus Hall, chairman of the Communist Party of the United States.*

"[Michael] Eisner just stared at me. Then he said, 'General Motors is going to have you killed.' That was the last time I was in Los Angeles." *1995: Describing the response of Michael Eisner, head of the Disney Studios, to his film* Roger and Me.

"I spent the first 35 years of my life in Flint, Michigan. That's enough to give anyone an edge for the rest of their life." *1996*

"All wisdom comes from growing up in Flint. The rest of the ideas just come from reading *Entertainment Weekly*." *1996*

"It's the evil of two lessers." *1996: On the presidential race between Clinton and Dole.*

"Where was Linda Tripp when I needed her?" *1998: After Lee Weinstein, Nike's head of public relations, phoned him and asked, "What would it take to have a couple of scenes removed from the movie?" referring to Moore's film,* The Big One, *which is critical of Nike and its labor and marketing practices.*

"One day he came to Flint. We took him around all day, and he had to have a nap. I remember him taking a nap on my couch. I looked at him thinking, 'There's Dr. Spock, sleeping like a baby, right on my couch. It's kinda cool.'" *On a visit by Dr. Benjamin Spock to his hometown.*

"I'm crazy from the '70s and '80s. I got so high, I'm still loaded. Now, for me, a nice afternoon is sneaking a couple of cigarettes in the house. My wife is afraid that I'm going to get into the [Rock and Roll] Hall of Fame and that I'm going to die, so she's going to have to give the speech." *1999*

MIKE MORITZ
(Silicon Valley Venture Capitalist)
"Look at our companies [in Silicon Valley]. Maybe they've produced 100,000 jobs or 150,000. But what kind and for whom? Jobs that 250 million people in this country aren't qualified to apply for. Jobs for guys out of MIT and Stanford. Jobs that in many ways gut the older industries in the Midwest and on the East Coast. Are the benefits of these jobs passed down? I don't know. What are we investing in? Companies that enable people to work harder and longer—anyplace, anytime. You can be reached on a ski lift, on a beach, or on a plane. Why is that good for people's lives?" *1999*

MARK MORRIS
(Dancer & Choreographer)
"What I thought would freak me out was getting older, but I like it. I mean, my back hurts right now, and my neck—this happens to every dancer with time. Otherwise, I don't feel any different from when I was 2, except I have a slightly larger vocabulary and more body hair." *1995*

TONI MORRISON
(Nobel Prize–Winning Writer)
"I want to take them all in my arms and say, 'Your baby is beautiful and so are you and, honey, you can do it. And when you want to be a brain surgeon, call me—I will take care of your baby." *1990: Offering her babysitting services to black teenage mothers.*

"I called someone at the Nobel Committee and I said, 'Look, if you're going to keep giving prizes to women—and I hope you do—you're going to have to give us more warning. Men can rent tuxedos. I have to get shoes. I have to get a dress." *1993: On winning the Nobel Prize for Literature in 1993.*

"Race is the least reliable information you can have about someone. It's real information, but it tells you next to nothing." *1998*

"I was reading some essay about the 'Black Family' and the writer went into a comparison between one of my novels and *The Cosby Show*. That's like comparing apples and Buicks." (1998)

MORRISSEY
(Singer)
"You react instantly. Your body obeys this sense of attack within your mind. It's great. You should try it on a waiter." *1994: On getting into fistfights.*

LISA MORTMAN
(Spokesman for Crunch Fitness)
"People are seeking out a kinder, gentler life experience and they want soothing fitness. Attendance in yoga has matched—and in some cases surpassed—our traditional step and hi-low aerobics classes." *1998: On celebrities in the entertainment business (such as the obviously soulful Madonna, Sting, Jennifer Aniston, Beastie Boy Mike Diamond, Paula Cole, Morisa Tomei, Willem Dafoe, and others) seeking a new "spiritual oneness."*

RICHARD MUHLBERGER
(Art Museum Director)
"You get a hard-on when you look at it." *1990: Telling how pornography differs from art.*

ANNE PLESHETTE MURPHY
(Editor of Parents Magazine)
"There's an old joke: 'Why does it take 10,000 sperm to fertilize one egg? Because none of them will stop to ask for directions.' Women know men won't ask for help on unfamiliar turf. Without role models for taking care of kids, even the most liberated man can metamorphose into Ward Cleaver." *1998*

DANNY MURPHY
(Musician)
"I just thought, 'Oh, brother. Another weird gig." *1993: On how he felt when he learned his group Soul Asylum was to play a twenty-minute set at the White House.*

EDDIE MURPHY
(Actor)
"Being the best is a fucking drag." *1992*

"I'm never giving anyone a lift again." *1997: After he was pulled over by police after picking up a*

EDDIE MURPHY (CONT'D)

transvestite prostitute in a seedy area of West Holly-wood but he says he was merely furnishing trans-portation and advice.

"My heart breaks for people like this. I . . . told her to find another line of work. I've always felt bad for people in these situations, homeless, working the streets. I have given away hundreds of thousands of dollars to help out those who need the help most. . . . I don't care who they are. In the eyes of God, they are the same as me. . . . I can afford to help them. It's my way of paying back. . . . I want to help those who haven't been so lucky. . . . I see it as an act of kindness to someone on the bottom of the ladder and I thank God that I can afford to do it because I have been so successful." *1997: Explaining why he gave a transsexual hooker $1,000.*

BILL MURRAY
(Comedian)

"Men read in magazines that girls like men who are funny, so they try to be funny. Most aren't. Women are actually funnier by nature. They use a sense of humor in their life to make moments more bearable. Most men have no ability to laugh at themselves." *1999*

MICHAEL J. MUSTO
(Journalist)

"Sharon's hubby can breathe more easily, plus potential intruders will still stay away, since Sharon retains the scariest weapon of all—the ability to bore people to death with viewings of *Diabolique, Gloria,* and any number of fruity flicks." *1999: After reading a Sharon Stone press release announcing that following the Columbine High School shootings she had turned in all of her guns to the Los Angeles Police Department.*

N

DIMITRI NABOKOV
(Author's Son)

"He didn't think it would ever be published. He was on the way to the incinerator with it when Mother stopped him." *1998: On the attitude of his father, Vladimir Nabokov, toward his book* Lolita, *before it was published in 1955.*

GRAHAM NASH
(Musician)

"I spent many years thinking that I was not good because I was still alive." *1990*

LIAM NEESON
(Actor)

"When I got to Hollywood, this fat man with a cigar asked what I'd done, and I said I'd got some good reviews in *Of Mice and Men.* And he took the cigar out of his mouth and said, 'You played a mouse?' " *1994*

"You have these people in therapy 25 years because, what, their moms didn't cuddle them? I'm sorry. Get a fucking life." *1998*

"Helen [Mirren] taught me there's more to life than meat, vegetables and potatoes on a plate. Literally, I had my first Chinese meal with her." *1999: Describing the importance of actress Helen Mirren, his former lover.*

"At the end of the day, you know something? It's just a movie." *1999: On the movie* Star Wars: Episode 1—the Phantom Menace, *in which he stars.*

KATE NELLIGAN
(Actress)

"The world I dreamed to be part of when I started ceased to exist. It's not about acting, technique, art. It's about effects. I wouldn't become an actor again if I could choose. I'm too bright for a career that runs out. I thought I'd spend my life telling good stories to an intelligent public. I must have been out of my fucking mind." *1994*

CRAIG T. NELSON
(Actor)

"I never had a chance to meet the football coach at the University of Arizona [in the 1960s] because I was in drama and the two just didn't mix. Back then, we were busy smoking dope and painting, while they were busy on the football field smoking dope and hitting each other." *1990*

"I'm really getting dumber, and it's beginning to make me mad. What do I mean? I have no idea." *1993*

LANA NELSON
(Daughter of Singer & Musician Willie Nelson)
"If Mama were alive right now, I know she'd be wondering what ever happened to her other eight and a half hours." *1991: On hearing that a woman said she had sexual intercourse with Willie Nelson for nine consecutive hours.*

WILLIE NELSON
(Singer & Musician)
"I'm not saying it didn't happen. But you would've thought I'd remember at least the last four or five hours." *1991: Commenting on the story told by a woman who said she had sexual intercourse with him for nine consecutive hours and that he consummated the act with a backward somersault with her still attached. Nelson later told an interviewer that this was the only true story ever written about him.*

"You can't put a melody to this shit." *1991: When asked if he'd write a song about his IRS problems.*

"It keeps me from killing people." *1995: On why he smokes marijuana.*

"Since he's quit drugs, he's very boring. He's reliable and all that shit. He shows up, he sings good. Who needs that?" *1995: On his good friend Waylon Jennings.*

"If I could have found 'they,' I would have killed that son of a bitch a long time ago." *1995: Responding to Forrest Sawyer's question, What if they just told you to quit [recording]?*

"If I knew I was going to deal with them, I made sure I was stoned." *1998: On dealing with the Internal Revenue Service.*

"A wise man, Ray Price, told me recently that there's one thing he's learned in life. In fact, he called me on the phone to tell me this, and I said, 'What is it?' He said, 'Money makes women horny.'" *1998*

"I was doomed to go to hell by the time I was 7. I had been told that if you smoke cigarettes and drink beer, you're going to hell. And by 7, I was gone." *1999*

THE NEW REPUBLIC
(Magazine)
"Look at the photographs (which are all that matter, anyway) of these dizzy, overdone people, arriving in their shared belief in the sanctity of glamour and in their instantly obsolete silks to congratulate one another on being in one another's company: you will not see images of power or beauty, you will see only images of frantic, amoral, moneyed emptiness. So pity the planet's icons. They do not understand that there is nothing in the world less real than a party. And *Time*, which went to all this trouble—Muhammad Ali! Mikhail Gorbachev! Raquel Welch!—to prove that it is just the company's beard for *People*." *1998: Commenting on the 75th anniversary gala held by* Time *magazine.*

BOB NEWHART
(Actor & Comedian)
"[As a commencement speaker] you don't have to be intelligent, you just have to create the impression. This can usually be accomplished by [making] a reference to Kafka, even if you've never read any of his, or her, works." *1994*

"How can you tell if you've been robbed by an Asian gang? Your dog is gone but your kid's math homework is done." *1995*

"Laughter gives us distance. It allows us to step back from an event over which we have no control and deal with it. . . . It helps distinguish us from animals. No matter what hyenas sound like, they are not actually laughing." *1997*

"I'm not sure I'm up to answering that question." *After an audience member asked him what he thought of Viagra.*

PAUL NEWMAN
(Actor)
"Lust. And respect. And forgiveness. And persistence." *1998: Paul Newman, on the key to his forty-year-old marriage.*

RANDY NEWMAN
(Composer, Musician & Singer)
"It's actually an improvement on Goethe's version. I've tightened up the structure, plus it's in English." *1993: On his musical version of Goethe's* Faust.

HELMUT NEWTON
(Photographer)
"I used to always carry chains in the trunk of my car because you never know when you'll need them. You know, you go out in the streets of Paris and you might want to chain a model to a fence." *1991*

MIKE NICHOLS
(Director)
"I was just deeply confused—the way you are when the real world seems to echo your inner world." *1998: When his wife, TV journalist Diane Sawyer, tipped him off about the Monica Lewinsky story. Nichols had just completed filming* Primary Colors, *the story of a Southern governor's run for president that is nearly derailed by charges of womanizing.*

"The whole point of marriage—the thing that makes it a marriage—is that nobody will ever know what goes on in it. It's the ultimate private event. And that's the power of a marriage. When you contemplate your friends' marriage or your parents' marriage, you're curious, but you don't really know. And that's a very important element in the movie and in life. We don't know—thank God, at last there's something we don't know." *1998: Emphasizing that his film* Primary Colors *is about all marriages, not just about the marriage of the first couple of the United States.*

"I don't think they [the Clintons] will see it, just as I wouldn't see it if I were, God forbid, in such a situation. But in my own fantasy I often think about them seeing it. Because I like them so much, I would hope that they would be able to see past some of the specifics and would know how much the movie loves them and feels for them." *1998: On* Primary Colors, *based loosely on the political and private lives of Bill and Hillary Clinton.*

"Moralizing is America's special contribution to gossip." *1998*

"Most celebrities are basically left alone [by the press]—unless they marry or have an affair or divorce. They are most interesting when mating." *1998*

"Satire is heartless, and I'm not sure that this is a moment for heartlessness. I think that, in the polls, American people have answered from their hearts, and what they've said is, 'Private life is private.' The fact that *everybody* lies about sex is foremost, I think, in everyone's mind. The thing about satire is that it presents something closed, a conclusion. What interests me more is embodied in a line that I like from *The Philadelphia Story:* 'The time to make up your mind about people is never.'" *1998: On why he considers his film* Primary Colors *a "comedy-drama" rather than a "satire."*

"I've been in hotels and had people say, 'Here's a package, Mr. Sawyer.'" *1998: On the attention he receives as the husband of star journalist Diane Sawyer.*

JACK NICHOLSON
(Actor)
"Violence is a bad habit. Kiss a tit, it's an X. Hack it off with a sword, PG." *1992: On the movie rating system.*

"Don't you think Gary Hart would be the best candidate to run against Bush? And why isn't he there? Because he fucks, that's why." *1992*

"After my first screen test, the director said, 'I don't know what we can use you for, but if we ever do need you, we'll need you real bad.'" *1992*

"Such is the price of fame. People start poking around in your private life, and the next thing you know, your sister is actually your mother." *1995*

"You just don't find scripts that leave much room for the actor. They're all about plot." *1995*

"Women find men boring, and men have no morality. If men get the feeling that women want them to wear green ears, they will wear them. And they'll say, 'I'm just my own man,' all the while they're

84

wearing 'em. And this, incidentally, is my thumbnail sketch of American marriage. A woman sees a man; she likes him. Now she jumps on this thing and rides it to some kind of standstill. Then she changes it and trains it, and to the exact degree that she's able to do this, she disrespects him." *1996*

"John Huston used to say, 'We can make movies good and we can make 'em bad. Bad is just more expensive.' I'm from the late '50s, '60s underground American film movement that honestly believes you can make any movie on any subject for any price. What's hard to do is change what is formally acceptable to a movie audience." *1996*

"I'm not a doomsday philosopher, but if you want to talk about what's really tough, I can't respect a society that can't keep guns out of schools. I don't care if you've gotta put thirty adults with guns down there to do it." *1996*

"The only thing wrong with turning 60 is there's no guarantee you'll be alive till you're 160. You know what I'm saying?" *1996*

"In 1972 I eliminated all years from my life. I don't keep track of anything by years or weeks. I call it my living experiment." *1998*

SARAH NICKLES
(Editor)
"We all have different standards for what passes as honesty. From faking an orgasm to fixing the World Series, who is to judge which is the more serious crime?" *1997: In her introduction to,* Lying, Cheating & Stealing: Great Writers on Getting What You Want When You Want It.

KIM NOVAK
(Actress)
"It was not that he thought actors were cattle. He thought that actors should be treated as if they're cattle. That's a whole different thing." *1996: On working for Alfred Hitchcock.*

KRIST NOVOSELIC
(Musician)
"If it hadn't been heroin, it would have been booze or cappucino. Drugs were just a small part of

Kurt." *1994: The bassist for the band Nirvana on the suicide of Kurt Cobain.*

DEBORAH NORVILLE
(Radio & TV Announcer)
"Television is in my future, despite everyone who says I definitely have a face for radio." *1991*

O

KEITH OBERMAN
(Newsman)
"He has gone from being an idiot with a modem to an idiot with a modem and a TV show, on the most irresponsible network in America." *1998: On gossip specialist Matt Drudge, who gained notoriety on the Internet.*

CONAN O'BRIEN
(TV Host)
"A college in the Netherlands is offering a course on Madonna. Not surprisingly, the final exam is oral." *1997*

"Scientists announced yesterday that life actually originated on the ocean floor. And the Mafia announced that's also where life ends." *1997*

"There's no going back now that people know there are all these mathematical geniuses running around there." *1998: The Boston native on why the* Good Will Hunting *town has become the hot locale for movies and TV projects.*

"George Michael was arrested for performing a lewd act in a public rest room where gay men are known to hang out. The most embarrassing part is, he was arrested by the cop from the Village People." *1998*

"According to a new survey, the first thing men notice about a woman is her eyes. Then, when her eyes aren't looking, they notice her breasts." *1998*

"I've never had a job as long as this one. The only thing that I've done as long as this show in my life was elementary school. This will be the first time I'm seen by people who are fully awake. It could be a disaster. I think one of the reasons our show has stayed on the air is when a comedy bit goes dangerously

CONAN O'BRIEN (CONT'D)

awry or we do something that's over the line, people aren't sure in the morning whether they actually saw that or not." *1998: On* Late Night's *5th Anniversary Primetime Special.*

"In 1993, the year we went on the air, Julia Roberts married Lyle Lovett, Prince changed his name to a weird symbol, and Michael Jordan quit the Bulls to play baseball. So, as you can see, we were hardly the year's biggest mistake." *1998: On* Late Night's *5th Anniversary Primetime Special.*

"Sharon Stone said that recent media speculation about whether she's pregnant is an invasion of the most private part of her body. Stone said that part of her body is reserved for her husband, her gynecologist and the people who see her in the movies." *1998*

"Tonight is our 1,000th show. Which means my dad owes me twenty bucks." *1998*

"Woody Allen said that because of Soon-Yi he no longer sees his psychiatrist. Allen said, 'Instead, I see my psychiatrist's daughter.'" *1999*

"In a recent interview, Celine Dion vehemently denied that she's anorexic. However, Celine did admit that her music is one of the leading causes of bulimia." *1999*

SINEAD O'CONNOR
(Singer)

"You're a sleazeball, and nobody would fuck you if you were dying, and your mother sucks cocks in hell." *1992: To a salesman in a New York electronics store when he refused to allow her to return a $300 camera lense she had purchased earlier.*

"Poor Mike Tyson . . . He's only a little tiny baby, and all of these people are trying to kill him. . . . If he looks for solace in the arms of lots of women, what do you expect him to do? . . . That woman who is suing him is a bitch. I don't care if he raped her. . . . She used him. She's a disgrace to women as far as I'm concerned." *1992*

"The church created what happened to me; the church is responsible for this attitude in my country that led to the attitudes of my parents that led to the pain inside them that led to what happened to me and my brothers and my sister." *1993: Explaining why she tore up a picture of Pope John Paul II on a TV show—to call attention to child abuse.*

"Do you know the difference between love and like? Swallowing or spitting." *1993*

ROSIE O'DONNELL
(Actress & TV Talk-show Host)

"When I was a child, I believe I blamed it on the dog. I had a dog named Happy, and every time I farted I would say it was Happy." *1993: On the benefits of having a dog.*

"I think that the people who are going into a $7.50 movie to sit with popcorn in a darkened room full of 200 strangers and are gonna look to be guided morally in their life are in the wrong place." *1996*

"She sleeps with her trainer. I ignore mine." *1996: Comparing herself with Madonna.*

"Whenever anyone tells me to lose weight, I always laugh, like I could, but I'm just keeping it on because I like to." *1997*

GARY OLDMAN
(Actor)

"Someone once said that actors are all a bunch of sissies dressed up in frocks. That's not far from the truth." *1994*

"Well, he was one of the most famous people in the world. Certainly, the most famous composer. He was a star—Beethoven." *1994: Explaining the historical importance of Beethoven.*

JACQUELINE KENNEDY ONASSIS
(Celebrity)

"I don't get it. I did everything right to take care of myself and look what happened. Why in the world did I do all those push-ups?" *1994: On learning she had cancer.*

OZZY OSBOURNE
(Singer-musician)

"I've been branded the Godfather of Heavy Metal, and I'm not sure how I should take that. I suppose I should start speaking Italian or something." *1991*

"I've been to therapists and in my opinion, most were more fucking crazy than I was." *1993*

"My favorite place to be is my house. It's what I work for. . . . I watch TV a lot and adore my dogs. Over in England, I like to take them out and sit on an old log." *1999*

SCOTT OSTLER
(Columnist)

"*Titanic* will be underawarded because the boat itself will get screwed. It should be best actor. Take away the boat and what have you got? *Beverly Hills 90210* with an older wardrobe." *1998: On his predictions for the Oscars.*

"The *Titanic*'s character development was marvelous, the evolution from carefree bon vivant to brooding down-'n'-outer. It achieved what most actors never truly convey: vulnerability." *1998*

"Why did God choose Texas? Possibly because people there are experienced UFO travelers and won't try to bring too much carry-on luggage." *1998: On the Hon-Ming Chen Cult, which believed God would land in a Dallas, TX, suburb at the end of March.*

PETER O'TOOLE
(Actor)

"The only exercise I take is walking behind the coffins of friends who took exercise." *1998*

"These days I only share my bed with my books. I wouldn't want to live with anyone again. There would be hair and fluff and face powder, and I don't want that about the place." *1999: On his preferences at age sixty-seven.*

RONN OWENS
(Radio Talk-show Host)

"What is *soft core* anyway? Does that mean no penetration? Does that mean no erection? Then it's just like marriage!" *1996*

P

AL PACINO
(Actor)

"All I really need is a room. That's all I live in, is a room. I rarely go out of my room. I don't venture out that much, so my ideal would be to live in a big house with a large family and have my own room." *1996*

CAMILLE PAGLIA
(Author)

"Men have created the world that allows me to be free and allows me to write this book. I think strong women can admit the strength of men. It's only weak women who deny it." *1990: After the publication of her book* Sexual Persona.

"This prospect is too horrible for words. I cannot bring myself to believe it. . . . The cutesy role model who set American women back 20 years wants to play a real woman who helped us forward? It's too depressing. How do you film a poet anyway?" *1998: Commenting on the prospect of actress Meg Ryan playing poet Sylvia Plath in a movie.*

SHALON PAIGE
(High School Moviegoer)

"It was long ago and far away and about people we never met. We don't know about those concentration camps, but I do hear a lot of Jew jokes." *1994: Paige, fourteen, after a group of students from Castlemont High School in Oakland, CA, were heard laughing during a showing of* Schindler's List.

GWYNETH PALTROW
(Actress)

"Everyone is making all this fuss over Brad (Pitt), but I'm telling you, Morgan Freeman is the sexiest man alive. You heard it here." *1995*

"There are a lot of shitty things about being famous, and amazing things, too. But one of the best things is when you're in the street and you see a kid coming toward you, a girl going through her teenage angst and she'll see you and her whole mood changes. It's a pretty amazing power—to be able to make somebody feel good. It's sweet." *1998*

SARAH JESSICA PARKER
(Actress)

"I didn't used to like sex. . . . But now let's just say I'm satisfied. Let's just say I'm very happy currently. Oh, let's just say Matthew [Broderick] is great. Let's just say Matthew knows how to treat a woman." *1993*

TREY PARKER
(Co-creator of TV's South Park*)*

"One day, I think I was three or four, I guess I had a problem with flushing the toilet. Like I would go poo and then wouldn't flush it. And my mother would yell at me and yell at me. And so my dad—the geologist on *South Park* is my dad—my dad said, 'Well, Trey, you need to flush the toilet because if you don't, Mr. Hankey is going to come out and kill you.' And I'm like, 'What do you mean?' And he goes, 'Well, it just sits there, and you flush it. But if you don't he'll come to life, and he sings a little song, and he kills you.'" *1998: On the inspiration for the creation of one of the show's characters, Mr. Hankey, the Christmas Poo, a stool specimen wearing a sailor hat and speaking with the voice of a castrato ventriloquist.*

DOLLY PARTON
(Singer & Actress)

"I'm not offended at all because I know I'm not a dumb blonde. I also know I'm not a blonde." *1992: On dumb blonde jokes.*

"I've been showing my ass for years. In fact, I've never known a Parton who hasn't shown their ass." *1993*

"I'm proud of my tits. We've made each other rich and famous. It's part of the whole Dolly Parton persona. I not only don't play 'em down, I play 'em up. I'm not interested in taking them away, I want more! I was offered all kinds of money to just show one of them. But I'm not interested to put them on the table. I'll just keep pushing them up, pulling them around. I don't know if they carried me or I've carried them. But I'd rather jack 'em up than jack 'em down." *1993*

"I had this idea to do a series called *High and Mighty* about a country singer that has a near-death experience, then becomes like a gospel singer. But everybody's afraid to touch anything that's religious because most of the people out there (in Hollywood) are Jewish, and it's a frightening thing for them to promote Christianity. But that's all right, 'cause now I'm going to do that *High and Mighty* as a TV movie of the week." *1994*

"Most people spend so much time looking natural, when somebody like me takes less time to look artificial." *1994*

"It's amazing how healing money can be." *1994*

"I was caught sucking a sow. I was about three years old, and we had a sow who had fewer pigs than she had nipples . . . so I fell in with the pigs. . . . Some have suggested that there could be some connection between that incident and the way I developed later in life." *1994*

"There I sat, trying to be holy, praying for forgiveness for things I couldn't put my finger on, repenting for things I *had* put my finger on." *1994: On attending church when she was young.*

"I couldn't get my hair big enough or 'yaller' enough. Couldn't get my skirt tight enough, my blouses low enough. Couldn't get my boobs to stand up high enough. . . . Believe it or not, I thought I needed falsies." *1994: On her early singing career.*

"He told me that I couldn't act. I said: 'Well, that's no news to me. You didn't hire me because I could act, you know.'" *1994: On working with director Herbert Ross on* Steel Magnolias. *Parton told Ross that if he were any kind of director he'd make it look like she was acting.*

"I was in the movie business before Elvis was the king of rock and roll and little Richard was the queen." *1995*

"Even though it's controversial, I'm honored. There's no such thing as baaaad publicity." *1997: On her namesake Dolly the cloned sheep.*

"I have to honestly say that most of the stuff [the tabloids] write has a little grain of truth. They've told a lot of stuff about me that's true. They've told a lot of stuff about me that ain't true. And I don't admit or deny any of it, because what I ain't done, I'm capable of doing." *1998: On stories in the tabloids.*

VICTOR PELEVIN
(Author)

"Yellow journalism and crime stories cover it in all its stinking width and breadth. And if sometimes it has some depth, usually it's the depth of a grave.'" *1997: On everyday life in Russia as a topic for literature.*

"I don't want my readers to learn anything from what I write. A good book should take you on a trip, not to a class." *1997*

SEAN PENN
(Actor & Director)

"I wanted a healthy child and all that. But I found out the moment that she was born and I saw that she was a girl, that I had expected a boy. It's hard to imagine that you can make a girl—particularly after all the hell girls put us through. And there she is, and I thought to myself, Jesus, man, if this were a little boy, I'd look down and say, 'Hey, man, we got things to talk about.' But I'm looking at this little girl and saying, 'Shit, like I've never understood one of you in my life. You got some shit to tell me.' So that was that experience." *1991: On the birth of his daughter.*

"Let's face it, we have an insane fascist in the White House." *1991: On George Bush.*

"My code was never that I was above the law—it's just that it was beneath me." *1995*

"Guns are a necessity, living where and how I live. But I'm pretty much a hypocrite with guns: I want to be the only one who has 'em." *1995*

"I figure you can be in love with anybody, at random—an old lady with yellow teeth, an old man, a sheep." *1995*

"Cigarettes are the greatest, most enjoyable of all living hells." *1995*

"People can be real ignorant. In fact, it's one of the most pervasive talents in this country." *1995*

"Paparazzi. These are wildly dysfunctional people. They tend to have mustard from a week ago smeared on their collar, or they're big guys with really high voices. Another man follows you everywhere you go and alters your life in the negative with behavior that's vulturesque. Nothing you can do about it. For four years of marriage, that was my life, twenty-four hours a day." *1995: On his marriage to Madonna.*

"I guess this means you tolerate me, you really tolerate me." *1996: Accepting an award for best actor honors at the Independent Spirit awards.*

"That was madness. A handgun is never accurate at that range." *1997: Admitting that on the day he married Madonna, he'd fired a pistol at a helicopter full of paparazzi flying overhead.*

"I'm not alcoholic. I'm just a big drinker, and there's a difference." *1999*

"If you want entertainment, you get a couple of hookers and an eight ball." *1999*

ROSIE PEREZ
(Actress)

"One thing I will never do is use a body double. It's like saying, 'I'm too good to be naked in a movie, but the bitch down the street can do it for me.'" *1994*

ANNE PERKINS
(U.C. Davis Graduate Student & Researcher)

"If is very difficult to look at the possibility of lesbian sheep because if you are a female sheep, what you do to solicit sex is stand still. Maybe there is a female sheep out there really wanting another female, but there's just no way for us to know." *1990: On her study of sexuality among sheep.*

VALERIE PERRINE
(Actress)

"I think it's a very healthy thing to hit the person you love. I hit and I've had it done to me." *1990*

"Minks are mean little critters. Vicious, horrible little animals who eat their own. They're not beavers. I wouldn't wear a beaver. I'd rather have a mink coat made of mean little critters that are killed in a very nice way and treated nicely for their short, mean lives, so that I could be kept warm." *1990*

LUKE PERRY
(Actor)

"I will not refuse to do something because of the fear of looking bad or stupid. I mean, Jesus Christ, I did *Buffy, the Vampire Slayer*." *1993*

JOE PESCI
(Actor)

"Joe Pesci doesn't exist. I see myself on a talk show, I'll say, 'I like that guy. He's honest. Yes, he's a good actor. Who the hell is he?' " *1993*

CASSANDRA "ELVIRA" PETERSON
(Actress)

"During October I have to work every minute of every single day. I'm kind of like the turkey at Thanksgiving: everybody wants a piece." *1991*

TOM PETTY
(Musician & Singer)

"That would incredibly compromise my undoing." *1991: On why he doesn't do commercial endorsements.*

"If you really wanna see somebody's old pants, it's all right with me." *1995: On the Rock and Roll Hall of Fame and Museum.*

MICHELLE PFEIFFER
(Actress)

"I guess the most wisdom I've gained is realizing I don't really know that much." *1994*

"I don't think people should live together for the rest of their lives, suppressing frustrations. Fidelity is possible. Anything is possible, if you're stubborn and strong. But it's not that important." *1995*

LIZ PHAIR
(Singer)

"I'm really excited [about] Viagra. If older men are getting a lot of sex and they feel really good about their erections, I have the feeling the world will be a nicer place." *1998*

JULIA PHILLIPS
(Writer & Producer)

"We shoot in and around the San Francisco area for the summer. The worst is Berkeley, which is the black part of town." *1991*

RIVER PHOENIX
(Actor)

"I was completely celibate from ten to fourteen." *1991*

ROB PILATUS
(Lip Syncher)

"Musically, we are more talented than Bob Dylan . . . than Paul McCartney. Mick Jagger . . . his lines are not clear. He don't know how he should produce a sound. I'm the new modern rock and roll. I'm the new Elvis." *1990: Pilatus, half the duo of Milli Vanilli, who lip-synched the songs sung by others.*

"If you are going to be a star you have to have special hair." *1990*

"Fabrice and I—I think we are big talents. We can sing as good as any other pop star in the Top Ten. But I have to go through this again and again, till I get cancer in my stomach and die." *1990: Fabrice Morvan and Pilatus formed the group Milli Vanilli.*

"I am schizophrenic and have drug-induced psychoses. But other than that, I'm fine." *1994*

"I feel like a mosquito being squeezed. The last two years of our lives have been a total nightmare. We've had to lie to everybody. We are true singers but that maniac Frank Farian would never allow us to express ourselves." *1990: Frank Farian produced Milli Vanilli and admitted that Pilatus and Morvan never sang a note on their album, which sold seven million copies and won them a Grammy in 1989— which they returned in 1990.*

"We just hope [our fans] understand that we were young, that we just wanted to live life the American way." *1990*

"I mean, I've been through one suicide, I don't want to go through another one." *1993: Pilatus finally committed suicide in April 1998.*

STEVEN PINKER
(Author)

"Gossip is a favorite pastime in all human societies because knowledge is power. Knowing who needs a favor and who is in a position to offer one, who is trustworthy and who is a liar, who is available (or soon to become available) and who is under the protection of a jealous spouse or family—all give obvious strategic advantages in the games of life . . . the social equivalent of insider trading." *1998: Pinker is the author of* How the Mind Works.

DAVID PIRNER
(Singer)

"I met Bill Clinton. I think my aspirations are higher than his." *1995*

BRAD PITT
(Actor)

"They say when a dog sticks his head out a car window, it puts him in a state of constant euphoria. I can understand." *1992*

"I really don't like vampires all that much. I find them to be full of shit, frankly." *1993*

"I say to myself, 'You shoulda got more sleep last night. You should floss more.'" *1996: On what he thinks when he looks in the mirror.*

"I wound up in a giant chicken costume, making clucking sounds, trying to lure customers into an El Pollo fast-food restaurant." *1996: On one of his early jobs.*

"Reporters ask me what I feel China should do about Tibet. Who cares what I think China should do? I'm a fucking actor. I'm here for entertainment, basically, when you whittle everything away. I'm a grown man who puts on makeup." *1997*

"I'd date me!" *1998: Assessing his looks.*

ROBERT PLANT
(Singer)

"I think I could actually live the way I'm living now without sex. For about another half an hour." *1994*

"I think I'm prone to panic. I've become obsessively Virgo. I like to comprehend more or less everything around me—apart from the creation of my music." *1994*

SIDNEY POITIER
(Actor)

"They are making pictures where people get killed and nobody cries." *1997: Telling what's wrong with movies nowadays.*

IGGY POP
(Singer)

"Things like vacuuming the house and folding my clothes also surprise me, but the biggest mindblower is when I pull out my American Express card. It's only a green one. I haven't gone for the gold yet. I used it the other day in Beverly Hills, and the girl at the cash register said, 'Oh, why, I haven't seen one of these in years. A green card, how quaint.'" *1990*

"I like to lick girls' sweaty armpits in the summer. The smell really turns me on, especially if they have hair." *1996*

"The only thing I ever thought might kill me off was clean living. I thought, 'How am I going to listen to that horrible noise I make without a gram of coke and a couple of double Jack Daniels?'" *1996*

PAULA PORIZKOVA
(Model)

"The last place I want to be is in the country. There are too many trees." *1992*

MICHAEL PORTNOY
(Performance Artist)

"Soy is protein and life and energy. And bomb is explosive and propulsive. All art should be soy bombs." *1998: Portnoy jumped on the stage at the 1998 Grammy Awards and danced while Bob Dylan performed. Portnoy had painted the words "Soy Bomb" on his torso.*

"If you can get me into the Oscars, I'll take it from there." *1998*

MONICA POTTER
(Actress)

"I seriously wanted to be a nun for a while. Couldn't you just see it? I'm not sure how interested I was in the help-people part of it. I just liked the shoes." *1998*

PAULA POUNDSTONE
(Comedienne)

"I have the largest gospel music collection in the world, probably, for an athiest." *1993*

PAULA POUNDSTONE (CONT'D)

"I've been looking for a project that I could still be on medication to do, and this has medication written all over it." *1999: On her UPN animated series,* Home Movies.

MAURY POVICH
(TV Talk-show Host)

"None of the daytime talk shows would be on the air if the states of Florida, Texas and California didn't exist. That's where every weird person alights." *1993*

EMILY PRAGER
(Fashion Writer)

"Some people will undoubtedly consider it frivolous to mention fashion and killing in the same sentence." *1994: Describing how the young killers of Mogadishu and Kigali uphold the treasured African tradition of "warrior fashion."*

LISA MARIE PRESLEY
(Celebrity Daughter & Wife)

"Michael is a true artist in every facet of its nature. [He is] extremely aesthetic and very, very romantic. This is who he truly is despite degrading comments made in the past by certain larva. Michael, as well as myself, have been severely underestimated and misunderstood as human beings. I can't wait for the day when all the snakes who have tried to take him get to eat their own lunch and crawl back in the holes from which they came. We know who they are and their bluff is about to be called." *1995: On her husband, Michael Jackson.*

"He's an artist. He resculpted himself." *1995: On husband Michael Jackson's reconstructive plastic surgery.*

RICHARD PRICE
(Novelist & Screenwriter)

"Wonderful means change it. Fantastic means change it. Terrific means change it. Thank you means you're fired." *1998: On the way screenplays are evaluated by film studio executives.*

JASON PRIESTLEY
(Actor)

"George Bush is the most qualified man to run this country. He used to be head of the CIA!" *1992*

LINDA PROAPS
(Writer)

"Eric proceeded to unbutton her pink satin nightshirt, and she went through the physical motions of making love to him. As he reached his climax, Stacy gasped. Eric mistook her reaction as proof of his sexual prowess. In fact, Stacy's reaction had nothing to do with Eric. She had figured out why everyone insisted the tax conformity bill was revenue neutral." *1991: In the novel* Capital Punishment.

RICHARD PRYOR
(Comedian)

"Two things people throughout history have in common are hatred and humor. I am proud that, like Mark Twain, I have been able to use humor to lessen people's hatred." *1998: On being chosen by the John F. Kennedy Center for the Performing Arts in Washington, D.C., as the first recipient of the new annual prize named for Twain.*

MARIO PUZO
(Writer)

"People always ask me about *The Godfather*, about whether it's my favorite book. . . . The more money I make from it, the better book I think it is." *1997*

Q

JOE QUEENAN
(Writer)

"Having to sit there and listen while this K-mart Joe Cocker mutilates *You Send Me* is like sitting through a performance of *King Lear* with Don Knotts in the title role." *1996: On listening to Michael Bolton.*

"Being introduced to Joe Piscopo and Dan Aykroyd and only later discovering the existence of Adam Sandler and Chris Farley is like . . . learning about the Black Plague only to find out . . . that there's something called the Blacker Plague." *1996*

ANTHONY QUINN
(Actor)

"I really don't think death exists. I think it's just a change that you go through." *1990*

COLIN QUINN
(Comedian)

"Illness prevented Barbra Streisand from performing a duet with Celine Dion at the Grammy Awards this week. At the last minute, Streisand developed a violent allergic reaction to sharing the spotlight." *1998*

R

LEE RADZIWELL
(Celebrity Sister)

"I won't eat anything with eyes. I love fish; I understand them. I love the way they move and shimmer. I love being a fish." *1992*

LUISE RAINER
(Actress)

"He was very normal. He played the violin and did not talk about the theory of relativity." *1988: Rainer, eighty-seven, who won Academy Awards in 1936 for* The Great Ziegfeld *and in 1937 for* The Good Earth *remembering meeting Albert Einstein during a visit to Princeton in 1938.*

"I am a freak of nature. I am 87! And I am proud of it." *1988*

BONNIE RAITT
(Singer)

"I don't know about you, but winning a Grammy sure helped me get laid." *1991: To Don Henley of the Eagles.*

DAN RATHER
(TV News Anchor)

"Uh . . . it must be terribly lonely for both of them." *1991: After commenting on "the terrible loneliness" of the pilot of an F-15 and then being informed that the F-15 has a crew of two.*

"I have worked stripped to my waist in 115 degree temperatures for minimum wage with no benefits, thank you very much. And that was work. We worked from early dawn 'til well after dark moving dirt. Now that's real work. This passion of mine, it takes hours, it takes time, it takes some juggling the schedule around. But listen, I have worked for a living, and this beats working any day of the week." *1999: On how happy he is to be part of the* 60 Minutes II *team at CBS.*

TED RAWL
(Author & Cartoonist)

"SATs are all that matter, but don't come off like a jerk. I was a lowly assistant, so I didn't make admissions decisions. Nevertheless, I was the applicants' first contact, and if someone was a total, unadulterated jerk, the file would gather dust in the bottom of my lower desk drawer. I once picked up the line and the idiot started yelling, 'What the hell is going on with my application?' A lot of callers treated me like pond scum. It was worse than working at Wendy's." *1998: Recalling his experience working in the admissions office at an Ivy League University.*

"If you have nothing better to do, squander your parents' money on college tuition. But college is a scam. All it trains you to do is work for somebody until you croak. We don't live in a Buddhist society, so we're not coming back anytime soon. Don't do anything that leads to becoming a corporate drone." *1998: Advice to current high school graduates.*

HELEN REDDY
(Singer)

"I've been a man many times. That is what I'm trying to atone for now." *1991: Reddy, whose song "I Am Woman" made her a star in the 1970s, believes in reincarnation.*

ROBERT REDFORD
(Actor)

"I get asked all the time what I do when I'm not making films. . . . I said to myself, 'You're not doing anything, why not cobble?'" *1990*

KEANU REEVES
(Actor)

"Once I cried over beauty, once I cried over pain, and the other time I cried because I felt nothing. I can't help it, man. I'm just a cliché of myself." *1991*

"Vampires, submission, domination, rape, bestiality, guilt, Biblical overtones, Satan, God, Christian motifs, the dead, undead, blood, murder, revenge, opera, classicism and oral sex." *1992: On what the movie* Dracula *is about.*

STEVE REEVES
(Movie Muscleman)

"When your arms are bigger than your head, something is wrong." *1998: Commenting on the beach scene in Venice, CA.*

ROB REINER
(Actor & Director)

"Tom (Cruise) likes to jump out of planes. He likes to race cars. He likes to ride on motorcycles. He likes to climb rocks. He likes white-water rafting. And now he likes this aerobatic stuff. Let's just say there's not a drop of Jewish blood in him." *1994*

PAUL REISER
(Actor)

"My friends come over and we do Gregorian chants. We do this in robes eating fish sandwiches." *1995*

"I was reading this article about Sting, and it was like a big bulletin that through yoga he can make love for eight hours. I've actually discussed this with a lot of women who went, 'Who wants that?' First of all, who has eight hours free—you know what I mean?" *1995*

DON REO
(TV Producer)

"We're going to go out on a limb and say that education is good." *1996: On messages in his college-based sitcom,* Pearl.

BURT REYNOLDS
(Actor)

"There are two things I've learned in life: You should never race a guy named Flash and never bring a girl named Bubbles home to meet your mother. Both of which I've done, by the way." *1992*

"I've done almost 50 movies—I've had a relationship with four actresses. They all lasted almost seven years, except my first marriage [to Judy Carne], which lasted an hour and a half." *1992*

"I thought the chances of my being here were that of there being a Richard Simmons, Jr." *1998: Speaking at the Film Critics Circle Awards in New York where he was nominated for an award for best supporting actor.*

"I am so superstitious about the Oscars. I'm trying to remember what underwear I had on when I won a Golden Globe so I can wear it again." *1998: On what he'd wear to the Oscar ceremonies.*

"I told them, 'Look, I can do this. I can still fall; I just can't get up.'" *1998: On insisting on doing one of his own stunts on a recent acting job.*

CHRISTINA RICCI
(Actress)

"She said, 'You don't have to be interesting. It's their job to make you interesting." *1999: Relating Courtney Love's advice on dealing with the media.*

"Basically, I'm like a whore. I'll give people whatever they want so they'll like me." *1999*

"It's really interesting how she romanticizes a way of dealing with emotions and people that's so different than what we're given in films and stuff." *1999: On her favorite book, Ayn Rand's* The Fountainhead.

ANNE RICE
(Author)

"I think sleeping in coffins is fine. What's wrong with that? When it comes to ingesting blood, I can't recommend it." *1999*

KEITH RICHARDS
(Musician & Singer)

"I don't suppose Joshua took his band and walked around Jericho and blew a few trumpets and the wall actually fell down from that. It was probably some cats inside Jericho who were saying, 'Jesus, those guys are playing good—open the back door and let them in.' That's how I think Jericho's walls crumbled. It's like the Iron Curtain now." *1992*

"Probably blue jeans and rock 'n' roll had (the biggest) effect on undermining the Iron Curtain. . . . It's (rock 'n' roll) a beautiful armor-piercing weapon, man." *1992*

"Do you need a mudfest every 25 years? I don't know. My claim to fame is that I wasn't at the first one, and I ain't going to be at the second one. It was mud and bad acid." *1994: On Woodstock.*

"The devil doesn't bother me, it's God that pisses me off. Him and his rain. You wait until I meet the motherfucker. Doesn't he know who we are? We're the Rolling Stones!" *1995*

"Passing the vodka bottle. And playing the guitar." *On what he does to stay fit.*

"If you're lucky enough to be a father, you learn a whole new kind of love. Because basically love, to a guy without children, it's just another word for 'fuck.' It's a very confusing thing to guys, because love is something that you only really learn when you've got to nurture something in yourself." *1995*

GERALDO RIVERA
(TV Personality)

"I think we're doing a better show. Sex is easy; sex is cheap; sex always gets an audience. So if you are not doing sex, you have to work harder to be provocative without being salacious, to be hot without pandering. Now we're clever as opposed to naughty." *1990: Describing his TV show* Geraldo.

"I was tame compared to some other programs. I never put freaks on. I never put on armless, legless, bellyless lovers of tall, skinny purple people. I've always been a lightning rod, attracting far more scrutiny, far more critical comment than anybody else. It's almost as if I'm the metaphor for all that ails TV, and it doesn't matter what I'm really doing. Rather than do your homework and criticize specific programs, you just criticize Geraldo as intellectual investigation of the generic. It's a pain in the butt." *1990: On critics of* Geraldo.

"I was a cheater. I was a cheater. That was my drug. I don't drink. I don't do drugs. My drug was women and sex and whatever you call it. What a cheater does is to cheat. A cheater cheats . . . A cheater cheats when a cheater has the opportunity, not when it's appropriate—[that's] when the cheater cheats . . . when you have the opportunity . . . Back to what I said about a cheater. That's what a cheater does. That was my drug . . ." *1991*

"The Jewish people, for their tiny numbers, have done superbly. I mean, they don't need me. They have Albert Einstein. They have, you know, everybody—Maury Povich." *1991*

"I refused to look in the mirror until it was finished. Then I was horrified. I recognized myself, but I wasn't at all sexy or dashing." *1991: On how he had himself fitted with prosethetic fat for a special program on fat people.*

"I rowed us to a secluded spot. . . . Right there, the estranged First Lady of Canada lent new meaning to the term 'head of state.' " *1991: On his alleged relationship with Margaret Trudeau in his autobiography* Exposing Myself.

"Hey, calling me a rapist? I feel totally violated. . . . This is a terrible blow to my credibility." *1991: On an allegation of Bette Midler that he groped and molested her and committed "interview rape."*

"I just want to make sure that all the kids out there who are saying, 'Hey, mommy, I want to be like Geraldo,' and their mommy is going to say, 'How can you do like that, look at him, he's out there doing that and promoting sex and stuff?' I want to say, 'Look, ma, Geraldo wears condoms.' " *1992*

"It's easy for Barbara Walters to hold an HIV-positive infant. But to hug a gay man who's HIV-positive on television—as I've done—is not easy." *1992*

"A good story needs to have meat, a unique angle and heat." *1993*

"Bill Moyers could do a story about a dog urinating, and you would all say how elegantly he phrased it. I could get an exclusive interview with Jesus and half the people would say I was too tough on him. The other half would say I was too easy on him. I don't ever expect to be the critics' darling." *1994*

"The biggest practical result is that most Americans now know that in Spanish the 'G' is pronounced 'H.' " *1994: On how his contributions to television have changed society.*

"How can you not look at Barbara Walters and see those great tits?" *1998*

"She's exactly my type. She's got balls, that woman." *1998: On news reporter Christiane Amanpour.*

JOAN RIVERS
(Comedienne & TV Host)

"Never tell (your daughter) about your sex life—or lack of it. It's ugly to see pity in a daughter's eyes." *1994*

"She was so hairy—when she lifted up her arm, I thought it was Tina Turner in her armpit." *1994: On Madonna.*

"You leave money?" *1995: Responding to Howard Stern's statement that he does things in bed with women that drives them crazy!*

"If you don't want gays in the military, make the uniforms ugly." *1996*

"The only way to get back at them is to litter. Go over there and litter. Spit. Blow your nose on the sidewalk." *1997: After she was barred from broadcasting her radio talk show from a hotel in Palm Beach, FL, because of zoning laws in the city.*

"I don't mean to sound bitchy. She may turn out to be fabulous. There may be more to her than dimples and boobs." *1999: After her cable TV show's coverage of the celebrity arrivals at the Oscars was bumped off the air for half an hour by ABC's new Oscar special, hosted by actress Geena Davis.*

JULIA ROBERTS
(Actress)

"I think wings are sexy. I bet if you walked outside and looked carefully at people around you, you could immediately tell who has wings and who doesn't." *1998*

"I've never discussed it before. As a child, I used to bite my toenails off, you know, instead of clipping them with clippers. I was very limber." *1999*

VITO ROCCO
(Film Director)

"At least nobody will walk out." *On his first movie,* Ciao Mamma, *which is seven seconds long.*

CHRIS ROCK
(Comedian)

"You got to kind of live like a bum to be a successful stand-up. But the bigger you get, the less free time you have to let your mind just wander. In order for me to be a good stand-up, I got to pretty much do nothing all day." *1998*

"You got a black Michael Jackson?" *1998: To a Harlem shopkeeper after being shown a portrait of a black Princess Diana.*

ROY ROGERS
(Singer & Actor)

"After I visit the Roy Rogers & Dale Evans Museum every morning to meet folks and pose for pictures, I rush home to watch *Guiding Light*." *1993: On how he spends a typical day.*

STAN ROLAND
(Saxophonist)

"I couldn't believe Clinton didn't inhale pot till I heard him play the sax." *1993*

RAY ROMANO
(Actor & Comedian)

"My daughter names her toes. *That's Judy, that's Julie.* . . . It's so cute. But if Granddad names his toes, all of a sudden it's a *tragedy*." *1995*

"He's a little obsessive-compulsive. But we don't make fun of it. We don't want to insult any obsessive-compulsive people because if they start writing letters, they don't quit. Send the letter, check the stove. Send the letter, check the stove. Send the letter, check the stove." *1996*

"Once in a while my wife complains about my jokes. I just tell her to go cry into a big bag of money." *1998*

"The second day of rehearsal my manager called me and said, 'They decided to go in another direction.' I said, 'Tell me what direction. I'll meet them there.'" *1999: Remembering being fired from* News Radio *before it ever aired.*

MICKEY ROONEY
(Actor)

"I lost my hair because of tennis and ping pong. I was the Southern California ping pong champion for five years. But I took too many showers . . . You can't take 15 showers a day for 11 or 12 years and not have something happen to your hair. No one else in my family is bald. And no one else played tennis." *1993*

"Age is nothing more than experience, and some of us are more experienced than others." *1998: On being seventy-seven.*

AXL ROSE
(Singer)
"I've done regression therapy all the way back, just about to the point of conception. I kind of know what was going on then." *1993*

ROSEANNE
(Actress)
"This is not a democracy. It's a queendom." *1990: Addressing the staff of her television show.*

"Me and my husband found a foolproof method of birth control. Every night before we go to bed, we spend an hour with our kids." *1990*

"I think myself and my husband, Tom Arnold, should be the final word on what is obscene. We're cooler than Jesse Helms and we've actually had sex in the past decade." *1990*

"This town is a back-stabbing, scum-sucking, small-minded town, but thanks for the money." *1990*

"The biggest misconception about me is that I'm fat." *1991*

"We don't go for any diets 'cause it doesn't help you, and you just end up getting fatter and fatter. We're both fat because we dieted. That's the truth." *1991: Commenting on her weight problems and those of her husband at the time, Tom Arnold.*

"You are a cock-sucking pinhead. . . . You're a butt-rammer from the word go. You fucking bitch. Fuck you, you smarmy little tight-assed prick. . . . Try using KY next time. . . . P.S. You are not in a position to understand or criticize anything about heterosexuals." *1991: From a letter faxed nine times to Matt Roush of* USA Today, *who's transgression was that he did not like Tom Arnold's [Roseanne's husband] HBO special.*

"When was the last time you thought anything was fun? A dour, skinny creep like you reviewing comedy is akin to a blind baboon reviewing great art." *1992: In a letter to* L.A. Times *television critic Howard Rosenberg who wrote an unfavorble review of Tom Arnold's HBO special.*

"I approached reading his review the way some people anticipate anal warts." *1992: On* L.A. Daily News *critic Ray Richmond, who didn't like Tom Arnold's sitcom,* The Jackie Thomas Show.

"My whole career is guided by God, so that's why I don't have to answer to any earthly shit." *1993*

"I used to be a feminist, until the first time Tom grabbed me by the hair, threw me up against the wall and fucked me in the ass." *1993: On her husband, Tom Arnold.*

"I don't think women want to be equal to men. I think we would need lobotomies to do that." *1993*

"The way I think about it is that anybody can have sex with anything. The person you're having it with doesn't do anything to make you one way or the other. If you want to go over there and have sex with that lamp post, you can do that, too." *1994*

"I don't think I can play someone that ain't as famous as me." *1994: On rumors that she'd play Mae West in a movie.*

"We did try for a couple of years, but we found out that one of us has to have a penis." *1994: On attempts to get pregnant with Tom Arnold.*

"I'd like to be one of those people who can completely accept what they look like, but there aren't many of those. And none of them are women. And none of them are in Hollywood." *1994*

"Oh, honey, there'll be prenuptial agreements up the ying-yang from henceforth." *1995: On her scheduled Valentine's Day wedding to ex-bodyguard Ben Thomas.*

"I think women should be more violent, kill more of their husbands. I like the fight. If people are comin' at you, you don't just sit there and lay down and go, 'Oh, bless you.' That's not in the human

ROSEANNE (CONT'D)

arsenal. To say that women shouldn't do that is to say women aren't human." *1995*

"I gave Clinton an extraordinary amount of money to help get him elected because I felt he was better than whoever he was running against. . . . I feel as though I elected Bill Clinton. Not only did he not call to thank me, but he has never invited me to the White House. It was a snub to me and my constituency." *1996: On her extraordinary amount of $1,000 given to the winning 1992 presidential candidate.*

"Dead ones." *1996: On what kind of women get noticed as artists.*

"Computers scare me. I think they're satanic." *1996*

ROSEANNE: "Too bad you were on the wrong side in the O. J. trial."

BALD MAN: "I was?"

ROSEANNE: "Aren't you Robert Shapiro?"

BALD MAN: "No, I'm Dick Vitale."

ROSEANNE: "Oh." *1997*

"I am the most qualified person to host a talk show. I've got five kids by three men. I came from a trailer park where I was a Jew passing as a Mormon in Salt Lake City. My brothers and sister are homosexuals and my younger sister is a recovering anorexic. I was reunited with my long-lost daughter, whom I gave up for adoption and who was found by *The National Enquirer*. I am a woman who has multiple personalities, several of whom don't even know they're famous!" *1998*

"Albert Einstein . . . he was one of 'em. And Ed Sullivan." *1999: On her childhood idols.*

"My hope is that gays will be running the world, because then there would be no war. Just a greater emphasis on military apparel." *1999*

"I told them I'm not giving them any more money. I said, 'Get a fucking job or find husbands.'" *1999: On her relationship with her three daughters.*

GARY ROSEN
(TV Spokesman)

"Quite frankly, we are surprised that Madonna is stunned by anything." *1996: The spokesman for television tabloid* Hard Copy *on the singer's outraged reaction to the show's broadcast of a home video of her and new baby Lourdes.*

LIZ ROSENBERG
(Publicist for Madonna and Cher)

"I think Madonna called her a c— once, but I'm sure she meant it in the nicest possible way." *1999: On Madonna's opinion of Cher.*

ROGER ROSENBLATT
(Writer & Critic)

"Mr. [Bret Easton] Ellis may be the most knowledgeable author in all American literature. Whatever Melville knew about whaling, whatever Mark Twain knew about rivers are mere amateur stammerings compared with what Mr. Ellis knows about shampoo alone." *1990*

JANE ROSENTHAL
(Film producer)

"Compare producers to plumbers—it's only when things get backed up that anybody notices." *1998*

PHIL ROSENTHAL
(Columnist)

"The guy sells cotton underpants for $20—and people think his *ads* are obscene?" *1995: On Calvin Klein.*

DAVID LEE ROTH
(Singer)

"The reason why rock critics all like Elvis Costello is because rock critics all look like Elvis Costello." *1993*

"The '80s was a very different time—a condom was a small apartment. Who knew?" *1994*

MICKEY ROURKE
(Actor & Boxer)

"I don't got no future really as a boxer, but I do it because I have a good time." *1992*

"He's very intelligent and very generous in giving me his time and helping me do my thing. I do roles that are urban-type roles. He knows that stuff." *1992: On his friend, John Gotti.*

Like An Actor With Amnesia
Or A Director Without A Penis
You Make Me Cry
Like An Orphaned Baboon
Chained to the Dyke Saleslady
At Bloomindales
In N.Y.C. At Xmas Time.
1994: One of the poems composed by Rourke for a collection of poetry.

BRIAN ROUTH
(Performance Artist, aka Harry Kipper)
"People always point their finger at performance artists and say they're a bunch of sickos. But we're not the ones who are sick. I think it's just the opposite." *1991: Routh appears onstage dressed only in his underwear and a baby's bib and tells Bible stories using stuffed animals and a doll—he strangles the doll and then whips himself with a cat-o'-nine-tails.*

NICHOLAS ROYLE
(Novelist)
"Yasmin grinned and writhed on the bed, arching her back, making a noise somewhere between a beached seal and a police siren." *1997: In his book* The Matter of the Heart. *This passage was partly responsible for Royle's being awarded the Bad Sex in Fiction Prize by the* Literary Review *magazine of London.*

SAUL RUBINEK
(Actor & Director)
"Gambling goes on [at film festivals.] And where there are gamblers there's disappointment; where there's disappointment there's desperation; where there's desperation there's fear; and where there's fear there's an atmosphere that isn't healthy." *1998: Rubinek premiered his directorial debut,* Jerry and Tom, *at the Sundance Film Festival.*

"Sundance is a way for independent filmmakers who have been isolated from the realities of the business to get a taste of it. Sometimes you're kicked in the ass, sometimes you're given a French kiss." *1998*

RITA RUDNER
(Comedienne)
"They're used to pain and they're used to buying jewelry." *1994: On why men with pierced ears make great husbands.*

"Personal ads are dangerous. You have to separate the ones who are lying from the ones who are hallucinating." *1994*

"In high school, I didn't make the cheerleading team because we had to write our own cheers for the tryouts, and I don't get that excited. I wrote, 'If we win, we win. If we lose, we lose. Really, you can deal with it.'" *1995*

"It's hard being a woman. It's like being a female impersonator every day." *1998*

RUPAUL
(Female Impersonator & Actor)
MILTON BERLE: "You know, forty years ago, when I was on TV, I used to wear gowns myself."

RUPAUL: "Is that right? You used to wear gowns, and that's funny—now you wear diapers." *1993: At the* 10th Annual MTV Music Awards *where the two stars were presenters.*

"We have to tell these kids what condoms taste like." *1993: On sex education in the public schools.*

"People always say, 'Should I call you he or she?' When it's like, 'It don't matter, as long as you call me.' You can call me he or she, or you can call me Regis and Kathie Lee." *1994*

"I got to actually concentrate on acting instead of sitting around worrying if my face is cracking." *1995: On finally getting to play the part of a guy in the made-for-television movie* A Mother's Prayer.

"The point of my whole image is really making fun of celebrities. It's making fun of this Madison Avenue concoction of what femininity is. You know, wigs and high heels have nothing to do with what a woman is. It's true! People ask, 'Why do you dress like a woman?' I don't dress like a woman. I dress like a drag queen." *1997*

SALMAN RUSHDIE
(Author)

"I always felt I had the problems of rock & roll without the music or the groupies." *1999*

KURT RUSSELL
(Actor)

"Why are people attracted to each other? Because they can make a good baby. It's instinct. We call it chemistry. . . . The doe knows the stronger the buck she has, the stronger the offspring. All men face that. All the time, every day. The male knows what the male should do." *1991*

WINONA RYDER
(Actress)

"If anyone ever calls me quirky again, I think they should be shot. . . . I'm not precocious, and so I don't know why people call me precocious. Yeah, they should be shot, too." *1991*

"I feel my best when I'm happy." *1991*

"During dinner he used the word 'cognitive' twice in five minutes." *1994: Giving evidence that her boyfriend, rocker David Pirner of Soul Asylum, is "well read."*

"He's a great guy. . . . Every time you think he's senile, he's not." *1994: On Timothy Leary.*

"I guess I don't have the cleavage." *1998: On her fifteen-minute wait for drinks at a bar in Cannes, France.*

"I was never like an overnight sensation. I'm just kind of there. Certainly there's nothing Leonardoish about me right now." *1999: On why the paparazzi don't hound her.*

S

MORT SAHL
(Comedian)

"I hear (Oliver) Stone is going to film the life of Simon Wiesenthal. That's the good news. The bad news is that Kevin Costner is going to play Hitler." *1994*

PAT SAJAK
(TV Host)

"You know one of my pet peeves? I've never told anyone this. People who have a lot of money, not many letters up there, they don't know the puzzle and there are a lot of blank spaces, they're spinning that wheel and calling letters at random, instead of buying a vowel. I've seen more people lose a game without buying a vowel." *1997*

AIR SAMUELS
(Comedian)

"Some friends called me up. They said, 'Move to California where a man can live like a king.' So I did. But I didn't know they was talkin' about Rodney." *1992*

ADAM SANDLER
(Actor & Comedian)

"I was in New Hampshire with my family at a pizza place. The kid working there goes, 'Hey, you look like Adam Sandler.' I said, 'Yeah, I know.' He goes, 'What's your name?' I go, 'Adam Sandler.' And he goes, 'Whoa, that's a coincidence.'" *1999*

SUE SARA
(Spokesperson for Apple Computer's Asia-Pacific Division)

"We did not want to offend anyone." *1998: On her company's decision to pull images of the Dalai Lama from an advertising campaign in Asia for fear of angering China.*

SUSAN SARANDON
(Actress)

"Gore, you were breast-fed—so I guess breast-feeding is no guarantee that one won't turn out twisted." *1993: To Gore Vidal.*

"I think it's very hard to be naked in a scene and not be upstaged by your nipples." *1995*

"I was told I had an overabundance of original sin." *1995: On the troubles she experienced in a parochial school in the third grade.*

DIANE SAWYER
(TV Journalist)

"Do you think the pope liking your sausage gets you a special place in heaven?" *1999: Interviewing a butcher asked to make Polish sausage for the pope.*

"Her legs." *1999: On what she admires most about Barbara Walters.*

HEIDI SCHANZ
(Actress & Model)

"It's all pretty disgusting. I once got word through an agent that some producers felt I was the best actress they had seen for a part, but they couldn't imagine wanting to have sex with me. I wanted to go back there and rip the toupees off their heads." *1998: On dealing with studio executives who have the final say in casting after she tried to get a role in a TV series.*

CLAUDIA SCHIFFER
(Model)

"I think [Prince] is a very sexy singer. I would go out to dinner with him in a minute." *1993*

DR. LAURA SCHLESSINGER
(Radio Talk-show Host)

"There are three types of men in the world. One type learns from books. One type learns from observation. And one type just has to urinate on the electric fence." *1998*

"In my 20s, I was my own moral authority. The inadequacy of that . . . is painfully obvious today." *1998: The fifty-one-year-old nationally syndicated self-help radio guru, after losing her legal battle to bar an Internet site from displaying nude photos taken of her in the 1970s by a former boyfriend.*

PAUL SCHRADER
(Screenwriter & Director)

"I don't know what is more appalling, the conservatives' hypocrisy or the entertainment industry's sanctimony. The reality is, we've worked so hard at making audiences dumber, they have actually become dumber." *1997*

ARNOLD SCHWARZENEGGER
(Actor)

"Read my lips. No more fat." *1990*

"It makes no sense to create a computer genius by 12 and then he has a heart attack at 13." *1990: Speaking to Wisconsin fitness experts on why schools should stress physical fitness.*

"I look down on people who are waiting, who are helpless." *1990*

"I was always dreaming about very powerful people, dictators and things like that." *1990: On his childhood fantasies.*

"The only thing that makes me nervous is when I don't get my own way." *1990*

"People need somebody to watch over them. . . . Ninety-five percent of the people in the world need to be told what to do and how to behave." *1990*

"The key thing is to let the mind, like the body, float. And then when you need to hit hard, you're ready with all your energy. That's why I always say to people, 'Don't think!' That doesn't mean you shouldn't have a brain, but there's a part of us that likes to go through life instinctively and not make decisions. You free yourself and don't analyze everything and interpret or misinterpret." *1991*

"Jim Cameron and I have just decided backstage that we're going to do another *Terminator*. The title will be *The Sperminator*. I'LL COME AGAIN!" *1991*

"That's what separates leaders from followers." *1991: Responding to a Terminator 2 crew member's complaint about how Arnold humiliated him on the set.*

"Everybody in this country has the freedom to say what he or she wants to, but I sometimes think there is too much of that commodity for my taste." *1992*

"Of course in *Terminator*, when I saw myself die." *1993: When asked if he ever cries in movies.*

"I only play the Terminator. You married one." *1994: To Tom Arnold, husband of Roseanne.*

"I hate pants. This is something I have inherited from my father. He despised pants, and my mother was never allowed to wear them at home. I still feel that way, and neither my mother nor Maria is allowed to go out with me in pants." *1998*

"My friend, the director of *Titanic*, James Cameron and I, made three movies together—*The Terminator*, *Termintor 2* and *True Lies*. That was, of course,

ARNOLD SCHWARZENEGGER (CONT'D)

during his early, low-budget, art house period." *1998: Speaking at the Academy Awards ceremony*
.

MARTIN SCORCESE

(Director)

"In order to get the picture made I had to learn how to make a movie. I didn't learn how to make a movie in film school. What you learned in film school was to express yourself in pictures and sound. But learning to make a movie is totally different. That's the people with the production board, the schedule. That means you gotta get up at five in order to be there, you gotta feed the people." *1998: On the making of his film* Mean Streets *in 1972.*

WILLIAM LEE SCOTT

(Actor)

"She can hardly get through an open door without explicit instructions." *1999: On the intellect of his fellow* Black and White *cast member Claudia Schiffer.*

KRISTEN SCOTT-THOMAS

(Actress)

"You grin a lot and go, 'I can't believe I'm meeting you.' He's totally charming and used to dithering females. And yes, I was one of them." *1998: On first meeting Robert Redford, her costar in* The Horse Whisperer.

STEVEN SEAGAL

(Actor)

"Two monks were crossing a bridge. One asked the other, 'What is Zen?' The second monk picked up the first and threw him in the river, telling him to swim in it, become one with it, and not ask about it because words don't mean shit." *1991: An explanation of Zen Buddhism.*

"I just care about bringing joy into this world in my little way." *1997*

SEAL

(Singer)

"I'd never been to that part of the equator before." *1991: On his first visit to Japan.*

GEORGE SEGAL

(Actor)

"They don't want to clutter our little minds." *1999: On why actors seem to be the last to see scripts.*

JERRY SEINFELD

(Comedian)

"If there was no such thing as masturbation, most men would not know that anything could happen." *1993*

"Screw the Smithsonian. I want to keep it for myself." *1998: When asked if his TV show's living room set might go to the Smithsonian Institution to join Archie Bunker's chair when* Seinfeld *ended its nine-year run in May 1998.*

"Should I make you cry? This is a comedy show, after all. It's not good to have the audience crying." *1998: To the audience viewing the taping of his final show.*

"I *love* being back in New York. L.A. to me is like Vegas—but the losers stay in town." *1998*

KATHY SELF

(Celebrity Friend)

"If you haven't had a chocolate-covered dwarf in your shower, you haven't lived." *1992: On her relationship with actor Herve* Fantasy Island *Villechaize.*

TERRY SEMEL

(Warner Bros. CEO)

"A sign of a good executive is someone who doesn't return phone calls." *1998*

DAVID SEMLER

(Cinematographer)

"We were assembled to meet Her Majesty and Prince Philip, and when she got to me, she asked what exactly I did in the movie [*Dances with Wolves*]. I said I was director of photography, to which she replied, 'Oh, how terribly interesting. Actually, I have a brother-in-law who is a photographer.' I replied, 'Oh, how terribly coincidental. I have a brother-in-law who's a queen.' She moved on without saying another word." *1991*

CHRISTOPHER SERRONE

(Actor)

"I lead a double life. I'm fighting pimples and I'm an actor." *1990*

TUPAC SHAKUR
(Rapper)

"This guy Romeo from the Bloods falls for Juliet, a female from the Crips, and everybody in both gangs are against them." *1995: On how Shakespeare has influenced his lyrics.*

"They lock the jail there, so you can't move around. It's like, in jail it's a whole different thing, it's like how we should be in life." *1995: On life in jail.*

GARY SHANDLING
(Actor & Comedian)

"I used to think I was safe using a condom; now I'm using the Club." *1994: Referring to Lorena Bobbitt slicing off her husband's penis while he slept.*

"I wouldn't know if it's a 'cult' exactly. I do know that the guys who went on the Hale-Bopp comet were big fans." *1998: On his cable TV show,* The Larry Sanders Show.

"I learned most of my comedy at a French cooking school. Hence, the heavy use of butter. All I know for sure is, there's a very, very, very bitter after-taste." *1998*

"I am afraid of many things but I force myself to do them. I went to Magic Mountain, and I looked at the bungee jump and I thought, This is the devil's work. I did think for a moment, I should do it, it will make me more courageous. But no. There's a line. The roller coasters scare me, too. As does dating. It's those three things: bungee jumping, roller coasters and dating. And the idea of dating with my hands up in the air is the ultimate frightening experience." *1998*

"It bothered me, looking at hair and thinking that was important. I've grown past that. I now think it's the kind of hair you have inside that matters." *1999*

ARTIE SHAW
(Musician & Bandleader)

"Maybe I should drop dead—it would be a good career move. Look what it did for Glenn Miller." *1992*

BOB SHEEHAN
(Auctioneer)

"When she wasn't praying, she was needle-pointing. So she had a lot of time to needlepoint." *1999: As he presided over a Texas auction of items once owned by missing atheist activist Madalyn Murray O'Hair, including framed needlepoint pieces.*

GAIL SHEEHY
(Writer)

"Did Gorbachev change the world or did the world change him? I took as my premise the second interpretation." *1990: In her paradoxically entitled book,* The Man Who Changed the World: The lives of Mikhail S. Gorbachev.

CHARLIE SHEEN
(Actor)

"I'm more comfortable killing than making love." *1992*

"I'm a foot guy, you know. Terrible foot fetish. I'm not saying 'terrible' as in 'bad,' I'm saying it's just tremendous." *1994*

"How does fucking Francis Ford Coppola, one of the greatest filmmakers of our time, see Keanu Reeves' work, see what we've all seen, and say, 'That's what I want in my movie'? How does Bertolucci see that and say, 'That's my guy'? Emilio [Estevez] and I sit around and just scratch our fucking heads, thinking, 'How did this guy get in?' I mean, what the fuck?" *1994*

"It's starting to add up." *1995: In a videotaped deposition shown at the Heidi Fleiss trial, in which he admitted paying Fleiss more than $53,000 for call girls.*

"There was a voice. Not like drug-induced voices, but there was a voice that kept telling me this will not work." *1996: On his decision to divorce his wife of five months, Donna Peele.*

"I've always been one of those guys given the gift of realistic recognition. I just rely on my instincts, you know? I suppose that's what's kept me alive, kept me successful from time to time. Kept me in touch with some semblance of reality. And . . . I've found God. I did. I got saved a couple of months ago." *1996*

CYBILL SHEPHERD
(Actress)

"Everybody hates to hear how hard it is to be beautiful, but I can tell you that because of the way I look, I know people are watching my lips move and aren't hearing what I am saying. It makes you understand prejudice." *1993*

"Beauty has been far more of a help than a hindrance throughout my life, but it's had its negatives. I've spent a lot of my life watching other people watch me." *1995*

BROOKE SHIELDS
(Actress & Model)

"Just finding the quintessential female role that encompasses strength and vulnerability is just not easy to find." *1993*

"He's not a gifty-jewelry person. He'll buy you a car. He'll get your house painted, or you'll come back and your garage will be de-spidered." *1995: On the endearing qualities of Andre Agassi.*

"Smoking kills. If you're killed, you've lost a very important part of your life." *1997*

PAUL SHIMKONIS
(Topless Bar Victim)

"It was like two cement blocks hit me." *1998: On a suit he filed against Clearwater, FL, topless bar Diamond Dills, for injuries he claims to have sustained at his bachelor party in an encouter with generously proportioned stripper Tawny Peaks.*

TALIA SHIRE
(Actress)

"I'm here on behalf of the ozone layer." *1992: At a rally for Democratic presidential-nominee candidate, Jerry Brown.*

"If you vote for anyone other than Jerry Brown, you are voting for planetary death." *1992*

PAULY SHORE
(Actor & Comedian)

"Everyone likes to be an idiot once in a while, and that's what I'm here for." *1992*

"Is Arkansas in Tennessee?" *1992: On a road trip while passing through Arkansas.*

"People over 25 are so intense. They're into being intelligent and stuff." *1993*

"I just, like, found something no one else was doing and just, like, kind of like having your own thing. . . . That's, like, the most important part about stand-up comedy. It's no, like, oh my God, tell me this funny joke. You know, it's about who's telling the joke that makes it funny. It's having your own thing, and that's basically being yourself. People appreciate that, and people identify with that." *1993: On how he developed his act.*

ELIZABETH SHUE
(Actress)

"I had a hard time letting go of *Leaving Las Vegas.* I still visit red-light districts in every city I go to." *1996: Shue starred in the film* Leaving Las Vegas.

BARBARA SHULGASSER
(Moviegoer)

"What can you say about a movie that glorifies a fascist whore?" *1997: After watching* Evita.

BRUCE SILVERMAN
(Advertising Executive)

"If I were the head of a tobacco company, I'd say, 'God bless *Titanic.*'" *1998: Silverman, directed California's antismoking media campaign and was upset by the smoking of the main stars of* Titanic.

ALICIA SILVERSTONE
(Actress)

" 'Just be what you are': I still haven't figured that one out." *1997*

"When I get lonely, I want to be alone. I like to indulge in my loneliness so I can figure out that I'm not really lonely." *1997*

"When I was little, I was more sexual than I am now. Why? I don't know. The cart left before the horse." *1999*

GENE SIMMONS
(Musician & Singer)

"It has good food, good service, and very good chandeliers to swing from." *1994: On the wonders of Chicago's Ritz-Carlton Hotel where his group, KISS, stays.*

"All things American, from movies to rock 'n' roll to comic books to KISS to Fourth of July fireworks, critics never got any of them. But we are an example of the American way. It's of the people, by the people, for the people. That's why hamburgers rule the world. All the food critics can say, 'Ah yeees but eet eez not filet mignon.' Not only don't I especially like filet mignon, I can't even fucking *spell* it! Hamburgers, hot dogs, Coca-Cola, yes!" *1996*

"Past a certain point, your senses in and of themselves are the be-all and end-all. The Greeks only went as far as 'I think, therefore I am.'" *1996*

"The whole idea of people singing about their misery and getting paid for it—there's a contradiction right there. I mean, once you get paid for it, shut up. You have nothing to be miserable about anymore." *1996*

"Once I saw Superman and the Vikings on TV having fun, getting the money and getting the girls, I thought I was on the wrong team. There was not a single person running around having fun who had a beard. They all looked miserable, and never got the broads." *1997: On why he left an ultra-devout Jewish sect to became a rock star with KISS.*

"Here's the religion: Nobody dies; nobody comes back; there's no father of God, no cousin of God, no God. Just worship us. I make fun of the whole thing because, let's be honest here, we just plug instruments into amplifiers and make a lot of noise and hopefully entertain people. I live unbelievably better than anybody can imagine. You can be as ugly as I am and still get laid more than the best looking guy. 'Cause I'm in KISS. So if any one of us has the balls to moan, just pie us." *1998: On starting his own religion and on the success of his band.*

"We wanna go where no other band has gone. Toys and games? You bet your ass. KISS Cola. KISStianity." *On his band's plans for the future.*

"We are living testament that the intelligentsia and the critics mean absolutely less than fucking zero. I'm sick of musicians saying, 'I don't care what you wanna hear, I'm gonna play whatever I want 'cause I'm an *artist.*' You're an artist? Paint my house, bitch!"

"When I look in the mirror, I see a powerful and attractive man. Nobody else sees it, but I don't give a shit." *1999*

"We are like cockroaches; we will never go away." *1999*

RICHARD SIMMONS
(Fitness Guru)

"I believe there is a thin gene and a fat gene, some genes in between, and a 501 gene." *1996*

"I look good in white." *1996: One of the reasons he wants to study for a medical degree.*

CARLY SIMON
(Singer & Songwriter)

"I have a faucet dripping in my mind all the time with melodies." *1990*

"President Kennedy, as usual, I love you!" *1996: To President Bill Clinton, after singing for him at a campaign rally.*

PAUL SIMON
(Singer & Songwriter)

"Not everything in the play happened, but it is more or less true. I remember the story from when it happened, but I can't remember exactly what I remember." *1997: The* New Yorker *called his musical,* The Capeman, *about a Puerto Rican teenager who stabbed two white kids to death on Manhattan's West Side in 1959—two years into the original Broadway run of* West Side Story—*the "first instance of Broadway imitating life imitating Broadway imitating life."*

FRANK SINATRA
(Singer)

"It's amazing what a broad will do for a buck." *1995: Responding to Shirley MacLaine's stories about him in her book.*

"Another birthday." *1996: When asked on the eve of his eighty-first birthday what gift he'd like.*

PETER SINGH
(Impersonator)

"I don't smoke dope. I don't drink bourbon. All I want to do is shake my turban." *1990: Singh is a Pakistani-born Elvis imitator.*

JOHN SINGLETON
(Movie Director)

"Those who attributed the violent acts to my film probably voted for Ronald Reagan, who created the climate in which teenagers shoot each other for gold chains and sneakers." *1992: On objections to his film* Boyz N the Hood.

"If AIDS was a natural disease, it would have been around 1000 years ago. I think it was made in order to kill undesirables. That would include homosexuals, intravenous drug users and blacks." *1993*

GENE SISKEL
(Film Critic)

"Little girls who wear glasses in movies always tell the truth. Little boys who wear glasses in movies always lie." *1995*

ROB SITCH
(Film Director)

"All that money, all that hype, you never want to forget why we really got into the film industry . . . and that's to meet Cameron Diaz." *1998: The director of* The Castle, *which premiered at the Sundance Film Festival.*

CHRISTIAN SLATER
(Actor)

"It was more of a woman, actually, than an imaginary friend. It was kind of a love affair. There was one specific pillow, but different pillow cases. . . . I've graduated to a much bigger pillow. I've actually graduated to a human now. Works much better." *1992: On his first love—a pillow.*

"Rage seems to be much easier to drum up than laughter or happiness. I'm one of the lucky guys. I get patted on the back for being insane." *1993*

"I'm in a relationship with myself. And God. Me and God. That's it." *1999: On his dating status.*

GRACE SLICK
(Singer)

"If animal research is so great, why are people still getting sick?" *1993*

"Extrapolating information from animal to man is the silliest goddamn science I ever heard, except for some of the silly things they did in the Middle Ages." *1993*

"This is nothing but a bunch of doddering goddamned old people." *1996: On the Jefferson Airplane's induction into the Rock and Roll Hall of Fame.*

CURTIS SLIWA
(Guardian Angel & TV Talk-show Host)

"She looks like she got hit in the face with a bag full of nickles. She's so ugly she looks like Captain Bligh looking for Ahab." *1992: Speaking about Chelsea Clinton.*

BOB SMALE
(Musician)

"Poys, our sponsor is in da audience tonight so I vant you to pee on your toes." *1990: Smale toured fifteen years with Lawrence Welk and was recalling Welk's speech to the band.*

ANNA NICOLE SMITH
(Model)

"I coulda married him four years ago, if I'd just wanted to get rich. But I didn't." *1994: On her husband, eighty-nine-year-old Texas oil millionaire Howard Marshall II.*

"I take care of him in a sexual way—I do my wife duties." *1995: On her relationship with her husband.*

KEVIN SMITH
(Screenwriter & Director)

"I have a slim chance of getting a screenplay nomination. But I would die happy if I got one. It would cut down on the amount of sex I have to beg for." *1998: The* Chasing Amy *writer/director on his Oscar possibilities.*

PATTI SMITH
(Singer)

"When I was just starting out reading my poetry, I used to clear my throat and spit at the beginning of a reading, and some of the auditorium people got all agitated about that, so then I did it even more. . . . A local New Jersey newspaper nicknamed me The Keeper of the Phlegm. I still like to spit when I perform. Somehow it sets the mood right off." *1998*

WILL SMITH
(Actor & Singer)

"I don't know what my calling is, but I want to be here for a bigger reason. I strive to be like the greatest people who have ever lived. Like Jesus . . . I'm in the middle of this movie thing and loving it, but Malcolm X [and] Muhammad Ali achieved a higher level of personal greatness." *1998*

SNOOP DOGGY DOG
(Rapper)

"A role where I can play an attorney or something high fidelity instead of a gang member." *1995: On the kind of part he would like to play in the movies.*

SUZANNE SOMERS
(Actress & Fitness Expert)

"The woman who wrote the story thought of me the whole time she was writing the script. She had bought one of my Thighmasters, and whenever she would be trying to think, she put it between her knees and she would exercise." *1994: On her relationship with Renee Longstreet, who wrote the screenplay for a Sommers' TV movie.*

STEPHEN SONDHEIM
(Composer)

"Yeah! Show the tits! Nipples! Sell tickets!" *1994: Backstage at the Tony Awards watching a video clip of a bedroom scene from his Tony-award winner for best musical* Passion.

BARRY SONNENFELD
(TV Producer)

"I fear flying. . . . Every time I step out of an airplane, I consider it a failed suicide attempt." *1998*

TABITHA SOREN
(MTV reporter)

"[Who] is 'the loneliest monk?'" *1993: After interviewing Bill Clinton, who said he once dreamed of playing saxophone with jazz great Thelonius Monk.*

"His favorite Beatle was Paul and he likes Michael Bolton. I mean, how hip is he, really?" *1993: On Bill Clinton.*

"When I'm talking about the war in Bosnia, I won't be wearing a bustier." *1995: On dressing appropriately for a news broadcast.*

SISTER SOULJAH
(Rapper)

"I mean, if black people kill black people every day, why not have a week and kill white people?" *1992*

"I am white America's greatest nightmare. Why? Because I'm competent. I'm intelligent. I'm articulate. I'm compassionate. I'm selfless. And I'm attractive. Six things they don't want to see in one person." *1993*

"I didn't feel spiritually connected to whether or not Colin Powell ran for president. . . . I'm not just one of those people who is just looking for a black face in a high place." *1996*

PHIL SPECTOR
(Record Producer & Songwriter)

"The first thing to do is to make sure he is dead. I don't trust him. . . . Albert Goldman was truly an evil man. He knew the least yet was the most vain about his opinion. In Goldman's case, death was not an end, but rather a very effective way of cutting down on the pollution." *1994: On the death of Albert Goldman, who wrote unflattering biographies of Lenny Bruce, Elvis Presley, and John Lennon.*

"You don't tell Shakespeare what plays to write, or how to write them. You don't tell Mozart what operas to write or how to write them. And you certainly don't tell Phil Spector what songs to write or how to write them, or what records to produce or how to produce them." *1996*

"I wonder how Michael Jackson started out as a black man and ended up as a white girl." *1999*

"In my next life, I want to come back as either a proctologist, so I can deal with all the assholes I meet, or as a matador, so I can deal with all the bullshit." *1999*

TORI SPELLING
(Actress)

"Trust me. I walked in and it was like flies on shit—too many fans." *1993: On why she can't visit Disneyland anymore.*

TORI SPELLING (CONT'D)

"I used to cry reading the Internet." *1998*

"My butt fascinates me. . . . I mean I like it so much that when I dance, I'm always looking back at it." *1998*

"Sometimes when I'm alone, I put on 6-inch heels and wear nothing else and dance around in front of the mirror and do my little stripper dance." *1999*

HAYLEY SPICER
(Celebrity Look-alike)

"I feel like Barbie, everyone calls me Barbie, I love Barbie. The main difference is she's plastic and I'm real. There isn't any other difference." *1993*

STEVEN SPIELBERG
(Producer & Director)

"According to my mom, I'm such a big shot that she's threatening to have her uterus bronzed." *1994*

"There's no way for me to be closer to her except to live insider her. Which I've already done." *1997: On his mom.*

"Fortunately, my boat didn't have to sink." *1998: Discussing directing the water sequences of* Amistad *and why he didn't have to worry about any comparisons of his film with* Titanic.

"You gain yourself. You're reborn every time you make a movie." *1998: On what he likes best about the filmmaking process.*

"I stayed up at night fantasizing about how I could get myself off this picture short of dying. I was out of my mind for a while. So I went to [Sidney] Sheinberg and [Richard] Zanuck and [David] Brown and said, 'Let me out of this film.' Dick pulled me aside and called me a knucklehead, said, 'This is an opportunity of a lifetime. Don't fuck it up.' And Sid said, 'We don't make art films at Universal, we make films like *Jaws*. If you don't want *Jaws*, you should work somewhere else.'" *1998: Remembering how he wanted to pull out of making the movie* Jaws *after six months in troubled preproduction.*

"I never took LSD, mescaline, coke, or anything like that. But I went through the entire drug period. . . . I would sit in a room and watch TV while people climbed the walls." *1998: On his early years as a filmmaker in Hollywood in the 1970s.*

"I have never made a movie that I consider immoral. I've never made a film that I could say, 'You know, I wish I hadn't made that picture because it led people astray.' And I'm real proud of that." *1999*

"Take a deep breath and hold it till they call your name. If you win, let it out fast. If you lose, let it out slow. Just be sure to breathe." *1999: Advice to Oscar nominees.*

MICKEY SPILLANE
(Writer)

"One fan used to write me personal letters and I never knew who she was till she said something about her son, the President. And that was Mrs. Carter." *1990*

"Over the course of a book I probably throw away five pages. I write the ending first, so I know where I'm going, but I don't know how I'm going to get there. It's like sex. There's this long troubled part that builds up and builds up and bang!" *1990*

BENJAMIN SPOCK
(Physician & Best-selling Author)

"Right from the start, the book said, give your children firm, clear leadership, ask them for politeness and cooperation. Respect your children, but ask them for respect also." *Describing his best-selling* Book of Baby and Child Care, *which sold 50 million copies.*

"The good things you do in this world outlast you. When someone says to me, 'You helped me raise two fine children,' that's plenty for me. I can die in peace." *1998: Spock died in March 1998.*

JERRY SPRINGER
(TV Talk-show Host)

"I've been everything you can't respect—a lawyer, a mayor, a news anchor, and a talk-show host. If I sell used cars, I've done the whole cycle." *1995*

"I know it sounds hypocritical, but you have to protect the reality of your show. You can't let people make up stories on talk shows. You have to set some standards." *1996*

"We are mostly silly entertainment. Our show by definition is about outrageous people and outrageous relationships. Almost every one of these subjects is something I wouldn't endorse. But that's not the issue. The issue isn't about what I like: it's about what's outrageous. By this standard, half the sitcoms would be off the air. And certainly the news would have to be off the air." *1996: Defending the fine content of his TV show.*

"The show is stupid. I know that. But it's OK, one hour a day, to be that way." *1998*

"If you're over 100, we send you to Oprah." *1998: Joking about his guests' IQs.*

"To a certain extent, I'm saving the American taxpayers a lot of money, especially on the defense budget. My theory is when the rest of the world sees us, they no longer want to take us over." *1999*

DUSTY SPRINGFIELD
(Singer)
"I used so much hair spray that I feel personally responsible for global warming." *1995*

ANNIE SPRINKLE
(Porn Star & Performance Artist)
"If more people had sex toys, the world would probably be a much more peaceful place to live in." *1990*

"I don't think being obsessed with sex is any stranger than being obsessed with stamp collecting." *1991*

KELLY SQUIRES
(Writer)
"'Don't let your zipper do the talking!' Those were the inevitable words that my father would say to me each time I left on a date." *1997*

SYLVESTER STALLONE
(Actor)
"People think I've got the IQ of a hockey score. My vocabulary is larger than 90 percent of the writers I've met." *1990*

"That's very important [lying on your resume]; you must lie." *1991: In a speech to students at the University of Virginia.*

"I have a full-on street fight with that canvas. I go to war." *1991: On his painting technique.*

"Charlie Chaplin's and Valentino's stuff. I go back—I'm a traditionalist. I'm tired of me." *1991: On the memorabilia he enjoyed on the walls of his Planet Hollywood restaurant.*

"I find it incredible to come to France and to be understood and appreciated so fully, it just makes my heart so incredibly special." *1992: On being decorated by the French Culture Ministry for his contribution to the arts.*

"The Duchess of York is one hell of a lady. I knew she was a married woman, but I'd heard the marriage was in trouble. . . . We went out with two friends the next night and had such a good time, we made another date for the following evening. It was the beginning of something special between us." *1993*

"I do believe in reincarnation, but I wouldn't want to come back as a woman. Too complicated and I would hate to have to deal with men like myself. No, I'd like to come back as a crow." *1993*

"I got very jealous when I saw *Basic Instinct*. 'Damn, I could do this. Why aren't I doing this?'" *1994*

"I had a couple of scenes where the wind was so cold, my face was swollen shut. I couldn't articulate—and I don't articulate that well anyway." *1993: On filming* Cliffhanger.

"I despise heights. Maybe it's because of my second marriage. Brigitte [Neilsen] was built like a mountain. Even Edmund Hillary couldn't climb her." *1993*

"Politically correct? I don't know . . . but it felt great." *1994: On arriving at the grand opening of his restaurant in Hong Kong in a rickshaw drawn by four female models.*

SYLVESTER STALLONE (CONT'D)

"We were talking the other day, and she was all upset because some magazine gave out her age. Like them, I didn't realize that she gave birth to me 35 years before she was born." *1995: On his mother.*

TONIANN STALLONE

(Actor's Sister)

"People think that he is really a jerk. It's kind of sad in a way." *1990*

PAUL STANLEY

(Musician & Singer)

"I don't think there is 'adult rock.' Rock 'n' roll is music that originates in your crotch, not in your cranium. If you spend too much time thinking about it, you're not making it." *1992*

"Sting made the cover of *GQ*. Why can't I? I've got more clothes than Sting!" *1993*

"Women and huge crowds—it's the life. Anybody who tells you otherwise is either ungrateful or confused." *1993*

"I can't tell you how many people have come over to me, looking like the last person you'd expect, and said, 'I'm a corporate lawyer. I was totally influenced by you guys.'" *1993: On the influence of his band, KISS.*

"[Kurt Cobain's] last act was great. He blew his head off. The only thing is, he couldn't come back for an encore." *1996*

"Actually, it's Kaddish Is So Swell." *1996: On the meaning of the acronym KISS.*

MAURICE STARR

(Producer)

"I have to say that most white families have as much talent as the New Kids on the Block." *1990: Starr was the inventor, producer, and manger of the New Kids on the Block.*

RINGO STARR

(Drummer)

"Yes, I wrote the drums." *1997: On sharing the songwriting credit for* Really Love You *with Paul McCartney.*

"In the music business, you are allowed to drink, and you are up all night, and you are allowed to take drugs—it's part of it. But, you know, we must always remember that the highest suicide rate is among dentists." *1998*

"Right now I'm shlepping to Boise, Idaho. That's what happens to old legends." *1999: After a fellow dinner guest commented on the honor of meeting a member of the famed group.*

CHRISTINA STEAD

(Novelist)

"If all the rich men in the world divvied their money amongst themselves, there wouldn't be enough to go around." *1990*

DANIELLE STEEL

(Novelist)

"She was wearing a blue dress the same color as her eyes that her father brought back from San Francisco." *1990: Writing in her novel* Star.

DAWN STEEL

(Hollywood Producer)

"I do call people I like 'asshole.' It's a term of affection to me. I have also in my life called people 'fuckhead' or 'fuckface' but never 'motherfucker.' Do you understand the difference? For me there was a big difference." *1993*

BARRY STEIGER

(Comedian)

"Billy Graham has described heaven as a family reunion that never ends. What must hell possibly be like? Home videos of the same reunion?" *1997*

ROD STEIGER

(Actor)

"Thought is like a snowball. The longer you live, the more it melts." *1998*

"What you don't know will scare the shit out of you." *1998*

"In the fifties, I went to see this analyst. It was the vogue. I told him, 'Now, look, before we go into this—I have to be free to create; I have to be free to do things. I have to be free to get up when I want, sleep with anyone I want, do what I want to do. I can't be regimented; I have to be free!' And he said, 'That's fine. Just be careful you don't become a slave to freedom.'" *1998*

"Success means controlling your own time. If you can gain control over 60 percent of the time in your life, you are really successful. Time is the most important currency, but once you spend it, man, it is gone." *1998*

"Man is cursed with the ambition to be the best hunter in the tribe. When a guy came home to the village covered with blood, there was no argument when he asked for a gourd of water or a piece of ass." *1998*

"If I could find a way to have sex with myself that was as exciting as it is with a lady, I'd live in a white tower and never come out." *1998*

"Surprise is the lubrication of adventure." *1998*

GLORIA STEINEM
(Editor & Writer)
"There was one lunch where a woman who was 50-something was telling about an affair she was having with a guy 20-something and saying how much nicer young men were. And there was this little silence, and then someone said, 'Of course they're nicer. We were their mothers.'" *1994*

"Turning 50 was the end of an era, the era in which a woman is still a sexual, reproductive commodity. Turning 60 is more like a beginning. I'm free. . . . It used to take two years of wild passion before I became friends with a lover. Now it's immediate. A part of my brain is free." *1995*

"At my graduation, I thought we had to marry what we wished to become. Now you are becoming the men you once would have wanted to marry." *1995: In a commencement address at Smith College.*

DARCEY STEINKE
(Writer)
"Was it the bourbon or the dye fumes that made the pink walls quiver like vaginal lips?" *1994: From the book* Suicide Blonde.

HOWARD STERN
(Radio Talk-show Host)
"Was he carrying a TV?" *1992: On hearing that a black South African had won the New York City Marathon.*

"To have sex with her, he's the strongest heterosexual out there. I'm gay, compared to him." *1993: On Tom Arnold and Roseanne.*

"I set my goals low. I'm in an industry of idiots, and I'm king of the idiots." *1993*

"First of all, he has thick white makeup on, like Bozo. . . . It's so thick you feel like you could take a hunk of it off and stucco a wall. . . . And his nose is wrapped like a mummy's except at the tip. At the end of his nose the tape is unraveling, so it just sort of hangs. The oils from his hair are now dripping onto his face. I want to stand up and call 911— 'We've got a melting Michael Jackson . . . Over.'" *1995: On meeting Michael Jackson.*

"Our view of society is somehow that we're all public television viewers, when in fact we're all watching The Gong Show." *1996*

"Ninety-nine percent of my thoughts are sexual. I'm convinced I'm not different than any guy. It's our penises controlling our brain. . . . You're hearing it straight from a guy's head, exactly what he thinks about sex." *1997*

"Television has changed. Standards have gone to an all-time low, and I'm here to represent it. It's a miracle; I prayed to God for this." *1998: On his plans to launch a syndicated TV show, which committed to air opposite* Saturday Night Live *on twelve stations.*

JANE STERN
(Critic)
"People really love to see rich people drown in a big way." *1998: On the popularity of the film* Titanic.

JON STEWART
(Actor & Comedian)
"My first sexual experience was in the back seat of a car—only I was in the front seat, driving." *1995*

JON STEWART (CONT'D)

"To all those people who said my show wouldn't last, I have only one thing to say: Good call." *1995: On the final* Jon Stewart Show.

"Accused stalker Athena Rolando apparently hoisted herself through a window of Brad Pitt's home, where she was shocked to discover that hers wasn't the only bedroom covered with wall-to-wall pictures of Pitt." *1999*

"There is a fine line between flirting and stalking. I learned to tone [myself] down, so I flirt." *1999*

ROD STEWART
(Singer)

"Always remember that the greatest thing you can say to a girl—it's always been my killer line—is 'Hello, darling, what have you got in that basket?' You try it next time. 'Hello, darling, what have you got in that basket?' It just leaves a lot of things open. Basket? Here's the key. We always have to guess what's in the basket—if you get my drift. And the longer we have to wait to see what's in the basket, the better." *1991*

"I know I'm singing a lot better now than ever. I hate to say it, but I am knocked out listening to my own voice, which I never used to be." *1992*

"I've been tamed. I've put the last soldier in the barrack, my last banana in the fruit bowl." *1993*

"Plenty of lead still in the old pencil, you know." *1995*

"Anything Sam Cooke did I would do . . . apart from getting shot in a hotel room by a hooker." *1995*

"I wouldn't take her anywhere too fancy, in case she throws up. I wouldn't take her anywhere downtown, either. We'd go to the launderette and wash our delicates together. We'd compare underwear." *1995: When asked where he'd take Courtney Love on a date.*

BEN STILLER
(Actor)

"I've been practicing for it my whole life." *1998 On simulating masurbation for a film scene.*

STEPHEN STILLS
(Singer)

"Michael Bolton is one of the greatest singers to come along in 20 years." *1993*

ROGER STIM
(Singer)

"They may take away the freedom of speech, but they can never take away the freedom to shut up." *1991*

R. L. STINE
(Author)

"I had a very boring, normal childhood in a suburb of Columbus, Ohio. . . . I find that most people who work in horror had very boring, ordinary lives. Recently I met Wes Craven. . . . He is another quiet Ohio guy just like me." *1998*

STING
(Singer)

"We have to use birth control." *1991: The father of five giving advice to the human race.*

"I know I'm not trained for it, but I think I could bring something maybe to some Mahler songs." *1991*

"I've been doing yoga for a few years. It can make you have sex longer and better. I can only demonstrate it. I can't really verbalize it." *1993*

"I often stand in a stadium full of people and ask myself the same question: 'How the hell did I end up here?'" *1994*

"Every celebrity in my position gets a seedy book written about them. So there's one coming out about me saying that I've had sex and taken drugs. What a shock, you know?" *1996*

"Of course I've been in bed with several women at once. I'm a rock star, after all." *1996*

MICHAEL STIPE
(Singer)

"I would be pond scum. It's my spirit animal." *1999: On what kind of animal he'd be if given the choice.*

ERIC STOLTZ
(Actor)

"Films are made taking money into consideration above all. It's a business. Whereas, in theater it seems everyone knows you're not really going to make any money, so they actually try and make something memorable. . . . The plays that I've done in the past couple of years have been so rich that you could basically do them in a clown suit and the story would still resonate. I would say most films are unwatchable and most theater is unseen." *1998*

"One of the silly things about interviewing actors is that you give them these large questions. We don't know much about anything except how to say lines." *1998*

OLIVER STONE
(Writer, Director & Producer)

"What is history? Some people say it's a bunch of gossip made up by soldiers who passed it around a campfire. They say such and such happened. They create, they make it bigger, they make it better. I know guys in combat who made up shit. I'm sure the cowboys did the same. The nature of human beings is that they exaggerate. So what is history? Who the fuck knows?" *1991*

"I don't even know if I was born or who my parents were." *1992*

"I won't flatly deny that. If I admit to that (having a homosexual experience) then they'll (the government) really be on my ass! They're trying to nail me—well, I guess I've already done everything wrong in my life in their opinion." *1992*

"Did you get my erection on tape?" *1992: To a reporter for* US *magazine.*

"In America, in the late fifties and early sixties, we didn't see women. We didn't hang out with them. The dances were terrible. They would bring in the girls, in the back of the bus you would have a kiss, and that was all. Everything was illegal. You couldn't do anything. And we all had these sexual urges, and we couldn't alleviate them. It was a horrible time. I couldn't stand the sixties." *1992*

"New York was sadder in the fifties. We used to get chased by gangs. We tried to walk across the park and they'd always give us a hard time: Irish gangs, Puerto Rican gangs, and the Italians kids and the black kids. We were always getting into trouble." *1992*

"Anybody who's been through a divorce will tell you that at one point . . . they've thought murder. The line between thinking murder and doing murder isn't that major." *1994: Commenting on the O. J. Simpson case. Author John Irving responded, "Stone's remark is positively biblical in its stupidity."*

"I could take off tomorrow. I don't have to make a movie. I don't even have to pay fucking alimony. Fuck Clinton—I'm a deadbeat dad. She's got enough money to live out the rest of her fucking life; she doesn't do a thing. I'll just change my name. They'd never find me." *1994: On making movies, his divorce, his ex-wife, and responsibility.*

"In my life, I guess I've tried to be honest to some degree. I mean, my wife would say I wasn't. I did lie and cheat on her, so that is true." *1994*

"There was blood, there was screaming, there was forceps and there was me. And the lighting wasn't too hot either." *1995: On how his penchant for violence goes back to his "rugged" birth.*

"Actually, Nixon has always reminded me of my father. My father was a big Nixon supporter and so was I. I went to Trinity in New York and I had fights because I was a Nixon supporter." *1995*

"I want to be a quarterback. You know what a quarterback does—he just has to win. You have to get the team in the end zone. I think a lot of people don't understand directing. At the end of the day it's not just about the moves—you've gotta win, you've gotta get the ball in the end zone and beat the other team." *1996*

"Every time you open a movie, it's like running for office. . . . There is a thing that exists between fact and entertainment that's called 'drama'. . . . It's existed since the Greeks wrote about their kings and queens. I mean, look at Shakespeare. Did people sit around and say that he condensed three years into three days in *Julius Ceasar*? He didn't have to write an annotated script." *1996*

OLIVER STONE (CONT'D)

"I saw [Richard Nixon] once in Dallas when we were shooting *JFK*. We were shooting on a trailer—car shots—and he drove by in a limo waving to everybody on the crew like he was running for office. And nobody waved back at him. It was a strange moment. He criticized *JFK*, by the way, on *Larry King Live*." *1996*

"He was a Russian czar. I think that's a great copy line and I believe it." *1996: On Richard Nixon.*

"How can people in their right minds accuse film of corrupting people when children have as an example . . . the United States government selling weapons indiscriminately?" *1996*

"He has had sex with a chicken and with some of the world's most beautiful women." *1996: On why he finds Larry Flynt so compelling.*

"I give them away to one-night stands." *1998: On his awards.*

"The awkwardness of conspiracy theories still prevails in American politics, as I think we see in the murder of President Kennedy and the media's inability to sustain an ambiguous and unclosed investigation. It is reasonably clear from historical study that politics is power and people do kill one another if they want to acquire that power or, equally important, stop it. Kennedy, in 1963, like Alexander [the Great] long before him, was increasingly calling for radical change on several fronts— the USSR, Cuba, Vietnam. Looming ahead with his certain victory in 1964 was the specter of a Kennedy dynasty well into the 1970s. If nothing else, a motive for murder is evident." *1998*

"In our country, we find the fascinating coup d'etat planned against President Franklin Roosevelt in 1934 to have almost disappeared from the history books. You don't have to wonder why when you understand the power of the conspirators—J. P. Morgan Jr., Bernard Baruch, and Thomas Lamont, with the limited participation of General Douglas MacArthur—or the amazing ability of the media, which were then as now basically controlled by the powerful of this country, to vaporize the incident into the black hole of ridicule. Henry Luce's magazines trivialized the various testimonies at the time, and the incident was buried largely because Roosevelt himself was weathering a major storm and feared a revolution if these events were revealed. Thank God for the memory of the few men still around who do not so easily forget a coup d'etat, and thank God for the little-read Dickstein-McCormack congressional hearings into the affair." *1998*

SHARON STONE
(Actress)

"If I was just intelligent, I'd be OK. But I am fiercely intelligent." *1992*

"Listen, I have a four-minute sex scene with Michael Douglas in which I have three orgasms. What does that tell you?" *1992: On her role in* Basic Instinct.

"If you have a vagina and a point of view, that's a deadly combination." *1992*

"I'm very old fashioned. Occasionally I *do* wear underwear." *1992*

"One thing I find since becoming famous is that I get to torture a higher class of men than I used to." *1993*

"If I could get into it, it would be great. But you know, it don't mean a thing if it ain't got that schwing." *1993: On dating other women.*

"I've fallen in love with my horse." *1995*

"I find gambling boring. Here is a game you can play all night, and chances are you're gonna lose. No thanks. It sounds a little like Hollywood when you start out. I've been there, done that." *1995*

"Not in this lifetime." *1995: Recalling that Madonna wanted to give her a big French kiss during a Miami Heat game in 1994.*

"Someone once told me I have a mind like a bad neighborhood—I shouldn't go in there alone." *1995*

"I think that people who have fur coats from before, I don't know, what do you think? Is it wrong? If you have them and these animals have died already, shouldn't you wear them in honor of the animal that died?" *1996*

"My first exercise in charity was the patience I had with casting directors who spoke on the phone while I gave my audition." *1996*

"I have a couple of ex-boyfriends that I could actually see killing. That's probably why I'm so obsessed with abolishing the death penalty. I want to get clear options in advance." *1997*

"There was this shop selling brains. And a guy went in to buy one. They told him the male brains were $100,000, the female brains were $25,000. So the guy wondered at the price discrepancy. The salesperson said, 'Well, you see, the female brains have been used." *1998: At a roast for feminist author Betty Friedan. After hearing the joke, Friedan was said to have asked, "Who is Sharon Stone?" A friend said that "Ms. Stone is the Marilyn Monroe of our time." "Oh," said Friedan and went back to eating.*

"Generally, you have another actor to work with. I had a 6-year-old who, like, had to pee." *1999: On her* Gloria *costar Jean-Luke Figueroa.*

"She's very young and lives in rarefied air that's a little thin. It's like she's not getting quite enough oxygen . . . I would like to think that she will eventually spend her fame valuably." *1999: On Gwyneth Paltrow who did a parody of Stone on* Saturday Night Live.

BARBRA STREISAND
(Singer & Actress)

"He was getting turned on. I was embarrassed. . . . Every time I got a little hot, I yelled, 'Cut!' Where is it going to go? Is he going to take off all my clothes and we're going to screw on the floor? I'll never use it. So why go to those places?" *On directing romantic scenes with Nick Nolte during filming of* The Prince of Tides.

"How do you Republicans feel now that you've lost everything and are all losers?" *1993: To Senator Arlen Spector while the two shared a ride on an elevator. Spector replied, "Well, perhaps you haven't heard, but I won."*

"I owe my career to my mother. Because if she'd believed in me, I'd probably have been a typist." *1995*

"One thing's for sure: now when I look at *Funny Girl*, I think I was gorgeous. I was too beautiful to play Fanny Brice." *1996*

DONALD SUTHERLAND
(Actor)

"The casting agent for the first film I ever went up for said to me, 'The character as we see it is the guy next door. And to be absolutely truthful, you don't look like you've ever lived next door to anybody.' " *1993*

PATRICK SWAYZE
(Actor)

"Good-looking people turn me off. Myself included." *1992*

"There aren't many big words I don't know, know what I mean?" *1992*

"Cody dying was like my son dying. I never had a communication like that. . . . Not long ago, I was sitting by myself at Cody's grave. I found myself making all sorts of decisions, like, 'I will never allow myself to love like this again.' " *Describing the death of his dog, Cody.*

T

GAY TALESE
(Author)

"The Irish have been in the forefront of sexual repression for centuries. They drove James Joyce out of Ireland, and every other creative soul who might be dealing with erotica. . . . Irishmen always want to be policemen, and the Irish media want the President to climb up the hill on bloody knees like the Stations of the Cross. Italy is a very male country which has always been anticlerical. Men run Italy. They don't abide the church and aren't shocked by adultery. Ireland is a very female country run by suffering nuns." *1998: On the reason why Irish-American journalists are much harder on Bill Clinton than Italian-American politicians have been.*

QUENTIN TARANTINO
(Writer, Director & Actor)

"People ask me if I went to film school. And I tell them, 'No, I went to films.'" *1994*

"I have a lot of little theories, and one of them is that nobody really likes sports, so they act as if they do. I also feel that way about the Who. I don't think anybody really likes that band. Everyone thinks they're supposed to like the Who, so they just pretend." *1994*

"If you're making a movie and your big idea is that war is bad, why do you even need to make a movie? If that's all you're trying to say, just say it. It's only two words: WAR IS BAD." *1994*

"When I'm making a movie, everything else is secondary. Now movies are secondary—third-ary. Now it's be with my friends, do my taxes, learn another language, rearrange my apartment." *1994*

"To tell you the truth, I thought *Showgirls* was fucking great. I'm thinking about writing an article in *Film Comment* in complete and utter defense of *Showgirls*." *1996*

"*Mandingo* . . . is one of my favorite movies. *Showgirls* is the *Mandingo* of the '90s." *1996*

"I became an adjective sooner than I thought I was going to." *1998*

ELIZABETH TAYLOR
(Actress)

"They think because he's got a rich wife, why work? It's like asking, 'Why maintain your balls?'" *1992: On her husband, Larry Fortensky.*

"The first time I died it was overwhelming." *1992*

"One problem with people who have no vices is that they're pretty sure to have some annoying virtues." *1995*

"I'm on a diet right now, trying to lose weight, which I hate. But when you've been bedridden almost two years, it's impossible not to put weight on. When you're in pain, you crave sweets because sugar is an anti-depressant. It makes you feel better. And comfort food definitely comforts.

Sometimes I would be in so much pain that instead of sucking my thumb, I'd order some chicken and suck on some wings." *1996*

"Lucky bitch." *1997: On a veterinarian's suggestion that her pet Maltese, Sugar, lose a pound and a half.*

JUDY TENUTA
(Comedienne)

"This guy tells me, 'Judy, I practice safe sex.' Yeah, your idea of safe sex is when the cow doesn't kick you in the head." *1994*

JOHN TESH
(Musician)

"I would rather be hated and vilified than ignored." *1997*

RICHARD THOMAS
(Actor)

"I am a very controlling person, very crotchety. I even have moments of not being nice. Ultimately, to be able to just be a person—to have a marriage that came apart and a divorce and all the stuff that everybody else goes through—was just terrific in some ways." *1995: On how divorce was good for him.*

EMMA THOMPSON
(Actress)

"As far as I can see, from Sharon Stone's love scene in *Basic Instinct*, they molded her body out of tough Plasticine. She was shagging Michael Douglas like a donkey, and not an inch moved. If that had been me, there would have been things flying around hitting me in the eye." *1994*

"Talking to them? Darling, I would have slept with all of them that night, I was so thrilled." *1994: On accepting a compliment on how terrific she was with the American press in 1993 at the Academy Awards ceremonies where she won an Oscar.*

"I have always been beguiled by people who can use words, which is very confusing, because people who can use words don't necessarily know how to live life. In fact, people who use words best use words to keep life at bay. It's a great temptation." *1995*

"Kenneth is so tired even his sperms are on crutches." *1995: Answering a question about having children with her husband of six years, Kenneth Branagh. A short time after this statement was made, the couple announced their separation.*

"I really like human beings who have suffered. They're kinder. I mean, if you've suffered and done some work on it. Adolf Hitler suffered, and look what happened to him. All those years of being a tramp in Austria didn't really help out on the old compassion front." *1996*

HUNTER THOMPSON
(Writer)

"Crack is ruining the drug culture." *1990*

"Get that lesbian bitch out of here!" *1990: Shouted after freelance journalist Gail Palmer-Slater refused to get into his hot tub during an interview.*

"Get out of here or I'll blow your head off." *1990: Thompson's "corrected" statement of what he said to Gail Palmer-Slater.*

"Cover a war in a place where you can't drink beer or talk to a woman? Hell no!" *1990: On why he refused to cover the Gulf War.*

STELLA MARIE THOMPSON
(aka Divine Brown, Prostitute)

"Who the hell is Hugh Grant?" *1995: On being informed at the Los Angeles police station of the identity of her illustrious client.*

"It was the best five minutes' work ever." *1995: On her encounter with Hugh Grant.*

BILLY BOB THORNTON
(Actor & Director)

"I went bowling one night and ended up married. It was one of those deals." *1997: On his short-lived marriage at the age of twenty.*

LIZ TILBERIS
(Editor)

"We were all struck by how amazing it was to have seen the entire royal family file past us, with all the teenagers that we remembered as babies, and we all remarked on how good Princess Anne's legs were. But mostly we remembered Diana." *1998: The editor of* Harper's Bazaar, *describing a lunch she had with friends in London after attending the funeral of Princess Diana.*

MEG TILLY
(Actress)

"I have nothing intelligent to say." *1997: To reporters while on her way to the Oscar ceremonies.*

RICHARD TING
(TV Producer)

"When I was growing up, we always thought that the biggest movie star in China was [Cambodia's King] Sihanouk." *1998: The producer of* New York Adventures, *a romantic comedy series about immigrant Chinese shown in China but filmed in the United States, on the dull fare that characterized Chinese television programs until recently.*

TIFFANY TOWER
(Porn Star)

"I'm sick of them saying, 'Write something dirty.' But I have to be friendly. I just want to make a lot of money, then retire and get married and have a lot of kids and animals." *1994: On men who ask her to sign autographs.*

PETE TOWNSHEND
(Musician)

"I know how it feels to be a woman because I am a woman." *1990*

"It was the first time I realized I wanted to fuck a man." *1999: On seeing Mick Jagger perform for the first time.*

JOHN TRAVOLTA
(Actor)

"I always think nominations are the compliment. When it goes to the award, it becomes subjective—though I hope people will 'subject' my way." *1995: On his Academy Award nomination for best actor.*

ALEX TREBEK
(TV Host)

"Have you had any wild and wooly adventures as a gynecologist?" *1990: To a contestant on the game show he hosts,* Jeopardy.

"All right now, the clue is 'I Wanna Hold Your __,' Peter." *1992: On the game show* Jeopardy *when the contestants were Peter, Kevin, and Colleen.*

ALEX TREBEK (CONT'D)

"When I'm off the air I wear nothing. I like it, even though it frightens little children and dogs." *1998: When a member of the audience at a taping of* Jeopardy *in Berkeley, CA, asked him "Do you wear Perry Ellis when you're off the air?"*

"We like to pick a place synonymous with intellectual achievement. It's a cute little community. Kind of tight, kind of crowded—NO parking." *1998: On why one of the* Jeopardy *shows was taped in Berkeley, CA, home of the University of California. Supporters of the Stanford contestant on the show—Stanford and Berkeley are renowned rivals—rolled their eyes at Trebek's allusion to "intellectual achievement" in Berkeley.*

TREVANIAN
(Author)

"I suppose I just prefer dignity to wealth." *1998: The one-name author who wrote* The Eiger Sanction, Shibumi *and* Incident at Twenty Mile *on why he has never made a single promotional appearance. His books have sold five million copies.*

"I've had a few stalkers. But I deal with them in my own way. Let's just say they never stalk me twice." *1998: On his passion for privacy, when asked if any of his devoted fans have ever tried to find him.*

CALVIN TRILLIN
(Writer)

"Math was always my bad subject. I couldn't convince my teachers that many of my answers were meant ironically." *1995*

"Why is it that Henry Kissinger who was secretary of state and who holds a Ph.D. is called 'Dr. Kissinger' and George Schultz who was secretary of state and who holds a Ph.D. is called 'Mr. Schultz'? I concluded that Kissinger must have a podiatry practice on the side." *1999*

TRAVIS TRITT
(Singer)

"I watch *Cops* regularly, just to see if any of my relatives or band members are on it." *1994*

G. G. TRUDEAU
(Cartoonist)

"There is no denying that satire is an ungentlemanly art. It is rude. It is uncivil. It is lacking in balance and proportion. It has none of the normal rules of engagement. Satire picks a one-sided fight and the more its intended target reacts, the more its practitioner gains advantage. Unfair? You bet." *1991: The creator of* Doonesbury *on his craft.*

"[Florida Governor Jeb Bush] said he had only two words for me. 'Walk softly.' Now telling a cartoonist to walk softly is like asking a professional wrestler to show a little class. This is not a productive suggestion." *1999*

DONALD TRUMP
(Celebrity Businessman & Author)

"I like Ivana, but we've grown apart. Her level of arrogance has grown steadily worse in recent years. The bottom line is, I don't want to create another Leona Helmsley." *1990*

"My life is shit!" *1990*

"I wanted to see whether or not the great Louis XIV style, which I consider the most beautiful style, could work in a modern building. I didn't want to buy old columns, because they're cracked and broken. I wanted to have brand-new minted marble columns. . . . I've used all onyx. Onyx is a precious stone, many times more expensive than marble. And everyone agrees it is more beautiful. I don't believe there is an apartment like this anywhere in the world. The view, the solid bronze window frames, the fountain all brand-new and carved. Did you see the way the window shades go up and down, all remote? And they're bulletproof. . . . I don't care about material needs. I could be happy in a studio apartment with a television and a telephone." *1995: Showing off his digs in Trump Tower.*

"A place like Chicago should not have gambling. It would destroy the fabric of the city. The stores would die. The car dealerships would die. The landlords wouldn't get their rent because people will spend their money on the slot machines."

1996: On why he is starting a casino on a boat in Gary, IN, rather than Chicago.

"I'll always have myself!" *1997: Following his second divorce.*

"They know that I'm always here for them with advice and counsel should they need it." *1997: Offering his services to his estranged wife, Marla, and ex-spouse Ivana.*

IVANA TRUMP
(Celebrity Wife)

"I always stand by my man. This is why feminists aren't married and have no children. . . . A man is not going to put up with that nonsense. I'm a normal woman." *1990*

"I read a lot; about two books a month, and all the newspapers and magazines I can find—and that's a lot." *1995*

"I think women look up to me and, in a sense say, 'If Ivana can do it, so can I.' " *1993*

"The only time you don't need a prenuptial is if he has no children . . . and he's got a bad cough and a walker." *1995: On the art of divorce.*

"To my surprise, I find I have a great imagination. I don't say I am the Shakespeare, but it's not just about the beautiful people and the gorgeous yachts and the fabulous homes and lots of sex. I tried to put in more the feelings." *1997: On the novel about a Czech ingenue named Katrina, which Trump paid ghostwriter Camille Marchetta $350,000 to write for her.*

"Roffredo is the real thing; he has a real title and is the only importer of Ferraris in New York. Roffredo has a G-O-B. A real G-O-B." *Meticulously spelling out the remarkable fact that her latest boyfriend, Roffredo Gaitani d'Argona, has a job, a real job.*

IVANKA TRUMP
(Celebrity Daughter & Model)

"Dad, you've contributed so much to Atlantic City and Florida." *1996: At the fiftieth birthday party for her father, Donald.*

"Of course I'm in love with Leo, but I'm an adolescent, so it should be expected." *1998: On Leonardo DeCaprio.*

TANYA TUCKER
(Singer)

"I definitely want to be a better human and a better Christian and still kick their asses when I walk out on stage." *1994: On her spirituality and reputation as a hard worker and party girl.*

"To be honest, I haven't read it yet. I'm not really ready to read it. I'm not really a reader." *1997: When asked about her autobiography,* Nickel Dreams.

IKE TURNER
(Musician)

"The only time I ever punched Tina with my fist was the last fight we had." *1993: On life with his former wife, Tina Turner.*

TED TURNER
(Media Mogul)

"It's easy. You just kick a little foreign butt and, whammo, people are hooked." *1990: On his planned races against a Soviet sailboat to attract support for a round-the-world regatta.*

"People who know us say that we are two people who will enjoy each other—for as long as it lasts." *1990: On his relationship with Jane Fonda.*

"I don't let unauthorized autobiographies bother me." *1991*

"When you're living single and you want to throw your dirty clothes in the middle of the floor of your apartment, there's nobody there to say no, right? But when you take a roommate or a wife, then you've got to keep the stuff clean." *1992: On singleness and married life.*

"I have five children. If I were doing it again today, I would have no more than two. But, I mean, you can't shoot them, you know, that's the thing." *1992*

"We've got eight of them. Or seven. It's hard to keep track." *1994: On how many cable channels he owns.*

TED TURNER (CONT'D)

"The one piece of advice I can give you is to put on sunscreen and wear a hat." *1994: In a keynote address at commencement at Georgia State University.*

"I believe in a reasonable amount of 'right to bear arms.' But private citizens of the United States are not allowed to own nuclear weapons. I always wanted a nuclear weapon, if I could have gotten one. I'm every other kind of power, but I'm not a nuclear power." *1995*

"We have our entertainment networks everywhere but Africa. And we're talking about going into Africa with *Tom and Jerry* because Africans like cartoons, too. Trouble is, most of them don't have television sets or electricity." *1995*

"I feel like the Jewish people in Germany in 1942. I know exactly what it is to be rounded up and sent to the East somewhere." *1995: Complaining that the minority status of his network has prevented him from acquiring a major broadcast network.*

"I'd feel powerful if my kids got straight A's and my wife never got mad at me and I never got a case of diarrhea. As it is, power is a bunch of hooey." *1995*

"You're toast." *1996: Telling his son Teddy that he was being laid off from his managerial job at Turner Broadcasting.*

"When we were going out . . . I told her I didn't think [women] were equal, I thought they were different. Finally, we settled on their being 'roughly equivalent.'" *1996: On debating with wife Jane Fonda.*

"The United States has got some of the dumbest people in the world. I want you to know that. We know that." *1996*

"My son is now an 'entrepreneur.' That's what you're called when you don't have a job." *1997*

"There are too many nuts running around anyway, right? It's a good way to get rid of a few nuts, you know, you gotta look at it that way." *1997: On the mass suicide of members of the Heaven's Gate cult.*

"Having great wealth is one of the most disappointing things. It's overrated, I can tell you that. It's not as good as average sex. Average sex is better than being a billionaire." *1997*

"Are you really a Jew? You're the biggest goddamned Jew I've ever seen." *1998: On meeting the six-foot-seven CNN President Rick Kaplan.*

"People who think like us may be in the minority, but we're the smart ones." *1999: The father of five, promoting a one-child policy of population control.*

"If you're only going to have 10 rules, I don't know if adultery should be one of them." *1999: Suggesting that the ten commandments are "a little out of date."*

TINA TURNER
(Singer)

"Was he a good lover? What can you do except go up and down, or sideways, or whatever it is that you do?" *1993: On former husband Ike Turner.*

CYRINDA TYLER
(Former Wife of Singer Steven Tyler)

"He's embarrassed because he's no Tommy Lee—you know what I'm saying? The only big thing he has in the world is his career." *1999: On her intention to publish nude photos of the rock star.*

LIV TYLER
(Actress & Celebrity Daughter)

"I just want to sleep late, listen to music and go to the mall. And I still have slumber parties with my father [Aerosmith's Steven Tyler] where we do beauty treatments. It's really cool because he has all the good creams and stuff." *1997*

"We both wear the same size, and we'll just try on clothes for hours." *1998: On quality time with her dad.*

STEVEN TYLER
(Singer)

"I'd just like to give the tip to MTV for giving the finger to all of the right-wing liberals trying to unplug us." *1993*

"You have no idea how expensive it is to look this cheap." *1994*

"Good blues is like fucking. So much music today is more like masturbation. You need a little foreplay." *1994*

"My get-up-and-go has not gone up and went." *1994: On aging and performing.*

"I live for *canning* other people's *can'ts*." *1994*

"For a long time we were musicians messing around with drugs. These days, they're drug addicts who mess around with music." *1996*

"Stuffing coke up your nose 'till it bleeds is an acquired taste." *1997*

"The problem with journalists [is] they think that their opinions matter. That's the problem with most rock stars and musicians; they think that their opinions *really* matter. They don't. They're there for you to enjoy or throw out. That's why ears have holes in 'em; music can go in and out." *1998*

"*Patch Adams, Bambi*—I'm such an easy cry. I'm 70 percent woman." *1999*

U

RUDY UGLAND
(Horse Trainer)

"It takes drama away to know that the horse is acting." *1996: On "the greatest falling horse ever in pictures," Twister, who has taken falls in nearly fifty movies—but has never been nominated for a Patsy award—the animal equivalent of the Oscars.*

LARS ULRICH
(Musician)

"Wear what's in your closet. Probably the Symphony will be in black tie, and we'll be in black leather." *On his group's gig with the San Francisco Symphony.*

JOHN UPDIKE
(Writer)

"I don't like videos. There's something squalid about a video store. The people look furtive, like drug addicts, as they take them out in stacks of four or five. It's like people who drink alone. It's one thing to drink at a party, another thing to drink alone. One thing to go to an assembly hall and watch big

illusions, another thing to take them home in a little can." *1996*

"I wouldn't have read it otherwise." *1998: On reading Tom Wolfe's* A Man in Full *for a* New Yorker *review in which he panned the book.*

V

JACK VALENTI
(Entertainment Executive)

"Homicide rates and crime generally have been going down for the last three or four years, especially in big cities. Should television get the credit for that, too?" *1998: One of the architects of the TV content ratings system, after former talk-show host Steve Allen took out full-page newspaper ads blaming the "sex, filth, violence and sleaze" for such problems as violent crime and teenage pregnancy.*

DEAN VALENTINE
(UPN Network Head)

"I think Jamie hasn't met a nasty remark or a half-truth that he didn't like." *1999: On his Warner Bros. counterpart, Jamie Kellner.*

JEAN-CLAUDE VAN DAMME
(Actor)

"I've got a talent to act. No matter what any newspaper says about me, I am one of the most sensitive human beings on earth, and I know it." *1992*

"I'm very proud of my butt. What you can do is . . . contract the butt hard for 15 seconds, then release. I mean hard! Do this 20 times a day and you won't be able to walk. But you'll look like Van Damme. *1992*

"At night, when a woman drinks coffee, and she's got coffee breath, and she talks to you . . . , that's very exciting." *1994*

"Feel my butt. If you were healthier, you could have a butt like mine." *1995: Giving advice to Lori Petty, star of* Tank Girl. *Van Damme was trying to get Petty to stop drinking alcholic beverages and to take vitamins instead.*

"I don't want to talk for eight hours to get a simple fuck, like people are doing. A lot of guys talk to a

JEAN-CLAUDE VAN DAMME (CONT'D)

woman to get laid. I do it to get married." *1995: Van Damme was married four times.*

"A guy like me, a guy like Mel Gibson, a guy like Tom Cruise, a guy like Stallone, they can walk on the street and twenty girls, thirty, forty, they want those guys. They just have to . . ." *1995*

"If I have a date, if I spend time with a woman, I want to get married." *1995*

"Are you telling me, is it possible for a movie star to be faithful? Or a man to be faithful? Man loves to chase, my friend, until the day he really finds love. And love is very rare. If you want to talk about women and marriage, we have to talk seven or eight days." *1995*

"I was good. I was on time." *1995: Discussing his pre-Hollywood occupation as a pizza delivery man.*

"I wish she would come back alive for just one day—me and her, on the beach, nobody else . . . I would give all the money I have to have that dog back." *1996: Remembering his third wife's dog, Buffy.*

"L.A. is a city of dreams and everyone wants to have the biggest dick, so they make movies." *1996*

MAMIE VAN DOREN
(Actress)

"He drools a lot. He has such active glands." *1990: On Warren Beatty.*

DICK VAN DYKE
(Actor)

"Today, if you're not an alcoholic, you're nobody." *1990*

EDDIE VAN HALEN
(Musician)

"To me, making music is a very from-the-heart-and-soul kind of deal, and I have no idea what I'm going to be playing tonight. . . . I have no idea what the hell I'm doing; it's like there's somebody up there pulling the strings for me. It's not calculated, is what I'm saying. I don't know what the hell I'm doing." *1991*

"I don't do anything consciously, really. Dweezil Zappa interviewed me for some Japanese magazine the other day, and he asked me, 'So what were you thinkin'?' I don't think, man, I really don't." *1995: On the inspiration for his tenth album,* Balance.

"Believe it or not, when I stopped drinking—October 2, 1994—that same week, I started limping." *1997*

"The only thing I have to say is they're both full of shit, and I said it then. There's nothing new to add." *1998: On two previous lead singers with his band, David Lee Roth and Sammy Hagar.*

"I know the guy too well. Why should I read a book that's probably half fiction. What do you think—he's going to have something *nice* to say about me? And I don't give a fuck, because he knows and I know and the man upstairs knows what went down." *1998: When asked if he'd read David Lee Roth's autobiography,* Crazy from the Heat.

"Sometimes you've got to taste shit before you know how good a steak is. Aw, but even all the shit was pretty good." *1998: On the troubles he's experienced with his group Van Halen over the years.*

ERIC VAN HOFFMAN
(Writer)

"Gerald leaked sex appeal like a rutting moose. And like Rasputin, Gerald didn't need to look for women—they flocked to him like buzzards to a dead carcass." *1990: In his novel* Venom and Blood.

VANILLA ICE
(aka Robby Van Winkle, Rapper)

"I don't know all the certain words to word it." *1991: On the difficulties of writing his autobiography.*

"People need to know I'm not in this for the money. I'm in this for more, like, the girls." *1991*
"If I had a choice to either make money or be respected, I'd definitely go for the money." *1991*

"I've been checking out churches—Catholic, Baptist. I haven't decided on any religion yet. But definitely, God is in my life." *1995*

"What am I here for? What is my purpose in life? This is horrible. I'm the butt end of every joke!" *1998*

GUS VAN SANT
(Movie Director)

"I read the first act and thought, 'OK, this is great, but there probably won't be a second act.' Then I read the second act and thought, 'OK, but there won't be a third act.' And by the end, the script knocked me out." *1998: On why he eventually decided to direct the script he'd read*—Good Will Hunting.

STEVE VAN ZANDT
(Musician & Actor)

"To be white and sound that black you had to be Italian." *1997: Saluting the blue-eyed-soul pioneers the Rascals.*

VINCE VAUGHN
(Actor)

"For me, the guy who's the coolest is the biggest nerd because he's not interested in being cool, and to me, that's cool. It's the cool guy who's trying oh-so-hard to be cool, with the moves and everything . . . Guys like that, I just think 'Man, just lay it down and take a nap.'" *1998*

GORE VIDAL
(Writer)

"Every Presidential candidate, even Reagan, claimed to have read [my book] *Lincoln*. He probably colored it—we had a version for them to color." *1995*

"Truman [Capote] could not tell the truth about anything. He was a psychopath, and the lies would get crazier and crazier, and I'd watch his face as he told them, and there was a kind of rictus going on, as though he was out of control, orgasmic." *1995*

"I don't want people in ghettos. I'm a universalist. I think people should intermingle. Once you get the idea that there's such a thing as gay sensibility, then you've got to say that there's such a thing as straight sensibility. It's just hopeless. But if other people are going to proscribe people belonging to a nonexistent category, one must fight back with every weapon." *1995*

"What on earth is that [gay fiction]? Does that mean the book only hangs out with other books?" *1995*

"She confessed that rage made her orgasmic. I forgot to ask her if sex ever did." *1995: On his mother.*

"When I was a child, I wished my mother would die, but then, most people who knew her well felt that way about her. She was actively malevolent." *1995*

"I'd never work for you. You distorted Kennedy, you distorted Nixon, and you lack the one quality a director needs most—talent!" *1996: Responding to Oliver Stone's request that Vidal work with him on a motion picture.*

"One reason we get so much sex in politics is that we're forbidden by our corporate ownership to discuss anything of a political nature. In this representative government that we pretend we have, the only thing we can talk about is taxation." *1998*

"We can't really discuss, say, the power of the insurance companies, who have kept us from a national health system that's found in every other decent country. Unfortunately, the Clintons tried to change this part way, without attacking the real enemy. So that gave the insurance companies—who are really the piggy banks of corporate America—time to smear the Clintons." *1998: On Hillary Clinton's claims of a right-wing conspiracy against her husband.*

"The meekness of the American people startles me. There are almost no labor unions and everyone is terrified of striking. Perhaps they've been so beaten down by mandatory urine tests and such things—the intrusion of government that drives all these Montana-men mad.

"The average person is concerned with keeping what he earns and doesn't have anything but skepticism for politicians—because he knows that the government is wholly owned. And it's owned by a class of people we rarely see, except when there is someone really stupid, like Nelson Rockefeller. He didn't seem to realize that you don't run for president when you can buy it." *1998*

"Along with being a radical reformer by nature, I see all kinds of possibilities out there. Luckily, I

GORE VIDAL (CONT'D)

have a satirist's eyes. I get a great deal of joy out of all the absurdity that my native land provides." *1998*

"Let's just say each of us is eager to have plausible deniability for the other." *1998: On his relative, Vice President Al Gore.*

"I would much rather have the children of the United States know about oral sex than listen to Oral Roberts." *1998: During a conversation with radio talk-show host Michael Krasny.*

"There is a notion abroad now that something called gay is a separate race, entirely. Well, I don't think that. I'm a universalist. I believe everybody is everything. Lucky ones get to do everything and some people prefer one thing to the other." *1998*

BRUCE VILANCH
(Comedian)

"As the evening goes on, you basically have a room that fills up with losers. If you win, you're backstage soaking in the glory." *1998: Explaining why jokes made early on in the Oscar awards ceremony get more laughs than jokes made later.*

VURY VITTACHI
(Writer)

"What is the Hong Kong definition of a pervert? A man who prefers women to money." *1998*

"Of course, Hong Kongers are terrible at sex. The British are considered the least sensuous people in Europe, and the Cantonese the least sensuous in Asia. Being half-and-half, this place is by definition going to be a disaster. There isn't even any sex in the sex centers here." *1998*

HAL VOGEL
(Wall Street Analyst)

"There is little merchandising upside. It is not really an action movie, but a love story against the backdrop of boat and iceberg. And look at the story line: I heard it didn't have a happy ending." *1997: Musing about the unpromising box-office prospects for* Titanic.

W

DONNIE WAHLBERG
(Singer)

"We're being immortalized in plastic. We even have some rubber on our head." *Wahlberg, a member of the New Kids on the Block, commenting on dolls based on the group.*

MARK [MARKY MARK] WAHLBERG
(Rapper & Actor)

"The only thing I can't do is grab my penis. I'll get into trouble. I do come out in boxer shorts for a number about safe sex." *1992: On his act.*

"They're all talented singers. That's why I couldn't stay in the group. I couldn't sing." *1992: On the singing group New Kids on the Block.*

"Sometimes I feel I can't be with no girl. She might bring me down from all this. She might mess me up, she didn't really help me get here. And I ain't had no time for nonesky." *1992*

"It's not that big a thing for me. After all, I've pulled my pants down in front of millions of people millions of times." *1992: On seeing posters of himself in his underwear advertising Calvin Klein briefs.*

"My beauty secret is I try to bathe at least once every—six days—changing underwear and socks." *1992*

"Being a little pimple-faced, ugly kid, knowing that women want you—that's a great feeling." *1993*

"People seemed to really enjoy it when I was in my underwear and nothing else, but you gotta move on." *1995*

"It's like you become, what's the word, *neurotic.* Thinking about what other people think about you. Then worrying about it. Then just trying to be yourself. This shit is so complex. Sometimes I'm like, just let me go back to running around in my underwear." *1996: On the actor's life.*

TOM WAITS
(Singer)

"Do you know how many teardrops it takes to fill up a teaspoon? A hundred and twenty, actually. I tested it. I was very sad and I thought, I'm going to make some use of it, so I held a spoon at my cheek and I cried. This is my science project for the year." *1999*

CHRISTOPHER WALKEN
(Actor)

"I don't think I'm damaged. I think I'm strange. I'm happy being strange." *1994*

"I've never really confused movies with life, and I really don't believe anyone but a few very sick people do either." *1996*

"I'm not going to say it, but I think I was in it." *1999: When asked to name the worst movie ever made.*

JOE WALSH
(Singer & Musician)

"A whole bunch of us are complete idiots, but kids need something to identify with." *1991*

WANG JIAN
(Computer Programmer)

"This is about gangs? Hmm, I guess America really does have social problems." *1999: After hearing Washington's National Symphony Orchestra perform works from* West Side Story *in Beijing's Great Hall of the People.*

WANG SHUO
(China's Most Popular Novelist)

"In China, if you don't have a wife and a family and a job, then you're a hooligan. If you're not a hypocrite, then you're a hooligan. According to Chinese standards, all Americans are hooligans." *1997*

JOHN WATERS
(Director)

"She was a real Catholic saint. Now I think I have someone to pray to. I'm not saying that with any irony at all." *1994: On Jacqueline Kennedy Onnasis.*

"I don't dislike animals, but I don't have a problem if they test medicines or even cosmetics on them. Eyeliner has been important in my life. If 10 chickens have to die to make one drag queen happier, so be it!" *1997*

"Big-budget Hollywood romantic comedies are the genre I loathe. I try not to ruin it, but I start squirming and fuming, and I can feel all the people around me loving it, and I almost have to be taken away on a stretcher." *1998*

"If someone vomits watching one of my films, it's like getting a standing ovation." *1999*

BILL WATTENBURG
(Radio Talk-show Host)

"I never touch the door handles in rest rooms anymore. I always wait for somebody else to open the door before I'll leave. I've waited twenty or thirty minutes in there sometimes before leaving." *1990: The weekend host on San Francisco's KGO Radio explaining his hygenic habits.*

CHARLIE WATTS
(Drummer)

"I think it's an awful drink, to be honest with you." *1998: The drummer for the Rolling Stones, on Pepsi-Cola, which uses the band's 1971 single "Brown Sugar" in a TV commercial.*

DAMON WAYANS
(Actor & Comedian)

"I wanted to be just like him, except for the drug habit, the failed marriages, the temper and the guns." *1998: Saluting Richard Pryor, who received the Kennedy Center's Mark Twain prize.*

KEENAN IVORY WAYANS
(Actor & Comedian)

"When you see poor people running into a store and coming out with food, that's not a riot. That's just people fulfilling their needs. What you saw was people celebrating. It was as festive as the Olympics." *1993: On the Los Angeles riot of 1993.*

"I have a philosophy about problems. Fix the ones you can fix, and fuck the rest." *1994*

SIGOURNEY WEAVER
(Actress)

"They really did tell me I had no talent and I'd never get anywhere. I should get all my money back from that place." *1998: On the Yale School of Drama.*

STEVEN WEBBER
(Actor)

"The endless vanity that is allowable—it's frightening. You get used to being a brat." *1998: On being in the movie business.*

SANDI WEINTRAUB
(Roommate of Director Martin Scrocese)

"Marty was tempestuous, volatile, passionate. He breathed, ate and shat movies. We never ever looked at a movie and thought, 'Oh, wow, what a great career move for him.' I told him about my dreams, and he would tell me about the movie he had seen the day before." *1998: On life with film director Scorcese, with whom she lived for four years in the 1970s when he began making films.*

ROB WEISS
(Director)

"I didn't kill anybody—but I'm not gonna say I didn't. You know what I'm saying?" *1993*

RAQUEL WELCH
(Actress)

"I was asked to come to Chicago because Chicago is one of our 52 states, and the mandate we've now been given on the prochoice issue is that we have to pick up the pieces. . . . In 52 states across the nation, we have to bail water out of the boat." *1993*

"People are so constipated these days. They never speak their minds anymore." *1994*

MING-NA WEN
(Actress)

"This is the only awards show where people show up with their real dates." *1996: At the annual Gay and Lesbian Alliance Against Defamation media awards in Los Angeles.*

JAN WENNER
(Publisher of Rolling Stone)

"He knew all of the major celebrities of his time. And he was a friend of movie stars. He may have had to leap across rows of seats to meet them, but he knew all the big ones. Like Telly Savalas." *1992: On the words he wants written on his tombstone.*

"It's awesome to see somebody who looks like me . . . given this tremendous burden. I feel it all the more, because I could be in those shoes." *1993: On the election of Bill Clinton as president.*

"I don't want any more stories about condoms that don't mention the word *penis.* I want to see penises in this magazine." *1996: To the editorial staff of* Men's Journal.

ADAM WEST
(Actor)

"Alone and undisturbed for nearly a minute, I reveled in the power and isolation and beauty of the character." *1994: On playing Batman on TV.*

RILEY WESTON
(Actress & Writer)

"It's like you walk in, and go, 'Oh God,' and roll your eyes and say, 'Duh?' " *The thirty-two-year-old writer for the adolescent drama* Felicity, *on how she passed herself off as a nineteen-year-old, on the teen roles she was being offered.*

ESTHER WILLIAMS
(Actress & Swimmer)

"Well, obviously, with those pontoons, she could certainly float!" *1994: On teaching fourteen-year-old Elizabeth Taylor to swim.*

ROBIN WILLIAMS
(Actor & Comedian)

"I couldn't imagine living the way I used to live. Now people come up to me from the drug days and go, 'Hi, remember me?' And I'm going, 'No, did I have sex with you? Did I take a dump in your toolbox?' " *1992*

"I want to thank my father, up there, the man who when I said I wanted to be an actor said, 'Wonderful, just have a backup profession, like welding.' " *1998: In his speech after receiving the Oscar for best supporting actor in* Good Will Hunting.

"No one ever says, 'I was named Sid. I had a small shop. I was miserable.' " *1998: On how people talk about their past lives.*

"Your culture is interesting. We are fascinated by your people. We sometimes journey south and learn of your ways." *1998: On visiting Southern California.*

KEVIN WILLIAMSON
(Screenwriter)

"I guess I was a bit troublesome as a kid. Like, in school, when we had to write a sentence on the blackboard and then diagram it. I would write stuff like, 'The baby on the meat hook jerked.' " *1997: Williamson is the screenwriter of* Scream *and* Scream 2.

MALCOLM WILLIAMSON
(Master of the Queen's [Elizabeth II] Music)
"[Andrew] Lloyd Webber's music is everywhere, but so is AIDS." *1993*

BRUCE WILLIS
(Actor)
"Start having babies. Nothing will get you straightened out faster than that." *1994: Willis, the father of three daughters, offering unsolicited advice to newlywed Michael Jackson.*

"You can print this caveat at the end of the interview if you want. If I have offended anyone during the previous discourse in which I reflected on how I feel about any number of things in the world: (A) I had no idea what I was saying or that they would print it. (B) It was my personal opinion and does not reflect the opinion of any group or organization. Take it or leave it at that. (C) Go fuck yourself." *1996: Ending his interview with* Playboy *magazine.*

"You can't undo the past . . . but you can certainly not repeat it." *1998*

GORDON WILLIS
(Cinematographer)
"Francis's attitude is like, 'I'll set my clothes on fire—if I can make it to the other side of the room it'll be spectacular.' You can't shoot a whole movie hoping for happy accidents." *1998: The director of photography for* The Godfather, *on the odd behavior of director Francis Ford Coppola, during the making of the film.*

BRIAN WILSON
(Musician, Singer & Composer)
"I've always thought my dad never should have had kids." *1991*

"Leading us into the bathroom, he pointed to the toilet. Carl and Al turned away, grossed out. Dennis and I were amazed. 'Fourteen inches!' Mike erupted in laughter. 'I think it might be the world's largest turd!' " *1991: In his autobiography,* Wouldn't It Be Nice.

CARNIE WILSON
(Singer)
"I love clean guys with a nice smell. God! I'm like a dog. I'll run after them." *1993*

"I can be sexy being heavy, and if you don't like that, then shove it up your ass." *1993*

OPRAH WINFREY
(TV Talk-show Host)
"I'm on a diet." *1993: After declining dessert in a San Francisco restaurant. Winfrey dined on a dozen oysters, tuna tartare, crabcakes, stuffed calamari, salmon with mushrooms, and risotto with truffles.*

"I am defined by the world as a talk-show host. But I am spirit, connected to the greatest spirit." *1998*

DEBRA WINGER
(Actress)
"You know, he's swell—swell without being swollen." *1992: On Steve Martin.*

"The famous actress, the rock star, you never see them vomit or take a shit; you never smell their breath or their farts, or hear their snores and trip over their pee-stained underwear. . . . It's not a person you're thinking about; it's a plastic illusion." *1993*

REESE WITHERSPOON
(Actress)
"I did a scene with Paul Newman that took a lot of courage. I'm not going to say why, but it took a lot of courage and I just had to close my eyes and say, 'God, do it!' " *1998: On her courage during the filming of* Twilight.

TOM WOLFE
(Writer)
"It is such a burden to be right all the time." *1990*

"This is undoubtedly a good time in history, [but] so far we have been utterly unable to answer the question: 'Good for what?' " *1995*

"I think it's one of the great time-wasters of all time. We don't need another time-waster in America. I don't believe the Internet is going to change human nature in the slightest." *1998: On the Internet.*

TOM WOLFE (CONT'D)

"What people wear in the streets today is so bad—rags, practically. They look like they're fleeing before an invading army. Casual Fridays! It's crazy. Any man over 35 should wear a jacket and a tie. It just makes you look better. To see old men in October wearing shorts, it's ghastly." *1998*

"I think your soul is your relationship with other people." *1998*

"I went to a music store and bought quite a few tapes. They were of value in two ways. First, the music. And then the printed lyrics, which I must say, are considerably more idiotic than mine. I had to lift them a level or two." *1999: On prepping to write rap lyrics for his novel* A Man in Full.

JAMES WOODS
(Actor)

"Filmmaking, like sex, isn't a polite enterprise. It involves a lot of mess and sweat and tears, and the bottom line is, if somebody ain't screamin', you're not doin' your job." *1996*

LOUISE WOODWARD
(Nanny)

"People don't seem to be able to distinguish between celebrity and notoriety. They ask me to sign baseball caps, which I find ridiculous." *1998: The British nanny who was convicted of involuntary manslaughter for killing a baby in her care, on being a household name.*

ROBIN WRIGHT
(Actress)

"He's a rarity as a father. He's so there. . . . It's all about purity, honesty and that cliche—unconditional love. I always knew he was that way, though. He was that way with his dogs." *1992: On her husband, Sean Penn.*

ELIZABETH WURTZEL
(Author)

"Frankly, I have a tough time feeling that feminism has done a damn bit of good if I can't be the way I am and have the world accommodate it on some level." *1998: Wurtzel is the author of* Prozac Nation *and* Bitch.

"Who cares if Mary Jo Buttafuoco lives or dies? As far as anyone can tell, her consciousness is not much more than that of an alligator and must only fight its way out of the sewer. Only she is not fighting. And that is why I am sorry she isn't dead." *1998*

NAN WYATT
(TV News Anchor)

"Being dead doesn't necessarily take you off the air here." *1997: On KMOX radio in St. Louis, which continues its regular broadcasts of Richard Evans's* A Thought for the Day, *even though he has been dead for twenty-six years.*

NOAH WYLE
(Actor)

"Women are the only reason I'm not gay." *1996*

X

SUANJUN XIE
(Intellectual & Dissident)

"The problem with China is that instead of adopting Christ's ideals, too many Chinese think they are Jesus Christ themselves." *1999: The convert to Christianity, now living in New York.*

Y

MARTIN YAN
(Celebrity Chef)

"What happened to you in the thousand years before the Chinese opened any restaurants? What did you eat?" *1998: The star chef of the TV series* Yan Can Cook *to an audience at the Jewish Community Center in Hong Kong.*

JONATHAN YARDLEY
(Writer)

"Let's make the stamp in honor of the real Elvis. In the middle should stand the King himself, decked out in sequins. His eyes are glazed, his mouth sags and his flesh has the texture of lard. To his side is a huge pile of pills. Above him are the words: *Elvis Presley, 1935–1977: American Role Model.*" *1992*

WALTER YETNIKOFF
(President of Sony's CBS Records)

"I'm very spiritual. I commune with my higher power, I connect spiritually with my inner self . . . then I go out and I try to fuck people." *1990*

ALAN YOUNG
(Actor)

"Ed was in show business two weeks when they changed his name and castrated him. Happens to many of us." *1995: On his costar in the TV show* Mister Ed, *who was a horse.*

NEIL YOUNG
(Singer)

"I think she could play an excellent hooker and I think she'd take that as a compliment. Hookers have got a lot of soul." *1993: On Sandra Bernhard.*

SEAN YOUNG
(Actress)

"God would have been merciful if he had given him a little teeny penis so that he could get on with his life." *1990: On actor James Woods.*

"He fired me from that movie because, basically, whenever we were both onscreen you looked at me and not him—well it all comes back later. He became a fool wearing a yellow shawl. . . . He was a weenie. A real little weenie." *1991: On almost playing the role of Tess Trueheart opposite Warren Beatty in* Dick Tracy.

HENNY YOUNGMAN
(Comedian)

"I was coming out of a fish restaurant the other day, and a hooker walked up to me. She said, 'I'll do anything you want for $50.' I said, 'Paint my house.'" *1992*

JESSICA YU
(Filmmaker)

"What a thrill. You know you're entering new territory when your outfit costs more than your film." *1997: After winning an Oscar for her short-documentary film* Breathing Lessons.

Z

FRANK ZAPPA
(Musician & Singer)

"He told me he liked my records, especially *Bongo Fury*." *1990: After interviewing Czechoslovakian President Vaclav Havel.*

RENEE ZELLWEGGER
(Actress)

"People are always asking me what it's like to kiss Tom Cruise and I have to admit I don't remember!" *1998: Zellwegger starred opposite Cruise in* Jerry Maguire.

"When I first moved to L.A. and I saw limos, I honestly thought President Clinton was in there. Or maybe Steven Spielberg. Now I know it's just some little actress." *1998: On her success in Hollywood.*

"I was in love—love—with Paul McCartney. He was my prototype male. I didn't have any boyfriends, but every guy I thought was attractive basically looked like him. Well, him or Speed Racer. You can see the similarity, can't you?" *1998*

MARIA ZOLOTUKHINA
(Russian Sociologist)

"Fun is not a Russian concept." *1996: On the difficulties faced by the creators of a Russian version of* Sesame Street.

JOHN ZORN
(Musician)

"You up there! Shut the fuck up and listen to the music!" *1997: Addressing Czech Republic President Vaclav Havel and his pal Secretary of State Madeleine Albright at the Knitting Factory, a New York Jazz club. Albright and Havel, who were sitting in the balcony, were having an animated conversation during Zorn's performance.*

DAPHNE ZUNIGA
(Actress)

"In acting class, they tell you to think of something sad to help you cry. But after a while, thinking of Grandma under the tractor didn't work anymore. That's when I knew it was time to leave." *1996: Explaining her departure from the TV program* Melrose Place.

PART TWO

POLITICS
&
POLITICIANS

POLITICS & POLITICIANS

A

RACHEL ABRAMS
(Wife of Elliot Abrams, Former Assistant Secretary of State)
"I know something about Hillary and Bill Clinton right now. I know how their stomachs churn. . . . I know their inability to sleep at night and their reluctance to rise in the morning. . . . I know all this, and the thought of it makes me happy." *1994: On scandal accusations involving the first couple.*

BELLA ABZUG
(Congresswoman & Activist)
"She is a person who vibrates in her own right." *1996: On Hillary Rodham Clinton.*

ROBERTA ACHTENBERG
(San Francisco Board of Supervisors)
"I think it says that Bill Clinton is interested in looking at all people—in their qualifications and in their breath." *1993*

JEFF ACKERMAN
(Editor, Nevada Appeal)
"Except for the degree of pleasure they provide, lawmakers and prostitutes might actually have lots in common." *1997: Ridiculing state lawmakers for proposing a "fact-finding" mission to tour one of the state's legalized brothels. The legislators canceled the trip.*

ROGER AILES
(Political Media Consultant)
"He's a weenie." *1990: On Senator Paul Simon of Illinois, who beat an Ailes client in an election.*

MADELEINE ALBRIGHT
(Secretary of State)
"At times, Warren Christopher seems almost life-like." *1997: On her low-key predecessor.*

"One of my role models, Xena, the Warrior Princess, comes from here." *1998: After naming Dean Acheson as an exemplar—in New Zealand, home of Lucy Lawless, who portrays Xena.*

"See what happens when you let men into the cabinet." *1999: After Health and Human Services Secretary Donna Shalala pointed out that the two women were discussing Kosovo policy while, nearby, Housing and Urban Development Secretary Andrew Cuomo was complimenting Agriculture Secretary Dan Glickman on his shoes.*

HENRY ALDRIDGE
(North Carolina State Representative)
"People who are raped—who are truly raped—the juices don't flow, the body functions don't work, and they don't get pregnant." *1995: Arguing against state-funded abortions for rape victims.*

LAMAR ALEXANDER
(Secretary of Education & Presidential Candidate)
"I'm not from Washington, D.C. I was there long enough to be vaccinated but not to be infected." *1996*

"Sometimes there'll just be better places to live than a place with low wealth and high needs. If you're living in an area with a bad school, you move to a place where there's a better school." *1996: Explaining his ideas on what parents of children who attend poorly funded urban or rural schools should do to solve their problems.*

DORIS ALLEN
(Speaker of the California State Assembly)
"Do I let a group of power-mongering men with short penises tell me what to do. Well, I don't know. What am I supposed to do?. . .These men have a real problem. They can't be doing it from logic and truth. Logic and truth don't dictate a recall. Certainly not from the party. So what else can it be? They can't help it if they were born with shortcomings." *1995: On proponents of her recall election. Allen later resigned as speaker to focus on fighting a recall campaign.*

WOODY ALLEN
(Actor & Director)
"If I were Clinton I would have gone in front of the American people and said, 'Yes, I'm having an

WOODY ALLEN (CONT'D)

affair with this woman. My wife is still behind me, so it's really none of your business—and if this is not OK with you, fine, get yourself a new president." *1998: On how he would have handled the Clinton-Lewinsky matter if he were the president.*

THE AMERICAN OXONIAN
(Magazine of American Rhodes Scholars)

"Bill Clinton writes that the biggest family news is he and Hillary have become empty nesters. Also Hillary turned 50. He says he likes being married to an older woman, but wishes their daughter wasn't so far away. He still loves his job, but says that how Washington views the world, spends its time and treats people is often another matter. Bill writes that seeing friends eases the pain of the empty nest. . . ." *1998: Item in the winter 1998 edition of the publication.*

ALDRICH AMES
(Former CIA Agent & Spy)

"If I can keep my failings in perspective, I believe I can hold my head up high and feel like a normal and decent member of our species in all the critical respects." *1997: Ames spied for the Russians and provided them with the names of twenty-eight agents working in various countries for the United States. Many of those agents were subsequently eliminated by the Russians.*

TERRY ANDERSON
(Hostage)

"Goodbye!" *1991: In answer to the question put to him by reporters following his release in Lebanon, "What was the last thing you said to your kidnappers?"*

PRINCESS ANNE
(of Great Britain)

"The definition of developing and developed countries sometimes worries me. If we consider that Britain and the United States are fully developed, we have some worries." *1996*

GEORGI ARBATOV
(Russian Foreign Policy Expert)

"It is difficult to act as a great power when you constantly beg for aid." *1998: On Russia's worsening economic state.*

IAN ARKATOV
(Political Consultant)

"He's like Velcro for dog-doo." *1990: Commenting on former governor Jerry Brown of California.*

DICK ARMEY
(GOP House Majority Leader)

"Barney Fag." *1995: Referring to Rep. Barney Frank, D-Massachussetts, an openly gay member of Congress. Frank replied, "There are a lot of ways to mispronounce my name. That is the least common."*

"Maybe we ought to take another look at the amount of money we're spending on education." *1996: When asked how he would make up for the revenue lost by cutting the gasoline tax.*

"I know this is going to come as a big surprise to you, but I have been a longtime fan of Boy George's music." *1996: After comparing Bill Clinton to a "Karma Chameleon."*

"Say what you want about the president, but we know his friends have convictions." *1996: After Jim Guy Tucker and James and Susan McDougal were found guilty of Whitewater-related crimes.*

"If it were me who had documented personal conduct along the lines of the president's, I would be so filled with shame I would resign." *1998: To a group of Coppell High School students in suburban Dallas. "I could not let those children think the president is a good role model," Armey said later to reporters.*

"If I were, I would be looking up from a pool of blood and hearing [my wife asking], 'How do I reload this thing?'" *1998: Explaining what would happen if he were in President Clinton's scandalous position.*

PETER ARNETT
(Journalist)

"They gave me the list. I asked these questions. The producers took the tape and I was gone. I was the face." *1998: Claiming he should not be blamed for CNN's retracted story alleging the United States used poison gas in Laos during the Vietnam War.*

B

JAMES BAKER
(Former Secretary of State)

"This is a delightful surprise to the extent that it is a surprise and it is only a surprise to the extent that we anticipated." *1990: On a Kohl/Gorbachev German reunification agreement.*

"Fuck 'em. They didn't vote for us." *1992: On Jewish voters.*

"You know you're out of power when your limousine is yellow and your driver speaks Farsi." *1993*

RUSSELL BAKER
(Journalist)

"Torrents of words poured out of him. . . . He canvassed the spectrum from the magisterial arrogance of Charles de Gaulle, to poverty in India, to his youthful career as a rural Texas schoolteacher. Always, however, the talk came back to his admiration for President Kennedy. . . . In the middle of the monologue he surreptitiously, without interrupting the word flow, sent a note out to his secretary asking, 'Who is this I'm talking to?' " *1997: Remembering the time he went to interview then Vice President Lyndon Johnson in Washington.*

ALEC BALDWIN
(Actor)

"Sexual promiscuity has always been the medicine of choice for the chief executive of the United States. What would you rather have him do: take drugs? Drink?" *1998: Dismissing the allegations of misbehavior concerning Bill Clinton.*

"Campaigning and raising money with Clinton or Gore and those guys. I refuse to do it. Those guys want to sleep in the Oval Office, sleep in the mansions, it's about access. I think political activism has negatively impacted my career. I wish I had been more like Danny Glover, aggressively steering my career more toward a box-office franchise kind of career, doing the 'Lethal Weapons,' and having those successes over and over and over again. And you say to yourself, that's a guy that's generated enough economic good will in the community to be able to do some of the other things he wants to do." *1999*

JAMES BARCIA
(Congressman)

"(Ted Nugent has) earned the respect and administration [*sic*] of millions of adults and young people. . . . He still finds the time to blow your mind with what I think is some of the greatest music in decades." *1993: Nugent donated $1,000 to Barcia's campaign.*

MICHAEL BARONE
(Columnist)

"He is passing up the chance to be another Fiorello LaGuardia in order to be another Phil Donahue." *1992: On Jesse Jackson's decision to host a television talk show rather than run for mayor of Washington, D.C.*

MARION BARRY
(Mayor of Washington, D.C.)

"Just take lemon juice and lots of water." *1990: Advising a drug dealer, Charles Lewis, on how to pass a drug urine test.*

"I'm the luckiest man in the world. The Lord's on my side." *1990: Words spoken to his female companion in a hotel room only moments before he was arrested for smoking crack cocaine.*

"Bitch set me up!" *1990: Words spoken about his female companion in a hotel room only moments after he was arrested for smoking crack cocaine.*

"It reminds me of what happened in Germany during the period when citizens were abrogated—their rights were abrogated—in a totalitarian kind of state." *1996: On the D.C. financial control board's decision to fire its human services director.*

"One reputation I don't have is for stealing money from the public." *1999: The outgoing mayor reflecting on his sixteen-year tenure in a farewell news conference.*

JACQUES BARZAGHI
(Campaign Advisor to Jerry Brown)

"The fish swim, then go up the river. To mature. Before a meal you have a cocktail. During the meal, with the entree, you probably have a rosé. For your meat, you might have red wine. Then with the fish, a white wine. With your dessert, champagne.

JACQUES BARZAGHI (CONT'D)

But at the end, the bottom line, you drink a glass of pure water. And he [Jerry Brown] is that glass of water. One day it will be time for that glass of water. We don't know when. But it will be pretty soon." *1992*

"We are not disorganized. We just have a kind of organization that transcends understanding." *1992*

"What really makes Jerry tick, what really makes him run, is the sense of the suffering he is experiencing. It's really real for him." *1992*

"Jerry didn't say boo. He was sitting with a look of green on his face." *1992: On how Brown behaved when former presidential candidate David Duke talked to Brown about the flat tax proposal, on a USAir flight between Pittsburgh and Washington D.C.*

EVAN BAYH
(Governor of Indiana)

"In the words of George Bernard Shaw . . . 'Two roads diverged in a wood, and I—I took the one less traveled by.' " *1992: Calling for educational excellence at a meeting of the Education Commission of the States.*

ROBERT BECKEL
(Political Consultant)

"The political landscape is littered with the bodies of people who predicted Bill Clinton's demise." *1998: On initial predictions that the president could be fatally damaged by the Monica Lewinsky allegations.*

DAVID BECKWITH
(Spokesman for Vice President Dan Quayle)

"We've long had hopes of converting Leonard Bernstein to the Republican Party. But it's about time to give up." *1992: Upon hearing that Quayle's office had sent a fund-raising letter to the composer, who died more than a year earlier.*

PAUL BEGALA
(Presidential Advisor)

"Like we say in Texas, if goofy ideas ever go to $40 a barrel, I want the drilling rights to Dick Armey's head." *1998: A Clinton advisor on House Majority Leader Armey's suggestion that Clinton resign.*

"I feel like I spent the last year in Imelda Marcos's closet." *1999: The retiring Clinton aid, when asked by radio host Don Imus if he would return to the White House if another "shoe drops" during the president's remaining scandal-plagued tenure.*

"I never promised to be the one loading Buddy and Socks into the U-Haul." *After announcing his resignation in order to teach.*

RICHARD BELZER
(Actor)

"A week before Lincoln was shot he was in Monroe, Maryland. A week before Kennedy was shot he was in Marilyn Monroe." *1999: Adding a new comparison between assassinated presidents Lincoln and Kennedy.*

BILL BENNETT
(Secretary of Education)

"I say, too bad about foreign films. If they can't make it, tough. I stopped going at the same time I threw away my black turtleneck. . . . I went to those Bergman things and felt bad, and felt good about feeling bad, and the '80s was good medicine for that." *1992: On why foreign films don't succeed commercially in the United States.*

"If parents cannot see that there is a problem with a man in office who they would not trust alone with their own daughter, then they have a problem." *1998: On President Clinton's popularity despite allegations of sexual impropriety.*

JACKIE BENNETT
(Deputy to Kenneth Starr)

"You're 24, you're smart, you're old enough, you don't need to call your mommy." *1998: To Monica Lewinsky, when she wanted to call her mother during a deposition.*

LLOYD BENTSEN
(Senator)

"If Jerry Brown is the answer, it must be a very peculiar question." *1992*

SANDRA BERNHARD
(Comedienne)

"Maybe if Clinton had just completely lost it and cried hysterically the speech would have been more appealing. I think he should've consulted his drama coach and just gone for it. A half-assed statement doesn't have the punch that a good cry does—even Nixon cried. He should've just gone for it, just in terms of drama and excitement for the country." *1998: On the Clinton apology speech.*

GEOFFREY C. BIBLE
(CEO of Philip Morris)
"There's an interesting question you should ask the public-health people. What do you think smokers would do if they didn't smoke? You get some pleasure from it, and you also get some other beneficial things, such as stress relief. Nobody knows what you'd turn to if you didn't smoke. Maybe you'd beat your wife. Maybe you'd drive cars fast. Who knows what the hell you'd do?" *1998: On the benefits to society from people smoking cigarettes.*

JOSEPH BIDEN
(Senator)
"Tens of hundreds if not thousands of people will die." *1993: Warning what would happen without outside intervention in Bosnia.*

"This is about guns. Bang-bang. Shoot-shoot. Guns." *1994: In a rhetorical flourish while speaking on the maneuverings in the Senate over a crime bill.*

MR. BLACKWELL
(Fashion Critic)
"She looks like a sheep dog in drag." *1999: On Linda Tripp, who topped his annual worst-dressed women list.*

LINDA BLOODWORTH-THOMASON
(Friend of President Clinton)
"Hollywood people are more genuine, more calm, childlike in their sincerity. They openly say they want to be stars. Washington is a more hysterical town . . . filled with people who want to be stars, but cover it up." *1993: On being asked which is a phonier town, Hollywood or Washington, D.C.*

PAUL BODEN
(Coalition on Homelessness)
"I think there's a couple of levels where it's just bizarre." *1999: On a plan supported by San Francisco*

Mayor Willie Brown to provide that city's panhandlers with machines to accept credit-card and ATM donations.

CHASTITY BONO
(Daughter of Mayor & Congressman Sonny Bono)
"It's definitely a hell of a lot more rewarding than making records." *1996: On her career as a gay activist.*

"The problem with my father is that he is hypocritical. While he has had gays and lesbians working for him and has always appeared accepting of me, his voting record on gay and lesbian issues has been totally atrocious. How can I respect him for that?" *1997*

"I was always daddy's girl—or daddy's boy, I don't know." *1998: On her relationship with her famous father, Sonny Bono.*

"Aside from being a lesbian, I'm pretty boring." *1998*

MARY BONO
(Congresswoman and Widow of Sonny Bono)
"Did you see *Happy Gilmore*? He wanted to be tough for hockey so he went up in front of a batting cage and stood there and let the baseballs kind of hit him. I guess that's what I need to do. Toughen up my skin." *1998: On how she handles criticism while campaigning to fill the congressional seat once held by her husband.*

"What has been most interesting to me today is to watch all of these lawyers attack other lawyers for what it is lawyers do—whatever it is." *1998: The California member of the House Judiciary Committee on the impeachment hearings.*

SONNY BONO
(Mayor of Palm Springs, CA & Congressman)
"I'm not the slick, articulate talker that most politicians are, but what I say, I mean. I feel confident that the public is ready for a non-politician politician." *1990*

"I've been in D.C. a few times. Nobody fell over backward when I said I would like to try to go for the Senate." *1990*

"That was kind of a thrill. I did see it as some sort of recognition." *1990: On an invitation he received to*

SONNY BONO (CON'T)

ride in Vice President Dan Quayle's car after a political rally in Los Angeles.

"Do I have any foreign policy experience? No. Did I have experience before writing a song? No. Producing a show? No. Running for mayor? No." *1991: Announcing that he'd run for the US Senate in 1992.*

"As far as free thinking, I would probably be the most free thinker." *1991: Contemplating a run for the U.S. Senate.*

"The job has to do with the larger issues of life and the welfare of mankind." *1991: On his job as mayor of Palm Springs, CA.*

"It was as if I was pulled by an unseen force like the mysterious voice in *Field of Dreams* that says, 'If you build it, he will come.'" *1991: On how he felt when he first saw a "For Lease" sign in a building that became Bono's restaurant.*

"I have written 10 hit songs and I know this: You're not in tune with California Republicans." *1992: To GOP primary opponent Tom Campbell.*

"For me to sit in this car and say, 'OK, here's what a senator does, boom, boom, boom'—I think that's political rhetoric. . . . I think what you've got to look for is the horsepower of the guy to deliver what he says he's gonna deliver." *1992: While running for the GOP nomination for senator from California.*

"Everyone in this room is probably smarter than me, but I know that years ago my father taught me you can't spend more than you make." *1992*

"I've never been qualified for anything I'm good at." *1992*

"We have hundreds of agencies; some of them we don't even need. I bet you could take an agency and just put an efficiency expert in there and you could come out with a lot of bureaucratic waste." *1992*

"I like him a lot. He's very straight ahead, very direct, almost what I call a street person. . . . I've greeted President Reagan, President Bush, and I've greeted him. And he was the most earthy, with a lot of humor." *1992: On Dan Quayle.*

"I gave Newt a metaphor to use. I said to him, 'Once in a while a metaphor comes into your life and it's a magical time. It's like having your first hit record.'" *1995: On meeting Newt Gingrich during his first week in Congress.*

"In many cases, the media—the *Washington Post* for instance—is determined to keep me in the category of being a doof. But those things have never bothered me." *1995*

"Boy, it's been flying in this room like I can't believe today. . . .We have a very simple and concise bill here, and I think it would be to everyone's pleasure if we would just pass this thing. And now certainly everyone has demonstrated their ability in legal knowledge, and wouldn't it be nice now if we vote on this thing and move on." *1995: After debating a crime bill at a committee meeting. Chuck Schumer (D–NY) replied, "I'd say, to the gentleman, he talks about legalese. We're making laws here, not sausages. We have to talk about the law. That's what we're here to do."*

"She's not my type, let's put it that way. She wouldn't pass the test. Yes, the Bono Test." *1995: On Hillary Clinton.*

"I guess it's not illegal, 'cause he's still the president." *1995: When asked by David Letterman for his opinion on Whitewater.*

"I chose to go skiing, and that was the wrong choice." *1996: After he needed eleven stitches to close a facial gash he suffered when he collided with another skier near Big Bear Lake in California.*

"The guy looks like he's out of gas." *1996: On Senator Strom Thurmond, ninety-three.*

"Let me put it this way: I made a living as a singer, and I'm not a singer." *1996: Describing himself as a "non-politician" in politics.*

"I have been in the arts for 30 years. That has been my occupation. I know of no one in 30 years in the arts who has been assisted by the

NEA. So I don't see where the NEA is this amazing contribution to mankind." *1997: Supporting a proposal to do away with the National Endowment for the Arts.*

RICHARD BOUCHER
(U.S. Ambassador to Cyprus)
"Talk about results. If you don't have results, talk policy. If you don't have policy, talk facts. If you don't have facts, talk process. You always have process." *1995*

WILL BOYD
(Seventh Grade Student)
"It isn't looking very impressive. They're banging their books and stuff." *1998: After observing lawmakers screaming at each other during a school trip to the Illinois state capitol.*

MARK BRADEN
(Ex-counsel for the Republican National Committee)
"Unless, of course, he was struck by lightning on his way to Damascus and he decided to tell the truth out of the goodness of his heart, but there doesn't seem to be much goodness in his heart, so I don't think that's going to happen." *1999: On Harvard Professor Alan Dershowitz's claim that Clinton shouldn't testify at his Senate impeachment trial.*

ED BRADLEY
(TV Journalist)
"Was he aroused?" *1998: Probing question put by Bradley to Kathleen Willey when she detailed her encounter in the Oval Office with President Clinton in 1993 during which, she said, the president placed her hand between his legs.*

NICHOLAS BRADY
(Secretary of the Treasury)
"Don't worry about it. It always looks dark at the bottom of a recovery." *1991*

"We have light bulbs around. And that level of light bulb accumulation per family in the United States over the last two or three years has reached a level which is traditionally its low, and it's going to turn around again. . . ." *1992: On why he foresaw an economic recovery just around the corner.*

THOMAS BRAY
(Editorial Page Editor, Detroit News)
"We felt that many of the columns seem too content-free." *1996: On his decision to drop a column written by Hillary Rodham Clinton.*

JOE BOB BRIGGS
(Columnist)
"But the scariest thing of all [about the Senate Judiciary Committee hearings on the confirmation of Judge Clarence Thomas] I thought, was one of the facts that kept coming up again and again, and none of the commentators ever mentioned it. It threatens the future of this country more than anything else that came out of the hearings. I need to scream it out before it's too late: Oral Roberts University has a law school! Now we're talking scary." *1991*

"Has it ever occurred to anybody that the only people left in America who think sexual behavior is a campaign issue are reporters?" *1992*

"Has it ever occurred to anybody that the only people not having sex in America are reporters?" *1992*

DAVID BRINKLEY
(TV Journalist)
"I wish to say that we all look forward with great pleasure to four more years of wonderful, inspiring speeches, full of wit, poetry, music, love and affection, plus more goddamned nonsense." *1996: On President Clinton, during Brinkley's final election night broadcast. Brinkley was not aware he was on the air when making this remark.*

"Among things I admire, almost near the top is creativeness, and everyone in this group has it. It shows in your work, it shows in your thinking, and it shows in your speech, what you do, what you write, what you say. And it's one reason this group is so terrific. Bill Clinton has none of it. He has not a creative bone in his body. Therefore, he's a bore, and will always be a bore." *1996: Addressing his ABC News colleagues—Peter Jennings, Hal Bruno, Cokie Roberts, Lynn Sherr, Jeff Greenfield, and Sam Donaldson—just before ABC signed off its election night coverage.*

DAVID BROCK
(Journalist)

"I didn't go searching for the story. It found me." *1998: The author of the "Troopergate" article that first appeared in* The American Spectator *and helped launch the Paula Jones harassment suit and the Monica Lewinsky scandal. Brock made this statement in an open letter of apology to President Clinton.*

JAMES BROLIN
(Actor)

"He's the most fun president we've ever had. I think we can all agree about that. The fact is, the job is getting done, and he's enjoying himself." *1998: On President Bill Clinton.*

HAMILTON BROWN
(Former Secret Service Agent)

"We do our jobs chiefly with our eyes, not our ears. No one's ever talked a president to death." *1998: The executive secretary of the Association of Former Agents of the U.S. Secret Service, expressing doubt that agents subpoenaed by Kenneth Starr would have paid attention to any incriminating conversations between the president and others.*

JERRY BROWN
(Governor of California & Mayor of Oakland, CA)

"I had been a former governor." *1990*

"You are neither hot nor cold so I vomited you out of my mouth. That's what I say about moderates." *1991*

"This is Jerry Brown. Thanks for calling. And please do everything you can to assist and be an active member in the insurgent campaign to take back America. To speak to a live human being, dial zero." *1992: Taped message on the Jerry Brown for President office phone in Santa Monica, CA.*

"Some people think I act kind of strange." *1992*

"This is an Empire State." *1992: Campaigning in New Jersey, the "Garden State." When corrected, Brown replied, "Although we are physically in New Jersey, we are spiritually in New York. . . ."*

"Good question. I think I did once. But it wasn't my money." *When asked by a student at Medgar Evers College in Brooklyn if he had ever given anyone a $1,000 campaign contribution.*

"So I guess what's goose for—what is it?—what's sauce for the goose is goose for the gander or something." *1994*

"A baby smiles and a flower grows." *1997: Campaign slogan for Brown during his successful quest to become Oakland's mayor.*

KATHLEEN BROWN
(California State Treasurer & Sister of Jerry Brown)

"Jerry has to feel comfortable about what he does and says because if he doesn't, it won't be authentic." *1992*

"Guys, you're going to hear some pretty terrible things during this campaign. You're going to hear that I'm Jerry Brown's sister. That's how bad it's gonna get." *1994: To her campaign workers during her campaign for the Democratic nomination for governor of California.*

VICKY BROWN
(Official at Madame Tussaud's Museum in Sydney, Australia)

"We were finding that every time we went past Bill Clinton, the zipper was down." *1998: On why staffers sewed closed the fly on the presidential mannequin.*

WILLIE BROWN
(Speaker of the California State Assembly, Mayor of San Francisco)

"For San Francisco, losing Willie Brown would be like losing its water supply. The Speaker tucks a lot of stuff away for the city, and without much fanfare." *1990*

"Sorry, I'm busy. I'll call him back in 1993. Maybe . . . Did I say 1993? I'll call him back in 1995." *1992: Answering a call from Reverend Jesse Jackson's secretary. Brown was upset because Jackson appeared in his assembly district and asked for donations to his [Jackson's] Rainbow Coalition. "He was trying to take money from my people and that isn't kosher," said Brown.*

"All of those people who say they couldn't go to work for Clinton were never invited in the first place and I should know because I'm one of them." *1992*

"He's too principled!" *1995: After hearing President Bill Clinton's speech in Sacramento in which the president called for an examination of affirmative action in order to see if it is working and fair.*

"Those white boys got taken, fair and square." *1995: On California State Assembly Republicans, after he maneuvered to appoint his own successor and cleared the way to run for mayor of San Francisco.*

"You ought to challenge him every day in every way. You should read ahead of him. You ought to do what you do best to terrorize professors you don't like, and I guarantee he will be a basket case by the end of the term." *1995: Speaking to students at California State University, Hayward, advising them on how to combat and harass a professor who sponsored the California Civil Rights Initiative, a measure that would end affirmative action programs in California.*

"Anybody who's willing to hang upside down like a bat for hours at a time is my kind of guy. I realize it's a stretch but it sells me." *1996: Newly appointed police chief Fred Lau attempted to join the police force in 1970 but was too short. So he started a series of stretching exercises, including hanging upside down for long periods. Eventually he got into the department, not because he got taller, but rather because the civil service decided the height limit was discriminatory and abolished it.*

"They offered me either the Queen or the Lincoln (bedrooms). Being from San Francisco—the Queen intrigued me. But I'm doing the Lincoln. He cut me loose." *1996: Describing his choice of accommodations after being invited by President and Hillary Clinton to spend the night at the White House.*

"Can't give it to you—her husband'd kill me." *1996: When asked by a journalist who was the beautiful woman he was seen dining with in Sacramento.*

"I chose the Lincoln Room as the place where I would hang my hat. I didn't tell him which room, by the way, before I got to Washington. I wanted to be able to prove to you that I was there. I didn't want no inventory made of anything. Because, I want you to know, I took everything out of the Lincoln Room that had 'White House' on it that wasn't tied down. I mean, I took everything." *1996: On his overnight stay at the White House as a guest of his friend, Bill Clinton.*

"Never make deals with Republicans that screw Democrats. Make deals with Republicans that screw Republicans. . . . Any time they've ever dealt with me, when they have left the table, they have left most of what they came with on the table. And I have left with everything I came with and what they left. That's the way to deal with Republicans." *1996*

"We must ensure that every school kid has an opportunity to do exactly what Willie Brown has been able to do." *1996: On education.*

"I hope that when they do an audit of the city and county of San Francisco that I am in a country that doesn't have extradition." *1996*

"What an experience to tell my constituents of my experience in public housing." *1996: On sleeping at the White House.*

"This is definitely not a one-man show. It's a one-man credit, though." *1996: On his San Francisco administration.*

"I don't care about your idiot kids." *1996: To Professor Glenn Custred who believes that university admissions should not be based on race but purely on academic achievement. Brown disagreed.*

"Hey, if you can't take people's money and then screw 'em, then you've got no business being in the business." *1996: When asked how he could authorize a lawsuit by the city against tobacco companies that had donated to his campaign.*

"The California party was horse shit. The Tennessee party had Hootie and the Blowfish. The New York party had Billy Joel. The D.C. party had the Coasters. And we didn't have anyone. There were no stars there but me. . . ." *1997: Complaining about the California party in Washington, D.C., during presidential inauguration week.*

"His boss may have needed choking. It may have been justified." *1997: Objecting to the firing of Golden*

WILLIE BROWN (CONT'D)

State Warriors all-star guard Latrell Sprewell for attacking his coach, P. J. Carlesimo. Sprewell choked Carlesimo and threatened his life. As a result Sprewell was fired by the Warriors and given a one-year suspension by the NBA.

"I don't even know his name . . . some Latino gay guy . . . He was recommended to me by (Supervisor) Susan Leal. [Turning to an aide] What's the guy's name?" *1997: On the appointment of a new city park commissioner in San Francisco, demonstrating how he seeks out the very best talent for city jobs in San Francisco.*

"I just got new carpeting in here, and I don't want any blood on it." *1997: Scolding San Francisco 49ers campaign manager Jack Davis after he and rival political consultant Robert Barnes had a fist-swinging brawl in the mayor's office.*

"His father was, frankly, the standard by which all mayors should be measured. To receive this award as a new mayor is more than I could hope for." *1997: Gracefully accepting the Richard J. Daley award during the conference of mayors in San Francisco.*

"I do not intend to lose the Super Bowl. As long as I have the 49ers as a sponsoring team, the Super Bowl will be in San Francisco, whether it's in the city or not." *1998*

"The quality of our water is superior to anything else we produce in the city." *Suggesting San Francisco bottle and sell its own water, which comes from the Hetch Hetchy Valley in Yosemite National Park.*

SAM BROWNBACK
(Senator)

"So no raise money, no get bonus?" *1997: During a hearing on China's role in campaign fund-raising.*

PATRICK BUCHANAN
(Presidential Candidate)

"[He's] an 85-year-old chain-smoking communist dwarf." *1992: On Chinese leader Deng Xiaoping.*

"I don't want to be charged with child abuse." *1992: On why he didn't want to debate Vice President Dan Quayle.*

"Bill Clinton's foreign policy experience is pretty much confined to having had breakfast once at the International House of Pancakes." *1992*

DALE BUMPERS
(Former Senator)

"You say, 'He should have thought it all out beforehand.' And indeed he should, just as Adam and Eve should have." *The former Arkansas senator, in his Senate defense of President Clinton.*

NINA BURLEIGH
(Correspondent)

"The president's foot lightly, and presumably accidentally, brushed mine once under the table. His hand touched my wrist while he was dealing the cards. When I got up and shook his hand at the end of the game, his eyes wandered over to my bike-wrecked, naked legs. And slowly it dawned on me as I walked away: He found me attractive. I'd be happy to give him (oral sex) just to thank him for keeping abortion legal." *1998: The former White House correspondent for* Time *magazine in an essay for* Mirabella *magazine on Clinton's attractiveness to women.*

BARBARA BUSH
(Former First Lady)

"I rarely hug guns." *1990: While flinching at a combat rifle during a photo opportunity with United States troops in Saudi Arabia.*

"My speech is nothing. I'm just going to remind people of what George Bush has accomplished." *1992: Explaining what she would say at the Republican National Convention in Houston.*

"One thing I can say about life with George Bush—he may not be able to keep a job, but he's not boring." *1995*

"I don't miss one darn thing. I loved being the wife of the president, but anyone who wants something that's gone, or that they can't have, is stupid. I hate it when people whine about something they can't have." *1996: When asked if she missed the White House.*

"It's very disappointing and hurtful. How come nobody ever thought I had an affair with anyone?" *1998: On the sex scandals tainting the White House.*

GEORGE BUSH
(President of the United States)

"Repeat after me—substance tomorrow!" *1990: Responding to reporters' questions about the substance of his proposals on a reunified Germany.*

"I'm President of the United States and I'm not going to eat any more broccoli." *1990*

"If anyone figures that out, call me." *1990: After seeing the movie* Field of Dreams.

"What do you call it? Suddenly gone blank—in terms of when you bring a guy back and he no longer is in the Army." *1990: Trying to remember the word* demobilize.

"And the look on his face, as the man who was in jail and dying, or living—whatever—for freedom, stood out there, hoping against hope for freedom." *1990: Commenting on Vaclav Havel, President of Czechsolvakia.*

"It's full-time work. It's very interesting. You meet interesting people. It's very important. It's exciting. You live in a beautiful White House. After supper, guess who we walk with? Millie! So it's not all hard work." *1990: Describing his job to Chicago school children. Millie was the First Dog.*

"I read so much sometimes I start to read backwards, which is not very good." *1990*

"So, I'm glad you asked it because then I vented a spleen here." *1990: Defending his China policy.*

"I see this glass not half empty, but half full and more." *1990: Responding to a reporter's question if the Cold War was over.*

"How was the actual deployment thing?" *1990: To astronauts on the space shuttle* Atlantis.

"And for you missile crews, the pointy end is up, and keep 'em in the grass." *1990: During a visit to the Strategic Air Command in Omaha, NE.*

"Kuwait is a country that has been aggressed against." *1990*

"You're burning up time. The meter is running through the sand on you, and I'm now filibustering."

1990: To a reporter's question about the Iran-Contra scandal.

"Well, I'm going to kick that one right into the end zone of the secretary of education. But, yes, we have all—he travels a good deal, goes abroad. We have a lot of people in the department that do[es] that. We're having an international—this is not as much education as dealing with the environment—a big international conference coming up. And we get it all the time—exchange ideas. But I think we've got—we set out there—and I want to give credit to your Governor McWherter and to your former governor Lamar Alexander—we've gotten great ideas for a national goals program from—in this country—from the governors who were responding to, maybe, the principal of your high school, for heaven's sake." *1990: Responding to the question of a high school student in Knoxville, TN: "I was wondering, do you have plans to get ideas internationally to improve education."*

"We'll win the war on drugs because you have what a longtime resident of Orange County, John Wayne, had—true grit." *1990: To a group of school children at the Santa Ana Bowl in Orange County, CA.*

"The great American writer, Mark Train." *1990*

"And I don't want to see this used to eventually—like real soon—raise taxes on the American people." *1990: On a congressional proposal for a tax cut.*

"And, you see, I think there's some real reasons—Asian reasons, if you will—Cambodia and Japan—that we should retain relations with China. . . . I tell you, one of the criticisms that gets me a little, and I vowed—I didn't tell you my New Year's resolution was not to let it get to me—but it's the idea that I don't care about human rights." *1990: Defending his China policy.*

"I think that the arrows have been flying, front, back, sideways, but that's what I get paid for." *1990: On his reversal on a tax increase.*

"Chevy Chase has arrived." *1990: After stumbling into a sign at ceremonies marking a Transportation Department campaign against drunk driving.*

GEORGE BUSH (CONT'D)

"If we get into an armed situation, he's (Saddam Hussein) going to get his ass kicked." *1990: During a White House meeting with members of Congress.*

"A new world of freedom lays before us." *1990*

"We have a big ocean between us and the ah, the ah, the ah, Western Europe." *1990*

"Have a very good time at this museum we're very proudful of." *1990*

"Read my hips." *1990: To reporters following him while he was jogging.*

"Only just yesterday, it seemed that we celebrated the last Super Bowl victory. And now here we are." *1990: To members of the San Francisco 49ers during their visit to the White House one week after winning the Super Bowl.*

"I'm girding up my loins to go into battle to beat back the tax attempts I think are coming, because I think the American people are fed up with it." *1990*

"All those factors come together from a pure foreign-policy standpoint to help the understanding of others about what I do, proudly did, had to do." *1990: On the invasion of Panama.*

"I expect in this job I'll make plenty of mistakes but I don't want to make the wrong mistakes." *1990*

"Good way to go to jail." *1990: When asked if he'd like to make a prediction about the outcome of the 1990 elections.*

"I'm just doing my job as president of the United States. I'm not preparing anybody for anything." *1990*

"They're gonna do it over my dead veto. Or my live veto. Or sump'un like that!" *1990: On suspicions that Democrats might try to raise income tax rates.*

"Obviously, when you see somebody go berserk and get a weapon and go in and murder people, of course it troubles me." *1991: On a mass murder in Texas.*

"Terminator's kind of a pussy, isn't he?" *1991: Commenting on Arnold Schwarzenegger, whom he called 'Terminator,' after playing volleyball with him.*

"It's how Julian Caesar ordered four or five beers." *1991: Holding up his fingers in a "V" sign to reporters and asking if they knew what it meant.*

"When I need a little free advice about Saddam Hussein, I turn to country music." *1991*

"Nobody said it was going to be easy, and nobody was right." *1991*

"I think I've got to do better in making clear what the message is, and I think I can do better. But I think there's so much noise out there that I've got to figure out how to make clearer that we are for the things that I have advocated that would help." *1991: On his economic recovery program.*

"I'm down here to learn about orange juice." *1991: During a trip to Florida.*

"You might argue, technically, are we in a recession or not. But when there's this kind of sluggishness and concern, definitions, heck with it." *1991*

"Play horseshoes. I read, I read a bunch of books . . . I've read, oh, I think 12 books since March. . . . But easy reading—Dan Jenkins and other relaxed treatises, you know, detective stories or something like that.

"Watch TV quite a bit. I watch the news, and I don't like to tell you this because you'll think I'm into some weird TV freak here, but have a set upstairs that has five screens on it. . . . Barbara accuses me of being too much—not too much, but plugged into TV too often, I put it that way. Love sports, though . . . Love to watch a football game . . . Take a rest to relax, read some to relax . . . I love watching movies. . . .

"Love fishing—that's real relaxing for me— real relaxing.

"But I think competitive sports still—tennis and golf and once again horseshoes." *1992: On his hobbies.*

"I mean a child that doesn't have a parent to read to that child or that doesn't see that when the child is hurting to have a parent and help out or neither parent there enough to pick the kid up and dust him off and send him back into the game at school or whatever, that kid has a disadvantage." *1992: On child rearing.*

"Part of the great success was the fact we have an all volunteer army, and part of the all—the military. And part of the rationale is people will have more to say in what they want to do. So a mother—I want to be part of this. I can respect that and understand it." *1992*

"Get the families involved. Help them learn to read—teach their kids to read and all of that. So this program and, gosh, your all's participation in it. I think sends a strong message to the rest of the country that parental involvement is real important. I worry, and I think everyone here does, about the pressures on family. So please stay involved and give these kids the extra ounce of energy and teaching and stuff that comes only from family." *1992: While touring a Head Start facility.*

"I just wanted to get a little attention." *1992: After he vomited and collapsed during a state dinner in Japan.*

"And let me say in conclusion, thanks for the kids. I learned an awful lot about bathtub toys—about how to work the telephone. One guy knows—several of them know their own phone numbers—preparation to go to the dentist. A lot of things I'd forgotten. So it's been a good day." *1992: At a Head Start center in Catonsville, MD.*

"R and E." *1992: Referring to "research and development."*

"I'm all for Lawrence Welk. Lawrence Welk is a wonderful man. He used to be or was, or wherever he is now, bless him. But you don't need $700,000 for a Lawrence Welk museum when we've got tough times and people in New Hampshire are hurting." *1992: Campaigning in New Hampshire while Lawrence Welk was still among the living.*

"So far it did not reverberate in the negative there. The signature is being checked through the master computer, which is located someplace else, and we'll get an answer back after we leave." *1992: On writing a check in a supermarket.*

"Get this [economic plan] passed. Later on, we can all debate it." *1992: Speaking to New Hampshire legislators.*

"While the press is here, was there—did the Democratic governors meet, and is there any feeling that we shouldn't press to try to get something done by March 20th? Do we—is there—can anyone—is there a spokesman on that point? Because what I would like to suggest—not that you'd have to sign every 't' and 'i' but that we urge Congress to move by that date. And if that date isn't good, what date? Is there feeling on that one?" *1992: To the National Governors' Association.*

"All I was doing was appealing for an endorsement, not suggesting you endorse it." *1992: To Colorado Governor Roy Romer.*

"Because I'm a little bit tired—well, I'll give you an example, I'll give you an example. This state of Tennessee had 6,700 Reservists and Guardsmen volunteer—one community of 1,000 had eighteen people—this is the volunteer state, people are still very proud of the fact of this—of Desert Storm. And there is a national pride there, there's a pride in having a strong America. That's my position—a strong America, and having led a very triumphant and very important war over there." *1992*

LINDA YU OF WLS-TV, CHICAGO: "You were here in Chicago last week and everybody wants to know when you went to Billy Goats, did you really like the 'cheezboygers, cheezboygers?'"

PRESIDENT BUSH: "It's your pronunciation I like. Yes, I did. I did. And I got a bum rap. Somebody said I asked for French fries; I didn't. That was the guy that owns the place sitting next to me saying, chips only. Before I even got my mouth open. But, boy, I loved it. I had two 'cheeseburgers.'"
Linda Yu: "Cheezboygers." *1992*

"Ours is a great state, and we don't like limits of any kind. Ricky Clunn is one of the great bass fishermen. He's a Texas young guy, and he's a very competitive fisherman, and he talked about learning to

GEORGE BUSH (CONT'D)

fish wading in the creeks behind his dad. He in his underwear went wading in the creeks behind his father, and he said—as a fisherman he said it's great to grow up in a country with no limits. . . ." *1992: On Texas.*

"Somebody—somebody asked me, what's it take to win? I said to them, I can't remember, what does it take to win the Super Bowl? Or maybe Stein-brenner, my friend George, will tell us what it takes for the Yanks to win—one run. But I went over to the Strawberry Festival this morning, and ate a piece of shortcake over there—able to enjoy it right away, and once I completed it, it didn't have to be approved by Congress—I just went ahead and ate it—and that leads me into what I want to talk to you about today." *1992*

"Total mistake—policy, political, everything else . . . Policy because it simply did not do what I thought—hoped it would do: control this—control—get this economy moving. There were some good things about it, so I can't say—shouldn't say—total mistake. But it was—spending caps is good, getting the spending caps is good, keeping the government going as opposed to shutting down for whatever number of days it would have taken—that was good. But when you have to weigh a decision, in retro-spect—have the benefit of hindsight—I would say both policy and politically, I think we can all agree that it's drawn a lot of fire." *1992: On the 1990 budget agreement.*

"Hey, hey, nihaoma. Hey, yeah, yeah. Heil, heil—a kind of Hitler salute." *Greeting tourists at Lafayette Park on his way home from church. Nihaoma is Mandarin for "How are you?"*

"I guess if I had 90-90 hindsight . . . I'd certainly rethink our position." *1992: On his administration's arming Saddam Hussein early in his term.*

"You cannot be president of the United States if you don't have faith. Remember Lincoln, going to his knees in times of trial and the Civil War and all that stuff. You can't be. And we are blessed. So don't feel sorry for—don't cry for me, Argentina." *1992*

"I think in politics there are certain moral values. I'm one who—we believe strongly in pluralism . . . , but when you get into some questions there are some moral overtones. Murder, that kind of thing . . ." *1992*

"I've told you I don't live and die by the polls. Thus I will refrain from pointing out that we're not doing too bad in those polls." *1992*

"'With frequent changes laws and institutions must go hand in hand with the progress of the human mind. As that becomes more developed, more enlightened, with new discoveries were made, new truth discovered, matters of opinions change is certain of that. Institutions must advance also to keep pace with my times.' If I've ever heard an eloquent plea for term limits, that's it." *1992: Reading from an inscription engraved inside the Jefferson Memorial.*

"Blame the Congress, because we've got the best health care plan there is. And it does not socialize medicine in this country. It preserves the quality of care. It gives health care and access to all and it does it without reducing the quality of American education." *1992*

"We've set these six education goals to reach by the year 2000, and when today's third-and fourth-graders will be taking part in this event—this aca-demic decathlon—by then—and you all know these goals—our kids are going to—one of them, the first one—our kids will be—start school ready to learn." *1992: To the winners of the Academic Decathlon in a Rose Garden ceremony.*

"I never heard of them. But I know that rap is the music where it rhymes." *1992: On rapper Ice Cube.*

"Heckuva guy. I had a hard time relative . . . to somebody whose wingspan with his ears is wider than his total height." *1992: On Ross Perot.*

"It won't be—of course, we have submitted a bal-ance, but it won't be in two years. And we have sub-mitted budgets that get in it. We've got one right up there now that does that. And I think it's going to be five years." *1992: Responding to a question about whether he would submit a balanced budget to Congress if reelected.*

"We are going to keep pushing, because I think the six goals are sound—math and science, and nobody is too old to learn. It gets into your whole feeding of adult education. Tests—volunteer, but nevertheless standard, so a parent can tell how his or her kid adds up to others across the country. And these are good." *1992: At a question-and-answer session with schoolchildren in Marietta, GA.*

"I told him to keep this thing *secret*. I told him, I said, 'If I'm going to meet with you, never discuss it.'" *1992: Commenting on a story in the tabloid* Weekly World News *showing him with an extraterrestrial alien.*

"I see no media mention of it, but we entered in— you asked what time it is and I'm telling you how to build a watch here—but we had Boris Yeltsin here the other day. And I think of my times campaigning in Iowa, years ago, and how there was a— Iowa was kind of, I single out Iowa, it's kind of an international state in a sense and has a great interest in all these things—and we had Yeltsin standing here in the Rose Garden, and we entered into a deal to eliminate the biggest and most threatening ballistic missiles . . . and it was almost, 'Ho-hum, what have you done for me recently?'" *1992: Defending his accomplishments as president.*

"And I salute the secretary for this, and obviously—I wish that you had been with me, sir, when I was in Australia. They were on me about that—how can you treat a friend. I said, look, this is the law, this is what we should and must do, is to use those provisions of the law to enhance our agricultural exports. And it's not aimed at you, Mr. Australian foreign minister or whoever it was that was all over my case down there, it is the law of the land." *1992: Referring to the administration's international agricultural policy, during remarks to the Agricultural Communicators Congress.*

"And I know people are turned off from politics, but that doesn't mean that you withdraw and you pull away from it. If anybody should feel like withdrawing or pulling away from something, I could make a case for the Bush family. But I'm not going to do that, because I do believe in some of the stuff that I—you know, problems that I'm faced to solve, and I'm going to keep on saying what I believe. Yo." *1992*

"Yea, I think there's some social change going on. AIDS, for example, uh, is a, is a, uh, disease for, disease of poverty in a sense. It's where hopelessness is. It's bigger than that, of course, and the hopelessness that comes when you have AIDS inter—, interjecting with narcotics in some areas, not across the whole country. The whole country is doing pretty well in a lot of ways. More Americans at work than any time in the history of this country and a higher percentage of the work force, but I don't think there's quote a malaise unquote in this country. I think there are some serious problems out there, that your question is a very deep and philosophical one. And, of course, there are current sociological currents in this country that, that, uh, lead people to conduct their lives in some ways, but I am one who thinks that at various times in our history we have condoned some of the things we should have condemned. We have gotten away from values in school for one. Some of it is out of post-Watergate, post-Vietnam syndrome, where our kids were taught, for example, about Vietnam, that we were all immoral. My kids were taught that by a good, smart people, who agonized over the war, and look at Vietnam today. We go through cycles, it seems to me. So, yes, there's some underpinnings of discontent, but I don't think that should be used as an excuse for tolerating the use of narcotics." *1992: Appearing before the Association for a Better New York, in answer to the question, "Why do so many Americans want to use drugs? Is there some underlying cause in American life?"*

"You talk about the environment—take a look at that Arkansas River. And I'll have more to say about that in a minute. We've even seen some chickens along the way. Here's one back here. I can't figure out if that chicken is talking about the draft—I can't figure that out or maybe he's talking

GEORGE BUSH (CONT'D)

about that Arkansas River again where they're dumping that—I've got to be careful here—that fecal—some kind of bacteria into the river. Too much from the chicken." *1992*

"And also, if you haven't detected, I'm a little sore at the national media. Let me tell you something. Remember what Harry Truman said, 'They wouldn't know'—I better be careful. Well, I better not say that. I got the—they're mad at me anyway." *1992*

"I am absolutely—I'm driving down to the wire with—I've never felt more energetic. You weren't in this country at the time. And one of the things I'm a little upset about the media, about the national media—always separate out the local media, the photographers, the guys that carry the cameras, but it's these talking heads—and for a while, there was a spate of stories that George Bush is in bad health. We couldn't shake it. Doctor would go out and reveal health records and talk about—I have never felt about—I feel like a spring colt, going right down to the wire." *1992*

"We're enjoying sluggish times, and not enjoying them very much." *1992*

"Why don't you roll me under the table, and I'll sleep it off until you finish dinner." *1992: After vomiting on the Japanese prime minister during a state dinner.*

"Now it's back to the real world." *1993: On leaving the White House.*

"Too bad. The hell with them." *1995: On Washington eggheads who refused to believe that he truly enjoys country music.*

"I don't get out much anymore. I don't get asked out much anymore. It's amazing how many people beat you at golf now that you're no longer president." *1996*

"Unlike Churchill, I have no plans to shape history. . . . Socrates gave advice—and they poisoned him." *1997*

"Millie went paws up, and we're very sorry." *1997: On the former First Pooch, an English Springer Spaniel, who died in mid-May at the Bush's summer home in Kennebunkport, ME.*

"Had my chance. We did our bit. We did a lot of things right, some wrong." *1997: On his presidency.*

"Not even being dead? It's a terrible thing. It would be better if you were dead; then you couldn't see it as clearly." *1997: When asked how it feels to be memorialized in his new presidential library and museum at Texas A&M University.*

"The thing I miss most about the White House is the Marine Band." *1998: Confiding to Bill Clinton at a White House dinner serenaded by the 148-person band, known as "the president's own."*

GEORGE W. BUSH
(Governor of Texas)

"Then I misquoted, then I misspoke myself. I'm still exploring." *1999: Clarifying a story suggesting that he has decided to run for president.*

"Marijuana? Cocaine? I'm not going to talk about what I did as a child." *1999: The presidential hopeful, to a reporter asking if he had ever used drugs.*

ROBERT BYRD
(Senator)

"I hope this message will find its way to the right audiences in the . . . circles of those countries whose promises are hanging out." *1991: On nations who had not yet paid their pledged support for the Gulf War.*

C

PAT CADDELL
(Political Advisor)

"He's developing his thinking. I've never seen a politican go through an intellectual exercise like this." *1991: On Jerry Brown running for the Democratic presidential nomination.*

MINDY CAMERON
(Editorial Page Editor, Seattle Times)

"We were curious to see what the First Lady had to say to readers. Not that much, it turns out." *1996: On the paper's decision to drop a column written by Hillary Rodham Clinton.*

CARROLL CAMPBELL
(Governor of South Carolina)

"He's very good at seeing the train go, jumping on the caboose, and running from the caboose to the engine." *1996: On Bill Clinton.*

JOHN CARMAN
(Journalist)

"Most of us might say that the closest we've come to the criminally insane, aside from occasional contact with the Internal Revenue Service, is in the movies." *1992*

BILL CARPENTER
(Mayor of Independence, MO)

"The difference between rape and seduction is salesmanship." *1990*

DAVID CARR
(Newspaper Editor)

"People listen to 'The Body' and say, 'He is no moron.' But really, he is a moron." *1998: The editor of* Washington City Paper, *who worked with Jesse "The Body" Ventura who was elected governor of Minnesota.*

JIMMY CARTER
(President of the United States)

"Yesterday, a woman came up to me and said, 'If you still lust in your heart, Mr. President, I'm available.'" *1993*

"Quite often . . . these little guys, who might be making atomic weapons or who might be guilty of some human-rights violations or whatever, are looking for someone to listen to their problems and to help them communicate." *1994: On dealing with dictators.*

"I told him about my nickel a week. It didn't seem to make much of an impression on him." *1998: Remembering the reaction of a Chinese leader to Carter's weekly donation of 5 cents to missionaries in China when he was a child.*

"As one of the few leaders who have served in the White House, I have deplored and been deeply embarrassed by what has occurred there. I've also deplored and been embarrassed by the reaction to it, the overemphasis on it." *1998: Commenting on the Clinton–Lewinsky affair.*

JAMES CARVILLE
(Clinton Campaign Advisor)

"I'm a little like a piano player in a whorehouse. Somebody out there hums something, I try to pick it up." *1992*

"Dukakis fucked up because he didn't tell people what he was about. [The party] never said, 'I'm on your side.' I think any fucking fool could have turned that Pledge of Allegiance shit around. They coulda said, 'Look, George, lemme tell you something, pardner. In West Virginia, they had six kids who didn't say the Pledge, and they made them take castor oil. They castrated a Jehovah's Witness in Nebraska. And you know George, if you can't stand up for six kids in West Virginia, how you gonna stand up for workin' people? Now take your goddamn goofy Pledge of Allegiance issue and jam it up your stupid WASP ass!'" *1992: On how he would have handled the issue of the Pledge of Allegiance in the 1988 campaign.*

"Suzy—come on over here, front and center. Blow jobs for these boys, right now." *1992: The campaign manager for Bill Clinton, to "a young blonde intern sitting nearby" after he rounded up two male workers who had done some good research for the 1988 Frank Lautenberg campaign in New Jersey.*

"I can just hear my answers at the confirmation hearing. 'But Senator . . . I didn't know she was 17!'" *1992: On why he probably wouldn't get a Cabinet-level post.*

"Pat Buchanan wants to make English the national language—what's Strom Thurmond gonna do?" *1992*

"My slogan is, Don't get mad, don't get even, just get elected. *Then* get even." *1992*

"A ceiling fan messes up your sister's hairdo. Your brother-in-law is also your uncle." *1994: Describing how to tell if you are white trash.*

"Six months ago, the surgeon general said we should teach masturbation in school. I said to myself, 'Just

JAMES CARVILLE (CONT'D)

my luck! Thirty years after I graduated, they think of something I could have made an A in.'" *1995*

"The Republicans must love families, they have so many of them. I'm offering a reward to any Republican candidate who's left his wife for an older woman." *1996: On the marriages of the GOP candidates for the presidential nomination.*

"The only thing Perot ought to run for is a psychiatrist's office." *1996*

"Politics is show business for ugly people." *1996*

"Here I am: 56 hours of F's [at Lousiana State University]. It just goes to show you how far a stupid, ugly guy can go in this world. So all of you guys with zits and F's: Hang in there." *1996: In a commencement address at the University of Virginia in Charlottesville.*

"I went home and bit her." *1996: On being called a "rabid dog" by his Republican wife Mary Matalin.*

"I can sort of paraphrase what Dante said, that the hot blooded shall be judged differently from the cold hearted. . . . If the biggest thing I gotta deal with in my life is somebody fibbing to me about sex, I think I can deal with that pretty good." *1998: On the Clinton White House scandals.*

"What was it Ricky used to tell Lucy? I think the president's got some splaining to do. I think, to paraphrase Queen Victoria, she's not amused. I think the president's going to spend a little time in the woodshed here." *1998: On the Clinton White House scandals.*

"They forgot the rule of holes. And the rule of holes stated thusly is: When you've dug yourself into a hole, the first thing you do is stop digging. And these Republicans are intent on keeping on digging. . . ." *1998: On the Linda Tripp tapes and the falling public approval of the GOP.*

ALEX CASTELLANOS
(Political Consultant)

"Ordinarily, you would think this would inhibit the president's ability to carry out his agenda.

Fortunately, Clinton doesn't have one, so it really doesn't impair his ability to do anything." *1997: On the Supreme Court's ruling that Paula Jones can go ahead with her suit against Bill Clinton.*

JIM CHAPMAN
(Congressman)

"If I could have remembered the conversation, I would say that up until now, I thought that sigh of relief was because I agreed to support him on some issue." *1998: According to the Starr Report, Chapman was one of three members of Congress who President Clinton spoke on the phone with while being intimate with Monica Lewinsky.*

AL CHECCHI
(Politician)

"My candidacy is not for sale since I'm paying for it myself." *1998: Checchi spent $18 million of his own money in his unsuccessful run for the Democratic party's nomination for governor of California.*

"It's easier to teach economics to Democrats than compassion to Republicans." *1998*

SABBARUDDIN CHIK
(Malaysia's Minister for Culture, Arts & Tourism)

"Something different from the norm." *1998: On why tourists might find mass-circumcision ceremonies interesting.*

SUMMA CHING HAI
(Supreme Master of the Ching Hai Cult)

"The Clinton money is nothing. It's only $600,000 for God's sake!" *1997: Wondering aloud why anyone would object to her insignificant contribution to a Bill Clinton legal aid fund.*

"If I help a man who has some stress because of a flood, why would I not help a President who is stressed? If the American people would allow me, I would give him $2 million right now." *1997: On her humanitarian concerns for Bill Clinton.*

WARREN CHRISTOPHER
(Former Secretary of State)

"Having your portrait painted is a strange experience. At the same time, to anyone who has served in Washington, there is something oddly familiar about it. First, you are painted into a corner. Then you are hung out to dry. And finally, you are framed." *1999: At the unveiling of his portrait in the State Department.*

JOHNNY CHUNG
(Businessman & Contributor to the Democratic National Committee)
"I see the White House is like a subway—you have to put in coins to open the gates." *1997: On his $366,000 contribution to the Democratic National Committee between 1994 and 1996.*

"Please keep in mind that I didn't create this system. You did." *1999: Testifying before Congress on his role as intermediary for Chinese government contributions to the Democratic National Committee.*

JENNY CHURCH
(Journalist)
"The astrologer told him: 'Your moon is in Jupiter, your head is in Uranus.'" *1995: Commenting in the* Los Angeles Times *on the news that former Orange County, CA, treasurer Robert Citron relied on a mail-order astrologer and a psychic for his failed interest-rate predictions.*

CLARK CLIFFORD
(Political Advisor & Former Defense Secretary)
"Welcome aboard, we will tell more lies now." *1991: Clifford's words according to BCCI official Ahdur Sakhia when Sakhia introduced his successor to Clifford.*

BILL CLINTON
(President of the United States)
"You bet . . . That's the job I want. That's the job I'll do for the next four years." *1990: While running for reelection as governor of Arkansas, when asked, "Will you guarantee to us that, if reelected, there is absolutely, positively no way that you'll run for another political office and that you'll serve out your term in full?" The next year Clinton announced his candidacy for president.*

"I was just lucky, I guess." *1992: On why he wasn't drafted during the Vietnam War. A well-connected uncle successfully lobbied the draft board on Clinton's behalf.*

"If you want a perfect candidate, vote for somebody else." *1992*

"You know, I have acknowledged wrongdoing. I have acknowledged causing pain in my marriage. I have said things to you tonight and to the American people from the beginning that no American politician ever has." *1992: To Diane Sawyer on* 60 Minutes.

"I'll be there for you 'til the last dog dies." *1992*

"When I was in England, I experimented with marijuana a time or two, and I didn't like it and didn't inhale and never tried it again." *1992*

"I like to play the saxophone because you don't inhale." *1992*

"Where I come from, a cow pie means something else. . . . If I came home from the state of Wisconsin and said I ate a cow pie, they'd say, 'The presidency's not worth that, Bill.'" *1992: When a dairy farmer handed him a chocolate candy called a Wisconsin Cow Pie.*

"If I could wave my arm and make HIV-positive go away and all of you that have it, I would, so help me God I would, and I'd give up my race for the White House for that." *1992: In a speech at a gay fund-raiser in Los Angeles.*

"Nearly everyone will lie to you, given the right circumstances." *1992*

"You know, Bush is always comparing me to Elvis in sort of unflattering ways. I don't think Bush would have liked Elvis very much, and that's just another thing that's wrong with him." *1992*

"The chart you had was very moving." *1992: At his economic summit. The chart showed the difference in wages earned by college- and high-school-educated workers.*

"This is still the greatest country in the world, if we just will steel our wills and lose our minds." *1992*

"I think Mr. Darman has proved himself an expert on math not adding up." *1993: On criticisms of his*

BILL CLINTON (CONT'D)

economic plan by Bush budget chief Richard Darman, who disclosed in January 1993 that the federal deficit would be some $60 billion higher than expected.

"Gosh, I miss the Cold War. We had an intellectually coherent thing. The American people knew what the rules were." *1993*

"I've been criticized for doing more than one thing at once. . . . Would it be nice if you could pay your bills and not earn any money to pay them? I don't understand this whole—you can't do one thing at once. But anyway, that's what they say." *1993: During an appearance at a Cleveland shopping mall.*

"I don't eat much junk food." *1993: When asked about his taste for fast food.*

"I don't necessarily consider McDonald's junk food. I eat at McDonald's and Burger King and these other fast-food places. A lot of them have very nutritious food . . . chicken sandwiches . . . salads." *1993: Amending the previous assertion.*

"I'm real sorry this happened to you. I've wanted to do this ever since the first time I laid eyes on you." *1993: To Kathleen Willey, a Richmond, VA, socialite who worked as a volunteer in the White House and who had come to see the president to ask for a paying job. According to Willey the president pulled her to him and hugged her, then began fondling her breasts and placed her hand against his erect penis. She left the office after someone knocked on the door and interrupted the president's advances. Coincidentally, Willey's husband committed suicide on the same day as her encounter with Clinton.*

"Come on. Come on. Listen, goddammit. You can't do that. You can't bring me out here with the mayor and a congresswoman and push them back." *1993: Showing his temper to an aide who blocked Washington, D.C., Mayor Sharon Pratt Kelly and congressional delegate Eleanor Holmes Norton from joining him in a photo op with local construction workers.*

"Secretary Reich could almost live in there." *1993: Referring to the four-foot-ten-inch Secretary of Labor*

Robert Reich as they examined a Lego model of the White House.

"The prescription drug industry is spending one billion more dollars a year on advertising than they are on developing new jugs. Er, drugs." *1993*

"I am a lot like Baby Huey. I'm fat. I'm ugly. But if you push me down, I keep coming back. I just keep coming back." *1994*

"It was a real sort of Southern deal. I had AstroTurf in the back. You don't want to know why, but I did." *1994: Reminiscing about an El Camino pickup truck he once owned, while visiting a GM plant in Louisiana. Two days later Clinton told radio talk-show host Don Imus, "I carried my luggage back there—it wasn't for what everybody thought it was for when I made the comment, I'll tell you that. I'm guilty of a lot of things but I didn't do that."*

"I grew up in a little town in Arkansas that had a substantial Lithuanian population. So I grew up knowing about the problems of Baltic nations." *1994: Before his visit to Latvia, on foreign-affairs experience he gained in Hope, AR.*

"I wish someone had told me that before I showed up with a neutered cat." *1994: After being told President Harry Truman's advice on Washington: "If you really want a friend in this town, get yourself a dog."*

"Being president is like running a cemetery; you've got a lot of people under you and nobody's listening." *1995*

"I identify with Babe Ruth. He was a little overweight, and he struck out a lot. But he hit a lot of home runs because he went to bat." *1995*

"Close the door. She'll be in here for a while." *1995: To Secret Service officer Lewis Fox, who was posted outside the Oval Office, after Monica Lewinsky arrived for a presidential visit. When Fox's shift ended forty minutes later, she had not come out.*

"There are so many turkeys in Washington, I should pardon at least one." *1995: On why he spared the ceremonial White House turkey the day before Thanksgiving.*

"Every time somebody has made a charge related to the Whitewater issue, it's turned up dry. I've said before and I'll say again, if everybody in this country had the character that my wife has, we'd be a better place to live." *1996*

"Presidents have feelings, too." *1996: Referring to his irritation after a barrage of media stories questioning the credibility of first lady Hillary Rodham Clinton.*

"I'd love to play with you . . . sometime." *1996: To k.d. lang during her visit to the Oval Office. Clinton was referring to playing the saxophone with lang.*

"You know, if I were a single man, I might ask that mummy out. That's a good-looking mummy." *1996: At a Democratic party fund-raiser, on the subject of the frozen 500-year-old Inca "ice princess" on display at the National Geographic Society in Washington.*

"If I said anything which implies that I think that we didn't do what we should have done given the choices we faced at the time I shouldn't have said that." *1996*

"I'm just trying to be fair." *1996: While nibbling a cheeseburger, pirogi, cheese cornbread, barbecued pork, rice, and tandoori chicken at a Chicago smorgasbord.*

"In the fine arts we've been blessed with the exuberance of Italians in music, from Toscanini to Sinatra to Jon Bon Jovi." *1996: On the contribution of Italian-Americans to the nation's cultural life.*

"This is the last day of my last campaign. I will never seek office again, unless I go home and run for the school board some day." *1996: After winning reelection as president.*

"The last time I checked, the Constitution said, 'of the people, by the people and for the people.' That's what the Declaration of Independence says." *1996: Quoting the Gettysburg Address.*

"If you live long enough, one person you know couldn't help doing the wrong thing, yet you couldn't help liking him. They have some good qualities, they were loyal to you, but you knew they just couldn't do the right thing." *1997: On the human truths in the*

books of Walter Mosely that make him one of the president's favorite writers.

"I was the only man in the class for the longest time. And it was really fun." *1997: Remembering a yoga class he once took when he was in Yale Law School.*

"I felt a special relationship to Elvis Presley because he was from Mississippi, he was a poor white kid, he sang with a lot of soul. He was sort of my roots." *1997*

"Almost makes you want to go to jail out here, doesn't it?" *1997: On viewing Bellver Castle, a fourteenth-century fortress that was once a prison, in Palma de Mallorca, Spain.*

"It's the same old stuff. I'm not worried about it." *1997: Referring to the fund-raising videotapes that were lost and then found and turned over to a Senate committee investigating political fund-raising.*

"It is not an improper relationship and I know what the word means. . . . The relationship was not sexual." *1998: When asked about his alleged affair with Monica Lewinsky.*

"It means that there is not a sexual relationship, an improper sexual relationship, or any other kind of improper relationship." *1998: When asked about his alleged affair with Monica Lewinsky.*

"I don't know any more about it than I've told you, and any more about it, really, than you do. But I will cooperate. The charges are not true. And I haven't asked anyone to lie." *1998: When asked about his alleged affair with Monica Lewinsky.*

"I did not urge anyone to say anything that was untrue." *1998: To interviewer Jim Lehrer of PBS's NewsHour on the Monica Lewinsky scandal.*

"I want you to listen to me. I'm going to say this again. I did not have sexual relations with that woman, Miss Lewinsky. I never told anybody to lie a single time. Never. These allegations are false, and I need to go back to work for the American people." *1998: Denying an alleged affair with a then twenty-one-year-old White House intern Monica Lewinsky.*

BILL CLINTON (CONT'D)

"I'm just getting warmed up." *1998: To a woman in a reception line in the White House in early March who, when she finally came face to face with him, whispered to him, "Don't let the bastards get you down."*

"Yes. And I like to see them concentrated here." *1998: After a wildlife tour in Botswana, when asked if a Democratic president can admire an elephant, symbol of the Republican party.*

"If I was there, I would give you a big kiss. But then you'd have to sue me." *1998: To his lawyer Robert Bennett, who had called to tell him a federal judge had dismissed Paula Jones's sexual harassment lawsuit against him.*

"This is the only thing every year, no matter what else happens, I know I will do right." *1998: As he prepared to blow the whistle starting the annual White House Easter Egg Roll, which included 30,000 children and adults.*

"I'm a very schmaltzy person, so I get all choked up when I come here. I keep imagining whether I'm standing someplace where John Lennon was and all that." *1998: During a fund-raising luncheon at the Dakota, the New York apartment building where John Lennon lived and was killed.*

"No one concerned about fighting crime would even think about saying, 'Well, three years from now we're going to throw out the criminal code and we'll figure out what to put in its place.'" *1998: Denouncing a proposal by the National Federation of Independent Business to scrap the existing tax code by 2001 and replace it with a flat tax or a national sales tax.*

"Indeed, I did have a relationship with Ms. Lewinsky that was not appropriate. In fact, it was wrong. It constituted a critical lapse in judgement and a personal failure on my part for which I am solely and completely responsible." *1998: Admitting his improper relationship with Monica Lewinsky.*

"I was not contrite enough. . . . I have repented." *1998: Begging for forgiveness at the White House prayer breakfast on September 11, 1998.*

"I'm having to become quite an expert in this business of asking for forgiveness." *1998: In a speech on Martha's Vineyard marking the thirty-fifth anniversary of Martin Luther King's I Have a Dream Address.*

"I let you down. I let my family down. I let this country down. But I'm trying to make it right." *1998: Speaking to an audience in Florida just before the release of the Starr Report.*

"It is in the hands of Congress and the people of this country—ultimately in the hands of God. There is nothing I can do." *1998: On the House vote in October to begin an impeachment inquiry.*

"I loved *Road Kill.* I had to read it to make sure it wasn't a biography of me." *1998: In a jacket blurb for a new mystery novel by Kinky Friedman.*

"I deplored the innocent people they were tormenting and traumatizing." *1998: Speaking of the lawyers for Paula Jones.*

"I'd give anything in the world not to have to admit what I've had to admit today." *1998: During his videotaped grand jury appearance.*

"My goal in this deposition was to be truthful, but not particularly helpful." *1998: During his taped deposition.*

"We could give it all back to you and hope you spend it right." *1999: To supporters in Buffalo, NY, expressing his belief that the government is in a better position than the public to decide how to spend the budget surplus responsibly, preferably on Social Security.*

"This dog is limping but going." *1999: To adoring fans in New Hampshire.*

"Sometimes I feel like the fire hydrant looking at a pack of dogs." *1999: To an Interior Department gathering.*

"What I hope is that she will be permitted to go on with her life, and I hope it'll be a good life." *1999: Attempting closure following the Monica Lewinsky interview with Barbara Walters.*

"I ask you literally to go get down an atlas and look at the map." *1999: Selling U.S. airstrikes in Kosovo to the American people.*

"Let me tell you, through it all, I still believe in a place called . . . Hell." *1999: Joking about his impeachment ordeal at the annual Gridiron Dinner.*

"I do not regard this impeachment vote as some great badge of shame." *1999*

"I hate it when people blame someone else and don't take responsibility." *1999: Discussing with Virginia students the problems he sees with American youth that may have led to the high school shootings in Littleton, CO.*

"No. 53! I mean, what does a guy have to do to make the top 50?" *1999: In mock anger that his impeachment due to the Lewinsky sex affair didn't rank in the top 50 stories of the century compiled by the Newseum, a journalism museum.*

"If she's successful, I'll happily go to the Senate spouses' meeting if that's part of the job." *1999: On the possibility of the first lady being elected to the Senate.*

HILLARY RODHAM CLINTON
(First Lady)

"We've just screwed all these people!" *1993: To her husband Bill upon learning at a White House reception that thousands of people outside might not get to see the first family.*

"I thought you were real people." *1993: Dis-inviting a crowd of spectators to a White House reception after the swearing-in of Supreme Court Justice Ruth Bader Ginsburg, when she learned they were members of the press.*

"Well, everything." *1994: When asked what food President Clinton likes best.*

"The White House is just like a box of chocolates. Pretty on the outside but inside there's lots of nuts." *1995*

"My theory is, don't do it before you're 21—and then don't tell me about it." *1995: On teens and sex.*

"My mother took some offense [at columnist William Safire's accusation], because being called a congenital liar seemed to reflect badly on her and my late father." *1996*

"We were always answering questions on the fly, especially during the '92 presidential campaign." *1996*

"I apparently remind some people of their mother-in-law or their boss or something." *1996: On why some people can't stand her.*

"Shortly before I arrived, I had one of my conversations with Mrs. Roosevelt. She thinks this is a terrific idea." *1996: Joking about her much discussed conversation with "guru" Jean Houston, during a speech at a conference on families.*

"How could you be so damn stupid? How could you do that?" *1996: To husband Bill in front of White House aides. She wanted him to rise above his preoccupation with bills that were pending in Congress and to behave more presidentially.*

"Hair to me has always been the one part of my body that I had control over. I could not grow any taller. I could not lengthen my legs. I could not make my eyes have perfect vision—there was nothing else I could really do. But my hair has always been a source of great amusement for me." *1997*

"I'm not about to start caring about things that I've never cared about because it's not appropriate in somebody else's mind for me to continue to care about what I've always cared about." *1997: Rejecting suggestions that she occupy herself with uncontroversial issues during her husband's second term.*

"We're trying to get everyone in a good mood." *1997: Telling viewers on the* Rosie O'Donnell Show *that she and the president want Americans to cheer up.*

"I like men who are kind of rough on the outside, but have hearts of gold." *1997: On the* Rosie O'Donnell Show, *when informed that Oscar the Grouch, the Sesame Street character, had a crush on the first lady.*

"Sometimes I'll look at my husband and he'll be doing something really official and important and I'll think, my gosh, he's the president and we live in the White House." *1997*

HILLARY RODHAM CLINTON (CONT'D)

"In our country we expect so much from the woman who is married to the president." *1997*

"I have to confess that it has crossed my mind that you could not be a Republican and a Christian." *1997: Addressing the National Prayer Breakfast.*

"That's part of the continuing saga of Whitewater . . . the never-ending fictional conspiracy that honest-to-goodness reminds me of some people's obsession with UFOs and the Hale-Bopp comet some days." *1997: Denying any White House attempt to get hush money to former Associate Attorney General Webster Hubbell.*

"I have talked to my husband about everything, but I don't, you know, ever talk about my conversations with my husband. But I can state unequivocally that, as my husband has said, these are false allegations." *1998: On allegations that her husband had an improper relationship with Monica Lewinsky.*

"This is—the great story here for anybody willing to find it and write about it and explain it—is this vast right-wing conspiracy that has been conspiring against my husband since the day he announced his candidacy for president. A few journalists have kind of caught on to it and explained it. But it has not yet been fully revealed to the American public. And actually, you know, in a bizarre sort of way, this may do it." *1998: Explaining the feeding-frenzy of the media following allegations that her husband had a sexual relationship with a White House intern, Monica Lewinsky.*

"You must take very good care of this goat!" *1998: To Senegalese villagers upon hearing that they had named a billy goat "Bill Clinton."*

"I'm tired of all these wussy guys wringing their hands." *1998: On why she decided to go on the* Today Show *to defend her husband against allegations he'd had an affair with White House intern Monica Lewinsky.*

"Don't confuse having a career with having a life. They are not the same." *1998: Delivering Howard University's commencement speech.*

"I think a lot of this is prejudice against our state. They couldn't be doing this if we were from some other state." *1998: Blaming her husband's legal and ethical difficulties on the fact that he is from Arkansas. Earlier she blamed his difficulties on a "vast right-wing conspiracy."*

"All things considered, actually, it wasn't too bad." *1998: Responding to a reporter's question, "Did you have a nice summer?"*

"I was on the cover of *Vogue* magazine. I don't need any resolutions." *1999: When asked if she made any New Year's resolutions.*

"Part of growing up is learning how to control one's impulses." *1999: Introducing her husband, Bill, at a gun-control press conference.*

"It's probably a contradiction, like all things—men, women, night, day." *1999: Commenting on a ceiling painting of a deep-blue sky and stars inside an Egyptian temple she visited during her tour of North Africa.*

"And what is so amazing is that Bill has not been defeated by this. There has been enormous pain, enormous anger, but I have been with him half my life and he is a very, very good man. We just have a deep connection that transcends whatever happens." *1999: On her husband's infidelities.*

"We like to lie in bed and watch old movies—you know those little individual video machines you can hold in your lap?" *1999: On nights with her husband.*

"You know in Christian theology there are sins of weakness and sins of malice, and this was a sin of weakness." *1999: On her husband's affair with Monica Lewinsky.*

"I was thinking of when Peter betrayed Jesus three times and Jesus knew it but loved him anyway." *1999: Making a biblical comparison with her marriage to President Clinton.*

BEN COHEN

(Co-founder of Ben & Jerry's Homemade, Inc. & Member of Business Leaders for Sensible Priorities)
"The United States is now, literally, in an arms race with itself." *1999: Reacting to President Clinton's proposed increase in the military budget.*

RICHARD COHEN
(Political Columnist)

"I hope Clarence Thomas gets to hear Clinton's case." *1998: On Kathleen Willey's allegations against the president.*

SILVIO CONTE
(Congressman)

"And a-one, and a-two, and a-three . . . and a $500,000. What are they going to do for an encore? Earmark funds to renovate Guy Lombardo's speedboat or restore Artie Shaw's wedding tuxedo?" *1990: On a government plan to restore Lawrence Welk's boyhood home in Strasburg, ND.*

MICHAEL COONEY
(Attorney)

"To forcibly remove a politician from public office, one has to meet a much higher standard of dishonesty." *1991: To residents of Santa Barbara, CA, demanding the resignation of a city councilman who switched price tags on items he was buying at a store.*

KATIE COURIC
(Today Show Host)

"I, for one, hope my kids are watching *Barney*." *1998: On her show's coverage of the alleged presidential sex scandal, including details not necessarily suitable for children.*

ALAN CRANSTON
(Senator)

"I decided I wanted to live as long as possible and that the human race would be better off if people lived longer." *1992*

H. R. CRAWFORD
(Washington, D.C., City Council Member)

"Here is one of the most politically powerful people in the country, suddenly without a job, no pension, no retirement. I thought it was most fitting that he get at least a nice, fine car." *1991: Crawford headed a committee that raised money to buy former Washington Mayor Marion Barry a $25,000 car.*

NORMAN CHRISTOPHER
(Town Commissioner of Mardela Springs, MD)

"I forgot no one was working. Everyone had Buckwheat's birthday off." *1992: On why he had* trouble contacting employees on Martin Luther King Day.

MICHAEL CROWLEY
(Journalist)

"From his earliest years, Joe Kennedy has been trying to fight off the reasonable suspicion that he's not as sharp as, say, the average butter knife." *1997*

RANDY CUNNINGHAM
(Congressman)

"[They are] the same ones that would put homos in the military." *1995: Slamming supporters of a measure to make the military comply with water-pollution laws.*

"[It's] just not natural, unless maybe you're Barney Frank." *1998: Describing a rectal cancer treatment procedure he received by referring to gay Congressman Frank from Massachusetts. Cunningham later apologized for the remark.*

MARIO CUOMO
(Governor of New York)

"These are human beings. This disturbs me. I don't know why." *1990: On why he signed a bill banning the tossing or bowling of dwarfs.*

"What am I disapproving of? Their judgement? God forbid! I mean, what am I disapproving of? Their sincerity? Their enterprise? Their energy? Their independence? Their willingness to sacrifice? The little glimmer of Don Quixote in their souls? Their individuality? Their David complex? Their willingness to take on the great fight? If I were to criticize them for that, I would be declaring invalid everything I've tried to be. Would you have me condemn myself?" *1992: On whether he disapproved of those writing his name on New Hampshire primary ballots.*

D

ROBERT DALLEK
(Historian)

"He was a principled scoundrel." *1998: The biographer of Lyndon B. Johnson, summing up the character of the late president.*

LISA DALLOS
(Spokesperson for George *Magazine)*
"She does have unique political experience. I'll have to speak to the powers that be." *1998: When asked about Monica Lewinsky having put "anything at George" on her list of dream jobs. John F. Kennedy Jr. edited the magazine.*

EUGENE DALY
(Journalist)
"Dan Quayle may not be able to spell potato but Clinton has had even more trouble with tomatoes." *1992*

ALFONSE D'AMATO
(Senator)
"Let me into Latvia!" *1990: During a mission to the Soviet Union, while standing at the border of Lithuania.*

"Those guys could screw up a two-car funeral procession." *1991: On federal banking commissioners.*

RICHARD DARMAN
(White House Budget Director)
"I have no idea what White House statement was issued, but I stand behind it 100 percent." *1990*

"He didn't say that. He read what was given to him in a speech." *1992: Replying to complaints that Bush had broken a promise to environmentalists.*

GRAY DAVIS
(Governor of California)
"Most voters want you to win the governorship, not buy it." *1998: California's lieutenant governor and candidate for the Democratic party's nomination for governor. He raised only $4 million for his campaign.*

PATTY DAVIS
(Presidential Daughter)
"It was like for years every morning I had been walking out of the house with this button on saying, 'Hi, my name is Patti and my mother is very controlling and my father just bombed Libya.'" *1998: In a speech at a New York College. Mom and Dad are Nancy and Ronald Reagan.*

DENNIS DECONCINI
(Senator)
"When I met Mother Teresa—I believe it was in 1986 in this city—I was introduced to her and told her what state I came from . . . and the first thing she said was, 'How is my friend Charles Keating?'" *1990*

"We're finally going to wrassle to the ground this gigantic orgasm that is just out of control." *1992: On the Constitutional amendment to require a balanced budget.*

TOM DELAY
(Congressman)
"Here's a flower child with gray hairs doing exactly what he did back in the '60s—he's apologizing for the actions of the United States. Wherever he went. It just offends me that the president of the United States is, directly or indirectly, attacking his own country in a foreign land." *1998: The House Republican whip after President Clinton expressed regret about America's involvement in the African slave trade.*

"He's very quick to apologize for other people's mistakes, but he won't apologize for his own, and it comes back to character." *1998: Criticizing Clinton's remarks about slavery during his Africa trip.*

"Money is not the root of all evil in politics. Money is the lifeblood of politics." *1998: The House majority whip, opposing campaign reform proposals that he and other Republican leaders said would violate the right to freedom of speech.*

WALTER DELLINGER
(Acting U.S. Solicitor General)
"The least costly treatment for any illness is lethal medication." *1997: Urging the Supreme Court not to establish a constitutional right to physician-assisted suicide because of the danger of abuses.*

MIKE DEWINE
(Senator)
"Sorry for the crowding, but welcome to coach class." *1998: DeWine (R-Ohio), chairman of the subcommittee on antitrust, to seven airline executives squeezed around a single witness table.*

JOHN DINGLE
(Congressman)

"As they say in *Hamlet*, 'There's something fishy in Denmark.'" *1993*

CHRISTOPHER DODD
(Senator & Democratic National Committee Co-chairman)

"There's value in listening to people." *1995*

"We've got a strong candidate. I'm trying to think of his name." *1996: On Elliott Close, who unsuccessfully opposed GOP Senator Strom Thurmond, ninety-three, in South Carolina.*

"Actually, most people wanted to know whether or not Bob Dole had experimented with beer during Prohibition." *1996: Joking about revelations of youthful pot-smoking by politicians and White House aides.*

BOB DOLE
(Senator & Presidential Candidate)

SENATOR DOLE: "The media have a role to play, and I do not think the media are wrong all the time."

SADDAM HUSSEIN: "Neither are they always right."

SENATOR DOLE: "I always say they are wrong all the time, especially given that they attack me. [But] I am not talking about myself." *1990: During a talk with Saddam Hussein in Iraq in the spring of 1990.*

"There they are. Look at them—See No Evil, Hear No Evil, and Evil." *1991: On being shown a photograph of ex-presidents Carter, Ford, and Nixon at the 1981 funeral of Anwar Sadat.*

"[Public television viewers are] 'affluent, highly educated, the movers and shakers, the socially conscious and the well informed.' What about the rest of us?" *1992: Speaking against federal funding for public television.*

"Life is very important to Americans." *1993: When asked whether American lives are more important than foreign lives.*

"Dave Gergen would probably stay. . . . The furniture, Al Gore—things like that would probably go." *1994: Senate Minority Leader Robert Dole on what he would change if he were in the White House.*

"We kind of wonder sometimes what we're doing here." *1994: On himself and his fellow senators.*

"Every time I look at Strom Thurmond, I'm inspired. . . . When I see him eat a banana, I eat a banana." *1995*

"He's in the right wing of the Capitol. But to get there you gotta take a right, then you take another far right, and then you go to the extreme right, and he should be right there." *1995: Offering to help the Tonight Show staff track down Sonny Bono's office.*

"The wind doesn't bother me. I'm in the U.S. Senate." *1995: Campaigning on a breezy day, on C-Span.*

"My cholesterol's lower than Clinton's, my blood pressure's lower than Clinton's, my weight is less than Clinton's. I am not going to make health an issue." *1995: Dole, seventy-two, on the age factor in the '96 presidential race.*

"If anybody can tell me precisely what the 1994 election message was, I'll eat their hat." *1995*

"I will not tolerate intolerance." *1996*

"We do have thousands and thousands and thousands of people—and they're all on my short list for vice president." *1996: To Republican lawmakers after wrapping up the party's nomination for president.*

"Like a lot of people in this audience, the war came." *1996: In a speech at a rally after the California primary.*

"If something happened along the route and you had to leave your children with Bob Dole or Bill Clinton, I think you'd probably leave your children with Bob Dole." *1996: In a campaign speech.*

"We're trying to get good pictures. Don't worry very much about what I say." *1996: On the campaign trail.*

"Beats me." *1996: When asked by a reporter what important quality he would most want voters to know about him.*

"We know it's not good for kids. But a lot of other things aren't good. Some would say milk's not good." *1996: On tobacco. Tobacco companies have contributed*

BOB DOLE (CONT'D)

$385, 000 to his campaign. Dole refused to back legislation to have the FDA regulate tobacco.

"It's all about the future. That's where we're headed in this country." *1996*

"Probably." *1996: On whether he would be rooting for the National or the American league in baseball's All-Star game.*

"You always feel a little older in the morning. By noon I'll feel about 55." *1996: Celebrating his seventy-third birthday.*

"My mother used to wash our mouths out when we used four-letter words with soap." *1996*

"I'm going to be like Nomo—I'm going to pitch a no-hitter from now until Nov. 5. The Brooklyn Dodgers had a no-hitter last night, and I'm going to follow what Nomo did." *1996: In a speech in a Los Angeles suburb, referring to Hideo Nomo, the Dodger who pitched a no-hitter against the Colorado Rockies in Denver the night before.*

"Everyone in this audience, whether you agree with me or not, this is America." *1996: On the campaign trail.*

"I'm running for president of the United States, because I believe that—with strong leadership—America's days will always lie ahead of us. Just as they lie ahead of us now." *1996: On his vision for America.*

"Tomorrow will be the first time in my life I don't have anything to do." *1996: In his concession speech.*

"There's nothing left to do but go out and get rich." *1996: After losing the 1996 presidential race.*

"You can always get the truth from an American statesman after he has turned 70, or given up all hope of the presidency." *1997: At a Washington symposium in honor of George McGovern's seventy-fifth birthday.*

"I walk by very fast." *1998: On the fact that his apartment at the Watergate complex is in the same hall as Monica Lewinsky's.*

"You read what Disraeli had to say. I don't remember what he said. He said something. He's no longer with us." *1998: On the challenge of keeping a politician's private life separate from his public life.*

"We're going to buy that place, and I'll be giving tours on weekends." *1999: After expanding his Watergate apartment by combining it with the unit next door, which had been vacated by its previous tenant, Monica Lewinsky.*

SAM DONALDSON
(TV [ABC] Newsman)

"If he's not telling the truth, I think his presidency is numbered in days. This thing isn't going to drag out. . . . Mr. Clinton—if he's not telling the truth and the evidence shows that—will resign, perhaps this week. . . ." *1998: Predicting the imminent demise of Bill Clinton on January 25th, 1998.*

ROBERT DORNAN
(Congressman)

"Every lesbian spearchucker in this country is hoping I get defeated. Every abortionist doctor is hoping I get defeated." *1992*

MAUREEN DOWD
(New York Times Reporter)

"President Clinton returned today for a sentimental journey to the university where he didn't inhale, didn't get drafted, and didn't get a degree." *1994: Reporting on Bill Clinton's return to Oxford University.*

FREDERICK DOWNS
(Author & Veteran's Bureau Official)

"Is it gas? Is it cabbage? Is Iran going to enter the war against Iraq?" *1990: Explaining the kinds of complex questions he asks himself about American foreign policy in the Middle East.*

MATT DRUDGE
(Internet & TV Journalist)

"Those Supreme Journalist types seem to think the news has to be Terribly Sobering. I don't." *1998: On the difference between* The Drudge Report *and other publications.*

MICHAEL DUKAKIS
(Presidential Candidate & College Professor)
"I teach my mistakes." *1996: A professor of state and local government at Northeastern University in Boston.*

"You have to teach politics, how to get things done in a political environment. But then I always begin my courses by saying, 'If I knew anything about politics, I wouldn't be here.'" *1996*

"Not quite hard enough, huh?" *1996: At the Democratic National Convention, in response to a woman telling him that she had worked for him in 1988.*

"I teach at UCLA. You have to excuse me, but if I don't get the car back to my wife (Kitty), she's going to kill me." *1998: At the California State Democratic convention, explaining how he wound up on the podium of the gathering in Los Angeles and why he didn't have time to field questions from reporters.*

DAVID DUKE
(Louisiana Gubernatorial Candidate, Congressional Candidate & Former KKK Wizard)
"That's the kind of cheap shot a little worm like you would make. . . . You could use a little plastic surgery yourself." *1991: To CNN commentator Michael Kinsley who asked him if he'd ever had a chemical face peel.*

"Skeletons in my closet? I don't even have a closet." *1999: Declaring himself the front-runner to replace Representative Robert Livingston.*

KACY DUKE
(Monica Lewinsky's Former Fitness Trainer)
"I could have achieved more if Monica didn't cheat." *1999*

JENNIFER DUNN
(Republican)
"Steve's been a famous football player. I'm a single mother. We're an example of the diversity that we want to see in our party." *1999: On why she and Representative Steve Largent of Oklahoma were chosen for the GOP response to the State of the Union.*

CHARLES DUPLESSIS
(Navy Spokesman for the USS Eisenhower)
"Diplomacy? Yes, it was 95,000 tons of diplomacy that convinced Saddam." *1998: Referring to the amount of water that the nuclear-powered ship displaces.*

DR. CHARLES P. DUVALL
(Former President of the American Society of Internal Medicine)
"If you were trying to sell Chevys to the Japanese, you'd probably be stressed, too." *1992: On why President George Bush vomited and collapsed during a state dinner in Japan.*

ROBERT DUVALL
(Actor)
"They think if this chunky little Monica Lewinsky girl can get him, what about me?" *1999: Robert Duvall, the actor, chastising the president's feminist friends.*

E

EDWIN EDWARDS
(Former Governor of Louisiana)
"Currency per se is not illegal. . . . The federal government prints cash every day." *1998: After the FBI seized some $400,000 in cash from his home and safety-deposit box, money it says Edwards extorted from San Francisco 49ers owner Edward DeBartolo as the price of a casino license.*

BARBARA EHRENREICH
(Social Commentator)
"He screws up, she covers up. Then they bond over it. I don't see what's so great about that." *1998: On the Clintons.*

JOYCELYN ELDERS
(Former United States Surgeon General)
"If I could be the 'condom queen' and get every young person who is engaging in sex to use a condom in the United States, I would wear a crown on my head with a condom on it. I would!" *1994*

"Women, for the most part, use their power, prestige and position to try to make a difference in the lives

JOYCELYN ELDERS (CONT'D)

of people, to make the world a better place. Men, on the other hand, look at power in terms of money and control." *1995: On how things would be different if we had a Senate full of women.*

ELIZABETH II
(Queen of England)

"Sorry, I don't do that." *1998: Excusing herself from an autograph-seeker in Kuala Lumpur. The queen was visiting Malaysia to close the Commonwealth Games.*

HARVEY ENGLANDER
(Political Consultant)

"He could easily become a singing Dan Quayle." *1993: Upon learning that Sonny Bono planned to run for lieutenant governor of California.*

JUDITH CAMPBELL EXNER
(Mistress)

"I was 26 and in love. Was I supposed to have better . . . judgement than the President of the United States?" *1996: On her affair with JFK.*

F

JERRY FALWELL
(Minister)

"The only thing we know is he must be male and Jewish." *1999: Acknowledging he does not know who the Antichrist will be, but providing what information he does have about the biblical figure who will spread evil prior to the Second Coming of Christ, which the reverend expects within ten years.*

LOUIS FARRAKHAN
(Minister, Nation of Islam)

"There is no better example of crucifixion in the modern era than Marion Barry." *1990*

"You saw the tape. They said, 'Mr. Mayor, we're going to read you your rights.' Well, the day's soon coming when we're going to read white folk their rights." *1990: On the arrest of Mayor Marion Barry of Washington, D.C.*

"It's a great honor for me . . . to get to know the only government in the world that is run according to God's laws." *1996: In Iran.*

JAMES FARRINGTON
(Mayor)

"Justice is done. It has prevailed." *1998: After his ace-high flush won a poker game to decide a runoff for mayor of Estancia, NM, between two candidates who tied in the regular election.*

DANTE FASCELL
(Congressman)

"You have 535 opinions. Actually, you have 635, because you have to count the Senate twice. Each senator has two opinions." *1990: On the variety of opinions in Congress.*

FRANK FASI
(Mayor of Honolulu, HI)

"You are entitled to your opinions, but as far as I am concerned, you can go to hell! Take your complaints and shove them up your big fat nose." *1990: Responding to a vacationing Philadelphia police officer who said he saw drunks, drugs, and prostitutes in Hawaii.*

DICK FEENEY
(Congressional Aide & Lobbyist)

"You can always tell the difference between a dog and a lobbyist—because when you finally relent and open the door and let them in, the dog will stop whining." *1996*

ANDREW FERGUSON
(Author & Speechwriter)

"If people know or suspect [Bill Clinton]'s a sleazeball, which many of them obviously do, it may turn out that having a sleazeball for a president isn't such a big deal." *1996*

SARAH FERGUSON
(Duchess of York)

"I move out for the night or go away for the weekend." *1998: On what she does when ex-husband Prince Andrew has a date over.*

GEORGE FERNADES
(Defense Minister of India)

"I don't know why India and Pakistan should be seen as blowing each other up when nuclear weapons in the hands of the United States and China are seen as stabilizing factors." *1998*

GERALDINE FERRARO
(Vice Presidential Candidate)
"I haven't gotten the tape of Paula Jones, so why would I get the tape of this? I can't assess what's real and what's not real. And I don't want to." *1998: When asked if she had seen and heard the allegations of Kathleen Willey on* 60 Minutes. *She said she was out having dinner and missed* 60 Minutes *and that she had no interest in seeing the tape of Mrs. Willey's interview.*

GENEVIEVE FIELD
(Co-founder of the Online Magazine Nerve*)*
"Having an affair with an older man or an older woman is a learning experience. But I do think Monica learned a different lesson than most people do. The biggest crime of all is that more people know her name than know Madeleine Albright's." *1998: On Monica Lewinsky's fame.*

MARLIN FITZWATER
(Presidential Press Secretary)
"I know I'm being set up. I'm not going to look there—not for a million dollars. Not on your life. I don't do dolls." *1990: After reporters placed on the White House podium a replica of an anatomically correct doll that Vice President Quayle brought back from South Africa.*

"This strategy represents our policy for all time. Until it's changed." *1990*

"I'm sick of all you lazy bastards." *1992: Speaking to reporters in the White House Communications Agency, inferring that their stories did not reflect truth as he saw it.*

"It's been a very good trip, with the exception of the tear gas." *1992: Trying to make the best of a visit to Panama during which President Bush was forced to flee an anti-American protest rally.*

GENNIFER FLOWERS
(Mistress)
"They don't have a page that broad." *1992: On why Hillary Clinton couldn't "bare her butt in any magazine."*

"I gave Bill a huge piece of my heart for many, many years. Now it appears that the man I loved . . . was cheating on me, too. Left and right." *1994: Responding to new allegations that President Clinton had extramarital affairs.*

"I am not a bimbo, golddigging SOB that came in here trying to destroy a man. I was trying to cover my own rear end." *1994: On the taped conversations she had with Clinton.*

"I had taken a journalism course in high school, and I thought 'How hard could it be?' Not hard at all, it turned out." *1995: On beginning her career in journalism.*

"It sort of surprises me at this point with all of the problems and the scandals and the 'Gates' that have come up during his terms, that he would be foolish enough to do something like this at this point. You think the boy would learn." *1998: On initial allegations that President Clinton carried on an affair with a White House intern.*

"He was thinking with another head." *1998: In response to Larry King, who asked what may have motivated President Clinton to have an alleged sexual affair with Monica Lewinsky, a former White House intern.*

LARRY FLYNT
(Publisher)
"There's nothing that changes people's moral outlook like money." *1998: After he agreed to pay hundreds of thousands of dollars to four women for their stories about their affairs with Representative Robert Livingston (R-Louisiana), prompting him to announce his resignation on the eve of becoming Speaker of the House.*

"He considers himself a real Romeo. He makes Bill Clinton look like Mary Poppins." *1999: On Robert Livingston, who gave up the House Speaker–designate job and resigned his seat as the magazine was about to reveal his extramarital affairs.*

"Bob Livingston told the *New York Times* that I was a bottom feeder. That's true. But when I got down there, look what I found." *1999*

"It's not money, it's not politics—it's who controls the pussy that controls the world." *1999*

"Smut is my vocation; politics is my hobby." *1999*

MARK FOLEY
(Congressman)
"I worked as a dishwasher. I cleaned toilets. My grandmother came from Poland. She made 28 beds

MARK FOLEY (CONT')

a day in a Travelodge. She cleaned 28 toilets a day . . . I was a wrecker, an auto mechanic. I worked at a golf course. Now I am a proud member of the United States Congress. No job is beneath me." *1995*

BETTY FORD
(Former First Lady)

"Why in the world would this able man want to run for public office?" *1992: Introducing senatorial candidate Tom Campbell in Los Angeles.*

RICHARD FORD
(National Wizard of the Fraternal White Knights of the KKK)

"We're jokesters!" *1990: On the sense of humor of members of his organization.*

WENDELL FORD
(Senator)

"Well, I'm not nigger rich, either." *1995: Responding to the statement by a caller he was chatting with on a radio program in Louisville. The caller said, "I'm not near as rich as yourself, Senator." When Ford responded with this statement, the caller explained, "I said 'not near as rich as you.'"*

WYCHE FOWLER
(Senator)

"Students don't vote. Do you expect me to come in here and kiss your ass?" *1992: To young volunteers campaigning for deficit reductions. Fowler denies making the statement, but the volunteers insist he did.*

BARNEY FRANK
(Congressman)

"If they don't cut the crap, something's going to happen, and I'm going to happen it." *1990: Threatening to expose closeted gay Republicans.*

"It looks like a recipe book with 15 ways to cook spinach. But it's still about spinach. This is still about sex." *1998: On the list of fifteen possibly impeachable offenses presented to the House Judiciary Committee by Republican investigative counsel David Schippers.*

"He lies by being technically accurate. I wish he would stop it. He's not 14 anymore, trying to outsmart the principal." *1998: On President Clinton's evasions about Monica Lewinsky.*

"I just want to say that the assertion that this was bipartisan is just silly. If this is bipartisanship, then the Taliban wins a medal for religious tolerance." *1998: On the vote by the House Judiciary Committee to make public a transcript of President Clinton's grand jury testimony in the investigation conducted by the Whitewater independent counsel, Kenneth W. Starr.*

"I have become the go-to-guy on genitalia." *1998: On the many queries he's fielded about the Monica Lewinsky affair and Sen. Trent Lott's comments comparing homosexuals to alcoholics and kleptomaniacs.*

"If Bob Barr caught fire and I was holding a bucket of water, it would be a great act of discipline to pour it on him. I would do it, but I'd hate myself in the morning." *1999: Discussing his least favorite fellow congressman, a Georgia Republican.*

AL FRANKEN
(Comedian & Author)

"Having Al D'Amato head up an ethics investigation is a little like getting Bob Dornan to lead a mental health task force." *1996*

"There's cuts in both NASA and Medicare that Gingrich . . . [was] proposing . . . 30% of Medicare costs are incurred . . . in the last year of . . . life, and NASA spends billions . . . on astronaut safety, so my idea was to shoot the elderly into space." *1996*

"I went to the inaugural balls. . . . For $50,000 you could waltz with Hillary, for $25,000 you could tango with Tipper, and for just $25 you could get a lap dance from Janet Reno." *1997*

"No, because I'm a Democrat." *1999: When asked if he ran for public office if he might be afraid of Larry Flynt looking into his private life.*

BETTY FRIEDAN
(Author & Activist)

"It's a complete misuse and misreading of feminism and the women's movement to put people's private sexual behavior as a priority. The women's movement is about public policy that will affect the lives of women. This other stuff is nonsense, even if it's true. It's not important. [Even if] somebody in a high position makes an advance to a woman in not such a high position, if she says no and he walks away, what's the big deal? Whose lives are affected?" *1998: On the sexual misconduct of the president.*

LINDAY FURNEY
(Ohio State Senator)
"If it has tires or testicles, you're going to have trouble with it." *1992*

G
PETER GABRIEL
(Singer & Songwriter)
"I don't think one should look to the president for spiritual leadership." *1998: On the Clinton scandals.*

JOAN GALLO
(City Attorney, San Jose, CA)
"The confusion about betting limits is that we refer to it as betting limits." *1997: Explaining why there is confusion in local card clubs and on the city council over betting limits in the cardroom clubs.*

BILL GATES
(Businessman)
"As long as they are going to steal software we want them to steal ours." *1998: On the popularity of pirated Microsoft software in China. Gates said that piracy gets the users used to Windows, and that they will ultimately become customers.*

DANIEL GECKER
(Attorney for Kathleen Willey)
"The first order of business was to retain her privacy. We lost that. So, is it better to lose your privacy and have money, or lose your privacy and not have money?" *1998: On reports that he tried to sell his client's story to a book publisher or tabloid newspaper after she was subpoenaed by independent counsel Kenneth Starr.*

DAVID GEFFEN
(Businessman)
"Let me put it this way: I am delighted to have a relationship with the president of the United States. I can't tell you I don't value that greatly. But, I mean, you know, I'm not blown away by anybody." *1998*

RICHARD GEPHARDT
(Congressman)
"Is this on C-SPAN?" *1993: While watching Congressman Dan Rostenkowski carousing in a conga line with a tablecloth draped over his head and Representative Charles E. Schumer toss M&Ms into the air while dancing and then catch them in his mouth without missing a beat. These and other Congressmen were carousing at a two-day "conference" held at Johns Hopkins University celebrating the alleged end of Congressional gridlock.*

"Partisanship inflames all debates, all motives are suspect and nothing is below the belt. Last Congress, the House of Representatives was run with the dignity of the World Wrestling Federation." *1999*

DAVID GERGEN
(Presidential Press Secretary)
"Everybody here is bending over triple-backwards to ensure that we handle this straight up." *1994: On the White House and the Whitewater scandal.*

KATHLEEN GINGRICH
(Mother)
"She's a bitch." *1995: Whispering her son Newt's opinion of Hillary Rodham Clinton to Connie Chung in a CBS interview, after Chung assured her the comment would be "just between you and me."*

"I think it will be quite a while before I do any more whispering." *1995*

NEWT GINGRICH
(Speaker of the House)
"He's their flake, but our savior." *1992: On Jerry Brown, candidate for the Democratic nomination for president.*

"Maybe we need a tax credit for the poorest Americans to buy a laptop. Now, maybe that's wrong, maybe it's expensive, maybe we can't do it. But I'll tell you, any signal we can send to the poorest Americans that says, 'We're going to get into a twenty-first-century,

NEWT GINGRICH (CONT'D)

third-wave information age, and so are you, and we want to carry you with us,' begins to change the game." *1995: On solving the problem of poverty in America with laptop computers.*

"If combat means living in a ditch, females have biological problems staying in a ditch for 30 days because they get infections . . . males are biologically driven to go out and hunt giraffes." *1995: In a lecture to students on why most women are not suited to traditional military combat.*

"They are socialists. Oh, they may not technically believe in government ownership, they just believe in government control on a grand scale—most of them do." *1995: On the people who write newspaper editorials.*

"I'm not a natural leader. I'm too intellectual; I'm too abstract; I think too much." *1995*

"People assume I'm some right-wing, out-of-touch Neanderthal who doesn't get it. I mean, I'm *adopted!* Both of my fathers are *adopted!* I mean, give me a break!" *1995*

"It was a great experience for me." *1996: On meeting Mickey Rooney.*

"He's not going to feel your pain because he's not going to cause your pain." *1996: On Bob Dole as president.*

"Let me just start by saying somebody I wanted to introduce to all of you, a good friend of mine and a good friend of Bob Dole's—somebody who many of you will recognize—Kent Steffes, who won the first gold medal ever given in the Olympics for beach volleyball, from California, is right here with us. You know, Kent is an example of what freedom is all about. A mere forty years ago, beach volleyball was just beginning. Now it is not only a sport in the Olympics, there are over thirty countries that have competition internationally. There are some thirteen states with twenty-five cities in America, and there's a whole new world of opportunity opening up that didn't even exist thirty years ago or forty years ago. And no bureaucrat would have invented it, and that's what freedom is all about." *1996*

WILLIAM GINSBURG
(Attorney for Monica Lewinsky)

"I was taking Monica to the airport with me for a ride (because) she was going stir crazy. And the media—I know it wasn't the guys from the networks—were right up against my rear bumper. They had a van in front of me holding me back, and they had two vans on the side swooping in and out to get pictures. I told my driver to slow down to 35 or 40 miles an hour on the freeway because I didn't want an accident. While we were parked at the Dulles airport, the reporters and photographers jumped out of their car, pushed their cameras against the window and began to take pictures, rocking the car. Then one photographer, referring to Monica, said, 'Look at the cunt, she's enjoying this.' And that was it. I opened my door, and kicked the guy right on his ass. Then the guy walked up and put a camera a foot from my face and I swatted it away and said, 'Get out of here.' Then when I went around to the gate, I turned around and saw those damned photographers giving themselves high fives for getting a reaction out of me." *1998: On the difficulties of protecting his client from the press.*

RUDOLPH GIULIANI
(Mayor of New York City)

"This is a reciprocal relationship." *1999: Explaining that although other regions benefit from the business and culture centered in his city, New York benefits by shipping them its trash.*

"I'm going to say, 'I've never lived in Arkansas, I've never worked in Arkansas, I've never been to Arkansas, but I love Arkansas. In fact, I love it so much I'm going to be running for the Senate. And do you know how I'm going to prepare for it? I'm going to come here and take a vacation.'" *1999: At a fund-raiser announcing that he was going to Arkansas—this was one week after Hillary Clinton announced she would seek a Senate seat from New York.*

APRIL GLASPIE
(U.S. Ambassador to Iraq)

"We have no opinion on the Arab-Arab conflicts like your border disagreement with Kuwait. The issue is not associated with America. President Bush is an intelligent man. He is not going to declare an economic war against Iraq." *1990: Speaking with Saddam Hussein one week before his invasion of Kuwait.*

JOHN GLENN
(Senator)

"There is still no cure for the common birthday." *1997: Glenn, seventy-five, announcing that age was the important factor in his decision not to run for another term.*

"With all due respect to my good friend Senator Leahy, I know the Great Lakes. I've traveled the Great Lakes. And Lake Champlain is not one of the Great Lakes." *1998: On Senator Leahy's bill authorizing marine-research funds—normally allocated for colleges in states that border the Great Lakes and the oceans—for Vermont colleges.*

SETH GODFREY
(Jerry Brown Delegate from California to the Democratic National Convention)

"I spent a month there [North Korea], after studying in Moscow. It was a clean country, and the people looked well-fed. I couldn't judge anything else." *1992*

BERNARD GOETZ
(Political Candidate)

"There is something wrong with the process when good people don't run for office." *1998: Goetz, who shot four black teenagers on a New York subway in 1984, on his plans to run for mayor of New York in 2001.*

"I would like to see some type of vegetarian diet offered as an alternative in the New York public school system. I think circumcision shouldn't be allowed in the city of New York. And I think that generally there should be the death penalty for the first violent sexual offense. Those are personal things that are important to me." *1998: On the issues he will push when he runs for Mayor of New York in 2001.*

LUCIANNE GOLDBERG
(Literary Agent)

"She kept it as a souvenir. How sick is that?" *1998: The woman who advised Linda Tripp to record phone conversations with Monica Lewinsky, on the dress the former intern claimed bore physical evidence of a sexual encounter with President Clinton.*

WHOOPI GOLDBERG
(Actress & Comedienne)

"If things don't work out, he can take center square on my new program." *1998: On Hollywood Squares, tentatively offering President Clinton a position.*

AL GOLDSTEIN
(Pornographer)

"Larry [Flynt] in terms of being a pornographer doesn't impress me. But as a torchlight for journalism, he's magnificent. I have a pin I wear that says POLITICIANS GIVE PROSTITUTES A BAD NAME." *1998: On Larry Flynt's search for mistresses of politicians.*

BARRY GOLDWATER
(Senator & Presidential Candidate)

"Every time I see him, I get sick to my stomach and want to throw up." *1991: On journalist Bill Moyers.*

"I look back on my 30 years in the Senate and I think I can truthfully say that after 12 years I'd about shot my wad." *1992*

MIKHAIL GORBACHEV
(Former Soviet Premier)

"I don't think Mr. Onassis would have married Mrs. Khrushchev." *1997: When asked, "What effect on history do you think it would have made if, in 1963, President Khrushchev had been assassinated instead of President Kennedy?"*

AL GORE
(Vice President of the United States)

"One of the things we've all been learning on the subject of sexual harassment is what goes on inside the mind of a victim which sometimes leads that person to keep silent about it and to continue maintaining a facade of friendship and an outward relationship so long as that secret is kept." *1991: On the accusations of Anita Hill against Supreme Court nominee Clarence Thomas.*

"As Socrates said 2,500 years ago, 'Man must rise above the earth to the top of the atmosphere and

AL GORE (CONT'D)

beyond, for only thus will he understand the earth in which he lives." *1998: Gore awoke one night at 3:00 A.M. and sat bolt upright in bed and thought: "Let's send a satellite into space that would beam back sun-washed images of the whole Earth—something more majestic than the tight shots seen on the Weather Channel.*

"It's clear that cracking the genetic code would be of significantly less benefit if we allow our moral code to become cracked as well." *1998: Proposing a federal ban on genetic discrimination in the workplace.*

"I really can't think of a clearer demonstration of the contrasts between Democratic policies and Republican policies than what happened under Scar compared to what happened under Simba." *1998: Equating GOP environmental policy to the scorched-earth practices of the Lion King villain Scar.*

"He must have been bitten by a squirrel as a child." *1998: On why Washington Republican Senator Slade Gorton is critical of the Endangered Species Act.*

"The New Hampshire primary is rich in traditions. First and foremost, there is pandering." *1999: In a speech honoring the Library and Archives of New Hampshire's Political Tradition.*

TIPPER GORE
(Wife of the Vice President)

"I don't know what he's like when I'm not around." *1999: When asked if husband Al is different when she's not around.*

BETSY GOTBAUM
(New York City Commissioner of Parks and Recreation)

"I'm not thrilled that people use Pelham Bay Park to dump dead bodies; but I do hope everyone understands these aren't crimes against park visitors. . . . Knowing how New Yorkers respect their parks, I can't help suspecting the culprits are out-of-towners." *1992*

REVEREND BILLY GRAHAM
(Preacher)

"I forgive him, because I know the frailty of human nature. He has such a termendous personality that

I think the ladies just go wild over him." *1998: Saying he would forgive President Clinton if the president were found to have had sex with a former White House intern.*

PHIL GRAMM
(Senator)

"Arguments are often made on the floor of the Senate that have been rejected in the Soviet Union." *1990*

"If federal control of child care makes sense, why didn't we tear down the Berlin wall to get into East Berlin?" *1990*

"People will be hunting Democrats with dogs by the end of the century." *1993*

"It's all true. We *are* space aliens. I'm amazed that it's taken you so long to find out." *1994: Responding to the June 7 edition of the* Weekly World News *supermarket tabloid, which says a dozen U.S. senators have been "exposed" as space aliens.*

"The idea that Pat Buchanan wants to engage me on economic issues is laughable. I never duel with unarmed men." *1995: On his rival for the GOP presidential bid.*

"Mama's got a .38 Special, and she knows how to use it!" *1996: Speaking about his wife's pistol-shooting expertise to a forum for gun owners.*

"At the end of the interview, I walked out with Wendy and helped her on with her coat and said to her, 'As a single member of the faculty, I would be especially interested in you coming to Texas A & M.' . . . Wendy looked up at me and said, 'Yuck.'" *1996: Recounting his first meeting with Wendy Lee, who was to become his wife.*

"When the voter speaks, I listen, especially when the voter is saying someone else's name." *1996: Bowing out of the presidential race after coming in fifth in the Iowa GOP caucuses.*

"I repeated the third grade but I know the fifth is not as good as the first." *1996: On finishing fifth in the Iowa caucuses.*

"I don't want him to look back 20 years from now, when he's lancing boils or doing wills . . . and say,

'I wonder if I could have been a big rock star?' " *1996: Explaining why he and his wife, Wendy, are allowing their twenty-one-year-old son to take a year off to try his luck as a singer & songwriter before encouraging him to pursue a professional degree.*

"I think it's sort of like it must be having babies—you've got to forget how hard it was before you're willing to do it again." *1998: After he spent millions running for president in 1996 but captured not a single delegate in the GOP primaries, when asked if he plans another bid in 2000.*

BOB GRANT
(TV Host)

"My hunch is that he [Ron Brown] is the one survivor; I just have that hunch. Maybe it's because, at heart, I'm a pessimist." *1996: Remark made before Brown's body was recovered from a plane crash scene and while a survivor was believed to exist. Grant was subsequently fired from his radio job.*

ALAN GREENSPAN
(Chairman of the Federal Reserve Board)

"I've been able to string more words into fewer ideas than anybody I know." *1998: At a Senate hearing.*

BRYANT GUMBLE
(TV Personality)

"The controversy about the Kennedy assassination isn't over by a long shot." *1992*

MIKE GUNN
(Michigan State Senator)

"If guns are outlawed, how can we shoot the liberals?" *1996*

CARL GUNTER
(Congressman)

"Inbreeding is how we get championship horses." *1990: On why he believed incest should not be an exception in legislation banning abortions.*

H

ALEXANDER HAIG
(Nixon Presidential Advisor)

"This town is in a panic mode. There is too much negative negabobbing." *1990: On Washington, D.C.*

"I don't think of this as helping Castro—I think of it as burning his crops." *1992: On his habit of smoking Havana cigars.*

RICHARD HALVERSON
(Senate Chaplain)

"Gracious Father, investigative reporting seems epidemic in an election year—its primary objective to defame political candidates. Seeking their own reputation, they destroy another's as they search relentlessly, microscopically for some ancient skeleton in a person's life. Eternal God, help these self-appointed vacuum-cleaner journalists to discover how unproductive and divisive their efforts are." *1992*

ARGUS HAMILTON
(Humorist)

"Many Americans would like to see the front ends of horses sent to Washington for final assembly." *1996*

"Can't anybody write about the Clintons without mentioning genitals?" *1996: On William Safire calling Hillary Clinton a "congenital liar."*

SUSAN HAMMER
(Mayor of San Jose, CA)

"If anybody doesn't think there's any there here, I invite them to come down and spend an hour downtown visiting some of our neighborhoods." *1994: On people who believe that in San Jose there is no there there.*

ERNEST HANCOCK
(Gun-rights Activist)

"They just like their guns. And in Arizona, gosh darn it, that's normal." *1996: On his familiarity with all twelve of Arizona's "Viper Militia" members.*

TOM HARKINS
(Senator)

"Forget about that nonsense!" *1997: At a Democratic party fund-raising dinner that included small businessmen, CEOs of large corporations, and many lobbyists, commenting on the alleged scandals in Democratic fund-raising in the past.*

GARY HART
(Senator)

"I got linked to people whose behavior was, in my judgement, much worse than mine, people who were

GARY HART (CONT'D)

involved in sexual harassment for instance. Yet my picture was on the post office wall along with the rest of them." *1998: The former senator and candidate for the 1988 Democratic presidential nomination, remembering being suddenly bumped from the nomination race when allegations of his affair with model Donna Rice surfaced in the media.*

"If you're dealing with something as serious as the future of the presidency, maybe you don't have to be first." *1998: Criticizing the news media for what he sees as their practice of rushing to print allegations about President Clinton's alleged sexual misconduct.*

"The people never really spoke out in 1987; I was out of the race within a week. I don't think the American people watching that unique event ever really formed a solid opinion." *1998: Lamenting his quick exit from the race for the Democratic party's presidential nomination after allegations of his affair with model Donna Rice were printed in the media.*

SID HARTMAN
(Sports Columnist)

"All I know is that Mr. Clinton's ratings keep on going up, so maybe you people should find something else . . ." *1998: When asked on a sports talk show for his thoughts on Tara Lipinski.*

ORRIN G. HATCH
(Senator)

"I think he has a very charming approach. . . . Wherever he goes, especially young people—a large group the President had a little difficulty with when he was running for president—and especially women, and I think mature males, they say they go for Dan Quayle very well." *1992*

"What a jerk." *1998: On President Clinton's admission of his improper relationship with Monica Lewinsky combined with an attack on Ken Starr.*

"I'm convinced someday there will be a president who announces his program in less than 15 minutes. I don't care if he's Democrat or Republican, I'm going to support him." *1999: On President Clinton's seventy-seven-minute State of the Union address.*

ANNE HECHE
(Actress)

"Sure, Clinton disengaged himself from changing the sodomy laws. The guy got off the hook. He still let himself be photographed with Ellen and me, and that was a fucking important moment." *1998: Describing the courage of Bill Clinton.*

ANTHONY HEDLEY
(Chairman of the Hong Kong Council on Smoking and Health)

"Having a smoking section in a restaurant is like having a nonurinating section in a swimming pool." *1998: On the ubiquitous nature of secondhand smoke. He was commenting on a plan for compulsory nonsmoking sections in larger restaurants.*

HOWELL HEFLIN
(Senator)

"Ballroom dancing has been around in various forms since early civilization, and it has been a crucial factor in the development of mankind." *1991: Introducing a resolution to establish National Ballroom Dance Week.*

"I mistakenly picked up a pair of my wife's white panties and put them in my pocket while rushing out the door to go to work. Rather than take a chance of being embarrassed again, I'm going to start buying colored handkerchiefs." *1994: After reaching into his pocket during a lunch with reporters, and pulling out a pair of women's underwear.*

HUGH HEFNER
(Editor & Entrepreneur)

"The man does have a character problem, that's rather evident. . . . That he found it appropriate to lie about his situation raises some very real questions, but sex is the one subject in America that everyone lies about—to their girlfriends, their wives, themselves." *1998: On the Clinton scandals.*

MICHAEL HELLON
(Chairman of the Arizona GOP)

"He has co-opted so much of our agenda. You might say he's the most articulate spokesman we have for Republican issues." *1999: On President Clinton's policy initiatives as voiced in the State of the Union message.*

JESSE HELMS
(Senator)

"Let me adjust my hearing aid. It could not accommodate the decibels of the senator from Massachusetts. I can't match him in decibels, or Jezebels, or anything else apparently." *1993: After Sen. Ted Kennedy made a loud and impassioned speech in favor of allowing foreigners with AIDS to have U.S. residency.*

"There have been 248 different U.S. senators in the 18 years and five months I have been there. None, none, has been more capable than Dan Quayle." *1994*

QUESTION:"What kind of valve did they put into your heart?

HELMS: "What they call a pig valve, because it comes from a pig. Every time I pass a plate of barbecue, I cry. It might be one of my relatives." *1995*

"Kim Jong the Second." *1995: Referring to Kim Jong Il, leader of North Korea.*

"The Foreign Relations Committee has had the honor of welcoming the distinguished prime minister of India, and I wish to bring her to the floor." *1995: Introducing Prime Minister Benazir Bhutto of Pakistan in the Senate.*

MARSHALL HERSKOVITZ
(TV Producer)

"The scandal is really a referendum on sexual morality in the country. Those people whose sexual morality accepts the possibility of complexity and ambivalence in a marital relationship have not judged Clinton as badly as those who see marriage as a monolithic simple entity. And in Hollywood, marriage is often not seen as a monolithic simple entity." *1998: On why the president retains his popularity in Tinseltown.*

CHARLTON HESTON
(Actor & President of the National Rifle Association)
"There are plenty of liberals out there with weapons. I also think there are more conservatives in the Hollywood closet than there are homosexuals." *1998*

"We don't trust you with our 21-year-old daughters. And we sure, Lord, don't trust you with our guns." *1998: The newly elected president of the NRA, sending a message in his inaugural speech to President Clinton.*

CARL HIAASEN
(Author & Journalist)
"I ought to be circumspect . . . [but] here goes: Dave, have you completely lost your marbles?" *1998: The* Miami Herald *columnist blasting Herald publisher David Lawrence for briefly considering a run for governor of Florida.*

JUDGE LEON HIGGINBOTHAM
(Federal Judge)
"The other thing is what is on Auschwitz. He who does not know the lessons of history will be doomed to repeat its worst mistakes." *1998: While appearing before the House Judiciary Committee holding hearings on charges against President Bill Clinton. Higginbotham, a legal scholar, told the committee that the words of the American philosopher George Santayana were on the gate at Auschwitz (they were not) and then mangled one of the most familiar phrases of Santayana regarding history.*

JIM HIGHTOWER
(Radio Commentator)
"I see Bill Clinton as thixotropic—something like ketchup, that starts out as a solid until you apply a little heat. Then it becomes a liquid." *1994*

HISPANIC LINK
(Newspaper)
"I'd heard the rumor, and now it's confirmed. When Bill Clinton launches his presidency, Hispanics will have no balls." *1993: On the rumor that there would be no inaugural eve galas in Washington for Hispanics in January.*

JOSEPH HOEFFEL
(Political Candidate)
"It was certainly a successful campaign—except that we didn't win." *1996: On losing a House race in Pennsylvania by eighty-four votes.*

HULK HOGAN
(Professional Wrestler)
"When Jesse won I said to my wife, 'My God, I'm 10 times more popular than him. People know Hulk

HULK HOGAN (CONT'D)

Hogan like they know McDonald's and Chevrolet.'" *1998: On his intention to run for president in the year 2000 after he learned that former professional wrestler Jesse "The Body" Ventura had been elected governor of Minnesota.*

"Jesse's victory proves that people want a real man in power to lead, not a play plastic puppet like other politicians. I'd love to get him in the ring one time before he becomes president." *1998: Hogan played good guy to professional wrestler Jesse "The Body" Ventura's bad guy in the ring.*

ERNEST HOLLINGS
(Senator)

"You should draw a mushroom cloud and put underneath it, 'Made in America by lazy and illiterate Americans and tested in Japan.'" *1992: Responding to Japanese criticism of American work habits. Later Hollings said, 'I'm glad I said it.'*

"Everybody likes to go to Geneva. I used to do it for the Law of the Sea conferences, and you'd find these potentates from down in Africa. Rather than eating each other, they'd just come up and get a good square meal in Geneva." *1993*

"The only time, perhaps, in the military that government doesn't work is when some—called one time, two times, three times, four times, five times—did not answer the call and said 'I'd rather sit in the classroom.'" *1995: Said while wearing the Bronze Star, he won during World War II, criticizing Texas Senator Phil Gramm's call for cuts in government spending, including benefits for veterans. Gramm received five draft deferments while studying at the University of Georgia in the 1960s.*

SENATOR HOLLINGS: "What's the outside limit, since you've studied it in detail, about each percent and how many kids are going to stop smoking and how many thousand for every 10 cents and so forth—what's the outside limit—if I'm sitting as a member of a tobacco company, which I don't have any in South Carolina, but let's assume I was a board member and say, 'Well, they've reached the outside limit here and we'll just declare Chapter 11 and keep on making Kraft foods and Ritz crackers and move this operation to Beijing, China—they seem to like it over there—and business is business and we tried to be the good citizen and say rather than pay the lawyers, because that's all we've been doing—we just won another case up in Indiana this past weekend, so we haven't lost one yet—and we thought we'd be the good citizen and get better advertising and a better credibility for our corporate endeavor here?'

"But since they're going that route, what's the outside figure that you think—you know, like Kansas City here, to go as far as we can go without just turning over the apple cart and having a bunch of bankruptcies, the farmers are not cared for, the children may stop smoking but then they may on the other hand come around and start advertising otherwise, so you'd just—you'd have chaos in a way? But what would be—you say $1.50, and assuming the city council and the state legislature is not going to add any—suppose they add $1.50? How does that fit?"

MR. SUMMERS: "Senator Hollings, there's no certain way to answer that question." *1998: An exchange between Senator Hollings, Democrat of South Carolina, and Treasury Secretary Lawrence Summers about the extent to which an increase in cigarette prices would lead to a reduction in teenage smoking.*

"Kiss my fanny." *1998: To the suggestions from his foe, Rep. Bob Inglis, that they agree on a contract ensuring a civil campaign. Hollings later won reelection.*

BEN HOM
(San Francisco Mayoral Candidate)

"If I'm elected I will end homeliness in San Francisco." *1995: Hom lost.*

THE HONOLULU STAR
(Newspaper)

"Each moment shared with the president helps remind the rest of the nation and the world that there's another side of the planet out here." *1990: On a visit by President Bush to Hawaii.*

ART HOPPE
(Columnist)

"I'm for [the flat tax] as long as it's graduated." *1996*

DENNIS HOPPER
(Actor)

"Make some money, have a life, come back, kick ass." *1998: In a letter to outgoing House Speaker Newt Gingrich.*

JEAN HOUSTON
(Guru of Hillary Rodham Clinton)

"I consider myself a philosopher, and I'm called by whatever they want to call me because nobody can quite figure out what I do." *1996*

"Hillary expressed reverence and respect for Gandhi's life and works, almost drawing his and her own life together with her words. . . . She said he too was profoundly misunderstood, when all he wanted to do was help others and make peace." *1996*

DAVID HOWARD
(Civil Servant)

"You have to be able to see things from the other person's shoes, and I did not do that." *1999: Howard resigned his position in Washington, D.C., city government after colleagues complained about his use of the word* niggardly.

FRANK HSIEH
(San Francisco Mayoral Candidate)

"I have just one word to describe the Marina master plan—*no good!" 1991*

WEBSTER HUBBELL
(Attorney)

"He was dead serious." *1998: The disgraced friend of President Bill Clinton, remembering that Clinton suggest he work in the Justice Department and pursue two important national questions: Who killed JFK and whether UFOs are real.*

ARIANNA HUFFINGTON
(Political Commentator and Writer)

"I think our tolerance of political platitudes has increased. I call it the guffaw threshold. We need to guffaw more at what politicians say." *1998*

LOWELL HURST
(Watsonville, CA, City Councilman)

"While we don't want to look a gift horse in the mouth, I believe this is a Trojan Horse that has a lot of smoke and mirrors and will cause a domino effect to fall on other agricultural land." *1993: Before casting a vote against developing a seventy-acre apple orchard next to the town.*

HENRY HYDE
(Congressman)

"It's an onerous, miserable, rotten duty, but we have to do it." *1998: The chairman of the House Judiciary Committee, on why the House needed to proceed with an impeachment inquiry in October.*

"I came here thinking I could change the world. Now my only ambition is to leave the room with dignity." *1998*

"Keep your eyes open and your mouth shut." *1998: His advice to House Judiciary Committee members as they prepared to review independent counsel Kenneth Starr's report on President Clinton.*

"The statute of limitations has long since passed on my youthful indiscretions." *1998: Admitting to an adulterous affair in the 1960s after it was reported by the online magazine* Salon.

"Does the rule of law—have you been to Auschwitz? Do you see what happens when the rule of law doesn't prevail? Now I don't leap from the Oval Office on a Saturday afternoon to Auschwitz. But there are similarities when the rule of law doesn't obtain, or when you have one law for the powerful and one for the non-aristocratic." *1998: Striving for profundity while holding hearings on charges against President Bill Clinton.*

"I sort of feel that we have fallen short in the respect side because of the fact that we represent the House, the other body, kind of blue-collar people." *1999: Describing himself and his fellow members of the House of Representatives during his appearance before the Senate in the Clinton impeachment trial. The "blue-collar" House members earn $136,700 per year. The median family income in the United States is $42,300.*

I

HAROLD ICKES
(White House Deputy Chief of Staff Under President Clinton)

"I like Bill Clinton. Do I think he's a total idiot? Yes." *1999*

JAMES INHOFE
(Congressman)

"The refugees, in spite of the fact it is a horrible thing that some 3,000 of them have lost their lives, still when you look at the refugees, I was shocked to find out, as perhaps you were, that they are very well off, considering they are refugees." *After a fact-finding trip to the Balkans. "In spite of" those deaths, Inhofe said the children "are all wearing Nikes and were very well dressed."*

WALTER ISAACSON
(Author & Editor)

"His sensitivity is such that if he reread his own memoirs, he'd be outraged that they're not favorable enough." *1992: On Henry Kissinger.*

MICHAEL ISSIKOFF
(Newsweek Reporter)

"I don't know if I wanted to kill myself, but I won't deny certain homicidal impulses." *1997: Issikoff had the Monica Lewinsky story before anyone else but was scooped by the* Washington Post *when his editors postponed its publication.*

MOLLY IVINS
(Columnist)

"Weaker than bus-station chili." *1998: Evaluating the character of President Bill Clinton.*

J

REVEREND JESSE JACKSON
(Minister)

"He [Saddam Hussein] feels ignored." *1990: Said after a four-hour talk between Jackson and Hussein.*

"Let's hug a Russian. Let's hug until the fear comes out." *1990: Said at the "Friendship Games" in Seattle, WA.*

"Last week I had an awful experience. I stood there in the gallery of the U.S. Senate, denied the right to take part in the discussion. It was an awful and agonizing feeling. I stood there and watched a hundred senators debate our civil rights. I saw people like Hatch from Utah and Dole from Kansas—I saw them pull off their gloves and start screaming at the top of their voices, 'You are attacking white males! You are attacking white males!' " *1990: Describing what he saw while watching a Senate debate on the 1990 civil-rights bill.*

"Only people who are brain dead forget the past." *1990*

"Those that tried to bury [Anita Hill] too soon are like those that tried to bury Jesus too soon. She was buried on Friday but by Sunday, the stone was rolled away and there was new life and new hope and resurrection. So her crucifixion by that all-white upper-middle-class and wealthy male Senate will not last very long." *1991: On the Clarence Thomas Hearings.*

"Whenever I speak, it's prime time." *1996: On why he wasn't given a prime-time speaking slot at the Democratic National Convention.*

"The bottom line is, make our youth efficient English speakers so they can be competitive—ain't that the real point?" *1997: After reversing his condemnation of the Oakland school board's plan to recognize Ebonics, or black English, as the primary language of black students.*

"It's one thing to punish a man. It's another thing to take away his dignity." *1997: Commenting on Dennis Rodman's eleven-game suspension in the NBA after kicking a photographer in the groin.*

"I think he should not invest in gun manufacturers, and shouldn't invest in liquor companies, and shouldn't invest in tobacco companies." *1999: Testifying before the House Ways and Means Committee and providing advice after President Clinton proposed to "save Society Security" by having the government buy up some 4 percent of the stock market.*

TED JENNINGS
(New Mexico State Senator)

"It's my personal belief that if they're not rehabilitated after 15 years, kill 'em." *1995: On what to do about incorrigible prison inmates and criminals.*

GENERAL SHENGDE JI
(Chief of China's Military Intelligence)

"We like your president." *1996: To Democratic donor Johnny Chung before General Ji deposited $300,000 in Chung's Hong Kong bank account so Chung could pass it on to President Clinton's reelection campaign.*

ROSS JOHNSON
(California State Representative)
"Everybody's sacred cow is now coming home to roost." *1990: On the budget crisis in California.*

KELLY JOHNSTON
(Spokesperson for the National Food Processors Association)
"It is an insult to the integrity of American business and to the intelligence of the American public to imply that any industry contributes to Congress to buy votes." *1998*

P. J. JOHNSTON
(Spokesman for San Francisco Mayor Willie Brown)
"The mayor wouldn't actually live there. It would be more a ceremonial residence, perhaps a sort of Camp David." *1996: On Brown's interest in having Nimitz House, the Yerba Buena Island mansion an official residence for San Francisco's mayor. The 8,000-square-foot house was to be included in areas obtained by the city of San Francisco when the Navy pulled out of Yerba Buena and Treasure Islands in 1997.*

PAULA JONES
(Political Litigant)
"I have not come this far to see the law let men who have done such things dodge their responsibility." *1998: Announcing her decision to appeal the dismissal of her sexual-harassment lawsuit against President Clinton.*

"I was from the country." *1998: On the* Roseanne Show, *explaining why she didn't suspect Clinton had ulterior motives in inviting her to a Little Rock, AR, hotel room in 1991.*

"People didn't take me serious." *1998: Thinking differently.*

"He may think, 'Well, since I'm not president now, I . . . can get rid of her or hurt her family." *1999: Explaining to a British magazine her fears of post-presidential reprisals from Bill Clinton.*

TOM JONES
(Office of Housing in San Francisco)
"Just because the majority of the people in a neighborhood don't want something, it doesn't mean they shouldn't get it." *1991*

K

JOHN KASICH
(Congressman)
"If the B-2 is invisible, just announce you've built 100 of them and don't build them." *1995*

"I like Pearl Jam—and I have a personal relationship with God. But I think he likes Pearl Jam, too." *1997*

"If you're looking for something bigger and better, it ain't coming." *1999: Announcing his plans to run for president.*

"If I ever told my wife I left without burying this dog, we'd be divorced. Get me a shovel." *1999: To Linda Kaiser of New Hampshire, who organized a coffee social for Kasich. When Kaiser realized she was short on ice, she jumped into her car and backed out the driveway, running over and killing her thirteen-year-old family dog. After the event, Kasich insisted on helping bury the dog. "I can't imagine Elizabeth Dole or George W. Bush burying my dog," Kaiser later said.*

DONALD KAUL
(Columnist)
"Didn't he know that Buddhist monks' robes don't have pockets?" *1997: On Al Gore's fund-raising appearance at a Buddhist temple in Los Angeles.*

"Bill Clinton is Eddie Haskell [of the old *Leave it to Beaver* fame]; we don't expect much from him. We don't really believe the cockamamie explanation he produces to escape blame, but we don't care much either. He's lowered our expectation below outrage. So long as he doesn't screw up the economy or cut Social Security, we'll put up with him." *1997: On the phenomenon of Bill Clinton's continued high-approval rating among the public despite the rumors and accusations of scandal around him.*

GARRISON KEILLOR
(Author & Comedian)
"It is to the Republicans' great credit that they have managed to keep the word *impeachment* floating in the air for so long. This is a feat, considering that polls point in the opposite direction. They have accomplished it in a statesmanlike manner by announcing

GARRISON KEILLOR (CONT'D)

again and again, even when not asked, that when the time comes to consider impeachment, they will do so, and meanwhile they reserve judgement. This is sort of like your brother-in-law saying that although you're probably in perfectly good health, there is an ashenness in your complexion that suggests terminal liver cancer, and God forbid it should happen, but if it does, he would like to have your lake cabin." *1998: On the Clinton White House scandals and the Republicans.*

"I suppose that Monica Lewinsky, in her pain, has promised herself never again to get romantically involved with a sitting President. And I imagine it has dawned on Mr. Starr that he may go down in history as a rather small and obsessive figure who spent $40 million for a stained dress. And I imagine that by now all of the Monicas in America wish they were Cheryls or Ambers. And the President's reference to a hot-blooded amour as an inappropriate relationship does a real disservice to the English language. But otherwise, this story is without real import." *1998*

MICHAEL KELLY
(Journalist)

"Watching Bob Dole campaign for the Presidency is a curious and dislocating experience, like showering clothed or eating naked. It isn't unpleasant, but you can't escape the sense that the thing is at odds with itself." *1996*

JACK KEMP
(Vice Presidential Candidate)

"The vice president gets blown up." *1996: On why he refused to see the hit movie* Independence Day.

"As Lady MacBeth said to her guilt-stricken husband, 'Me thinks thou doth protest too much.'" *1997: In an op-ed piece in the* Wall Street Journal *dismissing ethics charges against Newt Gingrich. The play is* Hamlet, *and the character is Gertrude speaking to her son, not her husband, and the quote is 'The lady doth protest too much, methinks.'*

NANCY JO KEMPER
(Minister)

"Jesus would puke." *1998: The member of the Kentucky Council of Churches, on the state legislature's* decision after lobbying by some pastors to lift a ban on concealed weapons in houses of worship.

MURRAY KEMPTON
(Journalist)

"A gentleman does not abase himself or crawl or cry in public. President Bill Clinton's eyes well up at card tricks, and he never travels except to crawl wherever he lands. Senator Bob Dole used to show some potential for gentility, until . . . he wept over Nixon's casket, and he has since sunk further from crying in public to crawling in public for the Reverend Pat Robertson. . . . The last gentleman departs with [Colin] Powell, and we must rummage among those who have willed themselves into loutishness." *1995*

JOE KENDALL
(Federal Judge)

"If the activity and consequent damages continue, when all the dust clears, all the assets of the union, including their strike war chest, will be capable of being safely stored in the overhead bin of a Piper Cub." *1999: Ruling that the Allied Pilots Association will have to pay hefty damages to American Airlines to offset the cost of the pilots' illegal "sickout."*

GEORGE F. KENNAN
(Diplomat & Author)

"Tell your children, and your children's children, that you lived in the age of Bill Clinton and William Cohen, the age of Madeleine Albright and Sandy Berger, the age of Trent Lott and Joe Lieberman, and you too were present at the creation of the post-cold-war order, when these foreign policy Titans put their heads together and produced . . . a mouse.

"We are in the age of midgets. The only good news is that we got here in one piece because there was another age—one of great statesmen who had both imagination and courage." *1998: The architect of America's containment policy after World War II, on the expansion of NATO following the collapse of the Soviet Union.*

JIM KENNEDY
(Special Advisor to the White House Counsel)

"Ken Starr's backup plan." *1998: Revealing the name that White House insiders had given to a newly discovered asteroid a mile wide that is headed for Earth and might pass as close as 30,000 miles in the year 2028.*

JOE KENNEDY
(Congressman)

"As one of the few politicians who admits to both having inhaled and having enjoyed it, of course, I support it." *1992: On using marijuana for medicinal purposes.*

"You have a nice day!" *1998: Representative Joseph Kennedy's less-than-eloquent exit line as he ended the news conference at which he announced possibly the first-in-history voluntary retirement of a Kennedy from politics.*

JOHN F. KENNEDY JR.
(Magazine Editor)

"If you guys are going to be inhumane to my wife [by shadowing her constantly] then YOU SHOULDN'T PET MY DOG!" *1997: Kennedy was dining in a New York eatery and left his dog outside tied to a pole. Upon seeing one of the paparazzi covering the Kennedy's petting his dog, John John ran outside and denounced him with this non-sequitur.*

"With my wife beside me, I am really a happy man. I thank God every day that he's let me touch love with my hand." *1997: In an interview that may have lost something in the translation with Italy's* Chi *weekly magazine.*

"I was under that very desk 35 years ago, and I could tell you there was barely room for a 3-year-old." *1998: On his doubts about the Clinton White House sex scandal.*

"Anyone who's in the magazine business thinks about advertisers when they write about something. And anyone who says they don't is a liar." *1998*

BOB KERREY
(Senator)

"I don't know how many of you have ever seen *The Wizard of Oz,* which takes place in Kansas, just south of Nebraska. Dorothy clicks her heels and says, 'There's no place like home.' It won't be that easy for us." *1992: Speaking to a small crowd at the Christa McAuliffe Planetarium in Concord, NH.*

"Guys whose testosterone levels are dropping and they don't know what else to do." *1995: The Nebraska Democrat and Medal of Honor recipient, describing people who join paramilitary groups.*

"Clinton's an unusually good liar. Unusually good." *1998: On President Bill Clinton.*

"Did you ever think we'd see the day where the president would sit there and say, 'Oh, good, they're changing the subject to Vietnam'?" *1999: At the annual Gridiron Dinner, after getting a laugh from President Clinton with a wisecrack about draft-dodging.*

SERGEI KHRUSHCHEV
(Son of Nikita Khrushchev)

"I will not vote for Democrats—it's too dangerous for the country." *1999: On his political persuasion, just before he became an American citizen.*

CRAIG KILBORN
(TV Talk-show Host)

"President Clinton spent the day on the phone with friends, who said that while he seemed upbeat, he didn't end his conversations with his trademark, 'Oh, God, yes!' " *1998: On reports that Clinton was intimate with Monica Lewinsky while talking on the phone.*

"Like all low-budget porn, the audio was terrible, and it took way too long to get to the good parts." *1998: Analyzing the Clinton testimony on video.*

"It's the day after Bill Clinton's historic Ejaculation Proclamation." *1998: Referring to Clinton's televised apology.*

LARRY KING
(TV & Radio Talk-show Host)

"These days there are almost no good guys, no heroes, and even the villains are extra villainous. As for Bill Clinton, all I can say is that the president's best friends are his enemies." *1998*

PETER KING
(Congressman)

"It's painful to see the leader of the free world go through a perpetual 12-step program." *1998: On Clinton's apologies.*

HENRY KISSINGER
(Former Secretary of State & National Security Advisor)
"Me." *When asked at* Time's *seventy-fifth anniversary bash to name a man who's changed the course of events over the last seventy-five years.*

NANCY KISSINGER
(Wife of Henry Kissinger)
"We're both very absent minded. We've gotten our anniversary right only once and that was because the office reminded us." *1990: On what she has in common with her husband.*

JOE KLEIN
(Political Journalist & Author)
"A pretty good president in a pretty dull time. Can you imagine how dull the '90s would have been if we didn't have Clinton?" *1998: The* New Yorker *magazine correspondent whose novel* Primary Colors *is about a philandering Southern politician who strongly resembles Bill Clinton, evaluating his performance in office.*

EDWARD KOCH
(Former Mayor of New York City & TV Judge)
"People have misconceptions about me. They thought I was going to end up in a hospital in despair. But I looked 20 years younger. I look like a Greek god." *1990: On life after leaving political office.*

"It's not as exciting as a case I had on *The People's Court* involving a python that swallowed a Chihuahua." *1999: On the presidential impeachment trial over which his judicial colleague William Rehnquist presided in the U.S. Senate.*

TED KOPPEL
(Newsman)
"Look, tell him that I know when I get a direct answer and I know when I get bullshit and this is bullshit." *1999: On* Nightline *during an interview with Serbian soldiers. After the network got angry e-mails, producer Richard Harris wrote a response, defending Koppel by citing "the lateness of the hour, that children would not be watching*

and that the word was used only at the end of a long and frustrating exchange with the Serbs."

CHARLES KRAUTHAMER
(Journalist)
"Heart and soul . . . will get you nowhere when you've lost your way and your mind." *1996: Discussing Republicans running for the GOP presidential nomination in 1996.*

WILLIAM KRISTOL
(News Analyst)
"My prediction is that . . . [the House] may fail to report out articles of impeachment." *1998: On November 8, shortly before the House reported out articles of impeachment.*

BOB KRUEGER
(Texas State Senator)
"Was it Shakespeare who said, 'Hasta la vista, baby'?" *1993*

DENNIS KUCINICH
(Congressman)
"A fundamental principle of democracy is that one should never ask how a law or kielbasa is made." *1997: Kucinich, D-Ohio, is a vegetarian.*

WILLIAM KUNSTLER
(Attorney)
"Abraham Lincoln's assassination turned out to be a pretty good thing. Lincoln was a pretty bad guy, you know." *1992*

KUWAITI MAN
(Unidentified)
"We give special thanks to Mr. Bush and all the Allies: the British, the French, the Egyptians, CNN." *1991: Giving thanks after the Gulf War.*

L
ANTHONY LAKE
(National Security Advisor)
"I will try to follow the advice that a university president once gave a prospective commencement speaker. 'Think of yourself as the body at an Irish wake,' he said. 'They need you in order to have the party, but nobody expects you to say very much.'" *1995: In a commencement speech at the University of Massachusetts, Amherst.*

SAUL LANDAU
(Radio Commentator)

"Clinton will be known as the education president—the sex education president." *1998*

BERNARD LANDRY
(Quebec's Finance Minister)

"Ask a first violinist and a first basemen how much they make, and you will have your answer." *1999: On why his province will fund the Montreal Symphony but not a new park for the Expos.*

NATHAN LANE
(Actor)

"Want to get rid of Saddam Hussein? Put him on the NBC fall schedule." *1998: After his low-rated sitcom* Encore! Encore! *was pulled from NBC's schedule.*

JEREMY LARNER
(Political Speechwriter & Screenwriter)

"In politics, you can get to an even deeper level of truth when you fictionalize, and on film you can alter truth forever." *1998: Larner wrote Robert Redford's film,* The Candidate.

PATRICK LEAHY
(Senator)

"For the Midwestern states, the Great Lakes is all they have." *1998: The Democratic senator from Vermont after Congress reversed itself on his bill designating Lake Champlain as one of the Great Lakes, on why his measure evoked such a negative reaction from Ohio to Minnesota.*

JAY LENO
(TV Talk-show Host)

"And guess what he found in the glove compartment? His draft notice!" *1994: On Bill Clinton showing up at a Mustang owners' rally in his beloved 1967 Mustang.*

"This year's elections are like a horse race. Everybody runs in circles. They end up exactly where they started. And when they're done, manure is everywhere." *1994*

"He says he had no idea she was a prostitute, or he wouldn't have done it. And today the prostitute said, 'Hey, I didn't know he was a Congressman or I wouldn't have done it either.'" *1994: On Congressman Ken Calvert, a Republican from Corona, CA, who had a prostitute in his car when he was stopped by police.*

"[Dan] Quayle went in for an appendectomy. . . . He said he hopes that, with luck, someone will step forward with a donor appendix." *1995*

"Politics is just show business for ugly people. The hors d'ouevres are worse, but it's basically the same thing." *1995*

"If Colin Powell doesn't hear it, how the hell did Sonny Bono hear it?" *1995: After hearing Powell say being a successful politician requires "a calling that I do not yet hear."*

"Poor Russia. They've got a president with low popularity, no foreign policy, who can't keep his hands off women. Well, they wanted an American style of government." *1995*

"According to a new study, sex can make you smarter. President Clinton is a Rhodes scholar." *1995*

"Boy, that sounds like the real Clinton health care plan." *1996: On a magazine report that the more sex you have, the longer you will live.*

"Gingrich, Dole and Clinton. You get the feeling as each day passes that they're the nonessential employees?" *1996: On the budget impasse in Washington.*

"Bill Clinton says that he will be going to Bosnia. You know visiting Bosnia is the second scariest thing for an American President . . . other than having Oliver Stone make a movie about you." *1996*

"The theme of Clinton's State of the Union address was the Age of Possibility. I thought, for Clinton, the Age of Possibility was when a girl turned 18." *1996*

"Only in our system would a guy worth $400 million spend $25 million for a job that pays $200,000 and call himself a financial expert." *1996: On GOP presidential candidate Steve Forbes.*

JAY LENO (CONT'D)

"According to the agriculture department, according to a recent survey, Americans are eating four times as much Mexican food as they did twenty years ago. Four times! No wonder there's a hole in the ozone layer!" *1996*

"Hillary asked the Senate, 'Look as long as you've got the president under oath, I'd like to ask him a couple questions about that Paula Jones thing.'" *1996*

"It was the biggest suicide in San Diego since the Republicans nominated Dole." *1997: On the mass suicide of Heaven's Gate cult members.*

"The Kennedys are like the dinosaurs in 'The Lost World': They have big teeth . . . breed like crazy, and wherever they go, women are running and screaming." *1997*

"I guess Clinton spent days training the dog. In fact to teach the puppy to play dead, he's having the dog watch videos of Al Gore." *1998*

"It's amazing how little some people know about our presidents. Like, today they asked Monica Lewinsky who the first president was and she said, 'You mean for the country or, like, me personally?'" *1998*

"It's a good thing Clinton didn't go to Vietnam. It's obvious he's a terrible shot." *1998: Commenting on Monica Lewinsky's stained dress, used as evidence to prove she and President Clinton had a sexual encounter.*

"This guy [Bill Clinton] never really got out of high school. He's like a ninth-grader, quoting the Bible to say it's all right. Politics is the only business where, if you play around, your wife has to defend you. If he weren't a politician, his clothes would be all over Pennsylvania Avenue and his car would be on fire in the driveway. You know that movie *City of Angels*, where the guy gives up heaven for sex? That's Clinton." *1998*

"Last night they had the Miss Teen USA Pageant. Or as Clinton calls it, the Home Shopping Network." *1998*

"The Republicans on the House Judiciary Committee drafted articles of impeachment. And as always when drafted, Clinton left the country." *1998*

"I had a big Bill Clinton weekend. I gave in to my shame." *1998*

"Instead of impeachment, people are calling for the President to be censured. Have you heard about that? Censure. Do you think that will work? How about neutering?" *1998*

"Clinton is visiting the Holy Land where he plans to visit Bethlehem. Clinton in Bethlehem, well, good luck trying to find a virgin for the Christmas pageant now." *1998*

"As of today, Baghdad has surpassed New York for the number of potholes in the city." *1998*

"In Toronto, Canada, there is a museum that displays nothing but different types of contraceptive devices. Of course, here in America we call that the Kennedy Compound." *1999*

"Monica Lewinsky said today, if they make a TV movie about the scandal, she wants Neve Campbell to play her. . . . President Clinton said today, if they get Neve Campbell to play Monica, he'll play himself." *1999*

"Congress wants to give itself an increase of $5,000 a year. That's just jealousy. They saw how much Clinton and Gore were getting from the Chinese, and now they want a raise too." *1999*

ADRIAN LESTER
(Actor)

"You don't think Abraham Lincoln was a whore before he was a president? . . . He did it all just so he'd get the opportunity, one day, to stand in front of the nation and appeal to 'the better angels of our nature.'" *1998: The British actor and instant amateur American historian played the role of "Henry Burton" in the film* Primary Colors.

DAVID LETTERMAN
(TV Talk-show Host)

"[Governor Bill] Clinton outspent the other candidates by at least 2-to-1 . . . on Valentine's Day gifts." *1992*

"Earlier, Dan Quayle indicated that he would run for president in 1996. And today he announced that if he loses, he would run again in 1997." *1994*

"You look at some of these races around the country and you say to yourself, 'Boy, it's just a damned shame somebody has to win.' " *1994: On the fall election campaign.*

"Every time Gore led a round of applause [during Clinton's State of the Union speech], Clinton tossed him a herring." *1996*

"I'm not sure he should have done this. Through his State of the Union Address tonight, President Clinton kept referring to Hillary as 'the defendant.' " *1996*

"Yesterday, Bill Clinton confirmed that he is having financial problems, but he said he didn't run for this office for the money. Well no, I think it's clear to everybody that he's in it for the chicks." *1996*

"He's just gonna lay low until the fighting is finished. You know, just kind of like what he did in the 60s." *1996: On the president's election strategy.*

"The race for the White House is going along pretty smoothly. Bob Dole, now more confident than ever, is very optimistic that he's going to get the nomination. In fact, he's so confident that, according to his campaign manager, sometime in the middle of next week, he is actually scheduled to smile." *1996*

"Sunday will be the 130th anniversary of the death of Abraham Lincoln, and Senator Bob Dole was talking about it. He says he reflects on the death of Lincoln a great deal. I think Dole should because it was Dole that night who said, 'Abe, I got theater tickets. I can't use 'em. You want 'em?' " *1996*

"Dole in the last couple of weeks has been saying some very interesting things about cigarettes and tobacco. A couple of days ago, he said smoking tobacco is like drinking milk: some can, some can't. This doesn't sound like a guy who's running for President, this sounds like a guy who's auditioning for *Forrest Gump II*." *1996*

"On the bright side for Bob Dole, unlike most people who leave the Senate early, he's not going to jail." *1996*

"Smoked a joint and nailed a campaign worker—I'm sorry, that's how President Clinton celebrated." *1996: One of his "Top 10 Ways Bob Dole Celebrated the Fourth of July."*

"They're getting ready for President Clinton's inauguration in a couple of weeks. They're already planning the gala celebration down there in Washington. . . . And one of the bits of entertainment they'll have down there is a show just here in New York City, 'Bring in 'Da Noise, Bring in 'Da Funk,' performing. It's nice, I think that's a nice little treat for the Clintons while they're waiting for someone to 'Bring in 'Da indictment.' " *1997*

"According to the White House, President Clinton is changing his diet now. And, I'm thinking, this is amazing because I thought the guy was starting to look a little heavier around the middle, you know, but it turned out his pockets were just full of Indonesian cash." *1997*

"Are you all excited about the Presidential Inauguration next week? . . . Hillary Clinton will be wearing a gown designed by Oscar de la Renta. We still don't know what Clinton's date will be wearing." *1997*

"President Clinton will be playing himself in a TV movie right here on CBS. President Clinton has one disappointment and that is that he didn't really have to sleep with anybody to get the part." *1997*

"During President Clinton's first administration, there were 938 people visiting the White House, spending the night at the White House. Three categories: you had celebrities, of course; you had campaign supporters; and one night stands." *1997*

"The First Family was in town over the weekend to celebrate Chelsea's 17th birthday, and they went to see *Rent*, the Tony Award-winning show. *Rent*—you know, it's a musical based on the Lincoln Bedroom." *1997*

"Here's how it works: $50,000 for a ride on Air Force One, and for another $50,000, President Clinton will help you join the Mile High Club." *1997: On contributions to the Democratic National Convention.*

DAVID LETTERMAN (CONT'D)

"You know for the last three days, President Clinton, since the operation, has been showing up to work every day at the White House. He's got a cast, he's got a wheelchair and he's got a note from his doctor. Coincidentally, now, in 1968, that's exactly how he showed up at his draft board." *1997*

"You folks hear about this story—kind of interesting, kind of sad, I guess, in a way. From my home state of Connecticut . . . a kid, really a kid, a 17-year-old kid, working at McDonald's restaurant, was selling marijuana at the drive-up window in the happy meals. . . . I'm thinking about it though, marijuana and cheeseburgers—seriously, that is one-stop shopping for President Clinton." *1997*

"Anthony Lake, the nominee for director of the C.I.A., has taken himself out of the running to be the chief of the C.I.A. . . . So, let's see, that's six rejections for President Clinton. Well, seven if you count Paula Jones." *1997*

"You know one of the requirements for the Heaven's Gate cult was castration. And I'm thinking, 'Well, geez, maybe that should be a requirement for the Kennedys.'" *1997*

"Ladies and gentlemen, here's bad news for U.S. Congressman Sonny Bono. Sonny Bono has been accused of sexually harassing a college intern on his staff. In the beginning, I don't think many people took Sonny Bono seriously. But now, sexually harassing an intern? He sounds Presidential." *1997*

"Here's an interesting anthropological study that has just been published. Apparently now, chimpanzees frequently are unfaithful to their mates. It is not uncommon for them to sneak off from their own tribe and have an affair with a member of another clan. It's so interesting, they're doing a film about it—I believe it's called *Kennedys in the Mist*." *1997*

"Ladies and gentlemen, earlier tonight on VH-1, one-hour special—'Bill Clinton: Rock-n-Roll President' . . . You know what it is: for an hour, Bill Clinton has got his albums there and he's talking about his albums. Originally, VH-1 wanted Hillary to be on the show, but you know, she's destroyed all of her old records." *1997*

"Let me get this straight, now. If you commit adultery, you can't be Chairman of the Joint Chiefs of Staff. But you can be Commander in Chief." *1997*

"Today, by the way, in the world of history is the 25th anniversary of the Watergate break-in. . . . You know what that Watergate thing did? It started that annoying trend: anytime there's a political scandal, they add the suffix '-gate' on to the end of the scandal. For example, Clinton alone, he's had 'travelgate,' 'filegate,' 'Whitewatergate,' and then this Paula Jones mess I guess is 'tailgate.'" *1997*

"Whitewater prosecutor Kenneth Starr has now started investigating the sexual history of President Clinton. Wow! Finally something that doesn't involve Hillary." *1997*

"President Clinton is continuing now his South American tour. . . . While President Clinton is gone, Vice President Al Gore attended a summit meeting to study 'El Niño.' Well, President Clinton heard about this, got very excited and now is calling together a summit meeting to study Elle MacPherson." *1997*

"Everybody is happy down there in Washington, D.C., our nation's capital. President Clinton has a dog now. He's going to spend the next three years training a dog, that's what our President is going to do. And it's crazy down there. He is running around, eating everything in sight, jumping up on secretaries, and they're having problems with the dog, too." *1997*

"According to a medical study now, the size of a man's brain shrinks with age faster than a woman's brain. So if you think about this, President Clinton, now here's a guy who's 50 years old and then I thought, 'Oh, it doesn't make any difference there either because this guy's not exactly thinking with his brain.'" *1998*

"Say what you will about President Clinton, he is a pretty shrewd man, and he has now got a brand-new story for this whole thing. Clinton is now telling close friends and associates that he and Monica Lewinsky . . . were practicing for the two-man luge." *1998*

"It's Lincoln's Birthday and President Clinton is doing what he can to commemorate Lincoln's birthday, so instead of taking the interns to the Oval Office, he's taking them into the Lincoln bedroom." *1998*

"People are still talking about the 75th anniversary of *Time* magazine. . . . And to commemorate they had a big party, they had their own whoopdee-doo over at Radio City Music Hall. Man! The celebrities! It was star packed. . . . President Clinton, of course, was at the party and they sat him at dinner next to Sean Connery, the original 007. All night long, and I guess this was a little embarrassing for people around them, Clinton was begging Sean Connery to introduce him to 'Pussy Galore.'" *1998*

"President Clinton, now that the sexual harassment suit is behind him, he wants to get Social Security taken care of because President Clinton feels he understands the needs of the aging. Well, that makes sense because between Paula Jones, Monica Lewinsky and Kathleen Willey, he's aged about a hundred years." *1998*

"President Clinton held a press conference to announce the name of his dog, Buddy. You know, if I'm that dog, I'm going to be a little nervous, because I believe most of President Clinton's buddies are in jail." *1998*

"It looks like President Clinton has avoided war. You've got to hand it to him, he hasn't done that since the '60s." *1998: On problems between the United States and Iraq.*

"Good news for out-of-towners visiting New York City. Mayor Rudolph Giuliani is doing everything he can to make New York City a nicer, friendlier, gentler kind of city. You know what I think has made the biggest difference for this 'friendly' campaign for New York City? Those signs in the backseats of New York City cabs that read, 'Thank you for not urinating.'" *1998*

"President Clinton's approval rating has dropped . . . you know what that means. Time for another sex scandal." *1998*

"I'm beginning to think that the whole impeachment thing was Clinton's idea—so he could get rid of the Republicans." *1998*

"Hillary Clinton took a ride on a camel out into the Sahara desert. And I'm thinking to myself, 'What a coincidence because her husband, President Clinton, is also between humps.'" *1999*

BARBARA LEWINSKY
(Mother)
"I would say, 'You are a butthead.'" *1999: On what she'd tell President Clinton if she met him.*

MONICA LEWINSKY
(Former White House Intern)
"I'm going to the White House to get my presidential kneepads." *1995: To a friend, describing a special relationship she had with someone in the White House.*

"If I ever want to have an affair with a married man again, especially if he's president, please shoot me." *1997: During a taped phone conversation with Linda Tripp.*

"I hope you all know how very sorry I am that so much attention was brought to the building." *1998: In a note to Watergate residents upon her move.*

"I'm really sorry for everything that's happened. And I hate Linda Tripp." *1998: As she wrapped up her grand jury testimony on August.*

"I'm kind of known for something that's not so great to be known for." *1999: Turning away an autograph seeker at the Los Angeles airport.*

"I wouldn't dream of asking Chelsea and Mrs. Clinton to forgive me. But I would ask them to know that I am very sorry for what happened and for what they've been through." *1999: On her affair with President Clinton.*

"I need to have the means to take care of myself for the next few years. Therapy is not cheap." *1999: On why she agreed to cooperate in her biography, written by Andrew Morton, for which she was paid $1.5 million.*

MONICA LEWINSKY (CONT'D)

"Mommy made a big mistake." *1999: On what she would tell her children about her affair with President Clinton, in answer to a question from Barbara Walters.*

"You can be anything in this world but fat." *1999: On her weight problem.*

"I knew that I was never going to talk about this publicly." *1999: Talking about her affair with President Clinton on primetime TV.*

"Sex is like eating. . . . Sometimes you have fast food, and sometimes you eat a gourmet meal." *1999: During a British interview.*

"It reminded me of *The Diary of Anne Frank.*" *1999: Describing her meetings with prosecutor Kenneth Starr's deputies.*

"Now there's a dress more famous than my dress." *1999: On the pink Ralph Lauren gown Gwyneth Paltrow wore to the Academy Awards.*

"With what's been going on in Kosovo, he's been on my mind a lot more. . . . It's like if you smell someone's perfume it reminds you of that person." *1999: Proclaiming that she thinks a lot about President Clinton but is no longer in love with him.*

"I certainly am not going to go through and reenact for you verbally what was going on and what my feelings and emotions were at the time." *1999: To radio host Terry Gross on Fresh Air on NPR. Gross had asked Lewinsky how she and President Clinton had "clicked at an incredible level" during a sexual diversion while he was on the phone with a congressman. Lewinsky then walked off the show in midconversation.*

"It's getting serious out there. I just hope it doesn't go nuclear." *1999: On her concerns over the crisis in Kosovo.*

MONICA LEWINSKY
(Legal Secretary)

"Like I'm in a Rod Serling story and someone has usurped my name." *1998: The Manhattan legal secretary, on how it feels to endure the alleged presidential sex scandal.*

MICHAEL LEWIS
(Journalist)

"The vice president's conversation is littered with *franklys* and *to-be-honest-with-yous* and *it-is-my-understandings,* all of which translated into civilian English as 'I'm never going to tell you the truth about anything, so why on earth are you asking?' " *1996: On Al Gore.*

JOHN LEYDECKER
(Californian)

"If this is not Bill Clinton's idea of heaven, I don't know what is." *1998: After spotting a partially unlit neon sign in front of a restaurant that read INTERN HOUSE OF PANCAKES.*

ROBERT LICHTER
(President of the Center for Media & Public Affairs)

"The Lewinsky scandal is like the Hope diamond. It attracts people and destroys everyone that comes into contact with it. The President's moral standing is destroyed, the political process is suspended and the press, instead of filtering out the fire hydrant of information in the information age, is like a dog urinating on it." *1998*

"We thought that nothing could top the O. J. Simpson story, and this proved us wrong." *1999: Reporting that the evening newscasts by the three big broadcast networks featured 1,502 stories on the Monica Lewinsky scandal, surpassing any other subject in 1998.*

G. GORDON LIDDY
(Former Watergate Burglar)

"If I can go from burglar for the government to talk-show host, you can go from entertainer to congressman." *1995: To freshman Congressman Sonny Bono.*

RUSH LIMBAUGH
(TV & Radio Talk-show Host)

"There he stands, looking down at his notes, trying to remember how he feels." *1992: On President George Bush at the Republican National Convention.*

"I tell people don't kill all the liberals, leave enough around so we can have two on every campus; living fossils, so we will never forget what these people stood for." *1995*

ARTHUR S. LINK
(Historian)

"I've read a lot of history in my life and I think that aside from Saint Paul, Jesus and the great religious prophets, Woodrow Wilson was the most admirable character I've ever encountered." *1998: Link spent thirty-five years editing the papers of America's twenty-eighth president, Woodrow Wilson.*

"I believe God created me to do this. Not many people in this day and age would think there was such a thing as a divine call, but I do, and I had it." *1998: On editing the Woodrow Wilson papers.*

"Most of the Hitler and Stalin scholars I know are depressed people." *1998: Comparing his work on Woodrow Wilson, which he said was "uplifting and a joy," to work by other scholars.*

ROBERT LIVINGSTON
(Congressman)

"I guess I didn't think of the impact of a million bucks. I just can't believe that somebody would do that to me. Welcome to the big leagues. Welcome to the world of Larry Flynt. I just didn't think it possible that he would do what he did." *After his resignation from Congress on the eve of his becoming Speaker of the House, because of his fears that Flynt was planning to publish the details of Livingston's past indiscretions.*

"I want to assure everyone that these indiscretions were not with employees on my staff, and I have never been asked to testify under oath about them." *1998: In his resignation speech before Congress during impeachment hearings on President Clinton. Livingston admitted that he had "on occasion strayed from my marriage."*

RICHARD LLAMAS
(Tourist)

"God almighty, take the vote and get it over with." *1999: Shouting from the Senate gallery during the impeachment trial of President Clinton. He was removed from the chamber and arrested.*

CAROLYN LOCHHEAD
(Columnist & Reporter)

"Lying about your personal life never carries over to lying about policy. You really can sleep with dogs and not wake up with fleas. Republicans really were going to throw babies, old ladies and puppies in the street and you stopped them. Never mind that you signed their legislation that you insisted was going to result in this." *1998: Summing up the philosophy of the Clinton presidency.*

"The message [of the film *Primary Colors*] is, personal integrity bears no relation to integrity. Crudeness is just quaint Southern charm. Predatory behavior is simply a joyous lust for life. *Primary Colors* is a kind of *Titanic* in reverse. . . . Only Hollywood could turn the Clinton administration into a paragon of virtue and idealism." *1998*

"You must not lose if you're a likeable fellow who cares about the little guy. Because of your high ideals, which boil down to pandering to every conceivable voter constituency, the country would be terribly deprived if you lost. Therefore you are justified in doing anything to win, no matter how sleazy. This, the movie tells us approvingly, is the Clinton legacy. No other groundbreaking Clinton policy, aside from school uniforms, compares. This is why, ultimately, Hillary stands by her man." *1998: On the theme of the film* Primary Colors.

JOHN LOGAN
(Boston Voter)

"We're not voting for pope. He's a bozo and a drunk, and all that. But he's our bozo." *1994: On why he voted for Senator Edward Kennedy.*

TRENT LOTT
(Senate Majority Leader)

"I think it is beginning to have an impact on . . . the president and on his ability to deal with many very important issues for the future of our country—from Social Security to what's going on in Iraq and now what's going on in Kosovo." *1998: On the continuing Clinton sex-scandal investigations in Washington.*

"What do Monica Lewinsky and Ken Starr have to do with scheduling business in the Senate?" *Responding to White House Spokesman Mike McCurry.*

TRENT LOTT (CONT'D)

"It looks like they are hiding something." *1998: Deep thoughts after President Clinton invoked executive privilege to prevent certain aides from testifying before a grand jury.*

"Since there've been so many bits of bad news and his poll numbers went up, since this appears to be good news for the president, I presume the political numbers will go down." *1998: Predicting lower approval ratings for the president after the dismissal of the Paula Jones case.*

"Quite frankly, these little boo-boos, where you're hitting a KLA headquarters, where you're killing innocent citizens, I think is hurting the image of the military, which is unfair." *1999: Arguing that mistakes in NATO's bombing of Yugoslavia, including hitting the Chinese embassy and killing scores of civilians, are damaging U.S. prestige.*

COURTNEY LOVE
(Singer & Actress)

"Impeach someone for adultery? That's so retarded. I can't believe you're actually asking me that question." *1998: When asked if she thought President Clinton should be impeached.*

BUZ LUKENS
(Congressman)

"It's been an unexciting and dull campaign. With me in it, it's no longer dull." *1992: On his decision to run for reelection to the House after he was convicted of having sex with a minor.*

M

GLORIA MACAPAGAL-ARROYO
(Philippine Senator)

"He was always dating the foxiest girls in our dorm." *1995: Remembering her college classmate, President Bill Clinton.*

MADONNA
(Singer & Actress)

"Dr. King, Malcolm X, freedom of speech is as good as sex." *1990: A rap to encourage voting in the 1990 election.*

"If you have an intimate relationship with somebody, I don't care if it's the bellboy or the president of the United States, shut the fuck up." *1998: Advice to Monica Lewinsky.*

"Does she change her hair a lot?" *1999: Discussing the first lady.*

BILL MAHER
(Comedian & TV Talk-show Host)

"*Independence Day* is a blockbuster. Washington is flattened and the First Lady dies. President Clinton called it the 'feel-good hit of the summer.'" *1996*

"The Kennedys have proved that if you stick together as a family, you can get through adversity and tragedy and then make a fortune selling your mom's old crap." *1996*

"I guess we all remember where we were when Michael Kennedy was killed—I was at a New Year's Eve party." *1998*

"In five years, people will think Monica Lewinsky was the chick who used to date Seinfeld." *1998*

"[Hurricane Bonnie] probably won't hit Martha's Vineyard. But just in case, Hillary Clinton tied down the President's dinghy." *1998*

"Monica Lewinsky's lawyers told her she would get off scot-free, and she asked, 'Who's Scott Free?'" *1998*

"A rear admiral had to resign today because he had an adulterous affair with a defense contractor. Here's how you know your husband is having an affair with a defense contractor—you find motel receipts for $19 trillion." *1998*

"Paula Jones said she always told the truth and the President never did. And that's why the more he lies the smaller her nose gets." *1998*

BILL MAHER
(San Francisco Supervisor)

"The [San Francisco] Board of Supervisors is a testament to the success of the policy of getting the mentally ill out of institutions and on the streets." *1991*

NELSON MANDELA
(President of South Africa)

"There's one regret I've had throughout my life—that I never became the heavyweight boxing champion of the world. I would like my friend, Evander Holy-field, to know that today, I feel like the heavy-weight boxing champion of the world." *1998: After becoming the first African American ever to receive the Congressional Gold Medal.*

IMELDA MARCOS
(Widow of Former Philippine President Ferdinand Marcos)

"In a way, the longer he's gone, the more perfect he becomes." *1998: On her late husband.*

"Perception is real, truth is not. I'm not fighting for money and possessions. I'm fighting for something more precious. I pray that as we enter the cyber age—the Age of Transparency—the facts and the truth will out." *1998*

"If you know how rich you are, you are not rich. But me, I am not aware of the extent of my wealth. That's how rich we are." *1998: Claiming that her family has more than $800 million in secret bank accounts abroad, which she would give to the poor if she won in the May election.*

"Justice delayed is justice denied." *1999: After filing a petition with the anti-graft court to release some $570 million from frozen Swiss bank accounts. She said she will use the money to help President Estrada "save our economy and save the poor."*

"We own practically everything in the Philippines." *1999: Claiming her family owns 500 billion pesos [about $13.1 billion] worth of stock, while official records put the Marcoses' total income from 1965 to 1984 at only 16 million pesos.*

GABRIEL GARCIA MARQUEZ
(Author)

"The first thing you notice about Bill Clinton is how tall he is." *1999: On meeting the American president.*

"Clinton, born and raised in Arkansas, a Southern state, applauded the notion and professed himself happy to be a Caribbean." *1999*

JUDITH MARTIN
("Miss Manners")

"The general discourse had been getting cruder and cruder. Privacy and discretion had almost disappeared from the general public usage before the scandal. Now the salacious nosiness has been carried to this logical conclusion; there's been a reaction on the side of propriety. Now, this is a society that has had nonstop television confessions for 20 years, people vying to get on and reveal everything they can. With this story, what a pleasant surprise—people are reacting by saying, you know, we really shouldn't be discussing this." *1998: Said just prior to Bill Clinton's televised confession of his improper relationship with Monica Lewinsky.*

VANESSA MARTINEZ
(Fourteen-year-old Student)

"He seems like an average type of man. He's not, like smart. I'm not trying to rag on him or anything. But he has the same mentality I have—and I'm in the eighth grade." *1992: After Dan Quayle visited Bret Harte Middle School in South Central Los Angeles.*

MARY STUART MASTERSON
(Actress)

"He's a terrific president. I've met him. He never hit on me." *1998: On what she thinks of Bill Clinton as president.*

MARY MATALIN
(Political Consultant)

"James is a very good man—a patriot and a corporal in the Marine Corps, which makes him the highest ranking military man in the Clinton administration." *1993: Describing her fiancée, James Carville.*

"Sleeping with them is one thing. Liking them is another." *1994: The Republican political consultant and wife of Democratic political consultant James Carville, on Democrats.*

"Everyone in D.C. should smoke pot and they'd make better decisions." *1994*

"When I leave the hospital, the first thing I'll do is have a martini and cigarette in the parking lot. It's not like I plan to get tanked in the parking lot. I'll hand her off to James before I inhale." *1995: On what she'll do after having her baby.*

"There's a new study—I love this study—that your brain actually shrinks while you're pregnant. So

MARY MATALIN (CONT'D)

there's a definitive explanation for the stupidity that sets in when you have a baby. Your brain goes back to normal size, unlike your feet, which stay big, and your breasts, which actually end up permanently smaller. . . . I'd say the brain death is one of the biggest surprises. I remember sitting on the front porch with my new infant in my arms, crying hideously, while singing to her: 'You are my sunshine, my only sunshine . . .' What is that about?" *1998*

"My husband helps a lot (with raising our child), since he has the maturity of a 2-year-old. He's a perfect playmate. He has an office at home and our daughter answers his phone." *1998*

"I'm happy to report that I have not been beaten to a bloody pulp." *1999: After a false newspaper story was spread on the Internet suggesting that her husband, Democratic consultant James Carville, had been arrested for assaulting her.*

TERRENCE MCAULIFFE
(Chief Fund-raiser for Bill Clinton)
"What do you want me to do with our donors, take them out . . . and pistol-whip them?" *1999: To critics of the special treatment the White House and Democratic party give to financial contributors.*

BARRY MCCAFFREY
(Federal Drug Czar)
"This is not medicine. This is a Cheech and Chong show." *1997: Ridiculing claims that marijuana can relieve illnesses, which led to the passage of ballot initiatives in California and Arizona allowing its therapeutic use.*

JOHN MCCAIN
(Senator)
"No one can 'out-Oprah' Bill Clinton." *1996*

"I enjoyed shooting rockets and dropping bombs and shooting off guns. Nobody in their right mind wouldn't enjoy that." *1998: Describing his tour of duty in the Navy during the Vietnam War—where he was an enemy prisoner.*

"He'll be a chapter in American history; those of us who follow him will be footnotes." *1998: On Barry*

Goldwater, after the death of the 1964 GOP presidential nominee.

EUGENE MCCARTHY
(1968 Presidential Candidate)
"I get these invitations to speak on some campus and find that the students don't really want me, don't know what it's all about. But there's always about 10 faculty people who invited me and want me to talk about the old days." *1996*

ELIZABETH MCCAUGHEY
(Lieutenant Governor, New York)
"This is the essence of McCarthyism. Go back and look at what Joe McCarthy did. It's exactly the same." *1996: On Governor George Patakai's forcing her to take taxis to public events.*

DAVID MCCULLOUGH
(Historian & TV Host)
"I'm asked, how does he differ from Bill Clinton? Well, that could be a long answer. I'll tell you this: if Harry Truman ever took a sip of bourbon, he swallowed, and he didn't care who knew about it." *1997*

MIKE MCCURRY
(President's Press Secretary)
"But two Huangs don't make a right." *1996: On the two John Huangs who often visited the White House.*

"We may do dumb things from time to time, but we are not certifiably insane." *1997: Commenting on allegations that the White House was behind an IRS audit of the tax returns of Paula Jones.*

"He asked if it was, in fact, an April Fool's joke." *1998: On the president's reaction when his lawyer, Robert Bennett, called to tell him the lawsuit by Paula Jones had been dismissed on April 1, 1998.*

"The use of a two-syllable vulgarity by the chairman was rather ambitious." *1998: On GOP committee chairman Dan Burton calling President Clinton a "scumbag."*

"Maybe there'll be a simple, innocent explanation. I don't think so because I think we would have offered that up already." *1998: In March, on the unfolding Monica Lewinsky scandal.*

"Sometimes not knowing the answer—even though that puts you in a tough postion, too—is better than consciously misleading people." *1998: During his final press briefing in October on his strategy of deliberately not asking the president about the Lewinsky scandal.*

"Quite a bit, but I'm going to go out and make people pay to hear it." *1998: When asked what he had learned about how the White House works.*

"Bill Clinton should wake up every single morning and thank the Lord for women." *1998: Speaking at the University of Virginia. He was referring to female voters, of course.*

"He is an enormously gifted and richly qualified leader for our nation but someone who is exasperatingly stupid in his personal life." *1998*

"There were times when I took my briefing book and threw it against the wall." *1998*

"For someone who loves the presidency and loves that White House and is a student of it, that will hurt him a lot forever when he's down in Little Rock at his library." *1999: On President Clinton's impeachment by the House of Representatives.*

JAMES MCDOUGAL
(Friend of the First Family)
"What irritates me is the constant self-comparison to Eleanor Roosevelt. We didn't get any Eleanor! We got Evita!" *1996: On Hillary Clinton.*

"I think she's found it isn't pleasant to suffer." *1996: On the political education of Hillary Clinton.*

"I wouldn't go to the bank on that." *1997: The former business partner of President Clinton, when asked after receiving a three-year prison sentence whether he believed the Clintons would be exonerated in the Whitewater scandal, as he insisted during his trial.*

"I was just tired of lying for the fellow." *1997: On why he changed his story to say that President Clinton was involved in the wrongdoing.*

"The institution I'm going to is coeducational, and I think there's an excellent chance I might get to see Hillary there." *1997: McDougal, who cooperated in the investigation of the First Couple, on the eve of beginning his term in the federal penitentiary in Lexington, KY.*

"They were like tornadoes moving through people's lives. I was left in their wake. And I had company." *1998: On Bill and Hillary Clinton.*

"Since I spent much of this decade dealing with lawyers and journalists, I like to say that I've improved my associations by joining the criminal class." *1997*

"I don't want to die in prison." *1997: In a moment of rare self-pity.*

"I think I left my mark, even a small one." *1998: Before he died after suffering a heart attack while in solitary confinement in prison.*

SUSAN MCDOUGAL
(Friend of the First Family)
"If the Clintons have helped me or the White House has helped me, then God help us all because I'm about to go to jail." *1996: Before being imprisoned for refusing to testify about the Clintons before a grand jury.*

"That I hate the independent counsel and I want them dead and their children dead? That one?" *1999: The Whitewater figure in an outtake from an interview with ABC's Diane Sawyer, responding to Sawyer's question about what message she wanted to deliver. McDougal's attorneys said the clip was taken out of context.*

EILEEN MCGANN
(Wife of Presidential Advisor Dick Morris)
"I'm not happy about what he did and sometimes I think about dismembering him, and good friends have offered to help me dig up the back yard and bury him." *1996: After her husband became embroiled in a sex scandal.*

"We are in the middle of a terrible, terrible trauma, and that seems to get lost in the overanalysis of people who don't know me and don't know Dick." *1996*

CYNTHIA MCKINNEY
(Congresswoman)
"When the military brass were on Capitol Hill saying that our reasonable belt-tightening had resulted in an

CYNTHIA MCKINNEY (CONT'D)

impotent military, I guess I did not fully understand the scope of the problem. With $50 million worth of Viagra, the entire military industrial complex will be locked, cocked, and ready to rock." *1998: On reports of Pentagon requests for money for Viagra.*

HENRY MCMASTER

(Chairman of the South Carolina GOP)

"If you're in a popularity contest with someone who's giving away money, it's hard to win—and that's all he does." *1999: Appraising President Clinton and his State of the Union speech.*

DICK MELL

(Chicago Alderman)

"Why would you trade the third most powerful man in this country for a freshman who couldn't find his ass with both hands." *1994: Summing up Representative Dan Rostenkowski's reelection message.*

JIM MERRILL

(Political Consultant)

"If you took Gumby and spent a quarter of a million dollars, he would also reflect well in the polls." *1996: On Steve Forbes's GOP presidential nomination campaign.*

TANYA METAKSA

(National Rifle Association Lobbyist)

"Many importers are going to be out on the street. . . . You can't return these firearms to the place you bought them like you return a shirt to Macys." *1998: On President Clinton's ban on fifty-eight types of assault rifles.*

DEE DEE MEYERS

(White House Press Secretary)

"Since January, I've been asked often if I was surprised by allegations that the President had an affair with a 21-year-old intern. I wasn't. After all, as the Clintons are quick to point out, they've been accused of everything from adultery to drug running to murder. What surprised me in this case was this: It was true. I never believed that Bill Clinton would risk his presidency—a job he had studied, dreamed about and prepared for since he was a kid—for something so frivolous, so reckless, so small." *1998: The former Clinton press secretary, on Clinton's admission of wrongdoing.*

"The President's relationship with Monica Lewinsky was so reckless as to seem pathological. He knew the consequences of getting caught, but he went ahead. For 18 months. In the West Wing of the White House." *1998*

"Yes, Bill Clinton is a big flirt. He flirts with me. He flirts with women. He flirts with pets."

CAROL MIGDEN

(California State Assemblywoman)

"I got a lezzie event back in San Francisco I'm co-hosting tonight." *1998: The San Francisco assemblywoman telling reporters why she left the California State Democratic party convention early to head back to her hometown.*

DENNIS MILLER

(Comedian)

"I find a lot of what [Rush Limbaugh] says makes sense. Some of it's kind of elitist crap, though. As an entertainer, I consider him in the same realm as the World Wrestling Federation: a big, fat guy making people laugh." *1996*

"Bob Dole made an appearance on MTV to try to get across to a younger audience. Hey, the guy's 72—he could go on *Matlock* and get across to a younger audience." *1996*

"Yesterday, Mike McCurry announced that he is stepping down as White House press secretary. Then, out of force of habit, he denied it." *1998*

"After the capture of three U.S. soldiers, President Clinton warned Serbia that the U.S. 'takes care of its own.' That's true, Bill, but I don't think a job at Revlon is what those three soldiers need right now." *1999*

"NATO air strikes reportedly hit a hospital in Belgrade this week. A NATO spokesman explained the error by saying the hospital looked exactly like the Chinese embassy." *1999*

ZELL MILLER

(Former Governor of Georgia)

"You won't find average Americans on the left or the right. You'll find them at Kmart." *1999: Lamenting how politicians often fail to gauge what their constituencies really care about.*

ANDREA MITCHELL
(Reporter)

"Did the markets go up or down?" *1998: Upon hearing erroneous rumors that her husband, Federal Reserve Chairman Alan Greenspan, had suffered a heart attack.*

GEORGE MITCHELL
(Senator)

"This is the most blatantly, flagrantly, obviously unconstitutional proposal that I've seen since I've been in the Senate. . . . This phony argument that we ought to be treated just like everybody else." *1991: On a proposal to apply the Occupational Safety and Health Act and the Fair Labor Standards Act to Congress.*

MAHATHIR MOHAMMAD
(President of Malaysia)

"I have seen CNN showing President Clinton hugging Monica Lewinsky at least 1,000 times already. I think the hugging happened only once." *1998: Equating CNN's coverage of the Clinton scandals with CNBC's coverage of opposition rallies in Malaysia. He berated the foreign media for spreading the idea that there has been constant social unrest since the arrest of his former deputy, Anwar Ibrahim.*

MONICA L. MONICA
(Candidate for Congress)

"I was Monica long before the other one was." *1999: The candidate for a Louisiana House seat vacated by Representative Robert Livingston, the onetime speaker nominee who quit after admitting adultery.*

MICHAEL MOORE
(Documentary Filmmaker)

"It really gets me, these people who grew up in a blue-collar, working-class family and try to forget where they came from. Today Clinton said if he were Joe Sixpack, he'd want to pursue the Paula Jones case. Hey, you *are* Joe Sixpack. Do you think because you went to Oxford and Yale that doesn't make you Joe Sixpack? That's where you come from. That's who you are." *1998*

DICK MORRIS
(Presidential Advisor)

"It basically required the ability of an academic and the canniness of a drug pusher." *1996: The former Clinton advisor, who resigned in a sex scandal involving his relations with a Washington hooker, on how to succeed as a political consultant.*

"I have a foot fetish. Do you find that weird?" *1996: Sharing his sexual fantasies with a hooker.*

"Deep down inside I'll bet that they miss me—I miss them." *1996: After hearing White House officials say they were "happy" he is no longer there.*

"The president is a little weird. He has, like, skin that absorbs what you're thinking." *1997: In a guest lecture to political science students at New York University.*

"A lot of times in your own life, I'll bet, when you're fighting with someone, you might be stuck on a position. You might be saying 'yes' and they're saying 'no,' and you're fighting with each other. And then, if you take the time and trouble to ask them, 'What are you worried about, why do you say no?' or 'Here's why I say yes,' and then you say to them, 'Well, you want us to have dinner tonight, and I said I can't do it at 6:30.' Well you don't care about 6:30, you just wanna have dinner, so 'How 'bout eight o'clock?' 'Great, that's fine,' and it all works out and the fight is over. And that's kind of what we do with polls." *1997: Explaining, in a lecture to political science students at New York University, what presidential advisors really do.*

"The central goal of my life is to persuade Eileen McGann to come back to me, and the only way I can is by changing and persuading her that I've changed." *1997*

"What's going to be his downfall is that he'll have nothing to do in '98, '99 and 2000. And Bill Clinton with nothing to do is an ugly sight." *1997: On his former boss Bill Clinton.*

"If he did anything wrong, he would still believe he didn't do anything wrong. This man could walk in and pass a lie detector test." *1997: On Bill Clinton's powers and problems.*

"I didn't do any of the fund-raising. I just did the fund spending." *1997: Alleging that he had nothing to do with scandals involving the fund-raising efforts for the president during the 1996 presidential campaign.*

DICK MORRIS (CONT'D)

"Somebody once asked me if I put Clinton and (Vice President Al) Gore in an embarrassing position by asking them to raise all this money, and I said, 'Yes, president and vice president.'" *1997*

"There are a thousand things, not including oral sex, which could have gone on, which fell well short of adultery. . . . Let's assume that some of the allegations that Hillary sometimes—not necessarily being into regular sex with men—might be true. Let's assume that this is a guy who has been sexually active for a long time, and then got it that as president . . . he'd have to shut himself down. You would then expect a variety of things which would be quasi-sexual in nature but which would fall short of it. . . . Phone sex might be one of them; fantasies might be one of them. . . . Those all could be real things without actually committing adultery." *1998: On the Clinton White House problems.*

"It's going to be Custer's Last Stand for the Democrats in November. They will absolutely be obliterated." *1998: The ex-Clinton aide and pundit, on September 14, just before a big Democratic victory in the polls.*

MARIO MORROW
(Political Consultant)

"The Republicans would like to portray him as a lunatic, except that he's rich. When you're rich, you know, you're just eccentric." *1998: The Michigan political consultant on Democratic gubernatorial nominee Geoffrey Fieger, who gained fame as Jack Kevorkian's lawyer and became known for slinging insults, such as calling the Republican incumbent "dumber than Dan Quayle and twice as ugly."*

ROBERT MOSBACHER
(GOP Campaign Chairman)

"Georgette is not one of the idle rich. Oh no. She actively spends and consumes. What I'm about to tell you is the absolute truth. I was in the Forbes 400 list until the very year I married Georgette." *1992: On his wife.*

"The other night we went out, and I said, 'If the stock market plunges as low as your neckline, this country is in big trouble.' She said, 'Don't worry. I know what's holding up my gown, which is more than I can say for the stock market.'" *1992*

"This woman is single-handedly keeping the U.S. economy afloat. If you factor out Georgette, we're actually in a depression." *1992*

PATRICK MOYNIHAN
(Senator)

"If you don't like this country, why don't you pack your bags and go back where you came from?" *1990: Speaking to an outspoken student at Vassar College where he lectured. Moynihan later denied making the remark and returned the $1,000 lecture fee.*

FRANK MURKOWSKI
(Senator)

"Coke's 130-year-old secret is more secure than our nuclear weapons research." *1999: Complaining about the Clinton administration's alleged failure to safeguard top-secret weapons information at Los Alamos National Laboratory.*

N

RALPH NADER
(Activist & Green Party Candidate for President)

"I don't believe in belonging to a party, because I'm a citizen advocate first and foremost. You want some garlic?" *1996: In a conversation with a journalist.*

THE NATION
(Newspaper)

"[Governor Bill] Clinton is in front of the pack and perhaps unstoppable except by an obstacle of his own erection." *1992: From a story on the race for the Democratic party's presidential nomination.*

WILLIE NELSON
(Singer & Musician)

"It's ridiculous to treat a man that way, much less the president of our country. If there's anything else important going on, we're missing it. We'll hear about it next generation." *1998: On the media, Ken Starr, and the Clinton scandals.*

LARRY NEWMAN
(Secret Service)

"With Kennedy, of course, it was a free-for-all. And with Johnson, too. Then comes Nixon, and every guy immediately saw the change. You wouldn't go into Nixon's office and say, 'Boss, I've got a couple babes for ya.' On the other hand, if you wanted to discuss the kind of stones used in the Great Wall, you'd be in there for three hours." *1998: Newman retired from the secret service in 1983 after twenty years of protecting the presidents.*

BAI VAN NGUYEN
(Agricultural Officer in Vietnam's Quang Tri Province)
"Floods may kill more people, but at least we'd have water." *1998: On the severe drought that has hit his province.*

MIKE NICHOLS
(Director)
"It's a drama because it gets real upsetting toward the end. There are strange emotions when you begin to think, 'Fuck, [the film] is about us, not the [politicians], and what's happening to us, and do we mean this to be happening to us?' For centuries we have said, 'He [the president] was a great man. Unfortunately, he couldn't keep his zipper closed. Nobody has ever yet put the two together and wondered, 'Does that come with it? What if it's one thing, not two things? A passion for people is expressed sexually too. We know it from real-life Democrats.'" *1998: On his film* Primary Colors.

JACK NICHOLSON
(Actor)
"I supported Gary Hart because he fucks. I support President Clinton and always will be on his side because he is someone who fucks. . . . I don't trust any guy who doesn't." *1998: On his political preferences.*

RICHARD NIXON
(President of the United States)
"I have often thought that if there had been a good rap group around in those days I might have chosen a career in music instead of politics." *1990: On choosing a career in the late 1940s.*

"They like froth; I'm a person of substance." *1990: On why the media was so tough on him.*

"Anybody who thinks that Japan is going to export democracy to China must be smoking pot." *1990*

"If I could find a way to get him out of there, even putting a contract out on him, if the CIA still did that sort of thing, assuming it ever did, I would be for it." *1991: On how to get rid of Saddam Hussein.*

"Paul Tsongas is too responsible to be president." *1992*

"That's bullshit!" *1992: Responding to allegations in the film* JFK *that the military conspired to kill Kennedy.*

"You want a wife that's intelligent, but not too intelligent." *1992: On the perfect wife for a politician.*

"I regret that I can't be there in person, but I understand Elvis may be standing in for me today." *1993: In a telephoned address to a party at the Nixon Library and Birthplace. Revelers attended a joint birthday celebration for Nixon and Presley promoted by the library.*

LYN NOFZIGER
(Political Consultant)
"He's not only not a typical politician, he's not a typical person." *1992: On Jerry Brown of California.*

PEGGY NOONAN
(Speechwriter for Presidents Reagan & Bush)
"One of the things I have noticed lately about rich people is the perfection of their ears. . . . I'm noting, in exclusive restaurants, at editorial board meetings where the perfectly dressed politician comes to speak, all these perfectly smooth round ears, unflawed by a stray hair, a mole, a wen, an imperfection of any sort. . . . I'm at a celebratory lunch at Le Cirque, and to my right is a famous movie producer—two big perfect pink sea shells on the sides of his head." *1990*

"My generation, faced as it grew with a choice between religious belief or existential despair, chose marijuana. Now we are in our Cabernet stage." *1996*

"It was the worst inaugural address of our lifetime, and I think the only controversy will be between those who say it was completely and utterly banal and those who say, 'Well, not completely and utterly.'" *1997: On Bill Clinton's inaugural address.*

SAM NUNN
(Senator)
"General Perestroiski." *1990: Addressing General John Piotrowski, commander of the U.S. Space Command.*

O
CONAN O'BRIEN
(TV Talk-show Host)
"According to a poll, the most popular New Year's resolutions are losing weight and spending less. Which also happens to be President Clinton's '96 campaign slogan." *1996*

"Last year, women in Washington, D.C., made more money than women anywhere else in the country. Although that's all expected to change, now that Dick Morris is out of the picture." *1997*

"*George* magazine printed a list of the country's '20 Most Fascinating Political Men' and President Clinton was not on it. The weird part is, Janet Reno was." *1997*

"Sixty-six percent of Americans think that President Clinton had an affair with Monica Lewinsky. . . . Apparently, the other 34 percent think he just had an affair with her dress." *1998*

"Yesterday was 'National Clean Off Your Desk Day.' Or as President Clinton refers to it, 'Hose off the DNA Day.'" *1999*

"Hillary Clinton was principal for a day at a New York City middle school. Apparently the kids loved it, because they could all fool around and she had no idea that anything was going on." *1999*

SINEAD O'CONNOR
(Singer)
"Does impeachment mean they're gonna turn him into a peach? If so, can I eat him?" *1999: In a letter to the* Irish Times *concerning "this Bill Clinton nonsense."*

THOMAS OLIPHANT
(Columnist)
"Jerry Brown's behavior gives hypocrisy a bad name." *1992*

P. J. O'ROURKE
(Journalist)
"Amazing how well-meaning, how virtuous, how *good* people in authority always are. I guess good people are just naturally attracted to government." *1995*

"Compared to the Clintons, Reagan is living proof that a Republican with half a brain is better than a Democrat with two." *1998: On the achievements of the two presidents.*

"You know how there are always these foreign countries that are mad at America—Iraq, Serbia, Afghanistan and so forth? They just can't stay mad anymore. Because whenever Saddam Hussein, Slobodan Milosevic or Osama bin Laden think of the leader of the free world, the commander in chief of the American armed forces, the most powerful man on earth, all they will picture is Bill in his tighty whities, giving the national flag pole a hanky yank in the Oval Office. They're busting up. They're doing spit takes in those little bitty cups of coffee in Afghanistan. They're blowing slivovitz out their noses in Belgrade. It's worth firing dozens of Tomahawk missile 'Lewinsky distractors' into the local terrorist camps to keep entertainment like this in the White House. Doubtless that was Bill's whole motivation for asking Ambassador Richardson to give Monica a job at the U.N." *1998: On the revelation that President Clinton had phone sex with Monica Lewinsky.*

BILL OWEN
(Governor of Colorado)
"Colorado has so many national treasures that we would not want to steal the only one Arizona has to offer." *1999: After the postal service printed millions of stamps, which it plans to destroy, misplacing the Grand Canyon in his state.*

RONN OWENS
(Radio Talk-show Host)
"Democracy is gained through McDonalds and Kinkos and not through force." *1998: Supporting President Clinton's trip to China and the means by which democracy will eventually undermine the authoritarian regime in China.*

P

BOB PACKWOOD
(Senator)

"A little more than Francis of Assisi and a little less than Wilt Chamberlain." *1995: On the amount of sex recorded in his diaries.*

"I don't remember all of the women I've made love to. How can I remember all of the women I've kissed?" *1998: Recalling that it was a kind of out-of-body experience for him to read what some women said he'd done to them when he'd served in the U.S. Senate.*

"For the life of me, I can't figure out why people thought that was a sordid story. It is a kind of tender moment." *1998: Recalling an allegation that after a party he danced with a young staff member, had sex with her on the rug of his office, and lay naked with her for an hour and a half afterward.*

"I am offended at myself." *1998: Recalling some of the groping, kissing, and chasing women he'd been accused of and claiming he was too drunk at the time to remember exactly what happened.*

"My bones tell me she did not." *1998: Analyzing whether Monica Lewinsky had a sexual relationship with President Clinton.*

"I think they [President Clinton and Kathleen Willey] were both right. She may have accurately described what happened. And the President may have thought, I didn't do anything wrong. Both of them would tell their version of it and be telling the truth. Both of them could take a lie-detector test and both of them would pass." *1998: On the alleged sexual encounter between the president and Willey.*

"He's the kind of lawyer that if you were indicted for murder, found guilty and hanged, you'd still think you had a good defense." *1998: On attorney Jacob Stein, who represented Packwood in an ethics investigation.*

CAMILLE PAGLIA
(Author)

"Leftism . . . is a white, middle-class citadel where people have these bizarre visions in their minds of the victimized working class. Here's [an] example that comes out of them: 'Black teenagers lack self-esteem.' . . . This is condescending, paternalistic, PC-elitist garbage. The people in this country with the strongest self-esteem are black teenagers. The people with the weakest self-esteem are white liberals, all those therapists and social workers. . . . PC is a degenerate form of what was once progressive leftism. It's a feel-good thing where you think compassion is the ultimate principle of life. If you could just feel sorry enough, somehow that's going to be the answer. Well, I think that any kind of politics based on compassion is ridiculous. It should be based on justice and dignity." *1996*

"I don't want a cold fish! I want someone in the White House who would love to have sex with 10 different people in 3 days." *1998: On why she is uncritical of President Clinton despite allegations of his numerous affairs.*

"The fanatic overprotection of women is fast making us an infantile nation. We need to treat sex with greater realism and imagination. Women should be taught not that they are passive wards of the state but that sex is a great human comedy where the joke is always on us." *1998*

"The president has become Nero crossed with Howdy Doody. And the independent counsel has become a bumbling Mr. Magoo in a Godzilla mask." *1998: On the White House sex scandal.*

REVEREND IAN PAISLEY
(Political Activist)

"When I heard he was coming, I said, 'Lock up all of the women!' "*1998: A leader of militant Protestants opposed to the Northern Ireland peace accord, on President Clinton's canceled plan to visit the British province.*

LEON PANETTA
(Congressman, White House Chief of Staff)

"You know, if it happened to you or me, what the President is going through, we'd probably have jumped in the Potomac a long time ago." *1998: Explaining what would happen if he were in Clinton's position as the Lewinsky scandal began to unfold.*

LU PARKER
(Miss USA)

"[Senator Strom Thurmond] is an absolute southern gentleman. Needless to say, he is 92 years old and spunkier than most 25 year olds I know." *1996*

DOLLY PARTON
(Singer & Actress)

"He's a horny little toad, too." *1998: Describing the president on TNN.*

WILLIAM PASCOE
(Political Director of the American Conservative Union)

"Any time you have Republican leaders citing the Bible as the foundation for their beliefs and Democratic leaders citing the American Psychiatric Association, I think we win." *1998: Rejecting arguments that the GOP may pay a political price for criticizing homosexuals.*

"I'm watching for the same reason you watch a car race—you keep watching in the morbid hope that someone is going to wipe out in the fourth turn." *1999: On the Senate impeachment trial.*

CHARLES PEACOCK
(Politician)

"I'm a politician, and as a politician I have the prerogative to lie whenever I want." *1994: An ex-director of Madison Guaranty, the Arkansas S&L at the center of Whitewater, explaining why he had lied about writing a check to help cover a Clinton gubernatorial campaign debt.*

ROSS PEROT
(Presidential Candidate)

"The total national debt was only $1 trillion in 1980, when President Reagan took office. It is now $4 trillion. Maybe it was voodoo economics. Whatever it was, we are now in deep voodoo, I'll tell you that." *1992*

"Most people give up when they're about to achieve success. They quit on the one-yard line. They give up at the last minute of the game, one foot from a winning touchdown." *1992*

"China is a huge country, broken into many provinces." *1992: In response to a question on foreign policy.*

"I would prefer you not put me in a category with Howard Stern." *1994: On beginning a new syndicated radio talk show.*

"I will cut the grass, I will take out the trash, I will sleep under the bridge." *1996: On what he'd be willing to do if asked by his Reform party to run for president.*

PRINCE PHILIP
(of Britain)

"I wasn't a revolutionary or an anti-social being. I went to school and said, 'You teach me.'" *1998: On a visit to McAteer High School in San Francisco.*

MICHELLE PHILLIPS
(Singer)

"Balkans are people, too!" *1999: On the crisis in the Balkans.*

DOUGLAS PIKE
(Scholar)

"I understand politics in Hanoi better than I do at Berkeley." *1997: The director of U.C. Berkeley's vast Indochina Archive, which was forced to move to Lubbock, TX, after administrators refused to fund the institution any longer.*

KRISTIE PRANTIL
(Internet Marketing Worker in Washington)

"Look, Clinton's a handsome guy, the most powerful man in the free world—give me a break, women are throwing themselves at him. People like to think of Clinton as a typical guy, a smart guy for sure, but deep down, sort of an average Joe. In a way, this is proof of that: this is how an average Joe would act if he were in that powerful office." *1998: A twenty-three-year-old's perspective on the Clinton female problems.*

Q

MUAMMAR QADDAFI
(Libyan Dictator)

"Thailand is a country in Asia. It was an English colony. Thais guard Queen Elizabeth, a special guard of Thais—Gurkhas." *1993: A comment made after accusing the Thai government of supporting U.S. charges that Thais are helping to build a chemical-weapons plant in his country. Thailand never was a colony, does not guard the queen, and does not have Gurkhas.*

"Tell her that I love her. And that if she loves me, she should wear something green at her next press conference. I shall be watching and hoping." *1996: Telling an American reporter of his love for State Department spokeswoman Margaret Tutwiler.*

DAN QUAYLE
(Vice President of the United States)
"But then, everybody had to come from some-where." *1990: At the dedication of a memorial and museum on Ellis Island.*

"I'm convinced that the president's correct and courageous decision to do what he had to do in Panama will not be of long-term consequence in a negative sense." *1990: On President George Bush's decision to invade Panama.*

"One word sums up probably the responsibility of any president, and that one word is *to be prepared.*" *1990*

"I'm going to be a vice president very much like George Bush was. He proved to be a very effective vice president, perhaps the most effective we've had in a couple of hundred years." *1990*

"Dick and I have something in common. That is that we both overmarried." *1990: On Defense Secretary Dick Cheney.*

"Why do you think it is that the people of Nicaragua had a chance to vote for freedom and democracy and the people of Cuba never had the chance to vote for freedom and democracy? The reason is very elementary: In Nicaragua we supported the democratic resistance; in Cuba we abandoned the resistance. Let us not make that mistake again." *1990*

"I've never seen a joke told in his presence that he didn't get." *1990: On President Bush's sense of humor.*

"For NASA, space is still a high priority." *1990*

"Quite frankly, teachers are the only profession that teach our children." *1990*

"Marilyn and I had a one-minute conversation one time whether I would even perhaps, maybe, some time, run myself [for president] in 1988. And in this one-minute conversation, I just dismissed it, said no, not this time. George Bush is there, we'd have to take two years away from the family." *1990: On a conversation with his wife.*

"It is a unique profession and, by golly, I hope that when they go into the teaching field that they do have that zeal and they do have that mission and they do believe in teaching our kids and they're not getting into this just as a job or a way to put food on the table." *1990: On the importance of teachers and teaching.*

"We offer the party as a big tent. How do we do that within the platform, the preamble to the platform or whatnot? That remains to be seen. But that message will have to be articulated with great clarity." *1991*

"More than 20 centuries have passed since the Constitution was ratified." *1991*

"The morale of troops on the home front is just as important as the morale of troops likely to be blown up at any moment." *1991: Speaking of his trip to a National Guard Armory in Grand Rapids, MI, following his morale-boosting trip to U.S. troops in Saudi Arabia.*

"It's wonderful to be here in the great state of Chicago." *1991*

"I think especially in her position, a highly successful professional woman, it would be a real exception to have an *unwed child.*" *1992: Commenting on Murphy Brown, television's most famous single parent, who did have an "unwed child."*

"I stand by all the misstatements that I've made." *1992*

"It's time for the human race to enter the solar system." *1992*

"When I have been asked during these last weeks who caused the riots and the killing in L.A., my answer has been direct and simple: Who is to blame

DAN QUAYLE (CONT'D)

for the riots? The rioters are to blame. Who is to blame for the killings? The killers are to blame." *1992: On the Rodney King riots in Los Angeles.*

"What a waste it is to lose one's mind. Or not to have a mind is being very wasteful. How true that is." *1992: Speaking to the United Negro College Fund.*

"Bobby Knight told me this: 'There is nothing that a good defense cannot beat a better offense.' In other words a good offense wins." *1992: Comparing the offensive capabilities of the Warsaw Pact with the defensive system of NATO.*

"I should have remembered that was Andrew Jackson who said that, since he got his nickname 'Stonewall' by vetoing bills passed by Congress." *1992: Confusing Andrew Jackson and Thomas Jackson.*

"Marriage is probably the best anti-poverty program there is." *1992*

"That's fine phonetically, but you're missing just a little bit." *1992: To Trenton, NJ, sixth grader William Figueroa, after the youngster correctly spelled the word potato, which Quayle thought was spelled potatoe. Figueroa responded, "It showed the rumors about the vice president are true—that he's an idiot."*

"We will be asking them to join with us. I'm also going to ask them to help us to change the Congress. It's not just enough to change the president if we want to change America." *1992*

"Illegitimacy is something that we should talk about in terms of not having." *1992*

"If Ross Perot runs, that's good for us, and if Ross Perot doesn't run, that's good for us." *1992*

"Hawaii is a unique state. It is a small state. It is a state that is by itself. It is a—it is different than the other 49 states. Well, all states are different, but it's got a particularly unique situation." *1992: When asked whether Hawaii's universal health coverage could serve as a national model.*

"It's the best book I've certainly read. And he goes through it; he starts around the turn of the century up through Vietnam. And it's a very good historical book about history." *1992: Commenting on Paul Johnson's* Modern Times. *"There's a lot of good stuff on Lenin and Stalin," he added.*

"Are they taking DDT?" *1992: Asking staff members at a hospital in New York about their AIDS patients. Staffers explained that DDT was a pesticide and that Quayle probably meant AZT.*

"I told him I will come into Alabama and campaign for him, or campaign against him—whatever way will help. He hasn't decided which." *1994: On what he told Charles Barkley, who said he might run for governor of Alabama as a Republican in 1998.*

"Feburary and Noverber." *1996: Spelling of the months of the year on his WWW Home Page.*

"There's a lot of viewers in England at that time." *1996: Suggesting that Bob Dole should offer defeated rival Pat Buchanan a 4 P.M. slot to address the Republican convention in San Diego.*

"You need to take these life-threatening drugs seriously, and get them on the market." *1997: Trying to give the George Bush administration the credit it deserved for getting faster federal approval of "life-threatening drugs."*

"Some day, somewhere, we're going to wake up—and this isn't just to scare people—we're going to wake up and someone is going to launch a nuclear weapon somewhere." *1997: Warning of the consequences of not controlling the proliferation of nuclear weapons.*

"A pock on both their houses." *1997: Describing his take on the public view of both Democratic and Republican parties.*

"Let me just be very clear that the Republican Party will select a nominee that will beat Bill Clinton." *1998: When asked about whether he will run for president in 2000.*

"One-third of the children today are born into homes without families." *1999: On the social ills caused by the antiwar sentiments of the '60s generation.*

"It's going to be different for me this time around, running for President. . . . I will be in control." *1999: On his prospective bid for the presidency.*

"I've wanted to be president for a long time." *1999: Announcing on* Larry King Live *that he will run for president in 2000.*

"I hope that we don't try to use this as an excuse to go and take away guns." *1999: The announced presidential candidate, following the massacre of high school students in Littleton, CO.*

"If Gore invented the Internet, I invented spell-check." *1999*

MARILYN QUAYLE
(Wife of Vice President)
"Bill Clinton gives a lot of lip service to women." *1992*

JAMES QUELLO
(Former member of the Federal Communications Commission)
"I read *Playboy* now for the same reason I read *National Geographic*—to see fascinating places I'll never get to visit." *1997: Quello was eighty-two when he made this statement.*

R

DAN RATHER
(TV News Anchor)
"Tonight, Chuck Robb's ship came in. But it simply docked at the—well, his ship came in, period." *1994: On election night, providing a "Ratherism" on Senator Charles Robb's defeat of Oliver North.*

"If you're ordinarily watching *Teletubbies* at this hour, you probably shouldn't watch this." *1998: Introducing the Clinton-testimony video on a news program.*

ELIZABETH RAY
(Mistress)
"I still don't know how to type." *1998: Ray, who became famous in the 1970s for her $14,000 a year job working for Congressman Wayne Hays, an Ohio Democrat, on planning a comeback as a stand-up comedienne.*

MAUREEN REAGAN
(Daughter of the President)
"Women, more than men, know that all men are flawed. We don't necessarily like it, but we're sort of used to it." *1996: The California political analyst and daughter of the former president, on why women overwhelmingly voted for Bill Clinton, despite their awareness of his character flaws.*

RONALD REAGAN
(President of the United States)
"A citizen of our country and . . . the victim of an accident." *1990: Identifying Gene Hasenfus, who was shot down over Nicaragua in 1986 in a plane delivering supplies to the Contras.*

"Nancy and I came here tonight because we share with cerebral palsy that each and every human life is sacred." *1990: At a charity fund-raiser.*

"Nancy and I are sorry to learn about your illness. Our thoughts and prayers are with you. God bless you." *1990: In a letter to Augusta Lockridge after she was blinded in the soap opera* Santa Barbara. *Lockridge is a fictional character.*

"Oh, dear, I could ask for help here. The name, I know, is very familiar." *1990: Trying to remember General John W. Vessey, the man he appointed Chairman of the Joint Chiefs of Staff in 1982.*

"There's something about . . . having a horse between my knees that makes it easier to sort out a problem." *1990*

"My problem with Bill [Casey] was that I didn't understand him at meetings. Now you can ask a person to repeat himself once. You can ask him twice. But you can't ask him a third time. You start to sound rude. So I just nod my head, but I didn't know what he was actually saying." *1990: On communicating with CIA Director William Casey.*

"I think much of the criticism [of former President Richard Nixon] was based on nothing at all." *1990*

"The world is a better place, a safer place, because of Richard Nixon." *1990*

"Maybe if I had gone to school without the distraction of football, I would have done well and

RONALD REAGAN (CONT'D)

made something of my life! I've recently lost my job, and before that I was in public housing for eight years." *1991: In a speech at George Washington University.*

LOU REED
(Singer & Musician)

"I think we're the first rock band to play inside the White House. It gave new meaning to the word *surreal*." *1998: Reed's band played at the White House during the visit of Czech Republic President Vaclav Havel.*

THOMAS REGALADO
(Miami City Official)

"There is no mayor in the city of Miami. I don't know what we'll do if Albania declares war on us." *1998: After a judge, citing "fraud and abuse," voided the results of the city's mayoral vote.*

WILLIAM REHNQUIST
(Chief Justice of the United States)

"You know, if I were thinking of retirement, I don't think you'd be the first person I'd tell about it." *1998: When C-SPAN interviewer Brian Lamb asked about speculation that he may retire soon.*

DAVID REHR
(Lobbyist)

"The tobacco industry had the attitude of an elephant hiding behind a telephone pole. Our view as beer wholesalers is that we're proud of our product—we're going to put the elephant out on the street." *1998: The key lobbyist for the National Beer Wholesalers Association explaining how his tactics differ from those of the tobacco industry lobbyists.*

ROBERT REICH
(Labor Secretary)

"Averages don't always reveal the most telling realities. You know, Shaquille O'Neal and I have an average height of 6 feet." *1994: Reich stands four feet ten inches.*

"I defy anyone to come up with a smaller, more efficient labor secretary. I can get by on 800 calories a day." *1995*

"I've captured the mood, the tone, the feel of the conversation, even if I got some of the words wrong. And that's the truth." *1997: Responding to criticism that parts of his autobiography entitled* Locked in the Cabinet—*particularly his putting words into the mouths of others—diverged widely from the truth.*

JANET RENO
(Attorney General of the United States)

"At this moment I do not have a personal relationship with a computer." *1998: Explaining how frustration with a new computer system sent her back to using pencil and paper.*

ANN RICHARDS
(Former Governor of Texas)

"Bill Clinton isn't the first man I've had to forgive, and he probably won't be the last." *1998: The former Texas governor, introducing the president at a San Antonio Democratic fund-raiser.*

BILL RICHARDSON
(Secretary of Energy)

"Whoever figured it out must've been smoking dope or drunk." *1999: On the security structure at the Energy Department—following revelations of more than a decade of Chinese spying.*

MARGARET RICHARDSON
(Chief of the I.R.S.)

"I'll be delighted to take your questions now, except any questions that relate to the fair-market value of long underwear." *1994: At a press conference, after reports that President Clinton took tax deductions for charitable donations of his underwear.*

GERALDO RIVERA
(TV Personality)

"There is, ladies and gentlemen, absolutely no possibility that a so-called semen-stained dress exists." *1998: On July 8, before Monica Lewinsky's semen-stained dress was produced as evidence against President Clinton.*

JOAN RIVERS
(Comedienne & TV Host)

"Nothing's inexcusable except what [Clinton] did to Chelsea. To know that she has a little brother or sister stuck to a dress somewhere . . ." *1998*

PAT ROBERTSON
(Minister & Politician)

"They just want to kill. They have a spirit of murder. Abortionists are worse than Ceausescu, worse than Stalin, worse than Hitler." *1990*

"From a public-relations standpoint, he's won. . . . They might as well dismiss this impeachment hearing and get on with something else, because it's over as far as I'm concerned." *1999: On his 700 Club television show, after president Clinton's State of the Union address.*

ROBBIE ROBERTSON
(Songwriter & Musician)

"Somebody told me an expression I had never heard before that seemed to sum everything up. I had asked about a friend of mine who had just gotten married but was fooling around, and another person said to me, 'Eatin' ain't cheatin'.' It seems this Arkansas philosophy was much more widespread than any of us knew. When the whole thing came up with Clinton, I thought he could just say, 'I'm from Arkansas—I don't know what you people do, but we have our own rules here.' I know that it's kind of silly, but it is so common in that area for people to behave that way." *1998: On the Clinton scandals.*

JOE ROCAMORA
(Political Scientist)

"It is the revenge of the masses. They are tired of being led by smart people." *1998: The head of the Filipino Political Policy Institute, on the victory of former actor Joseph Estrada in the presidential race.*

BARBARA RODGERS
(State Representative)

"Clinton is president of the state of Arkansas whether you like it or not." *1999: After losing on a state bill to fund renovations of the president's boyhood home.*

DOROTHY RODHAM
(Mother of Hillary Rodham Clinton)

"She is able not to over-emotionalize it." *1999: On her daughter's feelings toward the president.*

ROY ROMER
(Chairman of the Democratic National Committee)

"This was not a sexual relationship. It was a very affectionate relationship and I'm not trying to define when affection ends and sex begins." *1998: Describing the nature of his sixteen-year relationship with a woman eighteen years his junior.*

MICKEY ROONEY
(Actor)

"No, I'm not a fan [of Newt Gingrich]. I'm an American." *1996: Commenting on his first meeting with Newt Gingrich.*

DAN ROSTENKOWSKI
(Congressman)

"You walk on a mine field of eggs when you start doing that." *1992: On a proposal to ban Japanese car imports for five years.*

"You look at what they charged me with and what they found me guilty of and see if you can tell me they won, except for putting me in jail." *1996*

"What is it with you reporters about contrition? I mean what do you want? Do you want somebody to walk around with a crying towel?" *1998: Following his release from prison after serving thirteen months for mail fraud, declining to apologize during a radio interview in Chicago.*

JANI RUDDRAMA
(Founder of the Women's Temperance Movement in the Indian State of Orissa)

"To a large extent, we have succeeded in curbing drinking." *1998: Ruddrama's group allows women to chain their husbands to a post and beat them publicly as punishment for drinking too much.*

SITI HARDIJANTI RUKMANA
(Indonesian Minister for Social Affairs & Daughter of Former President Suharto)

"I hope all of these donations will teach the people and not make them lazy." *1998: On her concern about a food-relief program for needy people in northern Jakarta.*

APRIL RYAN
(White House Correspondent)

"He got stuck on one step: he couldn't cross that one leg over the other." *1999: On her more-or-less successful attempt to teach Vice President Al Gore "the Booty Call," a popular dance, aboard Air Force Two en route to South Africa.*

DREW RYMER
(Seven-year-old Student)

"Grandpa, how did a clown get to be governor?" *1992: To his grandfather, Tom Rymer, after viewing the "impressionist" painting of Jerry Brown in the Sacramento, CA, State Capitol building.*

S

MARGO ST. JAMES
(Former Prostitute & San Francisco Political Candidate)

"I'm pleased to be here. Nice to see so many familiar faces." *1996: Before speaking at San Francisco's Concordia Argonaut Club.*

PIERRE SALINGER
(Former White House Press Secretary)

"If what I said turns out to be wrong, it will probably be the biggest mistake of my entire life. If I do make that mistake, it'll be the first mistake I've made since the 1930s or the early 1940s." *1996: After he claimed to have secret documents proving a Navy missile brought down TWA Flight 800 off Long Island, only to be informed that the material had been on the Internet for months and had been debunked by the FBI.*

AL SALVI
(State Legislator, IL)

"I was told over and over again, 'Don't run, Al, this is David and Goliath.' I think they forgot David won." *1996: Salvi upset the favorite in the race to win the GOP nomination for a U.S. Senate seat.*

KHIEU SAMPHAN
(Cambodian Khmer Rouge Leader)

"Sorry, very sorry." *1999: Apologizing for the suffering and the one to two million deaths his regime caused the Cambodian people.*

"Let bygones be bygones." *1999: The former Cambodian head of state under the Khmer Rouge, after being promised amnesty from prosecution for genocide. Three days later, Prime Minister Hun Sen said Samphan and another defector may have to stand trial.*

SUE SARA
(Businesswoman)

"We did not want to offend anyone." *1998: Apple Computer's Asia-Pacific division spokesperson defending the company's decision to pull images of the Dalai Lama from an advertising campaign in Asia for fear of angering China.*

ALBERT SCARDINO
(Press Secretary to New York City Mayor David Dinkins)

"They don't understand that there is a new order running things. City Hall is no longer run by a bunch of tired old Jewish men." *1990: On critics of Mayor Dinkins's administration.*

ROBERT SCHEER
(Los Angeles Times Contributing Editor)

"It's sick. There was no blue dress and no semen stain, but America's mass media fell for the lurid details." *1998: On February 3, before Monica Lewinsky's semen-stained blue dress was introduced as evidence.*

DAVID SCHIPPERS
(Council for the House Judiciary Committee Republicans)

"Life was so much simpler before they found that dress, wasn't it?" *1998: Testifying before the committee on evidence in the Clinton scandals hearings.*

PAT SCHROEDER
(Congresswoman)

"I couldn't stand the Senate. Senators spend the first three months of every year ironing their togas." *1990*

"An extra chromosome is not a 'kick me' sign." *1993: Testifying in Congress in favor of legislation that would prohibit female genital mutilation. Nonscientist Schroeder was not aware that women do not have an extra chromosome.*

"[I'm going to] form a ladies' sewing circle and terrorist society." *1995: On her plans after retiring from Congress.*

"I always wanted to be cremated and made into a doorstop because basically what I want to do is hold doors open for people." *1998*

"It was really hard to listen to. It really is sexual assault if what happened happened. It makes my skin crawl. You get nauseous thinking, 'Yuck, I don't want to hear this.' " *1998: On hearing the accusations of Kathleen Willey against President Bill Clinton.*

"What are they going to do next? Go to Victoria's Secret to see if she wore underwear?" *1998: After independent counsel Kenneth Starr subpoenaed two Washington bookstores for records of books purchased by Monica Lewinsky.*

REVEREND ROBERT SCHULLER
(Minister)

"He did it with such passion and with his eyes locked on me. He lied. Blatantly. He's the third public man to do that to me—Nixon and Agnew lied to me, bluntly, boldly. And now Clinton." *1998: After meeting with President Clinton, who said he sought spiritual guidance.*

"I think he lied but doesn't know he did . . . he has to have a specialist check him out." *1998: Expressing concerns about President Clinton's early denials to him and other spiritual advisors of having sex with ex–White House intern Monica Lewinsky.*

CHARLES SCHUMER
(Senator)

"Well, Alison, it meant that he was very happy." *1999: Defining for his young daughter the Starr report's use of the word* aroused *in describing the reaction of President Clinton to Monica Lewinsky.*

BRENT SCOWCROFT
(National Security Advisor)

"I think it's quite possible it was a truthful statement." *1992: On George Bush's claim that he didn't actually oppose the Iran-Contra arms sale because he didn't know all the facts.*

HUN SEN
(Cambodian Prime Minister)

"Aids." *1998: On the legacy left by the United Nations Transitional Authority in Cambodia.*

"We should dig a hole and bury the past and look ahead to the 21st century with a clean slate." *1998: As he welcomed the surrender of two former henchmen of* Khmer Rouge leader, Pol Pot, the principal architect of autogenocide in Cambodia during the 1970s, when as many as 2 million Cambodians were murdered. Hun Sen was himself once a member of the Khmer Rouge.

F. JAMES SENSENBRENNER JR.
(Congressman)

"One of my jobs was to bring home money from D.C. to Wisconsin, but I didn't quite think it would be like this." *1998: On winning $250,000 in the Washington, D.C., lottery.*

"She did and he didn't." *1998: The House Judiciary Committee member on who had sex, according to Bill Clinton.*

VOJISLAV SESELJ
(Serbian Deputy Prime Minister)

"They can't accuse me of rape. If you look at what has been coming out of the slums of Kosovo . . . only a blind person could rape something like that." *1999*

DONNA SHALALA
(Secretary of Health and Human Services)

"The thing I noticed about fashion magazines as opposed to what people would describe as the more feminist publications is that they really celebrate beauty and brains. . . . Even the parties are about something important." *1994*

"Last night ABC exercised their First Amendment rights, and I think we're a better nation because they did." *1997: On the coming-out episode of the sitcom* Ellen.

REVEREND AL SHARPTON
(Minister, Politician & Activist)

"I've been indicted. I've been stabbed and now I've been sued. I've got every base covered for being a great civil rights leader." *1998*

CHRISTOPHER SHAYS
(Congressman)

"As Woody Allen said in *Bananas*, 'It's a travesty of a mockery of a sham.' " *1998: On the House leadership's treatment of campaign finance reform.*

DEREK SHEARER
(Ambassador to Finland)

"Historically, Finland and the United States have had friendly relations—especially in the cultural

DEREK SHEARER (CONT'D)

and economic realms, where there have been decades of interaction and mutual influence. To give a few personal examples: I first experienced the genius of Finnish architecture as a student at Yale, walking through the residential colleges designed by Eero Saarinen. My family's best dinnerware is by Arabia, a world-renowned Finnish firm. . . ." *1994*

MARIA SHRIVER
(TV Correspondent)

"You ever wanted to put one of those in the Oval Office?" *1998: To first lady Hillary Clinton, on being shown the cot that Thomas Edison kept in his laboratory for taking naps.*

BUD SHUSTER
(Congressman)

"I prefer to believe that they simply are misinformed." *1998: The Chairman of the House Transportation Committee rejecting charges from younger GOP colleagues that he trades lucrative highway projects for votes.*

ROGER SIMON
(Columnist)

"Bennett, who had been secretary of education without solving the problems of education and drug czar without solving the problems of drugs, now wants to write books on how to solve the problems of both. In America, this is what we call 'expertise.' " *1990: On William Bennett.*

ALAN SIMPSON
(U.S. Senator)

"You talk about democracy. Democracy is a very irksome and confusing thing. I believe your problem is with the Western media, not with the U.S. government, because you are isolated from the media and the press. The press is spoiled and conceited. All the journalists consider themselves brilliant political scientists. They do not want to see anything succeeding or achieving its objectives. My advise is that you allow those bastards to come here and see things for themselves." *1990: Speaking with Saddam Hussein during a visit to Iraq in the spring of 1990.*

"I never imagined I'd be sleeping with a 60-year-old woman." *1991: At the sixtieth birthday party for his wife.*

"Take [out] the word *Quayle* and insert the word *Bush* wherever it appears, and that's the crap I took for eight years. Wimp. Sycophant. Lap dog. Poop. Lightweight. Boob. Squirrel. Asshole. George Bush." *1992: Recounting how George Bush advised Dan Quayle on how to deal with Quayle jokes.*

"Politicians are the recipients of a great deal of finger pointing, and finger messages of all kinds." *1992*

"His life is bounding from precipice to precipice like a huge mountain goat, bridging crevasse after crevasse and people shooting at him with high-powered rifles and the other side crumbling as he lands, just like in the movies." *1998: On President Clinton's resilience.*

ROBERT SKLAR
(Scholar)

"You can't have a president playing the saxophone and talking about his underwear without some loss of dignity." *1997: Commenting on unpresidential movies about the presidency.*

HARRY SMITH
(TV Host)

"Let's talk about those disadvantaged children for a couple of seconds." *1996: Asking Hillary Clinton about her new book after prolonged questioning on Travelgate and Whitewater.*

PATTI SMITH
(Singer)

"When I look at the crucifixion of Clinton, I look at the crucifixion of my generation. They are finally nailing us for introducing new ideas about sexual mores, sexual freedom, personal freedom." *1998: On the Clinton scandals.*

WILL SMITH
(Actor & Singer)

"The President shouldn't have to answer questions from a dickhead about a cigar." *1998: On Bill Clinton's problems with Ken Starr.*

TONY SNOW
(Columnist)

"In most meetings, the key challenge is for members to stay awake." *1996: On his membership in the Council on Foreign Relations—an organization many believe to be a conspiracy to take over the world.*

BOB SQUIER
(Democratic Political Consultant)

"Can you believe it? The president I helped get elected is on trial for impeachment, and I can't stay awake." *1999: On the Senate impeachment trial.*

DIVESH SRIVASTAVA
(Aide to Indian Gangster-Politician Dharam Pal Yadav)

"It all depends on what you call crime. If it's a political crime, it's not really a crime." *1998: On the growing number of people with criminal records trying to win public office in India. Yadav faced twenty-five criminal charges, including six counts of murder.*

PETE STARK
(Congressman)

"Dear Lieutenant Colonel North,
I have heard your pathetic letter in which you refer to Representative Ron Dellums as an 'incredible security risk' and a 'very dangerous appointment' to the U.S. House Select Committee on Intelligence.

Frankly, Colonel, you are full of shit.

I find it incredible that anyone who would conspire to sell sophisticated weapons systems to the Ayatollah and the Iranian regime would even consider making such charges. . . ." *1991: In a letter to Oliver North.*

KENNETH STARR
(Independent Counsel)

"Daily." *1999: On how often he feels sorry that he didn't become dean of Pepperdine University's law school in 1997, when the position was offered to him.*

RONALD STEELE
(Journalist)

"But if politicians didn't name airports after themselves, who would? And if they waited a while to do so, who would remember them? The U.S. Postal Service has a useful rule: No one gets put on a commemorative stamp until he or she has been dead at least ten years (except Presidents, who just have to be dead). Not many politicians would risk that judgement of history. So they rush in with the chisels while the honoree is still alive." *1998: On the renaming of Washington, D.C.'s national airport in honor of Ronald Reagan.*

SHELBY STEELE
(Author)

"Most groups organized their identity, at least to some extent, around the source of their power. And for blacks, ironically, that meant organizing our identity around our victimization. . . . You get more and more tied into a victim-focused identity, and so, even as you enjoy the benefits of society, your screams of victimization grow louder." *1991: On the growing appeal of "victimhood" in America and demands for compensation.*

GEORGE STEPHANOPOULOS
(Campaign Strategist & Presidential Advisor)

"Some people compare me to John Kennedy, especially when I play under the president's desk during meetings." *1996*

"Is he telling the truth, the whole truth, and nothing but the truth? If he is, he can survive. If he isn't, he can't." *1998: As an ABC News commentator on revelations and denials of a White House scandal involving President Clinton and Monica Lewinsky on January 25.*

"I almost feel sorry for Newt Gingrich. President Clinton has an affair with a 21-year-old intern, and (Gingrich) loses his job." *1998*

"The only problem with law school was that when it was over I would be in real danger of becoming a lawyer." *1999*

TED STEVENS
(Senator)

"I had somebody tell me, 'Why do you Alaskans need handguns, anyway?' The next time you come up, Mr. President, I will let you catch a 200-pound halibut, and you bring it on board without a handgun. All right? You cannot very well carry a shotgun or a rifle over your shoulder and use your pole, but that is what people want you to do." *1991*

TED STEVENS (CONT'D)

"There's all these touchy-feely things out there . . . they want to spend money on." *1999: On why women don't support defense spending.*

MARTHA STEWART
(Entrepreneur)

"I'm going through eye-exercise therapy, strengthening my eyes. I'm supposed to . . . like, rest them." *1998: Explaining why her eyes were closed shut during an Al Gore speech.*

MARK STEYN
(Journalist & Film Critic)

"Constitutional scholars are divided as to whether Mr. Clinton has the legal authority to declare his pants a federal disaster area, but clearly they are." *1998: On Bill Clinton's female problems.*

JAMES STOCKDALE
(Vice Presidential Candidate)

"Who am I? Why am I here?" *1992: Opening statement at the vice presidential debate.*

SHARON STONE
(Actress)

"I just hate it. It's like *Fatal Attraction*. Ken Starr is Glenn Close." *1998: On "Monicagate."*

BARBRA STREISAND
(Singer & Actress)

"We elected him president, not pope." *1998: On the unimportance of the sexual encounters between the president and former White House intern Monica Lewinsky.*

LOUIS SULLIVAN
(Secretary of Health & Human Services)

"What you would have is a combination of the compassion of the I.R.S. and the efficiency of the post office." *1992: On how health care would be affected if it were nationalized.*

T

ROGER TAMRAZ
(Financier)

"Thank God we are a capitalist society, and there's nothing wrong in running after money." *1997: On contributing $300,000 to Democratic campaign committees in order to gain access to the White House.*

"I think next time I'll give $600,000." *1997: In response to a question by Senator Joseph Lieberman, D-Connecticut, as to whether Tamraz thought he got his "money's worth" for the $300,000. "Well, don't give out your phone number," Lieberman responded.*

EDWARD TELLER
(Physicist)

"A war without casualties cannot be as famous as a horrible war, but it is preferable." *1998: On the Cold War.*

ROSS TERRILL
(Author)

"Despite enormous differences in the Chinese and U.S. political systems, Mao's conduct may provide some insights into Bill Clinton's alleged problem. . . . Both Jiang [Qing, Mao's wife,] and Hillary Clinton knew the pain of seeing power act like an aphrodisiac on their husband. . . . Hillary Clinton sees a 'vast right-wing conspiracy' threatening her husband. Jiang saw a 'capitalist-road conspiracy' undermining her husband. . . . Filmed swimming feats were Mao's way of communicating a carefree, masterful image of himself to the people over the heads of his perceived enemies, a rough equivalent of Clinton looking the nation in the eye on TV and exuding sincerity." *1998: Stretching for an absurd but published analogy.*

SCARLET THOMAS
(Waitress at Champs Sports Bar & Grill in Oak Brook Terrace, IL)

"By the time he finishes defining [sex], I think I'll learn that I'm actually a virgin." *1998: The twenty-eight-year-old commenting on Clinton's hair-splitting definitions.*

EMMA THOMPSON
(Actress)

"It's a little bit like watching an assassination in incremental stages." *1998: Referring to President Clinton's White House problems.*

"You alpha males are like that. Your charismatic silverbacks will put it around. This is not new, and it's quite normal." *1998: On the string of allegations of sexual indiscretion by President Clinton and the reaction it's received in America.*

FRED THOMPSON
(Senator & Actor)

"I've still got a lot to learn about Washington. Thursday, I accidentally spent some of my own money." *1995*

"After spending a year in Washington, I long for the realism and sensitivity of Hollywood." *1996*

LAETITIA THOMPSON
(Presidential Questioner)

"I know the day that I die, they'll say, 'The woman who said, *Boxers or briefs?* died today.' " *1999: Regretting her 1994 question to President Clinton when she asked about his choice of underwear.*

TOMMY THOMPSON
(Governor of Wisconsin)

"He touched on every subject except his dog and the homeless—and he promised everybody something, so you've got to like it." *1999: The Republican governor on Clinton's 1999 State of the Union speech.*

STROM THURMOND
(Senator)

"If they are from South Carolina, I'm sure they are competent." *1996: When asked his opinion of the superstar rock band Hootie and the Blowfish.*

"When you bring in women it's always for the better. They are smart and we like to look at them." *1997: Thurmond, at the age of ninety-four became the longest-serving man in Congress on May 25, 1997, when he broke the forty-one years, nine months, and thirty-one day record set by Arizonan Carl Hayden in 1969. Thurmond said he was glad to have witnessed the coming of women to the House and the Senate, in this statement.*

"We've got some pretty women in here this time." *1999: At age ninety-six, looking forward to duty on the Senate Armed Services Committee with new member Mary Landrieu.*

"Honey, I was around for Y1K." *1999: The ninety-six-year-old South Carolina Republican, to a woman at the year 2000 ceremony on Capitol Hill.*

LIZ TILBERIS
(Editor for Harper's Bazaar*)*

"We were all struck by how amazing it was to have seen the entire royal family file past us, with all the teenagers that we remembered as babies, and we all remarked on how good Princess Anne's legs were. But mostly we remembered Diana." *1998: Describing a lunch she had with friends in London after attending the funeral of Princess Diana.*

JUDY BARR TOPINKA
(Illinois State Treasurer)

"I feel a little bit like Elizabeth Taylor's eighth husband. I know what to do, but I have to find a new and more interesting way to do it." *1999: Giving her inaugural speech in Springfield after several other constitutional officers had given theirs.*

KATHLEEN KENNEDY TOWNSHEND
(Politician)

"I definitely read the speeches before I give them. That's very helpful. I try to think about what I'm going to say before I say it. That also is useful." *1997: Maryland's lieutenant governor, who is generally considered one of the more outstanding of Robert Kennedy's children, describing the secret of her political success.*

JAMES TRAFICANT JR.
(Congressman)

"We let our government violate the rights of an old Nazi who is not a criminal." *1990: At a dinner honoring admitted Nazi Arthur Rudolph, who agreed to leave the United States after charges that he worked Jewish slaves to death during World War II.*

"I'm a jackass." *1990: On 60 Minutes.*

"In about ten years, you try and eat your Toyota." *1990: On why he is wary of Japanese trade policies and the loss of American jobs.*

"Madam Speaker [Barbara B. Kennelly, the Connecticut Democrat filling in as Speaker], the remains of 800 beagles and 1,700 tons of their radioactive urine and feces will be buried at a nuclear site in the State of Washington.

"The dead dogs have been in freezers since 1950. They were part of a study to assess the damage of radioactive fallout. The study is now conclusive: Radioactive fallout is fatal, and canines subject thereto died. But the point is, Madam Speaker, the funeral is going to cost $22 million.

JAMES TRAFICANT JR. (CONT'D)

"Tell me, are they going to ship the bodies by limo? Are they going to have gold tombstones for every hound?

"With 37 million people in America without health insurance, 9 million people unemployed, I would like to say that our Government is spending $22 million to erect a giant fire hydrant as a mausoleum to dead beagles.

"I think that says it all, Madam Speaker: America's domestic priorities have gone to the dogs." *1991*

"Mr. Speaker, space. The final frontier. The search for new life, new civilizations and now new toilets. That is right: NASA has a $30 million space toilet. You strap yourself in and 12 high-pressure jets aid your relief. . . . Mr. Speaker, I say it's time to call out the Roto-rooter man. . . . Beam me up, Scottie, nature is calling." *1993*

"Republican party, I wish you well. May you never be hated by Tonya Harding and never be loved by Lorena Bobbitt." *1994: Address to the House of Representatives.*

"Mr. Speaker, something does not add up. . . . Experts say, 'Don't worry, America. If the Federal Government shuts down, only nonessential workers will be furloughed. Now the dictionary says nonessential means not necessary. Now, if that is the case, did anyone around here ever stop to think that if Congress did not borrow money to hire nonessential workers, Congress would not have to borrow more money to pay nonessential workers and Congress would not have to shut down?

"Beam me up, Mr. Speaker. Maybe, just maybe, the Congress of the United States is a little nonessential." *1995*

"Mr. Speaker, the White House says NAFTA [the North American Free Trade Agreement] is creating new and exciting jobs. I did some research on those jobs: zipper trimmer, brassiere tender, jelly roller, bosom presser, chicken sexer, sanitary napkin specialist and pantyhose crotch closer machine operator. That is what I call exciting jobs, Mr. Speaker." *1997*

"Mr. Speaker, in 1993, Boris Yeltsin fell off a stage in Germany. In 1994, Boris could not get off his plane in Ireland. In 1996 Boris came up missing for seven consecutive days, unexplained, before an election. In 1997, he forgot about a meeting with Vice President Al Gore. Yesterday, he fired his entire cabinet. The White House says they are monitoring it . . .

"I say monitor this. Boris Yeltsin does not need monitors. Boris Yeltsin needs Alcoholics Anonymous. I say let us save our foreign aid and let us send some counselors over to take care of this guy." *1998*

"If the dress doesn't fit, we must acquit. If it's on the dress, he must confess." *1998: In a summary of the political landscape and the Clinton-Lewinsky affair.*

"Let us check this out: China gets $60 billion in M.F.N. [most-favored nation status] from Uncle Sam. Russia gets $15 billion in foreign aid from Uncle Sam. In exchange, Uncle Sam gets nuclear missiles pointed at our cities, two tape decks and three cases of vodka. Beam me up. I say our national security brain trust needs a proctologist on staff." *1998*

"Mr. Speaker, I think it is time to tell it like it is. When it comes to China, we have gone from 'Speak softly and carry a big stick' to 'Take the fifth and carry a toothpick.' Beam me up." *1998*

"Mr. Speaker, a new report says only 7 percent of scientists believe in God. That is right. And the reason they gave was that the scientists were 'super smart.' Unbelievable. Most of these absent-minded professors cannot find the toilet. Mr. Speaker, I have one question for these wise guys to constipate over: how can something come from nothing?

"And while they digest that, Mr. Speaker, let us tell it like it is. Put these super-cerebral master debaters in some foxhole with bombs bursting all around them, and I guarantee they will not be praying to Frankenstein. Beam me up here." *1998*

JOHN TRAVOLTA
(Actor)

"If it were the wish of the people, I would run [for president]. Short of that, I wouldn't do it. I'd have to feel like I could make a difference. Let's put it this way: I was a quarterback in high school, so I'd probably rather be the president [than the mayor of a small town or a senator]. If I'm going to take it on, I'd rather take on the whole kit and caboodle." *1998*

"Clinton's got a good sense of justice and fairness, and it almost hurts him. It hurts him because it opens him up to more scrutiny, and it hurts him emotionally. I think he does feel people's pain. He really, truly does." *1998*

"You have to be dead not to see that the film [*Primary Colors*] favors Clinton. The script was always kind to him. We're talking about kind to a character, but indirectly we're talking about kind to the president. I've always said that I think he'll be pleased with it, because more than anything it promotes what a decent fellow he is." *1998: Travolta plays the Clinton-act-alike Jack Stanton in the film.*

"I spoke to 5,000 people, including four presidents. The next day, I met with Clinton. He told me, 'Your program sounds great. More than that [the president said] 'I'd really love to help you with your issue over in Germany with Scientology.' " *1998: Recalling his travels around the country lobbying Scientology and President Clinton's offer to help him and his group in problems of alleged persecution they have with the German government, which considers them an insidious cult rather than a genuine church.*

"I was waiting for the seduction that I had heard so much about. I thought, 'Well, how could he ever seduce me?' And after we talked, I thought, Bingo! He did it. [Scientology] is the one issue that really matters to me." *1998: On the seductive powers of President Bill Clinton.*

RALPH TRAYMARK
(Part-time Minister & Retired Mechanic in Charlottesville, VA)
"We've known for years that he's a lying, cheating two-timer, and we don't need Ken Starr wasting taxpayer money to prove it." *1998: On the Monica Lewinsky allegations.*

LINDA TRIPP
(Government Worker & Informant)
"I'm not paranoid; I'm not delusional. I'm normal." *1999: Announcing on* Larry King Live *her belief that President Clinton's friends are trying to kill her.*

PAUL TSONGAS
(Senator)
"I came from a disadvantaged home—they were Republicans." *1992*

"I can speak with a southern accent. Unfortunately, it's Southern Ethiopian." *1992: On the influence of his time in the Peace Corps.*

"I want women . . . no, that's the other guy." *1992: Referring to Bill Clinton.*

U
MORRIS UDALL
(Senator)
"I learned the difference between a cactus and a caucus. A cactus has its pricks on the outside." *1991*

UNIDENTIFIED SOURCE
"Yeah, we got him home. . . . I don't think anyone saw him. And he didn't do anything *too* stupid." *1992: An unidentified aid to Congressman Joe Kennedy, after returning the intoxicated congressman to his Washington townhouse.*

V
DOROTHY VALLASIO
(Founder of the Hit the Trail for Quayle Club)
"The public is being programmed to think our vice president is a laughingstock. He's a human being." *1990*

JOHN VASCONCELLOS
(California State Assemblyman)
"I am embarrassed to be a Californian." *1990: On the failure of the state legislature to pass an acceptable budget. Vasconcellos was a member of the state's Committee on Self-esteem.*

"Men can be feelingful." *1991*

"Well, it begins with not simply a cultural bias about kids or the family; it begins with the assumptions about how we learn, how I learn. And whether . . . we are innately learners. If people believe that, then we address each other in ways that nurture that learning capacity, so we learn all of our lives—learn and develop who we are, how

JOHN VASCONCELLOS (CONT'D)

we get along, personal relations, analytical skills and all the rest. If we assume that kids only learn if we beat them up badly, they aren't inclined to learn on their own; then we end up screwing up badly. So the assumptions that [we have] about the nature of the child and his or her inclinations, and the process of learning to be inspired inform all the rest of it, that's really the starting point." *1992: Answering the question, "How can we create lifelong learners?"*

JESSE "THE BODY" VENTURA
(Professional Wrestler & Governor of Minnesota)
"We wasted them with wasted votes." *1998: After being elected governor of Minnesota as a third-party candidate, on critics who said a vote for him would be wasted.*

"Go to the Secretary of State's office. It says: live in the state for a year and be over 25. That's it. I think that's what the Founding Fathers wanted." *1998: On his qualifications to serve as governor.*

"I'll bet you they're never going to take the people lightly again." *1998: Commenting on his election as governor of Minnesota while running on a third-party ticket.*

"Oh, sheesh." *1998: When asked to provide details of his campaign proposal to cut taxes.*

"I asked them, I said: 'You know, I'm assuming this office, and all during the campaign I never used a note, I never used a prepared speech, ever.' And I asked those high school kids in Austin, 'Should I change?' And they said absolutely not. I'm not changing." *1999: Beginning his unscripted inaugural address and citing advice given to him by students in Austin, MN.*

"It wouldn't be too good if the governor knocks somebody down." *1999: On why he agreed to a contingent of bodyguards.*

"Tourism's gonna go up. People are going to come to Minnesota just to look at the people who voted me in." *1999: On one benefit of having a former professional wrestler as governor.*

"For running over reporters." *1999: On why he chose a full-size luxury sport-utility vehicle, the Lincoln Navigator, as his official car.*

"I have ways of persuading other than being diplomatic." *1999: On the tactics he planned to use on a trade mission to Hollywood, his first such trip.*

"My view is, to eliminate this cheating, or the possibility of it, why not let kids go to college and just be athletes while they're there? No classes. Let them simply play. Then when they're done, if they don't make it in the N.F.L., if they don't make it in the N.B.A., if they don't make it in pro baseball, whatever it might be, then give them their scholarship." *1999: Proposing that athletes should not be bothered by school work. He made the statement shortly after an apparent cheating scandal was exposed among University of Minnesota basketball players.*

"I never watched it." *1999: Commenting on Garrison Keillor's radio show.*

"Our government lies to us all the time." *1999: Asserting that Lee Harvey Oswald did not kill John Kennedy.*

TERRY VENTURA
(Wife of Jesse "The Body" Ventura)
"It's not my role to be like Hillary and try to rule the world." *1999: Explaining that she does not plan to use her first-lady role to adopt a political agenda as did Hillary Clinton.*

"I'm not stupid. I went to Wendy Ward Charm School. . . . I know how to walk, how to get in and out of a car without showing the world everything." *1999: On her readiness for her new role as Minnesota's first lady.*

GORE VIDAL
(Writer)
"He's got wonderful ideas [but] he actually doesn't do anything. I think that is now the requirement [for being president]." *1995: Discussing President Bill Clinton.*

"This will sound terrible in print, but I've met far too many presidents. I have no need of [meeting] another one. They're all alike. They're all paranoid. Goes with the job. It's a job that sort of drives people absolutely wacky. Fortunately, people who are rather wacky get into it." *1996*

"But it is a bum rap to say Albert [Gore] Jr. was caught at that Buddhist rally. The Gores pretend to be good Southern Protestants, but I tell you, every single Gore is a Buddhist. Why, when we're not running the South, we're meditating." *1998: On Vice President Al Gore.*

"One reason we get so much sex in politics is that we're forbidden by our corporate ownership to discuss anything of a political nature. In this representative government that we pretend we have, the only thing we can talk about is taxation." *1998*

"The meekness of the American people startles me. There are almost no labor unions and everyone is terrified of striking. Perhaps they've been so beaten down by mandatory urine tests and such things—the intrusion of government that drives all these Montana-men mad.

"The average person is concerned with keeping what he earns and doesn't have anything but skepticism for politicians—because he knows that the government is wholly owned. And it's owned by a class of people we rarely see, except when there is someone really stupid, like Nelson Rockefeller. He didn't seem to realize that you don't run for president when you can buy it." *1998*

GIULIO VIDON
(Australian Tour Guide & Presidential Fan)
"He would have been a great pope." *1996: After hearing President Clinton speak out against racism in Sydney.*

THE VILLAGE VOICE
(Newspaper)
"The One Thing the American People Will Not Forgive Is a Good Fuck." *1992: Headline for a story about allegations of extra-marital activities of presidential candidate Bill Clinton.*

DICK VITALE
(Sports Broadcaster)
"You're awesome, baby." *1996: Inscribing a copy of* Holding Court: Reflections on the Game I Love, *for Hillary Rodham Clinton, whose book tour for* It Takes a Village *brought her to the same store for simultaneous book signing.*

W

JOEL WACHS
(City Councilman, Los Angeles)
"If hypocrites could fly, this place would be an airport." *1996: On the speed at which a top-secret report on how to prevent leaks at city hall was leaked to the Los Angeles Times.*

CHARLES WALKER
(Corporate Tax Lobbyist)
"That's like a stud horse with no balls. . . . The purpose of the capital gains is to stimulate, but if you just give it to people who don't have much money, you don't get much stimulus." *1992: Describing the Democratic party's plan providing that the capital gains rate be reduced but the benefits should be restricted to people of the middle income ranges.*

BARBARA WALTERS
(News Correspondent)
"I found Monica warm and intelligent and very open. I told her, 'You are very alive.' And she said, 'Maybe that was the appeal.'" *1999: After meeting with Monica Lewinsky.*

"I would have tried to tell her that this was a relationship that had no future." *1999: On the advice she would have given Monica Lewinsky if the two had met during the intern's affair with President Clinton.*

JOHN WARNER
(Senator)
"I am pro-choice with limitations, pro-life with exceptions." *1990*

WASHINGTON TIMES
(Newspaper)
"Mr. Clinton [Bill Clinton, Governor of Arkansas] 44, says he will make his intentions clear by Labor Day. But the four-term governor insists he won't answer tough personal questions—like those about extra-marital affairs, illegitimate children, and having used drugs." *1991*

WEI JINGSHEN
(Democracy Activist)
"Perhaps President Clinton can thank his girlfriends for helping him deflect attention from his foreign-policy

WEI JINGSHEN (CONT'D)

mistakes, especially on China." *1998: The Chinese dissident, now in U.S. exile, on the American media's preoccupation with the president's private life.*

WILLIAM WELD
(Governor of Massachusetts)

"All that hair, all those teeth—you gotta run scared." *1993: On speculation that Representative Joe Kennedy will run against him in 1994.*

"There was the Rhodes scholarship, the Marshall scholarship, Harvard Law Review. My life is a tangled wreck of failures." *1997: Saying wryly that his losing bid for the U.S. Senate was not his first disappointment.*

ROBERT WEXLER
(Congressman)

"The President betrayed his wife. He did not betray the country. God help this nation if we fail to recognize the difference." *1998: Opposing a House impeachment inquiry.*

JOHN C. WHITE
(Chairman of the Democratic National Party)

"If you can't have a private elevator and be able to cash checks, I really don't see any reason to go through this rigamarole. If you don't have a policeman to stop traffic to let you walk across the street like you are somebody, how are you going to know you're somebody?" *1992: On serving in Congress.*

"They've already taken the sex and drinking out of politics. Hell, if they get this thing to where you can't exhibit a little sense of power—that's what drives this city." *1992*

JOHN WHITEHURST
(San Francisco Political Consultant)

"Less than a quarter of a percent of San Francisco voters are satanic followers, no matter what the national press says." *1997: Trying to explain away the birthday bash of Jack Davis, a powerful political player in San Francisco, which included "satanic debauchery."*

CHRISTINE TODD WHITMAN
(Governor of New Jersey)

"We have to get away from the perception that all we care about is whether or not Teletubbies are gay." *The Republican governor on her party's image problems.*

DOUGLAS WILDER
(Virginia Governor)

"The first black president will be a politician who is black." *1992*

KATHLEEN WILLEY
(Former White House Volunteer)

"He put his hands—he put my hands on his genitals." *1998: Describing an unwanted sexual encounter with President Clinton. "I did to (Willey) what I have done to scores and scores of men and women who have worked for me or been my friends over the years. . . . There was nothing sexual about it," President Clinton later responded to the allegation.*

"I thought, 'Well, maybe I ought to just give him a good slap across the face.' And then I thought, 'Well, I don't think you can slap the president of the United States like that.' " *1998: Describing her reaction when President Clinton allegedly fondled her during an Oval Office encounter in 1993.*

"My instincts told me he wasn't interested in chicken soup." *1998: On declining an alleged attempt by Bill Clinton to get her to drive to Williamsburg, VA, during the presidential campaign to bring him some broth for a sore throat.*

ROBIN WILLIAMS
(Actor & Comedian)

"Al D'Amato leading an ethics committee is [like] having Ray Charles lead a tour of the Louvre." *1996*

BRUCE WILLIS
(Actor)

"Bill Clinton and his wife did something that the country has to forever be indebted to them for, something the Republicans were unable to do for 45 years. And that is, bring about the downfall of the Democratic Party and make them look like the boobs they are. Here's a guy who ran on this platform of trashing Ronald Reagan and George Bush . . . This . . . clerk, this guy who never made more than $36,000 in his life in a year, running the government. OK, Bill! Here's the country! Turn it loose!" *1996*

GARRY WILLS
(Historian)

"The claim that 'mere sex doesn't matter' backfires on itself: if it did not matter, then he would have admitted to such an irrelevant thing from the outset instead of throwing a blanket of denial and distraction over the nation for more than half a year. His message as a result of this was less that 'sex doesn't matter' than 'truth doesn't matter.' Perjury may not matter, or be provable, but the larger betrayal was of a generation that prized itself on candor, on an openness about sex and authenticity." *1998: On the Clinton White House scandals.*

PETE WILSON
(Former Governor of California)

"In any audience, 20% listen, 20% let their minds drift, and 60% are actively engaged in sexual fantasies." *1994: On the importance of keeping political speeches short.*

OPRAH WINFREY
(TV Talk-show Host)

"When people say Monica set Clinton up, I think, I guess they weren't the 20-year-old I was." *1998*

HILLARY WINSTON
(Former White House Intern)

"I got some presidential M&Ms and a tote bag. That was about it." *1998: On reports that the president gave Monica Lewinsky gifts of clothing and poetry books.*

SUSAN WITKIN
(Journalist)

"The President is in San Francisco and things won't be the same until he leaves." *1992*

NAOMI WOLF
(Writer)

"If we decide to shrug off the idea of the CEO of the country sleeping with the staff, it will certainly give a green light to the corruption of meritocracy in general. Why, then, should we not tolerate judges who listen only to male attorneys, or doctors who only hire female nurses, or bluechip companies that hire only children of the rich? If we go that route, we will have workplace ethics that will become as degraded as those of other nations that see us as a bastion of fairness." *1998*

STEVIE WONDER
(Singer & Composer)

"I'm glad I'm blind and can't see it." *1998: On coverage of the Clinton scandals in the media.*

JANET WOODCOCK
(FDA Chief)

"This is not an aphrodisiac." *1998: On Viagra, the newly FDA-approved pill to treat male impotence.*

SUSAN WEBBER WRIGHT
(Federal Judge)

"Although it is not clear why the plaintiff failed to receive flowers on Secretary's Day in 1992, such an omission does not give rise to a federal cause of action." *1998: Dismissing Paula Jones's sexual-harassment lawsuit against Bill Clinton.*

"It appears that the president is asserting that Ms. Lewinsky could be having sex with him while, at the same time, he was not having sex with her." *1999: Finding President Clinton in civil contempt for falsely denying having intimate relations with Monica Lewinsky in his deposition in the Paula Jones case.*

"The record demonstrates by clear and convincing evidence that the president responded to the plaintiff's questions by giving false, misleading and evasive answers that were designed to obstruct the judicial process." *1999: Holding President Clinton in contempt of court for his testimony in the Paula Jones lawsuit.*

STEVE WYNNE
(President of Adidas)

"I don't believe you will encounter anyone smoking our shoes any time soon." *1996: In response to a request by Bill Clinton's former antidrug Czar Lee Brown, for a change in the name of Adidas's popular new shoe, Hemp.*

PAUL WYSOCKI
(Candidate for City Council in San Jose, CA)

"Lesbians and gay men give to the community over and over again." *1990*

Y

MA YING-JEOU
(Mayoral Candidate in Taipei, Taiwan)

"I think the best thing we can do now is maintain the status quo, without saying what the status quo

MA YING-JEOU (CONT'D)

is." *1998: Discussing the murky political waters involving China and Taiwan's future.*

MARIE YOCHIM
(President, DAR)

"There's nothing to apologize for. We have 150 employees. A lot of them are black and have been for years." *1990: On the non-discriminatory hiring policies of her organization.*

Z

JIANG ZEMIN
(President of China)

"This movie shows fully how people deal with the relationship between money and love, poverty and wealth, in the middle of a difficult situation." *1998: After seeing the film* Titanic *and stating how studying capitalist things could help his country.*

"That's venture capital, eh?" *1998: On hearing that* Titanic *had reaped nearly $1 billion globally.*

"You should not imagine that there is no ideological education in capitalist countries." *1998: Urging his Politburo comrades to see* Titanic *as a parable of class divisions.*

"This movie gives vivid descriptions of the relationship between money and love [and] rich and poor. . . . I don't mean to publicize capitalism, but [as the saying goes] 'Know thine enemy.' " *1998: On the opening of* Titanic *in China.*

VLADIMIR ZHIRONOVSKY
(Russian Politician)

"We, as individuals with high moral character, would prefer not to meet a person who still can't sort out his relationship with his secretary. In the traditions of Russian society, in such situations, one divorces the old wife and marries the secretary." *1998: Telling the Russian Parliament why Bill Clinton should not have visited Russia.*

PART THREE

SPORTS

SPORTS

A

VAL ACKERMAN
(President, WNBA–NBA Backed Women's League)
"David Stern and I talked about it. We're not letting Dennis play in both leagues." *1997: On cross-dressing Chicago Bulls forward Dennis Rodman.*

ANDRE AGASSI
(Tennis player)
"I've only scratched the iceberg." *1990: Assessing his career so far.*

"I saw a bunch of things I don't remember the names of, but I enjoyed them." *1991: Summarizing his sight-seeing in England.*

"I left at halftime." *1991: When asked what he thought of the musical* Les Miserables.

"You can never drive too far for Taco Bell, and you can never beat somebody too bad." *1992*

EMMANUEL AGASSI
(Father of Andre)
"He's 24. He could be a senator by now." *1994: Asked about his son's career.*

ROBERT ALEXANDER
(Golfer)
"It was a real shock to all of us, but there really was nothing we could do. We all thought to ourselves, 'Gee, that's a good way to go. He didn't suffer.'" *1991: Alexander of West Haven, FL, was playing golf with a group when buddy Donald DeGreve suffered a heart attack and died on the sixteenth green. His friends and playing partners covered DeGreve's body with a sheet right where he died, on the sixteenth green, and then played through.*

MUHAMMAD ALI
(Boxer)
"For years I've been telling people I was pretty good. But I've never been one to brag." *1991*

"I always liked to chase the girls. Parkinson's stops all that. Now I might have a chance to go to heaven." *1997: Calling his Parkinson's disease a blessing.*

"Go to Mecca, pray three times a day, and stay pretty." *1997: When asked about his plans for the future.*

"Don't make me laugh. Tyson don't have it. He don't have it." *1997: When asked if Mike Tyson could have beaten him.*

"Fighting is not the answer to frustration and hate. It is a sport, not a philosophy of life. I do not promote anybody become a professional boxer. I would prefer children use it as a springboard, not a career choice." *1999: On prizefighting.*

WOODY ALLEN
(Actor & Director)
"When asked why it is so important that the Knicks win . . . I can only answer that basketball or baseball or any sport is as dearly important as life itself. After all, why is it such a big deal to work and love and strive and have children and then die and decompose into eternal nothingness? [By now, the person who asked me why the Knicks winning is important is sorry]." *1998*

ROBERTO ALOMAR
(Baseball Player)
"I would advise everybody not to say that to Latin guys." *1997: The second baseman for the Baltimore Orioles, on the use of the word* motherfucker, *used allegedly by umpire John Hirschbeck in an argument with Alomar in 1996, which resulted in Alomar spitting in the umpire's face.*

SANDY ALOMAR
(Baseball Player)
"If it hadn't hit the scoreboard, it would have gone all the way around the world and hit me in the back of the head." *1997: The Cleveland Indians catcher after Oakland A's slugger Mark McGwire hit a 484-foot home run, the longest ever at Jacobs Field.*

FELIPE ALOU
(Baseball manager)
"I didn't feel sorry for me, and I know he didn't feel sorry for himself. But I felt sorry for him, and I

FELIPE ALOU (CONT'D)

think he felt sorry for me." *1999: The Montreal Expos manager recalling a chat with manager Tom Kelly of the Minnesota Twins, on trying to win with teams whose combined payrolls are less than what the Los Angeles Dodgers are paying pitcher Kevin Brown.*

DAVE ANDERSON
(Sportswriter)

"Siamese twins joined at the money clip." *1990: Describing the relationship of Mike Tyson and Don King.*

SPARKY ANDERSON
(Baseball Manager)

"You don't have enough smarts to straighten this out. This is unstraightable." *1995: The Detroit Tiger manager addressing his coaching staff on the woeful state of his team's pitching.*

"The World Series don't stay with me. The game stays with me. The game is the only thing that's important. The owners and players have to understand the game belongs to the fans. They lease it to us." *1995: On leaving the Tigers in October.*

TEDDY ATLAS
(Boxing Trainer)

"Our sparring partners were better than this guy. If he were in our camp, he wouldn't last." *1994: Corner man, Teddy Atlas to his fighter, Michael Moorer, between rounds in the heavyweight title fight between Moorer and forty-five-year-old George Foreman. Moorer was knocked out by Foreman in the tenth round.*

B

OKSANA BAIUL
(Ice Skater)

"I'm a Russian." *1997: Explaining to Oprah Winfrey that despite having had four or five drinks—and a blood alcohol content of 0.168 percent—she wasn't drunk when she had a high-speed crash.*

CHARLES BARKLEY
(Basketball Player)

"That's going to happen anytime you write a book, so I just have to deal with the heat." *1992: When he tried to block the publication of his own autobiography, entitled* Outrageous, *because he had been "misquoted" in his own book.*

"I told you white boys you've never heard of a '90s nigger. We do what we want to do. I'm going to be a little more vocal now. . . . And you've got two choices. You can kiss my behind. Or you can try and get me traded." *1992: When he was unhappy playing with the Philadelphia 76ers, complaining to sports reporters.*

"Japan makes the best car, Italians make the best clothes; why can't we be the best at something, too?" *1992: Explaining what's right about the Dream Team, the American basketball team in the Olympic Games.*

"I'm quitting this team for the swim team. I'm going to the pool as long as there are babes with no tops. You'll think I'm Mark Spitz before this week is over." *1992: At the Barcelona Olympic Games, after hearing that Monaco's women's swim team practices topless.*

"It was like I was president. No, not our president, sorry. A real president." *1992: On being a star in Spain during the Olympic games.*

"Everybody's complaining about pros in the Olympics. Why don't I hear anything about Steffi Graf or Jim Courier being here? Aren't they professionals? Don't they make millions of dollars? Are you telling me the track people aren't pros? I don't want to hear any shit out of them. The way I see it, a lot of people want to see us prove we're the best basketball players in the world. If other people don't like it, they can turn the fucking television off." *1992: On the true spirit of the Olympic games.*

"I miss America. I miss crime and murder. I miss Philadelphia. There hasn't been a brutal stabbing or anything here the last 24 hours. I've missed it." *1992: After the American Dream Team beat Lithuania by fifty-one points in the Olympic games.*

"You can't compare preseason to regular season. Preseason is just a way to screw fans out of money." *1992: Playing with the Phoenix Suns.*

"I can be bought. I have no pride. If they paid me enough money, I'd work for the Klan." *1992: When asked if he'd work for the 76ers again.*

"I heard Tonya Harding is calling herself the Charles Barkley of figure skating. I was going to sue her for defamation of character, but then I realized I have no character." *1994*

"There wouldn't be any such thing as Death Row, there'd be Death Week. If you killed somebody in a violent way, you would be dead within a week." *1994: On his position on violent crime and drugs if he held public office.*

"The players today . . . they're like [what] you see on TV: Kids killing kids and stuff like that. Kids in gangs. I think that's the generation of the young player that's coming to the NBA. Rebellious. Undisciplined. They speak for our society. I mean, if they didn't play basketball, they'd be the guys who'd be in gangs, who'd kill somebody." *1994*

"When I talk trash, I'm just having fun with it. I'm not trying to embarrass a guy. I don't say, 'I'm going to kill you.' Larry, Magic and Michael—these guys talked trash, but it was a friendly kind of trash. We didn't curse other players out. Every time we scored on a guy we didn't get in his face and stare at him. I think that's just wrong." *1994*

"People like to say we're all alike, but we're not. Some are on Earth and others, like him, are on another planet. He's achieved true greatness." *1994: On Justice Clarence Thomas.*

"The majority of poor people and minorities always vote Democratic. That's why they're poor and their options are limited." *1994*

"I know that I'm not a Democrat, because I don't think the Democrats have done a good job helping black people or poor people. . . . I guess the only thing left to me is to be a Republican." *1995*

"You guys should get a fucking life. That's why I hate fucking white people." *1995: Speaking to reporters.*

"Every kid I talk to thinks they're going to be in the NBA. I gotta be honest with you. You're not going to be." *1995*

"The NBA's in disarray—a white guy won the slam-dunk competition. We need to have another Million Man March." *1996: On teammate Michael Finley's loss to L.A. Clippers rookie Brent Barry.*

"Grandma, I *am* rich." *1996: On his response to his grandmother's complaint that Republicans were only for the rich.*

"I'm firing my mother . . . She had me too soon." *1996: Earning $4.7 million and complaining that he was too old for the NBA free-agent boom in 1996.*

"I think we should play all three of those teams today and then get the hell out of town." *1996: Charles Barkley of the U.S. Dream Team, after a bomb threat caused the evacuation of the team's hotel.*

"I didn't vote for either candidate. I respect Clinton but I can't vote Democratic. And Dole is the same age as my grandmother, and I don't want her to be president, either." *1996: On voting.*

"People are complaining that I'm working 40 minutes three days a week? What a great country." *1997: With the Houston Rockets, on worries he is courting injury by playing too many minutes.*

"I used to be a Chippendale. Now I'm a Clydesdale." *1997: On the effects of aging on his thirty-four-year-old body.*

"Heck, no. A guy threw a drink on me, and I threw him through a window. I was just mad I wasn't on a higher floor." *1998: When asked if the reason he quit drinking was a recently publicized altercation he had with a man in a ground-level bar.*

"I've got 500 channels on my dish, and he was on every one of them." *1999: Grousing about the coverage of buddy Michael Jordan's retirement.*

"Old basketball players just get older. They don't get better. This isn't golf." *1999: After his grizzled team was eliminated from the playoffs by the younger Los Angeles Lakers.*

MATTHEW BARNABY
(Hockey Player)

"I don't think anyone is smart enough to fall for that." *1998: The member of the Buffalo Sabres on his*

MATTHEW BARNABY (CONT'D)

team's response to Washington Capitals' coach Ron Wilson's attempt to goad the Sabres by calling them "chicken."

GARY BARNETT
(Football Coach)

"I think the only deception is if you knew you were deceiving them when you were doing it." *1999: Denying that he misled his Northwestern players when he sent team members an e-mail promising to lead them back to the Rose Bowl three days before accepting a new job as head coach at Colorado.*

SKIP BAYLESS
(Sportswriter)

"You need to be a criminologist these days to cover the Cowboys." *1997: On the alleged involvement of Cowboy players in another criminal case.*

DON BAYLOR
(Baseball Coach)

"No, I came into this game sane, and I'll go out the same way." *1992: When asked if he'd ever manage for Yankees owner George Steinbrenner.*

ROD BECK
(Baseball Player)

"I've never seen anyone on the DL with pulled fat." *1998: The Chicago Cubs closer on the physique that he says doesn't make him injury prone.*

DICK BELL
(Football Coach)

"Once we got around 70 I said, 'Let's go for 100.' Those deaf kids scored 40 points. They were excited and having fun." *1995: The first-year football coach at Cardinal Gibbons High School in Raleigh, NC, after his team defeated the Eastern North Carolina School for the Deaf, 100–42. ENCSD has only thirty-five males students, twenty-six of whom are on the football team. Bell left in his first-team offense for the entire game.*

RICK BENNER
(Basketball Team President)

"Let's say a player is on the court, and a girl on the sidelines decides she's had enough of this guy and throws a pompom at him. Wilder things have happened." *1993: After the team suspended a member of its dance team because she was dating a player, which is against team rules.*

HARRY BENSON
(Photographer)

"Of all the athletes I've photographed, basketball players are the most intelligent, baseball players are the most stupid. You go into a basketball player's house and you see books. You go into a baseball player's and you find *People* magazine." *1998*

YOGI BERRA
(Baseball Player & Coach)

"It's never happened in the World Series competition, and it still hasn't." *1990: Recalling Don Larsen's perfect game in the 1956 World Series.*

"Joe, I want to thank you for teaching me that the only way to do something correctly is to do it right." *1993: In an award presentation to Joe DiMaggio.*

"He's done more than that!" *1997: When asked if Tiger Woods had exceeded his expectations in winning the Masters Tournament.*

"I just wasn't the stereotypical Yankee. I was short and stubby and with my catcher's mask on, I looked like Hannibal Lecter. When I started with the Yankees, a reporter said that I didn't even look like I was a Yankee. That comment still hurts today. I'm kind of glad that reporters are not always accurate. I really have not said everything I've said. Back to my appearance. Lucky for me, you don't hit with your face." *1998*

CARMEN BERRA: "Yogi, when you die, where do you want to be buried, in Montclair, New York or in St. Louis?"

YOGI BERRA: "I don't know, Carmen, why don't you surprise me." *1998: An exchange between Yogi Berra and his wife.*

"It's over." *1998: On what he wants his gravestone to say.*

"If I had to do it all over again, I'd do it all over again." *1998: Reminiscing about his baseball career to the 1998 Little League World Series champions from Toms River, New Jersey.*

"It's over." *1999: Declaring an end to his fourteen-year feud with Yankees owner George Steinbrenner.*

"He was the greatest living ballplayer I've ever seen play." *1999: Describing his late teammate, Joe DiMaggio.*

LIU BIN
(Soccer Fan)

"We do it to let off steam. People at sports events want to hang loose." *1998: The Beijing fan explaining why he, and thousands of other fans, have taken to shouting torrents of vulgar abuse at football matches. The language is so crude that officials are trying to find a way to deal with what's been dubbed the "Beijing Curse."*

LARRY BIRD
(Basketball Player & Coach)

"There's more to life than basketball." *1996: When asked about the return of Magic Johnson to the sport.*

"He was one of two." *1999: When asked whether Michael Jordan was the best basketball player of all time.*

STEVE BLASS
(Sports Broadcaster)

"He should have been better, pitching on 3,195 days rest." *1995: The Pittsburgh Pirate broadcaster, on Buc replacement player Jimmy Boudreau, who last appeared professionally in 1986.*

BARRY BONDS
(Baseball Player)

"I ain't proud of no ring I ain't had nothin' to do with." *1996: Using a quadruple negative to describe world championship rings, of which he has none.*

JIM BOUTON
(Baseball Player)

"This is the third time I've wept today, and it's not even 2 P.M." *1998: The former New York Yankees pitcher, fifty-nine, to a reporter who called after the club invited him to play in an Old-Timers' Day game for the first time, lifting a ban imposed after he wrote a book,* Ball Four, *whose revelations angered some of his old teammates.*

BOBBY BOWDEN
(Football Coach)

"The defense had a job to do and just did it. Didn't have to coax 'em. Didn't have to beg 'em. Just said, 'Sic 'em.' With the offense, it's 'Please block that guy. Please catch the ball.' They're like that stinkin' cat. He just sits there, looks at you, scratches his ear. Ever tell a cat to sic 'em?" *1998: The Florida State football coach who was pleased with his defense but not his offense in a 30–10 victory over Southern Cal.*

RIDDICK BOWE
(Heavyweight Boxer)

"I'm really enjoying this entire ordeal." *1993: The world heavyweight champion commenting on the horde of autograph seekers who besieged him after he won his title in November 1992.*

BOB BRENLY
(Baseball Coach)

"He's so tough against us, they named a country after him." *1992: The San Francisco Giants coach talking about Astros pitcher Mark Portugal, who was 9–2 against the Giants.*

MARTY BRENNAMAN
(Sports Broadcaster)

"If Joe's dead, that explains a lot." *1998: On an erroneous report that his Cincinnati Reds radio broadcasting partner, Joe Nushall, had died.*

GEORGE BRETT
(Baseball Player)

"I know I'm fertile; I've got the checkbook to prove it. But getting a couple of girls pregnant probably gave me a sense that there's no sweat; I can have kids anytime I want. . . . I've had the security of knowing I'm a proven performer." *1990: The Kansas City Royals player on two former girl friends' abortions.*

DAVE BRISTOL
(Baseball Manager)

"If I had that bullpen, I would have slit her throat." *1995: The former major league baseball manager, in a speech in Albany, GA, referring to an incident in which Bobby Cox, manager of the Atlanta Braves, was arrested for assaulting his wife.*

WILLIE BROWN
(Speaker of the California State Assembly)

"I'm trying to get the French to invest in a new quarterback. This guy Grbac is an embarrassment to humankind. After that interception and that bonehead intellectual breakdown in the last game against Dallas, and we lost 20–17, he can't play in any stadium that I'm gonna assist to be built." *1996: While on a junket in Paris, commenting on 49er quarterback Elvis Grbac, who replaced Steve Young in a game against Dallas after Young suffered a concussion. Grbac threw two crucial interceptions, including one that set up the Cowboys' tying score before the game went into overtime. Grbac said later he wasn't prepared to play because he and his wife had been worried about the condition of their nine-month-old son, Jack, who suffers from spina bifida. The boy had recently undergone surgery to alleviate pressure on his spinal column and help him develop properly.*

JOEY BROWNER
(Football Player)

"It's not good for business if you care for a second whether blood is bubbling from a guy's mouth." *1992: The Minnesota Viking star on playing defense in the NFL.*

TERRELL BUCKLEY
(Football & Baseball Player)

"Everyone knows that Jim Thorpe was the best athlete of the first half century. Here I am, the best athlete of the second half century. They (the Packers) are really insulting me." *1992: After spurning the Green Bay Packers' contract offer and signing a minor league contract with the Atlanta Braves.*

JUD BUECHLER
(Basketball Player)

"It's difficult to read the paper in Chicago. There's stuff that's said that you're probably better off not knowing about." *1996*

JOHN BURKETT
(Baseball Player)

"That's a tough lineup. It's like you are facing All-Stars out there." *1993: The San Francisco Giant's pitcher after he was charged with a loss when he pitched for the National League in the All-Star Game.*

KEN BURNS
(Documentary Filmmaker)

"I finally figured out what ESPN meant, which is Every Sports Pundit's Nitpicks." *1995: On criticism of his baseball documentary by ESPN commentator Keith Olbermann.*

MIKE BURROWS
(British Bicycle Designer)

"It was wonderful. The scenery was unbelievable. The community was idyllic and the people were just beautiful. The whole town had nothing but beautiful people. I think there must have been an ordinance banning stupid, ugly people within city limits. . . . Then I came to Las Vegas and realized what they'd done with them all." *1998: Describing a trip in the United States that began in Marin County, CA.*

C

HERB CAEN
(Newspaper Columnist)

"The players don't have a picket line because they might soil their Guccis, but if they had to have one they could hire the homeless to walk it for them. Say, that's not a bad idea, all by itself. Since the whole dumb strike is simply about a bunch of rich people arguing over how to divvy up the billions, why don't the owners and players become partners? Man, do they deserve each other." *1994: On the baseball strike.*

ERNST CALIM
(Hot Dog Vendor)

"I have to say, I like the Yankee fans, and there is a good reason. They seem to buy more than the Mets fans." *1998: The Shea Stadium hot dog vendor after the Bronx Bombers played a game there due to structural problems that forced the closing of Yankee Stadium.*

ELDEN CAMPBELL
(Basketball Player)

"No, but they gave me one, anyway." *1991: The Los Angeles Lakers rookie forward, when asked if he had earned his degree from Clemson.*

PAT CAMPBELL
(Associate Counsel of the Major League Umpires' Assocation)

"I mean, if an umpire shot a player on the field, could he be terminated? I guess under those circumstances

I would have a tough time saying he couldn't." *1998: On what it would take to fire an umpire.*

TOM CANDIOTTI
(Baseball Player)

"I'm getting tired of seeing a guy cross first base and the next thing I know, he's headed for second." *1992: Reflecting on the number of errors made by his Dodgers teammates during the season.*

DYAN CANNON
(Actress)

"One night the referee called [a play] out of bounds, and it wasn't. So I got nuts and told him it was a bad call. He said, 'Dyan, I've seen your movies. They weren't all good.' And I thought, 'I won't mess with those guys again.'" *1997: On her experience watching a Lakers' game.*

JOSE CANSECO
(Baseball Player)

"Give him a couple million. He shouldn't have to take a second job to support himself or anything." *1990: The Oakland A's slugger on why Cincinnati pitcher Rob Dibble should earn more than $200,000 per year.*

"She's too old for me." *1991: When asked if he'd like to meet Queen Elizabeth, who visited the United States in May and attended an A's baseball game.*

"They can't complain about my contract. I'm one of the poorest guys in baseball." *1992: After Ryne Sandberg was given a $28.4 million contract for four years.*

"It's more relaxed here. It's an atmosphere I can relate to. In Oakland it was always win, win, win— and you get fed up with it." *1992: On being a member of the Texas Rangers.*

"I would clone Marilyn Monroe. Why waste time with baseball players? Why waste time cloning a guy?'" *1997: On cloning.*

CHIP CARAY
(Baseball Announcer)

"It's a partial sellout." *1998: The Atlanta Braves announcer, trying to put the best face on a paltry turnout at a home game.*

"I'm not Harry. And the best thing I could do to commit professional suicide would be to come out wearing big glasses, saying 'Holy Cow,' pronouncing people's names backward and singing 'Take Me Out to the Ball Game.' " *1998: New Cubs broadcaster Chip Caray, who said he'd lead his grandfather's traditional song during the seventh-inning stretch only if fans want it. Harry Caray died in February 1998.*

HARRY CARAY
(Baseball Announcer)

"Scott Bullett, as he takes left field, is getting congratulations from everybody. He and his daughter are parents of a new baby." *1995*

MARIAH CAREY
(Singer)

"I'm just a singer, not some magical baseball genie who can make or break someone's game." *1998: Responding to rumors that Yankee shortstop Derek Jeter was warned by boss George Steinbrenner that his romance with the singer was hurting his game.*

LOU CARNESECCA
(Basketball Coach)

"Hey, Mozart didn't write *Moonlight Sonata* every time out." *1990: The St. John's University basketball coach after his Redmen struggled to beat lowly Brooklyn College, 57–47.*

PETE CARRIL
(Basketball Coach)

"He has the shooting range. What he doesn't have is the making range." *1995: The Princeton basketball coach on why he wouldn't move freshman Steve Goodrich from center to forward.*

NORMAN CHAD
(Sportswriter)

"Have you heard the slogan NBC Sports uses at the end of its telecasts? 'Where America turns for the best in sports television—NBC Sports.' Oh, really? If NBC Sports had covered the discovery of America, it would have been in a commercial when Columbus hit land. I mean, what exactly does NBC do better than anyone else? I'll take Fox over NBC on the NFL. I'll take ABC

NORMAN CHAD (CONT'D)

on college football. I'll take CBS on basketball. I'll take CBS on golf and tennis. I'll take ESPN on *anything* over NBC. You watch NBC, it looks like SportsChannel Borneo. Its cameras are in all the wrong places, its analysts make all the wrong cases, its graphics are in all the wrong typefaces. And if some production assistant named Jason trips over the wrong extension cord, the whole network goes to black. NBC may be owned by GE, but NBC Sports shops at Radio Shack." *1995*

"I understand that he [Roy Firestone] interviewed Ken and Barbie and made them *both* cry. If ESPN ever starts thinking budget cuts, it could begin by losing one of the chairs on Firestone's set. He always ends up in his guest's lap anyway." *1995: On ESPN sports interviewer, Roy Firestone.*

"It (TBS) was okay when no one cared about the Atlanta Braves. But now that they've been good for several years, you can't help but notice that the superstation is filled with super-static. Skip Caray's so bad, I wish the South had won the war and seceded." *1995*

WILT CHAMBERLAIN
(Basketball Player)

"It's very simple. Since I traveled the world so much, especially throughout America, I knew my geography. I'd always ask, 'Where are you from?' And when she would answer, I'd pretend that I was from some small place close to it, and we would immediately be on common ground." *1991: Explaining the slick strategy he utilized in bedding (so he claims in his autobiography) 20,000 women.*

"Yeah, it's true—I'm just a lucky stiff." *1991: In an interview with Ross McGowan on KPIX, Channel 5, in San Francisco, when asked if he really slept with 20,000 women.*

MICHAEL CHANG
(Tennis Player)

"He can't cook." *1994: When asked if Pete Sampras had any weaknesses. Sampras had just eliminated Chang in the Wimbledon quarterfinals.*

NORM CHARLTON
(Baseball Player)

"If I can't talk you out of it or preach you out of it, I'll beat you out of it." *1995: The Philadelphia Phillie pitcher, on having a triple major—in political science, religion, and phys ed—while at Rice University.*

BRANDI CHASTAIN
(Soccer Player)

"Momentary insanity—nothing more, nothing less." *1999: On her unplanned gesture of ripping off her soccer jersey and exposing her sports bra after winning the Women's World Cup final.*

WILL CLARK
(Baseball Player)

Baseball Fan: "Hey, Will, what'd he say?"
Will Clark: "Nothin' educated." *1992: Exchange between a baseball fan and Clark of the San Francisco Giants. Clark had just spoken with Jose Canseco of the Oakland A's.*

ROGER CLEMENS
(Baseball Player)

"When I get home I'm going to have to try to bribe President Bush and get a set of his." *1996: The Boston Red Sox pitcher after calling from Fenway Park midgame to bid—unsuccessfully—on a set of John F. Kennedy's golf clubs at the Jackie Onassis auction.*

CHRIS CLEVENGER
(Football Player)

"I knew by that point to keep my helmet on on the sideline." *1998: The Former Notre Dame lineman during testimony in an age-discrimination lawsuit filed against the school by former offensive line coach Joe Moore, recalling what he said about the second incident in which Moore punched him in the face for an on-field mistake.*

KEITH CLOSS
(Basketball Player)

"I've apologized and it won't happen again." *1997: The Los Angeles Clippers rookie center, after missing practices to attend the funerals of his grandmother and his cousin.*

BUD COLLINS
(Sports Broadcaster)

"Two women on grass! It doesn't get any better." *1991: Commenting on the Steffi Graff–Gabriella Sabatini final match at Wimbledon in July.*

"I'm very thrilled and pleased. I'm looking forward to the embalming." *1994: On his election to the International Tennis Hall of Fame.*

DAVID CONE
(Baseball Player)

"The last time I was in this situation, my mom was washing my uniform." *1998: The Yankee pitcher, on dressing and playing in different places, after a fallen joint forced the team to move a game to the Met's stadium in April.*

JIMMY CONNORS
(Tennis Player)

"Three things happened over time. I think people began to look at me with different eyes. I was bad out there. It would be stupid to deny that. But people began to get a sense that that helped me play better tennis, give them a better show. I got married and became a father, and that changed me to a certain point. And, McEnroe came along. After that, just about anything I did was going to be OK." *1991: On his transformation from '70s bad guy to popular but aging champion.*

KEVIN CONSTANTINE
(Hockey Coach)

"They all need a lobotomy, and I mean that in the nicest way." *1994: The San Jose Sharks coach on the enthusiasm of Sharks fans.*

DAVID CORCORAN
(Baseball Fan)

"It doesn't make sense; there was a lot of alcohol consumed in the Bible." *1998: Objecting to a decision by Red Sox team officials not to serve beer at the Red Sox opener, which coincided with Good Friday and Passover.*

BOB COSTAS
(Sports Broadcaster)

"So if you walk by the dorms and hear anyone screaming *Oh, Canada*, it won't be the swimmers." *1996: Explaining during the opening ceremony broadcast that Canadian swimmers agreed to abstain from sexual activity during the Summer Olympics.*

JIM COURIER
(Tennis Player)

"I was just wondering if they've signed the NAFTA agreement or not?" *1993: During a changeover in the middle of a match against Andrei Medvedev, Courier turned to his coach, Jose Higueras, and asked this question. Courier's play and behavior on the court, fans and sportswriters noticed, was becoming increasingly bewildering.*

"At the moment, my best surface is my bed." *1994: The former world's No. 1–ranked tennis player, on his 1993–94 slump.*

"I know I'm good enough . . . and smart enough . . . and gosh darn it, people *like* me." *1994: At a press conference following his loss to Andrea Gaudenzi in an early round of the U.S. Open. Courier was borrowing words from comedian Al Franken's character, Stuart Smalley.*

MICHAEL CROUWEL
(Baseball Player)

"The only thing I know about it is that it's in New Jersey." *1992: The Philadelphia Phillie catching prospect, who was acquired from the Dutch national team, when asked about Philadelphia.*

BRIAN CUNNANE
(Basketball Coach)

"If it's true that losing builds character, then we have more characters than Disney and Warner Bros. combined." *1991: The assistant basketball coach of the U.S. Merchant Marine Academy, which went 3–23 for the 1990–91 season.*

LARRY CURRY
(Social Worker & Sports Psychologist)

"I felt he was very personable, very sensitive. . . . By and large he has the most strength and character of any individual in the professional athletes' department that I've worked with." *1998: Testifying before the Nevada State Athletic Commission on the fitness of suspended boxer Mike Tyson to compete again. Curry's clients include John Elway and the Denver Broncos.*

BOB CYZ
(Boxing Analyst)

"In a world-title fight, if I hit an opponent and his eye fell out of his head, I'd eat it before he could pick it up and put it back in." *1998: Explaining to New Jersey's State Athletic Control Board how the "performance blackout" that sometimes affects fighters led former heavyweight champion Mike Tyson to bite Evander Holyfield's ear during a 1997 bout.*

D

CHUCK D
(Rapper)

"Look at the NBA. In the late seventies, a lot of guys were coked up out of their minds, and a lot of them played great. But they were all burning out by the time they were 33. Then the NBA came up with a drug [testing] situation, and now these guys are making more money than ever [and] playing till they're 40. Maybe we [musicians] should think about something like that, 'cause our performance these days is definitely questionable." *1996: Public Enemy's Chuck D at a forum on possible solutions to drug abuse in the music industry.*

JOHN DALY
(Golfer)

"I couldn't care less about all those fiction stories about what happened in the year 1500 or 1600. Half of them aren't even true." *1996: On his lack of interest in world literature as a college student.*

MIKE D'ANTON
(Basketball Coach)

"We might not be big enough, but it's the size of the dog in the fight, or the fight of the size in the dog. . . . Whatever it is, we don't got it." *1999: On his team's dismal start.*

CHRIS DARKINS
(Football Player)

"The studying is a lot more words. The playbook is a lot more pictures." *1997: The Green Bay Packers' second-year running back, when asked to compare his academic work at Minnesota with learning football plays at minicamp.*

AL DAVIS
(Football Team Owner)

"Remember, they [the students] got in that park in the first place because he let them come there. He never stopped them from coming there and discussing things. What he didn't like was beaming it back [on TV] to your home in Baltimore." *1994: The Raiders' owner, at a press conference about city-shopping in such places as Baltimore, commenting on Deng Xiaoping and the Tiananmen Square massacre. Davis confessed that he was particularly "impressed" by Deng.*

CRAIG DAVISON
(Jogger)

"People say to me, 'I never find money when I run.' I say, 'You're running too fast.'" *1997: Davison says he has collected more than $5,170 in loose change since 1978.*

RALPH DELEONARDIS
(Baseball Umpire)

"I blew it the way I saw it." *1993: The minor league baseball umpire, after a disputed call.*

TIM DELL
(Replacement Baseball Player)

"When they strike again in August, are we guaranteed our jobs back?" *1995: The Milwaukee replacement player asking about future baseball strikes.*

ERIC DENNIS
(Athletic Director)

"I was shocked and surprised—I don't know how we scored a run." *1996: The athletic director at Robert Morris College of Chicago, on how he felt when he learned his school's baseball team had lost to St. Francis of Illinois 71–1.*

LUKE DE ROECK
(Sports Fan)

"To suggest that God really cares about the outcome of a sporting event is preposterous. Conservatively, 20 million people in the U.S. went to bed hungry on Super Bowl Sunday. A God who cares about the outcome of the Super Bowl is not a God I ever want to meet." *1998*

JIM DE SHAIES
(Baseball Player)

"I think everybody gets caught up in superstitions. But I don't put much stock in them—knock on wood." *1994*

GLENN DICKEY
(Sportswriter)

"For that kind of money she should have to live with Barry." *1994: On Sun Bonds, estranged wife of San Francisco Giant Barry Bonds. Sun was asking for monthly support of $130,899.*

GERALD DIGILIO
(Baseball Fan)

"We ain't trading it for nothing. We're selling it to the highest bidder. We didn't come down here to give anything to McGwire. He didn't come to Astoria to give us anything." *1998: DiGilio of Astoria, Queens, whose friend Johnny Luna recovered a ball hit by Mark McGwire, apparently his sixty-sixth home run, that was later ruled a ground rule double.*

ROB DIMAIO
(Hockey Player)

"They had to take a piece of bone out of my head in order to rebuild my nose. It was kind of a pain in the butt." *1998: The Boston Bruins' right wing, after undergoing two off-season operations on his nasal passages.*

TRENT DIMAS
(Gymnast)

"I carry a photograph of my dog, Sugar, everywhere I go. I look at the picture as a symbol of unconditional love. No matter what I do or how I do, Sugar will always love me. That gives me the courage and confidence to compete." *1993: The 1992 Olympic gymnast gold medalist on his dog.*

MIKE DITKA
(Football Coach)

"Sometimes I'm short with reporters because their questions aren't prevalent." *1990*

"They should put in a rule that when a receiver drops the ball he has to do the same gyrations as when he caught it." *1995*

"We spent more time on weaknesses." *1997: On taking over the 3–13 New Orleans Saints, after a conversation with his two predecessors on the team's strengths and weaknesses.*

"If there's anything you want to do, you can do it. And if you don't want to do anything, you can do that too." *1999: The former Bears' coach on why he loves Chicago.*

VLADE DIVAC
(Basketball Player)

"We all get heavier as we get older because there's a lot more information in our heads. Our heads weigh more." *1992: The Los Angeles Lakers' twenty-four year old center, who reported to training camp at 250 pounds, fifteen pounds more than the 1991 season.*

BUSTER DOUGLAS
(Heavyweight Boxer)

"I fell asleep. And right after I did, he did." *1990: On what happened to him after he sat down to watch Alex Stewart's heavyweight fight against Mike Tyson on December 8. Stewart was knocked down three times in the first round; the third knockdown ended the fight.*

ANGELO DUNDEE
(Boxing Manager)

"Mike Tyson is too short to be heavyweight champ." *1990*

DAN DUVA
(Boxing Promoter)

"He didn't go to Princeton for three years. He went to prison." *1995: On the intelligence of Mike Tyson's re-signing with Duva rival Don King.*

LOU DUVA
(Boxing Trainer)

"It's not a matter of life and death. It's more important than that." *1991: On Evander Holyfield's cancelled fight against Mike Tyson.*

"He's a guy who gets up at 6 o'clock in the morning regardless of what time it is." *1996: On Andrew Golota's attitude before his rematch against archrival Riddick Bowe, which Golota lost, again, because of a low blow.*

LENNY DYKSTRA
(Baseball Player)

"I'm going to drop you dude!" *1994: The Phillies outfielder to Pennsylvania state Senator Earl Baker*

LENNY DYKSTRA (CONT'D)

during a lunch at the Strafford Inn in Philadelphia. Dykstra, according to witnesses, was using "loud four-letter words" when the state senator objected and responded, "Would you please watch your language?" Dykstra responded with this quote. A maitre d' stepped in and restored order in the restaurant.

"Great trade! Who did we get?" *1992: When told that his team had dealt unproductive outfielder Von Hayes to the California Angels.*

E

MARK EATON
(Basketball Player)

"I think Jesus would have been a great basketball player. He would have been one of the most tenacious guys out there. I think he'd really get in your face—nothing dirty, but he'd play to win." *1992: Eaton is a born-again Christian.*

HARRY EDWARDS
(Sociologist & Advisor to the San Francisco 49ers)

"I'm saying the same things about race and sports that I was saying in '68, maybe a little less stridently. Only difference is then they called me a subversive and a revolutionary. Today, they call me a consultant and pay me a bunch of money to say it." *1998*

JONATHAN EDWARDS
(Triple Jumper)

"Sometimes I lie in bed at night and think: I jump into a sand pit for a living." *1995: Edwards was the holder of the world record in the triple jump.*

JACK ESPINOSA JR.
(Florida Judge)

"If this is the picture of life after baseball, it's not pretty." *1999: On sentencing New York Yankee Darryl Strawberry to eighteen months' probation for drug and solicitation charges.*

TODD EWEN
(Hockey Player)

"We got a new coach [Jacques Demers] and he said: 'See that little round, black thing? You're supposed to put that in the net.'" *1992: The Montreal right wing, when asked how he had scored two goals in a single game—an unusual feat for him.*

F

AMERICO FARIA
(Soccer Supervisor)

"Sex in itself is not a problem. The problem occurs when there are no limits . . . when there are abuses that lead to exhaustion." *1996: The Brazilian soccer-team supervisor on why the national team would be housed in hotels instead of university dormitories to cut down on temptation during the Summer Olympics in Atlanta.*

SUZY FAVOR
(Runner)

"I became disoriented and didn't know how many laps were left in the race." *1990: An excuse of the Wisconsin runner who competed in the 3.5-lap 1,500-meter race at the Goodwill Games in Seattle.*

BOB FELLER
(Baseball Legend)

"He couldn't hit a curveball with an ironing board." *1994: On Michael Jordan's bid to play for the Chicago White Sox.*

BOBBY FISCHER
(Chess Master)

"Shall we go to the toilets and prove it?" *1999: After denying to a Hungarian radio interviewer that he is Jewish. The live broadcast was cut short when Fischer broke into an impromptu anti-Semitic tirade, prompting the confused host to ask, "Aren't you Jewish yourself?"*

MIKE FLANAGAN
(Baseball Player)

"The first time I came into a game there, I got in the bullpen car and they told me to lock the doors." *1991: The Baltimore Orioles pitcher on playing in Yankee Stadium.*

SCOTT FLETCHER
(Baseball Player)

"People think if you're a Christian, you're wimpy and you don't care. Well, if you know God, you know that's wrong. That's way wrong. God is a winner. God never loses. That's why he's God." *1993*

GEORGE FOREMAN
(Boxer)

"I have not concentrated on being skinny." *1990: The 260-pound heavyweight fighter, known also as "the Great Wide Hope."*

"There'll be buffets everywhere. I'll grab me some legs of chicken, roasts of beef, porks of chop and chickens of liver." *1990: On his preparation for a heavyweight title fight in April 1991.*

"Remember when kids were running down the street with rags on their heads and senior citizens ducked back in the door? When I get through with [Holyfield], you're going to see senior citizens with rags on their heads and teenagers hiding behind the bushes. I'm going to eat him like he's a pork chop sandwich." *1991*

"If Larry Holmes and George Foreman got into the ring, the smell of Ben-Gay would be so great that nobody would want a ringside seat." *1994: Foreman, forty-five, on a future fight with Larry Holmes, forty-five, shortly after Foreman knocked out heavyweight champion Michael Moorer, twenty-seven, in the tenth round of their title fight.*

"I fixed it, you can believe that. I fixed it with a right hand." *1994: When asked if people might think his recent victory over Michael Moorer was fixed.*

"That's why I named my four boys George. To make sure I wouldn't forget." *1998: On the memory lapses that affect veteran boxers.*

"I was a preacher for 10 years before my second career in boxing. I had to counsel people. I saw accountants who couldn't remember numbers. I saw airline pilots who didn't know how to get to the airport. And every now and then I heard about a boxer with problems." *1998: On the memory loss and physical problems that affect veteran boxers.*

"Don't let Mike Tyson and those guys know it, but I was crying." *1998: On his daughter's high school graduation.*

"He did something stupid, and that's what he does best." *1999: On undefeated fighter Prince Naseem Hamed's performance in a victory over Paul Ingle.*

ROY FOREMAN
(Brother of Boxer)

"We've been trying to get Elvis. He's been dead long enough now." *1992: On brother George's next heavyweight fight.*

RUSS FRANCIS
(Football Player)

"[It's] the heartwarming story of a simpleminded Southern boy who leads a fantasy sports life. I kind of wish, though, that they had stuck with the original title: *The Terry Bradshaw Story*." *1994: The former NFL tight end, on the hit movie* Forrest Gump.

WALT FRAZIER
(Basketball Player)

"All of the guys should be in this room, paying homage to us." *1997: The New York Knicks' broadcaster and NBA all-time All-Star, on his disappointment that Michael Jordan and Charles Barkley skipped the media session for the league's fifty all-time greatest players.*

G

JOHN GAGLIARDI
(Football Coach)

"I have a lifetime contract, but they'd probably declare me dead if I started losing." *1998: The seventy-one-year-old football coach at Division III St. John's University in Collegeville, MN, whose 343 victories put him first among active coaches.*

MIKE GALLEGO
(Baseball Player)

It's unbelievable, believe me." *1990: After the A's swept the Boston Red Sox to win the American League pennant and before the A's were swept by the Cincinnati Reds.*

PHIL GARNER
(Baseball Manager)

"Even when he's below average, he's above average." *1997: The Milwaukee Brewers' manager on Seattle Mariners' fireballing lefthander Randy Johnson, who beat Milwaukee despite throwing a wild pitch, hitting two batters, and striking out only three.*

WILLIAM GATES
(Basketball Player)

"*Hoop Dreams* has done a lot for me. It got me into Michael Jordan's birthday party." *1995: The college basketball player and subject of the non-Academy-Award-winning documentary film.*

RICK GENTILE
(CBS Sports Vice President)

"He filled the Greg Gumble role very well." *1994: On TV host Greg Gumble's Olympic performance.*

JOE GIBBS
(Football Coach)

"In all defense of the president, I think he's come over to the Redskins' side. The reason why we were late, we were inside, and Barbara was trying to get the Hog nose off his face." *1992: The coach of the Washington Redskins, after visiting the White House, on President George Bush's conversion from the Houston Oilers to the Redskins.*

BRAD GILBERT
(Tennis Player)

"If it was a horse race they would have taken me in the back and shot me." *1995: Commenting on the way he played in the opening round of the St. Jude International tournament in Memphis in February.*

PHIL GILLICK
(Baseball General Manager)

"He likes to complain a lot [about] not playing, but that's what he does best. Not play." *1991: The Toronto Blue Jays' general manager on the oft-injured Mike Marshall, who was traded from the Boston Red Sox to the California Angels.*

JOE GIRARDI
(Baseball Player)

"We're going to have quite a universal staff. Cone is American. Pettitte is French. Irabu is Japanese. Wells is Martian." *1998: The New York Yankees' catcher commenting on the makeup of the 1998 Yankees team during spring training. Pitcher David Wells threw a perfect game in May.*

ROBERT GIST
(Attorney for Latrell Sprewell)

"Latrell's good name has been tarnished." *1998: On Sprewell's suit against the Golden State Warriors and the NBA for $30 million because of "excessive discipline" after Sprewell choked his coach.*

JERRY GLANVILLE
(Football Coach)

"Defense gets beat by mental errors. I don't believe you win a game with cerebral ideas. Your players have to know what they're doing. They have to react, not think." *1990*

"He was so fat he would've turned queer for a chocolate sundae." *1990: On an overweight player.*

KEITH GLASS
(Agent)

"Agents are like rats. We can adjust to anything." *1999: The agent for ten NBA players, on how he and his colleagues might react to the league's new collective bargaining agreement.*

BOB GOLIC
(Football Player)

"I roam the field from guard to guard." *1991: The Los Angeles Raider nosetackle, on his role.*

ANDREW GOLOTA
(Boxer)

"I stupid! I stupid! I stupid!" *1996: After losing a rematch with Riddick Bowe because of a low blow. Golota lost the initial match also because of a low blow.*

MARK GRACE
(Baseball Player)

"I was so mad, I started looking for him in the stands. I thought to myself, 'I'm going to find that limping SOB and kick his butt.'" *1999: The Cubs' first baseman, who says a rowdy fan at Wrigley Field once threw a crutch at him.*

STEFFI GRAFF
(Tennis Player)

"Blame it on the vampires." *1996: On storming out of a press conference at Wimbledon when quizzed about what looked like a love bite on her neck.*

CAMMI GRANATA
(Hockey Player)

"All your life you play hockey because you love it. And all of a sudden you realize, hey, I'm a girl, there's no place to go with this. You go to college and there is nobody at the games, and the guys are running you off the ice. It was like it was wrong for me to be good at hockey. And then you get a berth in the Olympic Games." *1998: After the U.S. Women's Hockey Team defeated Canada 3–1 in Nagano for the gold medal.*

HORACE GRANT
(Basketball Player)

"We're the Hatfields and the Catfields. Oh, I meant the Hatfields and the McCormicks." *1992: The Chicago Bulls' forward on the feud between Chicago and the Detroit Pistons.*

"At halftime my teammates wanted me to pee in a cup, like take a drug test." *1999: After he took a desperate half-court shot at the end of the first half in a game against the Nets, only to discover there were still six seconds left on the clock. Grant made up for his blunder by sinking the game winning shot at the close of the second half, with 16.6 seconds remaining.*

TIM GREEN
(Football Player)

"When I played, we didn't keep track." *1997: The defensive lineman for the Atlanta Falcons from 1986 to 1993, when asked how many concussions he suffered in his playing career.*

WILLIE GREEN
(Football Player)

"I was intimidated by going out there. You look around and you see all these great names, Vince Lombardi and all those guys. Then you see the fans—the fans can scare you, too, if you don't watch out. You go on out there and go, 'God, it's cold out here,' and then you see some guy with his shirt off." *1997: The wide receiver of the Carolina Panthers, on his first experience in playing against the Green Bay Packers in Green Bay, WI.*

WAYNE GRETZKY
(Hockey Player)

"At that age everybody thinks they know what's best. By the time you realize what your father was telling you was true, your own kids are telling you you're wrong." *1991: On eighteen-year-old hockey phenomenon Eric Lindros.*

"I just follow the Rams. Wherever they go, I go." *1996: On his trade from the Los Angeles Kings to the St. Louis Blues.*

"I can still play. I think I'll surprise a lot of people. You know the hardest part of being Wayne Gretzky is that I get compared to Wayne Gretzky." *1996*

"I was a boy that happened to love a game and got lucky, and the good Lord gave me a passion for it." *1999: While announcing his retirement from hockey.*

BOB GRIESE
(Football Player)

"That's why they're where they're at! I mean, that's why they're where they are!" *1996: Commenting for ABC on Northwestern's first touchdown in the Rose Bowl on New Year's Day.*

CALVIN GRIFFITH
(Football Franchise Owner)

"You and I should attend some of your classes." *1990: Upon running into equally hefty Craig Kusick, who taught high school phys ed.*

PRINCE ALBERT GRIMALDI OF MONACO
(Bobsledder)

"Bobsledding has been an incredible adventure for me. I've learned so much in terms of my personal development." *1997*

STU GRIMSON
(Hockey Player)

"That's so when I forget how to spell my name, I can still find my clothes." *1992: The Chicago Black hawks' enforcer, on why the Blackhawks' locker room features photos of each player above his stall.*

JOHN GROWNEY
(Bull Owner)

"He's probably the most famous person in northern California." *1994: The owner of Red Rock, a Pro Rodeo Hall of Fame bull who died in the spring at the age of eighteen in Red Bluff, CA.*

TOM GULLICKSON
(Tennis Coach)

"When Jim was at his best, his mental toughness separated him from the pack. When the guys he's competing against see him *reading* during changeovers, you can throw mental toughness out the window." *1994: The coach of the U.S. Davis Cup*

TOM GULLICKSON (CONT'D)

team, commenting on the troubled Jim Courier, who took up reading during changeovers in his tennis matches.

H

DOROTHY HAMILL
(Figure Skater)

"The really great competitors are not out there trying to figure out how to bump off the competition." *1995: Insisting that the Harding-Kerrigan controversy at attempted maiming was an isolated incident.*

ARGUS HAMILTON
(Humorist)

"The good news is, the USC Trojans won [the Rose Bowl game]. The bad news? The school announced it is moving the team to Nashville." *1996*

SCOTT HAMILTON
(Ice Skater)

"This is the healthiest person I know. He took care of himself." *1995: On the death by heart attack of two-time Olympic champion Sergei Grinkov, who was twenty-eight.*

RAY HANDLEY
(Football Coach)

"Things can build. Confidence can build. Momentum can build. These two things can be overrated." *1992: On the New York Giant's 1–3 record.*

TONYA HARDING
(Ice Skater)

"I made a mistake and I've paid for it. I'm still paying for it, literally, financially and mentally, and I mean it's taken a lot out of my life. I feel like I'm 30 instead of 24." *1995*

"O. J. Simpson has his image back. I have done everything anyone has asked of me. What I want is a chance to skate again. I want my image back." *1996*

"So, have you ever been kissed by a woman before?" *1996: To eighty-one-year-old Alice Olson, who Harding revived with mouth to mouth resuscitation.*

RON HARPER
(Basketball Player)

"If somebody did that on the Bulls . . . we would string him up, I think. I know Michael Jordan would hang him for sure." *1998: The Chicago Bulls*

player on the spate of throat-slitting gestures being made at opponents by NBA players.

JIM HARRICK
(Basketball Coach)

"At one time, yes, but I came right back and told him it was right. There's a difference in cheating. Cheating is a planned thing. Something happened, but in my mind, nothing grave." *1996: The UCLA men's basketball coach when asked if he had lied to the athletic director to conceal violations of NCAA rules, which, in addition to his alleged falsification of expense vouchers, got him fired November 6.*

SID HARTMAN
(Columnist)

"Isn't the big problem the umpires' lack of inconsistency?" *1996: Asking American League umpire Tim Tschida about the expansion of the strike zone.*

"All I know is that Mr. Clinton's ratings keep on going up, so maybe you people should find something else. . . ." *1998: When asked on a sports talk show for his thoughts on Tara Lipinski.*

CLEM HASKINS
(Basketball Coach)

"As much money as we make—and I understand the people who say it's too much—it's also not enough." *1997: The University of Minnesota basketball coach, on coaching salaries.*

SCOTT HASTINGS
(Basketball Player)

"This is the biggest ovation I've had since the last time I told my wife I was going to sleep on the couch." *1993: Hastings, of the Denver Nuggets, on scoring seven points and grabbing a season-high seven rebounds in a win over Charlotte.*

MICKEY HATCHER
(Baseball Coach)

"The last time they checked me for cork they X-rayed my head." *1994: The Texas Rangers' coach on an Albert Belle bat-corking incident.*

JUD HEATHCOATE
(Basketball Coach)

"I say this [his retirement] will enable me to finish my book. And people say, 'I didn't know you were writing a book.' I'm not. I'm reading one." *1995: The Michigan State basketball coach on his retirement.*

MARY HEGARTY
(Basketball Coach)

"Who are you, and where did you get those uniforms?" *1995: The women's basketball coach at Chapman University in Orange, CA, addressing her Panthers after they had committed twenty turnovers and trailed Cal Baptist 30–17 at halftime.*

RICKEY HENDERSON
(Baseball Player)

"The little things mean more than the big things to me. And that was one of the little things I cherished. And I didn't get it. And I was hurt. I really was hurt. It wasn't the money." *1990 : Henderson, of the Oakland A's, was upset because his new four-year $12 million contract did not include his receiving a Ferrari Testarossa if he set the all-time record for stolen bases.*

"During spring I keep a notebook. I go home every day and write something down. It's just something to do in spring to remind me of things. Spring training is a time when you *think* more. During the season, if you think too much, you'll be in a slump for a long time." *1998: Henderson, thirty-nine, on what he's learned in baseball.*

ALEX HENDY
(Boxer & Writer)

"Cheered by their words and with an altogether more positive attitude to boxing, I climbed the steps of the gym, quite in awe of these calm yet potentially explosive men. And I found myself recalling the words of Marlon Brando in *On the Waterfront*, 'I could have been a bartender.' " *1992*

KEITH HERNANDEZ
(Baseball Player)

"I think we're in deep trouble. I really do. I think we're all going to blow up and die. I really do, it's going to happen." *1993: The former New York Met, commenting on the state of the world.*

MARTIN HIGGINS
(Football Fan)

"If the Bills had had the ball-handling talent of Michael Jackson, they might have won." *1993:*

Higgins of Mill Valley, CA, commenting on the loss of the Buffalo Bills in the Super Bowl and the crotch-grabbing performance of Michael Jackson during the half-time show.

BOB HILL
(Basketball Coach)

"Beyond the hair, tattoos and earrings, he's just like you and me." *1995: On Dennis Rodman.*

DAVID HILL
(TV Executive)

"It was trick or treat, and we got tricked." *1995: The Fox Sports president after Mike Tyson canceled his fight with Buster Mathis Jr., claiming an injury.*

MARTINA HINGIS
(Tennis Player)

"I like to make presents to myself a lot." *1997: The big-hearted teen tennis sensation, on what she does with the money from her $10 million endorsement contract with an Italian clothing company.*

BILL HOLLAND
(Librarian)

"I think he [Dennis Rodman] is straight. He's too weird to be gay." *1996*

RORY HOLLOWAY
(Boxing Manager)

"Look around, you don't see no naked women running around." *1995: The co-manager of boxer Mike Tyson, commenting on the fighter's reformed personality during a barbecue at Tyson's home.*

LARRY HOLMES
(Boxer)

"I'm still capable of doing what I have to do. Even though I'm 43 years old, it would be like a 38-year-old man that they'd be fighting." *1993: The former heavyweight champion on why he wanted to fight Riddick Bowe, Lennox Lewis, or Tommy Morrison.*

SEAN HOLMES
(Snowboarder)

"If you can't ride baked, you shouldn't be riding." *1998: Commenting on Olympic gold medalist Ross Rebagliati's testing positive for marijuana at Nagano.*

MIKE HOLMGREN
(Football Coach)

"We can beat these guys, but it's not about out-smarting them or having a better scheme. Football is about kicking someone's ass. Football is about physically pounding the opponent. If you want to win this game, you have to beat the crap out of these guys." *1996: The coach of the Green Bay Packers, speaking to his team before they beat the crap out of the Super Bowl champion San Francisco 49ers in the NFC divisional playoff game.*

LOU HOLTZ
(Football Coach)

"You take the ball, you put it in the proper position, and then you squeeze the ball until you hear the ball go, 'Pssshhhhhhh.'" *1996: The Notre Dame football coach after his offense fumbled seven times in the season opener against Vanderbilt, on the advice he has given ball carriers to avoid such mistakes.*

BOB HOYING
(Football Player)

"I'm really happy for Coach Cooper and the guys who've been around here six or seven years, especially our seniors." *1993: The Ohio State quarterback, after a 23–17 victory over Indiana.*

KENT HRBEK
(Baseball Player)

"I'm working hard for the American dream and it's being taken away." *1993: The Minnesota Twins player complaining to the press about income tax increases. When he made the statement Hrbek was earning $3 million a year and hitting .231.*

BOBBY HULL
(Hockey Player)

"If you can pick women, you can pick cattle. You look for good angularity, nice legs and capacity." *1991*

BRETT HULL
(Hockey Player)

"I'll be sad to go, and I wouldn't be sad to go. It wouldn't upset me to leave St. Louis, but it would upset me to leave St. Louis. It's hard to explain. You'll find out one of these days, but maybe you never will." *1994: The St. Louis Blue right wing, on his obvious ambivalence about requesting a trade.*

GERRY HUNSICKER
(Baseball General Manager)

"The talent we would have to potentially give up would leave us with a team that Roger Clemens would not want to play for." *1998: The general manager of the Houston Astros, commenting on why he pulled out of the efforts to secure Roger Clemens for his team.*

BILLY HUNTER
(Executive Director of the NBA Players' Union)

"I guess we both blinked." *1999: On the labor agreement reached between the players and the owners.*

I

PETE INCAVIGLIA
(Baseball Player)

"People think we make $3 million and $4 million a year. They don't realize that most of us make $500,000." *1990*

ROBERT IRSAY
(Baseball Team Owner)

"Edelstein's a little Jewish boy and he doesn't know what he's talking about." *1990: The Indianapolis Colts' owner on the ESPN reporter Fred Edelstein.*

J

KAREEM ABDUL JABBAR
(Basketball Player)

"I have many fires in the iron." *1990*

BO JACKSON
(Football & Baseball Player)

"It takes the dignity out of college athletics when you have a guy playing football who can't spell football." *1990*

"My mind is always going, always spinning. I try to think of something to be the next Bill Gates." *1996*

LINDA JACKSON
(Cyclist)

"I'm 37 years old, 13 days younger than (winner) Jeannie Longo. This is probably one of the most disappointing days of my life. I've got to get on with my life. I've got a lot of aspirations, a lot of things I want to do . . . I want kids. First, I need a date." *1996: After failing to win an Olympic medal.*

PHIL JACKSON
(Coach of the Chicago Bulls)
"He lives three minutes from the Berto Center. We sent somebody to his house. He was sitting there having some Sugar Pops or Cap'n Crunch, and he said, 'I can't make it. I just can't get going. I can't.'" *1998: On what happened when Dennis Rodman didn't show up for practice.*

"It's more like being in special ed." *1998: On Dennis Rodman's missed practice following Game 3 of the NBA playoffs, when asked if handling him is like dealing with a kindergartner.*

"He didn't wrestle, did he?" *1998: After he learned that Dennis Rodman appeared at a wrestling show following the Bulls' victory over the Utah Jazz in the third game of the NBA finals.*

"It weighs about a pound. You can't clap your hands or touch anybody on the head. It's like a weapon, almost. And it gets caught on everything. It takes about three weeks to finally adjust to wearing it." *1998: On the downside of winning a NBA championship ring.*

SAMUEL L. JACKSON
(Actor)
"I love wearing the clothes. The golf course is the only place I can go dressed like a pimp and fit in perfectly. Anywhere else, lime-green pants and alligator shoes, and I got a cop on my ass." *1999: On playing golf.*

ANTAWN JAMISON
(Basketball Player)
"There's not much more to accomplish other than maybe winning a national championship." *1998: The North Carolina basketball star, on his decision to leave school early for the NBA.*

RYAN JARONCYK
(Baseball Player)
"I always thought it was boring." *1997: The Mets' first-round draft pick on why he retired from baseball at the age of twenty.*

DAVEY JOHNSON
(Baseball Manager)
"They've got a lot of guys you fear the most." *1995: The Cincinnati Reds' manager assessing the Atlanta Braves' lineup before his team was swept from the playoffs.*

"He's no different from anyone else, except that he's doing something no one else has ever done or ever will do." *1997: The Baltimore Orioles' manager, on the possibility of his benching Cal Ripken Jr.*

JOHNNY JOHNSON
(Football Player)
"I'm going to give 110 percent on every play. You can't give any more than that." *1995: The Illinois quarterback, on how he intended to perform next season.*

MAGIC JOHNSON
(Basketball Player)
"All the years I've been playing basketball, I've never been through stuff like this—never. I should have stayed retired, I guess." *1996: After his Lakers' co-captain went AWOL and point guard Nick Van Exel shoved a referee. One week after making this statement Johnson was suspended for three games for bumping a referee.*

"The main reason I'm disappointed in the young people in this league is because they look at Michael and they don't understand him. They see the greatest, but they don't know why he was so great. They miss the point. They don't remember or realize that when he first came into the league, all he did was drive and dunk on everybody. He worked hard to add a jump shot, the 3-point shot, the post-up moves, the passing, the defense, the leadership." *1999: On Michael Jordan.*

TIM JOHNSON
(Baseball Coach)
"Pressure was growing up in L.A. with $5 in your pocket and walking down an alley. A guy with a zip gun comes up to you and demands $25. Now that's pressure." *1994: The Montreal coach on the pressures of being interim manager when Felipe Alou flew to the Dominican Republic for his father's funeral.*

JUANITA JORDAN
(Wife of Michael Jordan)
"I see Michael doing a lot more car pooling." *1999: On her husband's future plans following his retirement.*

MICHAEL JORDAN
(Basketball & Baseball Player)
"I've always got room, even if it means my wife has to move or the kids have to go." *1992: When asked if he was in danger of running out of room to store all of his awards.*

"I am not out there sweating for three hours every day just to find out what it feels like to sweat." *1994: On his preparation for the Chicago White Sox spring-training camp.*

"I was pretty confident that I could make some kind of contact, and I did. You always think of the Mighty Casey stepping up with the bases loaded, and he strikes out. I just wanted to make contact." *1994: On his problems in major league baseball.*

"I don't think I've proved myself so I can make the team." *1994: On March 11, 1994, when his batting average (0 for 12) was .000.*

"The only message I can figure Phil Jackson is sending is that he's had way too much time between playoff games." *1996: Commenting on Phil Jackson's insistence that his team, the Chicago Bulls, watch the movie* King of Hearts, *in order to get the message of the movie before their first playoff game with Seattle.*

"I have big hands, so soap tends to slip out of my hands. I carry [big bars of] soap with me everywhere I go." *1996*

"I would never [commercially endorse] anything like Rogaine." *1997: On his philosophy of commercial endorsements.*

"Even though everybody gotta use them . . . they too small!" *1997: On why he will never make a commercial for condoms.*

"I've had a great time." *1999: Announcing his retirement from basketball.*

"I played it to the best I could play it." *1999: Announcing his retirement.*

"I never say never, but 95–99.9 percent, I'm very secure with my decision." *1999: Announcing his retirement, maybe for good.*

CHARLIE JUST
(Basketball Coach)
"We're so young, we've decided to dress only seven players on the road. We're pretty confident the other five can dress themselves." *1996: The women's basketball coach at Bellarmine College in Louisville, on his team's inexperience.*

DAVID JUSTICE
(Baseball Player)
"Don't believe the hype. There's some bad [dudes] in this league, and he ain't one of them." *1997: The Cleveland slugger after his team reached heralded Japanese pitcher Hideki Irabu of the Yankees for three homers and five runs in five innings.*

K

DONALD KAGAN
(Yale Dean)
"The batter is the hero. He begins at home, but his mission is to venture away from it, encountering various unforeseeable dangers. At each station opponents scheme to put him out by strength or skill or guile. Should they succeed he dies on the bases, defeated. If his own heroic talents are superior, however, he completes the circuit and returns victorious to home, there to be greeted with joy by the friends he left behind." *1990: Describing the true mythic structure of baseball.*

BRUCE KAUFMAN
(U.S. Lawnmower Racing Association Director)
"Who out there, while sitting on their lawn mower, hasn't thought of . . . strapping on a helmet, of going just a little faster and getting the grass cut just a little sooner?" *1997: On his 200-member organization's competitive season.*

JENNY KEIM
(Diver)
"This is the best thing that ever happened to me, except when I was born." *1992: Keim, thirteen, who took second place in the women's platform diving finals at the Alamo International diving championships in Fort Lauderdale.*

STEVE KERR
(Basketball Player)

"It's not like we're going to have unprotected sex with him. We're just going to play basketball." *1996: When asked if he was concerned or fearful about Magic Johnson's return to the NBA.*

"All those years, everyone thought the key was Jordan and Pippen. Who knew?" *1999: The former Bulls guard , now with the San Antonio Spurs, joking about going for his fourth consecutive championship ring.*

NANCY KERRIGAN
(Ice Skater)

"This is so corny. This is so dumb. This is the most corny thing I've ever done." *1994: The Olympic silver medalist during her post-Olympic appearance in a Disney World parade. Kerrigan had earlier signed a $2 million deal with Disney.*

DR. JACK KEVORKIAN
(Suicide Doctor)

"I'm going to walk up to Jack Nicklaus and tell him, 'If you don't win, I'm here.'" *1996: On being a spectator at the U.S. Open.*

VICTOR KIAM
(Football Team Owner)

"They can wiggle their waggles in front of her face as far as I'm concerned." *1990: The owner of the New England Patriots, referring to a fact that some of his players lewdly approached a* Boston Herald *female reporter in the locker room. Kiam referred to her as "a classic bitch."*

PARINYA KIATBUSABA
(Thai Kickboxer)

"So I would like to warn my opponent not to get distracted by my eyes or my smile." *1998: Kiatbusaba, a transvestite kickboxer from Thailand's northern Chiang Mai province, on how his looks can deceive opponents. Although Parinya, sixteen, appears fragile, local boxing experts say he is a terror in the ring.*

JENNIFER KIMBROUGH
(Assistant Basketball Coach)

"You know what coaching this team is like? It's like teaching a blindfolded person how to read." *1999: The assistant coach at Christway Academy, a tiny school in Duncanville, TX, whose girls' high school basketball team won only once all season, by forfeit, and lost one game 103–0.*

RALPH KINER
(Baseball Announcer)

"And this ball hit to deeeep right field. Way back. Waaaay back. Going . . . going . . . and it is gone . . . and is caught." *1991*

"Some quiet guys are inwardly outgoing." *1991: Reflecting on Bud Harrelson's laid-back style.*

BILLIE JEAN KING
(Tennis legend)

"Nobody knows I live here. Almost every single day that I go out people say 'Oh, what are you doing in Chicago? You playing in a tournament?' I mean, I'm 500 pounds overweight and I feel like saying, 'Does it look like I am?'" *1998: King, who has lived in Chicago since 1992, about the reaction of people when they see her on the street.*

DON KING
(Boxing Promoter)

"It's a grave injustice here. It's an injustice if it holds that Mike Tyson got knocked out. The fact is Buster Douglas got knocked out first." *1990: On the Douglas-Tyson fight, referring to a long count in Round 8 in which Douglas was given thirteen seconds to get up by the referee.*

"Only in America can a man survive . . . alleged involvement in national and international scandal. Not once, but three times." *1990: Thanking his lawyers. He was acquitted of charges of income tax evasion and fight fixing.*

"I've got a Ph.D. in Caucasianism." *1991*

"He's [Larry Holmes] mad at me because he has an Oedipus complex." *1991*

"He's three times seven and some. My responsibility is to teach, to talk, to advise, and to have a relationship with and give him a love and responsibility that he didn't have before. The day that Mike Tyson can be independent of anyone is the day that I look for. And you can never be independent if you're gonna keep the thing in his

DON KING (CONT'D)

mouth that he can suck on all the time, yunner-stan?" *1992: On Mike Tyson.*

"For a $100 million promotion, I would have fought for that promotion if Mike Tyson was going to jail the next day. See, that's the difference with me. I would have captured immortality in the promotion. Plus, Mike woulda went to jail a rich man, you know what I mean?

"And I'd have had some money, too, while he was gone." *1992: On promoting a fight for jail-bound Mike Tyson.*

"I don't want to get into that, but Mike's got a whole new set of banisters." *1992: When asked if Vincent Fuller would continue to serve as Tyson's lawyer.*

"We have a marriage, like a father and son." *1993: On his relationship with undefeated lightweight champ Julio Cesar Chavez.*

"McNeeley is a white kid who needs a break. . . . This is the American way." *1994: On why heavy-weight champ Oliver McCall's first defense probably would be against Boston's Peter McNeeley.*

"This time the Mexicans will win!" *1995: Promoting a fight between Julio Cesar Chavez and Pernell Whitaker in San Antonio, at the Alamodome.*

"You better not blow this fight, brother!" *1995: Fight promoter Don King, shouting from ringside at Oliver McCall, WBC heavyweight champion, after the sixth round in his fight against forty-five-year-old Larry Holmes in Las Vegas. Holmes dominated the first half of the fight, but McCall dominated the second half and won. The victory put McCall in the Mike Tyson sweepstakes. King was the promoter of both McCall and Tyson.*

"This night has been something we can all be proud of." *1995: After the eighty-nine-second Tyson-McNeeley fight.*

"No one asked the Kennedys to quit making money. Don't ask why Evander should quit because he has plenty of money. Ask how he can get more money with less effort." *1997: Responding to a reporter asking Evander Holyfield if he was participating in a* rematch with Mike Tyson primarily for the money a $35 million win or lose payday.

"I don't know why they stopped it. I have to see the replays before I can comment further." *1997: On the abbreviated Evander Holyfield–Mike Tyson fight, stopped by the referee after Tyson bit off part of Holy-field's ear.*

"Had they known I was Don King, I'm confident they never would have stopped me." *1998: After thieves in Mexico City relieved him of his watch, which he described as a "gaudy little thing that sparkles, nothing of significance."*

"June 6, D day. When we won." *1998: Promoting a fight between Henry Akinwande and Evander Holy-field at Madison Square Garden, while unaware of the meaning of June 6, D day.*

"I don't care what you think of me, look at my record." *1998: On Mike Tyson's suit against him alleging that King had "diverted" millions of dollars that should have gone to the fighter rather than the promoter.*

TOM KITE
(Golfer)

"I don't care what race he is. This doesn't matter to me. He's a golfer. He's a person. He's a great kid. He's a nice person. He's got very high standards. His parents did a hell of a job raising him. He's a nice kid. And when you see nice people do great things, it's pretty awesome." *1997: On Tiger Woods in the Masters Tournament.*

MARTY KLEIN
(Licensed Marriage & Family Counselor)

"Pornography does not breed crime. There are plenty of other activities that bring drugs and crime, like the San Francisco Giants, for instance." *1990: On protests of Palo Alto, CA's new adult bookstore.*

BOBBY KNIGHT
(Basketball Coach)

"People want national championship banners. People want to talk about Indiana being competitive. How do we get there? We don't get there with milk and cookies." *1994: The Indiana University basketball coach on the criticism that he's too rough on his players.*

"The Lord will be a hell of a lot happier if you pray and I talk." *1994: Interrupting a clergyman after growing impatient with the flattery of a man who was making a lengthy speech before his invocation.*

PHIL KNIGHT
(CEO of Nike)

"Americans don't want to make shoes." *1998: Explaining why he prefers to use cheap Indonesian labor to make his shoes.*

CHUCK KNOX
(Football Coach)

"Most of my clichés aren't original." *1992*

JOHN KONCAK
(Basketball Player)

"Remember the bar scene from *Star Wars* with all the animals? That's what it looked like." *1996: The Orlando Magic basketball player on being snowbound in a hotel with the cast of* Sesame Street Live.

TONY KORNHEISER
(Columnist)

"You should understand there is a difference between 'smart' and 'smart for an athlete.' Smart for an athlete refers to athletes who know *Hamlet* wasn't written for Mel Gibson." *1992*

BOB KRAVITZ
(Journalist)

"Somebody forgot to tell Shane Mack $8.1 million in American dollars will buy you two cheeseburgers and a large shake in Tokyo." *1995: Writing in the* Rocky Mountain News, *on Shane Mack's signing with a Japanese baseball team.*

DON KRESAL
(Runner)

"We're just everyday professional people who want to go out, put on a red dress and run." *1997: One of the 470 mostly male members of the Washington, D.C., Hash House Harriers who took part in this year's five-mile Red Dress Run, which featured everything from long-sleeved shifts to see-through negligees.*

JOHN KRUK
(Baseball Player)

"Lady, I'm not an athlete, I'm a baseball player." *1992*
"He can pitch when he's relaxed, and he'll be happy and relaxed here. If he isn't, we'll kill him." *1993: On the Philadelphia Phillies' new pitcher, Mark Davis.*

"They got books up there above the damn dugout, and I told 'em there ain't a fucking baseball team in the world that's got books in the dugout. But they don't listen to me. Same with throwing and batting. I like [star Wesley] Snipes and everything, but he couldn't hit a fucking building with that swing." *1996: On his role as a general manager in the movie* The Fan, *contrasting the movie with real life.*

ALAN KULWICKI
(Stock Car Racer)

"It's basically the same, just darker." *1991: On racing Saturday nights as opposed to Sunday afternoons.*

TERRY KUNZE
(Basketball Coach)

"We're so worried about someone fouling out that we have a new defense. All our players stand under the basket and yell, 'I hope you miss.'" *1992: On his Anoka-Ramsey Community College [MN] team.*

MICHELLE KWAN
(Ice Skater)

"When I was little I thought, 'Wouldn't that be wonderful to say I'm world champion.' It was one of my long, long, long-term goals, and I'm just 15. It hasn't hit my brain yet." *1996: On winning the World Figure Skating Championship at the age of fifteen in March.*

"I always look at my parents like they're so wise. But if they're so wise, how come they're not millionaires." *1998*

"I saw all those perfect 6.0s and I started thinking, 'What can I do to improve on this?'" *1998: On her flawless performance at the U.S. Figure Skating Championships in Philadelphia.*

L

RICK LANCELLOTTI
(Replacement Baseball Player)

"It's like they gave us a Mercedes without the keys. But at least we got to sit in it." *1995*

JEFFREY LANGE
(Football Fan & Snowballer)

"I think this whole situation could have been avoided if the snow wasn't there." *1995: Lange, twenty-six, at a press conference [accompanied, naturally, by his attorney], explaining the circumstances that led to his being photographed throwing a snowball at the field during a football game between the New York Giants and the San Diego Chargers. He said it was the fault of the stadium authorities for not removing the snow!*

TONY LARUSSA
(Baseball Manager)

"Don't you remember that I found a good new home for Jose Canseco?" *1992: At the Animal Rescue Foundation (in Concord, CA), to a little old lady who said to him, "I never knew you cared so much for homeless creatures."*

"I'd like to videotape one of these [replacement player] games and show our regular players what it was like when they used to want to play." *1995*

"Every time he opens his mouth he makes a fool of himself. Ruben is a village idiot." *1995: The Oakland A's manager commenting on the wisdom of player Ruben Sierra.*

"Down deep, he's proud of his record and enjoys it, but he doesn't really appreciate all the attention. Players are raised in a team sport to do whatever it takes to win, and all of sudden everyone is trying to get him to take four swings at a home run every day. That's not the way the game is played." *1998: The St. Louis Cardinals' manager on his phenomenal slugger Mark McGwire.*

TOM LASORDA
(Baseball Manager)

"I'm happy every day I pick up the paper, read the obituaries and don't find my name in it." *1995*

"To see the locker room empty makes me sad. I want them to come back. I miss Mondesi. Last spring I threw him 175 to 200 curveballs every day. I miss going out to dinner with Piazza and Karros. I call them Hall of Fame eaters." *1995: The LA Dodgers manager, on spring training without his regular players Raul Mondesi, Mike Piazza, and Eric Karros.*

"You don't have to speak English to be a genius. The first word I taught him was *great*. I told him, 'When people ask you how you're doing, Hideo, you just say *great*.'—which happens to be the truth." *1995: On his Japanese pitching sensation, Hideo Nomo.*

"He may speak Japanese, but the guy sure can eat Italian." *1995: On Nomo's love for Italian food.*

"I've had real good luck with guys from other countries who don't always look where they're supposed to before they throw the ball." *1995: On the windup of his Japanese pitcher, Hideo Nomo, who looks back toward center field during his windup motion. Fernando Valenzuela rolled his eyes heavenward before throwing a pitch.*

DAVID LEADBETTER
(Golf Coach)

"Her goal this year was to win five tournaments, which I thought was pretty ambitious for a rookie. But she's already won three. Like she says, 'I have no nervous.' " *1998: On twenty-year-old Korean phenomenon Se Ri Pak.*

JAY LENO
(TV Talk-show Host)

"How about Darryl Strawberry today! He got three hits . . . and that was before the game." *1995*

"If you think about it, baseball actually has a lot in common with the O. J. trial: (1) Attendance is down in both. (2) They both feature spoiled millionaires. (3) In both cases, you know somebody's gonna walk." *1995*

"Your two children, they can never skip school in their whole lives." *1995: To Cal Ripken Jr., who set the record for most consecutive baseball games played.*

"All NFL stadiums have provisions for millionaires. They're called locker rooms." *1995*

"According to a new sports survey, the most-used name for college football teams is *Tigers*. Anybody know the least-used name for college football? *Graduates*." *1997*

"Mike Tyson's going to ask the New York boxing commission if he can fight again. Gotta get back to work. Man's gotta eat." *1998*

"Last Sunday Chicago beat Utah 96 to 54. That's not a basketball game. That's like two Spice Girls comparing IQs." *1998*

SUGAR RAY LEONARD
(Boxer)

"Guys feared him. Now you hear guys saying, 'I can beat Tyson.' Before, you couldn't get a paragraph out of 'em." *1990: On Mike Tyson and his opponents.*

DAVID LETTERMAN
(TV Talk-show Host)

"Former Yankee Joe Pepitone was arrested for driving drunk in the Midtown Tunnel. If he's convicted he'll be re-signed by the Yankees." *1995*

"March 19th, mark this down, traditionally, that's the day the Mets are mathematically eliminated from the pennant race." *1996*

"The referee stopped the [Holyfield/Tyson] fight in the 11th round because Tyson was taking a pounding and the referee said he stopped the fight because Mike Tyson was incoherent. He apparently didn't talk to the guy before the fight." *1996*

"Dallas Cowboy Wide Receiver Michael Irvin broke his clavicle. . . . It's pretty serious. Doctors say it will probably be six to eight weeks before he can videotape one of his teammates having sex." *1997*

"How about that halftime show [at the Super Bowl]? You've got to give the NFL a lot of credit for coming up with James Brown to be part of the halftime show—the only guy in America with more arrests than the Dallas Cowboys." *1997*

"You know the Riddick Bowe saga? It turns out now the Marine Corps is saying that Riddick Bowe did not quit. The Marine Corps is saying that Riddick Bowe was tossed out. One the bright side, look at this—the guy spent 72 hours in a Marine Corps barracks tying the old record held by Madonna." *1997*

"I think now people are going to have to stop picking on Riddick Bowe because whether he quit, whether he was tossed out, it just doesn't make any difference. The important thing here—his military career lasted three days longer than President Clinton's." *1997*

"Yesterday, golfer Fuzzy Zoeller called a press conference to apologize to Tiger Woods again. . . . And Fuzzy pulled out of this week's golf tournament. You know, golf is a very strange game, golf. You make one bad joke, you may never play again. You murder two people, you get to play golf every day." *1997*

"Ladies and gentlemen, celebrity birthdays! Today, Dennis Rodman—36 years old. Happy birthday to Dennis Rodman, 36 years old. Dennis Rodman celebrated by taking a nice long walk and then he got a ride home from Eddie Murphy." *1997*

"Here's something funny and odd that happened to me yesterday. I had a couple of minutes so I renewed my subscription to *Sports Illustrated*. And today, complete surprise, absolutely free, I received the Frank Gifford tapes!" *1997*

"You know, Evander Holyfield is livid and I know how he feels. I get upset when somebody *talks* my ear off." *1997*

"I was thinking about this—there is only one way now Tyson can be given forgiveness for what happened out there in Las Vegas on Saturday night. There's only one thing this guy can do—he just has to step forward and admit simply that he's a flesh-eating zombie." *1997*

"Earlier today, Mike Tyson whispered an apology into Evander Holyfield's ear. Yeah, he had it with him in his hotel room." *1997*

"Every time I see the replay of 'Iron' Mike Tyson biting Evander Holyfield's ear off and spitting it on the canvas, I say the same thing to myself: 'Somebody misses prison food.' " *1997*

"Nutritionists tell you that you are what you eat, so now perhaps Mike Tyson will be a better fighter." *1997*

"The Jets won on Sunday, and the Giants won on Sunday. Pretty impressive. Coincidentally, Sunday, the temperature in hell was 32 degrees." *1997*

"Here now are the NFL matchups for the next weekend: you have the Patriots vs. the Jaguars, you have the Packers vs. the Panthers, you have the People vs. the Dallas Cowboys." *1997*

DAVID LETTERMAN (CONT'D)

"Don, shouldn't you be out fixing fights?" *1999: To surprise guest Don King.*

BOB LEWIS
(Horse Owner)

"When they plant me, I want my tombstone to read, 'Loving Husband, Adoring Father and winner of the 123rd Kentucky Derby.'" *1997: The California beer distributor and owner of Silver Charm, a thoroughbred horse. Despite his wish for immortality, Lewis did not run in the Kentucky Derby but his horse did and it won.*

CARL LEWIS
(Track & Field Legend)

"I was just trying to figure out how the hell all of you got in my dream." *1996: At the press conference after he won an unexpected gold medal in the long jump at the Olympic games in Atlanta.*

MITCHELL LIBONATI
(Hotel Worker)

"I have something he probably wants." *1997: To the security guard outside boxer Evander Holyfield's room, after he recovered a piece of Holyfield's ear that had been bitten off by Mike Tyson.*

PAT LIPINSKI
(Mother of Olympic Skater, Tara)

"We brought home a gold medal. What are we going to do? Go back and get one that looks just like it?" *1998: On why daughter Tara decided to turn professional after winning the 1998 Olympic gold medal in ladies' figure skating.*

"Don't you think it's a terrible thing for them to do to poor Tara? It's been like this for poor Tara. It's a terrible thing." *1998: Blaming the U.S. Olympic Committee for having Tara Lipinski's rival Michelle Kwan present Bill Clinton with a U.S. team jacket. The team representative was chosen by a vote of the athletes.*

ALTON LISTER
(Basketball Player)

"Why do you even want to talk about it? Let a dead horse sleep." *1991: The Golden State center, when asked about the Warrior's success in guarding Michael Jordan.*

STEVE LOTT
(Training Camp Manager)

"I'd say you don't know Robin [Givens]. . . . I don't know how Mike [Tyson] had the discipline to be with her and not beat her up all the time. If you were with her, you would have shot her four years ago. . . . Mike showed discipline and respect and everything he could. But she was an actress." *1992: On Mike Tyson and Robin Givens.*

SANDY LYLE
(Golfer)

"I don't know. I've never played there." *1994: When asked what he thought of Tiger Woods.*

M

JOHN MADDEN
(Sports Commentator)

SUMMERALL: "The 49ers haven't been shut out since 1977."

MADDEN: "Yeah, and they lost that game, too." *1995: Insightful commentary at halftime in a game between San Francisco and Carolina, with Carolina leading at the time, 13-0. Carolina won.*

PETER MAGOWAN
(Baseball Team President)

"This will be the most bladder-friendly ballpark in America." *1996: The San Francisco Giants president on the team's planned new stadium.*

KARL MALONE
(Basketball Player)

"Say what you will about Charles Barkley—when he tells you he's going to do something, he'll either do it, or he won't do it." *1998: The forward for the Utah Jazz, on Barkley, the Houston Rockets forward.*

ROGER MALTBIE
(Golfer & TV Golf Analyst)

"Grass isn't his best surface." *1996: After watching former tennis great Ivan Lendl hit five balls into a water hazard on the eighteenth hole of a celebrity golf tournament.*

SAOUL MAMBY
(Boxer)
"If you work in the post office, you can get killed just going to work." *1997: Dismissing the dangers of resuming his boxing career at age fifty.*

DWIGHT MANLEY
(Sports Agent)
"The commissioner of basketball probably wouldn't allow it." *1997: The agent for Dennis Rodman, when asked if the often troublesome star would clone himself if he could.*

MICKEY MANTLE
(Baseball Player)
"Many times Billy and I would just hang around the clubhouse. . . . Billy and I kept water pistols in our locker, and some nights Billy would fill his pistol and begin squirting water at me. Then I would get my pistol and fill it with water and I'd start shooting at him. This would go on for hours." *1991: Talking about his stimulating relationship with his old Yankee buddy, Billy Martin.*

"If I hadn't met those two at the start of my career, I would have lasted another five years." *1995: The liver transplant recipient on the effect his two New York Yankees teammates and comrades in wild living—Billy Martin and Whitey Ford—had on his career.*

"Don't be like me. God gave me the ability to play baseball and I wasted it." *1995: After receiving a liver transplant needed largely because of forty years of hard drinking.*

JOHN MARA
(New York Giants Executive Vice President)
"It really was the best field we've ever had. Except that it tore apart everywhere and kept changing colors." *1998: On the $1.2 million artificial turf installed at Giants Stadium that disintegrated within months due to a mysterious fungus-like growth.*

STEPHEN MARBURY
(Basketball Player)
"It's been 20 years, 20 long years waiting for this day." *1996: The Georgia Tech freshman, nineteen, after being picked by Milwaukee in the NBA draft.*

TED MARCHIBRODA
(Football Coach)
"I thought we probably played this week like I thought maybe we could have played last week, and I didn't even think we could play that bad last week if we played like this." *1992: After his Indianapolis Colts lost a second preseason game following a win in its first game.*

JOHN MARCHIONY
(Producer of the Computer Bowl)
"For this you don't have to be great at running or tackling. All you have to be is a geek." *1998*

DAVID MAYFIELD
(Football Player)
"There are no tattoos on my body that I'm aware of." *1994: The West Virginia defensive back, on reports that several Mountaineers had themselves tattooed on Bourbon Street before the Sugar Bowl game against Florida.*

TIM MCDONALD
(Football Player)
"You can put your head between your legs and walk away, or you can stand and fight back." *1995: The safety for the San Francisco 49ers, after his team's loss to the last-place Indianapolis Colts.*

ROGER MCDOWELL
(Baseball Player)
"The movie or the airport?" *1992: The Los Angeles Dodger reliever, when asked by a reporter if he had seen JFK.*

"I have to go to all the places he can't, to make sure he isn't there." *1994: On taking rookie bullpenmate Darren Dreifort under his wing.*

JOHN MCENROE
(Tennis Player)
"I don't know if I ever was a real bad boy, at least compared to the guys out there in music. But compared to the wimps in tennis, yeah, I'm probably still a bad boy." *1996*

MARK MCGWIRE
(Baseball Player)
"This is not ballet dancing, OK? Let's get that straight. This isn't ballet. We're soldiers marching

MARK MCGWIRE (CONT'D)

around." *1990: When he with A's manager Tony La Russa and teammates Steve Howard and Dave Stewart appeared in a special production of Tchaikovsky's* The Nutcracker.

"I thought you just showed up and voted. I didn't know there was a deadline." *1993: On why he didn't get to vote in the 1992 election—because he knew more about hitting home runs than he did about voter registration laws.*

"I hope you're here with me tonight, Roger." *1998: To the bat of Roger Maris, before he eclipsed Maris's home run record.*

"People have been saying it is bringing the country together. So be it. I'm happy to bring the country together." *1998: After hitting his sixty-second home run to set a new single season record in September.*

"Kiss Helen Hunt and meet the pope, now that's a great winter." *1999: On his off-season activities, which included a visit with Pope John Paul II during the pontiff's trip to St. Louis and an appearance on* Mad About You *as Jamie Buchman's romantic fantasy.*

JOHN MCKEON
(Baseball Manager)

"I've released plenty of players, but I've never released a pigeon." *1998: The manger of the Cincinnati Reds, on being asked to participate in a release of white doves on Opening Day.*

"Si." *1998: When asked during a discussion of the language barrier faced by visiting teams playing in Montreal if he spoke French.*

VINCE MCMAHON
(WWF President)

"In a very short time the World Wrestling Federation will be sports free!" *1991: On ESPN. McMahon corrected himself a moment later, saying that he meant the WWF would be "drug free."*

PETER MCNEELEY
(Boxer)

"I talked the talk and I walked the walk." *1995: After his eighty-nine-second loss to Mike Tyson.*

"I'll be back." *1995*

"You should come hang out with us. You're kind of thuggy." *1995: To Michael Sam, who he knocked out in five minutes in an October fight in Boston.*

DAVID MCWILLIAMS
(Football Coach)

"It's not a real sadness, but a football sadness. Not sad, sad, like if my cat was gone. It's not that kind of sadness." *1991: The Texas coach talking about the end of the Longhorns' series with Arkansas when the Razorbacks shift to the Southeastern Conference.*

RON MEYER
(Football Coach)

"It isn't like I came down from Mount Sinai with the tabloids." *1990: The coach of the Indianapolis Colts trying to figure out the fuss over his decision to start Jeff George at quarterback.*

ALYSSA MILANO
(Actress)

"What sport did you play?" *1999: To ex-NFL great Terry Bradshaw on* The Tonight Show.

MIKE MILBURY
(Hockey Team General Manager)

"It's too bad he lives in the city. He's depriving some small village of a pretty good idiot." *1998: The general manager of the New York Islanders, on Paul Kraus, the agent for a player who spurned several of Milbury's offers.*

JAMIR MILLER
(Football Player)

"Is a pile of cookies going to fall on him? That's the only way he'll get hurt." *1998: The Arizona linebacker, on why he should be paid as much as, say, the Nabisco CEO.*

OLIVER MILLER
(Basketball Player)

"I'm kind of scared about how the fans are going to accept me back. But who cares? They're just fans." *1996: On how he felt he'd be received in Toronto.*

RYAN MINOR
(Baseball Player)

"Does he know?" *1998: The Baltimore Orioles rookie after manager Ray Miller told him he was starting in place of third baseman Cal Ripken, bringing to an end Ripken's consecutive-game streak at 2632.*

DENNIS MITCHELL
(Sprinter)

"I'm Barcelona bound!" *1996: After winning the 100 meters at the Olympic track and field trials in Atlanta. The Olympic games were held later in Atlanta.*

KEVIN MITCHELL
(Baseball Player)

"I couldn't find a hotel room." *1994: Trying to explain why he was two days late in arriving for spring training in Florida.*

HUBERT MIZELL
(Columnist)

"Todd Marinovich, the . . . backup quarterback of the Raiders, gets a $100,000 bonus if he passes three drug tests a week during the NFL season. What's his fee for not committing murder?" *1991*

DOMINIQUE MOCEANU
(Olympic Gymnast)

"I read half of it, then I skipped through. I already know what it's about, though." *1996: The fourteen-year-old celebrity athlete commenting on her autobiography.*

GARY MOELLER
(University of Michigan Football Coach)

"If you're not Michigan or Ohio State, you don't play in this game!" *1993: Commenting on the Michigan-Ohio State game.*

HELEN WILLS MOODY
(Tennis Player)

"I wish I'd gone on with my education—I'd rather have been a biochemist than a tennis star." *1995: The star of the 1920s and the '30s won nineteen world singles titles—still a record.*

MICHAEL MOORER
(Boxer)

"In my mind I felt I was winning the fight." *1994: The former heavyweight world champion after George Foreman, forty-five, knocked him out in the tenth round of their heavyweight title fight. He was winning until Foreman caught him with a short right-hand punch that decked him for the count.*

HAL MORRIS
(Baseball Player)

"As Reds, I believe we have to observe the customary six-day mourning period." *1997: The Cincinnati Reds' first baseman on the death of Chinese leader Deng Xiaoping.*

TOMMY MORRISON
(Boxer)

"I don't mind being in a room full of snakes if the lights are on." *1996: On working with promoter Don King.*

"I've worked with thousands of sparring partners over the years, had 49 fights, and I've led a promiscuous lifestyle. So go fish." *1996: Telling reporters that there are several ways he might have contracted the AIDS virus.*

MSNBC
(Online News Service)

"American beats Kwan." *1998: Headline of news bulletin after Tara Lipinski beat fellow American Michelle Kwan for the Olympic gold medal in figure skating.*

"MSNBC apologizes for an error that may have been interpreted to state that U.S. figure skater Michelle Kwan was not American." *1998: Excerpt from the apology that was the subject of criticism by Asian-American groups who, among other things, objected to the way it assigned blame to glitches.*

HURAD MUHHAMAD
(Boxing Promoter)

"Great! That's the Italian city with the guys in the boats, right?" *1992: Discussing with another promoter the chances of a fight in Venezuela.*

N

CHRIS NABHOLZ
(Baseball Player)

"Everybody knows how to pitch to Darryl. You throw a curve when he thinks fastball, and a fastball when he thinks curve." *1991: The Montreal Expos' pitcher on pitching to Darryl Strawberry.*

MARTINA NAVRATILOVA
(Tennis Player)

"I've been in the twilight of my career longer than most people have had their career." *1993*

MARTINA NAVRATILOVA (CONT'D)

"Now that I've read up about Mona Lisa, I really want to see her up close. I've been in Paris over twenty times, but I have yet to go to the Loover." *1994*

QUESTION: "Tell me something you do that people would be surprised to learn."

ANSWER: "I only brush my teeth at night. I don't brush them in the morning." *1995*

ROGER NEILSON
(Hockey Coach)

"I was a little worried about the drinking, but they assured me they would be drinking anywhere they went." *1999: The Philadelphia Flyers' coach on allowing his players to spend a four-day break in New Orleans.*

GARY NELSON
(Athletic Director)

"His IQ is at least 50 points higher than anybody else's in our department." *1991: The Eastern Montana College athletic director on cross-country coach Dave Coppock, who showed up with the team a week early for a meet in Fargo, ND. Nelson blamed the mix-up on a change in the meet's traditional date.*

JOHN NELSON
(Journalist)

"The computerized commentator supposedly is capable of uttering 200 phrases, giving it a bigger vocabulary than Frank Gifford." *1992: Commenting on the* Joe Montana II Sports Talk Football *video game with continuous commentary.*

ROCK NEWMAN
(Boxing Manager)

"I would think Riddick would like to serve his country, but in some other capacity." *1997: The manager for Riddick Bowe, the former world heavyweight champ, on the boxer's decision to quit Marine boot camp after three days of training.*

NATE NEWTON
(Football Player)

"We've got a little place over here where we're running some whores in and out, trying to be responsible, and we're critcized for that!" *1996: The Dallas Cowboys' guard when asked about "the White House," a residence used by players for the Cowboys.*

JACK NICKLAUS
(Golfer)

"He has a mind like I had." *1997: On Tiger Woods's victory at the Masters Tournament.*

GREG NORMAN
(Golfer)

"I'm disappointed. . . . But I'm not going to run around like Dennis Rodman and head-butt somebody." *1996: After coming in second in the Masters Tournament—the sixth tournament he's lost in the last round.*

O

CONAN O'BRIEN
(TV Host)

"I read today that the Pope was a soccer goalie in his youth. Apparently, even as a young man he tried to stop people from scoring." *1996*

"As a big publicity stunt, Dennis Rodman married himself. Which is fine. I just don't want to hear about the honeymoon." *1996*

"Over the weekend, the Baltimore Orioles played the Cuban national team in Cuba. There was one weird moment when a Cuban player got thrown out trying to go from first to Miami." *1999*

HELGE OGRIM
(Norwegian Journalist)

"Norway is [not] desperate enough to recruit a convicted criminal from the U.S." *1997: On skater Tonya Harding's plan to become a Norwegian to compete internationally.*

SHAQUILLE O'NEAL
(Basketball Player)

"I can't really remember the names of the clubs that we went to." *1994: When asked if he visited the Parthenon during a trip to Greece.*

"I'm trying my hardest, but I can't have everything. I can't have the looks, the rapping ability and the scoring ability—*and* shoot the free throws. But I'm going to hit 'em one day." *1995: After missing 11 of 15 free throws against the Clippers.*

"I think it's time for new critics. I want to do something called *The Homeboy Review Network*. Me and one of my boys, we'd review movies for everyone, not just for Wall Street types like Siskel and Ebert do." *1996*

"One line was 'Somebody owes me $100,' and I said, 'Somebody owes me a—$100.' It added a little." *1996: On his artistic ad-libbing in the film* Blue Chips, *directed by William Friedkin.*

"One company wanted to bottle my sweat and sell it as cologne. They were going to call it EOS, Essence of Shaq. I'm no marketing genius, but I don't think millions of people want that." *1996: On endorsements and marketing.*

"It's not about the money. I just want to be young, have fun, drink Pepsi and wear Reebok." *1996: After signing a seven-year, $121 million deal to play with the Los Angeles Lakers.*

"He is the ugliest woman I have ever seen in my life." *1996: On Dennis Rodman.*

TOM OSBORNE
(Football Coach)

"I have to live enough years to use it." *1998: The former Nebraska football coach, upon being given a lifetime Nebraska fishing license.*

SCOTT OSTLER
(Journalist)

"The 49ers were so badly flattened that they didn't fly back to San Francisco, they were faxed." *1994: On the 49ers defeat at the hands of the Buffalo Bills.*

"Weather advisory: Hurricane Peter McNeeley downgraded to blowhard." *1995: On Mike Tyson's eighty-nine-second opponent.*

LEE OWENS
(Football Coach)

"It's always nice to take a trip to Louisiana. Unfortunately, we have to play a football game while we're down there." *1997: The football coach of Akron University, a perennial college football doormat, on the eve of the team's 56–0 loss to Louisiana State in Baton Rouge.*

RONN OWENS
(Radio Talk-show Host)

"Latrell Sprewell was so excited by the settlement that he choked back tears." *1999: On the the the reaction of the infamous Golden State Warriors player to the settlement of the NBA strike.*

P

SE RI PAK
(Golfer)

"I bought a house. I pay more taxes." *1999: The Korean professional golfer on how the winning of $872,170 in 1998 changed her life.*

ROBERT PARRISH
(Basketball Player)

"It's amazing what winning does for your reputation." *1992*

GARY PAYTON
(Basketball Player)

"People would have to cut their lifestyle, and they'd live like penny-pinchers." *1995: The Seattle SuperSonics' $2.7 million-a-year guard, on an NBA collective bargaining proposal.*

VINNY PAZIENZA
(Boxer)

"Tomorrow I'll be a little sore, but I'll be fine by the time the check clears." *1992: After defeating Luis Santana.*

SAM PERKINS
(Basketball Player)

"Is that before or after taxes?" *1990: The Los Angeles Lakers forward when asked how it feels to sign a $19 million contract while still a young man.*

LUIS POLONIA
(Baseball Player)

"The Yankees are only interested in one thing, and I don't know what that is." *1990: Criticizing his former team for using him mostly as a pinch hitter and designated hitter.*

BOOG POWELL
(Baseball Player)

"I don't remember it ever doing any good. But you looked cool." *1997: The former Baltimore Orioles'*

BOOG POWELL (CONT'D)

star used eyeblack under his eyes throughout his seventeen years in the major leagues.

BILL PULSIPHER
(Baseball Player)

"What does it hurt to ask? All they can say is yes or no, and I already know the answer." *1998: The left-handed pitcher for the New York Mets' Triple A club in Norfolk, VA, on his request that he be called up or traded.*

ELIZABETH PUNSALAN
(Ice Skater)

"Years from now we'll tell our kids. We made it to the Olympics, we had a good time, we skated like crap." *1994: Punsalan fell while skating with her husband, Jerod Swallow, in the Olympic ice dancing competition.*

Q

JOE QUEENAN
(Writer)

"Tiger Woods is a flashy public figure, but one of the reasons he has captured the public's imagination is that he is the first charismatic golfer since Lee Trevino. The other reason is that the public doesn't have much imagination." *1997: On why "Golf is not cool."*

R

PATRICK RAFTER
(Tennis Player)

"I'm still the same old sack of crap." *1998: The Australian tennis player, assuring his countrymen that his U.S. Open victory hasn't changed him.*

DENNIS RAPPAPORT
(Boxing Manager)

"I don't want to tell you any half-truths unless they're completely accurate." *1990: On why he doesn't want to talk about boxer Thomas Hearns.*

ROSS REBAGLIATI
(Snowboarder)

"I might have to wear a gas mask from now on, but whatever." *1998: After the Canadian snowboarder nearly lost his Olympic gold medal after testing positive for marijuana. Rebaliati attributed traces of the drug to his inhaling secondhand smoke.*

CALVIN (POKEY) REESE JR.
(Baseball Player)

"I wouldn't want that job. Of course, if I make four errors again, maybe they'll make me do that job." *1998: The Cincinnati Reds' shortstop made four errors subbing for Barry Larkin against San Diego, on the attendant assigned to clean up after an elephant that took part in Opening Day ceremonies.*

BRYANT REEVES
(Basketball Player)

"What happens to me next year will happen to me no matter what happens." *1995: The senior Oklahoma State center, when asked if his strong performance during the NCAAs might have bolstered his status in the NBA draft.*

JERRY RICE
(Football Player)

"That was my mistake; it was a bad decision. I think they played a trick on me. I was there five minutes. . . . It didn't take me long to put two and two together. I was blown away." *1998: On being found by police in the locked bathroom of a suspected brothel in Mountain View, CA. Rice said he'd heard from his 49er teammates that the establishment was a good place "to get a deep-tissue massage."*

NOLAN RICHARDSON
(Arkansas Basketball Coach)

"Where did most of the slave ships stop? In the South." *1998: On why there are so many good players in the Southeastern Conference.*

JIM RIGGLEMAN
(Baseball Manager)

"Maybe things got to get as bad as they can get before they can get better. But today they got as bad as they can get." *1997: After his Chicago Cubs broke the National League record for the worst start in a season by losing its first twelve games.*

FRANK ROBINSON
(Baseball Assistant General Manager)

"Well, I'm assistant general manager. That means I assist the general manager of the club." *1993: The assistant general manager of the Baltimore Orioles, telling a newsman just what an assistant general manager does.*

RACHEL ROBINSON
(Wife of Jackie Robinson, Baseball Legend)
"To tell the truth, he preferred football. . . . He'd watch for a few minutes then I'd hear him in there pacing up and down, talking to the set about strategy, or some mistake somebody'd made. Jack was really the first black manager, in our living room." *1997: When asked if Jackie liked watching baseball on television.*

CHRIS ROCK
(Comedian)
"[Psychiatric] doctors say that Mike [Tyson] is safe to return to the ring. Now, when he's outside the ring, doctors say he should be kept in a big steel cage." *1998*

ANIKA RODMAN
(Wife of Dennis Rodman)
"I am embarrassed and ashamed of myself for ever being married to him. Not only did he get tattoos, pierce his bellybutton and dye his hair like me, he is now dressing like me." *1995*

DENNIS RODMAN
(Basketball Player)
"She has $250 million, Mama!" *1995: Explaining to his mother why he dated Madonna.*

"All I know is, the NBA screwed me again. Other than that, I'm always winning." *1995: A few days before the San Antonio Spurs traded him to Chicago.*

"A lot of teams are afraid of the [Chicago] Bulls because of who the individuals are. They have to concentrate on so many people that they are skeptical about what they'll be able to do. They're so worried about how to play us that they forget to just play us." *1996*

"[My mother] was always strong. Her best move was to kick me out of the house. I wanted to just bum around, and she said, 'To hell with that.' It made me stronger, mentally and physically. I could've gone straight downhill." *1996*

"Fifty percent of life in the NBA is sex. The other fifty percent is money." *1996*

"I want to play my last NBA game in the nude." *1996*

"I fantasize about being with another man." *1996*

"She wasn't an acrobat, but she wasn't a dead fish, either." *1996: Describing the sex he had with Madonna.*

"Once you've had a total stranger ask you to fuck his wife while he watches, you're not going to be easily shocked. There's only one thing that shocks me: I'm still here." *1996*

"I just wanna be one of the 12 players on the floor." *1996: On his love of basketball.*

"It would have been a classic if I kissed him, but he probably would have sued me for slobbering all over him." *1997: After he tripped over a cameraman when he returned to the basketball court after an eleven-game suspension for kicking another lensman.*

"They say Elvis is dead. He's not dead. He's just a different color. He's 6 ft. 8 in., 225 lbs., plays basketball, and he's black." *1997*

"I'm about to do something that has never been done. Before next season, I am going to sign a $9 million or $10 million contract and tell the team, 'If I'm not worth it, don't pay me.' I'll play the whole year for free." *1997*

"The NBA won't say goodbye to me. They need me. The NBA is a cripple and I am the crutch." *1997*

"I wish I could put a diaper on all of them and burp them because I think they all have indigestion when it comes to the Chicago Bulls." *1998: Arguing that NBA referees and officials conspired to make his team lose against the Indianapolis Pacers in order to extend the best-of-seven series.*

"I'm not going to never win in the game of basketball, right? No matter what I do . . . No matter what I do for this league and for the game of basketball, I'm going to never win. And in a situation like this, when I'm playing for a minimum wage—I'm getting what, $250,000?—and I got 10 charities. I'm going to give $10,000 to each charity. That's $100,000. I'm getting paid $150,000 on top of that, and even with this, doing this right here, I'm still not going to win." *1999: On signing a contract with the Los Angeles Lakers.*

DENNIS RODMAN (CONT'D)

"You know, most psychiatrists call me a genius." *1999: When asked by NBC sportscaster Jim Gray whether he'd sought any professional help during his four-game absence from the team. Replied Gray: "Maybe they need a little help."*

PETE ROSE
(Baseball Legend)

"If I'd have been a cokehead, I'd probably still be managing the Reds. But I decided to bet on football, and that was the wrong thing to do. I'm a good citizen. I do a lot of positive things. I think I've been in the penalty box long enough. I try to stay away from baseball. I was a fighter on the field, but I'm not looking for a fight." *1998: In an impromptu speech to Cincinnati Reds' minor leaguers in Sarasota, FL. Rose was banned for life from baseball in 1989 for gambling. He visited the camp to see his son Pete Rose Jr., a Reds' minor leaguer.*

"Pay your taxes, by the way, and don't bet on Monday Night Football either." *1998: Advice to young baseball players in his unscheduled motivational talk to a Cincinnati Reds farm team—a violation of his ban from baseball.*

"I made the wrong mistakes." *1999: Insisting that had he been a drug addict rather than a gambler he'd be in the Baseball Hall of Fame today.*

NOLAN RYAN
(Baseball Player)

"I didn't have the heart to knock her down." *1992: On pitching to his wife, Ruth, at a Rangers' fantasy camp. She hit a fastball just above the fists and ground out to the mound.*

S
PETE SAMPRAS
(Tennis Player)

"I'm going to enter the ladies' event next year. Maybe I'll get lucky and win that." *1998: On his new strategy for winning the only Grand Slam tennis event that has eluded him, the French Open at Roland Garros.*

DEION SANDERS
(Football & Baseball Player)

"It's tough. You just sit there all day. I don't know how O. J. does it. I've got a lot of respect for the dude." *1995: The Cincinnati Reds' outfielder on the three days he had to spend in court where he faced three misdemeanor charges stemming from a confrontation with a security guard.*

"If I don't get booed, something's wrong." *1995*

"I'm not gonna say I told you so, but . . . well, you know what I'm going to say. I'm not saying anything. I'm just saying . . . you know. You know." *1996: On the Dallas Cowboys' playoff victory.*

"When you say I committed adultery, are you stating before the marriage of 1996 or prior to it?" *1996: Questioned in a hearing when his wife sued him for divorce.*

WIMP SANDERSON
(Football Coach)

"I've been here so long that when I got here, the Dead Sea wasn't even sick." *1992: The Alabama basketball coach, on lasting thirty-two years at the school.*

WARREN SAPP
(Football Player)

"I'd take a bullet for him—if it wouldn't kill me." *The Tampa Bay Buccaneers' defensive tackle on his devotion to the team's coach Tony Dungy.*

GLEN SATHER
(Hockey General Manager)

"He's been great at every level he's played at except the NHL, the Olympics and the world championships." *1999: The general manager of the Edmonton Oilers on his goalie, Tommy Salo.*

DANNY SCHAYES
(Basketball Player)

"I've long suspected that [Danny] Ainge had sex only once a year, on New Year's Eve." *1995: After learning that all five of teammate Danny Ainge's children were born in September or October.*

CURT SCHILLING
(Baseball Player)

"I can't throw one, so I did the next best thing. I bought one." *1993: The Philadelphia Phillies' pitcher on why he named his dog Slider.*

"The one creepy thought I have when he comes up there is the fear that he'll hit my best pitch back up the middle. He's the one guy in baseball who could hit a ball that goes in one side of you and out the other, and it would be going just as fast when it came out." *1998: On pitching to St. Louis Cardinals' slugger Mark McGwire, who hit fifty-eight home runs the previous year.*

JOE SCHMIDT
(Basketball Fan)
"It would be an honor to get HIV from playing Magic Johnson on an NBA court. He's one of the greats." *1996: A student at Western Kentucky University, he was asked if Magic Johnson's return to the NBA would put other players at risk.*

DANIEL SCHNEIDER
(District Court Judge)
"I am convinced he's smart enough to play with any dumb jock out there." *1995: The New Mexico district court judge, after ruling in favor of New Mexico basketball recruit Kenny Thomas, who sued the NCAA for declaring him academically ineligible.*

STEVE SCHNUR
(Football Player)
"You can't afford to miss classes; they know as soon as you don't come in that you are missing." *1995: The quarterback for Northwestern University's highly ranked football team, on the drawbacks of his team's newfound success after years of losing seasons.*

MARGE SCHOTT
(Baseball Team Owner)
"To our boys in the Far East." *1990: The owner of the Cincinnati Reds, dedicating the World Series to servicemen men and women in Kuwait. Later she tried to correct herself by dedicating the series to "Our boys in the Middle West."*

"I'm just making a visit to my money." *1992: At spring training camp.*

"Only fruits wear earrings." *1994: Explaining why she objects to players with pierced ears.*

"Wouldn't it be nice if we were all dogs?" *1996*

"We smoked a peace pipe with the Indians, right?" *1996: On why she'd rather see children smoke than take drugs.*

BUDD SCHULBERG
(Author)
"If you can't hit 'em, bite 'em!" *1997: On his interpretation of Mike Tyson's fighting philosophy in the ring with Evander Holyfield.*

"Never saw anything like it. Not even outside a saloon." *1997: After boxer Mike Tyson was disqualified for biting the ears of Evander Holyfield in their heavyweight title fight.*

VIN SCULLY
(Baseball Announcer)
"The seventh game of the World Series. If you spin the pages of history, boy, there's a lot of meat for you there." *1997: During the seventh game of the Florida Marlins–Cleveland Indians series.*

BRIANA SCURRY
(Soccer Player)
"Everybody does it. It's only cheating if you get caught." *1999: The goalkeeper of the U.S. Women's Soccer Team, admitting she bent the rules of the game during the crucial penalty shootout that cost China the Women's World Cup. Scurry failed to stand still as China's Liu Wing took her penalty shot.*

JOHN SEABROOK
(Journalist)
"Tara [Lipinski] is now endorsing Barbie dolls. Is there a logic in getting an ice queen with the body of a child to sell a child's toy with the body of a sexpot?" *1998: On the fifteen-year-old Olympic ice-skating gold medalist.*

GEORGE SEIFERT
(Football Coach)
"There was a lot of emotion at the Alamo, too, and they all died." *1995: The San Francisco 49ers' coach George Seifert on why anger over losing Deion Sanders to the Cowboys wasn't the sole reason for their 41–10 win over Atlanta.*

"This is a sad day for the fish and wildlife population. I'm here to announce my resignation as

GEORGE SEIFERT (CONT'D)
football coach of the San Francisco 49ers." *1997: On his plans to do a lot of hunting and fishing after leaving the 49ers.*

MONICA SELES
(Tennis Player)
"The only time (I get weighed) is when I do my insurance, and then I don't ever look at it because it is not a priority for me." *1996: Listed as five feet ten and a half inches, 145 pounds, in the tennis media guide, reacting to being pestered by the body-fat police since her return to the pro tour.*

PETER SELIGMAN
(Spokesman for the Professional Bowlers Association)
"Bowling's image has gotten away from Ralph Kramden. Today, it's more Michael Jordanesque." *1998: Optimistically assessing efforts to broaden bowling's appeal.*

RONALD SHAFTER
(Newspaper Editor)
"These days when I return to Ohio, I imagine that some of the highway signs have been erected in his memory. The ones that say: *Do Not Pass.*" *1995: The* Wall Street Journal *editor and 1962 graduate of Ohio State University, remembering legendary OSU football coach Woody Hayes, known for the run-dominated offense that brought his teams 258 winning games and thirteen Big Ten championships in twenty-eight years.*

MIKE SHANAHAN
(Football Coach)
"No. I made them." *1997: When asked by a reporter whether he was surprised at any of the Broncos' final roster cuts.*

SHANNON SHARPE
(Football Player)
"In the first quarter they tackle him for a two-yard gain, and it's, 'No, no, T.D.! You ain't getting nothing today, baby!' In the second quarter he gets a 10-yard gain, and they say 'It's all right, T.D., we'll give you that, but nothing else, baby!' In the third quarter he'll break one off for 25 and it's, 'Ooh, you running today, huh, T.D.?' And in the fourth quarter he's got 180 yards, and it's 'Yo, T.D., can you come to my charity golf tournament in July?'" *1999: The* Denver Broncos' tight end on the futile trash talk defenders aim at star running back Terrell Davis.

REVEREND AL SHARPTON
(Boxing Fan & Friend of Don King)
"In New York, where Mike [Tyson] and I come from, out in the harbor, they have a Statue of Liberty. And she's there for all the immigrants to come, and she stretches forth her hand. But we didn't have a statue for us, because we didn't come on Ellis Island. They brought us in the hulls of ships against our will. We came through the back door! But now we have a Statue of Liberation, who stands to tell black folks that you can make it if you try! Who rose from nothing to something! From the guttermost to the uttermost! From disgrace to amazin' grace! Brother Don King!" *1992*

"He's with the mob that marched with Martin Luther King and Hosea Williams in Alabama to make us free!. . . He's with the angelic mob, the black man's mob, the freedom mob—our champion Don King!" *1992*

BILL SHAW
(Football Player)
"The only thing the rest of us read was cards." *1996: The former Buffalo Bills lineman remembering teammate Jack Kemp as an avid reader.*

GARY SHEFFIELD
(Baseball Player)
"When you play with no sleeves, you can get rug burns. You don't want to risk injury." *1999: The Dodgers' outfielder after letting a ball fall to the artificial turf in Pittsburgh.*

ART SHELL
(Football Coach)
"This is no time for celebration. We're in a hole and we've got to keep digging." *1992: The Los Angeles Raiders' coach on his team's losing [4–6] record.*

BUCK SHOWALTER
(Baseball Manager)
"What was he doing with Miss Saigon?" *1992: The New York Yankee manager after being told that general manager Gene Michael had gone to see* Miss Saigon.

REVEREND MUHAMED SIDDEEQ
(Spiritual Advisor to Mike Tyson)

"I see Mike solving many of the world's problems." *1998: On why he thinks Tyson should have his boxing license reinstated by the New Jersey Athletic Control Board.*

TERRY SIMPSON
(Hockey Coach)

"Coaching is a funny profession. It prepares you to do nothing else." *1996: After being fired as coach of the Winnipeg Jets.*

HEATHER SINK
(Baseball Fan)

"I deserved it." *1998: The twenty-three-year-old from Chapel Hill, NC, on the booing she heard at an Atlanta Braves game after a foul ball hit into the seats eluded her grasp and bounced off her chin.*

SCOTT SKILES
(Basketball Player)

"If I had a dollar for every time somebody asked me that question—wait a minute. I do have a dollar for every time somebody has asked me that question." *1992: The Orlando Magic guard who earns more than $2 million a year, after being asked whether he was recruited by home-state Indiana before attending Michigan State.*

R. C. SLOCUM
(Football Coach)

"When I'm retired and sitting on my back porch, I don't want to say, 'I had the chance to go to New Jersey to play a big-time game against one of the best programs and one of the greatest coaches in college football on national TV, and I turned it down because I was afraid I'd get beat.'" *1998: The coach from Texas A&M on why he agreed to pit his Aggies, 9–4 last year, against perennial superpower Florida State in the August Kickoff Classic at Giants Stadium.*

KATHY SMITH
(Fitness Expert)

"I ate my vegetables as a child. I still love broccoli, carrots, asparagus and greens. I dislike okra, but I like her as a talk show host." *1996*

LEE SMITH
(Baseball Player)

"This is a class act. I don't even want to see 2,000 games, let alone play in them." *1995: The California Angels pitcher on Baltimore Orioles' shortstop Cal Ripken tying Lou Gehrig's major league record for most consecutive baseball games played [2130].*

ZANE SMITH
(Baseball Player)

"I'm not blind to hearing what everybody else hears." *1995: On rumors that he would be left off the post-season roster.*

SAMMY SOSA
(Baseball Player)

"There's nothing done. If it gets done, then it'll be done when it's done." *1997: The Chicago Cubs' slugger on the progress of his contract talks with the club.*

SHERRI SPILLANE
(Agent)

"Tonya didn't like Woody Allen's morals." *1995: The agent for Tonya Harding, on the reason why the former bad girl of ice skating turned down an offer to appear in a Woody Allen film.*

CHARLIE SPOONHOUR
(Basketball Coach)

"We're excited about the coming season—but, then, guys on death row are excited too." *1998: The St. Louis University coach on his team's prospects this season after the loss of a star guard to the NBA.*

LATRELL SPREWELL
(Basketball Player)

"No. That stuff happens." *1998: When asked if he was upset that his two pit bulls mauled his daughter. Sprewell was suspended for a year from the NBA for choking his coach.*

"It was all about the respect factor with me. It was all about P. J. [Carlesimo] disrespecting me as a man. You don't talk to people the way that P. J. talked to me. To have my pride and my respect and my manhood means more than any dollar amount." *1998: Explaining why he choked his Golden State Warriors' coach P. J. Carlesimo.*

LATRELL SPREWELL (CONT'D)

"I wasn't choking P. J. I mean, he could breathe. It's not like he was losing air or anything like that. I mean, it wasn't a choke, I wasn't trying to kill P. J. If you're choking someone, you don't get scratches. You get welts around your neck. It's not like I was going to sit there and kill the man. No, I would have stopped, definitely." *1998: Explaining exactly what he did to his coach, P. J. Carlesimo.*

"I've seen everybody say everything about me. It's like I've been in counseling watching TV." *Explaining what he's been doing during his suspension from the NBA.*

"I attacked him, but I don't know about getting away with it. I mean, to me, that's not getting away with it." *1998: Pointing out that his sixty-eight-game suspension from the NBA and the loss of $6.4 million in salary because of his mistreatment of his coach was truly not getting away with it.*

STEVE SPURRIER
(Football Coach)

"But the real tragedy was that 15 hadn't been colored yet." *1991: Telling Florida Gator fans that a fire at Auburn's football dorm had destroyed twenty books.*

GEORGE STEINBRENNER
(Baseball Team Owner)

"There isn't enough mustard in the United States to cover him, but when the time came to deliver he did." *1993: The owner of the New York Yankees, on Reggie Jackson's election to the Baseball Hall of Fame.*

"If I could get Yogi to come back, I'd bring him over with a rickshaw across the George Washington Bridge." *1999: As he apologized to former manager Yogi Berra to heal a fourteen-year rift in the hope that Berra will return to Yankee Stadium for Opening Day or Old-Timers' Day.*

DAVID STERN
(NBA Commissioner)

"You cannot strike your boss and still hold your job—unless you play in the NBA and are subject to arbitrator Feerick's decision." *1998: On an arbitrator's ruling easing Latrell Sprewell's punishment for choking his coach.*

ELVIS STOJKO
(Ice Skater)

"I was told to get in touch with my feminine side. I said, 'Buddy, I don't have a feminine side.'" *1998*

GREG STONE
(Basketball Player)

"It [*Old Yeller*] was sitting there, and there was nothing else to do, so I read it. That was the first time I finished a book. I'm working on my second now—*Everything I Need to Know I learned in Kindergarten.* It's sitting next to the toilet at home." *1992: The thirty-year-old basketball star at Santa Rosa Junior College in Santa Rosa, CA, on his academic accomplishments.*

JERRY STRICKLAND
(Boxer)

"It's a job. Right now you can get killed out in the street for free. I prefer if you hit me, I make some money." *1998: Strickland has been knocked out forty-six times since his first boxing match in 1968.*

RICH SWENSON
(Sled-dog Racer)

"The dogs . . . hear the music and they react to it. When I pick something like Creedence Clearwater Revival, they are up-tempo. When it's whiny stuff like Carly Simon or James Taylor, they're moody like they're saying, 'I don't want to be here.'" *1992: The five-time winner of the Iditarod dog sled race in Alaska, explaining how he motivates his dogs.*

T

BENEDICTE TARANGO
(Wife of Tennis Player)

"I don't regret anything. I'm a little hot-blooded, but that is my Latin temperament." *1995: The wife of tennis star Jeff Tarango, following her husband's default of a match at Wimbledon, slapped the French umpire Bruno Rebeuh, in the match.*

JEFF TARANGO
(Tennis Player)

"She's French. Women are emotional." *1995: Explaining why his wife slapped the French umpire for a match in which he defaulted and walked off the court, protesting what he believed were bad and biased calls by the umpire.*

"I lost my head, and my shorts came down; the gig was up." *1995: Explaining why he dropped his shorts after losing a match to Michael Chang in Tokyo.*

"I'm a very rational person. I definitely have probably a little Latin in me, but I don't. I'm an intellectual person who does not fly off the cuff without reason." *1995*

JIM TATUM
(Cyclist)

"When I get there, I'll tell you." *Tatum, seventy-six, who bikes 180 miles a week and regularly competes in bicycle races, when asked what old age is like.*

JOE THEISMANN
(Football Player & TV Announcer)

"The word *genius* isn't applicable in football. A genius is a guy like Norman Einstein." *1992*

DEBI THOMAS
(Ice Skater)

"I tell people I'm too stupid to know what's impossible. I had ridiculously large dreams, and half the time they came true." *1996: Thomas skated for the United States in the 1988 Winter Olympics and won a bronze medal. She graduated from Stanford and Northwestern Medical School and is now a surgeon.*

JOHN THOMPSON
(Basketball Coach)

"There's a hell of a lot of whites failing. I'm sick of us having to be perfect to get the job." *1998: The legendary Georgetown University coach talking about the lack of African Americans in sports management, during President Clinton's town meeting on race in Houston.*

"The process is a bitch." *1999: On his "draining" divorce proceedings, which led him to resign his coaching duties.*

ALBERTO TOMBA
(Skier)

"We will make a series of films like *Baywatch*, but in the mountains. And I am the star." *1996: The three-time Olympic gold medalist skier on his future cinema career.*

DICK TOMEY
(Football Coach)

"You won't find many football coaches with degrees from Princeton, Harvard and Stanford. Actually, you won't find many professors here with degrees from Princeton, Harvard and Stanford." *1996: The Arizona football coach on the hiring of brainy Homer Smith as an offensive coordinator.*

JEFF TORBORG
(Baseball Announcer)

"Wrigley Field—it sort of reminds you of some of the old ballparks." *1996*

JOSE TORRE
(Baseball Manager)

"When we lose, I can't sleep. When we win, I can't sleep. But when you win, you wake up feeling better." *1993*

MICHAEL TRANGHESE
(Big East Basketball Commissioner)

"Males are made differently. . . . Men compete, get along, and move on with few emotions, but women break down, get emotional." *1998: On why he wouldn't suspend rules for an injured male athlete as he had for a female.*

DONALD TRUMP
(Celebrity Businessman & Author)

"If it were just a great fight, everyone would have forgotten it. No one is going to forget this." *1997: Commenting on Mike Tyson's biting of both of Evander Holyfield's ears during their heavyweight championship fight.*

MONICA TURNER
(Wife of Mike Tyson)

"He's not perfect, but nobody is." *1999: On her husband, who is in prison for assaulting two motorists.*

NORV TURNER
(Football Coach)

"I've never thought to tell a guy not to hit the wall after a touchdown, so we'll put that in our preseason plans next year." *1997: After Washington quarterback Gus Frerotte injured himself after a touchdown by head-butting a wall.*

STEVEN TURNER
(Tennis Instructor)

"The funny thing is, every woman that I've ever taught always wants a stronger serve. They want

STEVEN TURNER (CONT'D)

more of a phallus, more of a phallic push in a phallic sense, not only genital, but phallus meaning the symbol of a phallus in the society: power! Women want more power, and so the serve presents that." *1999: Turner charges $130 an hour for lessons in Manhattan.*

MIKE TYSON
(Boxer)

"When white people first came to Africa, we owned the land and the white man had the Bible. When they finished, they had all the land and we had the Bible. So if there is a God up there, he don't like niggers." *1990*

"You know me. I talk it, I walk it. Losing's nothing, but I didn't lose fairly. . . . I knocked him out before he knocked me out." *1990: After losing to Buster Douglas.*

"I love women—my mother's one—and I respect them as well." *1991*

"I like to hurt women when I make love to them. I like to hear them scream with pain, to see them bleed." *1992*

"When I was hitting him with punches to the body, he was making noises. It was somewhat like a woman screaming." *1992: On his fight with Tyrell Biggs.*

"I'm in trouble because I'm normal and slightly arrogant. A lot of people don't like themselves and I happen to be totally in love with myself." *1992: On how people perceive him.*

"What else am I going to do, man, be a nuclear scientist?" *1993: On why he'd resume his boxing career when he got out of prison.*

"What do you think of Voltaire?" *1993: The first question the ear-chewing heavyweight fighter asked writer Maya Angelou [according to Angelou] when she visited him in prison, where he was serving a sentence for rape.*

"Now how would you rate the Eurocentrism of Tolstoy and, say, Charles Dickens, with the Afrocentrism of Richard Wright and James Baldwin?" *1993: Questioning Maya Angelou [according to Angelou] when she visited him in prison.*

"He was very awkward. He kept his head down. He was very difficult to hit. Eventually he would have gotten hurt. You know me. I'm a blood man. I'm glad they stopped it." *1995: On his eighty-nine-second fight with Peter McNeeley.*

"He's cute." *1995: On Peter McNeeley.*

"No offense, but I'd appreciate it if you'd put your clothes back on. After what I've been through, I think you can understand." *1996: To a woman who came up to him at a Manhattan club and stripped to her undies.*

"He had me all screwed up in jail, made me want to give everything away. Tolstoy was a square." *1996: On Leo Tolstoy, whose books Iron Mike read during time in prison on a rape conviction.*

"I would like to go to Europe and explore different situations. Before I'd go and visit dens of iniquity, stuff like that. There are places I could explore that are very positive, like the Louvre." *1996*

"This is not to be taken personally but I am just pissed off all the time." *1996: Following his second victory over Bruce Seldon.*

"I like to talk about what's happening out there. You can't do that with a dingbat." *1997: On why he married Washington, D.C., physician Monica Turner, on his preference for educated women.*

"He butted me in the first round and in the second round again. This is my career. I have children to raise. I have to retaliate. He butted me." *1997: Explaining how he sets an example for his children. In response to an accidental head butt he bit off part of Evander Holyfield's ear.*

"Saturday night was the worst night of my professional career as a boxer, and I am here today to apologize, to ask the people who expected more from Mike Tyson to forgive me for snapping in that ring and doing something that I have never done before and will never do again." *1997: Apologizing for biting Evander Holyfield's ears during their heavyweight title bout in Las Vegas.*

"Look at me. My kids will be scared of me." *1997: Pointing to a gash above his right eye caused by a head butt, and explaining why, in retaliation he bit both ears of his opponent, Evander Holyfield, in their heavyweight fight. Tyson lost by a disqualification.*

"When I was in prison, I was wrapped up in all those deep books—that Tolstoy crap. People shouldn't read that stuff. When we read those books, what purpose does it serve in this day and time?" *1997*

"I am not a stable person." *1997: In a candid confession on* Prime Time Live.

"I took boxing back to its raw form. Kill or be killed. The winner gets it all. That's what people want. And they paid me for it. People are afraid I'm going to unmask them for what they are. Hypocrites." *1998*

"Don't tell me about no fucking women's lib. How can a bunch of pussy-whipped men let their women parade around saying, 'All men are pigs. Us against them.'" *1998*

"I am no schizophrenic and no manic depressant. I'm just me. I represent people, pimps, whores, prostitutes." *1998: Testifying to his own good character before the Nevada State Athletic Commission, which voted 4–1 to restore his boxing license.*

"I have no self-esteem, but the biggest ego in the world." *1998: In an interview with psychiatrists who examined him and later pronounced him mentally fit to return to boxing after being banned for biting Evander Holyfield in the ring.*

"What the fuck was wrong with his grandmother?" *1999: When told that a young Japanese fan who'd come to Las Vegas to see him fight Francois Botha wanted to be like Tyson because his grandmother, on her death bed, told him to follow Tyson and to be like him.*

"A guy brought in some food the other day and he told me, 'Man, I'd love to be you.' I said, 'Please don't say that brother.' He said, 'I've got six kids and one paycheck.' I told him, 'I've got millions of dollars and no friends.'" *1999*

U

BOB UECHER
(Baseball Player)

"The highlight of my baseball career came in Philadelphia . . . when I saw a fan fall out of the upper deck. When he got up and walked away, the crowd booed." *1992*

JOHN URBANCHEK
(U.S. Men's Swimming Coach)

"They always say that the big thing they give their swimmers is turtle soup. Well, I guess the turtle soup this week is going to taste a little different, because they're missing some of the ingredients." *1998: Stated after a Chinese swimmer arriving in Australia for the World Swimming Championships was found to be carrying a thermos bottle filled with thirteen vials of human growth hormone—enough for the entire Chinese team for the entire meet. The swimmer and her coach were expelled from Australia, the growth hormone was confiscated, and the other Chinese swimmers did not do as well as they had in previous meets.*

WOODY URCHAK
(Baseball Coach)

"I predict we'll be more competitive against St. Francis this year." *1997: Robert Morris College's new baseball coach was brought in to rebuild a team that was 0–62 over the last two seasons, including a previous year's 71–1 loss to the College of St. Francis.*

V

ROBIN VENTURA
(Baseball Player)

"Pompons aren't going to help you score runs." *1998: The White Sox third baseman after pitcher Jaime Navarro complained about the lack of vocal support from his teammates during a shutout loss to Detroit.*

THE VILLAGE VOICE
(Newspaper)

"Billy Martin was the Elvis Presley of baseball." *1990: A subsequent letter to the editor disagreed with this evaluation and suggested that Billy Martin was "the Sid Vicious of baseball."*

PETE VUCKOVICH
(Baseball Coach)

"I was a victim of circumcision." *1997: The Pittsburgh Pirates' pitching coach, after being ejected from a game against the St. Louis Cardinals for arguing from the dugout with first base umpire Randy Marsh.*

W

STEVE WAGNER
(Sports Fan)

"I wonder how many of those football players who pray for a win 'only as a way to bring glory to God' give 10% of their paychecks to the glory of God." *1998*

DARRELL WALKER
(Basketball Player)

"I don't know why [Coach Ron Rothstein] just didn't tell me on the plane Monday. . . . Why couldn't he be a man? He probably thought I would have strangled his little butt, and maybe I would have." *1992: The Detroit Piston after player personnel director Billy McKinney told him he had been waived by the team on November 24, 1992.*

BILL WALSH
(Football Coach)

"It does have redeeming value, coaching at the college level—unless it's USC." *1992: On returning to coach Stanford University's football team.*

"His brilliant performances exhilarated all of us—and helped me purchase my new home." *1995: On Joe Montana's retirement.*

TYSON WALTER
(Football Player)

"I don't get paid to think like that; I get paid to do what they tell me." *1998: The Ohio State tackle, declining to speculate on why his team lost to Michigan State.*

CHARLIE WEATHERBIE
(Football Coach)

"I've never been booed for praying." *1997: The Navy football coach on the catcalls he heard when, after losing at Notre Dame, his players kneeled at midfield while the Irish marching band was playing.*

STEVE WEBBER
(Basketball Coach)

"It was a little different. It was like playing inside." *1992: The Georgia basketball coach after his Bulldogs played a game in the Louisiana Superdome.*

DOUG WEIGHT
(Hockey Player)

"We're big guys and the chairs aren't real strong. Some were broken while we were just sitting on them, playing cards." *1998: The U.S. Olympic Team member denying that some team members trashed their rooms after losing their last game at Nagano.*

BOB WEISS
(Basketball Coach)

"For a bunch of guys who would rather pass kidney stones than a basketball, it was pretty amazing." *1991: The Atlanta Hawks' coach on a game in which his often selfish players played as a team.*

DAVID WELLS
(Baseball Player)

"I wish my mom could have saw it." *1998: The New York Yankee pitcher on his one regret after throwing a perfect game on May 17.*

"New York has been very, very good for me. But, you know, I've been very good for New York." *1998*

RICHARD WESTGATE
(Police Chief)

"We don't have Secret Service up on the rooftops. This is baseball." *1999: The Jupiter, FL, police chief on plans to protect home-run king Mark McGwire.*

REGGIE WHITE
(Football Player & Ordained Minister)

"Homosexuality is a decision, it's not a race. People from all different ethnic backgrounds are living this lifestyle. But people from all different backgrounds are liars and cheaters and malicious backstabbers." *1998: The star of the Green Bay Packers and ordained minister, in a speech to the Wisconsin State Assembly, denouncing homosexuality as "one of the biggest sins in the Bible."*

"When you look at the black race, black people are very gifted in what we call worship and celebration. A lot of us like to dance, and if you do go to a black church, you see people jumping up and down because they really get into it." *1998*

"White people are blessed with the gift of structure and organization. You guys do a good job with building businesses and things of that nature. And you know how to tap into money pretty much better than a lot of people around the world." *1998*

"Hispanics are gifted in family structure. You see a Hispanic person, and they can put 20 or 30 people in one home." *1998*

"When you look at the Asian, the Asian is very gifted in creativity and invention. If you go to Japan or to any Asian country, they can turn a television into a watch. They are very creative." *1998*

TOM WHITTAKER
(Mountaineer)
"One of the things that really attracts me to mountaineering is its total pointlessness. So I've dedicated my life to it." *1998*

PAT WILLIAMS
(Basketball Team General Manager)
"Charles once told me he would write his autobiography as soon as he could figure out who the main character should be." *1992: The former 76ers general manager, on Charles Barkley's ghost-written autobiography.*

"I gave Gary a hockey puck once, and he spent the rest of the day trying to open it." *1992: On the possibility that NBA senior-vice-president Gary Bettman could become head of the National Hockey League.*

TED WILLIAMS
(Baseball Legend)
"I'm a real smart son of a bitch. I'm an old, dumb ballplayer and a real smart son of a bitch." *1999*

"Rogers Hornsby was some kind of guy. Everybody thinks, Oh, Hornsby—what a mean bastard. He treated me like a son, couldn't have been nicer. And he gave me the greatest single piece of advice on hitting that I ever got: Wait for a good pitch to hit." *1999*

"Pitchers are dumb. They don't play but once every four days. They're scratchin' their ass or pickin' their nose or something' the rest of the time. They're pitchin', most of 'em, because they can't do anything else." *1999*

RICHARD WILLIAMSON
(Football Coach)
"He had the MRI two weeks ago—MRI, did I pronounce that right?" *1991: The coach of the Tampa Bay Buccaneers, discussing the magnetic resonance imaging test given to wide receiver Bruce Hill.*

WILLIE WILSON
(Baseball Player)
"You mean we got to go with people." *1991: The Oakland A's outfielder, when told that the A's would be flying to Toronto on a commercial flight rather than on a charter.*

DAVE WINFIELD
(Baseball Player)
"I'm not an old codger that can't produce. I'm not just going to camp with just my bats." *1992: On playing for the Toronto Blue Jays at forty.*

"You get a bunch of guys on the bus talking trash, these are memories you never forget." *1996: Announcing his retirement after twenty-three years in the major leagues.*

TIGER WOODS
(Golfer)
"I'm a Cablinasian." *1997: Categorizing his racial makeup of Caucasian, black, Indian, and Asian.)*

"What we can learn from history is that we have learned nothing from history. And that's pretty important." *1998: After not winning the 1998 Masters Tournament.*

CHARLES WOODSON
(Football Player)
"People would come in and say, 'Let me get a Whopper with extra onions, extra pickles and no mayo,' and I'd be like, 'I'll make a regular Whopper. You deal with all that stuff in your car.' So they were getting it my way." *1998: The Oakland Raiders' cornerback and 1997 Heisman Trophy winner recalling his brief teenage career working at Burger King.*

BEN WRIGHT
(Golfer & TV Golf Analyst)
"Women are handicapped by having boobs." *1995: On why men play golf better than women as quoted*

BEN WRIGHT (CONT'D)

in a Delaware newspaper interview. Wright denied making the remark. "How does he know? He doesn't have any," responded Ladies Professional Golf Association Hall of Famer Nancy Lopez on the alleged remark.

RUTH WYSOCKI
(Distance Runner)

"In 1984 my shoe sponsor said it would take care of me for life. I guess I died in 1988." *1994: The former U.S. Olympic distance runner on her relationship with Brooks footwear company.*

Y

PETER YOUNG
(President of Australia's Synchronized Swimming Association)

"Why don't we do *Playboy*?" *1998: Recounting a suggestion by a team member to raise funds to prepare for the Sydney 2000 Olympics. Official funding has been slashed, forcing the swimmers to consider other sources of revenue.*

STEVE YOUNG
(Football Player)

"I think, to me, people expect now that I'll be able to put some kind of ensemble together—things that go together, things that make sense. . . . The problem now is that as I try to get into nicer suits I ask, 'Does this really go?' And I have the confidence that, you know what, I think, but I'm not sure." *1995: The San Francisco 49er quarterback who models for Macys, answering the question, What is your greatest fashion challenge?*

"I'm the Eighth Wonder of the World—a 32-year-old single Mormon." *1996*

"I've matured into soda now." *1996: Young abstains from alcoholic beverages and his teammates kidded him because he used to drink only milk.*

"I used to swim for a team at the Boys Club. But I can't open my eyes underwater. They finally told me to go home because I kept hitting the wall." *1998: When asked what sport he couldn't play.*

Z

MARIO ZAGALLO
(Coach of Brazil's World Cup Soccer Team)

"I'm in favor of sex before, after and even during the game." *1998: When asked how he felt about a ban on players' wives and girlfriends from team accommodations during the tournament.*

IVAN ZAMORANO
(Soccer Player)

"She thinks that now, and she has only seen me fully dressed." *1998: Chile's captain, upon hearing Madonna proclaim him one of the ten sexiest players at the World Cup.*

DON ZIMMER
(Baseball Manager)

"It just as easily could have gone the other way." *1990: The Chicago Cubs' manager, after his team went 4–4 on a road trip.*

NICK ZITO
(Horse Trainer)

"A lot of horses get distracted. It's just human nature." *1994: The trainer of the Kentucky Derby winner Go for Gin, on the importance of consistent workouts.*

FRANK URBAN "FUZZY" ZOELLER
(Golfer)

"There are two things that can happen when you hit a shot. You can hit a good shot—or you can hit a bad shot. Why wait?" *1994: On why he seldom hesitates before making a shot in golf.*

"You pat him on the back and say congratulations and enjoy it, and tell him not to serve fried chicken next year . . . or collard greens or whatever the hell they serve." *1997: Joking about the Masters' Champions Dinner in racially tinged comments about Tiger Woods, the first non-white to win one of golf's major championships.*

"I am relieved. It's over. I thought it was over three weeks ago. The only thing I'm upset about is that I had to buy his lunch." *1997: Following his lunch with Tiger Woods to discuss Zoeller's earlier remark about Woods' selection of a menu for next year's Masters' dinner banquet. Woods indicated at the lunch that he saw the matter as a racial incident and not as an innocent joke misinterpreted, as Zoeller had maintained.*

LAW
&
ORDER

A

VICTORIA GOTTI AGNELLO
(Daughter of Mafia Don John Gotti)
"My father is the last of the Mohicans." *1992*

"My father was a businessman. He was a good father. He came home every night for dinner at five." *1997*

VINCENTE PANAMA ALBA
(Former Member of the Young Lords Gang)
"You people have to use the technology. If the Young Lords had had fax machines and e-mail in our day, we would have brought the revolution for real." *1995: Speaking to students at Hunter College.*

JULIAN ALDARONDO
(Accused Cookie Thief)
"This is without doubt the most degrading and humiliating experience I have ever encountered and at this point I have no clue as to what is going on and am in a complete state of shock." *1998: After arresting Aldarondo in a movie theater in Oakland, CA, police forced him to listen to a police officer sing the Rupert Holmes' hit* Escape (The Piña Colada Song) *in the office of the theater where he had been handcuffed and taken after being accused of stealing a cookie from the Critics Corner Cafe before heading to the theater Being forced to listen to the song, Aldarondo claimed, was "the most degrading punishment" imaginable.*

LARRY AMOROS
(Comedian)
"New York is getting more and more hip. A drug dealer came up to me and said, 'Try this, it's angel dust,' and I said, 'It's green,' and he said, 'It's angel dust pesto.'" *1997*

KEITH ANTHONY
(Comedian)
"Three fucking months I'm unemployed. Three months. I'm watching TV for three months without cable. I watched so much fucking O. J. I thought *I* killed those people." *1995*

DONITA JO ARTIS
(Abusive Parent)
"You guys are so unfair." *1995: Artis, a twenty-four-year-old Pittsburgh, PA, mother, to a judge and prosecutors after being denied custody of her three-year-old son and sentenced to two to ten years in prison for beating him until he was blind, deaf, and unable to walk.*

B

BEN BAILEY
(Comedian)
"Crime is down in New York. Somebody told me the other day that in 1996 there were only 956 murders. I guess that's a good thing except there's some hit man who's depressed. Crime is down in New York. I've got to get my numbers up." *1997*

F. LEE BAILEY
(O. J. Simpson "Dream Team" Attorney)
"My God, Shapiro wanted O. J. to plead guilty! In fact he tried to have him plead guilty to manslaughter in which Bob Kardashian would be an accessory." *1995: Complaining about attorney Robert Shaprio's initial plan in the O. J. Simpson trial.*

"Johnnie Cochran bent over backwards to keep [Robert Shapiro] from embarrassing himself." *1995*

"I'm not Perry Mason; nobody is. Other lawyers whom I respect told me that given what I had to work with, it was good. Norman Mailer called me and said it was flawless. So I feel good." *1995: After his courtroom showdown with Detective Mark Fuhrman during the trial of O. J. Simpson.*

"Remember, Ito's wife is a cop. She will give him hell when there's an acquittal." *1995: On Judge Lance Ito.*

"This trial has spawned one of the great trial lawyers in America, and one who can lead and lead and lead to victory." *1995: Bailey on his colleague and fellow O. J. Simpson defense team member, Johnny Cochran. Cochran remarked, "I feel like a salmon" after hearing the statement.*

F. LEE BAILEY (CONT'D)

"It's only 1995. So we still have time for another trial of the century." *1995: Following the O. J. Simpson verdict.*

LOURDES BAIRD
(U.S. District Attorney)

"One does not seriously attack the expertise of a scientist using the undefined phrase 'butt-head.'" *1994: Dismissing Carl Sagan's libel suit against Apple Computer after the famed stargazer sued the company. He alleged it had changed the internal code name on a personal computer from 'Carl Sagan' to 'Butt-head Astronomer' after Sagan requested Apple to stop using his name.*

RALPH BALDWIN
(Municipal Court Judge)

"When I saw it put down on paper, it looked awful. It was stupid. When I thought about it, I thought, 'Oh my God, you fool.'" *1998: The Lakewood, WA, judge resigned after admitting to a newspaper report that at the end of a drunk driving case, he invited the lawyers to join him for "a cold one" and drove home with an open beer.*

FRANK R. BALL
(Police Chief)

"I'm not pregnant. Never have been." *1996: Ball of Brainerd, MN, was commenting on the movie* Fargo, *in which the Brainerd police chief is named Marge Gunderson and is seven months pregnant. The producer and director of the film insist that it is based on a real-life crime.*

"You might say this movie's put the name Brainerd all across the nation. So I say we should ride that wave. If you get some notoriety, you should make hay with it." *1996: Mixing metaphors and describing the importance of the film* Fargo, *which is partly set in Brainerd.*

MICHAEL BAND
(Public Prosecutor)

"Roy represents people who can afford him. You're basically innocent until proven broke." *1991: On William Kennedy Smith's high-priced defense attorney, Roy Black.*

DOMINIC BARBARA
(Attorney)

"The makers of Viagra should be liable for something like this. It's like giving a loaded gun to someone who has not been trained to shoot." *1998: The Illinois attorney threatening to sue Pfizer Inc. for negligence on behalf of a woman who said her seventy-year-old live-in partner's renewed vigor caused him to leave her in search of new conquests.*

VINCENT BARBIERI
(Father of O. J. Simpson Girlfriend Paula Barbieri)

"Maybe it's my daughter next." *1995: Concerned about his daughter's relationship with O. J. Simpson.*

"I am jumping with joy." *1995: After hearing his daughter had broken up with O. J. Simpson.*

ROBERT BARDO
(Murderer)

"I didn't kill Rebecca Schaeffer for fame. It's not like she's Julia Roberts or Madonna, you know what I mean? It's not like she's some big star." *1992: Bardo murdered actress Rebecca Schaeffer.*

DAVE BARRY
(Humorist)

"You're going to have to chip in a little extra to help offset the estimated $147 million business deduction that the [O. J. Simpson] defense team is claiming for suits." *1995: Answering a question on how the O. J. Simpson case might affect individual 1994 tax returns.*

PETER BART
(Editor of Variety*)*

"The bottom line, Laura, is that you spent 10 years researching and writing a screenplay that understandably no one wants to finance. . . . Judging from your script, Laura, your principal talent lies not in writing but rather in getting into trouble. And for that we are all paying a price. . . . Perhaps instead of teaching a course in screenwriting, you could actually take one." *1995: In an open letter to Laura Hart McKinny, described in the press as a screenwriter although she has never sold a script. McKinney, who teaches scriptwriting at the North Carolina School of the Arts, tape-recorded conversations with Detective Mark Fuhrman.*

JIM BAUGHMAN
(School Superintendent)

"I think I am a role model. I stood up and came clean about what I did and I'm going on with my life." *1993: The former San Jose Unified School District superintendent was forced to resign when it was learned that for eight years he falsely claimed he held a Ph.D. degree from Stanford University. He was later indicted for misappropriating school funds.*

BOB BERKOWITZ
(TV Host)

"It's called Courtus Interruptus." *1995: To a caller whose husband had lost interest in sex because of the O. J. trial, on CNBC's* Talk Back America.

NEAL BIGGERS
(Mississippi Judge)

"In my 20 years on the bench, I thought I'd seen everything. But this is the most sordid case I've seen." *1995: Sentencing a seventy-year-old man, who fathered two children with his granddaughter and conspired with her to kill her husband.*

DON BIZAR
(Probation Officer)

"They're more likely to call from the car phone if they're going to be late." *1998: The Federal probation officer whose charges include financier Michael Milken, on how the white-collar offenders he monitors differ from other ex-convicts.*

ROY BLACK
(Attorney)

"Will had to reluctantly admit that it was true, which has certainly helped him with dates since then." *1992: Joking about his client William Kennedy Smith's claim that he had sex twice in thirty minutes with Patricia Bowman.*

JOHN WAYNE BOBBITT
(Celebrity Crime Victim)

"Next month I'm supposed to make an appearance in a video store in Virginia and I'm going to pop in on her. We're still married, you know. I'm planning to just walk in on her with a bunch of flowers." *1994: On his hopes to reconcile with wife, Lorena, who cut off his penis.*

"It's a job. I used to work there before this happened. But I'd rather that my penis was not cut off at all." *1994: John Wayne Bobbitt, on his starring role in the adult video,* John Wayne Bobbitt . . . Uncensored. *Bobbitt, who expected to make more than a million dollars from the video, had sex with three different women.*

"I'd like to go out with her [Nancy Kerrigan]. She's a victim, too. She knows how it feels. I would have gone out with Nicole Simpson, but she didn't make it." *1995*

"I didn't realize at the time it was being unfaithful. I mean my wife didn't know I was seeing those two girls." *1995*

"It's like therapy. It makes me stronger." *1995: Pointing out the positive aspects of having his penis cut off.*

"I've had a lot of intuition since I've got my penis cut off." *1995*

"She was like retarded or something." *1995: On why his mother abandoned him when he was four.*

"You're not a celebrity. You didn't discover the polio vaccine. You're a guy who got his dick cut off." *1995: His lawyers responding to Bobbitt's statement, "I'm a celebrity now."*

"I could use the break. I'll kick back, read a couple of books and take it easy for a while." *1995: When threatened with jail for falling behind in his child-support payments.*

"I still have stitches in my public area." *1995: On his recovery from penis-enlargement surgery.*

"She's very sensitive." *1995: On why he had problems with his former wife, Lorena Bobbitt, who cut off his penis.*

"We were both attacked by a knife." *1995: Comparing himself to Nicole Brown Simpson.*

LORENA BOBBITT
(Penis Remover)

"I still have my American dream." *1995: Bobbitt, who cut off her husband's penis and then went back to a quiet*

LORENA BOBBITT (CONT'D)

life as a manicurist, wanted later to go on the lecture circuit and is open to serious, dignified proposals.

BONNIE BOBIT
(Editor)

"The crimes are deplorable, but the book is actually entertaining to read. It's a coffee-table book." *1998: The editor of the book* Death Row, *an annual compendium of people on death row in American prisons.*

SHIRLETHA BOXX
(Community Worker)

"While they were meeting with the mayor, there was a substantial decrease in drive-by shootings." *1990: A community worker closely involved with San Francisco Mayor Art Agnos's efforts in a Sunnydale housing project to decrease crime.*

"He was just a product of his environment. Psychologically, he wanted to go the right way, but his peers made him go physically the wrong way." *1990: On twenty-two-year-old Bernard Temple, sentenced to San Quentin Prison after being convicted of possessing an AK–47 assault rifle while on probation for sexually assaulting a fourteen-year-old girl.*

AL BOZA
(Miami Beach Police Spokesman)

"This was an exercise in how not to rob a bank." *1997: Commenting on a man's attempt to rob a bank one block from a police station and then hail a cab outside for his getaway.*

WALLACE (GATOR) BRADLEY
(Chicago Community Activist)

"I am speaking from the experience of being a former criminal." *1999: During a Chicago city-council hearing, on why he is an expert on the subject of police brutality.*

PAUL BRICKMAN
(Policeman)

"He took the position of an aggressive stance." *1997: Brickman, of the Metro-Dade (Florida) police, on a man shot by officers who mistook a sock on his hand for a gun.*

STEVE BRILL
(Producer & Editor)

"When it comes to arrogance, power and lack of accountability, journalists are probably the only people on the planet who make lawyers look good." *1997: Brill, who has sold his founding interest in* Court TV *and* The American Lawyer *magazine wants to start a journalism review.*

EARL BROADY
(Attorney)

"He's trying to assist Mr. Denny. That foot was there to protect Mr. Denny from further assaultive conduct by these other people." *1993: In the summation of his defense of his client Henry Keith Watson. Watson was accused of beating truck driver Reginald Denny during the Rodney King riot in South Central Los Angeles. Broady was attempting to explain what his client was actually doing in a videotape showing him standing over Denny with his foot on the fallen truck driver's throat.*

TOM BROKAW
(TV News Anchor)

"There is nothing that we can say or do that could possibly add to the drama of the moment." *1995: During the announcement of the not-guilty verdict in the O. J. Simpson trial.*

RHONDA BROWNSTEIN
(Attorney)

"It's a simple solution to a complex problem. The problem is, prisoners break rules. The solution is, torture them." *1997: Brownstein, a lawyer with the Southern Poverty Law Center, on the Alabama prison system's practice of punishing uncooperative inmates by handcuffing them to pillory-like metal bars for hours.*

DORIS BRYANT
(New York City Subway Token Clerk)

"I've stared down more gun barrels than the Lone Ranger." *1995*

RICHARD BRYDGES
(Attorney)

"She's just a typical little blue-haired lady." *1998: On his client, eighty-eight-year-old and 100-pound Virginia Davis, accused of beating to death a fifty-year-old man.*

DOUGLAS BUCHANAN
(Murderer)

"Get the ride started. I'm ready to go." *1998: Last words of Buchanan, executed for four murders in Virginia.*

GARRY BURRIS
(Convicted Murderer)

"Beam me up." *1997: The last words of the forty-year-old convicted killer, before being executed by injection in Michigan City, IN.*

JOEY BUTTAFUOCO
(Celebrity Adulterer & Actor)

"You can't talk to anybody. Prostitutes are all over the street. You walk by them, you're bagged." *1995: On his arrest for soliciting an undercover Los Angeles policewoman outside a convenience store.*

"This is a forum for anybody who has been jammed up by law enforcement . . . abused by the media, and who has been chewed up and spit out by the system." *1998: On his new talk show on cable television.*

MARY JO BUTTAFUOCO
(Wife of Joey)

"The little bitch got me!" *1992: The last words she said to herself before losing consciousness after being shot by seventeen-year-old Amy Fisher, a high school senior who'd been having an affair with Mary Jo's husband.*

"It could only happen to Joey! My husband is a friendly guy." *1995: Explaining why her notorious husband was arrested for soliciting prostitution in Los Angeles.*

BOB BUTTERWORTH
(Florida Attorney)

"People who wish to commit murder, they better not do it in the state of Florida, because we may have a problem with our electric chair." *1997: After a condemned man's black mask burst into flames as he was electrocuted.*

ROGER BYBEE
(Friend of Spies)

"This business of spying for East Germany—and doing it after the Cold War was officially ended! The Japanese soldiers who hid on the Pacific Islands all those years at least had the excuse of not knowing the war was over." *1997: Bybee was a college friend of Kurt Stand, who along with his wife and a friend, was arrested by the FBI for allegedly spying for East Germany before the Berlin Wall fell and trying to engage in espionage afterward.*

C

ROBERT CAHILL
(Judge)

"I seriously wonder how many men married five, four years would have the strength to walk away without inflicting some corporal punishment." *1994: On the eighteen-month prison sentence he gave a Maryland man for killing his wife, whom he found in bed with another man.*

MICHAEL CARNEAL
(Murderer)

"I guess it was because they ignored me. I had guns, I brought them to school, I showed them to them, and they were still ignoring me." *1998: Explaining to a psychiatrist why he shot eight classmates at Heath High School in Paducah, KY.*

ROBERT ANTHONY CARTER
(Murderer)

"Thank you for caring so much about me." *1998: Last words of Carter, executed for a murder at a gas station in Texas.*

ROSALIND CARTWRIGHT
(Psychologist)

"If we got charged with everything we dreamed about, we'd be in jail for most of our lives." *1995: The Chicago psychologist on allowing dreams as evidence in the O. J. Simpson murder trial.*

JAMES CASEY
(Deputy District Attorney)

"Sexual arousal or gratification can run a gamut of methods . . . so for counsel to hang his hat, if you will, on an erection is simply misleading and is a red herring." *1995: The Sonoma County [CA] deputy district attorney attacking the argument of an attorney defending a client against a lewd conduct charge.*

ROBERT CASSAR
(Leader of New York City Union of Parking Ticket Writers)

"I guess that shows that my guys do their job." *1997: On his car being towed because of $5,000 in unpaid tickets.*

DICK CAVETT
(TV Talk-show Host)

"If [O. J. Simpson] is acquitted, I will renounce my citizenship. And if I converse with him at a cocktail party, I will say, 'Well, there are so many people here who haven't murdered anyone, I think I'll go talk to them.' I'll also riot." *1995*

ROBERT CENTORINO
(Chief Prosecutor, Dade County, FL, State's Attorney Office)

"He has a much better voting record than a lot of living people." *1998: On rampant election fraud that produces such novelties as the late Manuel Yip of Miami, who voted six times, including three times in person, since his demise.*

MARK DAVID CHAPMAN
(Murderer)

"Please understand, Yoko, I wasn't killing a real person. I killed an image. I killed an album cover." *1992: The murderer of ex-Beatle John Lennon in 1980, on how he would explain his deed to Lennon's widow today.*

MATT CHRISTENSEN
(Police Sergeant)

"Bathroom gun safety and gun safety in general pretty much dovetail." *1997: On an eighteen-year-old man who accidentally shot his hand and knee while sitting on the toilet.*

ELSA CIAMPICALI
(Art Museum Docent)

"Robbers have a taste for money. Not for art." *1998: The volunteer docent at the National Gallery of Modern Art in Rome, on the theft of paintings done by Van Gogh and Cezanne, none of which she holds in high regard.*

MARCIA CLARK
(Prosecuting Attorney)

"This is the kind of nonsense that gives lawyers a bad name." *1995: Commenting on F. Lee Bailey's promise to deliver a key witness, Maximo Cordoba, against detective Mark Fuhrman, then failing to deliver on his promise after Cordoba claimed never to have spoken to Bailey.*

"Get a life." *1995: Said with a smile, to courtroom spectators who applauded when she appeared with a new hairdo.*

"What are we supposed to do, show him carrying the football?" *1995: Said after defense attorneys for O. J. Simpson objected to showing jurors a police mug shot of the accused murderer.*

"DNA testing is not only used to solve crimes, it has many other purposes. Some of you [jurors] talked about* Jurassic Park *and [how] they used it to make dinosaurs." *1995: Speaking to the jury in the O. J. Simpson trial.*

"Size small. I guess it's Mr. Bailey's." *1995: Responding to F. Lee Bailey's attempt to introduce a small glove, instead of an extra large one, as a stand-in for the one allegedly used by O. J. Simpson.*

"I'm sorry kiddo. I did everything I could." *1995: Prosecutor Marcia Clark, crying to Kim Goldman after the verdict in the O. J. Simpson trial.*

"Haven't we had enough DNA?" *1995: Said on Saturday, October 7, after the O. J. Simpson trial, when Sam Conti, owner of the Coconut Grove in San Francisco suggested that she and Chris Darden go to the DNA Lounge to listen to some late night blues.*

"Only in their dreams!" *1997: When asked by Barbara Walters if she thought O. J. Simpson's defense attorneys were really a "Dream Team."*

JOHNNY COCHRAN
(Defense Attorney)

"The prosecution was 'hoisted by its own petar' to quote Shakespeare." *1995: Commenting on the bad fit of the gloves recovered from the scene of the murder of Ron Goldman and Nicole Brown Simpson on his client, accused double-murderer, O. J. Simpson.*

"Kato the human being?" *1995: Checking that a reference by Arnelle Simpson to Kato was not a dog, but houseguest Brian [Kato] Kaelin.*

"Some people can't stand the truth." *1995: In his closing argument in defense of O. J. Simpson, stated while looking toward the family of murder victim Ron Goldman.*

"The prosecution is trying to portray Fuhrman as Mr. Hyde but he's really Dr. Jekyll." *1995*

"We chose to call it the credibility card." *1995: O. J. Simpson attorney Johnnie Cochran on suggestions that his client was acquitted because of the race card.*

"[The Mark Fuhrman tapes] are like Lay's potato chips—you can't put them down, and you can't eat just one." *1995: To Judge Lance Ito during the O. J. Simpson trial.*

"You can't tell by somebody's voice whether they sounded black . . . I resent that [as] a racist statement. This statement about whether he sounds black or white is racist and I resent it, and that is why I stood and objected. And I think it is totally improper that in America, at this time in 1995, we have to hear this and endure this." *1995: Insisting that it is impossible to distinguish the voice of a black person from a white person.*

"Don't be part of this continuing cover-up. Do the right thing, remembering that if it doesn't fit, you must acquit." *1995: In his summation to the O. J. Simpson trial jury, speaking of the ill-fitting and bloody glove found at Simpson's home on the morning following the murder of Nicole Brown Simpson and Ronald Goldman.*

"Your honor, I resent that tone. I'm a man just like you are, your honor. I resent that tone, your honor. I resent that tone, your honor." *1995: Cochran, apparently indicating to Judge Ito, that he resented his tone*

"This was a real heckuva trial, believe you me." *1995: Following the O. J. Simpson verdict.*

"The reaction to his [O. J. Simpson's] return doesn't seem very American. This is a country that traditionally takes people back who have fallen from grace. Richard Nixon left office in disgrace and was later welcomed at the White House. Spiro Agnew's bust was put in the Capitol this year. There are a lot of other examples, including Michael Milken. I don't look for sinister motives, but what is the difference between O. J. and others?" *1995: Following the O. J. Simpson verdict.*

"He's got his facts wrong—there was no ski mask." *1997: On rapper Ice-T's musical indictment of O. J*

Simpson and the American justice system in a video featuring images of gloves, gleaming knives, and a ski mask.

"The law is an effective tool for change. That's one reason I became a lawyer. I thought I could help society for the better." *1997*

"If you build a boat, it must float." *1998: Representing passengers of the Titanic at a mock trial held at a convention.*

ETHAN COEN
(Film Producer & Director)
"I could tell you, but then I'd have to kill you." *1996: The producer of the film* Fargo, *when asked where and when the crime that serves as the basis for his film actually occurred.*

MARSHALL COLEMAN
(Political Candidate)
"I used to think O. J. Simpson was a great guy, too." *1994: The independent senatorial candidate in Virginia, on why he saw fit to have Oliver North help him raise money in 1989, but later called North unfit for the Senate.*

CARTER COLLINS
(Wedding Photographer)
"He didn't even get to kiss the bride." *1995: On the arrest of just-married bridegroom Rufus Lawsen, in connection with a robbery.*

COOLIO
(Rapper)
"That's how it is in the inner city. I guess the police just missed me." *1998: After being arrested in Lawndale, CA, on charges of carrying a concealed weapon, possession of marijuana, having an expired driver's license, and driving his Humvee on the wrong side of the street.*

"I have friends who have prescriptions for it." *1998: On why police found marijuana in his truck.*

"I've been out of town. I was in Egypt." *1998: When his driver's license was found to have expired.*

"I go to shoot on Tuesday, so the gun's right here." *1998: When he was found to be carrying a concealed weapon.*

HARLON COPELAND
(Sheriff)

"What he does on his own time is up to him." *1992: The Bexar County (TX) sheriff, on a deputy charged with exposing himself to a child while off-duty.*

KATIE COURIC
(TV Host)

"There is only one word to describe this: *shameless.*" *1995: On the* Today Show, *without irony, after a* Today Show *report on people capitalizing on the O. J. Simpson scandal.*

BRUCE CUTLER
(Attorney for John Gotti)

"You can't walk the streets, you can't jog in Central Park. Let me tell you something: if John Gotti was in Central Park, not only could you jog there, you could live there." *1991*

"Sometimes ya haveta tell some white lies, you know? I mean, to avoid being impolite . . ." *1992*

D

JEFFREY DAHMER
(Serial Murderer)

"You don't forget your first one." *1992: On why he could remember so many details about his first victim, according to the police.*

MIKE DANIELS
(Hunt Club Manager)

"People are blaming what happened on guns. But the Oklahoma bombing was done with fertilizer and a pickup truck. An inanimate object didn't do this." *1998: The manager of the Richmond Hunt Club in McHenry County, on the schoolyard slayings in Jonesboro, AR.*

ALPHONSE D'ARCO
(Lucchese Crime Family Boss)

"Excuse me—which murder are we talking about?" *1992: While testifying in a murder-racketeering trial in which a dozen different "whacks" have been discussed.*

CHRISTOPHER DARDEN
(County Prosecutor)

"They said Marcia was going to ask me to get married, but apparently she got the $4.2 million and forgot all about me." *1995: The O. J. Simpson prosecutor joking about his rumored relationship with fellow attorney Marcia Clark.*

GRANGER DAVIS
(California Bar Patron)

"Because I'm drunk." *1998: Explaining why he was breaking California's new law against smoking in bars.*

RICHARD ALLEN DAVIS
(Convicted Murderer)

"They don't give the family no consideration . . . like the way they got in my face when I was going to court. . . . They're death dogs, man. They don't give a [expletive deleted], they're just looking for, a, you know, hype themselves up a little bit." *1996: On the media.*

MYRA DeCOURCY
(Church Parishioner)

"We have set up a 24-hour watch over the Holy Eucharist, and Satan doesn't like it so he's sending some of his bad people to get it." *1997: DeCourcy is a member of St. Charles Catholic Church in Picayune, MS, where guards were posted to make sure parishioners swallowed communion wafers because of fears that stolen wafers were being used in Satanic rituals.*

HARRY DEITZLER
(Lawyer)

"I hope that this doesn't ruin his career." *1997: On his client, Judge Joseph Troisi, who was charged with biting off a chunk of the nose of a defendant who had appeared in his courtroom southwest of Morgantown, WV.*

THELMA DE LA BECKWITH
(Member of the Southern National Party)

"Mostly real intelligent people are in it." *1990: On the type of person who belongs to their racist Southern National Party.*

JOHN DELANTY
(Chicago Policeman)

"They go down to the lake, they drink, get stupid and get killed." *1997: On the annual summer increase in pedestrians trying to cross Lake Shore Drive and getting hit by cars.*

PAUL DELO
(Correctional Center Superintendent)

"These guys are in here because they didn't think they'd get caught." *1990: Delo heads the Potosi Correctional Center in Missouri.*

MIKE DE NICOLA
(Comedian)

"I was reading crime was down 27 percent—yeah, I wish somebody would tell the muggers in my neighborhood. They're working overtime." *1997*

ALAN DERSHOWITZ
(Attorney & Law Professor)

"Defense lawyers like Bob Shapiro and others ought to be our heroes . . . because these lawyers shake up the system. They are the current-day gladiators. . . . Today Shakespeare would be writing about these lawyers. Because when he said, 'The play is the thing,' today the trial is the thing." *1994: Dershowitz joined Shapiro on the O. J. Simpson defense team.*

"He's probably up in heaven now suing God." *1995: On the death of attorney William Kunstler.*

"Yes, I would defend him. And I would win." *1999: Telling a group of Yale Law School students that, if he had the chance, he would defend Adolf Hitler.*

RAUL DIAZ
(Parapsychologist)

"He was lasered out by a remote-control device. He was zapped, just like that, right out of the twilight zone." *1995: On the alleged CIA plot against Colin Ferguson, who was subsequently found guilty of murdering six people on a commuter train.*

RISA DIMACALL
(NGO Officer)

"If (O. J. Simpson) had discovered a vaccine instead of being a football star, would people have lined up on the freeway to cheer him on? Our values are out of whack." *1995: The president of the board of officers of Las Casa de las Madres in San Francisco, following the O. J. Simpson verdict.*

PAUL DONNER
(Minister)

"I'm firmly convinced that Michael Carneal is a Christian. He's a sinner, yes, but not an atheist." *1997: The minister of the St. Paul Lutheran Church in Paducah, KY, on his parishioner, a fourteen-year-old high school student who shot to death three classmates who were participating in a prayer meeting.*

ROBERT DOWNEY JR.
(Actor)

"It's so cool—using a hair dryer again, good towels—and I can lock the door if I want." *1998: Upon his release from a four-month term in the Los Angeles County Jail for drug abuse.*

JAMES M. DOYLE
(Attorney)

"Most people come to me and say, 'Get me out.' She came to me and said, 'How can I make people understand I'm terribly, terribly sorry for what I did?'" *1998: The lawyer for Katherine Ann Power, who is in prison for her role in a 1970 Boston bank robbery by antiwar radicals in which a police officer was killed, after she stunned the parole board by withdrawing her request and tearfully apologizing to the victim's family.*

DOMINICK DUNNE
(Writer)

"I will never forget Nicole [Brown Simpson] and Ron [Goldman]. The autopsy photographs of their slit throats and open eyes will haunt me forever." *1995: Dunne covered the O. J. Simpson trial for* Vanity Fair *magazine.*

"My feeling is that he will never confess, because he has convinced himself that he did not do it. A close friend of his told me last week that if he took a lie-detector test now, he would pass it. I think there are people who knew the truth from him, in the immediate aftermath of the murders, but not since." *1996: On O. J. Simpson.*

"Never before has there been a national pariah like him. I honestly believe that under this constant rejection, not being allowed in his club, his neighborhood, stores and restaurants, he will eventually crack." *1996: On O. J. Simpson.*

E

MARC ELIOT
(Author)

"I heard Kato's testimony. I realized I was listening to a series of lies and I was shocked." *1995: Eliot, who collaborated with former Simpson houseguest Kato Kaelin on a book manuscript called* Star Witness/My Life with Nicole and O. J. Simpson: The Whole Truth.

F

JAN FAY
(Stepmother of Michael Fay)

"Michael's been through a very tough time in Singapore. And there's been a lot of publicity he's had to deal with." *1994: After police were called to the Fay home in Kettering, OH, to break up a fight between Michael and his father, George Fay. Michael was convicted of vandalism and imprisoned and then caned in Singapore earlier in the year. He said he was forced to confess to a crime he did not commit.*

MICHAEL FAY
(Expatriate Criminal)

"Let's not exaggerate." *1994: Saying that the caning he received for vandalism in Singapore was neither as severe nor as light as press reports had made out.*

MOHAMED AL FAYED
(Businessman)

"If I wasn't in a courtroom, I'd hang them all." *1998: At a court hearing to determine whether the paparazzi who chased Princess Diana and Al Fayed's son Dodi through a Paris tunnel contributed to the fatal car crash.*

RAUL FELDER
(Divorce Attorney)

"Maybe death can't take a holiday, but filing for divorce can." *1997: Felder refuses to file petitions for divorce or separation on Valentine's Day.*

"Mistresses are a direct function of the economy. There is no question about it. I can tell you how the economy is doing by how many mistresses come into my office looking for justice. I don't need no Greenspan." *1998: Pointing out the stock market boom has enabled more successful men to afford an illicit luxury.*

COLIN FERGUSON
(Murderer)

"There is no doubt in my mind. I am very fit for society." *1995: Ferguson murdered six people on a commuter train and made this statement to CNN talk-show host Larry King.*

LARRY FIELD
(Director of Corrections)

"Certainly, there's irony. But we're bound by the law, the same law he violated." *1995: The director of Oklahoma's Corrections Department, describing doctors' revival of convicted killer Robert Brecheen, who had overdosed on sedatives just hours before his execution.*

GLEN FITZERRELL
(Christian Activist)

"Whatever you conjure up in your mind when you hear the word *Christian*, these guys aren't it." *1997: Fitzerrell is the leader of Holy Nation, a weekly meeting of Christian gang members in Oak Park, IL.*

JAMES FLEETWOOD
(Judge)

"I leaned over and stared. I said, 'Surely, nobody would be so stupid as to wear the boots he stole to his trial.'" *1997: The Wichita, KS, judge presided over a trial in which a defendant accused of robbing a shoe store propped his feet, shod in stolen boots, on a courtroom table. He was convicted.*

"We sent him back to jail in his stocking feet." *1997*

MICHAEL FORTIER
(Friend of Murderer)

"If you don't consider what happened in Oklahoma, Tim was a good person." *1997: Testifying about his former Army buddy, Oklahoma City bomber and mass murderer Timothy McVeigh.*

TONY FOX
(Publicist)

"Kato is red hot in our mind. Everybody thinks this guy is an idiot, but he's not. I've heard a lot of people say he's a lot smarter than he makes out to be." *1995: On the future possibilities for stardom for Kato Kaelin.*

AL FRANKEN
(Comedian & Author)

"The only solution I can see is for white people to start committing more crimes." *1999: On highway patrol officers using race as a factor to pull over motorists.*

LAURA FREED
(Cat Owner)

"I hope this doesn't offend you—my cat's name is Nigger." *1991: Upon hearing this, Keovan Thompson—a black man—tried to choke Freed and then grabbed a knife and lunged at her roommate, Suzanne Lissette. Thompson was convicted of battery and placed on two years' probation and ordered to perform 100 hours of community service.*

LOUIS FREEH
(FBI Director)

"I put a quick stop to that—using draconian, lack-of-due-process methods." *1997: On a prank pulled by his young sons in the family home. The others goaded the three-year-old into setting off motion detectors wired to the FBI's Strategic Information Operations Center, which in turn summoned the police.*

MYRTLE FREEMAN
(Sex Shop Owner)

"It's so silly. It's just a little whatnot. Everything I have in here is just for novelty only. If we are going to go to all this trouble, I should at least heat them up. If you want them fried or baked." *1998: Freeman was visited by vice squad officers in Houston and ordered to stop selling edible underwear because her shop, "Condoms & More," does not have a food service license. She refused to pay the $200 food permit fee and stopped selling the underwear.*

SIDNEY FREUND
(School Superintendent)

"I wouldn't describe him as a sophisticated computer user." *1995: The Long Island school superintendent on a sixteen-year-old who e-mailed a bomb threat to his former school without disguising his name.*

PHYLLIS FRYE
(Criminal Attorney)

"Dressing up like a cowboy is a form of drag, isn't it? They feel sexier when they do it. They're acting out their fantasy of themselves. Some do it occasionally, some do it all the time. When you ask them about it, they say they're expressing their personality. It's as fetishistic as any cross-dressing. We call them transvestites." *1995: Frye, a criminal attorney in Houston, is a male transvestite activist, commenting on the cowboy clothing styles of Texans.*

MARK FUHRMAN
(New York City Marketing Executive)

"It's always the same joke, the off-the-cuff kind of stuff, like, 'I hope you're not a racist' and 'I'm not going to leave my gloves lying around when you're in the room!'" *1995: Describing the pitfalls of sharing a name with someone more famous than himself.*

MARK FUHRMAN
(Los Angeles Detective)

"This is what America's all about. It's not politicians and attorneys and celebrity athletes who murder people. These are the people who make the world go around and we ignore them." *1997: The former police officer, in Sandpoint, ID, where 1,000 people lined up to buy signed copies of his book* Murder in Brentwood.

HIROSHI FUJISAKI
(Judge)

"The amount of the award in this case may be considered insufficient rather than expansive when compared to life in prison or death." *1997: Denying O. J. Simpson a new civil trial and upholding a damage award of $33.5 million against Simpson for the deaths of his ex-wife and her friend.*

G

DANIEL F. GAETA
(Rapist)

"I'm sure she still likes me." *1994: On the fourteen-year-old girl he first attacked when she was eight, in a plea to the judge who had just sentenced him to twenty-five years in prison.*

GUADALUPE GARCIA
(Mother of Troubled Son)

"I think it was something he watched on television." *1997: Garcia, of McAllen, TX, on why her teenage son used a bomb threat to try to extort $10 million from police.*

WAYNE GARNER
(Chief of Prisons)

"We have 60 to 65 percent of our inmate population that truly want to do better . . . but there's another 30 to 35 percent that ain't fit to kill and I'm going to be there to accommodate them. My goal is for the prison experience not to be a pleasant one." *1996: Georgia's new chief of prisons, announcing that all inmates will perform daily chores even if it means digging unneeded ditches.*

JOHNNY FRANK GARRETT
(Murderer)

"I'd like to thank my family for loving me and taking care of me. And the rest of the world can kiss my ass." *1992: Last words before he was executed in Texas for killing a Catholic nun in 1981.*

BILL GATES
(Microsoft CEO)

"Would I have made sure that the camera work in this thing was decent? Would I have smiled a little bit? Absolutely." *1998: Explaining that he hadn't realized his videotaped deposition would be played in court.*

DARYL GATES
(Los Angeles Police Chief)

"I guess it gets down to one of my concerns about, again, that definition of casual user and what you do with the whole group. The casual user, if there is such a thing as a casual user, ought to be taken out and shot, because he or she has no reason for using drugs, and then we ought to direct our attention to those who really have an addiction problem." *1990: On casual drug users.*

DAVID GERLENTER
(Writer)

"We execute murderers in order to make a communal proclamation: that murder is intolerable. A deliberate murderer embodies evil so terrible that it defies the community. . . .

"Opponents of capital punishment tend to describe it as a surrender to our emotions—to grief, rage, fear, blood lust. For most supporters of the death penalty, this is exactly false. Even when we resolve in principle to go ahead, we have to steel ourselves. Many of us would find it hard to kill a dog, much less a man. Endorsing capital punishment means not that we yield to our emotions but that we overcome them. [Immanuel Kant, the great advocate of the death penalty precisely on moral grounds, makes this point in his reply to the anti-capital-punishment reformer Cesare Beccaria—accusing Beccaria of being 'moved by sympathetic sentimentality and an affectation of humanitarianism.'] If we favor executing murderers it is not because we want to but because, however much we do *not* want to, we consider ourselves obliged to." *1998*

WILLIAM GINSBURG
(Attorney for Monica Lewinsky)

"A number of people have said that based on my appearances on TV, I should become a TV commentator. And I have laughed. That is not my goal. But I would be happy to take over for Peter Jennings, if that opening ever occurs." *1998*

"Right now, all I see is a continuing dripping torture, as Dr. Lewinsky (Monica's father) puts it." *1998: On the seemingly stalled Kenneth Starr investigation of President Clinton.*

"You [the media] have your job to do, and I have mine—and working with you is part of my job. If you don't feed the bear, it will eat you. If you feed the bear, it won't eat you—it might even treat you reasonably. And if you overfeed the bear it comes back and defecates right where you live." *1998: On dealing with the media.*

BERNARD GOETZ
(Gunman)

"If I hadn't turned myself in, it would have been gone a long time ago. It would have been just one more messed up weekend in New York. There's a lot to be said for walking away." *1995: Goetz, forty-eight, who shot and wounded four young black men on a No. 2 train in New York City on December 22, 1984, commenting on his continued legal problems over the case.*

GOLDEN ACRES APARTMENT RESIDENT
(No Name Given)

"I don't remember exactly what all took place." *1991: The eighty-two-year-old resident of the Golden Acres apartments in Soldier's Grove, WI, testifying about prostitutes who turned up regularly at the apartment complex on the days when Social Security checks arrived. The memory of the elderly patrons about what the women did for money was somewhat fuzzy.*

FRED GOLDMAN
(Father of Murder Victim Ron Goldman)
"Murderer!" *1995: Shouted at O. J. Simpson as Goldman left the courthouse following the Simpson not-guilty verdict.*

RON GOLDMAN
(Murder Victim)
"If O. J. caught me with her, he'd probably kill me." *1995: In response to a question from a Brentwood, CA, clothier, Barry Zeldes, who asked on June 10, 1994, if Goldman was sleeping with Nicole Brown Simpson. Goldman and Simpson were murdered two days later outside her Brentwood townhouse.*

RICHARD GOLUB
(Attorney)
"The most important thing [when preparing for a divorce case] is to discover the other guy's assets. You have to find out how much there is and how to get it." *1999: The New York trial lawyer revealing the ethical code of divorce lawyering.*

AARON GORDON
(Manager)
"His whole life revolves around his dick. He loves Frankenpenis." *1995: Gordon manages the career of John Wayne Bobbitt.*

ARMAND GORDON
(Detective)
"He was having a bad day." *1997: The San Francisco detective commenting on a cook who shot to death a waitress after she berated him for cooking poached eggs, which weren't on the menu.*

MORGAN GORRONO
(Bar Manager)
"I was trying to be sensitive to the needs of my customers. My main complaint from customers is there are too many straight people here." *1997: Gorrono, manager of a gay bar in San Francisco violated a city anti-discrimination law when he ejected a heterosexual couple for kissing, though the bar allows kissing by gays.*

JOHN GOTTI
(Reputed Mafia Don)
"I gave youse $300,000 in one year. Youse didn't defend me. . . . You're plucking me. I'm paying for it. Where does it end? Gambino crime family? This is the Shargel, Cutler and who-do-you-call-it crime family." *1991: Speaking during a bugged conversation about the work of his defense team, Gerald Shargel, Bruce Cutler, and John Pollok.*

RUSSELL GRAHAM
(Sheriff)
"I'm looking for a guy with a beach ball on his head." *1997: Graham of the Lee County, FL, sheriff's office, on a bank robber whose mask was an inflatable ball cut with eyeholes.*

THOMAS J. GRASSO
(Murderer)
"I did not get my Spaghetti-O's. I got spaghetti. I want the press to know this." *1995: The convicted killer who was executed in Oklahoma, on his last meal's falling short of his expectations.*

DOUG GUNNELS
(State Representative)
"Call Michael Fay and ask him if he'd go over there and do that again and I bet he'd say no." *1995: The Tennessee state representative, on the efficacy of Singapore's corporal punishment laws. At least nine American states considered similar punishments, and Gunnels has sponsored such a bill in Tennessee.*

H

GREG HADLEY
(Businessman)
"Now I feel I'm at home." *1995: Hadley, who moved to Hong Kong from Chicago, expressing how he felt after robbers shot four people during a daytime jewelry heist in the colony's Central District.*

H. ELLIOT HALES
(Attorney)
"If all lawyers acted as well and as competently in proceedings as he did, we would have a great bar." *1998: The New York attorney on Paul C. Kurtz, who was arrested for impersonating a lawyer. Kurtz has allegedly fooled judges while representing as many as 100 clients.*

LLOYD WAYNE HAMPTON
(Murderer)

"It's one of the few times in my life I ever got what I wanted." *1990: Said after an Illinois court sentenced him to death.*

BOBBY HARRIS
(Murderer)

"If it does come down to dying, then I'll just have to die." *1990: Harris, a convicted murderer, is on California's death row.*

STEVE HARTNESS
(Private Investigator)

"All I can figure is, it was so intoxicating to them, they went insane." *1999: On thieves in North Carolina who stole $17 million but gave themselves away with big spending.*

PATTY HEARST
(Heiress & Former Client of F. Lee Bailey)

"When he sees a camera, normally he would just go right to it like crows to a shiny object or something." *1996: On watching lawyer F. Lee Bailey push reporters away on his way to jail for contempt of court.*

CHARLTON HESTON
(Actor)

"If there had been even one armed guard in the school, he could have saved a lot of lives and perhaps ended the whole thing instantly." *1999: The NRA president the day after the high school killings in Littleton, CO. Later reports indicated there was an armed guard at the school.*

JIM HEYWORTH
(TV Executive)

"We've had preliminary consumer surveys, and our audience feels it's not appropriate to pay to hear O. J.'s story." *1995: The president of Viewer's Choice, which claims to serve 60 percent of the 25 million American homes wired to receive pay-per-view.*

HENRY HILL
(Mobster)

"I don't have to worry about a call at 3 in the morning—someone saying, 'Meet me at the bar and bring a shovel!'" *1990: Hill, the man whose life the movie* Goodfellas *was based on, describing life in a federal witness-protection program.*

ABE HIRSCHFIELD
(Real Estate Mogul)

"I never hired nobody to kill him." *1998: After being charged with hiring a hit man to kill a longtime business partner.*

DARNAY HOFFMAN
(Attorney)

"He's a nerd, a geek, a peckerwood, a cracker." *1996: Bernhard Goetz' attorney, who said his client has a lot of faults, but that racism isn't one of them. A jury awarded $43 million in damages to one of four black youths shot by Goetz, the so-called subway gunman.*

DAVID HOIG
(Sheriff)

"He told us he was a genius!" *1995: The Alameda County (CA) sheriff's lieutenant commenting on the capture of kidnapper Joseph Guzman of Citrus Heights. Guzman kidnapped his former girlfriend. Police were able to secure his pager number and telephoned him. When Guzman answered, police traced the number and captured him a short time later.*

JEFFREY HOWORTH
(Murderer)

"I told you I would do it and I want a movie to be made for me after I kill everyone." *1995: Howorth, sixteen, of Macungie, PA, in a note he left in his room after murdering his parents and fleeing. He was captured later in Missouri.*

DONALD HUDSON
(Judge)

"It would certainly bring plea bargaining to a new and morbid level." *1997: The Kane County (IL) judge rejecting a request from a man charged with sexually assaulting a ten-year-old girl that he be granted a lighter sentence in exchange for being castrated.*

JOHN HURLEY
(Prison Warden)

"Believe me, we don't send out invitations to this place. They earn the right to be here." *1998: The warden of the new Supermax federal prison in Florence, CO, the country's most secure facility, which houses inmates considered unusually dangerous, including Unabomber Theodore Kaczynski.*

TERRY HUTMACHER
(Detective)

"It's still open to conjecture. It demands money and says he has a gun, but we have to spend some more time with it today." *1998: The Pearl River, NY, detective still trying to decipher a note handed by a would-be bandit to a bank teller. The note was unreadable and the teller consulted a colleague to help her read it. They finally figured out that part of the message was "I've got a gun." The would-be robber who had a bag over his head left while tellers were still trying to read his note. Police never found the robber nor could they decipher his note.*

I

ADAM ISMAIL
(Real Estate Owner)

"We inherited the planet from our ancestors 3,000 years ago." *1997: Ismail, Mustafa Khalil, and Abdullah al-Umari, three Yemeni men, in a lawsuit they filed against NASA for trespassing on Mars.*

LANCE ITO
(Judge)

"I would like to finish this case sometime this life-time." *1995: On the O. J. Simpson murder trial, as it entered its sixth month.*

"I'll see you all later." *1995: Closing the trial of the century with a polite goodbye.*

J

DR. CECIL JACOBSON
(Fertility Specialist)

"I knew my semen was safe because I haven't slept with anyone but my wife in our 30 years of marriage." *1992: Jacobson, who ran a clinic in Vienna, VA, was accused of using his own sperm to fertilize his patients and fathered as many as seventy-five children. Dr. Jacobson's patients apparently thought they were getting specially treated doses of their husband's sperm.*

ANTHONY JASENSKI
(Rotterdam, N.Y., Police Chief)

"I think putting the name of a funeral home on a paramedic vehicle would be distasteful, or the name of a massage parlor or a bar would be a conflict of interest." *1998: Jasenski, says there are limits on his offer to put advertisements on police cars to raise funds for equipment.*

TONY JENKYN-JONES
(Hong Kong Barrister)

"Love is a complex matter." *1998: Defending a man accused of procuring sex from his ex-girlfriend— by threatening to fax nude photographs of her to her workplace. The girlfriend reported him to police, but later wrote to the judge pleading for mercy for him.*

PETER JENNINGS
(TV News Anchor)

"I think you mean to refer to Marcus Allen, not Marcus Garvey." *1995: Correcting Cynthia McFadden during ABC's coverage of the O. J. Simpson trial.*

SUSAN JOHN
(Legislator)

"This will give me additional insights into the problem of drinking and driving." *1997: John, a New York lawmaker and sponsor of a "zero tolerance" bill for teen drivers, on pleading guilty to driving while impaired.*

CLARK JOHNSON
(Actor)

"If he's convicted, the judge should drop the theft charge and send him away for being stupid." *1996: Johnson, who plays a detective on television, on the theft suspect who stumbled onto the set of the TV show* Homicide *and surrendered to actors.*

JEFFREY JOHNSON
(Robber)

"Why are you talking about some witness, man? There was only me and her in the store." *1990: Johnson, suspect in a gas station robbery, representing himself at his trial and cross-examining a detective.*

LARRY JOHNSON
(Detective)

"We just put out third-hand information. We put it out for only one reason: We didn't want to sit on anything." *1990: Johnson is a member of the Knox County Sheriff's Department, TN.*

MIKE JOHNSON
(U.S. Border Patrol Pilot)

"I noticed he had white makeup on his face, a blue nose and a rainbow-colored wig." *1997: On an illegal border-crosser who evidently wanted to be seen and returned to Honduras.*

STEPHEN JONES
(Attorney)

"He's the same as any lawyer or news reporter." *1995: The lawyer for Oklahoma City bomber Timothy McVeigh, explaining why he would not pursue a mental-incompetence defense for his client.*

ROBERT JORDAN
(Police Applicant)

"What kind of a message does this send to children? Study hard, but not too hard?" *1997: Jordan was turned down for a job with New London, CN, because he scored too high on the written examination for the police department. He filed a federal lawsuit against the department alleging discrimination.*

K

KATO KAELIN
(House Guest)

"I've always had the same goal, to be in the entertainment field. I was never premed." *1995*

"I've tried very had to get a life after the trial. I hope that now everyone will, too." *1995*

"That's OK. I lived with a black guy." *1995: To a blonde who told him she preferred darker men than Kaelin.*

"I don't know how someone could sit and go, 'All right, the guy got popular because there was a murder' . . . I wasn't the only witness. There's been over, what? Like 300 witnesses already . . . It's this, for lack of a better word, destiny. . . . I always knew in my heart that something was going to be out there just for the world to notice me." *1995*

"Geez . . . I got a job." *1995: When he became the host of a two-hour afternoon talk show on KLSX-FM in Los Angeles.*

"I'm reading *The Tempest*. Somebody gave me a volume of the works of William Shakespeare, and this is the first play in the book. I'm trying to understand it. No, make that, 'I hath tried to understand it, speaketh yon Kato!' It's hard for me. It's difficult reading. But I'm gonna get it down. I hath tried to understand it." *1995: Announcing that his current reading material includes Shakespeare.*

"I know [the press] likes to rip into me. I don't worry about it. Whatever's happening is just coming from a higher source. I don't want to get all religious on you but . . . I mean, God. I believe very, very much in God. That's my life." *1995*

"People ask me if I'm sick of the attention. It's an honor." *1995*

THEODORE KACZYNSKI
(Unabomber)

"My occupation, I suppose, now is jail inmate." *Unabomber Kaczynski, responding matter-of-factly to a court question regarding his current profession.*

JAMES KALLSTROM
(FBI)

"I guess if you're a school kid, you could say that looks like a missile—or a cigar, or a pencil." *1997: Ridiculing conspiracy theorists' assertions that radar tapes show a missile streaking toward TWA Flight 800 moments before it exploded.*

LAUWRENCE KALUZNY
(Cross-dressing Bandit)

"I found out what pressure can do to a person. I never intended to hurt anyone. That's why I never used a real gun." *1998: Kaluzny lost his job as a security guard and turned to robbing banks while in drag. He was dubbed the "lipstick bandit" by police. He said he turned to crime because he was too ashamed to tell his wife he'd lost his job.*

ROBERT KARDASHIAN
(Attorney & Friend of O. J. Simpson)

"That's right. I was going to do it [plead guilty as an accessory to murder with O. J. Simpson]. I was going to plead with him." *1995: Kardashian, O. J. defense attorney and friend, on how strongly the prosecution implied he had been involved in disposing of O. J.'s bloody clothing after the double murders of Nicole Brown Simpson and Ronald Goldman.*

JOHN KAYE
(Public Prosecutor)

"You can't rush to judgment. There are some shocking things that happened here, but there may be a plausible explanation. At this point I can't think of one." *1997: The Monmouth County (NJ) prosecutor on a nineteen-year-old girl who gave birth at her high school prom and left the infant in a garbage can, where he was found dead. The girl then returned to the dance floor.*

PETER KEANE
(TV Attorney)

"I don't have long blond hair." *1995: Keane, an attorney who found a new career as an expert commentator on the O. J. Simpson trial, when a radio caller asked him, "You're profiting from the O. J. trial too—what makes you different from Kato Kaelin?"*

LISA KEMLER
(Attorney)

"A life is more valuable than a penis." *1995: Defending Lorena Bobbitt in a court address.*

R. GIL KERLIKOWSKE
(Police Commissioner)

"If it helps to calm the prisoners, that's fine with me. And if it shames them, that's OK, too." *1997: The Buffalo, NY, police commissioner after the department painted its cells pink because a study showed it would reduce aggressiveness among prisoners.*

BRENDA KERRIGAN
(Mother of Ice Skater Nancy)

"He's probably like most criminals. He's sorry because he got caught." *1995: On Jeff Gillooly's apology to Nancy for plotting to knock her out of the 1994 Winter Olympics.*

CASEY KING
(High School Student)

"He apologized, said he was sorry and was not shooting anybody in particular." *1997: King, a freshman in Pearl, MS, said fellow student Luke Woodham talked to one of the students hit when he began shooting people with a rifle, killing his former girlfriend and another student and wounding five others.*

LARRY KING
(TV & Radio Talk-show Host)

"If we had God booked and O. J. was available, we'd move God. There's nobody who wouldn't take a figure of this magnitude." *1995: On whether he would like an interview with O. J. Simpson. King was wrong. CNN, HBO, Request Television, Showtime's Event Television, and Viewer's Choice did not express interest in participating in an O. J. Simpson interview. NBC's* Dateline *did.*

"If O. J. Simpson had called the police and said, 'I lost it. I killed her. I'm sorry,' he'd have been out in five and had a show in eight. This country will forgive anything." *1997: On the willingness of Americans to give wrongdoers a second chance.*

RODNEY KING
(Beating Victim & Accused Spouse Abuser)

"I feel good and I'm going to Disneyland." *1996: King, thirty-one, after being acquitted of spousal abuse, reckless driving, and assault with a deadly weapon—a car—but convicted of hit-and-run driving for running over his estranged wife. He faced a year in jail and fines.*

STEVE KING
(High School Student)

"[He] was voted most likely to start World War III." *1998: The Thurston High School student describing fifteen-year-old Kipland P. Kinkel, who was charged with killing his parents in their home and fatally shooting two students after opening fire in his Springfield, OR, school cafeteria.*

JOYCE KITHIRA
(Deputy Principal of a Boarding School)

"The boys never meant any harm against the girls. They just wanted to rape." *1991: Kithira, deputy principal of St. Kizito's boarding school in Kenya, where seventy-one girls were raped and nineteen others died when a group of boys raided the girls' dormitory.*

JOEL KLEIN
(Attorney)

"Anytime you get tired of being a Jewish Yankee lawyer, you can come down here and be a Southern Baptist preacher." *1998: The head of antitrust in the*

JOEL KLEIN (CONT'D)

Justice Department, recalling a local man's response after he gave an impassioned closing argument before a Texas jury.

SUGE KNIGHT
(Head of Death Row Records & Prison Inmate)

"I want to know one thing—what killed Princess Diana, hard-core rap or liquor? Ask them that." *1998: On Seagram Co.'s decision to sever ties between its Interscope label and Death Row after he was sent to prison.*

ROBERT KOHL
(Attorney)

"In more than twenty years of practice, this was the first time an opponent in a divorce proceeding threatened Mr. Clair with physical harm following a conference with a judge." *1998: Referring to an incident in which New York attorney Bernard Clair was arrested for allegedly punching out a client's soon-to-be-ex, after the man began to throw a crumpled piece of paper at his wife outside the courtroom. Kohl said that Clair was only defending his client and himself.*

KUAN HSUI-CHIN
(Prostitute)

"They say we have no dignity. We don't steal. We don't cheat. What is undignified about that?" *1998: The licensed prostitute at the Buds of Grace brothel in Taipei, on the move by the city's mayor to shut down its eighteen legal brothels.*

WILLIAM KUNSTLER
(Attorney)

"Everyone's got an opinion [on the O. J. Simpson trial], as if all of this shit matters. They're legitimizing the legal profession, which is illegitimate." *1995*

L

ANGELA LAM
(High School Student)

"The coach gave us the answer key last year. He told us: everybody cheats, that's the way the world works and we were fools to just play by the rules." *1995: Lam, an eighteen-year-old captain of the Steinmetz High School Academic Decathlon team in Chicago, on the success of the team's coach, Jerry Plecki. Plecki's team finished second in Chicago in 1994 and first in 1995. Plecki resigned from teaching following Lam's revelation.*

BILL LANDRY
(Police Chief)

"He ordered a hamburger with no onions, and when he got his hamburger, it had onions on it." *1997: On why state official Carl Berthelot reportedly punched a Burger King manager.*

TOMMY LASORDA
(Baseball Manager)

"Freedom of speech is when you talk." *1998: Explaining to a congressional committee why the First Amendment should not protect flag burning.*

EARL LATHAM
(Prison Escapee)

"My name's not Earl Latham. It's Earl Smith." *1990: Latham escaped from the Maryland House of Correction and went to his mother's house. He told police his name was Earl Smith when they arrived at his mother's house. The police asked him to spell his last name and he couldn't. They took him into custody.*

TOBARIOS LAWSON
(Murderer)

"I want that dude, Cochran." *1995: The eighteen-year-old murder suspect, following the O. J. Simpson verdict.*

JAY LENO
(TV Talk-show Host)

"You can tell O. J.'s getting a little impatient; he keeps saying to Johnnie Cochran, 'Am I innocent yet?'" *1995*

"He kept talking and talking. I guess the director was scared to yell 'Cut!'" *1995: On O. J. Simpson's video telling his side of the story.*

"O. J. could be good marriage material: He's rich, he's famous, and he's learned the importance of picking up his socks." *1995*

"See, the new defense strategy is they are not murderers, they are just really bad shots." *1995: On Erik Menendez saying that he was suicidal and really meant to kill himself instead of his parents.*

"And there are reports that O. J. Simpson is out looking for work but he is finding it tough going. Nobody wants to hire him. I don't understand why, look at the guy, he's got a killer resume! I can't understand . . ." *1996*

"That certainly has worked well at 7-Eleven, hasn't it?" *1996: On Bill Gates predicting that future street lights will be equipped with security cameras to prevent crime.*

STEVEN LERMAN
(Attorney)
"The time of Mr. King's birthday party was spent discussing his cake—discussing his case." *1994: Lerman is one of a large group of attorneys who filed briefs in a Los Angeles court seeking $4.4 million in fees covering 13,000 hours of work for Rodney King. King was awarded $3.8 million in compensatory damages for a beating he received from a group of Los Angeles police officers. When a judge asked why Lerman sought payment for time spent at King's birthday party, as Lerman had requested, Lerman gave this reply.*

"To get out there and say that King was not some pervert took a lot of technique and craft." *1994: Lerman, Rodney King's first lawyer, was part of a group of some twenty-three lawyers asking for $4.4 million in legal fees to be paid by the city of Los Angeles, for 13,000 hours of work. The bill was $600,000 more than the $3.8 million King received in his judgement against the city.*

"Hey, I wasn't inventing the wheel here. All I am asking for is a day's wage for a day's work." *1994: Lerman requesting that the city of Los Angeles compensate him. Included in the bill presented by Mr. Lerman and the others for "a day's wage for a day's work" was $650 to attend King's birthday party, $1,300 to accompany King to the premiere of the film* Malcolm X, *$1,625 to appear with King at a theater production entitled* Mama, Why is L.A. Burning?, *and $975 to attend a meeting with two professors at the University of California at Irvine for King's "cultural enhancement" and "education."*

MARY KAY LETOURNEAU
(Child Molester)
"That's one of the ways he proposed to me. He said, 'I know we were together before this life and we had about 10 children.' And I felt that, too—we had at least that many." *1998: Letourneau, thirty-six, was sentenced to seven and a half years in prison for having sex with a thirteen-year-old boy who she says fathered her children in a previous life.*

DAVID LETTERMAN
(TV Talk-show Host)
"Less than 24 hours from right now, the O. J. Simpson trial officially begins, and there has been dissension among the defense team. You wonder if O. J. isn't saying to himself just about now, 'Maybe I should have called Jacoby & Meyers.'" *1995*

"Another setback today for Johnnie Cochran—O. J. told Cochran his arthritis is so bad he can't sign his check." *1995*

"O. J.'s hunt for the real killers continues. This weekend it will lead him to three days and four nights at Rancho Mirage Country Club in Palm Springs." *1995*

"The New York City drug dealers are offering the holiday crack gift pack: With a purchase of three vials, they toss in a New York Yankees cap." *1995*

"O. J. has been getting ready for his big trip to London. For the last couple of days, he's been going around the house practicing his British accent, saying things like, 'I can't find my bloody socks.'" *1996*

"Police have arrested the man who was pictured throwing snowballs at Giants Stadium. If convicted, he [may] face six months in jail and a $1,000 fine. If it turns out he was under the influence of alcohol or drugs, he'll be signed by the Yankees." *1996*

"F. Lee Bailey, as you know—why is it funny that this guy's in prison? Kind of entertaining that this guy's in jail! He's in prison serving a six-month sentence for contempt of court. He started, I guess, a couple of days ago. I thought this was kind of cute. Today, in the metal shop, they let F. Lee Bailey make his own vanity license plate. That's kind of cute—'SHYSTER 1.'" *1996*

"Speaking of attorneys, in an upcoming interview with Barbara Walters, former O. J. Simpson prosecutor,

DAVID LETTERMAN (CONT'D)

Chris Darden confirms the fact that he and Marcia Clark, co-prosecutor Marcia Clark, had an affair during the trial. Chris Darden had an affair with Marcia Clark. And I said, 'Congratulations, Chris, nice going. Too bad you didn't spend a little more time trying to nail O. J.!' " *1996*

"Victoria Gotti, the daughter of John Gotti and quite an author in her own right, has just published a new cookbook. Have you heard about it? I was thumbing through it earlier today. One of the recipes—something called 'Chicken Gotti.' Here's how it's prepared: the chicken is bound and gagged and then served tossed from a speeding car." *1997*

"On *Prime Time Live* Diane Sawyer reported on her two-day prison stay. She was locked up for 48 hours and now she's back on the street. You know, like real criminals." *1996*

"John Gotti's son-in-law has been arrested and accused of beating a guy with a telephone. . . . I believe the last words he uttered before the beating were, 'It's for you.' " *1997*

"O. J. Simpson now has been denied a second trial . . . It's not all bad news for O. J. Simpson, though. The judge told O. J., he said, 'Look, O. J., if you really want a second trial, all you have to do is go out and kill two more people.' " *1997*

"Apparently, O. J. Simpson is taking correspondence courses to become a lawyer. I think that's a great idea. He's going to save so much money on his next murder. . . . O. J. is a very complex man. First, he's going to find the real killers, then he's going to defend them." *1998*

RAYMOND LUC LEVASSEUR
(Prison Inmate)

"Lock yourself in your bathroom for the next four years and tell me how it affects your mind." *1998: Levasseur is serving forty-five years in the new federal supermaximum security prison in Florence, CO, where three-quarters of the inmates are locked alone in small cells for at least twenty-two hours a day, on the psychological toll it takes.*

DONA LINDER
(Neighbor of Terry Nichols)

"I thought, 'Oh boy, he's going to have a good lawn.' " *1995: On the quantities of fertilizer she saw her neighbor, Oklahoma City bombing suspect Terry Nichols, spreading two days after the attack. Federal agents believe that fertilizer was used to make the bomb.*

GERARD LIVERNOIS
(Pie Thrower)

"You're insane, your honor." *1999: After a judge sentenced him and two other environmental activists to six months in jail for hitting San Francisco Mayor Willie Brown in the face with pies.*

BOB LONG
(FBI)

"Apparently he's broke now. That's why he's searching for money in strange places." *1997: FBI spokesman Long, after the arrest of Winnetka, IL, commodities trader William Hertzog Thompson, who the FBI said admitted to robbing a bank, a convenience store, a bakery outlet, and three dry cleaners.*

ROBERT LONG JR.
(Attorney)

"We don't know whether it was because he was a highway patrolman or because Chris happens to be black or if this is something they do every now and then." *1998: The lawyer for North Carolina highway patrolman Chris Phillips, who is suing Taco Bell after being served nacho chips that he says an employee spit on; a laboratory analysis confirmed the presence of human saliva.*

M

RICHARD C. MACKE
(Admiral in the U.S. Navy)

"I think it was absolutely stupid. I've said several times, for the price they paid to rent the car, they could have had a girl." *1995: Macke, commander of U.S. forces in the Pacific, commenting on three American servicemen accused of raping a twleve-year-old girl in Okinawa. Macke was forced to take early retirement after the publication of his remark.*

CATHARINE MACKINNON
(Law Professor)

"Feminism stresses the indistinguishability of prostitution, marriage and sexual harassment." *1991*

"Compare victims' reports of rape with women's reports of sex. They look a lot alike. . . . In this light the major distinction between intercourse (normal) and rape (abnormal) is that the normal happens so often that one cannot see anything wrong with it." *1991*

"Taking rape from the realm of 'the sexual,' placing it in the realm of 'the violent,' allows one to be against it without raising any questions about the extent to which the institution of heterosexuality has defined force as a normal part of 'the preliminaries.'" *1992*

ROY MACMILLAN
(Potential Murderer)

"It would probably be to me more justifiable to assassinate the Supreme Court judges." *1995: McMillan, anti-abortion activist and head of the Jackson, MI–based Christian Action Group, when asked if he thought it would be justifiable homicide to execute the president.*

ELIZABETH HERNANDEZ MADDEX
(Robber)

"My mom always said, 'If you want something done right, do it yourself.'" *1997: Maddex, captain of the Rowland High School cheerleading squad, honor student, and teacher's pet, with two others, donned a ski mask and robbed a Bank of America branch in the Orange County (CA) city of Fullerton. They made off with $15,000. Maddex had previously worked as a teller at the bank.*

DONALD MAHLER
(Minister)

"When Jesus was asked about his support for the outcasts of the day, Jesus did not say, 'Let my attorney carefully review the matter before responding.'" *1998: The head of the gay and lesbian ministry at St. Paul the Apostle Church in Manhattan, criticizing Cardinal John O'Connor for what Mahler sees as a* clinical response in opposing a city proposal to give "domestic partners" some of the same rights as spouses.

NORMAN MAILER
(Author)

"The verdict was good for black emotion but terrible for whites. They now feel that black reactions are totally irresponsible. How can you live and work, whites will claim, with people who have no regard for facts, and don't live emotionally in our society, don't understand our feelings? Of course, blacks feel the same way about whites." *1995: On the acquittal of O. J. Simpson.*

DANIELE MALPELI
(New York Bicyclist)

"What planet am I on?" *1998: After New York City Parks Commissioner Henry Stern offered to waive a $1,000 fine issued to Malpeli for chaining his bike to a tree, in exchange for giving the tree a hug and an apology.*

CHARLES MANSON
(Criminal Conspirator & Prison Inmate)

"That's cool. I'm involved in too many things. I have a Web site I'm working on." *1997: Reacting to news that he had been denied parole for the ninth time.*

"Is Charles Manson crazy? Sure, he's crazy, mad as a hatter. You know, a long time ago being crazy meant something. Nowadays, everybody's crazy." *1995: Manson during an ABC News interview with Diane Sawyer, replying to Sawyer's question.*

ERNEST L. MARRACCINI
(Judge)

"You can have coffee and justice at the same time." *1998: The district judge in Elizabeth Township, PA, on temporarily setting up his court in the village cafe because of a fire at his office.*

KICA MATOS
(NAACP Official)

"It takes away from the individuality of the person." *1994: Criticizing the execution of three men in one day in Arkansas.*

NORMAN MAYO
(Concerned U.S. Citizen)

"If tobacco products can be required to have warning labels, why not dairy products? I think milk is

NORMAN MAYO (CONT'D)

just as dangerous as tobacco." *1997: Mayo, sixty-one, who sued the dairy industry for failing to warn consumers of the dangers of drinking milk, which he blames for his clogged arteries and a minor stroke.*

TONY McCARTHY
(Representative of Avon Silversmiths, Ltd.)

"It looks like an ordinary crucifix, but one tug will set it off—and it's loud." *1998: On the company's crucifix with a built-in alarm designed to protect the clergy from violence.*

LISA McCONNELL
(Oklahoma City Resident)

"You know, for a man like Tim McVeigh, who doesn't believe in the government, what a terrible way to be punished, to go through the justice system and see it really works." *1997: On the guilty verdicts against the bomber.*

PAT McKENNA
(Private Investigator)

"He couldn't find a mick in Dublin." *1995: Member of the O. J. Simpson defense team, refuting District Attorney Gil Garcetti's claim that the prosecution had discovered the Mark Fuhrman tapes.*

PAUL McKENNA
(Hypnotist)

"Police are probably looking for a criminal who doesn't smoke, is really slim and sleeps well at night." *1995: McKenna spoke after a thief broke into his car and stole a box of self-help tapes on how to give up smoking, lose weight, and beat insomnia.*

ALEC McNAUGHTON
(Attorney)

"He is the most dishonest person I've ever met, including all the criminals I've defended." *1997: On his former law partner Stephen Jones, who defended Timothy McVeigh.*

TIMOTHY McVEIGH
(Terrorist Bomber)

"Whether you wish to admit it or not, when you approve, morally, of the bombing of foreign targets by the U.S. military, you are approving of acts morally equivalent to the bombing in Oklahoma City." *1998*

MARC MEADOWS
(Mayor of East Lansing, MI)

"That there were that many people involved in a protest, not over human rights, poverty or racism . . . but because they won't be allowed to get drunk on a specific piece of the campus, is pathetic." *1998: After Michigan State students rioted to protest a new ban on drinking at a favorite gathering spot before football games.*

LYLE MENENDEZ
(Murderer)

"One of the things that makes this case difficult is we included my mom." *1995: In a taped conversation with Norma Novelli, author of* The Private Diary of Lyle Menendez.

ALBERT MESTEMAKER
(Judge)

"I believe the bonds of marriage might make an abuser think a little bit more before resorting to physical force. I believe strongly in family values." *1995: The Hamilton County (OH) municipal judge after sentencing a man to nine months' probation on the condition that he marry a girlfriend whom he'd punched in the mouth.*

DOUG MEYER
(Judge)

"I think what he needs—he needs a girlfriend, because if he doesn't, he's going to have bad dreams again. We'll let you arrange a dating service or something." *1995: Criminal Court Judge Meyer of Chattanooga, TN, on his decision to release rape suspect Vincent L. Cousin. Cousin claimed that voices told him to rape women.*

STEPHANIE MILLER
(Comedienne)

"The Menendez brothers don't have anything to worry about since murder is apparently legal in Los Angeles now." *1995: Following the O. J. Simpson trial verdict.*

BOB ANDERSON MITHCAM
(Judge)

"The court finds that this was an unprovoked, senseless killing. . . . We are living in times worse than Sodom and Gomorrah." *1998: The Florida judge confirming a death sentence for convicted killer Lawrence Singleton.*

IVAN MOFFATT
(Screenwriter)
"You can't convict $10 million." *1995: On the O. J. Simpson trial.*

RALPH MONACO
(City Attorney)
"We are looking for bright people, but we're not looking for people that are so bright to an extent that they're not going to be challenged." *1997: The New London, CT, city attorney, on why the local police department does not hire applicants who score "too high" on the entrance examination for the department.*

STEPHEN MONTOYA
(Attorney)
"I don't believe books should be banned, but I don't believe students should be forced to read them. I believe there is a First Amendment right not to read." *1998: Bold legal position taken by the attorney for a woman who wanted* Huckleberry Finn *removed from the required reading list in her daughter's high school.*

COLIN MOORE
(Attorney)
"Whether they agree or disagree with what Mr. Ferguson did, they would like to see that he has proper representation." *1995: Moore, a black Brooklyn lawyer, announcing that he would, at the behest of unnamed members of the black community, represent Colin Ferguson. Ferguson murdered six commuters and wounded seventeen others on the Long Island Railroad on December 7, 1993.*

BRENDA MORAN
(O. J. Simpson Juror)
"In plain English, the glove didn't fit." *1995*

JAMES MORGAN
(Cigarette Company President)
"If they are behaviorally addictive or habit-forming, they are much more like caffeine, or in my case, Gummy Bears. I love Gummy Bears . . . and I want Gummy Bears, and I like Gummy Bears, and I eat Gummy Bears, and I don't like it when I don't eat my Gummy Bears, but I'm certainly not addicted to them." *1997: The Philip Morris president testifying in a deposition, after being asked if cigarette smoking is addictive.*

DENNIS MURPHY
(Senior Deputy District Attorney)
"Every time he's had a difficulty with the court, the court has burned." *1995: On a man accused of setting fire to four courthouses in California to avoid being tried on a burglary charge.*

JOSEPH MURPHY
(Police Officer)
"I've heard of few self-defense cases where someone was shot in the back." *1997: The Chicago Police lieutenant on the defense offered by the lawyer for a man charged with murdering the son of a local alderman.*

N
CURT NAVARRO
(Detective)
"I asked, 'How did you learn this?' He said very quickly, 'I watched the *Jerry Springer Show*.'" *1999: The Hollywood, FL, police detective recounting the explanation a fifteen-year-old boy gave for repeatedly committing incest with his eight-year-old half sister.*

DAVID NELSON
(Manager)
"He's friendly, always smiling, ready to greet our customers. I mean, what kind of person would do this to him?" *1995: Nelson, a Big Boy's manager in Toledo, OH, on the theft of his restaurant's fiberglass Big Boy statue, which was dismembered and scattered around town, along with notes reading Big Boy is dead.*

"The long saga is over. We know who killed Big Boy. We can all rest a little bit easier." *1995: Nelson, after a group of college students confessed that they stole his 300-pound fiberglass restaurant pitchman, dismembered it with a hacksaw and scattered the remains.*

PETER NEUFELD
(Attorney & Dream Team Member)
"O. J. is entitled to enjoy the fruits of his liberty, the way the rest of us are. I think it's unconscionable that people are trying to deny him that." *1995*

INGRID NEWKIRK
(PETA Managing Director)
"Many violent criminals, including Jeffrey Dahmer, start as animal abusers. Feeding inmates bean burritos rather than baby back ribs would break the cycle of cruelty." *1995: Newkirk, managing director of People for the Ethical Treatment of Animals, arguing that vegetarian diets would make prison inmates less prone to violent misbehavior.*

TERRY NICHOLS
(Conspirator)
"I do forgive Lana for all the times she's broken my trust in her and caused me pain and suffering." *1998: Forgiving his ex-wife Lana for their divorce, in a letter to Judge Richard P. Matsch, his sentencing judge, explaining why he believes he should be given a break in the form of a short sentence. Nichols was convicted of conspiring with Timothy McVeigh to bomb the Oklahoma City federal building and killing 168 people, including nineteen children.*

"I know it may sound bold of me to ask this, but I'm thinking of my wife and children, not myself. More good comes from a complete loving family unit than a broken family with separated parents." *1998: In a letter to his sentencing judge, asking for a short sentence so his children won't grow up in a broken home.*

"That's the way I've been all my life. I don't like being the center of attention." *1998: Explaining why he didn't show more emotion than he did when victims and survivors of the Oklahoma City bombing testified at his trial.*

JONATHAN NOBLES
(Murderer)
"Silent night, holy night, all is calm, all is brigh—" *1998: Last words of Nobles, executed in midsong by a lethal injection.*

O
CONAN O'BRIEN
(TV Talk-show Host)
"During a lecture somewhere, Johnnie Cochran said he wants students to know that the law is an effective tool for change. Then he explained how he used the law to change a murderer into a golfer." *1997*

HENRYKA OLBROT
(Wife of Murder Victim)
"The math is extremely difficult. [The suspect] was just unable to do it." *1998: The widow of Andrzej Olbrot, a math professor at Wayne State University in Detroit, who was shot to death by a disgruntled graduate student.*

RONN OWENS
(Radio Talk-show Host)
"If I were, like, on trial for my life, and I could choose only one person in the entire world to confirm my story, yeah, I think I'd choose Rosa Lopez." *1995: Lopez was a housekeeper who testified in a pretrial deposition for O. J. Simpson.*

P
DIEGO PADRO
(Plaintiff)
"No one needs to improve their sex life [so much as] to die for it." *1998: The first Viagra user to sue Pfizer Inc., claiming the anti-impotency drug caused him to have a heart attack.*

GEORGE PALERMO
(Criminal Psychologist)
"Jeffrey Dahmer could best be described as an organized, non-social, lust murderer. He's not such a bad person, even though he did what he did." *1992: To County Circuit Judge Laurence C. Gram Jr., during Dahmer's trial in Milwaukee.*

ANTHONY PELLICANO
(Private Detective)
"If you found out the owner of *X* tabloid was a child molesting, sodomizing, woman-beating, dominatrix-loving fool, who cares? It won't stop the people at supermarket checkout counters from picking up tabloids." *1997: On reports that three unnamed celebrities had hired investigators to dig up dirt on tabloid editors.*

STEPHEN PERISIE
(Murder Plot Victim)
"She tried to be very cheap about this." *1995: Perisie, on his wife's $25 down payment on a $500 contract to kill him for his millions in lottery winnings.*

PAUL PETERSON
(Policeman)

"We appreciate the humor. But we don't appreciate the escape." *1997: Washington's Kent Police Department official, after three men escaped from their cell and left behind a Monopoly 'Get Out of Jail Free' card.*

TOM PETERSON
(Policeman)

"It just assures us that there is justice out there." *1998: The Winston–Salem, NC, officer on charges brought against Sidney Reuben Smith, who was caught when a bank teller recognized Smith's assumed name, date of birth, and Social Security number as those of the bank teller's deceased husband.*

KATHY PEYSER
(Reporter)

"She refused to be sworn in but did offer to play a quick game of Truth or Dare." *1996: On Madonna's court appearance as a material witness against a man accused of stalking her.*

PAUL PHILIP
(FBI)

"He kills people." *1997: The head of the FBI's investigation into Gianni Versace's murder, when asked about Andrew Cunanan's modus operandi.*

PETE PIERCE
(Deputy District Attorney)

"Call me a naive idealist, but I actually think this is an embarrassment to the district, and it's a fairly significant one, being the first congressman to wear a court's ankle bracelet." *1998: Said while running for the congressional seat held by Jay Kim (R-California), who was sentenced to two months' electronic monitoring for accepting illegal campaign contributions but is running for reelection anyway.*

NICHOLAS PILEGGI
(Author)

"These guys are tough. I mean, they were criminals under Stalin." *1996: On mobsters gaining a foothold in Brighton Beach, NY.*

EARL PITTS
(FBI Agent & Spy)

"It was expensive, dirty and a lot of crime, a lot of people, very congested." *1998: The ex-FBI agent jailed for spying, saying he did it because he was assigned to New York City.*

CHARLES PLUMMER
(Sheriff)

"You could also have target practice. That's a diversion. Give 'em guns and let 'em shoot." *1995: Plummer, the Alameda County (CA) sheriff, is a pioneer in the movement to ban weight-lifting equipment in prisons on the grounds that weights create super-cons who pose risks both in jail and later on the streets.*

STEVEN POLLACK
(Attorney)

"Why would he kill the cow that laid the golden egg?" *1991: During his summation in the case of a gambler charged with trying to kill another gambler.*

EDWIN POWELL
(Father of Police Officer)

"Actually, they did him a favor by using batons and not shooting him." *1992: The father of Laurence Powell, who faced a retrial on one count of beating Rodney King in Los Angeles. The elder Powell is a lieutenant in the Los Angeles County marshal's office.*

SISTER HELEN PREJEAN
(Anti-Death Penalty Activist)

"The key reason that the death penalty is not a deterrent is that the people doing the thinking and the people doing the murdering are two separate groups." *1996*

BOBBY PRINGLE
(Murderer)

"Whatever sentence I get won't matter because I lost my mother." *1990: Pringle's "last words" before sentencing in Prince George's County, MD, in July 1990. Pringle was convicted of killing his disabled mother by stabbing her more than seventy times.*

Q

LISA QUIÑONES
(Sister of Murder Victim)

"I heard love, honor. I didn't hear kill in any of that ceremony." *1998: Quiñones is the sister of a bride who was stabbed to death in Port Jervis, NY, allegedly by her new husband, at their wedding reception.*

R

MICHAEL RADELET
(Professor)

"Some people on death row want to embarrass the state and get a lot of publicity, to go out with a bang, so to speak." *1996: The University of Florida professor and death penalty expert, on convicted murderer John Albert Taylor choosing to die by firing squad in Utah.*

DANIEL RAKOWITZE
(Murderer)

"I just want everybody in New York City and the world to be happy and have a smile on their faces. If everybody smoked marijuana, there would be no violence in the world." *1990: Rakowitz murdered his girlfriend and boiled her body parts. He asked a New York judge to impanel a jury of marijuana smokers so he "could get a fair trial."*

NEIL RAMIREZ
(Deadbeat Dad & Santa Claus)

"Women are so evil." *1997: Ramirez was working as a Santa Claus in a Brooklyn shopping mall when his ex-wife served him with court papers accusing him of failing to pay child support for his son.*

ROY RAWERS
(Pricemart Merchandising Director)

"It doesn't matter what the law says. What matters is what the guy behind the desk interprets the law to say." *1997: On doing business in mainland China.*

STEVEN REINHARDT
(Federal District Judge)

"We view with considerable skepticism charges that reading books causes evil conduct." *1998: The judge of the 9th U.S. Circuit Court of Appeals, refusing to reinstate a black woman's lawsuit seeking to remove* Huckleberry Finn *from the required reading list at her daughter's high school in Arizona.*

FAY RESNICK
(Friend of Nicole Brown Simpson)

"Oh, God! Nicole was right. She said he was going to kill her and get away with it." *1995: After the O. J. Simpson trial verdict.*

"Saying I had breast implants is the only truth to come out of Johnnie Cochran's mouth during this entire trial." *1995: On the O. J. Simpson defense attorney's attempts to discredit her testimony.*

"Defense attorneys are great actors. I tell you, Johnnie Cochran deserves an Emmy." *1995*

RHOM ROBB
(KKK Grand Wizard)

"These are just attempts to give the Klan a bad name." *1990*

CHRIS ROCK
(Comedian)

"There were two white boys on the elevator up there. I got real scared." *1999: Rock, who is black, in the wake of the Columbine High School massacre.*

STEVEN ROGERS
(Police Officer)

"I was thinking about pleading not guilty, but I would have had to cross-examine myself in court." *1997: The police officer in Nutley, NJ, on issuing himself a $17 ticket for parking too close to a street corner.*

JOHN ROPER
(Policeman)

"It's not quite as bad as Elvis. At least we know this guy is alive." *1997: The Miami Beach police officer on the rash of alleged sightings of suspected killer Andrew Cunanan from around the country, including in an okra field in Arkansas.*

PHIL ROSENTHAL
(Columnist)

"He's all hair and tight jeans, as flaky as granola, as empty as Orange County's treasury. He has more tics than a stopwatch and . . . he had the look of a toddler in toilet training." *1995: On Kato Kaelin.*

SKADAVY MATH LY ROUN
(Interpol Director)

"My colleagues said, 'Why would any man want to sleep with young boys when we have a lot of young girl prostitutes available?' " *1997: Cambodia's Interpol director on the difficulty of curbing pedophile activities when his own officers don't understand the problem.*

S

JOHN SALVI
(Murderer)

"After [court] proceedings are through, I wish to have an interview with Barbara Walters within the year." *1995: Charged with murder in two shootings at Massachusetts abortion clinics, Salvi made this public statement following his arrest.*

ILICH RAMIREZ SANCHEZ
("Carlos the Jackal")

"My profession is professional revolutionary. The world is my domain." *1997: Identifying himself at the opening of his trial in Paris for killings linked to terrorist activities.*

MELISSA SARENANA
(Neighbor)

"He is dumber than a bag of hammers." *1999: Explaining why she was not surprised after a twenty-year-old neighbor was arrested in Reno, NV, in the killing of thirty-four wild horses for sport.*

SERGIO SARMIENTO
(Journalist)

"Whenever you want to accuse someone in Mexico of being dishonest, you just have to say he was a friend of Salinas and you don't need to say anything else." *1998: The Mexico City columnist and TV news director on the reputation of disgraced former President Carlos Salinas, many of whose relatives and friends have been charged with crimes.*

ANTONIN SCALIA
(Supreme Court Justice)

"Indeed, often I and my colleagues do not like . . . the results that we produce. . . . The system is really garbage in, garbage out." *1998: Commenting on those who criticize court decisions without fully understanding issues or statutes.*

BARRY SCHECK
(Attorney)

"Something is wrong. Something is terribly wrong." *1995: Attorney Barry Scheck in his summation to the jury in the O. J. Simpson case. Scheck was referring to the LAPD crime lab.*

DAVE SCOTT
(Taxi Driver)

"If you're caught in a foreign country with your pants down, that's what you get." *1995: On Michal Fay's return to his hometown after being flogged and spending time in a Singapore jail for vandalism.*

TONY SERRA
(Criminal Attorney)

"I used to say when you represent the criminal defendant, you've got to shoot him up—put him in the test tube and shoot him into your blood. You become him, you feel like him, you walk in his shoes, and you see with his eyes and hear with his ears. You've got to know him completely to know that nature of his behavior. But you have 'the word.' That is, you can translate his feeling, his meaning and his intellect as components that are relevant to his behavior into legalese, into the words of the law, or into persuasive metaphors. You take the clay of the person's behavior and you embellish it, you make it a piece of art. And that is the lawyer's creativity." *1998*

PATRICK SHANAHAN
(Judge)

"You have added new meaning to the word *contemptible*." *1997: The district court judge on sentencing Australian conman Nektario Zafiratos to five years in jail after he paid for his wedding reception with a check stolen from one of his guests.*

GARY SHANDLING
(Actor & Comedian)

"I just got a call from Lorena Bobbitt, who said, 'Even I wouldn't have cut off Frank Sinatra.'" *1995: The host of the 36th Grammy Awards, commenting on the decision by the television network to cut away from a speech by Frank Sinatra to show a commercial.*

"That's the saddest thing I've ever seen in my life." *1995: Commenting in all seriousness on the standing ovation given to Kato Kaelin by part of the audience on Comedy Central's* Politically Incorrect.

ROBERT SHAPIRO
(Attorney)

"The whole point of security is that nobody knows you have it. It's not to flash it around." *1995: Said*

ROBERT SHAPIRO (CONT'D)

with contempt in his voice, expressing his rage at Johnnie Cochran's Nation of Islam guards during the last days of the O. J. Simpson trial.

"I thought I would be leading a team of professionals. I was wrong." *1995: Robert Shapiro, head of O. J. Simpson's legal team, following the verdict of not guilty.*

"It was nothing but race, race, race. And why am I not reading that in the paper? All I hear is how great his summation was. Why do I keep reading this?" *1995: On the summation of his fellow defense attorney Johnny Cochran, at the close of the O. J. Simpson trial.*

"From day one, O. J. told me he was innocent, and I never doubted it. I never asked him to plead anything—other than not guilty." *1995: Speaking in direct contradiction to statements of attorney Robert Kardashian and F. Lee Bailey.*

"Not only did we play the race card, we dealt it from the bottom of the deck." *1995: On courtroom tactics of the Dream Team.*

PAULY SHORE
(Actor & Comedian)

"I am very sad that two innocent people are dead, but (the O. J. Simpson trial) has become a sitcom. Every time you turn it on, it's Judge Ito playing the role of Judge Ito and Kato playing the role of Kato. It's not about these two people. It's about what they're wearing." *1995*

ANDREW SIBEN
(Attorney)

"Katie might not be alive today if he did not help in her recovery. Without Mr. Esposito, this mystery might never have been solved." *1993: Siben, the attorney for John Esposito, who kept Long Island girl Katie Beers chained in a dungeon for two weeks, arguing for reduced bail because Esposito led police to Katie's cell.*

LINCOLN SIELER
(Attorney)

"They want to send a message to fellow cops that they don't have to deal with this." *1997: The lawyer for six Seattle policemen who sued three bank robbers for emotional distress suffered in a gunfight.*

O. J. SIMPSON
(Athlete & Accused Murderer)

"I loved her. Allways have . . . if we had a promblem its because I loved her so much. Recitly we came to the understanding that for now we wern't right for each other at least for now. Dispite our love we were diffearnt and thats why we murturally agreesd to go our spaerate ways. It was tough spitting for a second time." *1995: Simpson's mangled spelling and prose in his suicide note read by Robert Kardashian shortly after O. J. fled Kardashian's home with A. C. Cowlings in Simpson's famous white Ford Bronco. The actual uncorrected note was not published in any United States newspaper until September 1995.*

"If this jury convicts me, maybe I did kill Nicole in a blackout." *1995: To Johnnie Cochran after the jury had been picked for his trial.*

"I ran 2,000 yards in the snow. I can handle Marcia Clark." *1995: Boasting to friends that he was ready to testify at his murder trial.*

"I went with him to the cleaners before they closed, and his stuff wasn't ready. It was the weirdest thing to me. It was Willie Mays and his stuff wasn't ready." *1995: On Willie Mays, whose stuff wasn't ready.*

"I haven't really had a chance to breathe. Yesterday, it was a festive mood at the house. But at the same time, my kids don't have a mother. People don't seem to understand—I loved that woman." *1995: In a telephone interview broadcast by CNN on October 5, 1995, the day after he was acquitted of charges of double murder.*

"I will pursue as my primary goal in life the killer or killers that have slaughtered Nicole and Mr. Goldman." *1995: On Tuesday, October 3, 1995, following his acquittal for double homicide in a note read at a press conference by his son, Jason Simpson.*

"I don't think most of America believes I did it." *1995: O. J. Simpson following his acquittal for double homicide.*

"I've always found a way. I'm an American." *1995: Expressing confidence that he would find a job following his acquittal for double murder.*

"I still have my Ferrari, I still have my Bentley, I still have my home in Brentwood and my apartment in New York." *1995: Following his acquittal for double murder, when asked if his legal bills left him broke.*

"I wouldn't let the LAPD, (DA) Gil Garcetti and these people off the hook. I'd say, 'Hey, there still may be a killer out there. I know there is." *1996: During an interview on Black Entertainment Television cable network.*

"No, I did not commit those murders. I couldn't kill anyone and I don't know of anyone that was involved." *1996: During an interview on Black Entertainment Television cable.*

"I wouldn't characterize this as an argument. We were having a discussion." *1996: In deposition transcripts, commenting on a 1985 incident involving Nicole during which he smashed the windshield of a Mercedes with a baseball bat.*

"The shoes they had in court, that's involved in this case. I would have never owned those ugly-ass shoes. . . . Aesthetically I felt they were ugly." *1996: On Bruno Magli shoes.*

"The dogs were, you know, doing their 'do' around there, and this disgruntled ex-husband was going over there, picking up the dog do." *1996: Explaining why there was a shovel in his bronco in his special two-hour videotape on the Nicole Brown Simpson/Ron Goldman murders.*

"Hell, I figure I'm going to get blamed for everything." *1997: On why he refused to help those on board a twin-engine plane that crashed at Rancho Park Golf Course while he continued to play on the next fairway.*

"I can take people's shots. The Bible says I'm going to get it back seven times. The deeper they get into me, the more I get back down the line." *1997: On his critics.*

"Hey, buddy, can you spare $8.5 million?" *1997: Joking around on the golf course the day after his civil-trial jury found him liable for the deaths of Ron Goldman and Nicole Brown.*

"(Nicole) comes to me from time to time in my dreams, and it's always a positive dream. Occasionally I dream that I single-handedly solve the case." *1997*

"Even if I did do this, it would have been because I loved her very much, right?" *1998: On the murder of his ex-wife, Nicole Brown Simpson.*

"When I read the Bible—from Moses to Jesus to whoever you want to name, Job—they all went through similar things. And that's what the Bible was to me, a map that says, 'Things like this can happen in your life.'" *1998: Claiming that his hypothetical statement that if he'd killed his ex-wife he'd done it "because I loved her very much, right?" was taken completely out of context but that like the biblical Job, he has to bear such injustices.*

"A person is innocent until proven guilty . . . unless it's me." *1998*

"I've got a surprise for you!" *1998: Said just before he lunged at English television host Ruby Wax while holding a banana over his head as if it were a dagger. Wax was not amused.*

"I've heard 'em on those talk shows actually say it: 'A Jewish life has to be avenged.'" *1999: Telling Hard Copy why he thinks the media were interested in covering the murder of Ron Goldman.*

"I said, 'Man, why do you want to screw up your life? Take my car. You don't want to do this.'" *1999: On what he told the man who tried to rob him at gunpoint.*

LISA SLIWA
(Wife of the Founder of the Guardian Angels)
"Absolutely not. You've seen him. Look at him. I mean, he needs to be thrown in front of a couple of open fire hydrants and deloused. There's no way it would be love. It was for the organization." *1990: When asked if she married the Angels' founder Curtis Sliwa "for love."*

RICHARD SPECK
(Mass Murderer)
"If they only knew how much fun I was having in here, they would turn me loose." *1996: On videotape, mocking his imprisonment.*

TROY SPENCER
(Attorney)

"This young woman made contact with a very vulnerable element of our society—police officers—and drew them in." *1998: Explaining why his client, a Virginia cop suspended for exchanging sexy Internet messages with a minor, did what he did.*

HOWARD SPIRA
(Gambler)

"My father really should have worn a condom. He did not deserve Howard Spira as his son." *1991: After being sentenced to two and a half years in prison for attempting to extort money from George Steinbrenner.*

GERALD STANO
(Murderer)

"My attorney and my religious adviser will be passing out my last statement at the completion of the execution." *1998: Last words of Stano, executed for the murder of a hitchhiker in Florida.*

DAREN STAR
(Actress)

"The [Rodney King] riots in L.A. were really terrifying. It just felt like the end of the world. . . . *All the car phones were dead!" 1995*

HENRY STERN
(New York City Parks Commissioner)

"You might call them dog terrorists." *1999: Announcing stiff fines against those who allow their dogs to roam off-leash in the city parks.*

ROBERT STEUER
(Attorney)

"It's a different market." *1996: The Milwaukee lawyer, comparing the auction of Jackie Onassis's possessions with one he was arranging for the belongings of serial killer Jeffrey Dahmer.*

GEORGE STRICKLAND
(County Prosecutor)

"He taught applied economics, which I suppose is appropriate." *1997: The Lake County, IL, prosecutor on a high school teacher charged with exchanging good grades and excused absences to students for gifts and for letting him shoplift at stores where they worked.*

T

BERNARD TAPIE
(Politician)

"I have lied in good faith." *1995: French politician Tapie, speaking after his sworn alibi crumbled in court. Tapie was accused of fixing a match involving the Marseilles soccer club he owned in 1993.*

CLARENCE THOMAS
(Supreme Court Justice)

"I have no problems with Mississippi. You know why I like Mississippi? Because they still sell those little pickaninny dolls down there. And I bought me a few of them, too." *1992*

THOMAS THOMPSON
(Police Officer)

"You're sweating like a nigger." *1995: The Philadelphia police captain to a black officer on August 12, 1995. Thompson—who was reassigned—was a supervisor of a race-relations unit.*

PAUL TIMMENDEQUAS
(Brother of Murderer)

"The way we were raised and the household we grew up in has nothing to do with what he's done. I'm proud they found him guilty. Jersey has, what, lethal injection? Give me the needle." *1997: Timmendequas, whose brother Jesse was convicted of raping and killing seven-year-old Megan Kanka, on his lawyer's plea that the jury spare his life because of his nightmarish childhood, which included violence and sexual abuse by his parents.*

JEFFREY TOOBIN
(Attorney & Author)

"The defense table is like Thanksgiving from hell; they have to sit there with each other, but they can't stand it." *1995: On the team of attorneys defending O. J. Simpson.*

THOMAS TRUAX
(Misguided Paraglider)

"I thought it was a business center." *1997: Truax, a paraglider, landed in a field at a California prison, where he was immediately surrounded by fifteen deputies.*

WALTER TUCKER III
(Mayor, Congressman & Convict)

"Maybe I'll start a prison ministry—there's a lot of people in there who need to be saved." *1995: After his conviction for demanding and accepting bribes while mayor of Compton, CA, in 1991 and 1992.*

LEM TUGGLE
(Murderer)

"Merry Christmas." *1996: Tuggle's final words before being executed by lethal injection for a 1983 murder.*

ISAIAH TURNER
(City Manager)

"I don't want to tick off the animal lovers, but this is two steps short of ridiculous." *1999: The Richmond, CA, city manager after a jury awarded $255,000 to the owner of a dog that was killed by police.*

V

PHILIP VANATTER
(Detective)

"A knife is a very easy thing to dispose of. I have cases where I never found the body, so it's not unusual to not find the weapon." *1995: Explaining why it was not surprising that the O. J. Simpson case murder weapon has never been found.*

JOHN VAN EATON
(Unbiased Citizen)

"There was a colored family that lived here for more than 20 years. No one ever picked on them. We just didn't invite them over for lunch." *1995: The Eatonville, WA, resident explaining how the hometown he shares with Mark Fuhrman is not a racist place.*

ALFREDO VASQUEZ
(Detective)

"They say they didn't know it was a police building." *1996: The Key West, FL, detective commenting on three college students arrested for smoking marijuana after pot fumes wafted into the police station's air-conditioning system.*

WALTER VELTRONI
(Italy's Minister of Culture)

"The security system was adequate, but it did not foresee an armed robbery." *1998: Explaining the theft of two van Goghs and a Cezanne from Rome's National Gallery of Modern Art.*

ROBERT "JESUS BOB" VERNON
(Police Officer)

"Jesus was—as I like to say—a big moose . . . [not] a little twinkie . . . He was a masculine guy." *1991: Vernon, LAPD assistant chief in* The True Masculine Role, *a series of instructional videotapes.*

W

RICHARD WALSH
(Judge)

"If there's a lesson to be learned from this, it's that if you mess with your kids enough, they're going to beat your brains in." *1997: The Cook County, IL, Juvenile Court judge giving probation to a girl who clubbed her father to death with a baseball bat after years of alleged physical abuse.*

CAROL WARD
(Unhappy Taxpayer)

"Honey, from what I can see of your accounting skills, the country would be better served if you were dishing up chicken-fried steak on some interstate in west Texas, with all the clunky jewelry and big hair." *1997: Ward to IRS auditor Paul Dzierzanowksi during a tax audit of Ward.*

DOUG WATTS
(Advertiser)

"We factored the vandalism into their contract." *1995: Watts, of Gannett Outdoor Advertising, on the theft of several pairs of $40 khaki pants affixed to outdoor Levi's ads in New York and San Francisco.*

MARGARET WEITZMAN
(Wife of Celebrity Attorney)

"I never saw so many people in dark glasses and very short black dresses." *1995: The wife of O. J. Simpson's first lawyer, Howard Weitzman, describing Nicole Brown Simpson's funeral.*

BEN WHITE
(Advertising Executive & Poet)

"What'll we watch on the tube all day?
When we go to parties, what'll we say?
I was practically an expert on DNA!

BEN WHITE (CONT'D)

What'll we do without O. J.?" *Poetically lamenting the end of the O. J. Simpson trial.*

JOHN P. WHITLEY
(Former Prison Warden)

"When they start training deer to break into my house, rape my wife, and kill my daughter, then I'll get a gun and go out and shoot one." *1995: The former warden of Angola State Prison in Louisiana, who presided over four executions of inmates in Angola, but has a moral aversion to hunting.*

STEVE WILKOS
(Chicago Policeman & Jerry Springer Show Security Guard)

"Men take a few swings and wait for you to break it up. Women claw, scratch, pull hair and won't stop." *1998: On the raucous behavior of some of the Springer show's guests.*

KELLY WILLIS
(Police Department Spokesperson)

"If someone wants to be arrested by an officer with blue eyes and blond hair, it's not going to happen. We're not a drive-through restaurant." *1998: The Des Moines police department spokesman on Lisha Sue Little's refusal to be arrested by a black police officer after she was charged with several violations.*

RALPH WINTER
(Judge)

"I'm prouder of the title 'knucklehead' than any other one I've ever had." *1993: Winter, a federal judge and former clerk for the late Supreme Court justice Thurgood Marshall, recalling Marshall's pet name for his aides.*

EMIL WISNIEWSKI
(Murderer)

"I didn't want him to suffer because he was making funny noises and gurgling." *1990: Wisniewski, eighteen, of Greenfield, WI, telling police why he shot a gas station attendant a second time, killing him. The gas station attendant, shot twice in the head, lay unnoticed for several hours while customers at the station pumped free gasoline for themselves.*

CHARLES WOODS
(Sheriff)

"They're all going to wear shackles from now on." *1997: The sheriff of Henderson County, TN, after an inmate escaped from his arraignment by joining jurors filing out of the courtroom.*

DORTHA WORD
(Grieving Mother)

"They like that kind of entertainment." *1995: Detroit resident Word, on reports that a crowd watched while her thirty-three-year-old daughter was dragged from her car and beaten before jumping from a bridge to her death.*

Y

EMILIO YANNACONE
(Detective)

"That's probably the dumbest motive I've ever heard." *1997: The Key West, FL, detective, on a killing apparently triggered by two restaurant workers arguing over how to put silverware into a dishwasher.*

"He said the guy was very stubborn and wouldn't answer him." *1992: On a seventy-eight-year-old man who thought his roommate was ignoring him; in fact, the roommate had been dead for two months.*

ELAINE YOUNG
(Real Estate Agent)

"Invariably celebrities involved in some kind of infamous situation can get top dollar for their house." *1995: The real estate agent to the stars, on the cachet of notorious locations such as the Sharon Tate or O. J. Simpson homes.*

RICK YOUNG
(Police Officer)

"We must establish that a crime did in fact occur." *1998: The Glendale, CA, policeman on health-care worker Efren Saldivar's confession that he killed up to fifty terminally ill patients over the past decade.*

Z

PETE ZAFRIS
(Ice Cream Store Owner)

"I said, 'What are they going to steal, the ice cream?'" *1998: The owner of Emack & Bolio's Ice Cream & Yogurt,*

Pete Zafris, on why he hadn't installed a burglar alarm when building his Wilkins Township, PA, ice-cream store. A thief stole seventy-five three-gallon tubs, or $15,000 worth, of ice cream.

JIM ZAMORA
(Police Officer)

"We've had people bite off body parts of other people before, but I've never heard of anyone swallowing the body part." *1995: The Indiana police officer on a man arrested for biting off part of another person's ear during a barroom brawl, then swallowing it.*

JEFF ZUCKER
(TV Producer)

"A lot of legal experts who were using this case as oxygen over the last two years are going to be looking for something else to keep their lungs replenished.' 1997: The executive producer of NBC's* Today Show, *on the many legal commentators who made mini-careers out of O. J. Simpson's two trials.*

INDEX

Entries in **bold** represent people or publications that are quoted in this book.

ABC, 34, 96, 139, 160, 178, 189, 203, 205, 223, 231, 277, 283
abortion, 11, 142, 283
Abrams, Rachel, part II
Abzug, Bella, part II
Academy Award, 28, 63, 70, 117
accordion, 35
Achtenberg, Roberta, part II
Ackerman, Jeff, part II
Ackerman, Val, part III
Ackerman, Will, part I
acting, 26–27, 38, 41, 48, 55, 70, 72, 73, 82, 88, 94, 99, 121, 129, 273
Adams, Scott, part I
Adjani, Isabel, part I
adultery, 115, 120, 182, 186, 190, 191–92, 250
affair, 11, 16, 25, 61, 65, 73, 77, 84, 106, 111, 114, 134, 142, 149, 153, 155, 156, 162–64, 170, 173, 182–84, 186, 190, 194, 205, 208, 211, 267, 282
affirmative action, 141
Affleck, Ben, part I
Africa, 120, 156, 158, 163, 172, 186, 202, 256
Afton, Missouri, 48
Agassi, Andre, part III, 104
Agassi, Emmanuel, part III
Age of Possibility, 179
Age of Transparency, 187
Agnello, Victoria Gotti, part IV
Ahmad, Shannon, part I
Ailes, Roger, part II
Alabama, 198, 250, 252, 266
Alba, Vincente Panama, part IV
Albania, 200
Albright, Madeleine, part II, 65, 129, 163, 176
alcoholic, 89, 122, 260
Aldarondo, Julian, part IV
Aldridge, Henry, part II
Alexander, Lamar, part II
Alexander, Robert, part III
Alexie, Sherman, part I
Alexis, Kim, part I
Ali, Muhammad, part III, 37, 57, 83, 107
Alice in Wonderland (book), 26
aliens, 168

allegations, 18, 40, 55, 135, 136, 153, 156–57, 163, 170, 188, 190, 192–93, 195, 206, 209, 211
Allen, Doris, part II
Allen, Harry, part I
Allen, Jeff, part I
Allen, Woody, parts I, II, III, 19, 50, 68, 69, 70, 86, 203, 253
Allende, Isabel, part I
Alley, Kirstie, part I
Alman, Isadora, part I
Almond, Bob, part I
Alomar, Roberto, part III
Alomar, Sandy, part III
Alou, Felipe, part III
Altman, Robert, part I, 67
Amanpour, Christiane, 95
America, 21, 27, 31, 35, 55, 56, 60, 67, 79, 84–85, 107, 113, 123, 125, 127, 139, 140, 145, 158, 160, 166, 170, 172, 176, 180, 185, 194, 198, 202, 204–206, 208, 218, 223–24, 237, 241–42, 263, 265, 269, 273, 283, 290
American citizen, 177
American dream, 77, 234, 265
American Graffiti, 72
American League, 160
American Oxonian, The, part II
American press, 116
American public, 156, 175
American values, 79
Ames, Aldrich, part II
Amis, Kingsley, part I
Amis, Martin, part I
Amistad, 108
Ammondt, Juka, part I
Amoros, Larry, part IV
Amos, Tori, part I
Amsterdam, 31
anarchist, 27
Anderson, Dave, part III
Anderson, Loni, part I
Anderson, Pamela, part I
Anderson, Paul Thomas, part I
Anderson, Sparky, part III
Anderson, Terry, part II
Andrew, Prince, 162
Angels in the Outfield, 48
animal research, 106
animals, 18–19, 40, 45, 83, 89, 99, 115, 117, 125, 239

Aniston, Jennifer, 81
Anne, Princess, part II
Annis, Francesco, part I
Anthony, Keith, part IV
anthropologists, 69
antichrist, 23, 47, 162
Anton, Susan, part I
aphrodisiac, 206, 213
Apostle, The, 41, 283
Apple Computers, 58–59, 100, 125, 202, 243, 264
Arbatov, Georgi, part II
Argentina, 34, 146
Arizona, 17, 77, 82, 169, 170, 188, 194, 244, 255, 288
Arkansas, 104, 142, 147, 148, 151–52, 156, 166, 187, 196, 201, 211, 244, 248, 283, 288
Arkatov, Ian, part II
armageddon, 24
Armey, Dick, part II
Arnett, Peter, part II
Arnold, Tom, part I, 51, 97, 101, 111
Arquette, Patricia, part I
Arquette, Roseanne, part I
Arsenio Hall Show, The, 51
Arthur, Bea, part I
Artis, Donita Jo, part IV
Artist (Formerly Known As Prince), The, part I, 21, 27, 29, 37, 64, 75, 92, 99, 105, 109
Ashley, Elizabeth, part I
Ashman, John L., part I
Asner, Ed, part I
assassination, 78, 169, 178, 206
Associated Press, 13
Atkins, Chet, part I
Atlanta Braves, 221–24, 235, 253
Atlanta Falcons, 231
Atlanta Hawks, 258
Atlanta, 61, 72, 221–24, 228, 231, 235, 242, 245, 252–53, 258
Atlantic City, 119
Atlantis, 143
Atlas, Teddy, part III
Augustine, Mildred, part I
Auschwitz, 171, 173
Australia, 47, 140, 147, 257, 260
Austria, 117
Avital, Mili, part I

bachelor party, 44, 104
Backroads, part I
Bacon, Kevin, part I
Bailey, Ben, part IV
Bailey, F. Lee, part IV, 268, 276, 281, 290
Baio, Scott, part I
Baird, Lourdes, part IV
Baiul, Oksana, part III
Baker, Anita, part I
Baker, James, part II
Baker, Russell, part II
bald, 44, 96
Baldwin, Alec, parts I, II
Baldwin, Ralph, part IV
Bale, Christian, part I
Balkans, 174, 196
Ball, Frank R., part IV
Baltimore Orioles, 217, 228, 235, 244, 246–47, 249, 253
Baltimore, 38, 204, 217, 226, 228, 235, 244, 246–47, 249, 253
Band, Michael, part IV
Barbara, Domic, part IV
Barbie, 78, 108, 224, 251
Barbieri, Vincent, part IV
Barcia, James, part II
Bardo, Robert, part IV
Barker, Bob, part I
Barkin, Ellen, part I
Barkley, Charles, part III, 198, 219, 229, 242, 259
Barnaby, Matthew, part III
Barnes, Julian, part I
Barnett, Gary, part III
Barney (children's TV character), 75, 157
Barone, Michael, part II
Barry, Dave, parts I, IV
Barry, Marion, part II, 157, 162
Barrymore, Drew, part I
Bart, Peter, parts I, IV
Barzaghi, Jacques, part II
baseball, 12, 37, 48, 64, 86, 128, 160, 210, 217, 220–26, 228, 233, 235, 236, 239, 240, 243, 249, 250–51, 253, 257–58, 291, 293
Basic Instinct, 40, 109, 114, 116
Basinger, Kim, part I, 18, 70
basketball, 12, 210, 217–21, 223, 225, 228, 230, 232–33, 235–40, 243, 249, 250–51, 254, 258
Baughman, Jim, part IV
Bayh, Evan, part II
Bayless, Skip, part III
Baylor, Don, part III
Baywatch, 255
BBC, 18

Beach Boys, The, 67
Bean, Orson, part I
Beatles, The, 35, 53, 77, 78
Beatty, Warren, part I, 67, 73–74, 122, 129
Beck, Rod, part III
Beckel, Robert, part II
Beckwith, David, part II
Beckwith, Paul, part I
Bedelia, Bonnie, part I
Begala, Paul, part II
Bell, Dick, part III
Bellow, Saul, part I
Belzer, Richard, part II
Benchley, Peter, 26
Benigni, Roberto, part I
Benner, Rick, part III
Bennett, Bill, part II
Bennett, Jackie, part II
Bennett, Tony, part I
Benson, Harry, part III
Benson, Mildred Augustine Wirt, part I
Bensten, Lloyd, part II
Bergman, Ingmar, part I
Berkeley, 77, 90, 118, 196
Berkowitz, Bob, part IV
Berle, Milton, part I
Berlin Wall, 168
Bernard, Tom, part I
Bernhard, Sandra, parts I, II
Bernstein, Leonard, 136
Berra, Yogi, part III, 254
Berry, Halle, part I, 69
Bertolucci, Bernardo, part I
Beverly Hills Cop, 34
Bible, Geoffrey C., part II
Bible, The, 23, 76, 78, 99, 137, 180, 196, 225, 256, 258, 291
Biden, Joseph, part II
Big Bird, part I
Biggers, Neal, part IV
Bin, Liu, part III
Bird, Larry, part III, 21
Bismarck, North Dakota, 60
bitch, 78, 83, 86, 89, 97, 105, 116, 117, 165, 237, 255, 259, 267
Bizar, Don, part IV
Björk, part I
Black Plague, 92
Black Sabbath, 23
Black, Roy, part IV
Blackwell, Mr., part I, II
Blair, Virginia, part I
Blass, Steve, part III
Bleeth, Yasmine, part I

Bligh, Captain, 106
Bloodworth-Thomason, Linda, part II
Blount, Roy, Jr., part I
Bly, Robert, part I
Bob, Joe, part II
Bobbitt, John Wayne, part IV
Bobbitt, Lorena, part IV
Bobit, Bonnie, part IV
Boden, Paul, part II
Bodett, Tom, part I
Bolton, Michael, part I, 92, 107, 112
Bon Jovi, Jon, part I, 153
Bonaduce, Danny, part I
Bonds, Barry, part III, 22, 227
Bono, Chastity, parts I, II
Bono, Mary, part II
Bono, part I
Bono, Sonny, part II, 30, 159, 162, 179, 182, 184
boobs, 21, 56, 88, 96, 212, 259
Boogie Nights, 14
Book of Baby and Child Care, 108
books, 15, 17, 24, 31, 39, 50, 61, 63, 74, 101, 105, 114, 118–19, 123, 139, 144, 153, 203–204, 213, 220, 239, 254, 256–57, 265, 285, 288
Boone, Pat, part I, 20
Border Music, 63
Bosnia, 107, 137, 179, 184
Boston, Massachusets, 17, 85, 161, 185, 224, 227, 229, 230, 237–38, 244, 271
Boston Red Sox, 224–25, 229, 230
Boucher, Richard, part II
Bouton, Jim, part III
Bowden, Bobby, part III
Bowe, Riddick, part III, 227, 230, 233, 241, 246
Bowie, Angela, part I
Bowie, David, part I
Boxx, Shirletha, part IV
Boy George, part I
Boyd, Will, part II
boyfriends, 115, 129
Boyle, Lara Flynn, part I
Boyz N the Hood, 106
Boza, Al, part IV
Bradbury, Ray, part I
Braden, Mark, part II
Bradley, Ed, part II
Bradley, Wallace (Gator), part IV
Brady, Nicholas, part II
Brando, Marlon, part I, 33, 233
Brandy, part I
Bray, Thomas, part II
breasts, 13–15, 26–29, 36, 44, 49, 68, 77, 85, 152, 188

Breathless Mahoney, 27
Brenly, Bob, part III
Brennaman, Marty, part III
Brett, George, part III
Brice, Fanny, 115
Brickman, Paul, part IV
Bridges of Madison County, The,
   41, 63
Brill, Steve, part IV
Brinkley, David, part II
Bristol, Dave, part III
Broadway, 36, 70, 105
Broady, Earl, part IV
Brock, David, part II
Broderick, Matthew, 87
Brokaw, Sandy, part I
Brokaw, Tom, parts I, IV
Brolin, James, part II
Brooklyn, 39, 140, 160, 223, 285, 288
Brooks, Albert, part I
Brooks, El, part I
Brooks, Garth, part I
Brooks, Louise, 73
brothels, 133, 280
Brown, "Downtown" Julie, part I
Brown, Divine, 68, 117
Brown, Hamilton, part II
Brown, Helen Gurley, part I
Brown, Jackie, 49
Brown, James, part I, 11, 241
Brown, Jerry, part II, 29, 104, 114,
   134–36, 148, 165, 167, 193, 194,
   202
Brown, Kathleen, part II
Brown, Murphy, 40, 197
Brown, Tina, part I
Brown, Tony, part I
Brown, Vicky, part II
Brown, Willie, parts II, III, 137, 175, 282
Brownback, Sam, part II
Browner, Joey, part III
Browning, Stephanie, part I
Brownstein, Rhonda, part IV
Bruce, Lenny, 107
Bruni, Carla, part I
Bryant, Doris, part IV
Brydges, Richard, part IV
Buchanan, Douglas, part IV
Buchanan, Patrick, part II, 79, 149,
   168, 198
Buck, Peter, part I
Buckley, Terrell, part III
Buddhism, 46, 102
Buddhist, 19, 93, 123, 175, 211
Buddy (President Bill Clinton's dog),
   19, 136, 183

budget, 31, 102, 109, 125, 146,
   151, 154, 156, 158, 175, 177,
   179, 209, 224
Buechler, Jud, part III
Buffalo Bills, 233, 247, 252
Buffy Down Under (film), 51
Buffy the Vampire Slayer, 89
Bug's Life, A, 44
Bullock, Sandra, part I
Bulwer-Lytton Fiction Prize, 17
Bumpers, Dale, part II
Burger King, 152, 259, 280
Burke, Delta, part I
Burkett, John, part III
Burleigh, Nina, part II
Burns, Edward, part I
Burns, Ken, part III
Burris, Garry, part IV
Burrows, Mike, part III
Busey, Gary, part I
Bush, Barbara, part II
Bush, George W., 148
Bush, George, 24, 51, 70, 89, 92,
   142, 161, 184, 197–98, 203–204,
   213, 230
Bush, George, part II
business, 12, 15, 18, 22, 27, 42, 44,
   80–81, 88, 99, 110, 112, 125, 129,
   134, 141, 150, 154, 165–66, 172,
   175, 177, 179, 180, 185, 189, 222,
   264, 267, 276, 288, 292
Butler, Brett, part I
Buttafuoco, Joey, part IV
Buttafuoco, Mary Jo, part IV, 128
Butterworth, Bob, part IV
Bybee, Roger, part IV
Byrd, Admiral, 21
Byrd, Robert, part II
Byrd, Robin, part I
Byrne, David, part I
Byrne, Gabriel, part I
Byrum, John, part I

Caan, James, part I
Cabaret, 36
Caddell, Pat, part II
Caen, Herb, parts I, III
Cage, Nicholas, part I
Caesar, Julius, 113
Caglione, Don, part I
Cahill, Robert, part IV
Cain, Dean, part I
Caine, Michael, part I
California, 16, 20, 25, 35, 42, 51, 92, 96,
   100, 104, 118, 126, 133, 134, 137,
   138, 140–41, 150, 158–59, 161–62,

   166, 175, 179, 188, 190, 193, 199,
   209, 213, 222, 228, 230, 231, 233,
   242, 248, 253–54, 263, 270, 273,
   276, 281, 285, 292–93
Calim, Ernst, part III
Cambodia, 30, 45, 117, 143, 203, 288
Cameron, James, part I, 24, 51, 101
Cameron, Mindy, part II
Camp David, 175
Campbell, Carroll, part II
Campbell, Elden, part III
Campbell, Luther, part I
Campbell, Naomi, 79
Campbell, Pat, part III
Campbell, Tom, 138, 164
Candidate, The, 179
Candiotti, Rom, part III
cannibalism, 69
Cannon, Danny, part I
Cannon, Dyan, part III
Canseco, Jose, part III, 224
Capeman, 105
Capitol Gang, The, 19
Capitol Hill, 190
Caray, Chip, part III
Caray, Harry, part III
Carey, Ben, part I
Carey, Drew, part I
Carey, Mariah, part III
Carlesimo, P. J., 142, 253–54
Carman, John, part II
Carne, Judy, part I
Carneal, Michael, part IV
Carnesecca, Lou, part III
Carolina Panthers, 231
Carpenter, Bill, part II
Carr, Caleb, part I
Carr, David, part II
Carrey, Jim, part I
Carril, Pete, part III
Carroll, Lewis, 26
Carson, Johnny, part I, 69, 78–79
Carter, Helena Bonham, part I
Carter, Jimmy, part II
Carter, Nell, part I
Carter, Robert Anthony, part IV
Cartland, Barbara, part I
Cartwright, Rosalind, part IV
Carville, James, part II, 187–88
Casablanca, 41
Casey, James, part IV
Cash, Johnny, part I
Cassar, Robert, part IV
Cassidy, David, part I
Castellanos, Alex, part II
Casualties of War, 66

Cat in the Hat, The, 39
Cat on a Hot Tin Roof, 79
Catholic, 15, 60, 74, 123, 125, 270, 274
Cats, 12, 66
Caulfield, Holden, 77
Cavett, Dick, parts I, IV
CBS, 51, 70, 93, 128, 165, 181, 223, 230
celebrity, 13, 78, 108, 128, 265, 267, 293
celibacy, 49
censure, 180
Centorino, Robert, part IV
Central Park, 74, 270
CFO, 28
Chabert, Lacy, part I
Chad, Norman, part III
Chamberlain, Wilt, part III
Chang, Michael, part III
Chao, Victor, part I
Chapman, Jim, part II
Chapman, Mark David, part IV, 62, 67
Charles, Prince, 41, 58
Charles, Ray, part I
Charlie Brown Christmas, A, 76
Charlton, Norm, part III
Chasing Amy, 106
Chastain, Brandi, part III
Chavez, Julio Cesar, 238
cheating, 85, 232
Checchi, Al, part II
cheerleader, 71
Cheers, 71
Chen, Heng-Ming, part I
Cher, 25, 30, 55, 97, 98
Chi, Meilien, part I
Chicago, 25, 105, 118, 126, 143, 145, 153, 190, 197, 201, 217, 220, 222, 226–28, 231–32, 235–37, 240, 248–49, 253, 260, 266–67, 270, 275, 280, 285, 294
Chicago Cubs, 220, 223, 248, 253, 260
Chik, Sabbaruddin, part II
Child, Julia, part I
childhood, 25, 52, 63, 67, 98, 101, 112, 292
children, 11–13, 24, 32, 39, 45–46, 57–58, 68, 77, 95, 108, 114, 117–19, 124, 133–34, 143, 154, 157, 159, 172, 174, 176, 178, 184, 189, 197–98, 204, 207, 211, 213, 217, 240, 250–51, 256, 265, 277–78, 281, 286
chimpanzees, 22, 182
China, 71, 91, 100, 117, 125, 128, 142–43, 149, 162, 165, 172, 174, 193–94, 196, 202, 208, 212, 214, 288

Chinatown, 12
Chinese, 56, 82, 117, 125, 128, 142, 149, 151, 180, 186, 190, 200, 206, 212, 245, 257
Cho, Margaret, part I
Chong, Annabel, part I
Chopra, Deepak, part I, 80
Chow, Michael, part I
Christ, 70, 89, 128, 162
Christensen, Matt, part IV
Christian, 13, 18, 44, 93, 106, 119, 156, 228, 271, 272, 283
Christianity, 88, 128
Christopher, Norman, part II
Christopher, Warren, part II, 133
Chung, Connie, part I, 165
Chung, Johnny, part II, 174
church, 13, 15, 25, 51, 86, 88, 115, 146, 209, 259
Church, Jenny, part II
Churchill, Winston, 148
CIA, 134
Ciampicali, Elsa, part IV
Cicciolina, La, part I
cigarettes, 25, 80, 83, 137, 181
cigars, 169
Cincinnati, 14, 17, 221, 223, 229, 235, 244–45, 248, 250–51
Cincinnati Reds, 20, 221, 229, 235, 244–45, 248, 250–51
circumcision, 15, 150, 167, 258
civilization, 16, 170
Clancy, Tom, part I
Clapton, Eric, part I
Clark, Marcia, part IV, 270, 282, 290
Clark, Will, part III
Clay, Andrew Dice, part I
Clayton, Adam, part I
Clearwater, Florida, 104, 254
Clemens, Roger, part III
Cleveland, 152, 217, 236, 251
Clevenger, Chris, part III
cliché, 21, 93, 128
Cliffhanger, 109
Clifford, Clark, part II
Clinton, Bill, part II, 18, 22, 29, 58, 64, 66, 91, 98, 105, 107, 115, 126, 133–36, 139–42, 148–50, 156, 159–63, 170–94, 198–206, 209–14, 242
Clinton, Hillary Rodham, part II, 50, 84, 123, 138, 141, 163, 166, 169, 181, 183, 186, 189, 194, 204, 206, 210
Clooney, George, part I, 42
Closs, Keith, part III

CNN, 19, 21, 50, 120, 134, 161, 178, 191, 272, 279, 290
Cobain, Kurt, 42, 71, 85, 110
Coburn, James, part I
cocaine, 42, 135
Cochran, Johnny, part IV, 263, 290
Coen, Ethan, part IV
Coen, Joel and Ethan, 48
coffee, 39, 52, 121, 194, 266, 283
Cohen, Ben, part II
Cohen, Richard, part II
Cold Mountain, 45
Cold War, The, 143, 206, 267
Cole, Paula, part I, 68, 81
Coleman, Marshall, part IV
Collins, Bud, part III
Collins, Carter, part IV
Collins, Jackie, part I
Collins, Joan, part I
Collins, Michael, part I
Collins, Phil, part I
colonic irrigation, 29
Colorado, 17, 25, 145, 155, 160, 194, 199, 220, 276
Columbia University, 23
comedian, 12, 21, 24, 31–33, 37, 39, 48, 65, 68, 69–70, 77, 79, 83, 91–92, 96, 99–100, 102–104, 111, 116, 125–26, 129, 133, 167, 175, 186, 199–200, 217, 225
Compton, California, 49, 293
computers, 59, 77, 166
condoms, 38, 73, 95, 99, 126, 236
Cone, David, part III
Congress, 31, 44, 134, 138, 144–47, 150–51, 154–55, 162, 164–65, 168, 175, 179, 180, 185, 191, 198, 202, 207–208, 212
Congressional Black Caucus, 33
Connery, Sean, part I, 183
Connors, Jimmy, part III
Constantine, Kevin, part III
Constitution, 153, 197
Conte, Silvio, part II
Cook, Dane, part I
Cooke, Sam, 112
Coolio, part IV
Cooney, Michael, part II
Cooper, Alice, part I
Copeland, Harlon, part IV
Copperfield, David, part I
Coppola family, 27
Coppola, Francis Ford, part I, 103, 127
Coppola, Nicholas, 27
Corcoran, David, part III
Corea, Chick, 21

Corliss, Richard, part I
Cosby Show, The, 81
Cosby, Bill, part I
Costas, Bob, parts I, II, III
Costello, Elvis, part I, 98
Costner, Kevin
Costner, Kevin, part I, 24, 44, 68, 100
Couric, Katie, parts II, IV
Courier, Jim, part III
court, 11, 53, 187, 213, 220, 225, 231, 249, 250–51, 254, 270, 272, 274, 276, 279, 281, 283–85, 287–89, 291–92
Cox, Ronnie, part I
crack (cocaine), 135, 281
Cranston, Alan, part II
Craven, Wes, 112
Crawford, Cindy, part I, 22, 69
Crawford, H. R., part II
Crazy Horse Saloon, 12
Crichton, Michael, part I
crime, 85, 88, 121, 137–38, 154, 163, 205, 218–19, 238, 264, 266, 269, 271–72, 275, 278, 281, 287, 289, 294
Cringley, Robert X., part I
Crisp, Quentin, part I
critics, 13, 22, 32–33, 48, 75, 95, 98, 105–106, 188, 202, 210, 247, 291
Cronkite, Walter, part I
Crosby, Bing, 35
Crosby, David, part I
Crosby, Gary, part I
Crouwel, Michael, part III
Crow, Sheryl, part I, 21
Crowley, Michael, part II
crucifixion, 162, 174, 204
Cruise, Tom, part I, 21, 122, 129
Crystal, Billy, parts I, II
Cuba, 114, 197, 246
Culkin, Macaulay, part I
cult, 29, 103, 120, 180, 182, 209
culture, 12, 50, 63, 66, 79, 117, 126, 150, 166
Cummings, Alan, part I
Cunnane, Brian, part III
Cunningham, Randy, part II
Cuomo, Andrew, 133
Cuomo, Mario, part II
Curry, Larry, part III
Curtin, Jane, part I
Curtis, Jamie Lee, part I
Curtis, Tony, part I
Cusack, John, part I
Cutler, Bruce, part IV
Cyrus, Billy Ray, part I
Cyz, Bob, part III

D, Chuck, parts I, III
D, Mike, part I
D'Amato, Alfonse, part II
D'Anton, Mike, part III
D'arby, Terrence Trent, part I
D'Arco, Alphonse, part IV
Dafoe, Willem, 81
Dahmer, Jeffrey, part IV
Dakota, 12, 49, 154, 157
Daley, Richard J., 142
Dallas Cowboys, 241, 246, 250
Dallek, Robert, part II
Dallos, Lisa, part II
Daly, Eugene, part II
Daly, John, part III
Damon, Matt, 54, 125
Dando, Evan, part I
Dandridge, Dorothy, 21
Danes, Claire, part I, 64
Daniels, Mike, part IV
Danson, Ted, part I
Dante, 150, 162
Darden, Christopher, part IV
Darkins, Chris, part III
Darman, Richard, part II
Darwin, Charles, 64
dating disorder, 44
daughter, 11, 46, 64, 74, 80, 83, 86, 89, 92, 96, 98, 119, 120, 134, 136, 188, 199, 201, 203, 223, 229, 242, 253, 264, 282, 285, 288, 294
David, Larry, part I
Davis Cup, 231
Davis, Al, part III
Davis, Geena, 96
Davis, Granger, part IV
Davis, Gray, part II
Davis, Patty, parts I, II
Davis, Richard Allen, part IV
Davison, Craig, part III
De Cordova, Fred, 43
De Gaulle, Charles, 135
De La Beckwith, Thelma, part IV
De Mornay, Rebecca, part I
De Nicola, Mike, part IV
De Niro, Robert, part I, 77
De Palma, Brian, 66
De Roeck, Luke, part III
De Shaies, Jim, part III
death, 11–13, 21, 30, 35, 50, 58, 77, 82, 88, 92, 104–105, 107, 115, 140, 167, 181, 188, 207, 227, 232, 245, 253, 257, 266, 270, 271–76, 284, 286, 287, 288, 293–94
Declaration of Independence, 153
DeConcini, Dennis, part II

DeCourcy, Myra, part IV
Degeneres, Ellen, part I, 70
Deitzler, Harry, part IV
Delaney, Dana, part I
Delanty, John, part IV
DeLay, Tom, part II
DeLeonardis, Ralph, part III
Delillo, Don, part I
Deliverance, 56
Dell, Tim, part III
Dellinger, Walter, part II
Delo, Paul, part IV
DeMille, Cecil B., 51
democracy, 97, 178, 193–94, 197, 204
Democratic National Convention, 161, 167, 174
Democratic Party, 150, 158, 169, 170, 192, 211
Democrats, 141, 144, 150, 168, 177, 187, 192–93, 219
Dench, Judy, part I
Dennehy, Brian, part I
Dennis, Eric, part III
Denver, 25, 160, 225, 232, 252
Depardieu, Gerard, part I
deposition, 103, 136, 154, 213, 274, 285–86, 291
Depp, Johnny, part I
Derek, Bo, part I
Dern, Laura, part I
Dershowitz, Alan, part IV, 139
Desert Storm, 145
destiny, 60, 278
Detroit Tigers, 218, 240
DeWine, Mike, part II
diabetes, 15
Diamond, Mike, 81
Diamond, Neil, part I, 37
Diana, Princess, 13, 21, 35, 58, 74, 76, 96, 117, 207, 272, 280
Diaz, Cameron, 106
Diaz, Raul, part IV
DiCaprio, Irmelin, part I
DiCaprio, Leonardo, part I, 14, 28
Dick Tracy, 27, 129
Dickey, Glenn, part III
dictators, 101, 149
Die Hard 2, 20
Dietrich, Marlene, 73
DiGilio, Gerald, part III
Diller, Phyllis, part I
DiMacall, Risa, part IV
DiMaggio, Joe, 22
DiMaio, Rob, part III
Dimas, Trent, part III
Dingle, John, part II

Dinkins, Mayor David, 37, 202
Dion, Celine, 75, 86, 93
Dirk Digler, 14
disarmament, 51
Disney, 47, 78, 80, 225, 237
Disneyland, 53, 107, 279
Ditka, Mike, part III
Divac, Vlade, part III
divorce, 45–46, 51, 68, 79, 84, 103, 113, 116, 118–19, 250, 255, 272, 275, 280, 286
DNA, 194, 268, 293
Dodd, Christopher, part II
Doherty, Shannen, part I, 44
Dole, Bob, parts I, II, 166, 176, 181, 190, 198
Dolenz, Mickey, part I
dolls, 124, 163, 251, 292
Donahue, Phil, part I
Donaldson, Sam, part II, 139
Donner, Paul, part IV
Doonesbury, 118
dope (marijuana), 17, 22, 35, 82, 105, 200
Dornan, Robert, part II, 164
Douglas, Buster, part III, 237, 256
Douglas, Eric, part I
Douglas, Kirk, part I
Douglas, Michael, part I, 114, 116
Dowd, Maureen, part II
Downey, Robert, Jr., parts I, IV, 70
Downs, Frederick, part II
Doyle, James M., part IV
Dracula, 27, 93
Dream Team, 218–19, 263, 268, 285, 290
Drew, Nancy, 21
Dreyfuss, Richard, part I
Drudge, Matt, part II, 85
drug addict, 52
drugs, 14, 52–53, 59, 61, 65, 71, 80, 90, 95, 103, 106, 108, 117, 121, 125–26, 135, 152, 190–91, 204, 226, 228, 231, 244, 245, 248, 263, 274, 281, 286
Duchess of York, 109, 162
Duchovny, David, parts I, II, 69
Duesberg, Peter, 25
Dukakis, Michael, part II
Duke, David, part II
Duke, Kacy, part II
Dundee, Angelo, part III
Dunn, Jennifer, part II
Dunne, Dominick, part IV
Duplessis, Charles, part II
Durante, Jimmy, 20

Duva, Dan, part III
Duva, Lou, part III
Duvall, Dr. Charles P., part II
Duvall, Robert, parts I, II
Dykstra, Lenny, part III
Dylan, Bob, part I, 53, 90, 91
dysfunctional, 55, 57, 89

Eagles, The, 93
Easton, Bret Ellis, part I
Eastwood, Clint, part I
Eat, Drink, Man, Woman, 69
Eaton, Mark, part III
Ebert, Roger, part I, 25, 54
Ebonics, 33, 67, 174
economics, 56, 150, 196, 292
Edell, Dr. Dean, part I
Edmonton Oilers, 250
education, 26, 34, 48, 94, 99, 134, 141, 143, 146, 179, 189, 204, 214, 245, 281
Edwards, Edwin, part II
Edwards, Harry, part III
Edwards, Jonathan, part III
Ehrenreich, Barbara, part II
Einstein, Albert, 93, 95, 98
Einstein, Norman, 255
Eisner, Michael, 80
Ekbert, Anita, part I
Elders, Joycelyn, part II
Elfman, Jenna, part I
Eliot, Marc, part IV
Elizabeth II, part II
Ellis, Perry, 118
Elway, John, 225
Endangered Species Act, 168
endorsements, 90, 236, 247
Energy Department, 200
England, 16, 18, 30, 79, 87, 151, 162, 198, 217, 237
Englander, Harvey, part II
English, 17–18, 20, 23, 42, 56, 84, 148–49, 174, 176, 184, 196, 240, 285, 291
English, Paul, part I
environment, 143, 147, 161, 266
Ephron, Nora, part I
Espinosa, Jack, Jr., part III
ESPN, 74, 222–24, 234, 244
Estefan, Gloria, part I
Estevez, Emilio, part I
Eszterhas, Joe, part I
Eurocentrism, 256
Europe, 12, 124, 144, 256
euthanasia, 11
Evangelista, Linda, part I

Evans, Dale, 96
Evans, Robert, part I, 19, 33
Everett, Rupert, part I
Everhart, Angie, part I
Evita, 21, 59, 74, 75, 104, 189
Ewen, Todd, part III
executions, 48, 294
exercise, 11, 49, 76, 87, 107, 115, 148, 206, 266
Exner, Judith Campbell, part II
Eyes Wide Shut, 36, 57

Faber, J. P., part I
Fabio, 43, 58
Fairchild, Morgan, part I
Fairlie, Henry, part I
Faith, Adam, part I
Falwell, Jerry, part II
fame, 30, 39, 62, 74, 77–78, 84, 94, 163, 192, 264, 280
Fantasy Island, 24, 102
Fargo, 11, 60, 246, 264, 269
Faria, Americo, part III
Farian, Frank, 90
Farrakhan, Louis, part II
Farrington, James, part II
Farris, Linda Guess, part I
Fascell, Dante, part II
Fasi, Frank, part II
fast food, 34, 152, 184
Favor, Suzy, part III
Fawcett, Farah, 41
Fay, Jan, part I
Fay, Michael, part IV
Fayed, Mohamed Al, part IV
FDA, 160, 213
Feeney, Dick, part II
Felder, Raul, part IV
fellatio, 39
Feller, Bob, part III
Femina, Jerry Della, part I
feminism, 56, 128, 164
feminist, 32, 97, 115, 161, 203
feng shui, 56
Ferguson, Andrew, part II
Ferguson, Colin, part IV
Ferguson, Sarah, part II
Fernades, George, part II
Ferraro, Geraldine, part II
fidelity, 42, 107
Field of Dreams, 138, 143
Field, Genevieve, part II
Field, Larry, part IV
Fiennes, Ralph, 15
Figure Skating Championships, 239
figure skating, 219, 242

film, 12–13, 16–21, 24–26, 28, 32–33, 36–41, 44–54, 62, 65–73, 80, 84–87, 90, 94, 96, 98–102, 104, 106, 108, 111–16, 125–29, 133, 165, 179, 180, 182, 185, 193, 206–209, 214, 230, 247, 253, 264, 269, 281
filmmakers, 21, 99, 103
Fink, Barton, 48
first lady, 45, 153, 155, 186, 204, 210
Fischer, Bobby, parts I, III
Fishburne, Laurence, part I
Fisher, Amy, 267
Fisher, Carrie, part I
Fitzerrell, Glen, part IV
Fitzwater, Marlin, part II
Flanagan, Mike, part III
Fleetwood, James, part IV
Fleiss, Heidi, part I, 68, 103
Fletcher, Scott, part III
Flockhart, Calista, part I
Florida, 11, 92, 96, 118–19, 144, 154, 171, 217, 221, 228, 243, 245, 250–54, 258, 266–68, 275, 284, 288, 292
Flowers, Gennifer, part II
Flynt, Larry, parts I, II, 114, 164, 167, 185
Foley, Dan, part I
Foley, Mark, part II
Fonda, Bridget, part I
Fonda, Henry, 44
Fonda, Jane, part I, 62, 114, 119, 120
Fonda, Peter, part I
Foo Fighters, The, 50
football, 17, 27, 68, 71, 82, 144, 161, 199, 220–21, 223, 226, 229, 234, 240, 244, 247, 249–55, 258, 268, 271, 284
Forbes, Steve, 179, 190
Ford, Betty, part II
Ford, Harrison, part I, 77
Ford, Richard, part II
Ford, Wendell, part II
Foreign Relations Committee, 171
Foreman, George, part III, 218, 245
Foreman, Roy, part III
Forrest Gump, 13, 181, 229
Fortensky, Larry, 116
Fortier, Michael, part IV
Foster, David, part I
Foster, Jodie, part I
Fountainhead, The, 94
Fowler, Wyche, part II
Fox, Michael J., 26
Fox, Tony, part IV
Frampton, Peter, part I
France, 12, 39, 100, 109

Francis, Russ, part III
Frank, Barney, part II
Franken, Al, parts II, IV
Frankenstein, 208
Franklin, Aretha, part I
Franz, Dennis, part I
Frazier, Charles, part I
Frazier, Walt, part III
Freed, Laura, part IV
freedom of speech, 112, 158
Freeh, Louis, part IV
Freeman, Morgan, 87
Freeman, Myrtle, part IV
Freidan, Betty, 115, 164
French government, 12
French, the, 12–13, 39, 99, 103, 109, 114, 178, 221, 230, 244, 250, 254, 292
Freund, Sidney, part IV
Friar's Club, 37
Friedan, Betty, part II
Frye, Phyllis, part IV
Fuchs, Michael, part I
Fuhrman, Mark, part IV, 263–64, 268–69, 284, 293
Fujisaki, Hiroshi, part IV
fund-raising, 153
Funny Girl, 115
Furney, Linday, part II
future, 18, 50–51, 75, 85, 98, 105, 139, 160, 170, 185, 211, 214, 217, 226, 229, 236, 255, 273, 281

Gabor, Eva, part I
Gabor, Zsa Zsa, part I
Gabriel, Peter, part II, 16
Gaeta, Daniel F., part IV
Gagliardi, John, part III
Gallagher, Noel, part I
Gallego, Mike, part III
Gallo, Joan, part II
Gallo, Vincent, part I
Garcia, Annabelle, part I
Garcia, Deborah Koons, part I
Garcia, Guadalupe, part IV
Garcia, Jerry, part I, 68
Garfunkel, Art, part I
Garner, Leslie, part I
Garner, Phil, part III
Garner, Wayne, part IV
Garrett, Johnny Frank, part IV
Gates, Bill, parts II, IV, 11, 234, 281
Gates, Daryl, part IV
Gates, Henry Louis, Jr., part I
Gates, William, part III

gay, 13, 23, 46–47, 57, 62, 73, 78, 85, 95, 111, 123–24, 128, 134, 137, 142, 151, 157, 164, 212–13, 233, 275, 283
Gecker, Daniel, part II
Geffen, David, parts I, II
Generation X, 22
generation, 14, 22–23, 30, 42, 60, 72, 79, 192–93, 198, 204, 213, 219
genocide, 11, 67, 202
Gentile, Rick, part III
Georgia, 119, 164, 172, 190, 221, 243, 258, 274
Gephardt, Richard, part II
Gere, Richard, part I, 68
Gergen, David, part II
Gerlenter, David, part IV
Germany, 62, 120, 135, 143, 208–209, 267
Getty, Balthazar, part I
Gettysburg Address, 43, 153
Gibb, Robin, part I
Gibbs, Joe, part III
Gibson, Mel, part I
Gifford, Frank, 47, 241, 246
Gifford, Kathie Lee, part I, 42
Gilbert, Brad, part III
Gillick, Phil, part III
Gilligan's Island, 76
Gingrich, Kathleen, part II
Gingrich, Newt, part II, 138, 173, 176, 201, 205
Ginsburg, William, parts II, IV
Girardi, Joe, part III
Gist, Robert, part III
Giuliani, Rudolph, part II
Gladwell, Malcolm, part I
Glanville, Jerry, part III
Glaspie, April, part II
Glass, Keith, part III
Glenn, John, part II
Glover, Crispin, 39
Glover, Danny, part I, 135
God, 15, 19, 23, 29, 30, 34, 42–43, 47, 49, 51, 57, 64–65, 70–72, 75–78, 82, 84, 87, 93, 95, 97, 103–106, 111, 114, 120, 123, 126–29, 151, 154, 157, 162, 169, 171, 175–78, 185, 189, 199, 206, 208, 212, 226, 228, 231, 243, 256, 258–59, 263–64, 271, 278–79, 288
Godfather, The, 33, 86, 92, 127
Godfrey, Seth, part II
Goetz, Bernard, parts II, IV
gold medal, 166, 242, 248
Goldberg, David, part I
Goldberg, Lucianne, parts I, II

Goldberg, Whoopi, parts I, II, 37
Golden Globe Award, The, 48, 94
Golden State Warriors, 142, 230, 247, 254
Goldman, Fred, part IV
Goldman, Ron, part IV, 268–69, 291
Goldstein, Al, part II
Goldwater, Barry, part II
golf, 13, 50, 58, 73, 144, 148, 164, 217, 219, 223–24, 235, 241–42, 252, 260, 291
Golic, Bob, part III
Golota, Andrew, part III
Golub, Richard, part IV
Good Will Hunting, 85, 123, 126
Goodman, John, part I
GOP, 134, 138, 150, 159, 161, 168–70, 178–79, 188, 190, 192, 196, 202, 204
Gorbachev, Mikhail, part II, 83
Gordon, Aaron, part IV
Gordon, Armand, part IV
Gore, Al, part II, 55, 123–24, 159, 175, 180, 182, 184, 201, 206, 208, 211
Gore, Tipper, 46, 168
Gorrono, Morgan, part IV
Gossett, Louis, Jr., part I
gossip, 15, 84, 85, 113
Gotbaum, Betsy, part II
Gotti, John, part IV, 99, 263, 270, 282
Gould, Elliott, part I
Grace, Mark, part III
Graf, Steffi, part III, 224
Graffiti Bridge, 16
Graham, Barbara, part I
Graham, Reverend Billy, part II, 76, 110
Graham, Russell, part IV
Gramm, Phil, part II
Granata, Cammi, part III
Grand Canyon, 16, 194
grandfather, 14, 60, 72, 79, 202, 223
Grant, Bob, part II
Grant, Horace, part III
Grant, Hugh, part I, 41, 68, 117
Grasso, Thomas J., part IV
Grateful Dead, The, 46, 62, 66
Gray, John, part I
Gray, Spaulding, part I
Great Britain, 55, 76, 134
Great Lakes, 167, 179
greatness, 12, 107, 219
Greek army, 25
Green Bay Packers, 222, 226, 231, 234, 258
green card, 17, 91
Green, Tim, part III

Green, Willie, part III
Greene, Graham, part I
Greenpeace, 51
Greenspan, Alan, part II
Greer, Germaine, part I
Gretzky, Wayne, part III
Grey, Jennifer, part I
Grier, Pam, part I
Griese, Bob, part III
Griffith, Calvin, part III
Griffith, Melanie, part I, 59
Grimaldi of Monaco, Prince Albert, part III
Grimson, Stu, part III
Grippo, Nick, part I
Griscom, Nina, part I
Grisham, John, part I
Groening, Matt, part I
Grohl, David, part I
Gross, Terry, 184
Growney, John, part III
Guber, Peter, part I
Gulf crisis, 25
Gulf War, 117, 148, 178
Gullickson, Tom, part III
Gumble, Bryant, parts I, II
Gumble, Greg 230
Gunn, Mike, part II
Gunnels, Doug, part IV
Guns 'n Roses, 23
guns, 29, 156, 168, 174, 235, 264, 266, 268, 270, 277–78, 294
Gunter, Carl, part II
gynecologist, 86, 117

Haddad, Sharyn, part I
Hadley, Greg, part IV
Hagar, Sammy, 122
Hahn, Jessica, part I
Hai, Summa Ching, part II
Haig, Alexander, part II
Haines, David, part I
Hale-Bopp comet, 103, 156
Hales, Elliot, part IV
Hall of Fame, 80, 90, 224, 231, 240, 254
Hall, Arsenio, part I
Hall, Brad, part I
Hall, Gus, 80
Hall, Jerry, part I, 46
Halverson, Richard, part II
Hamill, Dorothy, part III
Hamilton College, 46
Hamilton, Argus, parts I, II, III
Hamilton, Ashley, part I, 43
Hamilton, Linda, part I
Hamilton, Scott, part III

Hamilton, William, part I
Hamlet (film), 47, 159, 176, 239
Hamlin, Harry, part I
Hammer, Susan, part II
Hampton, Lloyd Wayne, part IV
Hancock, Ernest, part II
Handley, Ray, part III
Handy, Bruce, part I
Hanks, Tom, part I
Hanoi, 44, 196
Hansen, Patti, part I
Hanson (musical group), 52
Hanson, Curtis, part I
Hanson, Zachary, part I
Happy Book, The, 63
Harding, Tonya, part III, 208, 219, 246, 253
Harkins, Tom, part II
Harper, Ron, part III
Harrelson, Woody, part I, 75
Harrick, Jim, part III
Harris, Bobby, part IV
Harris, Mark, part I
Harrison, George, part I
Harry, Debbie, part I
Hart, Gary, part II, 84–85, 114, 193
Hart, Mary, part I
Hartley, Nina, part I
Hartman, Sid, parts II, III
Hartness, Steve, part IV
Haskins, Clem, part III
Hastings, Scott, part III
Hatch, Orrin, part II
Hatcher, Mickey, part III
Havel, Vaclav, 129, 143, 200
Hawaii, 42, 53, 58, 162, 172, 198
Hawkins, Sophie B., part I
Hawn, Goldie, part I, 64
Hayek, Salma, part I
Hayes, Isaac, part I
Hayslip, Le Ly, part I
HBO, 21, 45, 97, 279
Hearst, Patty, part IV
Heathcoate, Jud, part III
Heaven and Earth, 53
heaven, 26, 29, 53, 61, 70, 100, 110, 143, 180, 184, 217, 271
Heaven's Gate, 120, 180, 182
Heche, Anne, part II
Hedley, Anthony, part II
Heflin, Howell, part II
Hefner, Hugh, parts I, II
Hefner, Kimberly, part I
Hegarty, Mary, part III
Helfgott, David, 75

hell, 16–17, 28, 38, 40, 62, 65, 67, 70, 83, 86, 89–90, 93, 109–110, 112, 117, 122, 137, 148, 162, 179, 219, 238, 241–42, 249, 255, 260, 263, 292
Hellon, Michael, part II
Helms, Jesse, part II, 97
Helmsley, Leona, part I, 19, 118
hemp, 48, 52, 55, 75
Henderson, Rickey, part III
Hendrix, Jimi, 32
Hendy, Alex, part III
Henley, Don, 93
Henner, Marilu, part I
Hernandez, Keith, part III
heroin, 37, 76, 85
Herskovitz, Marshall, part II
Heston, Charlton, parts I, II, IV
heterosexual, 62, 111, 275
Hewitt, Don, part I
Heyworth, Jim, part IV
Hiaasen, Carl, part II
Higginbotham, Judge Leon, part II
Higgins, Martin, part III
high school, 15, 26, 59, 65, 68, 99, 143, 155, 163, 180, 199, 208, 210, 229, 231, 237, 271, 276, 279, 285, 288, 292
Hightower, Jim, part II
Hill, Anita, 167, 174
Hill, Bob, part III
Hill, David, parts I, III
Hill, Grant, 45
Hill, Henry, part IV
Hillary, Edmund, 109
Hingis, Martina, part III
Hinkley, John, 16
Hirschfield, Abe, part IV
Hispanic Link, part II
Hispanics, 171, 259
history, 25, 28, 60, 62–63, 92, 113–14, 127, 147–48, 167, 171, 176–77, 182, 185, 188, 198, 205, 251, 259
Hitchcock, Alfred, 85
Hitler, Adolf, 55, 100, 117, 146, 185, 201, 271
HIV, 95, 151, 251
hockey, 109, 137, 230, 231, 259
Hoeffel, Joseph, part II
Hoffman, Darnay, part IV
Hoffman, Dustin, part I
Hogan, Hulk, part II
Hoig, David, part IV
Hole, 77, 114, 150, 180, 203, 252
Holland, Bill, part III
Holland, Dexter, part I
Hollings, Ernest, part II

Holloway, Rory, part III
Holly, Buddy, 19
Hollywood Boulevard, 79
Hollywood, 16, 18–19, 21, 28, 32, 34, 36, 43–44, 48, 50, 55, 61, 64, 68, 78–79, 82, 88, 97, 108–110, 114, 122, 125, 129, 137, 167, 171, 185, 207, 210, 285
Holmes, Larry, part III
Holmes, Sean, part III
Holmgren, Mike, part III
Holocaust, 49
Holtz, Lou, part III
Holyfield, Evander, 74, 187, 225, 227, 238, 241–42, 251, 255–57
Hom, Ben, part II
homosexuality, 35, 258
Hong Kong, 109, 124, 128, 170, 174, 275, 277
Honolulu Star, The, part II
hookers, 57, 89
Hootie and the Blowfish, 141, 207
Hoover, J. Edgar, 55, 80
Hopkins, Anthony, part I
Hoppe, Art, part II
Hopper, Dennis, parts I, II
Hoskins, Bob, part I
House Judiciary Committee, 137–38, 164, 171, 173, 202–203
House of Blues, The, 24
House of Representatives, 165, 173, 189, 208
Houston Astros, 234
Houston Oilers, 230
Houston, Jean, part II, 155
Howard, David, part II
Howorth, Jeffrey, part IV
Hoying, Bob, part III
Hrbek, Kent, part III
Hsieh, Frank, part II
Hubbell, Webster, part II, 156
Hudson, Donald, part IV
Huffington, Arianna, parts I, II
Hugo Boss, 57
Hull, Bobby, part III
Hull, Brett, part III
human beings, 92, 113, 117, 121, 157
human race, 112, 157, 197
Humperdinck, Englebert, part I
Hunsicker, Gerry, part III
Hunt, Helen, 244
Hunter, Billy, part III
Hunter, Holly, part I
Hurley, Elizabeth, part I
Hurley, John, part IV
Hurst, Lowell, part II

Hussein, Saddam, 15, 114, 144, 146, 159, 167, 174, 179, 193–94, 204
Huston, John, 85
Hutmacher, Terry, part IV
Hutton, Lauren, part I
Hwang, David Henry, part I
Hyde, Henry, part II
Hynde, Chrissie, part I
hypocrisy, 101, 194

Ice-T, part I
Ice Cube, 146
Ickes, Harold, part II
Idaho, 110, 273
Idol, Billy, part I
Iglesias, Julio, part I
Illinois, 133, 139, 207, 226, 235, 264, 272, 276
illiteracy, 51
immortality, 12, 238, 242
impeachment, 137, 139, 154–55, 173, 175, 178, 180, 183, 185, 189, 194, 196, 201, 205, 212
implants, 14, 16, 67, 77, 288
impotent, 17, 190
Imus, Don, part I, 136, 152
Incaviglia, Pete, part III
Indecent Proposal, 54
India, 46, 75, 135, 162, 171, 205
Indiana University, 64, 238
Indianapolis Colts, 234, 243–44
Indians, 11, 26, 78–79, 217, 251
infidelities, 156
Information Age, 166, 184
Ingham, Michael, part I
Inhofe, James, part II
Internal Revenue Service, 83, 149
Internet, 18, 24, 50, 85, 101, 108, 127, 160, 188, 199, 202, 292
Iowa, 147, 168
Iran-Contra, 143
Iraq, 159–60, 166, 183, 185, 194, 204
Ireland, 115, 195, 208
Irish, 46, 113, 115, 178, 194, 258
Iron Curtain, 94
Irons, Jeremy, part I
Irsay, Robert, part III
Irving, John, 113
Isaacson, Walter, part II
Isaak, Chris, part I
Ismail, Adam, part IV
Issikoff, Michael, part II
Italian, 17, 30, 33, 46, 55, 68, 86, 115, 123, 153, 233, 240, 245
Italy, 27, 56, 68, 115, 177, 293

Ito, Lance, part IV
Ivins, Molly, parts I, II

Jabbar, Kareem Abdul, part III
Jack Dawson, 28
Jackie Award, 53
Jackson family, 57
Jackson, Bo, part III
Jackson, Janet, part I
Jackson, Jesse, 135, 140, 174
Jackson, Katherine, part I
Jackson, La Toya, part I
Jackson, Linda, part III
Jackson, Michael, part I, 51, 65, 68, 79,
    92, 96, 111, 127, 233
Jackson, Phil, part III, 236
Jackson, Reverend Jesse, part II
Jackson, Samuel L., parts I, III
Jacobson, Dr. Cecil, part IV
Jagger, Mick, part I, 23, 25, 42, 46,
    50–51, 65, 90, 117
jail, 41, 271, 287
Jakes, Tina, part I
James Bond, 26
Jameson, Jenna, part I
Jamison, Antawn, part III
Japan, 28, 102, 143, 145, 161, 172, 193,
    218, 259
Jaroncyk, Ryan, part III
Jasenski, Anthony, part IV
Jaws, 26, 41, 108
Jazz Singer, The, 39
jazz, 25, 107
Jenkyn-Jones, Tony, part IV
Jennings, Peter, part IV, 139
Jennings, Ted, part II
Jennings, Waylon, part I
Jeopardy, 21, 117–18
Jesus Christ, 128
Jewish, 15–16, 43, 67, 87–88, 94–95,
    105, 120, 128, 135, 162, 202, 207,
    228, 234, 279, 291
Jews, 11, 15–16, 21, 49
Jian, Wang, part I
Joan of Arc, 15
Jobs, Steve, part I
Joel, Billy, part I
John F. Kennedy Center, 92
John, Elton, part I
John, Susan, part IV
Johnson, Clark, part IV
Johnson, Davey, part III
Johnson, Don, part I, 54
Johnson, Jeffrey, part IV
Johnson, Johnny, part III
Johnson, Larry, part IV

Johnson, Lyndon B., 157
Johnson, Magic, part III, 37, 221,
    237, 251
Johnson, Mike, part IV
Johnson, Ross, part II
Johnson, Tim, part III
Johnston, Kelly, part II
Johnston, P. J., part II
Joint Chiefs of Staff, 182, 199
Jolie, Angelina, part I
Jones, Grace, part I
Jones, James Earl, part I
Jones, Paula, part II, 81, 140, 150, 152,
    154, 163, 180, 182–83, 186, 188,
    191, 213
Jones, Stephen, part IV
Jones, Tom, parts I, II
Jones, Tommy Lee, 26
Jong, Erica, part I
Jordan, Juanita, part III
Jordan, Michael, part III, 86, 219, 221,
    228–32, 235, 242
Jordan, Neil, part I
Jordan, Robert, part IV
journalism, 42, 88, 155, 163, 167, 266
journalists, 115, 121, 156, 169, 189,
    204, 266
Judaism, 15
Judd, Ashley, part I
Judge Dredd, 29
Jupiter, 39, 151, 258
Jurassic Park, 35, 268
Just, Charlie, part III
justice, 155, 162, 173, 187, 200, 219,
    236, 280, 289, 292
Justice, David, part III

Kaelin, Kato, part IV
Kaczynski, Theodore, part IV
Kagan, Donald, part III
Kallstrom, James, part IV
Kaluzny, Lauwrence, part IV
Kansas, 23, 172, 174, 177, 221
Kardashian, Robert, part IV
Kasich, John, part II
Kaufman, Bruce, part III
Kaul, Donald, part II
Kaye, John, part IV
Keane, Peter, part IV
Keaton, Diane, 20
Keen, Sam, part I
Keillor, Garrison, parts I, II, 210
Keim, Jenny, part III
Keller, Helen, 30
Kelly, Chris, part I
Kelly, Grace, 13

Kelly, Michael, part II
Kemler, Lisa, part IV
Kemp, Jack, part II
Kemper, Margaret Trudeau, part I
Kemper, Nancy Jo, part II
Kempton, Murray, part II
Kendall, Joe, part II
Kennan, George F., part II
Kennedy, Douglas, part I
Kennedy, Edward, 185
Kennedy, Jim, part II
Kennedy, Joe, part II, 157, 209, 212
Kennedy, John F., 78, 92, 158, 177, 224
Kennedy, John F., Jr., part II, 158
Kennedy, Michael, 186
Kennedys, the, 22, 180, 182, 186, 238
Kentucky, 176, 242, 251, 260
Kerlikowske, R. Gil, part IV
Kerr, Steve, part III
Kerrey, Bob, part II
Kerrigan, Brenda, part IV
Kerrigan, Nancy, part III
Kesey, Ken, part I
Kevorkian, Dr. Jack, part III, 66, 80, 192
Khan, Chaka, part I
Khrushchev, Sergei, part II
Kiam, Victor, part III
Kiatbusaba, Parinya, part III
Kidd, Jodie, part I
Kidder, Margo, part I
Kidman, Nicole, part I, 62
kids, 22, 28, 31, 39, 44, 48, 68–69,
    80–81, 95, 97–99, 105, 113, 117,
    120, 125, 127, 141, 145–49, 157,
    159, 172, 194, 197, 209–210,
    219–21, 229, 231, 235–36, 248, 257,
    290, 293
Kiedis, Anthony, part I
Kierkegaard, 12
Kilborn, Craig, parts I, II
killing, 11, 41, 60, 83, 92, 103, 115, 128,
    186, 197, 219, 267–68, 274, 279,
    284, 286–87, 289, 292, 294
Kilmer, Val, part I
Kimbrough, Jennifer, part III
Kiner, Ralph, part III
King Lear, 92
King, Billy Jean, part III
King, Carole, part I
King, Casey, part IV
King, Don, part III, 218, 227, 238, 242,
    245, 252
King, Larry, parts I, II, IV, 114, 163,
    199, 209, 272
King, Martin Luther, Jr., 25, 57, 87,
    154, 157, 252

King, Peter, part II
King, Rodney, part IV, 13, 198, 266, 281, 287, 292
King, Stephen, part I
King, Steve, part IV
Kinney, Kathy, part I
Kipfur, Barbara Ann, part I
Kipnis, Aaron R., part I
Kirkland, Sally, part I
Kirn, Walter, part I
KISS, 25, 105, 110
Kissinger, Henry, part II, 118, 174
Kissinger, Nancy, part II
Kite, Tom, part III
Kithira, Joyce, part IV
Kitt, Eartha, part I
Klein, Calvin, part I, 98, 124
Klein, Joe, part II
Klein, Joel, part IV
Klein, Kevin, part I
Klein, Marci, part I
Klein, Marty, part III
Knievel, Evel, part I, 17
Knievel, Robbie, 17
Knight, Bobby, part III
Knight, Phil, part III
Knight, Suge, part IV
Knox, Chuck, part III
Koch, Edward, part II
Kohl, Herbert, part I
Kohl, Robert, part IV
Koncak, John, part III
Koons, Jeff, part I
Koontz, Dean, part I
Koppel, Ted, part II
Kornheiser, Tony, part III
Kors, Michael, part I
Kosovo, 58, 133, 155, 184–85, 203
Kove, Martin, part I
Kramer, Hilton, part I
Krantz, Judith, part I, 25
Krauthamer, Charles, part II
Kravits, Steve, part I
Kravitz, Bob, part III
Kravitz, Lenny, part I
Kresal, Don, part III
Kristofferson, Kris, part I
Kristol, William, part II
Krueger, Bob, part II
Kruk, John, part III
Kruk, Nicole, part I
Kuala Lumpur, 162
Kuan, Hsui-chin, part IV
Kubrick, Stanley, 36, 57
Kucinich, Dennis, part II
Kulwicki, Alan, part III

Kunstler, William, parts II, IV
Kunze, Terry, part III
Kushner, Malcolm, part I
Kuwait, 143, 166, 167, 251
Kwan, Michelle, part III
Kwiatkowski, Mark, part I

L.A. Clippers, 219
L.A. Confidential, 20, 52
L.A. Dodgers, 38
La Russa, Tony, 244
Lake, Anthony, part II
Lam, Angela, part IV
Lamas, Lorenzo, part I
Lamb, Brian, 200
Lancellotti, Rick, part III
Landau, Saul, part II
Landers, Anne, part I
Landry, Bernard, part II
Landry, Bill, part IV
Lane, Nathan, part II
lang, k. d., 50, 153
Lange, Jeffrey, part III
Lansing, Sherry, part I
Lapham, Louis, part I
Larner, Jeremy, part II
Larry Sanders Show, The, 103
LaRussa, Tony, part III
Las Vegas, 17, 45, 74, 104, 222, 238, 241, 256–57
Lasorda, Tom, part III
Lasorda, Tommy, part IV
Last of the Mohicans, The, 263
Late Night, 69, 86
Late, Late Show, The, 20
Latham, Earl, part IV
Latifah, Queen, part I
Lauer, Matt, 24
Lauper, Cyndi, part I
Lauren, Ralph, 184
Law, John Phillip, 43
Lawless, Lucy, part I
Lawson, Tobarios, part IV
lawsuit, 31, 141, 154, 175, 188, 213, 224, 277, 288
lawyers, 35
Le, Thuy Thu, part I
Leadbetter, David, part III
Leahy, Patrick, part II
Leary, Timothy, part I, 100
Leaving Las Vegas, 104
LeBlanc, Matt, part I
LeBon, Simon, part I
Lebowitz, Fran, part I
Lee, Spike, part I, 41
Lee, Tommy, 26, 120

Leigh, Jennifer Jason, part I
Lemmon, Jack, part I
Lenin, Vladimir, 23, 198
Lennon, John, 53, 62, 67–68, 107, 154, 268
Lennon, Sean, part I
Leno, Jay, parts I, II, III, IV
Leonard, Elmore, part I
Leonard, Sugar Ray, part III
Leoni, Tea, part I
Lerman, Steven, part IV
lesbian, 23, 126
Lester, Adrian, part II
Letourneau, Mary Kay, part IV
Letterman, David, parts I, II, III, IV, 40, 74, 76, 138, 241
Leung, Ivy, part I
Levasseur, Raymond Luc, part IV
Lewinsky, Barbara, part II
Lewinsky, Monica, part II, 51, 55, 65, 74, 84, 136, 140, 150, 152–56, 158, 160–61, 163–67, 170, 174, 176–77, 180, 185–87, 189–91, 194–95, 200, 202–203, 205–206, 209, 211, 213, 274
Lewis, Bob, part III
Lewis, Carl, part III
Lewis, Daniel Day, 11
Lewis, Jerry Lee, part I
Lewis, Juliette, part I
Lewis, Lennox, 233
Lewis, Michael, part II
Leydecker, John, part III
Liberals, 120, 169, 171, 184, 195
Libonati, Mitchell, part III
Lichter, Robert, part II
Liddy, G. Gordon, part II
Liebman, Wendy, part I
Life Is Beautiful, 20
life, 12–36, 40–43, 47, 49, 50–58, 61–74, 80–91, 94, 96, 100–105, 110–19, 123–26, 129, 138, 142, 147, 150, 153–54, 156, 160, 163–64, 169, 173–74, 178, 185, 187, 189, 191, 193, 195, 198–202, 204, 208, 211–13, 217, 219, 221, 227–30, 232, 235, 239, 247, 249–50, 259, 260, 264–68, 273, 275–76, 278–79, 281, 286, 289–92
Lillehammer, Norway, 19
Limbaugh, Rush, part II
Lincoln Bedroom, 55, 181
Lincoln, Abraham, 33, 178, 180–81
Linder, Dona, part IV
Link, Arthur S., part II
Lion in Winter, The, 43

Lipinski, Pat, part III
liquor, 19, 174, 280
Lister, Alton, part III
Literary Review, 99
Little Rock, Arkansas, 175, 189
Littleton, Colorado, 155, 199, 276
Livernois, Gerard, part IV
Livingston, Robert, part II
Lizer, Keri, part I
Llamas, Richard, part II
lobbyist, 162, 200, 211
Lochhead, Carolyn, part II
Locklear, Heather, part I
Logan, John, part II
Lolita, 82
London Evening Standard, 46
London, 46, 79, 99, 117, 207, 278,
    281, 285
Long, Bob, part IV
Long, Robert, Jr., part IV
Long, Shelley, part I
Longfellow, Pamela, part I
Longstreet, Renee, 107
Lopez, Jennifer, part I, 34
Lords, Tracy, part I
Loren, Sophia, part I, 42
Los Alamos, 192
Los Angeles County Jail, 41
Los Angeles *Daily News,* 44
Los Angeles Dodgers, 38, 160, 218,
    223, 240, 252
Los Angeles Times, 97
Los Angeles, 14, 24, 28, 31, 41, 44,
    48–49, 51, 74, 79–80, 82, 117,
    125–26, 151, 160–61, 164, 175,
    183, 187, 202, 211, 218–19, 222,
    224, 227, 230, 231, 243, 247, 250,
    266–67, 271, 273–74, 278, 281,
    284, 287
Lott, Steve, part III
Lott, Trent, part II
Louise, Tina, 76
Louisiana, 152, 161, 191, 247, 258, 294
Love Story, 19
love, 11–12, 14–15, 21–22, 24–28,
    33–35, 38–40, 42, 45–46, 49–50,
    53–58, 61, 66, 68–69, 71, 73–80,
    86, 89, 92–95, 102–103, 105–106,
    108, 111, 114–16, 119, 122, 124,
    127–29, 139, 144, 150, 153, 162,
    166, 172, 177, 184, 187, 195, 197,
    209, 214, 217, 227, 230–31, 235,
    237, 240, 249, 253, 256–57, 285,
    287, 290–91
Love, Courtney, parts I, II, 74, 94, 112
lover, 28, 47, 82, 111, 120

Lovett, Lyle, part I
Lowe, Rob, part I
Lukas, George, part I
Lukens, Buz, part II
lust, 71, 83
Lydon, John, part I
lying, 66, 99, 109, 185, 189, 209, 273
Lyle, Sandy, part III
Lynch, David, 39

Macapagal-Arroyo, Gloria, part II
Macdonald, Norm, part I, 70
Macke, Richard C., part IV
MacKinnon, Catharine, part IV
MacLaine, Shirley, part I, 20, 30, 68,
    69, 105
MacMillan, Roy, part IV
MacPherson, Elle, 79
Madden, John, part III
Maddex, Elizabeth Hernandez,
    part IV
Madison Avenue, 35, 99
Madison Square Garden, 238
Madonna, part II, 20–21, 24, 27, 63,
    67, 79, 81, 85–86, 89, 96–98, 114,
    186, 241, 249, 260, 264, 287
Magowan, Peter, part III
Maher, Bill, parts I, II
Mahler, Donald, part IV
Mailer, Norman, parts I, II, IV, 65,
    263, 283
Maine, 78, 148
Malcolm X, 107, 186, 281
Malibu, 79
Malone, Karl, part III
Malpeli, Daniele, part IV
Maltbie, Roger, part III
Mamby, Saoul, part III
Mamet, David, part I
Man in Full, A, 121
Mandela, Nelson, part II, 47
Manhattan, 70, 105, 184, 256, 283
Manilow, Barry, part I, 41
mankind, 138, 139, 170
Manley, Dwight, part III
manslaughter, 128, 263
Manson family, 78
Manson, Charles, part IV
Manson, Marilyn, part I, 33, 40
Mantle, Mickey, part III
Maples, Marla, part I, 25, 54
Mapplethorpe, Robert, 17
Mara, John, part III
Marbury, Steve, part III
Marchibroda, Ted, part III
Marchiony, John, part III

Marcos, Imelda, part II
Margulies, Julianna, part I
marijuana, 20, 55, 83, 151, 177, 182,
    188, 193, 233, 248, 269, 288, 293
Maris, Roger, 244
Mark Twain Prize, 125
Marquez, Gabriel Garcia, part II
Marraccini, Ernest L., part IV
marriage, 37, 42, 54, 59, 79, 83–85,
    87, 89, 94, 109, 116, 122, 151–52,
    156, 171, 185, 238, 250, 277, 280,
    283, 284
Marsalis, Branford, part I
Marshall, Howard, II, 106
Martha's Vineyard, 65, 154, 186
Martin, Billy, 243, 257
Martin, Dean, 13
Martin, Judith, part II
Martin, Steve, part I, 127
Martinez, Vanessa, part II
Maryland, 145, 207, 267, 280
Mask of Zorro, The, 45
Mason, Jackie, part I
Massachusetts, 157, 171, 178, 212, 289
Masson, Jeffrey, part I
Masterpiece Theater, 15
Masterson, Mary Stuart, part II
masturbation, 79, 102, 121, 149
Matalin, Mary, part II, 150
Matos, Kica, part IV
Mayfield, David, part III
Maynard, Joyce, part I
Mayo, Norman, part IV
McAuliffe, Terrence, part II
McCaffrey, Barry, part II
McCain, John, part II
McCambridge, Mercedes, part I
McCarthy, Eugene, part II
McCarthy, Jenny, part I
McCarthy, Tony, part IV
McCartney, Paul, part I, 23, 68, 90,
    110, 129
McCaughey, Elizabeth, part II
McConnell, Lisa, part IV
McCourt, Frank, part I
McCullough, David, part II
McCurry, Mike, part II, 185, 190
McDonald, Tim, part III
McDonalds, 57, 194
McDougal, James, part II
McDougal, Susan, part II, 134
McDowell, Roger, part III
McElhone, Natascha, part I
McEnroe, John, part III
McGann, Eileen, part II
McGrath, Bob, part I

McGraw, Ali, 19
McGwire, Mark, part III
McKagan, Duff, part I
McKellen, Ian, part I
McKenna, Pat, part IV
McKenna, Paul, part IV
McKeon, John, part III
McKinney, Cynthia, part II
McLaughlin Group, The, 64
McMahon, Ed, part I
McMahon, Vince, part III
McMaster, Henry, part II
McNally, Terrence, part I
McNaughton, Alec, part IV
McNeeley, Peter, part III
McNeil/Lehrer News Hour, The, 29
McQueen, Steve, 18
McVeigh, Timothy, part IV
McWilliams, David, part III
Meader, Vaughn, part I
Meadows, Marc, part IV
Meagher, Matt, part I
Mean Streets, 102
Means, Russell, part I
media, 38, 44, 62, 86, 94, 104, 114–15,
    119, 133, 138, 147–48, 153, 156,
    159, 166, 170, 191–193, 202, 204,
    212–13, 229, 252, 267, 270, 274, 291
Medicare, 164
Megadeth, 23
Mell, Dick, part II
Mellencamp, John Cougar, part I
Melrose Place, 68, 129
Memphis, Tennessee, 230
*Men Are From Mars, Women Are From
    Venus,* 49
Men at Work, 42
men, 21–22, 27–28, 31–32, 36, 38, 43,
    59, 60–61, 63, 68, 73, 77, 81–82,
    84–85, 87, 90, 97, 98–102, 109–111,
    114, 117, 123, 128, 133, 155–56,
    168, 175, 192, 199, 202, 211–13,
    232, 233, 251, 257, 260, 267, 272,
    274, 277–78, 283, 287
Menendez, Lyle, part IV
menopause, 61
Merrill, Jim, part II
Mestemaker, Albert, part IV
Metaksa, Tanya, part II
Methodist, 15, 33
Mexico, 44, 238, 251, 289
Meyer, Chris, 74
Meyer, Doug, part IV
Meyer, Ron, part III
Meyers, Dee Dee, part II
Miami, 114, 171, 200, 246, 266, 268, 288

Michael, George, part I, 47, 70, 85
Michigan, 16, 80, 192, 232, 245, 253,
    258, 267, 284
Mickey Mouse, 57
Microsoft, 11, 165, 274
Middle East, 54, 160
Midler, Bette, part I, 95
Midsummer Night's Dream, A, 48
Migden, Carol, part II
Milano, Alyssa, part III
Milbury, Mike, part III
millennium, 76
Miller, Dennis, parts I, II
Miller, Glenn, 103
Miller, Jamir, part III
Miller, Oliver, part III
Miller, Stephanie, part IV
Miller, Zell, part II
Milli Vanilli, 90
millionaires, 15, 239, 240
Milwaukee Brewers, 229
Minnesota, 149, 172, 179, 210, 218,
    222, 226, 232, 234, 264
Minor, Ryan, part III
Mirren, Helen, part I, 82
Mischer, Dennis, part I
misogynist, 35
Mission to Mars, 32
Mitchell, Andrea, part II
Mitchell, Dennis, part III
Mitchell, George, part II
Mitchell, Joni, part I
Mitchell, Kevin, part III
Mithcam, Bob Anderson, part IV
Mizell, Hubert, part III
Mizrahi, Isaac, part I
Moceanu, Dominique, part III
model, 11, 42–43, 50–52, 101, 128
Moeller, Gary, part III
Moffatt, Ivan, part IV
Mogadishu, 92
Mohammad, Mahathir, part II
Mona Lisa, 246
Monaco, Ralph, part IV
Monday Night Football, 72, 250
money, 16, 18, 24, 26–27, 31–32, 36,
    39, 45, 47, 51–52, 58–60, 66, 72, 75,
    77–80, 88, 92–93, 96–100, 105–106,
    109–110, 112–13, 117–18, 122,
    124–25, 134–35, 140–42, 150, 152,
    156–57, 161–63, 165, 173, 181, 187,
    190, 192, 194, 203, 206–209, 211,
    214, 218–19, 226–28, 232–33, 238,
    247, 249, 251, 254, 259, 268, 269,
    274, 277, 282, 292
Money, Eddie, part I

Monica, Monica L., part II
Monk, Thelonius, 107
Monopoly, 52, 287
Monroe, Marilyn, 36, 115, 223
Montana, 44, 123, 211, 246
Montana, Joe, 246, 258
Montoya, Stephen, part IV
Montreal Expos, 218, 245
Moody, Helen Willis, part III
Moonves, Les, 51
Moor, Colin, part IV
Moore, Darla, part I
Moore, Demi, part I, 46, 71
Moore, Michael, parts I, II, 191
Moorer, Michael, part III
Moran, Brenda, part IV
Morgan, James, part IV
Morris, Dick, part II, 189, 194
Morris, Hal, part III
Morris, Mark, part I
Morrison, Jim, 62
Morrison, Tommy, part III, 233
Morrison, Toni, part I
Morrow, Mario, part II
Mortman, Lisa, part I
Morton, Andrew, 183
Mosbacher, Robert, part II
Moscow, 60, 167
Moss, Kate, 38
Mother Teresa, 58, 158
mother, 21, 27, 32, 36, 39, 43, 71, 75,
    80, 84, 86, 88, 94, 101, 104, 110,
    115, 123, 136, 145, 155, 158,
    160–61, 219, 249, 256, 263, 265,
    280, 287, 290
movie star, 17, 67, 75, 117, 122
movies, 18–19, 25–26, 28, 33, 35–36,
    42, 47, 61, 71–73, 78, 85–86, 91, 94,
    101, 105–107, 113, 116, 121–22,
    125–26, 144, 149, 156, 204, 223, 247
Moyers, Bill, 95, 167
Moynihan, Patrick, part II
Mozart, 57, 77, 107, 223
MSNBC, part III
MTV Music Awards, 99
MTV, 69, 99, 107, 120, 190
Muhhamad, Hurad, part III
Muhlberger, Richard, part I
murder, 17, 146, 267, 273, 275, 286, 287
Murdoch, Rupert, 38
Murkowski, Frank, part II
Murphy, Anne Pleshette, part I
Murphy, Danny, part I
Murphy, Dennis, part IV
Murphy, Eddie, part I
Murphy, Joseph, part IV

Murray, Bill, part I
music, 12, 19, 21, 23, 26, 29, 30, 32–33,
35, 37, 46, 57, 59, 68, 70, 74, 76–77,
79, 86, 91, 100, 110, 120–22,
127–29, 134–35, 139, 144, 146, 148,
153, 193, 226, 243, 254
Muslim, 38
Musto, Michael J., part I

Nabholz, Chris, part III
Nabokov, Dimitri, part I
Nabokov, Vladimir, 82
Nader, Ralph, part II
NAFTA, 44, 225
NASA, 164, 197, 208, 277
Nash, Graham, part I
Nation, The, part II
National Enquirer, 15, 98
National League, 222, 248
NATO, 176, 186, 190, 198
Natural Born Killers, 70
Navarro, Curt, part IV
Navratilova, Martina, part III
Nazi, 62, 87, 207
NBA, 142, 174, 217, 219, 226, 229,
230, 232, 234–35, 237, 243, 247–49,
251, 253–54, 259
NBC, 47, 50–51, 69–70, 179, 223, 250,
279, 295
NCAA, 232, 251
Nebraska, 143, 149, 177, 247
Neeson, Liam, part I
Neilson, Roger, part III
Nelligan, Kate, part I
Nelson, Craig T., part I
Nelson, David, part IV
Nelson, Gary, part III
Nelson, John, part III
Nelson, Lana, part I
Nelson, Willie, parts I, II, 17, 42
Netherlands, 21, 85
Neufeld, Peter, part IV
Neverland, 79
New Hampshire, 100, 145, 154, 157,
168
New Jersey, 106, 140, 149, 198, 225,
253
New Kids on the Block, The, 110, 124
New Orleans Saints, 227
New Republic, The, part I
New York Knicks, 229
New York Times, 12, 67, 163
New York, 11–12, 16–18, 23, 29, 30,
41–43, 48, 52–53, 63–67, 69, 73–74,
76, 78–80, 86, 94, 102, 111, 113,
117, 119, 128–29, 138, 140–41, 147,

154, 157–58, 163, 166–67, 177–78,
180–81, 183, 188, 191, 194, 198,
202, 220–21, 228–29, 230, 232, 240,
243–44, 248, 252–54, 258, 263, 266,
273–75, 277, 280–81, 283, 287–88,
291–93
New Yorker, 25, 91, 105, 121, 178
New Zealand, 133
Newhart, Bob, part I
Newkirk, Ingrid, part IV
Newman, Larry, part II
Newman, Paul, part I, 67, 127
Newman, Randy, part I
Newman, Rock, part III
Newton, Helmut, part I
Newton, Nate, part III
NFL, 57, 222–23, 229, 240–41, 244–45
Nguyen, Bai Van, part II
Nicaragua, 197, 199
Nichols, Mike, parts I, II
Nichols, Terry, part IV
Nicholson, Jack, parts I, II, 20
Nicklaus, Jack, part III
Nickles, Sarah, part I
Nightline, 178
Nike, 75, 80, 239
Nirvana (band), 71, 85
Nixon, Richard, part II, 114, 199, 269
Nobel Prize, 64, 81
Nobles, Jonathan, part IV
Nofziger, Lyn, part II
Nolte, Nick, 51, 115
Noonan, Peggy, part II
Norman, Greg, part III
North Carolina, 220, 235, 264, 276, 282
North Dakota, 12
North Viet Cong, 29
Northwest American Indians, 26
Northwestern University, 251
Norville, Deborah, part I
nose job, 49, 71, 74
Notre Dame, 224, 234, 258
Novak, Kim, part I
Novoselic, Krist, part II
NRA, 50, 171, 276
nuclear weapons, 79, 120, 162, 192, 198
nude, 19, 31, 37, 45, 76, 101, 120,
249, 277
Nugent, Ted, 135
Nunn, Sam, part II
Nutcracker, The, 244
NYPD Blue, 45

O'Brien, Conan, parts I, II, III, IV
O'Connor, Sinead, parts I, II
O'Donnell, Rosie, part I

O'Neal, Shaquille, part III
O'Rourke, P.J., part II
O'Toole, Peter, part I
Oakland, California, 87, 140, 174, 217,
223–24, 233, 259, 263
Oberman, Keith, part I
O'Brien, Conan, 69, 85, 86, 194, 246,
286
Odd Couple, The, 20
O'Donnell, Rosie, 86, 155
Of Mice and Men, 82
Ogrim, Helge, part III
Ohio, 48, 112, 158, 165, 167, 178–79,
199, 234, 245, 252, 258, 272, 284–85
Ohlmeyer, Don, 47, 70
Oklahoma, 161, 248, 270, 272, 275,
278, 282, 284, 286
Olbrot, Henryka, part IV
Old Testament, The, 23
Oldman, Gary, part I
Oliphant, Thomas, part II
Olympic Games, 19, 218, 230, 242
Onassis, Jacqueline Kennedy, part I
One Lifetime Is Not Enough, 45
orgasm, 22, 85, 158
Orlando Magic, 239, 253
Osborne, Tom, part III
Osbourne, Ozzy, part I, 23
Oscars, The, 20, 28, 39, 51, 87, 91, 94,
121
Ostler, Scott, parts I, II
Othello, 43
Oval Office, 135, 139, 152–53, 173,
183, 194, 204, 212
Ovitz, Michael, 47
Owen, Bill, part II
Owens, Lee, part III
Owens, Ronn, parts I, II, III, IV
ozone layer, 104, 180
Ozzie and Harriet, 59

pacifist, 35, 67
Pacino, Al, part I
Packwood, Bob, part II
Padro, Diego, part IV
Paglia, Camille, parts I, II
Paige, Shalon, part I
pain, 11, 14, 24, 63, 86, 93, 95, 99, 116,
134, 151, 156, 166, 176, 206, 209,
227, 256, 286
Paisley, Reverend Ian, part II
Pak, Ri Se, part III
Pakistan, 105, 162, 171
Palermo, George, part IV
Palm Springs, California, 137–38, 281
Paltrow, Gwyneth, part I, 184

Panama, 144, 163, 197, 263
Panetta, Leon, part II
paparazzi, 89
Paris, 13, 29, 84, 222, 246, 272, 289
Parker, Lu, part II
Parker, Sarah Jessica, part I
Parker, Trey, part I
Parks, Rosa, 41
Parrish, Robert, part III
Parton, Dolly, parts I, II, 14
Partridge Family, The, 22
Party of Five, 29
Pascoe, William, part II
passion, 14, 93, 111, 118, 193, 203, 231
Passover, 225
Payton, Gary, part III
Pazienza, Vinny, part III
Peace Corps, 60, 209
Peacock, Charles, part II
Pearl Jam, 175
Pelevin, Victor, part I
Pellicano, Anthony, part IV
Penn, Sean, part I, 73, 128
Pennsylvania, 171, 180, 228
Pentagon, 190
People (magazine), 44, 220
Perez, Rosie, part I
Perisie, Stephen, part IV
Perkins, Anne, part I
Perkins, Maxwell, 63
Perkins, Sam, part III
Perot, Ross, part II, 44, 51, 114, 146, 198
Perrine, Valerie, part I
Perry, Luke, part I
pervert, 124, 281
Pesci, Joe, part I
Peterson, Cassandra "Elvira", part I
Peterson, Paul, part IV
Peterson, Tom, part IV
Petty, Tom, part I
Peyser, Kathy, part IV
Pfeiffer, Michelle, part I
Phair, Liz, part I
Philadelphia 76ers, 218–19, 259
Philadelphia Story, The, 84
Philip of Britain, Prince, part II
Philip, Paul, part IV
Philippines, 186–87
Phillips, Julia, part I
Phillips, Michelle, part II, 54
philosophy, 19, 125, 185, 201, 217, 236, 251
Phnom Penh, 30
Phoenix, River, part I
Pierce, Pete, parts II, IV

Pike, Douglas, part II
Pilatus, Rob, part I
Pileggi, Nicholas, part IV
Pinker, Steven , part I
Pirner, David, part I
Piscopo, Joe, 92
Pitt, Brad, part I, 67, 77, 112
Pitts, Earl, part IV
Pittsburgh, 136, 221, 252, 258, 263
Planned Parenthood, 38
Plant, Robert, part I
plastic, 14, 26, 30–31, 39, 49, 75, 79, 92, 108, 124, 127, 161, 172
Plath, Sylvia, 87
Playboy, 14–15, 19–20, 25, 34, 37, 51, 53–54, 57, 127, 170, 199, 260
playoffs, 219, 235
Plimpton, George, 29
Plummer, Charles, part IV
Plymouth Theater, 48
Pocahontas, 47, 78
Poitier, Sidney, part I
politician, 44, 137–38, 151, 157, 160, 178–80, 193, 196, 201, 203, 205, 212, 214, 292
politics, 22, 150, 179, 180
Pollack, Steven, part IV
polls, 51, 84, 146, 175, 190, 191, 192
Polonia, Luis, part III
polygamy, 79
pool, 65, 134, 170, 218
poor people, 16, 80, 125, 219
Pop, Iggy, part I, 23
Pope John Paul II, 65, 86, 244
Pope, the, 20, 25, 65, 86, 244, 246
Porizkova, Paulina, part I
porn star, 14, 71, 109
Portnoy, Michael, part I
pot (marijuana), 14, 29, 32, 37, 52, 65, 96, 159, 187, 193, 293
Potter, Monica, part I
Poundstone, Paula, part I
poverty, 20, 135, 147, 166, 198, 214, 284
Povich, Maury, 92, 95
Povich, Maury, part I
Powell, Boog, part III
Powell, Colin, 107, 179
Powell, Edwin, part IV
power, 18, 31, 52, 83, 84, 87, 90, 114, 120, 123, 126, 128, 133–35, 161, 172, 205–206, 212, 256, 266
Prager, Emily, part I
Prantil, Kristie, part II
pregnant, 46, 49, 56–57, 69, 71, 73, 86, 97, 133, 187, 221, 264
Prejean, Sister Helen, part IV

Presbyterians, 43
Presley, Elvis, 13, 22, 44, 63, 70, 107, 128, 153, 257
Presley, Lisa Marie, part I, 57, 79
press, 12, 16, 22, 44, 47, 51, 58, 66, 74, 82, 84, 145, 155–56, 166, 183–84, 189–90, 197, 200, 204, 212, 225–26, 230, 234, 240–42, 264, 272, 275, 278, 290
Preston, Billy, 30
Previn, Soon-Yi, 11, 12
Price Is Right, The, 18
Price, Ray, 83
Price, Richard, part I
Priestly, Jason, part I
Primary Colors, 84, 178, 180, 185, 193, 209
Prince, 16, 41, 58, 86, 101–102, 115, 162, 196, 229, 231, 287
Princeton University, 27, 93, 223, 227, 255
Pringle, Bobby, part IV
prison, 25, 153, 174, 189, 201, 227, 241, 255–57, 263, 266–67, 271, 273–74, 276, 280–82, 286, 292–93
privacy, 118, 165
Proaps, Linda, part I
proctologist, 21, 40, 54, 208
prostitute, 14, 22, 43, 49, 82, 117, 179, 280
Prozac, 128
Pryor, Richard, part I, 37, 125
Pulitzer Prize, 77
Pulp Fiction, 58
Pulsipher, Bill, part III
Punsalan, Elizabeth, part III
Puzo, Mario, part I

Qaddafi, Muammar, part II
quarterback, 22, 113, 208, 221–22, 234–35, 244–45, 251, 255, 260
Quayle, Dan, part II, 40, 50, 68, 136, 138, 142, 158, 162, 170–71, 180, 187, 192, 204
Quayle, Marilyn, part II, 62
Queen Victoria, 38, 150
Queenan, Joe, parts I, III
Queens, New York, 12, 227
Quello, James, part II
Quinn, Anthony, part I
Quinn, Colin, part I
Quinones, Lisa, part IV
Quixote, Don, 157

R.E.M., 25
racism, 51, 211, 276, 284

Radelet, Michael, part IV
Radziwell, Lee, part I
Rafter, Patrick, part III
Rainbow Coalition, 140
Rainer, Luise, part I
Raitt, Bonnie, part I
Rakowitze, Daniel, part IV
Ramirez, Neil, part IV
Randall, Tony, 39
rape, 53, 78, 93, 95, 133, 149, 203, 256, 279, 283–84, 294
Rappaport, Dennis, part III
Rather, Dan, parts I, II, 56
Rawers, Roy, part IV
Rawl, Ted, part I
Ray, Elizabeth, part II
Raye, Martha, 52
Razorbacks (University of Arkansas), 244
Reagan, Maureen, part II
Reagan, Nancy, 76
Reagan, Ronald, part II, 17, 37, 45, 50, 106, 158, 205, 212
Rebagliati, Ross, part III
recession, 144
Red Hot Chili Peppers, 20
Reddy, Helen, part I
Redford, Robert, part I, 54
Reed, Lou, part II, 23
Reese, Pokey, part III
Reeves, Bryant, part III
Reeves, Keanu, part I
Reeves, Steve, part I
refugees, 174
Regalado, Thomas, part II
Rehnquist, William, part II, 178
Rehr, David, part II
Reich, Robert, part II, 152
Reiner, Rob, part I
Reinhardt, Steven, part IV
Reiser, Paul, part I
religion, 15, 73, 105, 123, 224
Rembrandt, 22
Reno, Janet, part II
Reo, Don, part I
reporters, 24, 48, 117, 134, 139, 143–44, 161, 163, 166, 170, 174, 190, 201, 210, 218–20, 227, 245, 276
Republicans, 66, 136, 142, 150, 154, 156, 158–59, 161, 164, 168, 170, 179, 184, 187, 192, 194, 196, 198, 207–208, 212, 219
Resnick, Fay, part IV
revenge, 12, 22, 79, 93, 201
Revere, Paul, 17, 56
Reynolds, Burt, part I
Rhodes Scholar, 134

Ricci, Christina, part I
Rice University, 224
Rice, Anne, part I
Rice, Donna, 170
Rice, Jerry, part III
rich, 27, 35, 37, 45, 66, 74, 80, 88, 106, 110, 111, 113, 116, 160, 164, 168, 187, 192–93, 213–14, 219, 222, 238, 280
Richards, Ann, part II
Richards, Keith, part I
Richardson, Bill, part II
Richardson, Margaret, part II
Richardson, Nolan, part III
Richmond, Ray, 97
Riggleman, Jim, part III
Rivera, Geraldo, parts I, II
Rivers, Joan, parts I, II
Robb, Rhom, part IV
Robbins, Tony, 31
Roberts, Julia, part I, 72, 79, 86, 264
Roberts, Oral, 124, 139
Robertson, Pat, part II, 176
Robertson, Robbie, part II
Robinson, Edward G., 51
Robinson, Frank, part III
Robinson, Rachel, part III
Rocamora, Joe, part II
Rocco, Vito, part I
Rock and Roll Hall of Fame, 106
rock stars, 19, 66, 121
Rock, Chris, parts I, III, IV
Rockefeller, Nelson, 124, 211
Rodgers, Barbara, part II
Rodham, Dorothy, part II
Rodman, Anika, part III
Rodman, Dennis, part III, 33, 67, 174, 217, 233, 235, 241, 243, 246–47
Rogers, Roy, part I
Rogers, Steven, part IV
Roker, Al, 50
Roland, Stan, part I
Rolling Stone, 46, 72, 126
Rolling Stones, The, 30, 95, 125
Rolls-Royce, 38
Romano, Ray, part I
Romeo, 103, 163
Romer, Roy, part II, 145
Rooney, Mickey, parts I, II, 166
Roosevelt, Eleanor, 189
Roper, John, part IV
Rose Bowl, 220, 231–32
Rose Garden, 146–47
Rose, Pete, part III
Roseanne, 15–16, 51, 68, 72, 97–98, 101, 111, 175

Rosen, Gary, part I
Rosenberg, Howard, 97
Rosenberg, Liz, part I
Rosenblatt, Roger, part I
Rosenthal, Phil, parts I, IV, 44, 288
Ross, Diana, 37
Ross, Herbert, 88
Rostenkowski, Dan, part II, 165, 190
Rostenthal, Jane, part I
Roth, David Lee, part I, 122
Roung, Skadavy Math Ly, part IV
Rourke, Mickey, part I
Roush, Matt, 97
Routh, Brian, part I
Royle, Nicholas, part I
Rubinek, Saul, part I
Ruddrama, Jani, part II
Rudner, Rita, part I
Rukmana, Siti Hardijanti, part II
Rushdie, Salman, part I
Russell, Kurt, part I
Russia, 89, 134, 179, 208, 214
Russians, 134
Ruth, Babe, 152
Ryan, April, part II
Ryan, Meg, 87
Ryan, Nolan, part III
Ryder, Winona, part I
Rymer, Drew, part II

Sacramento, California, 141, 202
Sadat, Anwar, 159
Safer, Morley, 29
Safire, William, 169
Sahl, Mort, part I
Saigon, 252–53
Sajak, Pat, part I
Salinger, J. D., 73, 77, 114, 202
Salinger, Pierre, part II
Salt Lake City, Utah, 98
Salvi, Al, part II
Salvi, John, part IV
Samphan, Khieu, part II
Sampras, Pete, part III, 224
Samuels, Air, part I
San Antonio Spurs, 249
San Francisco Giants, 238
San Francisco, 27, 35, 77, 90, 110, 121, 125, 127, 137, 140–42, 144, 161, 172–73, 175, 186, 190, 196, 202, 212–13, 221–22, 224, 227, 234, 238, 242–43, 247, 251–52, 260, 266, 268, 271, 275, 282, 293
San Francisco 49ers, 142, 144, 161, 228, 234, 242, 247, 251, 252

San Jose, California, 165, 169, 213, 225, 265
Sanchez, Ilich Ramirez, part IV
Sanders, Deion, part III
Sanderson, Wimp, part III
Sandler, Adam, part I, 92
Sanger, Margaret, 38
Santa Fe, New Mexico, 73
Sapp, Warren, part III
Sara, Sue, parts I, II
Sarandon, Susan, part I
Sarenana, Melissa, part IV
Sarmiento, Sergio, part IV
Satan, 93, 270
Sather, Glen, part III
satire, 11, 55, 60, 84, 118
Saturday Night Live, 36, 70, 72, 111
Saudi Arabia, 142, 197
Saving Private Ryan, 62
Sawyer, Diane, part I, 84, 151, 189, 282–83
Sawyer, Forrest, 83
saxophone, 49, 80, 107, 151, 204
Scalia, Antonin, part IV
scandal, 133, 136, 140, 143, 153, 157, 165, 171, 175, 177, 180, 182–85, 187, 189, 191, 195, 205, 210, 237, 270
Scardino, Albert, part II
Scarlet Letter, The, 80
Schanz, Heidi, part I
Schayes, Danny, part III
Scheck, Barry, part IV
Scheer, Robert, part II
Schiffer, Claudia, part I, 33, 79, 102
Schilling, Curt, part III
Schindler's List, 62
Schippers, David, part II
Schlessinger, Dr. Laura, part I
Schmidt, Joe, part III
Schneider, Daniel, part III
Schnur, Steve, part III
Schott, Marge, part III
Schrader, Paul, part I
Schroeder, Pat, part II
Schulberg, Budd, part III
Schuller, Reverend Robert, part II
Schultz, George, 118
Schumer, Charles, part II
Schwarzenegger, Arnold, part I, 69, 144
Scientology, 13, 209
Scorcese, Martin, part I
Scott, Dave, part IV
Scott, William Lee, part I
Scott-Thomas, Kristen, part I

Scowcroft, Brent, part II
screenwriter, 11, 92, 101, 127, 264
Scully, Vin, part III
Scurry, Briana, part III
Seabrook, John, part III
Seattle SuperSonics, 247
Secret Service, 140, 152, 192, 258
Segal, George, part I
Segal, Steven, part I, 21
Seifert, George, part III
Seinfeld, 37, 102, 186
Seinfeld, Jerry, part I
Seles, Monica, part III
Self, Kathy, part I
Seligman, Peter, part III
Semel, Terry, part I
Semler, David, part I
Sen, Hun, part II
Senate Judiciary Committee, 139
Sensenbrenner, Rep. F. James, part II
Seoul, South Korea, 62
Serbia, 190, 194
Serra, Tony, part IV
Serrone, Christopher, part I
Sesame Street, 20, 129, 155, 239
Seselj, Vojislav, part II
Sex Pistols, The, 72
sex, 12–15, 18–19, 21–23, 27–29, 31–32, 34, 36, 39–40, 47, 49, 50–53, 55, 59, 65, 71–72, 74, 76, 84, 87, 89, 90–91, 93, 95–97, 99, 101, 106, 108–109, 111–12, 114, 116, 119–24, 126, 128, 139, 142, 150, 155, 157, 161, 164, 168, 170, 177, 179, 180, 183–86, 189, 191–92, 194–95, 201, 203, 206, 211–13, 237, 241, 249, 250–51, 260, 265, 277, 281, 283, 286
Sexiest Man Alive, the, 44, 45
sexual behavior, 18, 139, 164
sexual harassment, 18, 44, 154, 167, 169, 183, 283
Sexual Persona, 87
sexual revolution, 18
sexuality, 52, 53, 89
Shafter, Ronald, part III
Shakespeare, William, 31, 39, 43, 103, 107, 113, 119, 178, 268, 271, 278
Shakur, Tupac, part I
Shalala, Donna, part II, 133
Shanahan, Mike, part III
Shanahan, Patrick, part IV
Shandling, Gary, parts I, IV
Shangri-La, 35
Shapiro, Robert, part IV, 98, 263
Sharpe, Shannon, part III
Sharpton, Reverend Al, parts II, III

Shaw, Artie, part I
Shaw, Bill, part III
Shays, Christopher, part II
Shea Stadium, 222
Shearer, Derek, part II
Sheehy, Gail, part I
Sheen, Charlie, part I, 26
Sheenan, Bob, part I
Sheffield, Gary, part III
Shell, Art, part III
Shengde, General, part II
Shepherd, Cybill, part I
Shields, Brooke, part I
Shimkonis, Paul, part I
Shire, Talia, part I
Shore, Pauly, parts I, IV
show business, 15
Showalter, Buck, part III
Showgirls, 116
Shriver, Maria, part II
Shue, Elizabeth, part I
Shulgasser, Barbara, part I
Shuster, Bud, part II
Siben, Andrew, part IV
Sid and Nancy, 72
Siddeeq, Reverend Muhamed, part III
Siegfried and Roy, 68
Sieler, Lincoln, part IV
Silicon Valley, 35
Silkwood, 42
Silverman, Bruce, part I
Silverstone, Alicia, part I
Simi Valley, 45
Simmons, Gene, part I
Simmons, Richard, part I
Simon, Carly, part I
Simon, Paul, part I, 133
Simon, Roger, part II
Simpson, Alan, part II
Simpson, Nicole Brown, 265, 268–69, 275, 278, 288, 291, 293
Simpson, O. J., part IV
Simpson, Terry, part III
Simpsons, The, 50
Sinatra, Frank, part I
Singh, Peter, part I
Single Guy, The, 51
Singleton, John, part I
Sink, Heather, part III
Siskel and Ebert, 247
Siskel, Gene, part I, 41
Sitch, Rob, part I
60 Minutes, 93, 151, 163, 207
Skiles, Scott, part III
Sklar, Robert, part II
Slater, Christian, part I

Slick, Grace, part I
Sliwa, Curtis, part I
Sliwa, Lisa, part IV
Slocum, R. C., part III
Smale, Bob, part I
Smith College, 30, 111
Smith, Anna Nicole, part I
Smith, Harry, part II
Smith, Kathy, part III
Smith, Kevin, part I
Smith, Lee, part III
Smith, Patti, parts I, II
Smith, Will, parts I, II
Smith, Zane, part III
Smithsonian Institution, 102
smoke, 14, 32, 38, 40, 65, 75, 83,
    104–105, 137, 170, 173, 187, 248,
    251, 284
smoking, 17, 25, 31, 35, 37–38, 47, 66,
    79, 82, 104, 135, 137, 142, 159, 169,
    170, 172, 181, 193, 200, 213, 270,
    284–85, 293
Snoop Doggy Dog, part I
Snow, Tony, part II
Snyder, Tom, 20
Social Security, 154, 175, 183, 185,
    274, 287
Socrates, 55, 148, 167
Some Like It Hot, 36
Somers, Suzanne, part I
Sondheim, Stephen, part I
Sonnenfield, Barry, part I
Sony Pictures Classics, 21
Soren, Tabitha, part I
Sosa, Sammy, part III
Soul Asylum, 37, 81, 100
Souljah, Sister, part I
South Carolina, 80, 149, 159, 172, 190,
    207
South Park, 17, 88
South Park, Colorado, 17
Southern Methodist University, 33
Soviet Union, 158
Spago, 36
Spain, 153, 218
Speaker of the House, 163, 185
Speck, Richard, part IV
Spector, Phil, part I
Spelling, Tori, part I
Spencer, Troy, part IV
Spice Girls, The, 240
Spicer, Hayley, part I
Spielberg, Steven, part I, 26, 61, 129
Spillane, Mickey, part I
Spillane, Sherri, part III
Spira, Howard, part IV

Spock, Benjamin, part I, 81
Spoonhour, Charlie, part III
sports, 15, 68, 116, 144, 170, 218, 221,
    223–24, 228–29, 232, 240, 244, 255
Sports Illustrated, 37, 241
Sprewell, Latrell, part III, 142, 230,
    247
Springboro, Ohio, 48
Springer, Jerry, part I, 33, 62, 285, 294
Springfield, Dusty, part I
spring training, 230, 240, 245, 251
Sprinkle, Annie, part I
Spurrier, Steve, part III
Squier, Bob, part II
Squires, Kelly, part I
Srivastava, Divesh, part II
St. James, Margo, part II
St. Louis, Missouri, 128, 220, 231, 234,
    240, 244, 251, 253, 258
Stallone, Sylvester, part I, 29, 67
Stallone, ToniAnn, part I
Stanford University, 59, 118, 255, 258,
    265
Stanley, Paul, part I
Stano, Gerald, part IV
Star Trek: The Next Generation, 45
Star Wars, 82, 239
Star, Daren, part IV
stardom, 11, 273
Stargate, 17
Stark, Pete, part II
Starr Report, 150, 154
Starr, Kenneth, part II, 136, 140, 165,
    173, 182, 184, 203, 274
Starr, Maurice, part I
Starr, Ringo, part I
stars, 19, 21–22, 31, 36, 82, 99, 104,
    126, 137, 141, 156, 294
State Department, 150, 197
State of the Union Address, 161, 170,
    179, 181, 190, 201, 207
Stead, Christina, part I
Steel Magnolias, 88
Steel, Dawn, part I
Steele, Danielle, part I
Steele, Ronald, part II
Steele, Shelby, part II
Steiger, Barry, part I
Steiger, Rod, part I
Steinbrenner, George, part III, 146,
    220–21, 223, 292
Steinem, Gloria, part I, 52
Steinke, Darcey, part I
Stephanopoulos, George, part II
Stern, David, part III
Stern, Howard, part I

Stern, Jane, part I
Steuer, Robert, part IV
Stevens, Ted, part II
Stewart, Jimmy, 28
Stewart, Jon, part I
Stewart, Martha, part II
Stewart, Rod, part I
Steyn, Mark, part II
Stiller, Ben, part I
Stills, Stephen, part I
Stim, Roger, part I
Stine, R. L., part I
Sting, 81, 94, 110, 112
Stipe, Michael, part I
stock market, 174, 192, 272
Stockdale, James, part II
Stojko, Elvis, part III
Stoltz, Eric, part I
Stone, Greg, part III
Stone, Oliver, part I, 16, 53, 55, 70,
    123, 179
Stone, Sharon, parts I, II, 39, 49, 82,
    86, 115, 116, 206
Strategic Air Command, 143
Strawberry, Darryl, 228, 240, 245
Streep, Meryl, 36
Streisand, Barbra, parts I, II, 48, 71,
    93, 206
Strickland, George, part IV
Strickland, Jerry, part III
success, 24, 26, 28, 44, 46, 69, 70, 73,
    105, 114, 129, 145, 186, 196, 207,
    242, 251, 280
suffering, 21, 79, 115, 136, 189, 202, 286
suicide, 24, 42, 76, 80, 85, 90, 107, 110,
    120, 152, 158, 180, 223, 290
Sullivan, Ed, 98
Sullivan, Louis, part II
Sumerians, 13
Sundance Film Festival, 21, 46, 99, 106
Sun-ju, Kim, part I
Super Bowl, 57, 142, 144, 146, 226,
    233, 234, 241
Supreme Court, 150, 155, 158, 167,
    283, 289, 292, 294
Supremes, The, 37
surgery, 14, 30, 39, 40, 49, 75, 79, 92,
    161, 222, 265
Surinam, 60
Sutherland, Donald, part I
Swarm, The, 44
Swayze, Patrick, part I
Swenson, Rich, part III

Talese, Gay, part I
Taliban, 164

talk shows, 92, 109, 291

Tamraz, Roger, part II

Tapie, Bernard, part IV

Tarango, Benedicte, part III

Tarango, Jeff, part III

Tarantino, Quentin, part I

tattoos, 14, 16

Tatum, Jim, part III

tax, 42, 92, 134, 136, 143, 144, 154, 165, 172, 188, 200, 211, 234, 237, 264, 293

taxation, 123, 211

Taylor, Elizabeth, part I, 31, 50, 126, 207

television, 25, 30, 32, 34, 38, 40, 51, 57, 62, 69, 95, 97–99, 111, 117–18, 120–21, 135, 145, 159, 187, 197, 201, 218, 223, 249, 259, 267, 273, 277, 289, 291

Teller, Edward, part II

Tempest, The, 278

Ten Commandments, The, 51

Tennessee, 104, 141, 143, 145, 275, 278, 284

Tenuta, Judy, part I

Terminator, The, 101, 144

Terrill, Ross, part II

Tesh, John, part I

testimony, 164, 177, 183, 199, 213, 224, 272, 288

Texas, 17, 26, 87, 92, 103, 106, 135–36, 144–46, 148, 168, 172, 178, 196, 200, 223, 232, 237, 244, 253, 267, 270, 273–74, 280, 293

Thanksgiving, 72, 90, 152, 292

Thatcher, Margaret, 55

theater, 12, 21, 48, 73, 87, 112, 181, 263, 281

Theismann, Joe, part III

Thomas, Clarence, part IV, 139, 157, 167, 174, 219

Thomas, Debi, part III

Thomas, Richard, part I

Thomas, Scarlet, part II

Thompson, Emma, parts I, II

Thompson, Fred, part II

Thompson, Hunter, part I

Thompson, John, part III

Thompson, Laetitia, part II

Thompson, Stella Marie, part I

Thompson, Thomas, part IV

Thornton, Billy Bob, part I

Thorpe, Jim, 222

Thurmond, Strom, part II, 138, 149, 159, 196

Tibet, 91

Tilberis, Liz, parts I, II

Tilly, Meg, part I

Time (magazine), 83

Timmendequas, Paul, part IV

Ting, Richard, part I

Tinseltown, 171

Tiny Tim, 20

Titanic, 24, 28, 39, 45, 47, 51–52, 62, 68, 70, 87, 101, 104, 108, 111, 124, 185, 214, 269

tobacco, 104, 141, 160, 172, 174, 181, 200, 284

Today Show, The, 270

Tokyo, 239, 255

Tolstoy, Leo, 256–57

Tomba, Alberto, part III

Tomei, Marisa, 81

Tomey, Dick, part III

Tonight Show, The, 43, 244

Tony Awards, 107

Tony Brown's Journal, 25

Toobin, Jeffrey, part IV

Topinka, Judy Barr, part II

topless, 13, 28, 104, 218

Torborg, Jeff, part III

Toronto Blue Jays, 230, 259

Toronto, 57, 180, 230, 244, 259

Torre, Jose, part III

Tourette's syndrome, 74

Tower, Tiffany, part I

Townshend, Kathleen Kennedy, part II

Townshend, Pete, part I

Traficant, James, part II

Train, Mark, 143

Tranghese, Michael, part III

Travolta, John, parts I, II

Traymark, Ralph, part II

Trebek, Alex, part I

Trillin, Calvin, parts I, II

Tripp, Linda, part II, 80, 137, 150, 167, 183

Tritt, Travis, part I

Tropicana Hotel, 17

Truax, Thomas, part IV

Trudeau, G. G., part I

Trudeau, Margaret, 61, 95

True Lies, 36, 101

Truman, Harry, 148, 152, 188

Trump, Donald, parts I, III, 54

Trump, Ivana, part I, 45

Trump, Ivanka, part I

truth, 11, 16, 27, 42, 44, 86, 88, 97, 106, 116, 121, 123, 133, 139, 146, 152, 160, 163, 179, 184, 186–87, 192, 195, 200, 205, 213, 240, 249, 269, 271, 288

Tsongas, Paul, part II

Tucker, Tanya, part I

Tucker, Walter, III, part IV

Tuggle, Lem, part IV

Turan, Kenneth, 28

Turner, Ike, part I

Turner, Isaiah, part IV

Turner, Monica, part III

Turner, Norv, part III

Turner, Steven, part III

Turner, Ted, part I, 38, 44, 62

Turner, Tina, part I, 96, 119

Tuturro, John, 48

Twain, Mark, 92, 98, 125

Tyler, Cyrinda, part I

Tyler, Liv, part I

Tyler, Steven, part I

Tyson, Mike, part III, 74, 86, 217–18, 225, 227, 229, 233, 237–38, 240–42, 244, 247, 251, 253, 255

U.S. Women's Hockey Team, 230

UCLA, 161, 232

Udall, Morris, part II

Uecher, Bob, part III

UFO, 41, 87

Ulee's Gold, 44

Ulrich, Lars, part I

Unabomber, the, 69, 276, 279

United States, 18–19, 47, 51, 67, 74, 80, 114, 120, 124, 134–35, 139–40, 143–44, 146, 156, 158, 160–62, 164–65, 186, 203, 208, 212, 222–23, 254

Universal Pictures, 36

universe, 12, 19

University of Arizona, 82

University of California, 25

University of South Carolina, 80

University of Virginia, 109, 150, 189

Updike, John, part I

UPN, 50, 92, 121

Upper West Side, 48

Urbanchek, John, part III

Urchak, Woody, part III

Uruguay, 65

USA Today, 50, 97

Utah, 79, 174, 235, 240, 242, 288

Valenti, Jack, part I

Valentine, Dean, part I

Valentino, 109

Vallasio, Dorothy, part II

vampires, 91, 230

Van Damme, Jean-Claude, part I

Van Doren, Mamie, part I

Van Dyke, Dick, part I
Van Eaton, John, part IV
Van Gogh, Vincent, 22, 268
Van Halen, Eddie, part I
Van Hoffman, Eric, part I
Van Sant, Gus, part I
Van Zandt, Steve, part I
Vanatter, Philip, part IV
Vanilla Ice, part I
Vanity Fair, 25, 271
Vasconcellos, John, part II
Vasquez, Alfredo, part IV
Vassar College, 192
Vaughn, Vince, part I
vegetarian, 56, 178, 286
Veltroni, Walter, part IV
Ventura, Jesse "The Body", part II
Ventura, Robin, part III
Ventura, Terry, part II
Vermont, 167, 179
Vernon, Robert "Jesus Bob", part IV
VH1 Fashion Awards, 57
Viagra, 56, 58, 62, 83, 90, 190, 213,
    264, 286
Vicious, Sid, 72, 257
Vidal, Gore, parts I, II, 100
Vidon, Giulio, part II
Viet Cong, 53
Vietnam War, 53, 66, 151, 188
Vietnam, 16, 29, 53, 66, 114, 134, 147,
    151, 177, 180, 188, 193, 198
Vilanch, Bruce, part I
Village People, The, 85
Village Voice, The, parts II, III
Villechaize, Herve, 24, 102
Vitale, Dick, 98
Vitale, Nick, part II
Vittachi, Nury, part I
Vogel, Hal, part I
Voight, Jon, 59
Voltaire, 26, 256
Vuckovich, Pete, part III

Wachs, Joel, part II
Wagner, Steve, part III
Wahlberg, Donnie, part I
Wahlberg, Mark (Marky Mark), part I, 14
Waiting to Exhale, 68
Waits, Tom, part I
Walken, Christopher, part I
Walker, Charles, part II
Walker, Darrell, part III
Wall Street, 18, 124, 176, 247, 252
Waller, Robert James, 63
Walsh, Bill, part III
Walsh, Joe, part I

Walsh, Richard, part IV
Walter, Tyson, part III
Walters, Barbara, part II, 33, 58, 95,
    100, 154, 184, 268, 281, 289
war, 32, 35, 38, 40, 72, 98, 107, 109,
    116–17, 134, 143, 145, 147, 152,
    159–60, 166–67, 176, 183, 200, 206,
    224, 267, 271
Ward, Carol, part IV
Ward Cleaver, 81
Warner Bros., 121
Warner, Senator John, part II
Warsaw, 58, 65, 198
Washington Post, 48, 138, 174
Washington Times, The, part II
Washington, 18, 46, 48, 92, 125,
    133–38, 141, 148–50, 152–53, 157,
    160, 162, 168–69, 171, 173–74, 179,
    181–82, 185–86, 191, 194, 196, 200,
    203, 205, 207, 209, 211, 219, 230,
    239, 254–56, 287, 293
Watergate, 147, 160, 182–84
Waters, John, part I, 29
Waterworld, 34, 42
Wattenburg, Bill, part I
Watts, Charlie, part I
Watts, Doug, part IV
Wayans, Damon, part I
Wayans, Keenan Ivory, part I
weapons, 12, 114, 149, 171, 176, 192,
    196, 205
Weatherbie, Charlie, part III
Weaver, Sigourney, part I
Webber, Andrew Lloyd, 66
Webber, Steve, part III
Webber, Steven, part I
Wei, Jingshen, part II
Weight, Doug, part III
Weintraub, Sandi, part I
Weiss, Bob, part III
Weiss, Rob, part I
Weitzman, Margaret, part IV
Welch, Raquel, part I, 83
Weld, William, part II
Welk, Lawrence, 106, 145, 157
Wells, David, part III
Wen, Ming-Na, part I
Wendy Ward Charm School, 210
Wenner, Jan, part I
West Hollywood, 82
West Virginia, 149, 243
West, Adam, part I
West, Mae, 97
Westgate, Richard, part III
Weston, Riley, part I
Wexler, Robert, part II

White House, 36, 45, 51, 67, 81, 89, 98,
    136, 141–44, 148–59, 163, 165, 168,
    173, 176–77, 181–83, 185, 188–89,
    190–92, 194–95, 200–206, 208,
    212–13, 230, 246, 269
white people, 37, 46, 107, 219, 256, 273
White, Ben, part IV
White, John C., part II
White, Reggie, part III
Whitehurst, John, part II
Whitewater, 134, 138, 153, 156, 164,
    182, 189, 196, 204
Whitley, John P., part IV
Whitman, Christine Todd, part II
Whittaker, Tom, part III
whorehouse, 149
wife, 13–16, 18, 20, 23, 25, 32, 35–36,
    38–39, 47, 50–52, 54, 61–62, 68–69,
    73, 76–78, 80, 84, 92, 96, 103, 106,
    113, 116, 119, 120, 122, 125, 134,
    137, 142, 150, 153, 161, 168–71, 177,
    180, 187, 192–93, 197, 204, 206, 212,
    214, 220–22, 227, 232, 236, 249–50,
    254, 263, 265, 267, 273, 277–80,
    286–87, 288, 291, 293–94
Wild at Heart, 39
Wilder, Douglas, part II
Wilkos, Steve, part IV
Willey, Kathleen, part II, 139, 152,
    157, 163, 165, 183, 195, 203
Williams, Esther, part I
Williams, Pat, part III
Williams, Robin, parts I, II
Williams, Ted, part II
Williamson, Kevin, part I
Williamson, Malcolm, part I
Williamson, Richard, part III
Willis, Bruce, parts I, II, 80
Willis, Gordon, part I
Willis, Kelly, part IV
Wills, Gary, part II, 43
Wilson, Brian, part I
Wilson, Carnie, part I
Wilson, Pete, part II
Wilson, Willie, part III
Wilson, Woodrow, 185
Wimbledon, 224, 230, 254
Winfield, Dave, part III
Winfrey, Oprah, parts I, II, 218
Winger, Debra, part I
Winnipeg Jets, 253
Winston, Hillary, part II
Winter Olympic Games, 19
Winter, Ralph, part IV
Wisconsin, 56, 101, 151, 203, 207, 228,
    231, 258, 274, 294

wisdom, 24, 30, 80, 90, 240
Wisniewski, Emil, part IV
Witherspoon, Reese, part I
Witkin, Susan, part II
Wizard of Oz, The, 177
Wolf, Naomi, part II
Wolfe, Tom, part I, 63
women, 11, 14–15, 19, 21, 24, 27–28,
    30, 34, 38, 40, 46, 54–55, 60, 62,
    65, 68, 72, 75, 79, 80–81, 83–84,
    86–87, 94–95, 96–98, 112–14,
    119–20, 122, 124, 133, 137, 142,
    156, 162–64, 166, 170, 179–80,
    189, 190, 194–96, 199, 201–202,
    206–207, 209, 212, 217–18, 224,
    233–34, 236–37, 251, 255–57, 260,
    265, 274, 283–84
women's liberation, 75
Wonder Woman, 74
Wonder, Stevie, part II, 47
Wonderwall, 45
Wood, Randy, 23
Woodcock, Janet, part II
Woods, Charles, part IV
Woods, James, part I, 49, 129
Woods, Tiger, part III, 220, 238,
    241–42, 246, 248, 260
Woodson, Charles, part III
Woodstock, 13, 94
Woodward, Louise, parts I, IV
Word, Dortha, part IV

work, 11–13, 15, 18, 21, 24–30, 32–33,
    36, 44–47, 51, 55, 57, 63–65, 74–75,
    79, 82, 87, 90, 93, 95, 103, 108, 112,
    115–18, 123, 129, 133, 139, 140,
    143, 145, 147, 153, 167, 170,
    172–73, 180, 182, 185, 210, 217,
    219, 226, 240, 242, 263, 265,
    274–75, 281, 283
World Series, 85, 218, 220, 251
World Wrestling Federation, 165, 244
Wright, Ben, part III
Wright, Robin, part I
Wright, Susan Webber, part II
Wurtzel, Elizabeth, part I
Wyatt, Nan, part I
Wyle, Noah, part I
Wynn, Steve, part II
Wysocki, Paul, part II
Wysocki, Ruth, part III

Xena, 65, 133
X-Files, The, 41, 69
Xiaoping, Deng, 142, 226, 245
Xie, Suanjun, part I

Yale University, 37
Yan, Martin, part I
Yankee Stadium, 222, 228, 254
Yannacone, Emilio, part IV
Yardley, Jonathan, part I
Yeltsin, Boris, 147, 208

Yetnikoff, Walter, part I
Ying-Jeou, Ma, part II
Yochim, Marie, part II
yoga, 71, 74, 81, 94, 112, 153
Yosemite, 142
Young, Alan, part I
Young, Elaine, part IV
Young, Neil, part I
Young, Peter, part III
Young, Rick, part IV
Young, Sean, part I
Young, Steve, part III
Youngman, Henny, part I
Yu, Jessica, part I
Yugoslavia, 58, 186

Zafris, Pete, part IV
Zagallo, Mario, part III
Zamora, Jim, part IV
Zamorano, Ivan, part III
Zappa, Frank, part I
Zellwegger, Renee, part I
Zemin, Jiang, part II
Zen, 102
Zimmer, Don, part III
Zito, Nick, part III
Zoeller, Frank Urban "Fuzzy", part III
Zolotukhina, Maria, part I
Zorn, John, part I
Zucker, Jeff, part IV
Zuniga, Daphne, part I